The New York Times

SUNDAY CROSSWORD OMNIBUS VOLUME 13

Published in the United States by St. Martin's Griffin,
an imprint of St. Martin's Publishing Group

THE NEW YORK TIMES SUNDAY CROSSWORD OMNIBUS VOLUME 13.
Copyright © 2023 by The New York Times Company. All rights reserved.
Printed in the United States of America. For information,
address St. Martin's Publishing Group, 120 Broadway, New York, NY 10271.

www.stmartins.com

ISBN 978-1-250-89603-2

Our books may be purchased in bulk for promotional, educational, or business use.
Please contact your local bookseller or the Macmillan Corporate
and Premium Sales Department at 1-800-221-7945, extension 5442,
or by email at MacmillanSpecialMarkets@macmillan.com.

First Edition: 2023

10 9 8 7 6 5 4 3 2

The New York Times

SUNDAY CROSSWORD OMNIBUS VOLUME 13
200 World-Famous Sunday Puzzles from the Pages of *The New York Times*

Edited by Will Shortz

ST. MARTIN'S GRIFFIN
NEW YORK

Looking for more Sunday Crosswords?

The New York Times

The #1 Name in Crosswords

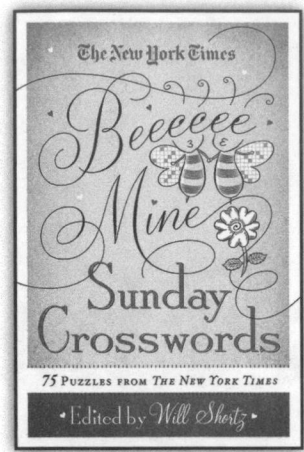

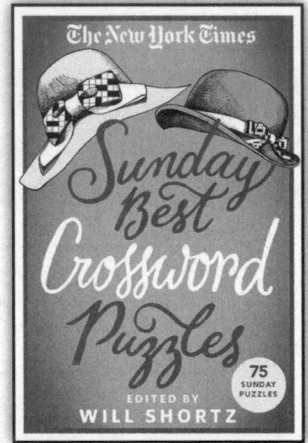

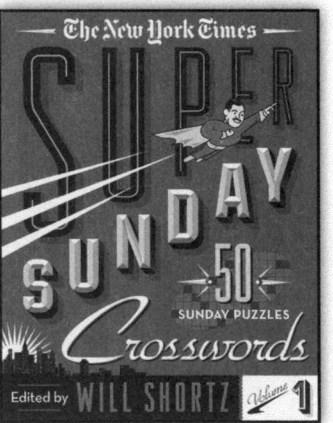

Available at your local bookstore or online at
us.macmillan.com/author/thenewyorktimes

 ST. MARTIN'S GRIFFIN

ACROSS

1 Up in the air
6 Memo abbr.
10 How many network sitcoms are rated
14 Floats
19 World capital once behind the Iron Curtain
20 Bubble tea flavor
21 One who might get a parade
22 Singer Goulding
23 Stoner movies?
25 Fired
26 Pioneer who lent his name to six U.S. counties
27 Île de la ___
28 At some point
30 Components of stoner movies?
32 Flooring wood
33 Furniture wood
34 Rubberneck
35 Certain Franciscan
36 Salsa variety
38 Chief Ouray and others
39 Came down to earth
40 Farrow with a Golden Globe
43 Tension in a stoner movie?
46 Stoner movie that flops at the box office?
48 Youngest Jetson
49 Wheat ___
51 "___ a dream . . ."
52 Rock's Brickell
53 Ancient Greek land that hosted the Olympics
54 ___ Calrissian, "Star Wars" role
55 Game's end
56 Blood flow aid
57 Set a good example, perhaps
58 Half of doce
59 Having two beats per measure, in music
61 Gives what for
62 Ending of a stoner movie?
65 Honeydew relative
68 Smooths
69 Peewee
70 The Horned Frogs of the Big 12 Conf.
73 Animal wearing red pajamas in a children's book
74 Make a jumper, say
75 Broadcasts
77 Piece on a1
78 Inter ___
79 Singer Chesney
80 Two tablets, maybe
81 Dog, for some
82 With 84-Across, like an audience during a stoner movie?
84 See 82-Across
86 After-hours convenience
87 ___ track (attack song)
88 Style to pick?
91 Splits lickety-split
92 Top-tier
94 Bottom-heavy fruit
95 Part of V.S.O.P.
96 Initials hidden in "jetway," appropriately
98 Bad actor in a stoner movie?
101 Certain Mexican-American
103 Lit
104 Like ornithologists' studies
105 TV host with the autobiography "Born a Crime"
107 Be behind the camera for a blockbuster stoner movie?

109 Very, in slang
110 Hella cool
111 James in both the Blues and Rock and Roll Halls of Fame
112 Certain godchild
113 Midlife crisis feeling
114 Big acronym in education
115 No longer gray, say
116 Woman's nickname that elides "Na"

DOWN

1 Adoption org.
2 Site of an annual May race
3 Unfindable, so to speak
4 Piccolo relative
5 Dance specialty
6 Squad bringing more than their B game?
7 Careful word choice, maybe
8 Fencing along a sidewalk
9 Samin ___, best-selling cookbook author
10 Terse email reply
11 Give a hard time
12 Kitchen work before cooking
13 Cupid, e.g.
14 Line on many a business card
15 HI goodbye
16 Item taken out of its packaging before it's sold
17 Window option
18 Notices
24 In worse health
29 Be short
31 Kiddie ride
33 Swirl
37 Density symbols
39 Bush
41 "That bothers me"
42 Lends a hand with contraband?
43 Command to a dog
44 "Encore!"
45 Davis Cup competition
46 "___ we?"
47 Back
50 Quality feigned by a humblebrag
51 Overstayed, e.g.
54 Film heroine who says "Somebody has to save our skins. Into the garbage chute, flyboy"
56 Orkney resident
58 Buckwheat noodles
60 Deploy
61 Repentance subjects
62 Dissident/writer Khashoggi
63 Big nonprofit that operates the Department of Defense Safe Helpline

64 One being taught a lesson
65 Maryland's ___ Barton Parkway
66 Set apart
67 The cutting of one's jib?
70 Travel kit contents
71 Shift from one dialect to another, depending on the social context
72 Strummed instruments, for short
74 Fratty feats
76 Center of the U.S. auto industry
77 Underhanded plan
79 Jewish snack
81 ___ the lily
83 Indignant denial
85 Big name in insurance
88 Tough H.S. science class
89 Scornful syllable
90 Subjected to a hostile takeover
93 Tips for journalists
95 First post-B.C. year
97 Befuddled
98 Rival of Ole Miss
99 Bard of ___
100 Not worth hashing out
102 Museo contents
103 Kind of seeds in health foods
106 Siamang or orangutan
108 Cause of a blowup, in brief

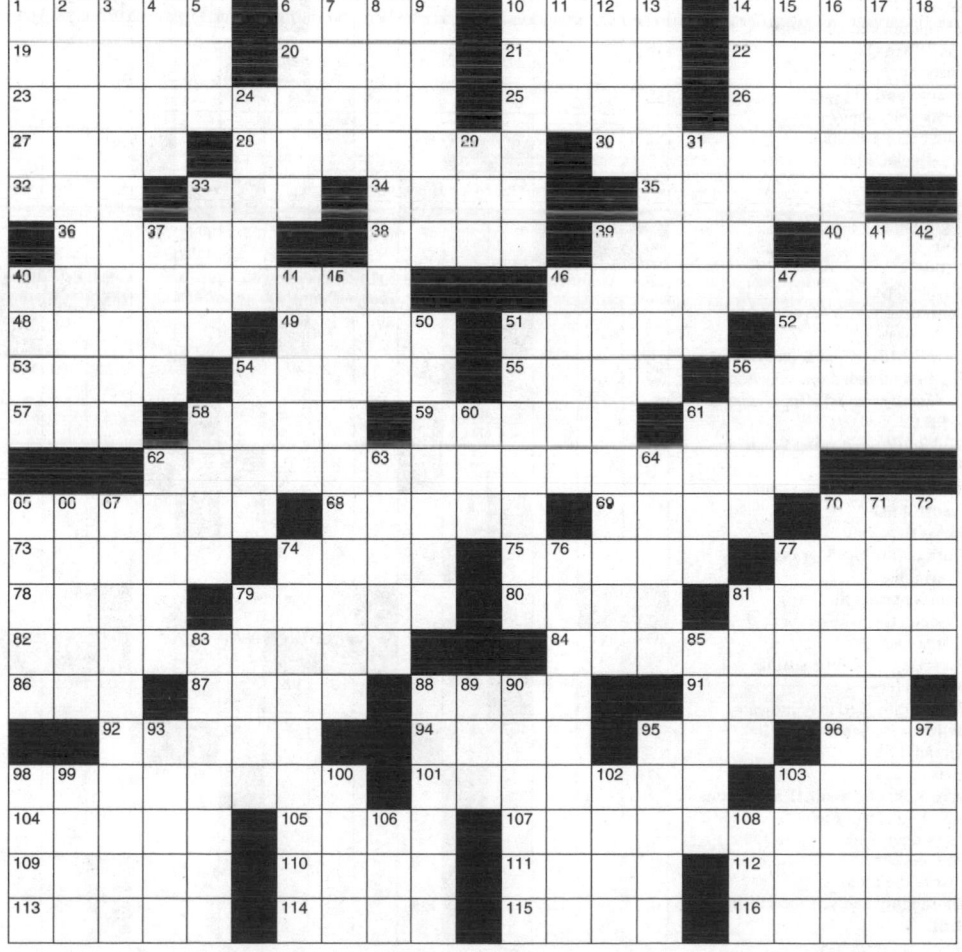

by Erik Agard

ACROSS

1 Exaggerated virility
9 Effortless assimilation
16 Alternatives to H.S. diplomas
20 Surgical removal procedure
21 What might raise the roof?
22 Come down, in a way
23 Line never said by 58-Across
25 Columnist Bombeck
26 Birth control option, briefly
27 "Please hold the line"
28 Shopping center?
29 Excerpt
30 Subjects of expertise
33 Lay an egg, say
34 Targets on "chest day"
35 Hollers
36 Line never said by 83-Across
41 Lobster ___ diavolo
42 Official language of a U.S. territory
45 Medical research org.
46 "Gotcha, man!"
48 December 31, e.g.
49 Diminutive for Theresa
52 Takes the plunge
55 Will who played Grandpa Walton on "The Waltons"
56 Big name in applesauce
58 Film villain who never said 23-Across, with "the"
61 Some purchasers of expensive gowns
64 Manhattan's ___ Stadium
66 The "E" in Q.E.D.
67 Noses out?
69 Counterpart of pitch
70 Prefix with -lepsy
71 Title for two Beatles
72 ___-Locka, Fla.
73 Try, in a way
75 Woodworker's tool
76 Digital image format
79 3:00
80 Willowy
81 Washer/dryer unit
83 Commander who never said 36-Across
86 Former Mississippi senator Trent
87 The first recorded one was noted by the Greek scientist Hipparchus in 134 B.C.
89 2014 hit film featuring Oprah Winfrey
90 Announcement from a band
92 Colorful fish
93 Surveillance aid
95 Word before check or drop
96 Overnighter
98 Chinese principle
99 TV detective who never said 121-Across
106 Exercise done while sitting
108 Wax holders
109 What a plus sign may indicate
110 Belief of Benjamin Franklin
114 Already: Fr.
115 Lhasa ___
116 May ordeal for some H.S. students
119 N.Y. engineering sch.
120 Pop singer Jason
121 Line never said by 99-Across
125 Last of the Stuarts
126 Thoroughly enjoyed something
127 Birth
128 Obstinate responses
129 "Oh, lordy!"
130 Corporations and partnerships, e.g.

DOWN

1 Secret society
2 Moving too quickly to be seen clearly
3 Half of an old crime duo
4 Croque-monsieur ingredient
5 Plural suffix?
6 Drinks in moderation
7 Post-___
8 Difficult kind of push-up
9 German artist Dix
10 "___ Love" (Cole Porter song)
11 G.I. grub
12 Without a buyer lined up
13 Seattle-based insurance giant
14 Least productive
15 Some beans
16 ___-Roman wrestling
17 British noble who never said 44-Down
18 Anastasia's love in Disney's "Anastasia"
19 Irritably answers
24 Purchase for a lorry
31 Blood-typing letters
32 Politician's goal
34 Impatient dismissals
35 London's ___ Park
37 All over again
38 Not yet rented
39 Varicolored
40 Like BFFs
42 Formative
43 Shade of green
44 Line never said by 17-Down
47 Iraq War danger, for short
50 Rest of the afternoon
51 Economizes
53 Common landscaping tree with acorns
54 Puts the kibosh on something
57 Active ingredient in marijuana
59 Sport making its Olympic debut in Tokyo in 2020
60 Number of Spanish kings named Carlos
62 Small boat, maybe
63 Angel
65 Head, slangily
68 Home to the Eads Bridge over the Mississippi: Abbr.
74 Suffer
77 Part of Caesar's boast
78 Las ___, Canary Islands
79 Opposite of kill
82 Elmer, to Bugs
84 "Sounds good to me!"
85 Many a northern Iraqi
88 Rubin ___ (classic illusion)
91 Try for a part
93 ___ Graham, Oprah's longtime beau
94 Former Penn State football coach
97 Go green, say
100 Standing
101 Hilarious joke, in slang
102 Titillating
103 Feudal estate
104 Cyrano de Bergerac's love
105 How paint is usually sold
107 Stuns
111 Shiraz native
112 #, to a proofreader
113 Performers in old-fashioned dumb shows
115 Stuck, after "in"
116 Buzzing
117 Stinky Le Pew
118 ___ Helens
122 Communication syst. for the deaf
123 Comp ___ (coll. major)
124 Crossed

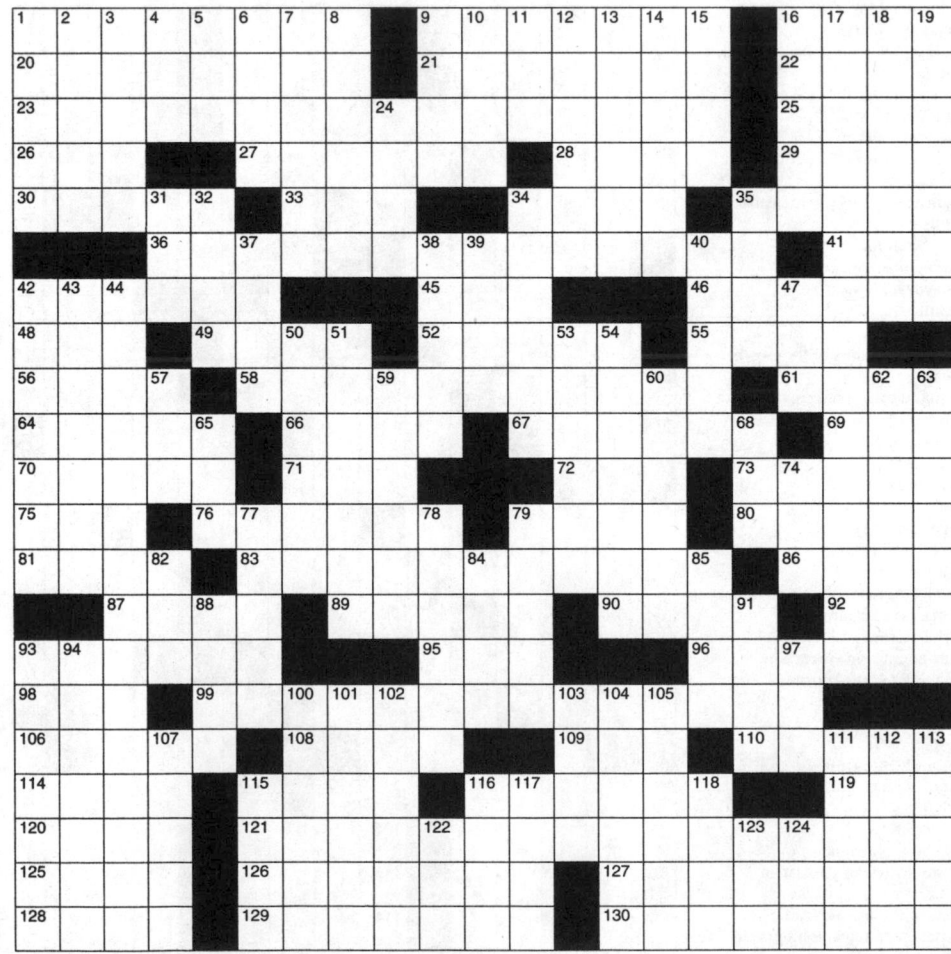

by Seth A. Abel

ACROSS

1 It was first officially designated in a 1966 Lyndon Johnson proclamation
11 Holders of tiny mirrors
19 Apple Store purchase
20 What studies show that men do more than women, conversationally
22 It might require a quick check
23 Star treatment
25 Male swan
26 Static, as an exercise
28 Access with a password
29 "Lord, show me ___"
31 World's largest cosmetics company
32 Post office?
33 Oscar winner Jared
34 Kitchen cabinet
35 Major academic achievements
36 "Yeah, whatever"
37 Having locks
39 Cocktail of tequila and grapefruit soda
41 Load
42 Specious arguer
45 Risk taker
47 One taking the bait
49 Like Earth's orbit
51 2019, zodiacally
56 Mine entrance
57 Calle ___, landmark street in Miami's Little Havana
59 Arcade game based on a film of the same name
60 "You listening?"
61 N.Y.U.'s ___ School of the Arts
63 Got by
66 Traces left by burning candles
67 Complete fool
69 Call of the wild
70 Catch a break?
72 Promote
73 Deli machine
76 Auditorium section beneath the balcony
78 Word before web or chocolate
79 Bundle
81 Heather has two, in a children's book title
82 Onetime U.S. soccer prodigy Freddy
85 Dates not found on the calendar
87 Hot sauce
89 Bank takeback
91 Great work
92 Without profit
93 Kid around
97 Owing
99 Greek goddess of the moon
100 Police, slangily
101 Negatively charged
102 Oppositely
104 Internet ___
105 Weapon with a distinctive hum
107 Classic play with a Delphic oracle
109 It's seen near Pennsylvania Avenue
110 Bright shade of red
111 Casino attraction
112 Buzzer beater?

DOWN

1 Kind of conservative
2 Put side by side
3 Something to champ at
4 It makes the earth turn
5 Finish with
6 Parts of a college app
7 Thomas Aquinas and others, philosophically
8 Inferior deities
9 Put forward
10 Number one on Rolling Stone's "100 Greatest Pop Songs" list
11 Polite
12 What "accommodate" is often inaccurately spelled with
13 ___ Dew (stylized brand name)
14 Stripped
15 Sinclair Lewis novel for which he received (but declined) the Pulitzer Prize
16 Parts of bluffs
17 Coaches
18 Nascar mishap
21 "My Neighbor ___," acclaimed animated film from Hayao Miyazaki
24 The "Tullius" of Marcus Tullius Cicero
27 Sci-fi weapon
30 Tied the knot
32 Org. for the Vegas Golden Knights
34 Sauce traditionally prepared in a mortar
35 Repeats mindlessly
38 Embarrassing sound when bending over
39 Fruits baked in wine
40 Tapped, as a cigarette
42 Delta Air Lines hub
43 Getting up there
44 Puckered fabric
46 Many a local volunteer
48 Ticker symbol?
50 Meanspirited person
52 Best
53 A ___ (based on logic)
54 Sinful
55 Brave deeds celebrated in verse
58 They're found among the reeds
62 Attacks vigorously
64 Goldman ___
65 An Emmy is awarded for the best one
68 Many action movie villains
71 White coat
74 Face-to-face interaction?
75 Recite from memory
77 Cable inits. for cinephiles
80 Muslim niqab, e.g.
82 Standard Windows typeface
83 Co-owner of Paddy's Pub on "It's Always Sunny in Philadelphia"
84 Not loose
86 Afrique du ___
88 Desiccated
90 "Pick me! Pick me!"
92 Agcy. created after the Manhattan Project
94 No longer interested
95 Placid
96 Scam artist
98 Between: Fr.
99 Begets
100 The birds and the bees, e.g.
102 Clothes dryer attachment
103 Gush
106 Part of a Twitter page
108 Private instructor: Abbr.

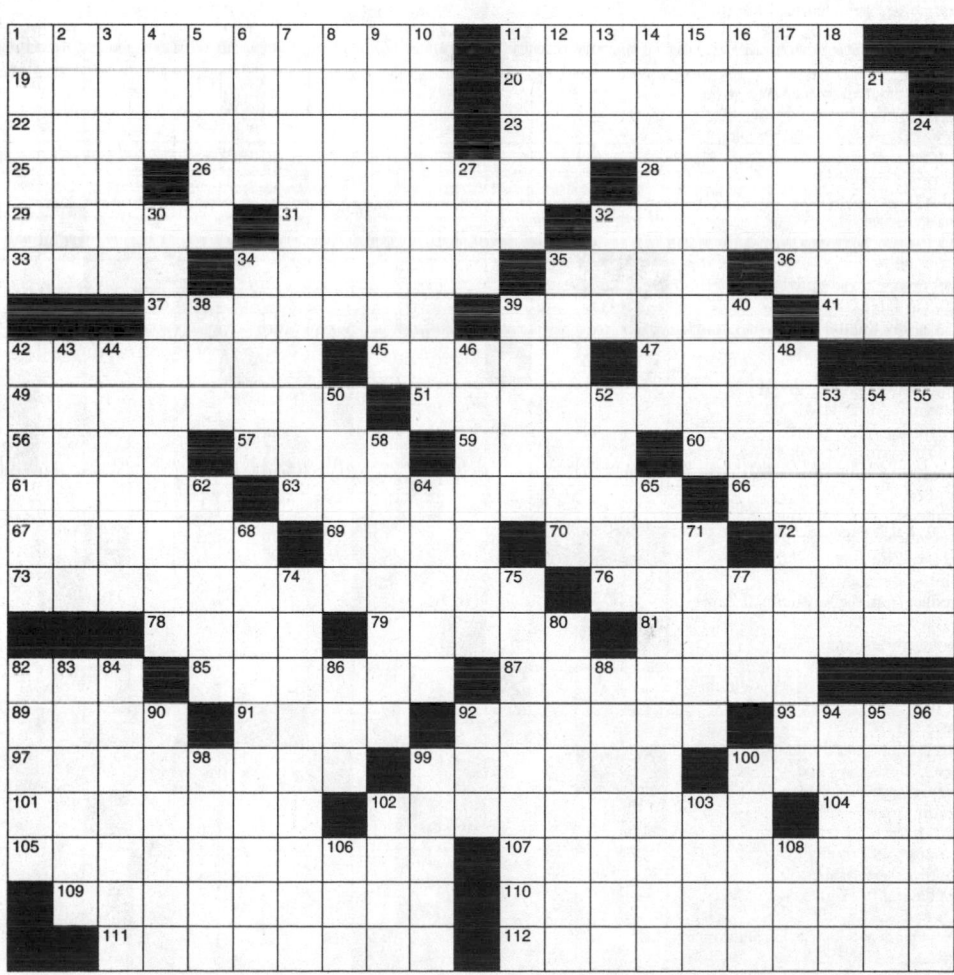

by Joel Fagliano

ACROSS

1 Word in Facebook and Disney Channel's original names
4 Ninny
8 Subj. of a National Historic Site outside Wall, S.D.
12 Ditties
17 Bridge component
19 Previously owned
20 Upshot of a story
22 Wolf howls, maybe
23 Org. concerned with grades
24 Certain warriors in Magic: The Gathering
25 One of three properties in Monopoly
26 Silver
27 Don at the Met
29 Cream and others
30 Attire that flaps in the wind
31 E, B, G, D, A or E
32 B-team
34 Sports team employee
36 Shell station?
38 Using without paying royalties, say
41 ___ amis (my friends: Fr.)
42 Part of Q.E.D.
43 Like a swished basketball shot
45 ___ volente (God willing: Lat.)
46 Aspire
47 Paroxysm
49 It "isn't so bad when you consider the alternative," per Maurice Chevalier
50 Designed to minimize drag
51 Cooked up
53 Being
55 What you will always be (but he or she isn't)?
57 Provincial capital south of a lake with the same name
59 Recurrent theme
60 Indication of good taste?
61 Famed furrier
62 Clip
64 Low-quality
66 Major name in network hardware
70 ___ Tin Tin
72 "If you can't imitate him, don't copy him" speaker
74 Introduce oneself
76 Fruit that, surprisingly, is slightly radioactive
79 Supporting role
81 Kind of spring found in a mousetrap
82 Reassuring words after an accident
83 Attacks
85 Fortitude
87 It's replicated during mitosis
88 URL ending
89 Winner's wreath
90 Product from the Royal Small Arms Factory
91 Sound while being tickled
92 Warm winter wear
94 Beatrix Potter's Mrs. Tiggy-winkle, for one
97 Pulse
98 "All ___ is but art, unknown to thee": Alexander Pope
101 Deeply ingrained habit
104 Leaning
105 Nails a test
107 Geniuses, informally
109 Impressive stylishness
110 Not having full rights, as a citizen
111 "Up and ___!"
112 Home team at Rice-Eccles Stadium
113 San ___, Calif.
114 Carpenter of note
115 Politician's core support
116 It's halfway around a diamond
117 Unsmiling
118 "Hey!"
119 Carrier with King David Lounges
120 Romulus, but not Remus, in ancient Rome

DOWN

1 Brutish sorts
2 "That happened?"
3 Signature
4 Some revealing beachwear
5 Caution
6 Things that most people have eight of
7 Bear necessities, for short?
8 Bank of China Tower architect
9 ___ Kaepernick, former N.F.L. QB
10 Confederate general with a fort named after him
11 Item carried in an academic procession
12 Bit of outerwear
13 Couple of high points?
14 Twice-monthly coastal phenomena
15 Suffix with defer or insist
16 About 5:00, directionally: Abbr.
18 Ray or Dave of the Kinks
21 Doris who won the 2007 Nobel Prize in Literature
28 "Gimme ___!" (Alabama cheerleader's repeated call)
29 Author Harte
33 Walk with a firm, heavy step
35 Staring a bit too long, perhaps
37 Bad tumble
38 Objects spinning in an orrery
39 Model for a bust at the Musei Capitolini
40 Continue
41 Knee-covering skirts
43 Nonwinner
44 Drug treatment for Muhammad Ali
46 Competitor of Sanyo and Bose
47 Add to the mix
48 Animation
49 Subject of a statue outside Boston's TD Garden
50 The two sides in chess, essentially
52 Arctic wear
54 Never to be forgotten
56 Trick-taking game
58 Talkaholics
63 What movie trailers do
65 What cibophobia is the fear of
67 Specialty of Muddy Waters and Blind Willie Johnson
68 Copy
69 Actress Chaplin of "Game of Thrones"
71 1998 Winter Olympics host
73 Teller?
75 Poetic direction
76 Majors
77 One way to run
78 New brother or sister
80 Flower for a 20th wedding anniversary
84 Bush
86 Bust supporter
89 Stieg who wrote "The Girl With the Dragon Tattoo"
90 Out of business
91 Somewhere to chill, paradoxically
93 Tricorder go-with
95 Nice finish, maybe
96 Sarcastic syllable
98 Gets warmer, so to speak
99 Jerks
100 Quaint contradiction
102 Eponymous cup maker
103 Thomas Cromwell, Earl of ___
104 Musical miscue
106 ___ eyes on (see)
108 Four-letter U.S. city with the highest population
109 Ruler units: Abbr.
111 Five Georges

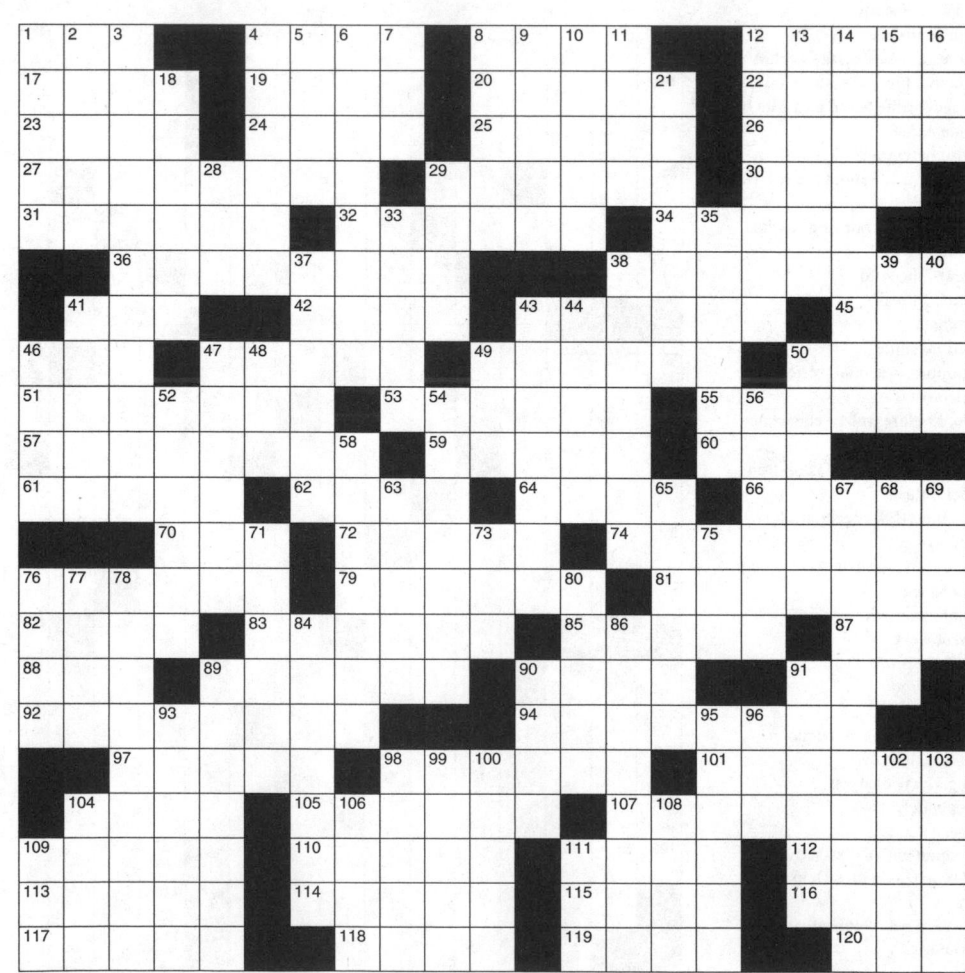

by David Liben-Nowell and Victor Barocas

ACROSS

1 Crawling marine mollusk
8 Victorious cry
14 At first, say
20 So-called "Crossroads of America"
21 Wife in F. Scott Fitzgerald's "Tender Is the Night"
22 Uprights, e.g.
23 Low end?
25 What sunblock blocks, briefly
26 Rushes
27 Hangout on "The Simpsons"
28 One of two for a buck?
30 Somewhat, slangily
32 Go astray
33 Part of town that may be dangerous
35 Tater ___
38 Extraterrestrial from the planet Melmac
40 Emphatic ending with yes or no
42 Bulging bicep, in slang
43 Raise
44 Wet
48 Agreement for exporting essential oils?
51 Raggedy ___
52 Around an hour after noon
54 Spend all weekend solving crosswords, say, with "out"
55 Dummkopfs
56 Movie-rating org.
58 Semi-essential part?
59 Driver of "BlacKkKlansman"
61 Most pallid
63 Exercise program done in formal attire?
66 Horse operas
68 Top squads
69 Sports page listings
71 Avoid cooked foods
75 Beyond prim and proper
77 Sturdily built friend on "Friends"?
79 Relative of a flute
82 Statement often starting "I . . ."
84 Egg head?
85 Train transportation
86 "Baby Blues" or "Rhymes With Orange"
87 PC key
89 Rita who played Anita in "West Side Story"
92 Setting for many Twins games: Abbr.
93 Spotted animal with a lot of sore spots?
96 Squirrels away
98 "What ___ ?"
99 Maestro's gift
100 ___ Rousey, first female fighter inducted into the U.F.C. Hall of Fame
102 Animal in un zoológico
103 First letter of "tsar" in Russian
104 Father of the Constitution
106 PC key
108 Extended family
112 Utterly useless
113 Totally abandon one's plan
114 Letter-shaped fastener
115 Laugh riot
118 Cause of a work stoppage at a shoe factory?
123 Tropical scurrier
124 Put on a pedestal
125 Charm
126 A cobbler might use one
127 Expunge
128 Word before shot or plot

DOWN

1 Some turban wearers
2 Film composer Morricone
3 Doe follower, in song
4 Breaks along the Panama Canal?
5 "Well, ___-di-dah!"
6 Commercial prefix with lever
7 "That's so-o-o gross!"
8 Is a willing participant?
9 Runs out of gas
10 Here, to Henri
11 Underworld boss
12 Troy story
13 Joan of Arc, at the time of her death
14 Fit for a king
15 Skin care brand
16 Attorney general under both Bush 41 and Trump
17 Santa ___ winds
18 ___ sauce
19 Symbol on a Mariners cap
24 ___ d'oeuvre
29 Slangy affirmation
31 Rare solo voice in opera
33 Arthur with a Tony
34 UnitedHealthcare competitor
35 Back-comb
36 Multi-time Pulitzer finalist, including for the volume "Lovely, Dark, Deep: Stories" (2014)
37 Meet on the down-low
39 Confines
41 Fixes up, in a way
43 Circuit board component
44 Fearsome snake
45 Stoned
46 Dumbstruck
47 Undiluted
49 Like Easter Island
50 Full of enthusiasm
53 Construction girders
57 Not without sacrifice
60 Call into question
62 Permeate
64 Shout from a lottery winner
65 Kid-lit character with the catchphrase "Thanks for noticing me"
67 In regard to
70 Big name in 2008 financial news
72 Jurisdiction
73 Stomach
74 Painful paintball mementos
76 Rapid movement of the eye from one point to another
78 Surrealist Tanguy
79 Groups in the quarterfinals, e.g.
80 Loses enthusiasm
81 Elicit a smile from
83 Last Oldsmobile ever produced
88 Sent
90 Pearl clutcher's cry
91 Bit of brewing equipment
94 "Sure thing, dude!"
95 Boatload
97 Untangle
101 "In your dreams!"
104 2016 film set in Polynesia
105 Reckon, informally
107 Section of a high school yearbook
109 Native Alaskan
110 Popular corn chip
111 What radio signals travel through, with "the"
112 Spring's opposite
113 Nongreen salad ingredient
115 Merest taste
116 Part of a sci-fi film's budget
117 French way
119 The Braves, on scoreboards
120 One of many extras in air travel nowadays
121 A little fun?
122 Letters on some luggage to New York

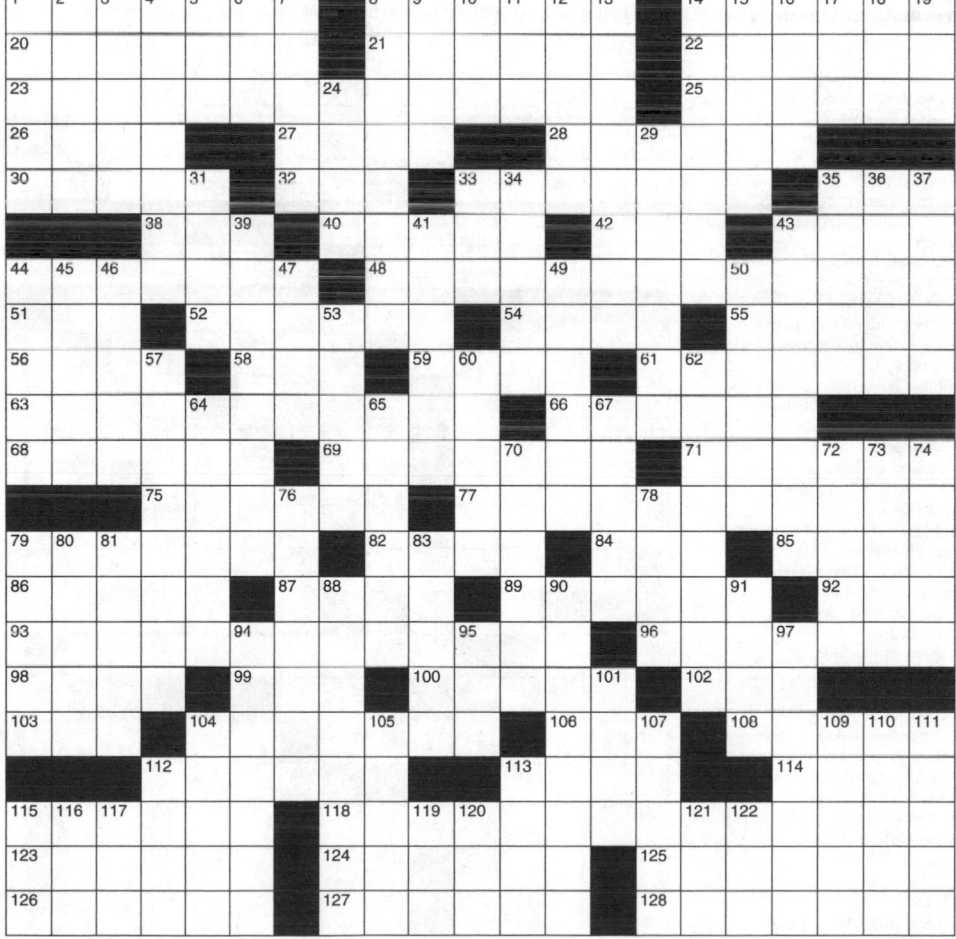

by Emily Carroll

HIDDEN TACTICS

Note: The center of this puzzle represents a 70-Down/55-Down, in which you can achieve a 122-Across by moving the 25-Across.

ACROSS

1 Cleaning product in a dangerous 2010s viral internet challenge
8 "Home" in a classic song
16 Jack of children's rhyme
21 "Agreed"
22 Escapes, as molasses
23 Irregularly notched, as a leaf
24 Protein found in hair and hooves
25 *See note*
27 Watson's creator
28 Pain for a tiler, maybe
30 Yearbook
31 Side represented by Δ
34 Adams and Elgort
35 Doctor's order
37 Dorothy's caretaker in "The Wizard of Oz"
40 Irritate
41 Irritable
42 Verify the addition of
43 Nabisco product with an exclamation point in its name
49 That guy's
50 Ill repute, to a Brit
52 Santa ___ winds
55 Some ovations
60 Become attentive
61 Succeeds
65 Cowboy flick
66 Eve's counterpart
67 What a plant may exude
69 Freak out
71 Treasure
72 When doubled, a Thor Heyerdahl book
73 Mother ___
74 [Grumble, grumble]
75 Pith holders
76 Set aside for now
78 Score elements: Abbr.
79 Digital message
80 Old gold coin
81 Map of Hawaii or Alaska, often
82 1974 Gould/Sutherland C.I.A. spoof
83 Lushes
84 Deteriorate with age
86 Cut into bits
88 Prevents, legally
89 Letters near an X-ray machine
90 People native to Tennessee and the Carolinas
92 "While I have you . . . ," in a text
95 Classic 1922 film subtitled "A Symphony of Horror"
98 Brown-headed nest appropriator
104 "Fighting" college team
107 Maker of pens and lighters
108 Sheer fabric
109 First commercial film shown in stereophonic sound
111 Key of Bizet's first symphony
116 Side represented by ○
117 87 is a common one
118 Conspicuous
121 Yuletide contraction
122 *See note*
125 Arrests
128 Outpost for an osprey
129 No longer needed for questioning
130 Senator Tammy Duckworth or former Senator Max Cleland
131 Symbol of directness
132 Arrived at, as an answer
133 Swollen area

DOWN

1 Hangout often near a pool
2 Glacial hue
3 Like Mount Kilimanjaro
4 Doe in "Bambi"

5 Polling fig.
6 French acceptances
7 Title 1962 film villain
8 Valentine heart, e.g.
9 Urban cacophony
10 Slate, e.g.
11 Touch up, as styled hair
12 Some airborne particulates
13 What dashes may represent in internet searches
14 Kind of reaction
15 Ike's W.W. II command
16 Veto on movie night
17 Figure in many a fairy tale
18 Mischievous
19 One-named singer with the 2002 No. 1 hit "Foolish"
20 Some cuppas
26 No longer edible
29 Computing acronym
32 Silicon Valley start-up V.I.P.
33 Baby fox
35 Unexceptional
36 Prefix with planet
38 St. Louis's ___ Bridge, the oldest span over the Mississippi
39 Biblical high priest
40 The "u" spelling of 50-Across, e.g.: Abbr.
43 Figures in the Sistine Chapel

44 Part of Africa or an orchestra
45 Your signature might be in this
46 Came down hard
47 Terrific
48 Chatter
51 City that hosted the 1974 World's Fair
53 Rare beneficiaries of royal succession
54 Together
55 *See note*
56 Dating-app distance metric
57 Stat
58 Lush
59 Son of Clytemnestra and Agamemnon
61 Enter incorrectly
62 Jawbone of ___ (biblical weapon)
63 How early Beatles songs were recorded
64 Best
66 Suffix on many an infomercial product's name
68 Self-inflicted ritual death of a samurai
70 *See note*
73 Leash
77 Dulce de ___ (confection)
82 Notice
85 ___ Luis Obispo
87 One of 24 in un giorno

88 Those: Sp.
90 Banned aerosol propellant, for short
91 Green: Prefix
92 Like some lenses
93 Wrong pipe, so to speak
94 Spends December through March (in)
96 Bit of judo attire
97 One-named singer with the 2014 hit "Chandelier"
99 Indianapolis-to-St. Louis dir.
100 "Phooey!"
101 Ape
102 Calls it quits
103 Boutique stock
105 Barbie's younger sister
106 Long (for)
108 Part of an M.A. program application
110 Religious sch.
111 Called out
112 Any of the Apennines
113 In ___ (grumpy)
114 War hawk
115 Situation after a leadoff single
118 Ball ___
119 Big org. in Saturday-afternoon TV
120 "Indiana Jones" setting
123 Half of a 1955 union merger
124 Singer's syllable
126 They'll sound sped up at 45 r.p.m.
127 French director Besson

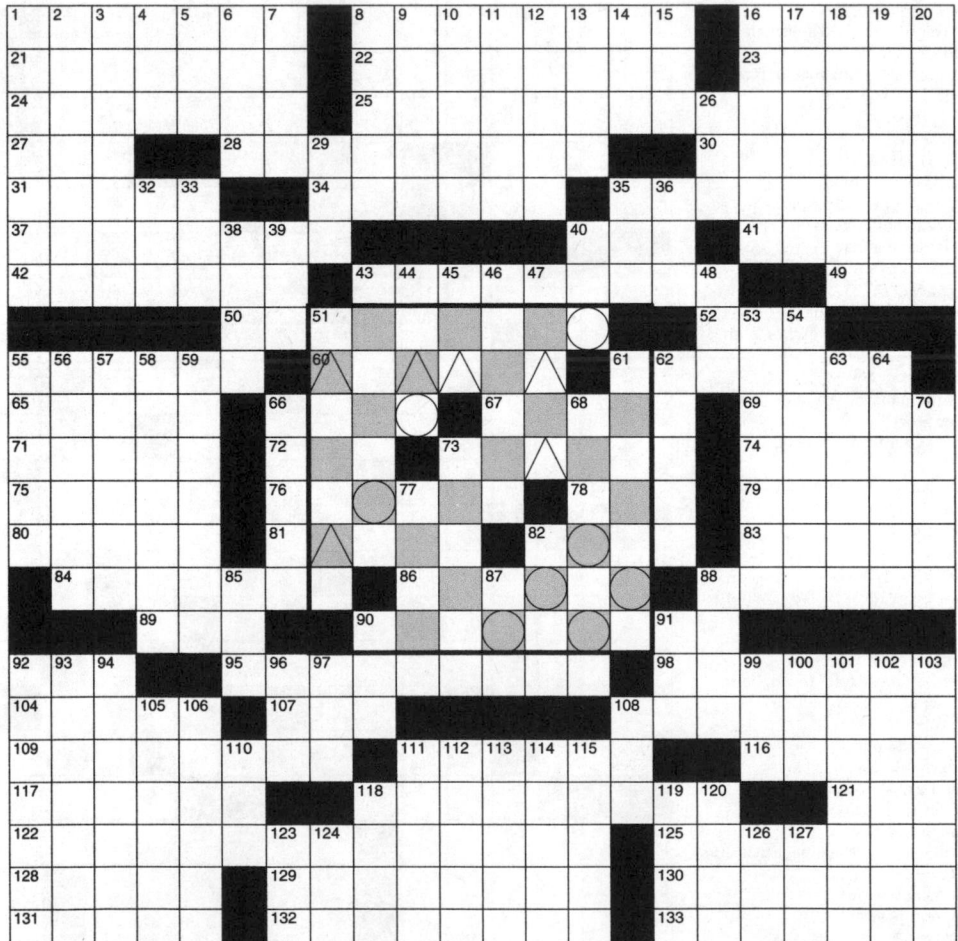

by Jack Reuter

ACROSS

1. Knock
4. Amped
9. Racket
13. Chocolate component
18. Humans' closest relatives
20. Alternative sweetener source
21. Trendy superfood
22. Coral formation
23. "Should I not use my oven clock?"?
26. "My turn! My turn!"
27. What bankers and prospectors both seek
28. Sends a Dear John letter
29. An arm and a leg
30. Soprano Fleming
31. Numerical prefix from the Greek for "monster"
32. Gloria, in the animated "Madagascar" films
33. Scrubs
35. The "Iliad" and the "Odyssey"?
40. ___ vu
41. Some spicy fare
43. Father of Zeus
44. Composer of "The Microsoft Sound," which, ironically, he wrote on a Mac
45. President-___
47. Its calendar begins in A.D. 622
50. Members of a flock
51. Put up
52. Give a ride to an Indiana hoopster?
55. Bargain-priced
56. New Year abroad
57. Teacher of the dharma
58. Orange juice option
59. "I can't take this anymore!"
61. The Kremlin, e.g.
63. "___ in the Underworld" (Offenbach opera)
65. Show impatience with, as an envelope
68. "Cool beans!"
70. ___ health
71. Pope's "___ on Solitude"
74. Shared spirit
75. Printer's low-ink alert?
78. How balloons are priced?
79. Round product with a wax wrapper
81. Unwanted looks
82. Less outgoing
83. Bygone monitor, for short
84. What no single speaker is capable of
86. Offerings in a bridal registry
88. Cause of an R rating
89. What a plumber did for a clogged drain?
93. Given a yellow card, say
95. Top of the Special Forces?
96. Little dippers?
97. Relish
98. Like a Tour de France rider on day 20 vis-à-vis day 10
99. Classical personification of ideal human beauty
101. Overlord, for the Battle of Normandy
104. Supereasy quiz question
105. World's shortest-reigning monarch?
107. Sphere of influence
108. Tweak, in a way
109. In no way reticent
110. Sketch out
111. Tries
112. Flotsam and Jetsam, in "The Little Mermaid"
113. Really like
114. Sign of a packed house

DOWN

1. Bust
2. Locale for a shrine
3. Personal favorite on an agenda
4. Least taxing
5. Colorful stone in a brooch
6. Flaps one's gums
7. Actress Mendes
8. What strawberries become as they ripen
9. Cover-up for a robbery?
10. Notoriously hard-to-define aesthetic style
11. Servings from a tap
12. La Baltique, e.g.
13. Big figures in 47-Across
14. Back to the original speed, in music
15. They usually include drinks
16. Relief
17. ___ Miss
19. Sole supporter?
24. "___ She Lovely" (Stevie Wonder song)
25. Neighbor of an Armenian
29. Some prom rentals
31. Scenic fabric
32. Improve gradually, say
33. Doing well (at)
34. Give a false impression of
35. Got taken for a ride
36. Unsolicited mentions online, in the press, etc.
37. "Meeeeeeeow!"
38. It makes you yawn
39. Shelfmate of Webster
42. One who gets take-out orders?
46. Subject of an annual festival in Holland, Mich.
48. Mini-program
49. Egyptian ___ (cat)
51. Derbies, e.g.
53. Spread out at a banquet?
54. Attire
55. Parts of a gymnastics routine
59. Calculation for an aerospace engineer
60. When doubled, "I agree!"
61. Alternative to a condo
62. Certain finish
64. Comparative in a wedding vow
65. Flinch or twitch, say
66. Computer guru, informally
67. Pops up in a flash?
69. Common sports injury site, briefly
71. Piquant bakery offerings
72. John who pioneered the steel plow
73. Messed up
75. Get bent
76. Green lights, so to speak
77. "Stop being such a baby!"
79. Old dentist's supply
80. Ingredient in insect repellent
84. 1st, 2nd, 3rd, etc.
85. Powerpoints?
87. Envelop in a blanket
90. "It's Not Easy Bein' Green" crooner
91. Opposites of 76-Down
92. Palais des Nations locale
94. Say for certain
97. Echolocation method
98. Bull, e.g.
99. Half of a children's game
100. Dastard's doings
101. Popular 2017 Pixar film set in Mexico
102. "Caboose"
103. Old Bond rival
104. Hit 2010s HBO series, familiarly
105. Late ___
106. Fish taco fish

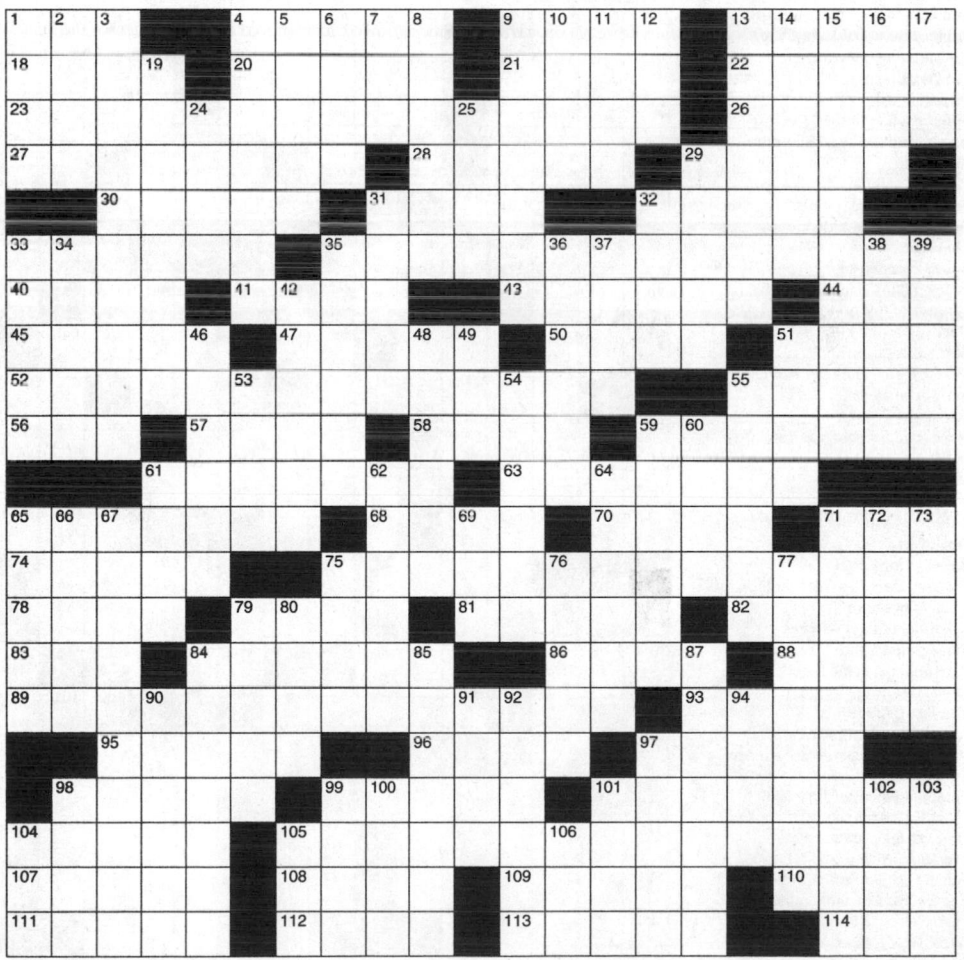

by Caitlin Reid

FIFTY YEARS ON

ACROSS

1 Org. whose workers can be a little frisky?
4 Meager
9 Charged
14 Picture framer's aid
17 Bad things for astronaut suits to have
19 Part of a broadcast feed
20 On the qui vive
21 Second-largest of the Hawaiian Islands
22 "However," in textspeak
23 Name of a sea first visited in 1969
25 Pot starter
26 World capital near the 60th parallel
27 What mattresses and spirits may do
28 Signs of nervousness
29 Good name for a fishmonger?
30 Gaming neophyte
31 Kind of diet
33 They don't keep their thoughts to themselves
36 Two tablespoons
37 W.W. II zone: Abbr.
38 End of a rope
40 Sean who played Rudy in "Rudy"
42 La-la lead-in
43 Certain seafood delicacy
44 Attention
45 Not as one
49 Appropriately palindromic reply to "Madam, I'm Adam"
50 Someone who might engage in a hobby with some frequency?
51 Bit of media hoopla
53 Words of Jesus
55 "Great" birds
57 Hillary who climbed Everest
59 The Notorious ___ (Supreme Court nickname)
60 Possible response to "No, you're not"
62 Skin care brand
64 Classic place to hide money
67 "Je t'___"
70 Suave competitor
71 Newsmaker of July 1969
72 Weeper of myth
73 Relating to the kidneys
74 Santa ___, Calif.
75 Where I go "when my baby smiles at me," in song
76 Bartender's supply
77 Necessity for going online, in brief
79 Passed
83 Loopy cursive letters
84 "There was no other choice!"
87 Deactivate
88 Request for a cold one
92 Bottom-dwelling fish that lack fins
94 "___ NewsHour"
95 Wizards, but not witches
96 Place to get a shot
97 Amenities at some hotels
100 Understanding
102 The last Pope Julius
103 ___ Stic (pen brand)
105 Hawk → snake → frog → insect, e.g.
109 Summer pest
110 Announcement of July 1969
115 "A-O.K. for launch!"
117 Do-nothing's state
118 Trojan warrior in the "Iliad"
121 What's gotten into your head
122 Represented in sheet music
123 1980s TV's "Remington ___"
124 Carol Brady and Camilla Parker Bowles, for two
125 Scruffs
126 Binoculars attachment

DOWN

1 Ticket issuers
2 Straddles
3 Long-distance traveler of 1969
4 800 things?
5 One putting on a show
6 "What goes up must come down" and others
7 Diarist Anaïs
8 Chef's hat
9 Mrs. Gorbachev
10 Totally
11 Some sound effects in westerns
12 Performer
13 Texter's sign-off
14 Achievement of 1969
15 Dictator
16 Rafter connectors
18 Unconventional home in a nursery rhyme
21 English football powerhouse, to fans
24 Strike caller
32 What 71-Across took in 1969, as represented literally in a corner of this puzzle
34 Regan's father
35 French comic actor Jacques
36 What 71-Across took in 1969, as represented literally in another corner of this puzzle
39 Third-largest of the Hawaiian Islands
41 Composer Charles
46 Domain of a municipal department
47 Extent
48 Wild party
52 Capital of South Australia
53 Dressed up
54 Dangerous substance that smells like bitter almonds
56 Receiver with a crystal
58 Org. with an Inspiration Award and an Award of Valor
61 So
62 Big inits. in news
63 Wrath
65 Nationality seen in most of Romania
66 Superman's father
68 Stat for which Hank Aaron holds the all-time record
69 Common Market inits.
78 Sport that players are not allowed to play left-handed
80 Nile biter
81 One waiting in line at an airport
82 Network with "Full Frontal With Samantha Bee"
83 Goes out
84 Apple on a desk
85 Pitch
86 Comes clean about
89 Member of a popular package delivery service
90 Mother of Hermes
91 Release
93 Tough job for a mover, maybe
95 "Peter Pan" dog
98 Access an account
99 Convinced of
100 Fuels (up)
101 Angered
104 ___ Weizmann, first president of Israel
106 Dirty mouth?
107 Economy
108 Test taker's downfall, perhaps
109 "The Maids" playwright Jean
111 Obstacles to teamwork
112 Very long time
113 "Illmatic" rapper
114 People with badges: Abbr.
115 Part of the foot between the toes and the ankle
116 Mr. Turkey
119 ___ mode
120 Mo. in 1962 in which J.F.K. gave his "We choose to go to the moon" speech

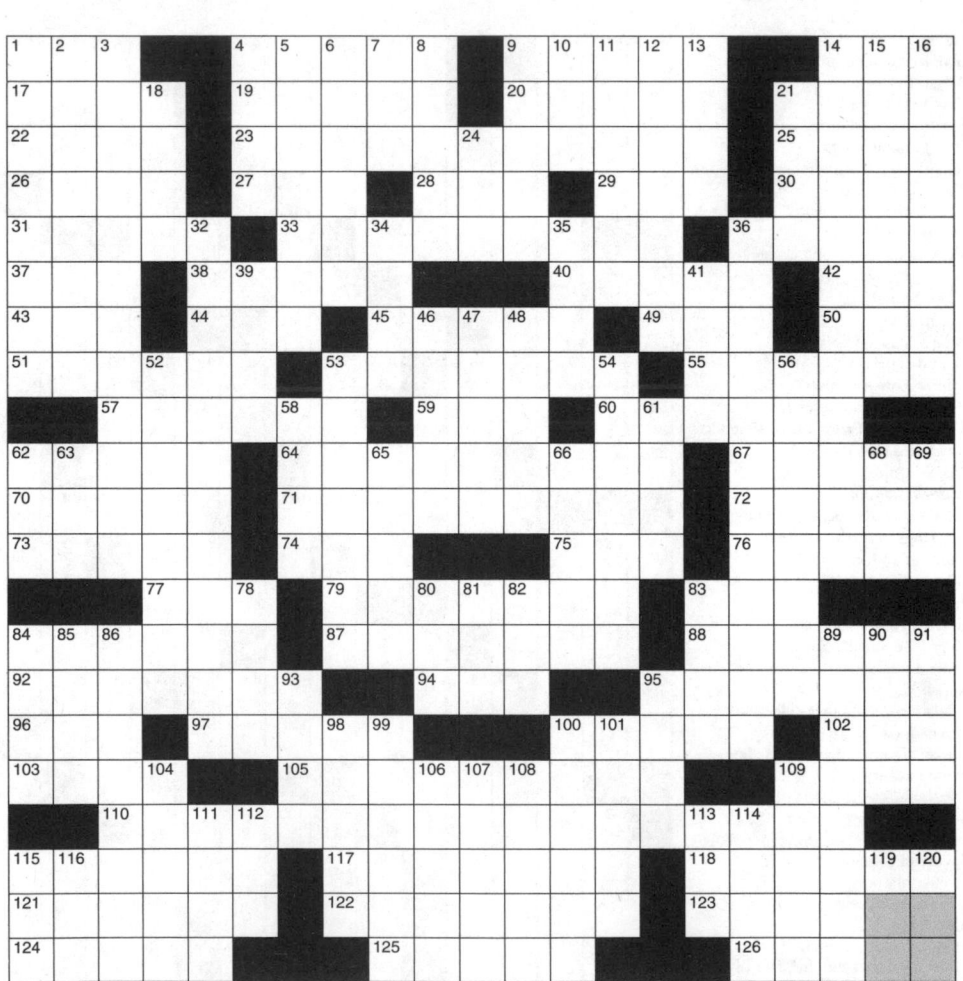

by Jason Mueller and Jeff Chen

ACROSS

1 Moth attractors
6 Rescue site for a polar bear
10 "Hold it right there!"
14 Word with grand or identity
19 Netflix crime drama set in a small town in Missouri
20 "Hahahahahaha!"
21 Blacken on the barbecue
22 Sun: Prefix
23 Change, as a hotel lock
24 Aura
27 Weasley family owl in the Harry Potter books
28 "You wish"
30 It's SW of the Pyrenees
31 "Give me an example!"
33 Designates for a specific purpose
35 Big things in D.C. and Hollywood
36 Source of the line "A Jug of Wine, a Loaf of Bread - and Thou"
37 Real nostalgia trip
40 Mobile
42 Mao-___ (Chinese liquor)
43 L.G.B.T. History Mo.
44 Bite-size chocolate candy
47 Home for doves and pigeons
48 Home for herons and egrets
50 "In case you didn't hear me . . ."
52 Group on the dark side of the Force
54 "Alas!," in Austria
55 Generally speaking
59 Not only that but also
60 Pompous pronoun
62 Vicuña product
63 Eye-catching print pattern
65 Creature slain in the Mines of Moria by Gandalf
66 "A Little Night Music" composer
70 Award for technological development since 1995
71 Shed, as feathers
73 Individually
75 Sometime collaborator with William Shakespeare, per the Oxford University Press
81 Deepest lake in the U.S. after Crater Lake
83 Place where musical talent may be wasted?
84 Assembly
87 Burns, in a way
89 Comics debut of 1963
90 Important topic in golf instruction
91 It's all downhill from here
92 Easy way that might lead to error
99 Printing measurement
100 Dead letters?
101 "It's bulls and blood, it's dust and mud," per a Garth Brooks hit
102 Enthusiastic enjoyment
103 Miss, say
104 Girl's name that's also a state abbreviation
105 Some laughable language mistakes - as found literally (in consecutive letters) in 24-, 37-, 55-, 75- and 92-Across
109 Small, rectangular candy
110 Cocktails with gin, vermouth and Campari
112 Gave the pink slip
113 Organism that grows on another plant nonparasitically
115 Bening with a star on the Hollywood Walk of Fame
116 Statistician Silver
117 Dog to beware of
118 Angioplasty inserts
119 Big 12 college town
120 Bounty hunter shot by Han Solo in "Star Wars: A New Hope"

DOWN

1 One-named singer with the 2017 #1 album "Melodrama"
2 Longtime Hyundai model
3 God, with "the"
4 First words
5 Business with perpetually high sales?
6 Glassy-eyed look
7 CPR administrator
8 Malek who won a Best Actor Oscar for "Bohemian Rhapsody"
9 Dimwit
10 Easily split rock
11 Which train goes to Harlem, in song
12 Something to dip in the water
13 Wedding agreement
14 Title movie role for Jim Carrey
15 "I found what you're looking for!"
16 Jane Jetson's son
17 Shrek's love
18 "For rent" sign
25 Beehive State bloomer
26 Occasion for a high school after-party
29 ". . . ___ mouse?"
32 Org. in a 1976 sports merger
34 Be on the court for tipoff, say
36 Précis
38 Bouillabaisse base
39 Myriad
40 Drink stirred with a spoon
41 Kind of alcohol used as biofuel
45 It borders the Suez Canal
46 Premium movie channel
47 Keto diet no-no
48 "The Jungle Book" boy
49 Chopped down
50 Place reached by boat
51 University in downtown Philadelphia
53 ___ Amendment, controversial 1976 Congressional measure
55 Stunned . . . just stunned
56 Alteration of a video game, in gamer lingo
57 "I like that!"
58 Chesterfield or reefer
61 Sleeve opening
64 What keeps athletic tape from sticking to the skin
66 "Go ___ Watchman" (Harper Lee novel)
67 Target of a spray
68 One of two in "The Grapes of Wrath"
69 Film-rating org.
72 "For shame!"
74 Like the verb "to be": Abbr.
75 Purchase for a celebration
76 Stable period from Augustus to Marcus Aurelius
77 Man, to Marcus Aurelius
78 Barely scratches (out)
79 Traitors
80 Pulitzer-winning W.W. II journalist
81 Russian rulers of old
82 Discovery of penicillin, e.g.
85 Built up gradually
86 It's skipped in the Gregorian calendar
88 Some track-and-field training
90 Propping (up)
93 Lead role in "Chicago"
94 November 13, e.g.
95 ___ school
96 Baby shark
97 "Days of Grace" memoirist Arthur
98 Corvette roof options
105 Women's rights pioneer Lucretia
106 End-of-semester stressor
107 Chapeau site
108 Bicker (with)
111 Kylo of the "Star Wars" films
114 Charlemagne's domain, for short

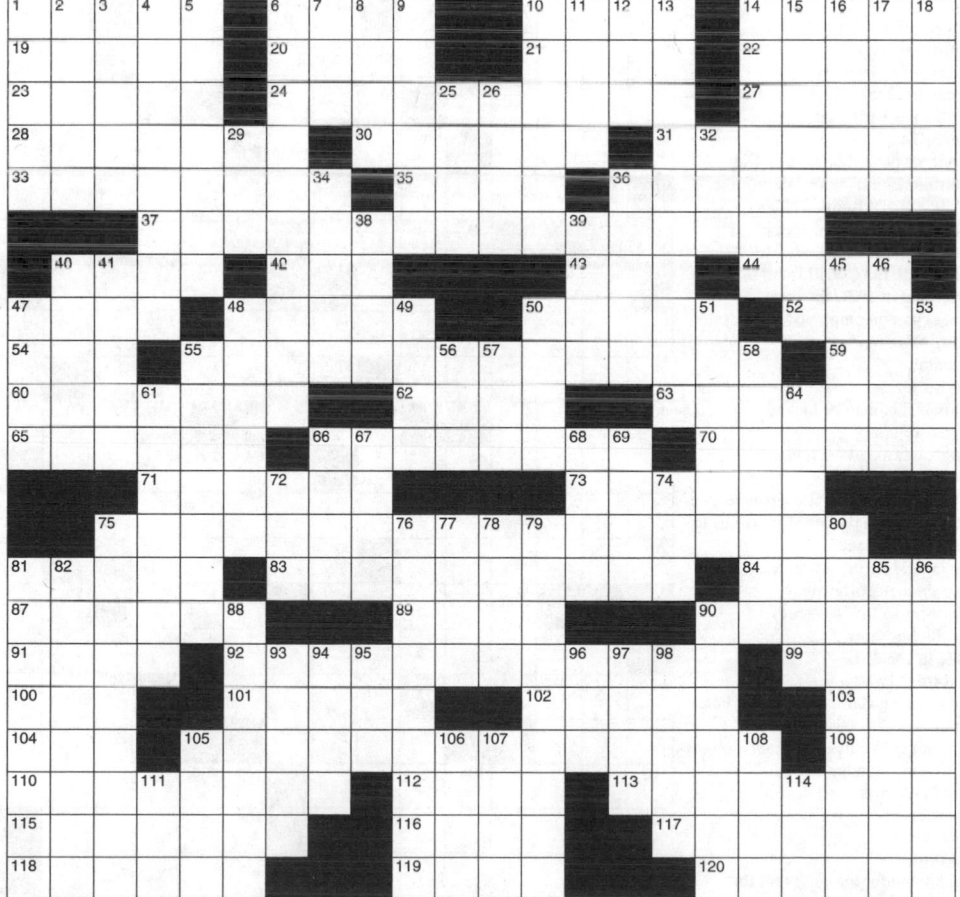

by Christopher Adams

ACROSS

1 Socializes (with)
6 With 20-Across, fire the whole staff
11 Most exorbitant
19 Showing more craft
20 See 6-Across
21 Artillery
22 With 105-Across, "What walks on four dino legs in the morning, four dino legs at noon and four dino legs in the evening?" and other riddles?
24 Genre for "Rush Hour" and "Lethal Weapon"
25 Oversupplies
26 The band Ben Folds Five, oddly
27 The "A" of BART
28 Any nonzero number to the zeroth power
29 "Little Women" sister
30 Pioneering silent director Weber
31 Bitter
33 Shopping binge
35 Says "Quack" instead of "Buzz"?
39 Like Cinderella's stepsisters
40 Like tennis player Anna Smashnova's name
41 "High-five!"
42 Melodic opera passages
45 Something a new parent might take
47 Audio engineer's device
51 Tables in an Old West saloon, e.g.?
55 "My Gal ___"
56 Admirer's words
57 Source of hand-me-downs
58 Unloading sign
60 The stuff of legends
61 Member of the Be Sharps, Homer Simpson's barbershop quartet
62 Kerfuffle
64 Olympic powerhouse in boxing
65 Confuse "stem" with "stern," e.g.
68 Claude ___, villain in "The Hunchback of Notre-Dame"
72 Some Dior dresses
74 Change to the Constitution first proposed in 1921, for short
75 Chess gambit employed by gangster Tony Montana?
78 Separate
80 Invite out for
81 Things that may be kicked
82 Verse, quaintly
84 English novelist McEwan
85 "Je t'___"
86 Claims that Louis XIV's palace is better than all the other buildings in France combined?
93 In the middle of, old-style
94 Parishioner's offering
95 Menaces to Indiana Jones
96 Really big show
98 Side in checkers
99 Not tread lightly
100 Advertising claim that usually has a catch
101 Animal with a flexible snout
102 "From my standpoint . . ."
105 See 22-Across
108 Most brave
109 Increase
110 Start to type?
111 Nickname for the capital of the Peach State
112 KFC order
113 Groups of stars

DOWN

1 Site of a 1920s renaissance
2 Relative of a guinea pig
3 Last innings, typically
4 Figures out
5 Sign of theatrical success
6 Subject of a fund-raiser
7 Thelma's road trip partner
8 Currency with a "zone"
9 Tempe sch.
10 Old game console, for short
11 Nickname
12 Aligned
13 Icelandic literary work
14 Where a tunnel opens
15 "You'll ___ for this!"
16 Extra couple of numbers?
17 Tea treats
18 Mobile home not much seen nowadays
19 Bygone N.Y.C. punk club
23 Informer
27 "___ longa, vita brevis"
30 Brings from outside with great effort
31 A in physics
32 Trig ratios
33 Pack rat
34 User of the Twitter handle @Pontifex
36 Target number
37 It's a blessing
38 Person who helps with a crash, informally
42 Large wardrobe
43 Finds hilarious, perhaps
44 Deduce
46 A doctor might check them
48 Together
49 Full-bodied Argentine wines
50 Word often said with a drawn-out "e" sound
51 Took shots
52 Single squat or crunch
53 Small goofs
54 Craft in a close encounter
59 54-Down genre
61 ___-compliant
63 Doomed to fail, for short
66 Motorcade head
67 Tender feelings
69 Debonair
70 La-la interval
71 Sierra ___
72 Friend of Athos and Porthos
73 Smear in print
76 "GoodFellas" co-star
77 Onetime fad item with replacement seeds
79 Culmination
83 Songs to be played at a concert
85 Gives the nod
86 Has because of
87 Portmanteau for a TV addict
88 Inc. relative
89 ___ to go
90 Some deals from dealerships
91 Whiz
92 Church toppers
93 Completely destroy
97 Approximately
99 Hammer part
100 Half-man/half-goat
101 "Toodle-oo!"
103 South, in Brazil
104 Texted question to someone who hasn't shown up yet
105 Automotive initialism
106 Louis XIV, e.g.
107 Key in a corner

by Will Nediger

ACROSS

1 Share on social media
5 Blackens
10 Screen org.?
13 William H. Bonney ___ Billy the Kid
16 Mathematician taught by Bernoulli
18 Most populous nation not in the U.N.
19 Best Actress winner of 1999 and 2004
22 It's just part of the act
23 Surname of Princess Leia
24 Midwest college town
25 "Curiouser and curiouser . . ."
28 Bother
29 Grand onstage
30 Place to swim or work out, informally
31 Business that has cut prices
32 Entertaining
34 Went over the limit, say
36 Major name in petrol
39 Language from which "jackal" and "jasmine" come
40 "La Traviata" composer
41 Jeer
43 Bit on a book jacket
46 Part of a three-in-a-row
47 Greasy in the Pro Football Hall of Fame
49 In-group at school
52 Preach the gospel
55 Rip off
56 Longtime "All Things Considered" host Robert
57 Screenwriter Ephron
58 Anchor, e.g.
59 Chinese liquor made from sorghum
62 "Consequently . . ."
63 Verbal alternative to a shoulder tap
65 Beginnings of ideas
66 Internet content typically viewed alone
68 Italian scooter brand
71 What 1 Down has that 1-Across lacks
73 Part of the resistance?
74 Some pickup info on rideshare apps: Abbr.
78 Stir
80 Man's name that means "my God"
81 What's depicted by the circled letters in 41-/49-Across
84 . . . in 52-Across
87 Rehearse a play from start to finish, in theater lingo
88 Swimmer in a Himeji Castle moat
89 Nursery floor hazard
90 Unfamiliar with
91 Informal "What if . . . ?"
93 Alter, as a manuscript
95 Bird's home
96 Bird's home
97 Places for speakers
98 Common people
102 Close up, say
104 Stylish ballroom dance
105 Investigation
106 . . . in 25-Across
112 Brown powder
114 French cake
115 Nashville university, familiarly
116 . . . and in 19-Across
117 Go to
118 Princess of Avalor, in children's TV
119 Machiavellian
120 Tape deck button
121 Oboes and saxes, e.g.
122 Aid for a detective

DOWN

1 Real pain
2 Reaction to pain
3 Berth place
4 Bowling
5 Cause of a supermarket parking mishap
6 Tripping
7 Expected
8 Serving with carrots and celery, maybe
9 Meander
10 Lighter-air link
11 Virtual people
12 Bitter, e.g.
13 Alternative to Times New Roman
14 Noncapital city whose name means "capital city"
15 City on the Nile
17 As (to)
18 Band with the 1983 #1 hit "Africa"
20 Far offshore
21 Kit ___
26 Dedicator of Iceland's Imagine Peace Tower
27 Ocelli
31 Challenges for movers
32 Habitually
33 ___ Nurmi, 1920s Olympic runner nicknamed the "Flying Finn"
34 Bud of baseball
35 Veep's boss
37 Subject of lessons at an island resort
38 Roman sun god
40 Team at an upscale restaurant
42 Brother
43 Cowboy's home, informally
44 Middle of the month
45 Best Play Tony winner with a geographical name
48 Jellied delicacies
50 Cry from Juliet
51 ___ club (annual show presenter)
53 Diaper, in Britspeak
54 Chef Lagasse
60 Crossword constructing, e.g. (no, really!)
61 AirPod pairing target
64 "Paradise Lost" tempter
65 Site of Jesus' crucifixion
67 Prefix with directional
68 Word with life or flak
69 Brand of markers
70 See the future with a crystal ball
72 Track meet divisions
73 Worth keeping around
75 Peacefully protests, as during the national anthem
76 Flier on a mission
77 Loses traction
79 Pristine places
82 Fairy tale alter ego
83 Crushed in competition
85 Pronoun in a picture rebus
86 Increase quickly
92 Mixing board
94 Wrongly predict, as an election
97 Dit's partner
98 Places for figureheads
99 Not express
100 Magazine that named Barack Obama its first-ever Person of the Year (2009)
101 Bit of sweat
103 "J. ___" (2011 Clint Eastwood biopic)
104 Missile first used in the Yom Kippur War
105 Non-Macs
106 Kind of mind
107 Suit
108 Number in brackets?
109 Without
110 Poet ___ St. Vincent Millay
111 Diana who was the first person to swim from Cuba to Florida without the aid of shark protection (2013)
113 Russian for "peace"

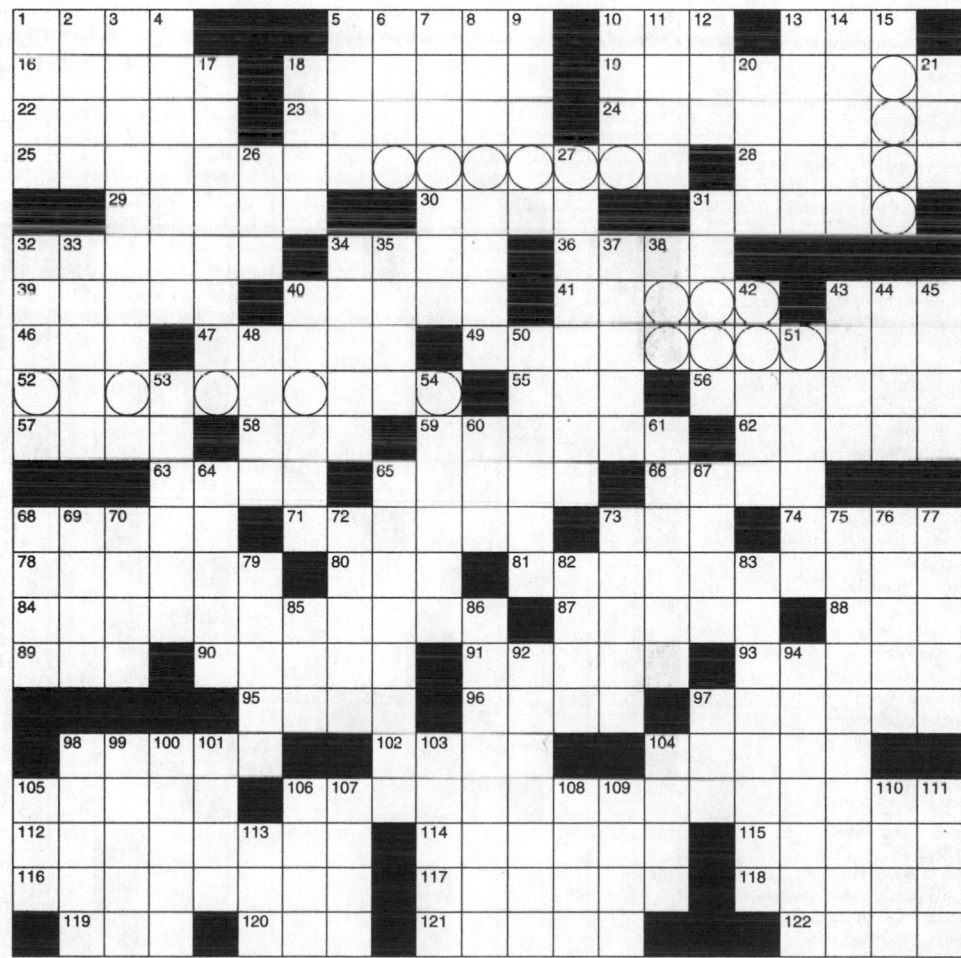

by Alex Eaton-Salners

ACROSS

1 Passes along, as a present
8 What 13-Down means in poker
14 Book in a mosque
19 Antarctic mass
21 Major British tabloid
22 Yogurt container words
23 Celebratory Native American feast
24 Drives around awhile . . . as suggested by this puzzle's shaded squares?
26 If's counterpart, in programming
27 "S.N.L." alum Cheri
29 Military alert system
30 Sow's home
31 Small criticism
32 Baa-dly needing a haircut?
34 "Today" co-host Hoda
36 Challenges for infielders
38 "De-e-e-eluxe!"
41 Cherry brandy
45 Certain rideshares
47 Deposit box?
48 Morning hour
51 Many a Stan Lee film role
52 Capital NE of Casablanca
53 Idris of "The Dark Tower"
55 Ones or tens place
56 0 0 0
57 Wafer brand
58 Hockey shot sound
59 Shots in the dark
61 Beginning of the Joint Army/Navy Phonetic Alphabet
62 Camera type, for short
63 Very funny person
65 Extremely cold
67 River through Pakistan
69 Sea creatures that may employ camouflage when hunting
71 Blood type system
72 Ones generating buzz in the music world?
74 Play at full volume
75 Super ___ (game series)
77 Help with a job
78 Wrath
81 Eco-friendly car introduced in 2011
82 Something the nose knows
84 ___ Pictures
86 First name on the Supreme Court
88 Quits a program
90 Dennis the Menace, e.g.
91 Burnt barbecue bits
92 Shooting stars, some think
93 Kind of salami
94 Pool components
96 Type units
97 Like going all in, maybe
98 Diamond pattern
100 Slowly, musically
102 Some are liberal
103 Meyers of late-night
105 Producer of brown eggs
107 Black ___
110 Arborist's tool
113 Laid, as a claim
117 "Spider-Man" director
118 Hit hard
119 1965 #1 Byrds hit . . . as suggested by this puzzle's shaded squares?
122 Australia's smallest state
124 Upstate New York city
125 Topic of Article I, Section 3 of the Constitution
126 Up-and-coming
127 Wrinkle treatment
128 Shaman, for one
129 Newspaper sections that often fall out

DOWN

1 Age
2 Romaine concern
3 Kicks things off
4 Land in the water
5 Mortgage org.
6 Mountains just south of Yellowstone
7 The Quakers and others
8 Celebrity socialite
9 Comedian Margaret
10 Mind
11 "___ quam videri," state motto of North Carolina
12 Strike on the head
13 See 8-Across
14 Home of the Marine Corps University
15 ___ Constitution
16 Individual curls, say
17 Slightly
18 It contains M.S.G.: Abbr.
20 1973 play featuring a sign with a burned-out "E"
25 Part of a king's guard
28 It charges to do some cleaning
32 Arrogant newcomers
33 Rebellion leader Turner
35 Swagger
37 Freud's first stage
39 Plays hard after working hard
40 Baker with the 1986 hit "Sweet Love"
42 Baker or dry cleaner, maybe
43 They multiply by dividing
44 Garden item that sounds like the plural of another garden item
45 Dispensers at banquets
46 Help (out)
47 Author of "The Lion, the Bear and the Fox"
49 Full of empty talk
50 Royals' org.
54 Teleported, in the Harry Potter books
60 Drop-down menu in online shopping
64 I as in Icarus
66 Something you might take a bow for in the theater?
68 Unapologetic
70 Squeaky mice, e.g.
73 Chasm
74 Jabber?
76 Whirlpool subsidiary since 2006
79 Place to lace up
80 "It's a snap!"
81 Summer Triangle star
83 The Notorious ___
85 Six Nations tribe
87 Leave off, as the last word of a
89 Line just above a total, say
95 Squid's ink holder
99 Latin rebuke
101 Accumulate
102 Up
104 Like a zero-star review
106 Savory taste
108 Coat that's hard to take off
109 Sports page fodder
110 Paycheck go-with
111 A plane might be flown on it
112 Judicial order
114 Pad site
115 ___ Rosso (Sicilian wine)
116 Kind of citizenship
118 Kind of tea
120 Cpl. or sgt.
121 Fwy., e.g.
123 Virginia Woolf's "___ Dalloway"

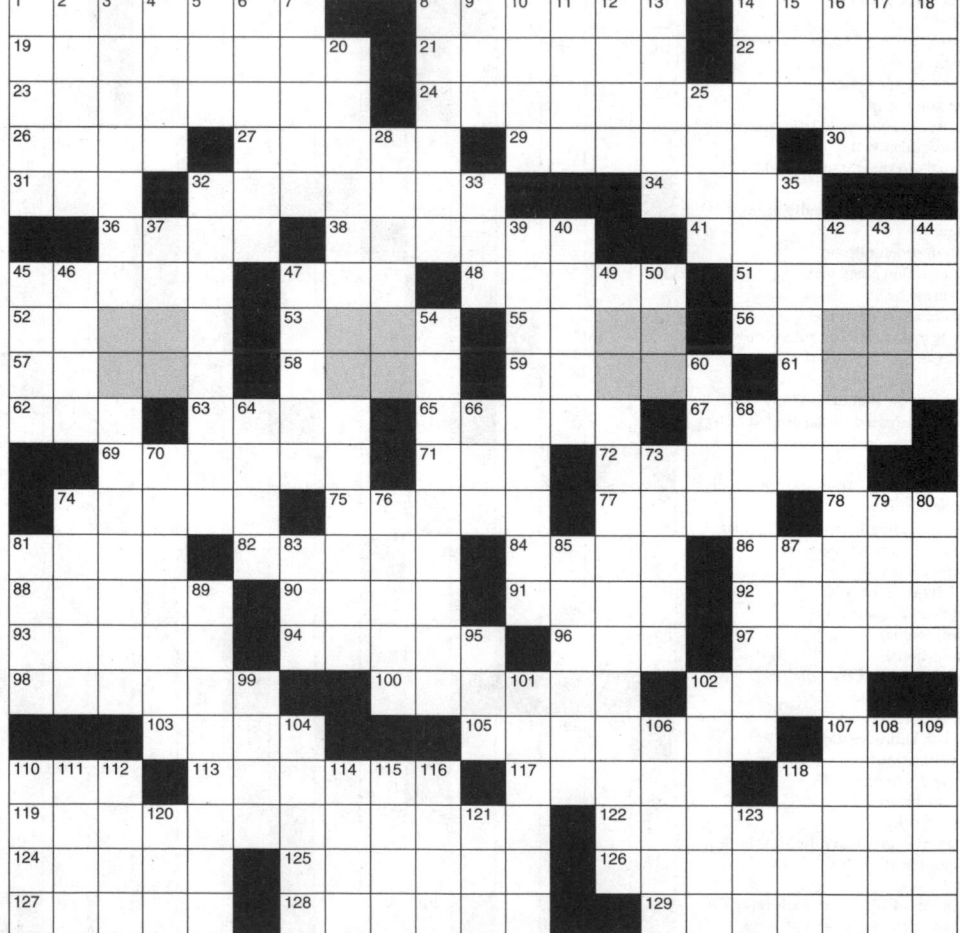

by David Steinberg

ACROSS

1 Literally, "commander"
5 Sights at Zion National Park
10 Didn't sink, say
14 Miles away
18 Where to find big bucks?
20 Jack who co-starred with Charlie Chaplin in "The Great Dictator"
21 Tepid greeting
22 Title film villain whose first name is Julius
23 When you can ice skate outside?
25 Poker player in the Old West after being caught with a card up his sleeve?
27 Checks' counterparts
28 Lamb offering
30 "Whew baby!"
31 "The Wizard of Oz" co-star
32 "Let's shake on it"
33 Edwin with the 1970 #1 hit "War"
34 Fling
37 Not for
39 Language in which "dd" and "ff" are treated as single letters of the alphabet
42 Interprets
45 ___ glance
46 Like the motion of the ocean
47 Curse
49 One going for big bucks?
50 Bad pun?
53 French greeting
54 Pea picker-upper
55 ___ bottle (topological curiosity)
56 Site of one of the 12 labors of Hercules
58 Manual part of an early printing press?
60 Cellar problem
62 Work with planes, maybe
64 Typically
65 "Westworld" airer
66 "The ___ of Christ" (classic work in Florence's Uffizi Gallery)
68 Dull-witted sloth in "Ice Age"
69 Profession since the Bronze Age
72 Leo, for example
73 Jerry, to Tom, in cartoons
77 Need for parents who weren't expecting twins?
79 One-named singer with the catchphrase "cuchi-cuchi"
81 Like some riyals
82 Barristers' wear
83 Surfer wannabe
85 Rookeries?
87 Singer Grande, to fans
88 Portuguese wine
90 "___, Macduff" (phrase from Shakespeare)
91 Consumes
92 City that becomes another city if you change both its vowels to A's
94 Perfume part
95 Japanese noodle
96 Suspiciously flattering, say
97 Emulated an Argonaut
99 "Stat"
101 Red letters?
103 Like a sonnet, in a way
105 Chronicler of Troy
107 Emmy-nominated actor for "Westworld"
111 Toothpaste aisle?
113 Illusionist's phrase illustrated by seven Across answers in this puzzle?
115 Informal negation
116 Pout
117 Wan
118 Famed orange troublemaker
119 D.C. nine
120 Brings up, say
121 ___ of all
122 Location of Cassius, who "has a lean and hungry look"

DOWN

1 Steed for a sheik
2 "___ Lisa"
3 Rustic poem
4 Bad news from Detroit
5 Queen Margrethe II, e.g.?
6 Din-din
7 It's après "après"
8 Grammy-winning songwriter Mann
9 School boards?
10 Many a mixer
11 Fare for Little Miss Muffet
12 Nice crossword experience
13 Thick (of)
14 Stick
15 Arrangement in which you buy three tires but get a whole set?
16 Anecdotal collections
17 Retirement account option, informally
19 "Game of Thrones" actress Chaplin
24 Foreign-language toast
26 Astrologist's reference
29 Tons
32 Pickle
33 "Dunno" gestures
34 Warmongers
35 Of use
36 Mumbai royal
38 Opinion, informally
40 Ballerina's cabriole, e.g.
41 Peace, in the Mideast
43 Poet who wrote "To His Mistress Going to Bed"
44 Run for, as office
46 Not ridiculous, as an argument
48 Order before "Fall out!"
51 0 0 0
52 Gleans
54 P.M. who took office in 2015
57 Brain area, jocularly
59 Ivy League newspaper name
61 Trick question
63 It's hard to hit
66 Big-circulation magazine originally titled So You're Going to Be Married
67 Get all tangled
69 Feature destroyed in the 2019 Notre Dame fire
70 Visit to baby Jesus?
71 Gradually diminished
73 Illusionist's phrase illustrated by three Down answers in this puzzle?
74 ___ bar
75 Perfect
76 Actress Spacek
77 Big smack
78 Lure
80 Pike
84 An alarm may interrupt it
86 Where Tokyo is
88 Scout's honor
89 Perennial London football powerhouse
93 Some inexpensive brews
96 Model of the solar system
98 PayPal money and the like
100 Stood
102 Onetime MS. accompanier
103 Volunteer's words
104 Donizetti's "Pour mon âme," e.g.
105 Lead
106 Symbols of might
107 Blinkers
108 Major city bisected by I-80
109 Opposite of "Too rich for my blood"
110 Farmer's purchase
112 French way
114 "Huh?"

by Matt Ginsberg

ACROSS

1 Volcanic residue
4 Iraqi, e.g.
8 Not working today
11 Top of the Alps?
17 Singer with the 2016 No. 1 hit "Cheap Thrills"
18 Ancient Iranian
19 Something dogs may pull
20 Only musical to win Best Picture since "Oliver!" in 1968
21 Early encyclopedist credited with coining "Home is where the heart is"
24 Adjusts, as an instrument
25 Reference aids for artists
26 Children's author Lowry
27 Nonkosher sammie
28 Tested
29 Phrase followed by "one two, one two"
32 English channel, with "the"
33 ___ Min Lee, victim in the podcast "Serial"
34 Archipelago nation in the Indian Ocean
35 Stage before pupa
36 Gchat transmissions, briefly
39 Accident-investigating org.
41 Big dealer in outdoor gear
42 Suggestion for a reading circle, informally
44 Fruit with a pit
46 Seek revenge on, in a way
47 Is a straight shooter
49 Some printer hues
51 Word after meal or before school
53 Put forward as a basis of argument
54 Takedown pieces, slangily
56 Charge (through)
58 Dryer residue
59 Dog sound
63 Sunbather in the tropics
64 Sources of weekly N.C.A.A. rankings
66 Looked at lasciviously
68 Work with feet?
69 Pretzel topping
71 Modern cousin of "Yay!"
72 Fear-inducing
73 Spanish phrase meaning "Enough is enough!"
76 "Pencils down!"
78 Huge mix-up
79 Soft-rock singer who received Kennedy Center Honors in 2016
82 Philanthropist Broad
84 Salacious stuff
85 Anonymous female, in court
86 Nurse in a bar
87 Train between N.Y.C. and Montauk
89 Crafty
90 Kind of acid
91 Inherited
94 Muffin ingredient
96 It's rigged
97 Protein in Wheaties
99 Bygone car model that's an anagram of GRANITE
103 Part of a diner display
104 It brings you closer to your subjects
105 "The 40-Year-Old Virgin" and "Knocked Up"
107 Mythical hunter turned into a stag
109 State bordering the Pacific
111 Establishment such as Crumbs and Whiskers or KitTea (both real!)
112 Avian diver
113 Not much
114 Conventional sort
115 Gets ready to pray
116 National Pizza Mo.
117 !
118 Future Ph.D.'s test

DOWN

1 Grp. with a pet project?
2 Buildings often outfitted with ladders
3 Lauds
4 Oscar nominee for "Gone Baby Gone," 2007
5 Measure of virality
6 Ritalin target, for short
7 It's full of hard-to-spell words
8 What a bitter person might try to settle
9 Retainer
10 Prez with the dog Fala
11 4-Across chief
12 All-in-one boxes
13 R.N.'s place
14 Foreign capital designed by two Americans
15 9+ for a game, e.g.
16 Program starting with the fifth year of college, informally
19 Like 100–1 odds
20 Popular gardening shoe
22 Early vintner, in the Bible
23 Music genre associated with the goth look
26 Baudelaire's "___ Fleurs du Mal"
30 Inch along
31 The common folk
32 Picnic side dish
34 Trucker with a transmitter
35 Stuff of legends
36 Futuristic tracking device
37 "Are we done here?," politely
38 Bust, maybe
40 Dines
42 Recycling ___
43 River mammal
45 Flow of one line of a verse to the next without pause
47 Music genre from Asia
48 Term of address from one girlfriend to another
50 IV, to III, e.g.
52 { }
55 Player of many an opera villain
57 Stun
60 Family name on a 1960s sitcom
61 Sorry
62 Bygone military punishment
64 ___ king
65 Fantasy series that inspired "Game of Thrones," briefly
67 What the thumbs-up emoji can mean
70 Took a course?
72 Kosher ___
74 Sleekly designed
75 Flared dress type
77 Spice Girl also known as Sporty Spice
79 Bob Marley, for one
80 Liqueur often mixed with water
81 Vacancy
83 One of the Avengers
85 Fill to absolute capacity
88 For all to see, in a way
91 Koala's tree
92 Marketing tactic
93 Australian band with the 1988 No. 1 hit "Need You Tonight"
95 "Ideas worth spreading" offshoot
97 Mistakes
98 Singular
99 Speck
100 Cleaning for military inspection
101 Happen again
102 In lockstep
104 Fervor
106 Lyft alternative
108 Nickname for a buddy
109 Bronx-born singer, familiarly
110 Bronx-born congresswoman, familiarly

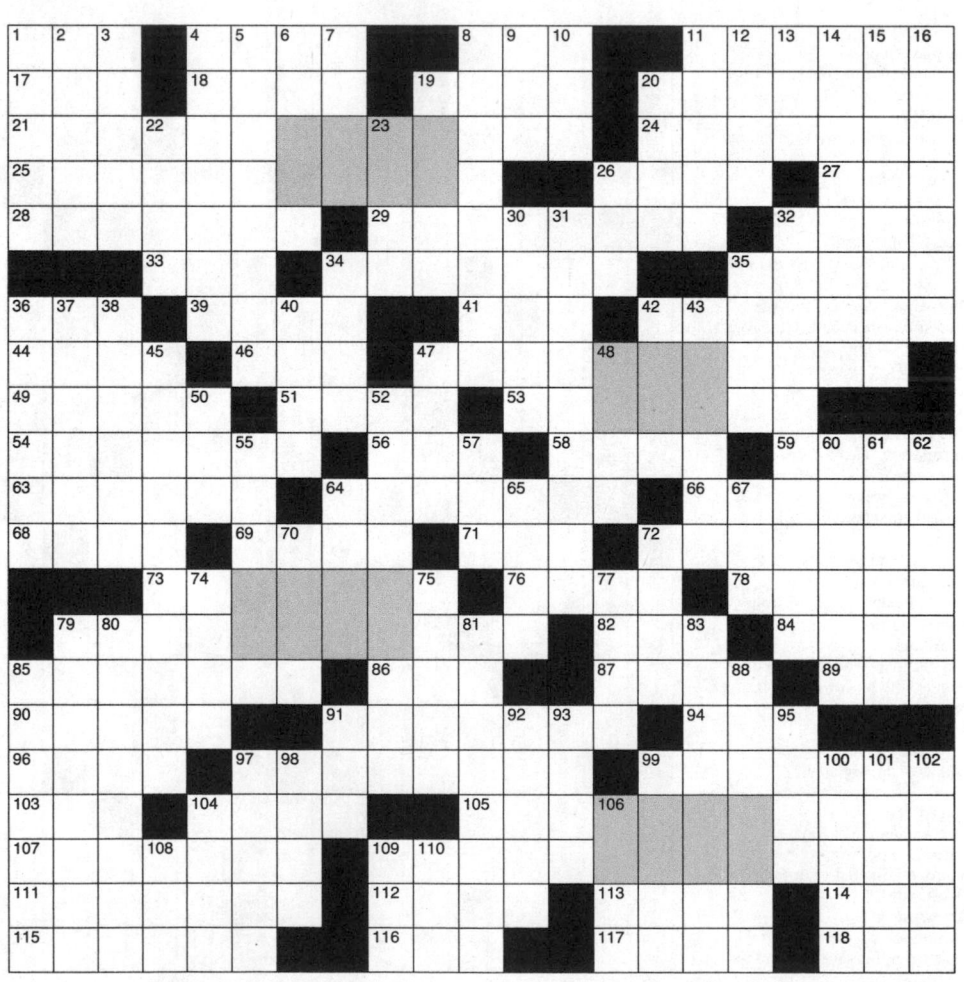

by Finn Vigeland

ACROSS

1 Well, for one
7 Longhair cats
14 For instance
20 Alternative to Martha Stewart Weddings
21 Caribbean island nation
22 Take in
23 . . . the guy who vows to take his Stetson to the grave
25 Baby Gap purchase
26 Famous conjoined twin
27 Figures
28 California's Big ___
29 TV's "___ Ruins Everything"
30 Lose control on the road
32 IV checkers
33 . . . the fraternity guy who wants to be a cardiologist
39 Levelheaded
40 Kind of furniture
42 Triumphant cry
43 Game lover's purchase
45 First word of "Jabberwocky"
47 Dated PC hookup
49 J. Carrol ___ (two-time 1940s Oscar nominee)
50 Traffic-stopping grp.?
51 . . . the guy who barely shows he's exasperated
56 . . . the guy who always shows up unannounced
58 Hugs, in a letter
59 Home of minor-league baseball's Aces
60 California's Santa ___ Mountains
62 Puts on TV
63 Show that NBC 62-Across, for short
64 Heaps
66 They follow springs by about a week
69 Sylvia of jazz
70 . . . the gal who delivered the greatest put-down ever
73 Small prevarications
76 Helicopter sounds
77 Permanent spot?
78 UPS unit: Abbr.
81 "Othello" provocateur
82 "Lethal Weapon" force, in brief
84 Prison division
85 "Well, well, well, whaddya know"
86 . . . the guy who takes aerial photos for the military
91 . . . the gal who loses it when pass plays are called
94 CPR teacher, maybe
95 Temporarily sated, with "over"
97 Critical campaign mo.
98 Source of some pressure
99 Place for trophies
100 Declaration
102 Singer with the 2009 #1 hit "TiK ToK"
106 Move a bit
108 . . . the gal who spends all day at the hairdresser
111 Rollaway
112 Word with club or cream
113 Aristocratic Italian name of old
114 Cartoonist Keane
115 Dance that might include a chair
117 West Coast summer setting: Abbr.
118 Dag Hammarskjöld's successor at the U.N.
121 . . . the guy who can't stop bragging about Bragg
125 Bit of trail mix
126 Underlining alternative
127 Creeped out?
128 Almost up
129 Exams given intradermally, for short
130 Actress Taylor of "Bones"

DOWN

1 Number one nun
2 Prolonged period of excessive imbibing
3 Soft blanket material
4 Ice cream eponym
5 Part of AARP: Abbr.
6 Note that sounds like an order to get with it?
7 Appalled
8 Big D.C. lobby
9 1995 crime film based on an Elmore Leonard novel
10 At the perfect time
11 Enthusiastic
12 Commercial suffix with Gator
13 Gained a lap?
14 ___ Paulo
15 Bit of art pottery
16 Staircase sound
17 "Star Trek" catchphrase said by Dr. McCoy
18 Far Eastern fruits that resemble apples
19 What a prefix or suffix gets added to
24 Sicily's Mount ___
31 Honey substitute?
34 Appear in print
35 Mouth, slangily
36 Con ___ (briskly, in music)
37 Talk like a tough, say
38 "Well, howdy"
41 Dieter's "I"
44 Picks up the bill
46 Unlikely handouts with beers
48 Court V.I.P.
51 Sea plea
52 Period of group activity, slangily
53 Addition to the family
54 Doth depart
55 Diamond brackets?
57 Dissenting vote
61 Swerves back
65 Cry like a baby
67 Large shrimp
68 See 72-Down
69 Parody
71 Pride Parade participants may be in it
72 With 68-Down, summer side dish
73 Shade for a field worker?
74 "Drawin' a blank here"
75 ___ vivant
78 Gambler's exclamation
79 Father of Enigma in DC Comics
80 Creamy beverage
81 Tagged, informally
83 Pitcher who famously claimed he was on LSD while throwing a no-hitter (1970)
87 And others, for short
88 Kind of bar
89 Renuzit target
90 It can be old or breaking
92 Sport ___
93 "Ocean's Twelve" role
96 ___ Terr., 1861–89
101 Maze explorer
103 Go downhill in a hurry
104 Part of a parka
105 Relaxing
107 High-grade
109 Auto dealer's offer
110 Auto owner's proof
113 Tip of Italy?
116 Field
119 Shoot down
120 Wile E. Coyote purchase
121 In good shape
122 Gambling parlor letters
123 Take steps
124 Sort of person who's blue: Abbr.

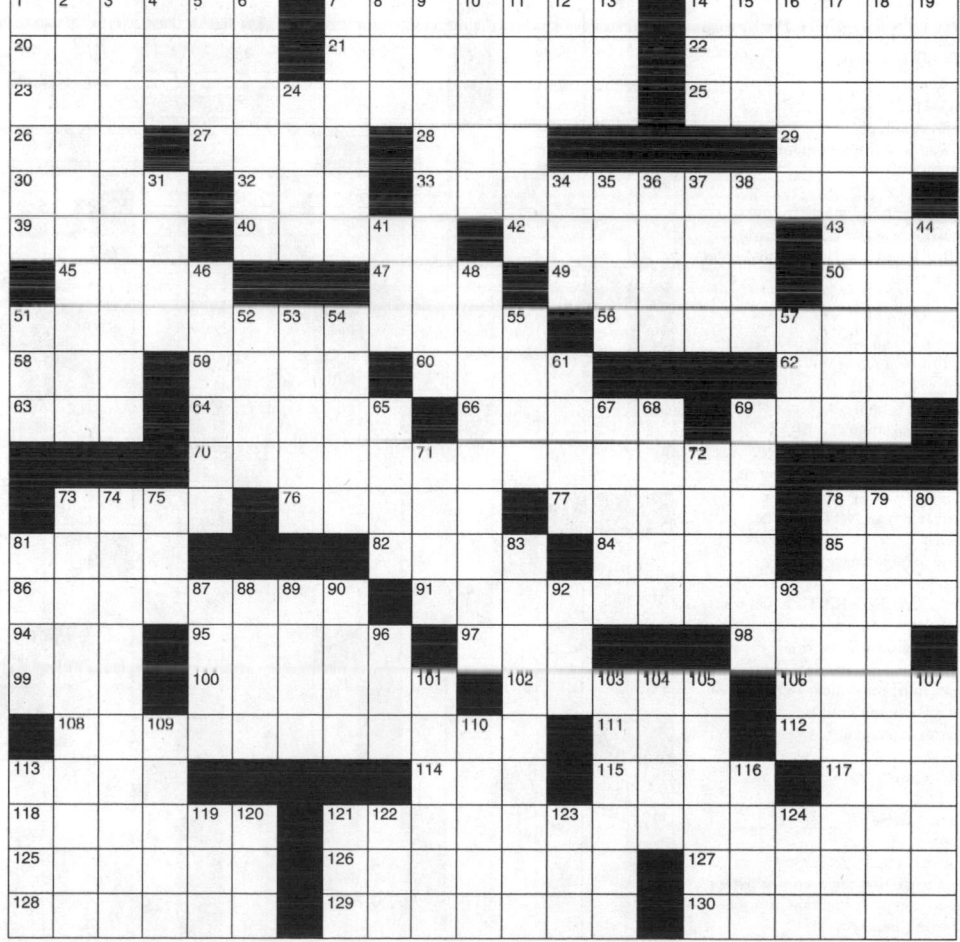

by Joe DiPietro

ACROSS

1 Cookbook amt.
5 "Careful where you watch this," in emails
9 Wonder Woman foe
13 Canned brand
17 "The ___ U Give" (2018 film)
18 Pro Football Hall of Fame locale
19 Sugar serving
20 Claimed
21 Pound who wrote "Literature is news that stays news"
22 Piece of cake?
23 Prop for a belly dancer
24 "As I Lay Dying" father
25 Something big in 1950s autodom
27 ___ Lane, home of the Muffin Man
31 Marine mollusks that cling to rocks
33 Symbol of strength
34 666, perhaps
36 Mimic
37 Yahoo!, but not "Yahoo!"
38 Trig calculation
39 It's a first
41 F.D.R.'s job-creating agcy.
42 Film monster originally intended as a metaphor for nuclear weapons
44 Zip
45 "Way to go, team!"
48 Fashion brand with a rhinoceros logo
49 Feature of many a state flag
50 Acclaimed 2017 biography subtitled "The Man, the Dictator, and the Master of Terror"
51 Childish comeback
53 Diplomacy
55 Called for
56 Major accidents
58 Taiwanese computer giant
59 ___ bull
61 Hoodwinks
63 "King Kong" co-star
64 Quattroporte and GranTurismo
66 Ballpark with the Home Run Apple
68 Are loath to
70 Issued
71 1980s TV ET
74 Emperor who, in actuality, played the lyre, not the violin
75 Suffix in Suffolk
77 Lady Vols' home: Abbr.
78 Sound investment?
81 Let the air out?
83 Posted warning near mountains
86 Lead-in to bargain or deal
87 Actress Foy of Netflix's "The Crown"
90 Notable Nixon gesture
91 Guzzles
93 Fort ___ (where Billy the Kid was killed)
94 More streaked, as marble
96 Principles
97 Eight things that most spiders have
98 Barack Obama's mother
99 Lacto-___-vegetarian
100 Black
101 Hole number
103 Vaulted
105 It's bedazzling
107 Stopper, of a sort
110 N.A.A.C.P. ___ Award
112 It's a tragedy when seen in close-up but a comedy in the long shot, per Charlie Chaplin
114 Co-star of 2011's "Bridesmaids"
115 Home of the Herald
117 Memo taker
118 Flanged fastener
119 Promgoer's concern, maybe
120 John of "The Addams Family"
121 Ring bearers?
122 It's not a good look
123 Handbook info, for short
124 Doctors' orders

DOWN

1 Upstart's goal
2 Istanbul's Grand ___
3 Perfect places for bowlers to aim?
4 Ring
5 Comment when you need a serious comeback at the end of a bowling game?
6 What a slug may leave behind?
7 Bygone cry of outrage
8 "You got that right!"
9 ___ Singer ("Annie Hall" protagonist)
10 French way
11 Estevez of "The Breakfast Club"
12 Whether to aim at 7 or 10, in bowling?
13 "Chop-chop!"
14 Disappointing news for a bowler?
15 Colt, maybe
16 City in Texas or Ukraine
26 Forces (upon)
28 Short end of the stick
29 Raising
30 Prepared
32 Smoky agave spirit
35 Big advertising catchword
37 Police rank: Abbr.
40 Like some poetry
43 "You didn't fool me!"
46 Geographical anagram of ASLOPE
47 Bring on
49 Material found in countertops
52 Birthstone of some Scorpios
53 Close kin, casually
54 Lotus-___ (figures in the "Odyssey")
56 Stroked
57 Code for the busiest airport in Australia
60 ___ blanc
62 Niña companion
65 Projected, as a film
67 First word across in the world's first crossword (1913)
69 Relates
70 Director Leone of spaghetti westerns
71 Pre-K group?
72 Knockout
73 Pace at which bowlers complete their games?
76 "Wheel of Fortune" option
78 Hip bowling enthusiasts?
79 Go from one state to another?
80 "Family Feud" option
82 Like some car air fresheners
84 Action-packed
85 What people who agree speak with
86 Like breast cancer awareness ribbons
88 Three-___ (long movies, once)
89 Highland language
91 Mix up
92 Changed like Ophelia in "Hamlet"
94 Modern activity banned in most high schools
95 Rodeo activity
101 Ben & Jerry's buy
102 Beloved: Lat.
104 Adele, voicewise
106 Quite a long time
108 Friendly femme
109 Bowlers' targets . . . 10 of which can be found appropriately arranged in this puzzle
111 "Gosh!"
113 When Bastille Day occurs
114 Major operation?
116 Prefix with -morphic

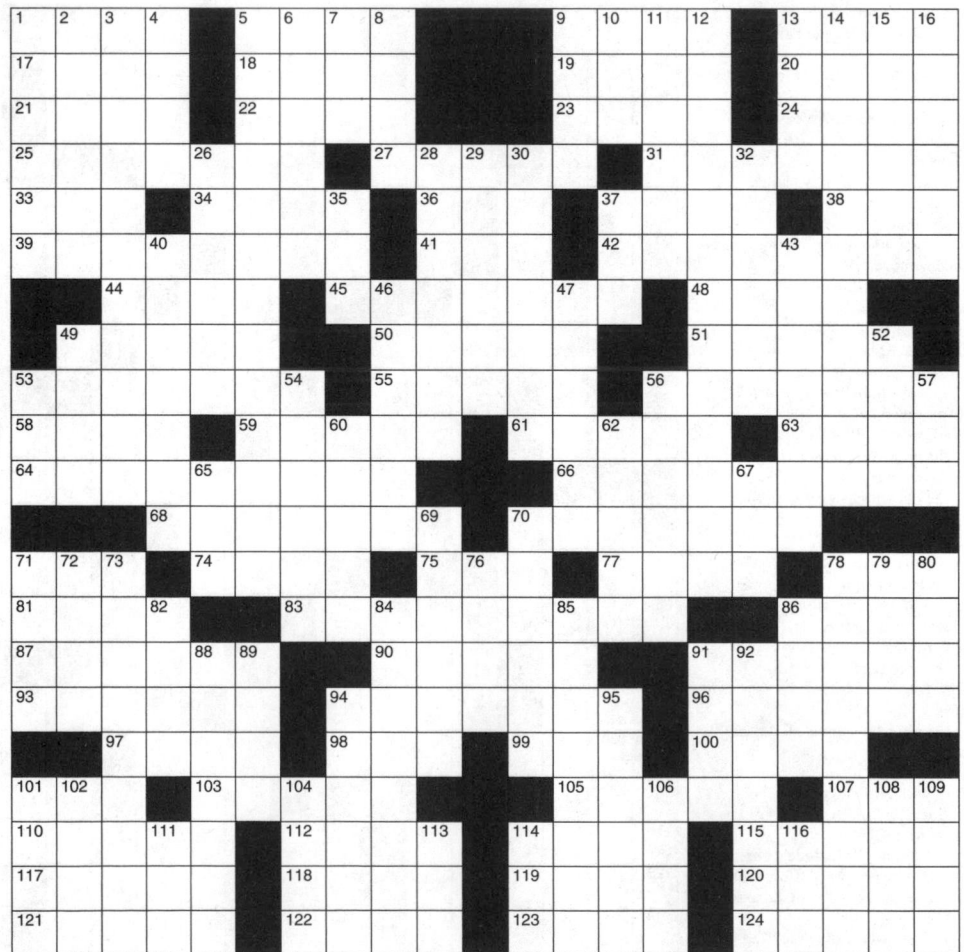

by Andrew Kingsley

ACROSS

1 Large decorative letter at the start of a chapter
8 Wood for crafts and rafts
13 Rapper Azalea with the 2014 hit "Fancy"
17 Farm stat
18 Weep for
19 Competitors in a classic advertising "war"
21 Salon bed acquisition, perhaps
22 Give a nudge
23 Discarded computers and such
25 Maintain the impression of well-being
28 [Grrr!]
29 General on Chinese menus
32 Put in order, in a way
33 Online instigator
35 "___ minute" ("Be patient")
36 Ancient region of Asia Minor
38 Lopes of R&B's TLC
39 Reconciled, as a couple
41 Ab-targeting exercise equipment
43 To the point
45 ___ Chex (old breakfast cereal)
46 With 12-Down, "Isle of Dogs" director
47 Work at a music school
49 When doubled, band with the 1984 #1 hit "The Reflex"
51 MGM rival of the '30s
53 Money handler on a ship
55 Amber, originally
56 Miniature spring bouquet
60 Pummel with snowballs, say
61 Roulette choice
63 "I believe," in Latin
65 Something that comes with a sock
66 Screen-minimizing key
67 Method for identifying mystery callers
70 M.L.B. stat
71 Downed
72 O'Connor's Supreme Court successor
73 Futuristic deliverer of packages
74 Flank or shank
75 Athlete's knee injury, familiarly
77 Bitter fruits
79 —
82 Material for classic hockey sticks
83 Bouquet offerers, maybe
84 Deep distress
85 Article in Paris Match
87 Animal mimic?
89 Response to "Who's there?"
91 Some cheesecake photos
95 Accelerated alternative to broadband
98 "Poppycock!"
100 Rainwater diverters
101 Diez menos nueve
102 "Au contraire!"
103 Hairstyling icon Vidal
105 What it is to kill a mockingbird, in "To Kill a Mockingbird"
106 "I feel the same way!"
108 Voltage-increasing electrical device
111 Animal mimic?
113 Ask too much
114 Brand in the dessert aisle
118 Character in "Grease" who sings "There Are Worse Things I Could Do"
119 Like many measuring cups and spoons
120 Doctor Doom and Galactus, to the Fantastic Four
121 Homer, for one
122 "Yecch!"
123 Puts to rest, as rumors

DOWN

1 2010s dance move involving dipping the head to the elbow
2 Inits. on 30 Rockefeller Plaza until 1988
3 Surgery sites, for short
4 Christmas Eve no-no
5 Large waterfalls
6 Slack-jawed
7 Distant correspondent
8 Oktoberfest locales
9 Mideast capital once known as Philadelphia
10 Tender ender?
11 Holy, in Latin phrases
12 See 46-Across
13 Treat to reduce swelling
14 Run amok
15 Flamboyant rock genre
16 Woman's name that's one letter off from a fragrant flower
18 Prepare, as pot roast
20 Roadside produce sellers
24 Cheese with a red covering
26 Top-drawer
27 Sammy with 609 career home runs
29 Bard's contraction
30 Cry a river
31 A quarter to four?
34 Ignore for the time being
37 Like xenon or neon
39 Popular moisturizing lotion
40 Subj. of Article 86 of the Uniform Code of Military Justice
42 Paint choice
44 Solved
48 Foe of Austin Powers
50 Dried chili peppers
52 ___-Aid
53 Tagliatelle topper
54 Reason for some bellyaching?
55 Got up again
56 Outer layer
57 Weapons that are about 3½ feet long
58 Five books of Moses
59 Whack
60 Fuel common in Scotland
62 Doc at a clinic
64 Red-headed friend of Harry Potter
67 Losing Super Bowl LIII team
68 Former leader of the Sinaloa drug cartel
69 Door openers for journalists
74 Family name?
76 "A bit of talcum / Is always walcum" writer
78 Set (down)
80 Chill in the air
81 Host of the Oscars, Grammys and Emmys
83 Apiarist's hazard
84 Oil painter's primer
85 One-dimensional
86 Act of self-aggrandizement
88 They might get collared
90 Like a jammed printer
92 KOA visitors
93 Waipahu wreath
94 Form 1099 fig.
95 Distinctive part of a zebu
96 Kind of button
97 Feature of many a Cape Cod house
99 Played (around)
103 Little brats
104 Muscat citizen
107 Pasta also called risoni
109 Lhasa ___ (dog)
110 Aid for getting a boat in the water
112 Little 'un
115 Many an alibi
116 This may shock you
117 It's twice twisted

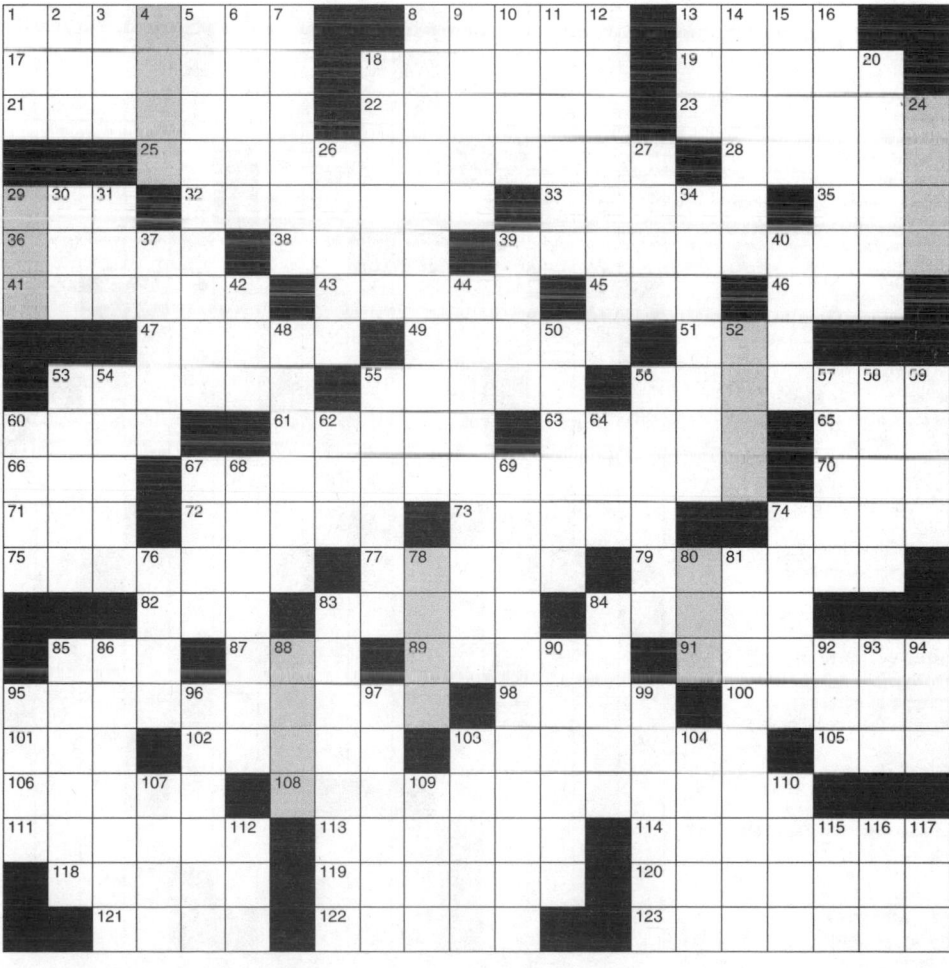

by Tracy Gray

18 NOW WEIGHT JUST A SECOND

ACROSS

1 Short strokes
6 Myriad
10 Habit
14 Pieces of work?
18 End of oyster season
19 Roof part
20 "___ Burr, Sir" ("Hamilton" song)
21 Vault
22 Cruise that specializes in baked alaska, e.g.?
25 Bona ___
26 Kim to Kourtney, or Kourtney to Khloé
27 Alma mater of George Orwell and Henry Fielding
28 Friend ___ friend
29 Quickly go through the seasons, say
30 Tiffany lampshade, e.g.
33 Like ambitious scientists?
37 Basic skate trick
38 "Yikes!"
40 Brewing one's morning coffee, e.g.
41 Verano, across the Pyrénées
42 Art ___
45 Cause of a shocking Amazon charge?
47 ___-V ("paste" on a PC)
48 Go wrong
49 How everyone on this floor is feeling?
55 Lead-in to -ville in children's literature
56 Beer, slangily
57 Trim, with "down"
58 Protected, as feet
59 "I saw ___ duck" (classic ambiguous sentence)
60 Long hikes
62 Refuse to admit
64 "My word!"
68 "Our lab studies regular dance moves rather than high-kicking"?
74 Architect Lin
75 Bankroll
76 Fire man?
77 "I see it now"
78 Lean
82 Garden plots
84 Indian title
85 The second "p" in p.p.m.
86 Summary of an easy negotiation?
91 Musician Brian
92 Option in an Edit menu
93 Loire filler
94 Coin in the Potterverse
95 Branch
96 Central region of the Roman Empire
99 Last in a series, perhaps
101 Terse summons
105 What a truck driver puts on before a date?
108 Massive weapon of sci-fi
111 The Oligocene, e.g., in geology
112 Big Apple airport code
113 Several of them could be used in a row
114 Dear
115 "___ nobis pacem" ("Grant us peace": Lat.)
116 The main food served at Walden Pond?
122 End ___
123 Alnico or chromel
124 ___ Minor
125 5×5 crosswords, e.g.
126 Pops up in France?
127 Co. heads
128 Rough amts.
129 Seize (from)

DOWN

1 What one does not do when sent to jail
2 Kind of battle
3 Like some customs
4 Word of advice
5 ___-mo
6 Quarrel
7 Capital of Punjab
8 State of stability
9 Tie the knot
10 Flavoring for snack peas
11 Galena, e.g.
12 ". . . ___ a lender be"
13 Purchase for Wile E. Coyote
14 Diminutive
15 Package deliverers of the present day?
16 Fancy gizmos
17 75+ person?
20 Regarding
23 Not many
24 The Phanerozoic, e.g., in geology
29 Words on an invoice
31 Faction
32 Apparently does
34 Mark indelibly
35 Old strings
36 Habitat for a mallow
39 Not go bad
43 & 44 Judge's mandate
46 Imperfect cube
49 Angle symbol in geometry
50 Having a long face, say
51 Request from
52 Fuss
53 Rough housing
54 Comics character often kicked off a table
55 Impulse
61 Diver's accouterments
63 Thirst (for)
65 Hogwarts potions professor
66 Was sore
67 MIX, for one
69 Voice role for Beyoncé in 2019's "The Lion King"
70 Had down
71 Serving at a pancake house
72 French dialect
73 Hastily
79 Shout from a lottery winner
80 Look after
81 ___ pool
83 Check out
86 Resting
87 One without a title
88 Do a star turn
89 "Great" place to be
90 GPS suggestions: Abbr.
91 Became less severe
97 Some brick houses
98 On the warpath
100 Leader in yellow journalism and an inspiration for "Citizen Kane"
102 Simple hydrocarbon
103 Native New Zealanders
104 ___ Rutherford, a.k.a. the Father of Nuclear Physics
106 Words to a dejected friend
107 Down
109 Domains
110 Airport grp.
116 The banker in the Beatles' "Penny Lane" never wears one in the pouring rain (very strange!)
117 Middle-earth quaff
118 Eponymous 2001 #1 album
119 Shade
120 Coal industry org.
121 Tree that starts fires?

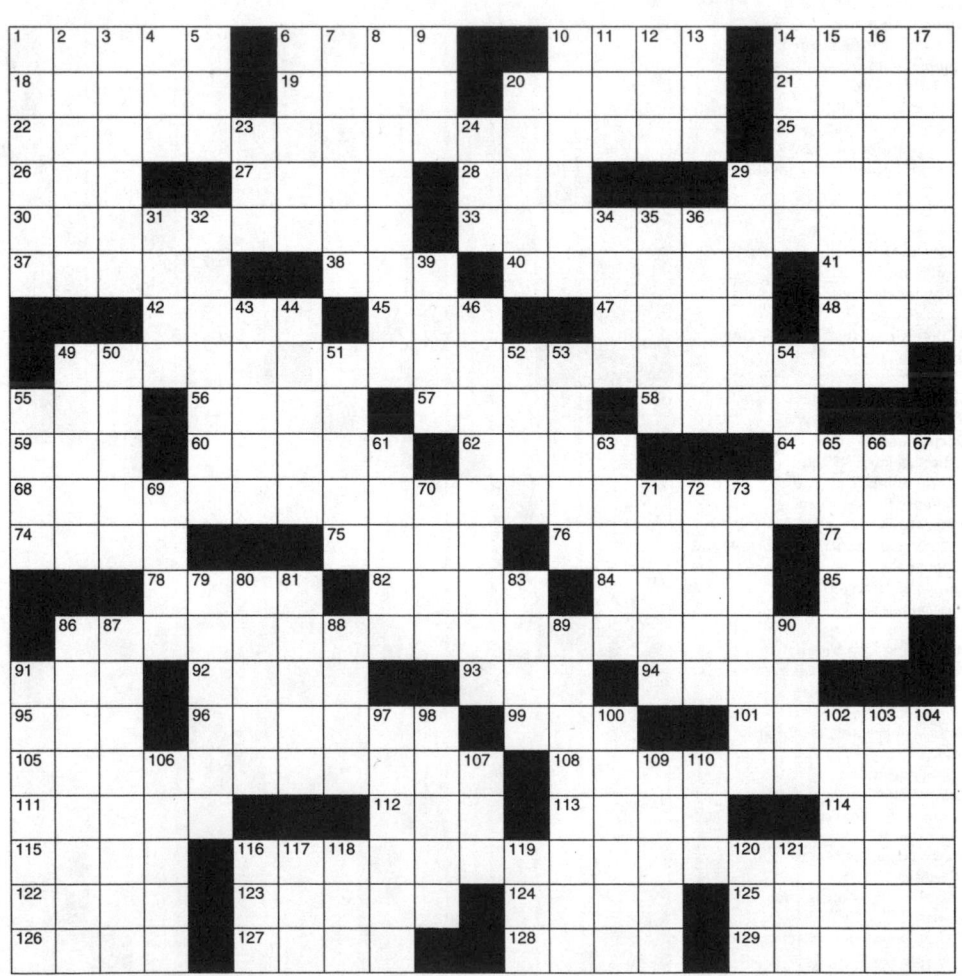

by Tom McCoy

ACROSS

1 What helicopter rotors do
5 "___ to Psyche"
8 Bartók and Lugosi
13 Seven Sisters school that went coed in 1969
19 Famous feature of the Florence Cathedral
20 Romulus, exempli gratia
21 It goes up with alcohol consumption
23 Cereal mascot since 1933
24 N.Y.C.-based dance troupe
25 ↑ Memoirist
26 Psalm 63 opening
28 Unable to choose
30 Blood drive worker
31 On the way
32 Many
34 Tactless
36 Marsh flora
38 Rapper Lil ___ X
39 ↓ Journalist and author
42 Maui setting: Abbr.
44 Downwind
45 Mimic
46 Quarry, e.g.
47 Raise one's spirits
49 Weighed on
51 Gangster's gun
52 Large print source
54 Org. for the Demon Deacons and Blue Devils
55 ↑ Sci-fi author
58 Observance on Yom Kippur or during Ramadan
61 H.S. class for future engineers, say
62 Spoke with a forked tongue
63 Guides of a sort
64 "From where I sit," briefly
65 Increases
66 Word appearing on only one current U.S. coin (the nickel)
67 Bit
68 Yonder
72 Medium on display at Brickworld
73 ↓ Famed rights advocate
75 Agcy. that supports entrepreneurs
77 Many a middle schooler
78 Sounds during a strep test
79 1976 hit whose title is sung just before the line "Take it easy"
84 Buenos ___
85 Sis's sib
86 Isn't in the black
87 Information on a game box
88 The so-called "winter blues," for short
89 ↑ Noted politician and orator
93 "Honor"-able org.
95 Gush
97 Largest cell in the human body
98 Got by
99 Yeats's homeland
101 Brings up
103 Award for Best Moment, e.g.
105 The "1" of 10−1, say
106 ↓ American composer and lyricist
109 Canyon maker
111 Kissers
113 "I can't understand this at all"
114 Half of a blackjack
115 Hideout
116 Star of the "Taken" film series
117 Wind ___
118 "Erie Canal" mule
119 Certain IDs

DOWN

1 MS. units
2 Site of the first Ironman race (1978)
3 Words accompanying "Uh-oh!"
4 Moved, as in a greenhouse
5 ___ pro nobis
6 Factor affecting a bond's rating
7 Took by threat
8 Actor on Time's list of the 100 most important people of the 20th century
9 California's ___ River
10 Reclined
11 Hex'd
12 Playing on both sides
13 "I ___" (sticker message)
14 "I'll take that as ___"
15 Parts of a portfolio: Abbr.
16 Iconic environmental book
17 Maker of the classic Radarange
18 Concludes one's case
22 "Ghosts" playwright
27 Forest mother
29 River through Dortmund
32 Model of vengeful obsession
33 Part of a Swiss bank account
35 One good at reading emotions
37 Boating hazard
40 Something a house might be built on
41 Epigrammatic
43 Brand in the dessert aisle
47 Clue collectors, for short
48 Grow a fondness for
50 Grub
51 Assoc.
52 Includes surreptitiously
53 Melds
55 Left on board
56 High percentage of criminals?
57 No longer green, say
58 Popular sans-serif typeface
59 Truism based on a line by Gertrude Stein
60 Major source of coffee beans
61 Mass-produced response?
63 Inspiration for a horror movie?
64 Nobelist Pavlov
66 Hammer feature
68 U.K. honours
69 Choreographer Twyla
70 Trio often heard in December
71 Northern borders?
74 Can't do without
75 Runners support it
76 Place of security
79 What causes a will-o'-the-wisp
80 Ann and Andy, notably
81 The King of Latin Pop
82 Popular sports news website
83 ExxonMobil abroad
85 Promise
86 Heavy responsibility
89 Comment following an unrepentant admission
90 Symbolic socioeconomic divider
91 Less bumpy
92 Suffix with sex or text
93 Get the show on the road
94 Número de Maravillas del Mundo Antiguo
96 Get one's hair just right
100 Bits of work
102 Something a cobbler may hold
104 "It's fun to stay at the ___" (1978 hit lyric)
107 Miracle-___
108 Org. for docs
110 Bit of animation
112 About one-quarter of a high school: Abbr.

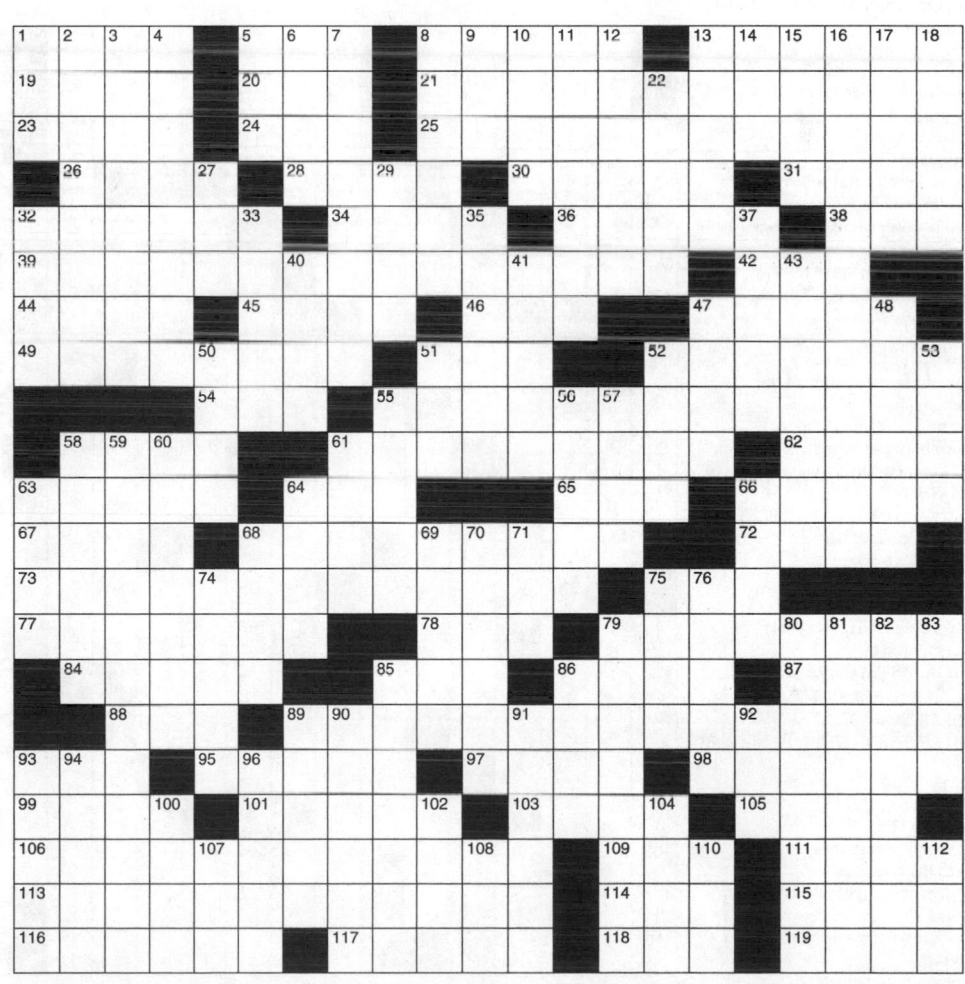

by Howard Barkin and Victor Barocas

ACROSS

1 Fasteners . . . or, if you change the fourth letter to an S, what the fasteners might be made of
6 It's lit eight nights in a row
13 Figure that denotes acidity
18 Less everyday
19 Humble expression of capability
20 Number that might be kept secret
21 Professional whose favorite movie line might be "There's no place like home"
23 Muse of astronomy
24 Dis-qualified?
25 Cyclops's "I"
26 "Uh-oh!"
28 Maker of the Acadia S.U.V.
29 Franchise with a series set in New Orleans
30 Singer ___ J. Blige
31 Weasel relative
34 South Asian garment
35 . . . "Here's looking at you, kid"
37 Not be attentive
38 President whose wife went on to become president
39 Unconfident utterances
40 . . . "I wish I knew how to quit you"
42 Not manually controlled
46 Foreign capital where W. E. B. Du Bois is buried
48 Do a little tidying
49 Lukewarm response
50 Arthropod appendages
51 Emitters of cosmic rays
53 Arctic coat
55 Typing sounds
56 "Well, aren't I clever?!"
57 Shaving mishap
59 One honored on March 8 per a 1977 United Nations resolution
61 . . . "Go ahead, make my day"
66 Less bronzed
67 Hated figure
68 Promote
69 Relative of the emu
70 Couleur in the middle of the French flag
72 Big maker of smartphones
74 Word between "stink" and "stunk" in "You're a Mean One, Mr. Grinch"
75 Hurry, quaintly
77 Place to get a knish
79 Obstetrics worker
80 Dwell
81 . . . "Get to the chopper!"
84 Recording device, for short
85 ___ planning
86 Part of N.S., in Canadian mail
87 . . . "Is this your king?!"
92 Fine deposit
93 Airport named for two Washington cities
94 Hurry
95 "This one's ___"
96 Caesar's "I"
97 Reaction to scritches, maybe
98 "___ the Explorer"
99 Things you might take a spin in
100 Stored
102 . . . "I'll have what she's having"
107 Low-carb diet creator
108 Piece of furniture that's at least a couple of feet wide
109 Best competitive performance, informally
110 Trials
111 Trick that's "pulled"
112 Doodling, say

DOWN

1 Mile High City athlete
2 Palm fiber
3 Drawer, say
4 Restructuring target
5 Sp. title
6 Term of address for a noble
7 Like some calories
8 Beyoncé film role
9 "Snakes ___ Plane"
10 Shaft of sunshine
11 Estimation from dating
12 Placed on a pedestal
13 Swedish name akin to Lawrence
14 Commercial suffix with Motor
15 2004 Nobel Peace Prize winner who founded the Green Belt Movement
16 Flower that's often yellow
17 Flower that's often purple
20 School district higher-up, informally
21 Like praises and arias
22 Story tellers
27 Half a pint
30 Firm-ly worded letter?
31 Bars that people walk into?
32 Actress Dawson
33 Clean (up)
34 French for "salt"
36 Humble homes
37 Incites to attack, with "on"
38 ___ saint
41 Witness's attestation
42 Makes a choice
43 Image Award org.
44 Children's playthings that help with spelling
45 Encourage to buy add-ons
46 Sound bites and such
47 Trolley sounds
51 Buddy
52 District 9, for short?
54 Alternatives to Targets
56 Swayed to the dark side, say
58 Danish coin
60 Ceaselessly
62 Exactly right
63 Half-frozen Italian dessert
64 Grooved on
65 Leaf blower alternative
71 Effective salesperson
73 Sp. title
74 Long truck
75 What goes in a box
76 Water
78 Overseen by
80 Anger
82 Receptacle for donations
83 Little 'un
84 Source of chocolate
87 One serving on a ship
88 Andean feline
89 Eventually
90 Enjoying a comedy
91 Stick-y pad?
93 Brewski
94 Like DC and MI
97 Calligraphers' choices
98 Twentysomethings, e.g.
99 Burkina Faso neighbor
101 Word before "home" or "the road"
103 School org.
104 Part of fwiw
105 Matrix character
106 Place to wear smocks

by Erik Agard

ACROSS

1 World capital with the historic Temple of Hercules
6 Responses to an offer, colloquially
11 ____ Dunphy, "Modern Family" matriarch
12 Slow Wi-Fi woe
15 Actor Don of old Hollywood
17 Uninteresting and self-absorbed
18 One-named electronic musician and D.J. with multiple Grammys
20 Paranoid types, slangily
22 Futon alternatives
23 Stand that an artist might take
24 Villainous brother of Prospero in "The Tempest"
25 E-sports enthusiast
26 Melt down, as fat
29 Occasion to sing "Dayenu"
30 Long narrative poem
31 Ice skating spot
32 Crew
34 Faux pas
35 Picasso's "____ Demoiselles d'Avignon"
36 Baseball hit just beyond the infield
37 "No kidding!"
39 Malawi-to-Kenya dir.
40 Element used in old television tubes
42 Creator of a philosophical "razor"
46 Best friend of Potter and Weasley
48 Banquet vessels
49 Speechify
50 One frequently saying "Sorry, I missed that"
51 Like classic Disney films
54 Golfer's vehicle
56 "No fighting!"
60 Geologic period
61 Eye roll accompanier, often
63 Muscle Beach sight
64 Their eggs are incubated by males
66 Eldest of the "little women" in "Little Women"
67 Wettish
69 It's always something
71 What may follow bigger or better
72 Farrah Fawcett's signature do
73 Sikorsky of aviation
74 "Message received"
76 Rabid enthusiast
77 Warrior, e.g., in yoga
78 Actress Roberts of "Everybody Loves Raymond"
80 Homeowner's need
82 Like most standardized tests
83 Tribe famous for weaving and sand painting
85 Crème de la crème
86 Really tickles
88 Russian ruler known as "the Moneybag"
90 It's in the bag
91 Fruit in an often-parodied William Carlos Williams poem
92 Dark forebodings
96 N.B.A. franchise whose mascot is the fireball Burnie
100 Kind of tuna
101 Troglodyte
105 Base of a column
106 Juul, e.g.
107 It can open a lot of doors for you
110 Historical role for Peter Lorre in "The Story of Mankind"
111 Party that might not start till midnight
112 Classic kids' game involving removal of body parts . . . with a hint to this puzzle's theme
113 Qatari leader
114 102-Down, affectedly
115 Minuscule, informally
116 "It is the ____, and Juliet is the sun"
117 Actress Cannon

DOWN

1 Top celebs
2 Red wine from France
3 Middle-distance runner
4 Nickname for an ESPN baseball commentator
5 Post production locales?
6 Weapons thrown by the Dark Knight
7 Volunteer's phrase
8 Sights on many music festival grounds
9 Seconded, so to speak
10 Karaoke selection
11 Gift that grows on you?
12 Fabulist
13 Semidomed church area
14 Secluded valley
16 Saint-____, capital of the Loire department
17 With wisdom
18 Wisecracking Marvel superhero
19 Experienced one
21 Worker at a recycling plant
27 British rocker Brian
28 Cry of terror
31 Contact electronically
33 Middle of a diamond
36 Hawks, e.g.
38 They might be hawked
41 Lament
43 Mobile home?
44 Ukulele accessory
45 Not much
47 Writer Anaïs
51 Fixed up
52 Old kingdom of Spain
53 Author Pierce of the fantasy series "The Song of the Lioness"
54 Way down
55 Response to tickling
57 "Hi, honey!" follower
58 Finishes
59 Urged (on)
62 "Now that was funny!"
65 Peace Nobelist who went on to become president
68 Outhouses
70 Well, I'll be dammed!
71 Drain
72 Treated meanly
75 Inclination
76 Brine-cured cheese
79 Classic Harlem ballroom, with "the"
81 Go (for)
82 Language from which "curry" comes
84 King who lent his name to a Bible
87 Like most oatmeal
89 Plant, as an idea, modern-style
91 Communist sympathizers, pejoratively
92 He was "thumb" critic!
93 Bishop's deputy
94 "Mercy!"
95 Metric of corporate success
96 Frenzy
97 Other side
98 Features of many malls
99 Part of an acacia tree
102 See 114-Across
103 Subj. of a "Delayed" sign
104 Speck
108 Decorative fish
109 "The Lord of the Rings" tree creature

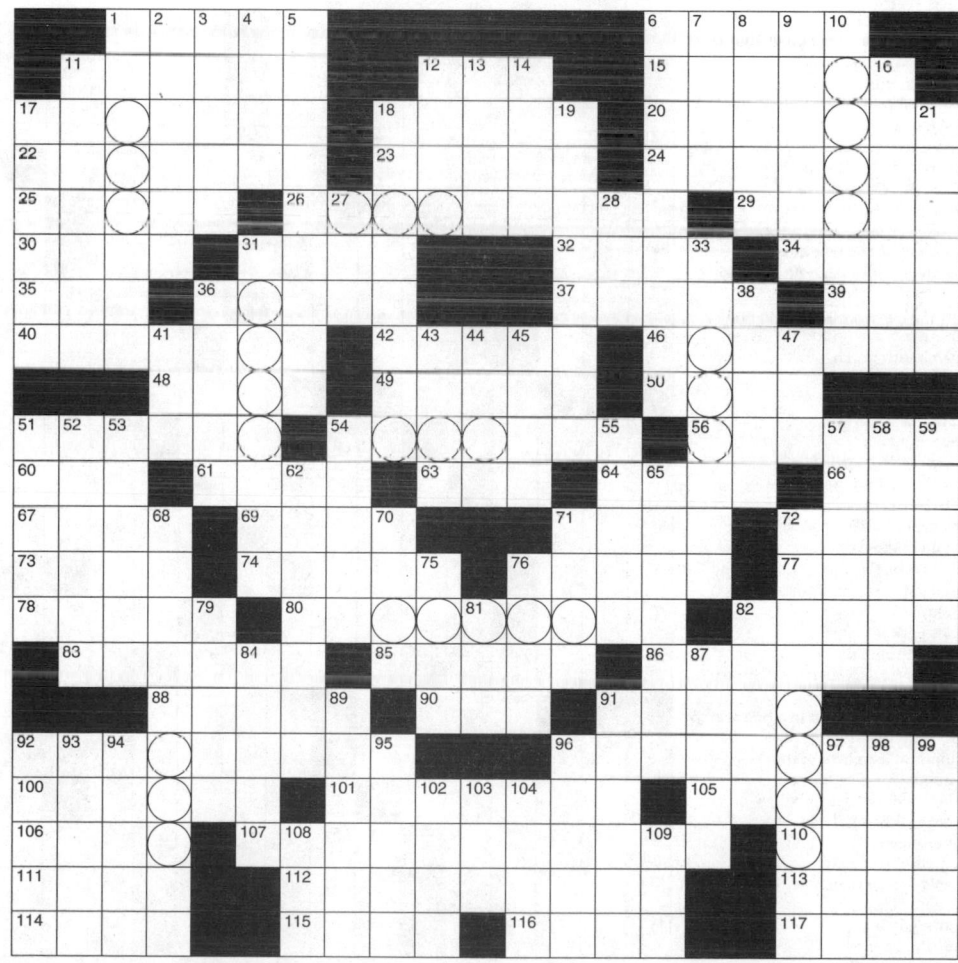

by Natan Last

ACROSS

1 Iraq War concern, in brief
4 An earl outranks him
9 Billiards maneuver
14 Exclaim "@#%!"
19 Tilling tool
20 QB defenders, collectively
21 Relating to a certain arm bone
22 ____ Kenyatta, president of Kenya starting in 2013
23 Something set by a stove
25 Year of the final flight of the Concordes
26 French-speaking African nation
27 Eyedropper, essentially
28 Submission to a record label, once
30 Rodeo loop
31 Accessory with a bass drum
32 Major fuss
33 Wedding bands?
34 Way out there
38 Hand over
39 Take a mulligan on
40 "<<" button: Abbr.
41 Ricochet like a hockey puck
43 To a certain extent, colloquially
45 Ad phrase indicating higher pricing tiers
49 Amtrak stop: Abbr.
50 Infomercial imperative
52 Pill bug, biologically
54 Intake suggestion, briefly
55 Unlock, to Shakespeare
56 Third-longest river in Europe, after the Volga and Danube
58 Tear to shreds
59 Partner of 46-Down in the frozen food business
60 Brown seaweeds
63 U.S. island owned almost entirely by billionaire Larry Ellison
65 Manic-looking, in a way
67 Neutral response from a therapist
68 Pattern once used for hospital volunteer uniforms, with a hint to this puzzle's theme
70 Loser of a beauty contest, in myth
71 Birds known to mimic car alarms and human speech
73 Graduate's "honor"
74 Carousel mount, to a tot
75 Mark of a scam artist
76 Hooked on
77 Laura of "Big Little Lies"
78 Emulate Johnny Appleseed
79 H, to Hellenes
80 "Ya dig?," in more modern slang
82 Get up in the face of
85 Emma Stone's role in "La La Land"
88 Protagonist in Toni Morrison's "Beloved"
90 Skate park features
92 Place for regulars
93 Handel's "____, Galatea e Polifemo"
94 Glenn Frey's "The Heat ____"
96 Bad thing to come up in a title search
98 Total failure
100 Important members of the community, so to speak
103 Where menisci are found
105 What socks usually do
106 Bitter green
107 Regards covetously
108 Display piece for tchotchkes
110 Virtual sticky
111 Battling it out
112 Boondocks
114 One of 11 in a Christmas carol
115 Provide an address
116 French novelist Zola
117 Bit
118 Company that once offered "the Thrift Book of a Nation"
119 Excited, with "up"
120 Foil alternatives
121 Meditative syllables

DOWN

1 Big fat lies
2 Where you might need to get a grip
3 In one's heart of hearts
4 Pop covers
5 Stopped a flight
6 Frosty encrustation
7 Its square equals its square root
8 Types who think school is too cool
9 They're kept under wraps for a long time
10 Nut extract used in skin care
11 Derisive chuckles
12 Didn't just hint at
13 Verdi's "____ tu"
14 Gold digger's goldmine
15 Alma mater of Tesla's Elon Musk
16 Jazzman Blake
17 Like a crowd when the headliner takes the stage
18 Pipsqueaks
24 Like some servings of Scotch
29 "You get the idea"
30 New Guinea port that was Amelia Earhart's last known point of departure
33 Large, purple Hanna-Barbera character
35 Campaign . . . or a campaign topic
36 Original N.Y.C. subway line
37 Non-pro
42 Heaps
44 Steamy
46 Partner of 59-Across in the frozen food business
47 Dairy sources
48 Biweekly occurrence, for many
51 Actress Fay of the original "King Kong"
53 Neuf + deux
55 Abbr. between * and #
57 Separation at a wedding?
60 What x's sometimes represent
61 Executor's charge
62 Pounce on, as an opportunity
63 The "two" in "two if by sea"
64 Portuguese-speaking African nation
65 What lettuce lends to a sandwich
66 Popular D.I.Y. site
68 Endeavor recognized by the César awards
69 Reid of "The Big Lebowski"
72 They come through when you need them most
74 Total stunners
77 Sketch out
78 W-2 IDs
81 Its closest neighbor is Andromeda
83 Mr. Wrong
84 All-vowel avowal
85 Carry some relevance for
86 Mode, on a menu
87 Scatterbrains
89 Neon marker
91 Is blinded by rage
95 Cent : euro :: ____ : krona
97 Modern, in Munich
99 Epic narrative
100 Tiny objections
101 What many a navel-gazer gazes at
102 Treatment for Parkinson's
104 Jag
107 Word repeated in "____ ou ne pas ____"
108 Lake bordered by four states and a province
109 Yarn
111 Just ducky
113 Person who might call you out

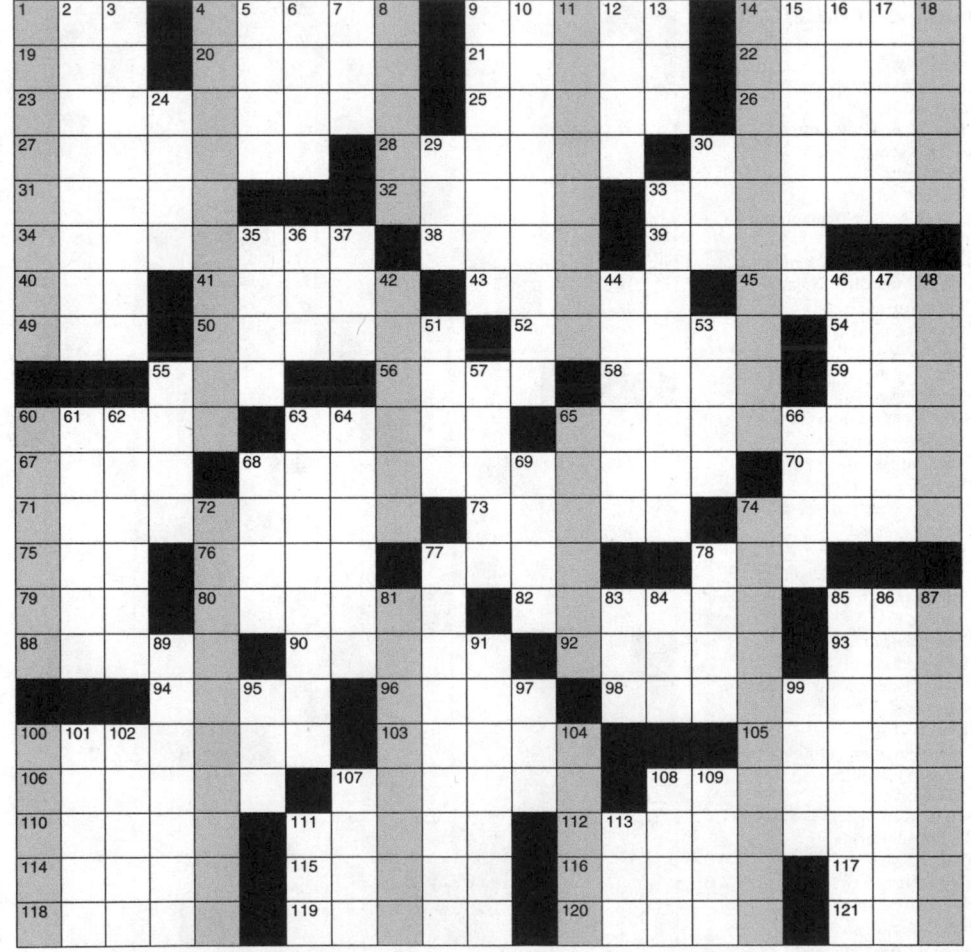

by Michael Paleos

ACROSS

1 Broods
6 "___ are the voyages of the starship Enterprise"
11 Long-billed wader
15 Idiosyncrasies
19 Brownie ingredient
20 Actor Tom of "The Dukes of Hazzard"
21 Indie singer/songwriter ___ Case
22 1980s U.S. Davis Cup team captain
23 Your apartment-mate, if you don't close the door before showering?
26 Self-involved
27 Blend
28 Expensive
29 Drumstick
30 Gets better
31 Your wish, maybe, when a rambunctious terrier puppy is first brought home?
36 Browning who directed "Dracula," 1931
37 Draw a bead on
38 Bring in
39 Songwriters' org.
42 Lady friend, in Florence
44 Great ___
45 See 88-Across
48 Soprano ___ Te Kanawa
49 Giant star
50 Tyrannic sort?
54 O. Henry?
56 Time and Tide
57 Zap
58 President pro ___
59 Giant flying turtle monster of film
61 "What greater gift than the love of a ___": Charles Dickens
62 But: Fr.
64 Not digital
66 Hankering
67 Monarch's inits.
68 It can cause shortness of breath
71 Sight at a gladiatorial fight
72 Fluffy neckwear
73 Chooses
75 Actress Grier of "Jackie Brown"
76 Location of Hephaestus' forge
78 Spoil, as a parade
80 Online reference about toilets?
82 Guys who pass out Halloween treats?
85 Greenhouse containers
86 Some fútbol cheers
87 Completely dominate
88 With 45-Across, what was once the world's fourth-largest inland body of water
89 Atkins dieters' no-nos
91 Rapunzel feature
92 Walked over
93 ___ syrup (natural sweetener)
95 Drummer Starkey
96 What outsiders think about the new hire?
103 Common baitfish
104 Terminal guesstimate, for short
105 Statistical tool for checking a hypothesis
106 Be a stool pigeon
109 "Mila 18" novelist
110 What the exhausted working woman wears to bed?
114 Man-to-man alternative
115 Lavish soiree
116 Ruffian
117 Singer Mann
118 Drink flavorer
119 Statuette that weighs 6 pounds 12½ ounces
120 According to
121 Become slick, in a way

DOWN

1 Grifter's game
2 Raced
3 Place to learn lessons in Lyon
4 Dye on a deck
5 Spade said to be excellent at digging up dirt
6 Pipsqueak
7 Football Hall-of-Famer Long
8 Flop that's one for the ages
9 Lecherous
10 Ordinal suffix
11 Emulate Edison
12 "Boring" shade
13 1950s White House nickname
14 Female badger
15 The Boar's Head, in Shakespeare
16 Russian artist Brodsky, the first painter awarded the Order of Lenin
17 It turns a hot dog into a Texas hot dog
18 Pick up on
24 Product that had sales of more than 300,000 on its first day in 2010
25 Michigan college
30 Biblical peak
32 Beat walker
33 Astrologer Sydney
34 Slowly eases (off)
35 Andrew ___, businessman-turned-politician
39 Pointy-eared dog
40 Tornado warning device
41 Early human
42 Early human
43 Michael Lewis best seller with the subtitle "The Art of Winning an Unfair Game"
44 Got results
45 Editor's stack of unsolicited manuscripts
46 Wapiti
47 All-vowel avowal
49 Publicist's concern
51 German city near the Belgian border
52 Tree knot
53 Textbook section
55 Bela Lugosi's role in "The Ghost of Frankenstein"
56 Word before bread or boat
60 Take care of, as a persistent squeak
62 Computation class in Cambridge
63 Part of A.P.A.: Abbr.
65 Truckful
69 Assembles
70 Out of whack
74 Fold-up beds
76 "Nations have their ___, just like individuals": James Joyce
77 Haul
78 Charles who wrote "The Cloister and the Hearth"
79 Bygone sister language of Latin
81 Valued asset for an employee
83 What some sailors bring back
84 Throat problem
85 Beautify
90 Gamers' embodiments
91 Whup
92 Adjustable feature of a typewriter
93 Off
94 Egg on
95 Cousin of penne
96 Slimeball
97 Painful sensation
98 Machu Picchu or Pompeii
99 Kingdom
100 What's left, in Paris
101 119-Across winner for both "Roots" and "Rich Man, Poor Man"
102 Wonderland cake message
107 Stead
108 Medieval stronghold
110 Go gray, say
111 Scene stealer
112 Corporate "a.k.a."
113 Chicken, in a Chinese dish

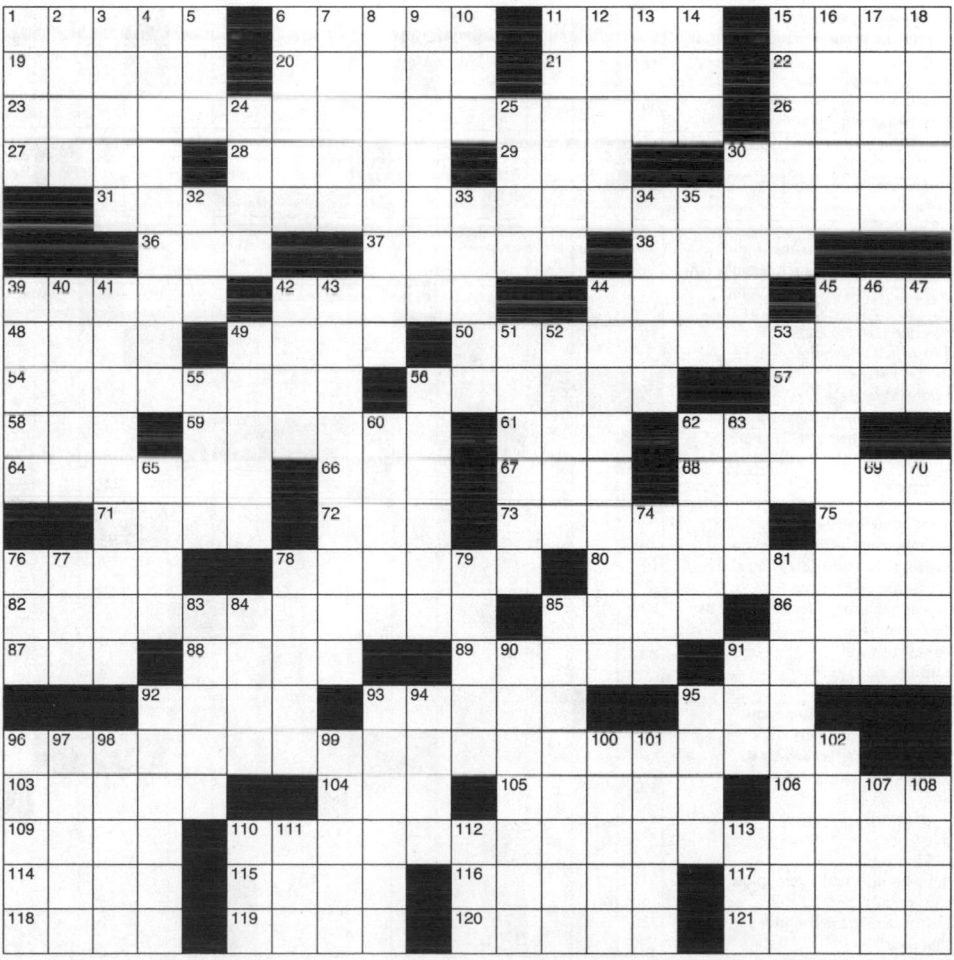

by Kristian House

ACROSS

1 "Hooked on Classics" company
5 Christina of "Monster"
10 Skins, so to speak
15 Silent
18 Last Supper item
20 Case study in many business ethics classes
21 Call on
22 "The Simpsons" character who holds a Ph.D. in computer science
23 Low singers, short on money, draw idly?
26 Place for a beer pump
27 Reaches a climax
28 High-class person?
29 Served in a certain cream sauce
31 Fleet runner: Abbr.
32 Boston's Liberty Tree, e.g.
34 Tennis player with a record 377 cumulative weeks ranked No. 1
36 First-rate
37 Works as an accountant for a Swedish aerospace company?
44 "Pearly Shells" singer
45 Like a llano
46 Put a stop to
49 Mlle., across the Pyrénées
50 Tangle
51 Airy areas of hotels
52 Urban intersectors: Abbr.
53 People who share an apartment with a Jordanian royal?
58 Rival of Havoline
61 Pec pic, say
62 1980s auto imports based on the Fiat
63 Turkish coin
64 Speed skater who won five golds at the 1980 Lake Placid Olympics
66 Not doff
69 Politico Liz
71 Unusual
72 Pocahontas's husband John
73 50,000-watt clear-channel radio station in Iowa for which Ronald Reagan was once a sportscaster
74 Sends to the canvas, for short
75 Designer Mizrahi shouts like a cowboy in a nonchalant way?
82 Citi Field player
83 Listens attentively
84 Man's name that becomes another man's name when a "C" is put in front
85 Life ___ (timesaving trick)
89 Events for special customers
91 Smooth and lustrous
93 Asian metropolis of 28+ million
94 Headline after an adolescent at a pool competition is made fun of?
97 Mughal emperor of India known as "the Great"
99 Nephew of Cain
100 Feminine side
101 Bit
102 Meteorological phenomenon
105 Mourning person, perhaps
109 Like triangles governed by the Pythagorean theorem
111 Stir
112 Matriculated students appear to be timid?
116 Couldn't stand?
117 John who invented a steel plow
118 Poles, e.g.
119 California mission founder Junípero
120 What's up?
121 More logical
122 Brownish gray
123 Fit together like matryoshka dolls

DOWN

1 Yuri Andropov headed it for 15 years, in brief
2 Opening in the theater, maybe
3 Legal grant to cross over someone else's land
4 ___ Genova, author of "Still Alice"
5 Rapper MC ___, formerly of N.W.A
6 Travel guide listings
7 One of the 11 official languages of Canada's Northwest Territories
8 Either brother who co-wrote "O Brother, Where Art Thou?"
9 Plants that yield a blue dye
10 Antonín who composed "Carnival Overture"
11 Host of the Olympics where golf returned after a 112-year hiatus
12 National School Lunch Program org.
13 Pepper dispenser
14 Cinematographic innovation of the 1970s
15 Raising Cain
16 Overturn
17 Unpleasantly humid
19 Thus
24 Mallorca o Menorca, por ejemplo
25 Socially awkward
30 Hearst-like film character
31 Interjects
33 It's more attractive the closer you are to it
35 Adorn
38 N.B.A. nickname until 2011
39 Something white rice lacks
40 Hay there!
41 Where the Nobel Peace Prize winner is announced
42 Money for a grand tour
43 Stiffly formal
47 Like binaural audio
48 Parts of college applications
50 Bean on the silver screen
51 Ship of mythology
54 Pac-12 player
55 Cry of dismay
56 Bemoan
57 Hoppy drink
58 Food item often prepared with lemon and garlic
59 Promo
60 Snack food brand that sounds like buried treasure
65 It may be a deal breaker: Abbr.
66 Gander
67 Some pipe joints
68 New York Titans' org. of old
69 Jackie of "Rush Hour"
70 Question that isn't a "wh-" question
72 Ned who composed "Air Music"
73 Sound heard at Churchill Downs
76 Alternatives to sleeper sofas
77 Quiet
78 The Collegiate School, today
79 Actress Sommer
80 50-50
81 Molt
86 Not out to lunch
87 Crib users
88 Captain played twice in film by Charles Laughton
90 Equine : horse :: cygnine : ___
91 Pub perch
92 "That's what you should do"
93 Jeans
95 Playwright Eve
96 Land on the Celtic Sea
97 Run up
98 Company that's had its moments
103 Draft classification
104 Small songbird
106 Composer Bartók
107 Biblical birthright seller
108 Send one's regrets, say
110 F.B.I. guys
113 Underground band
114 Direction from Belg. to Bulg.
115 "Krazy ___"

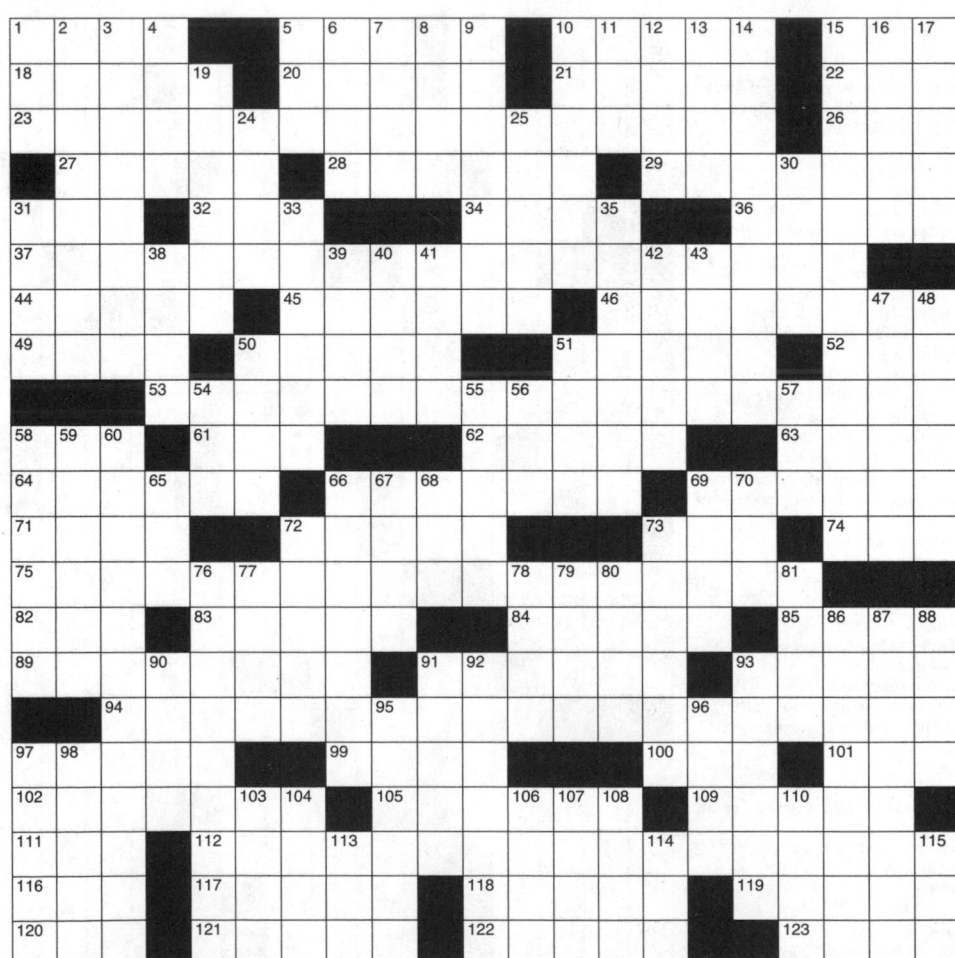

by Peter Gordon

ACROSS

1 Lack of this results in baldness
6 Alcohol
13 Scenes from action movies
19 Old foundation
21 1994 Jean-Claude Van Damme sci-fi thriller
22 Get back
23 Parenting: A+
25 Night demons
26 Maintain
27 Number of people in an office?
29 "Step ___!"
30 Bye word
33 Nervous stress
34 Chip-on-one's-shoulder outlooks, in slang
35 Taming wild horses: D−
40 Reflex messengers
42 Heavy metal
43 Some kitchen appliances
44 Wildlife conservationist's device
47 Union station?
49 Valet skills: B+
54 You can dig it
55 Spain and England in the 16th century
57 Like a sure bet
58 Watch chains
59 Do an old printing house job
60 Skills, in Sevilla
61 Heart
62 Hosting a morning news show: C+
67 Photo finish
70 First draft picks
71 It makes stealing pay off
75 "See you later!"
76 Cheerful
78 Norman Lear series star
80 Spots
81 Stuffing tip jars: D
83 Chip away at
84 Bottom line figure
86 Alternative to a Maxwell
87 Indy winner Luyendyk
88 Hot stuff
91 Employee efficiency: D+
95 Sorcerer
97 Much, informally
99 Supply-___ (economic theorist)
100 Growing room
101 Do a P.R. makeover on
103 16501–16511
107 Put on hold
109 Baseball skill: C
113 Protect, as freshness
114 What to do once you've made your bed, per a saying
115 Skirts
116 Nueva York, e.g.
117 Afterword
118 Bibliographical abbr.

DOWN

1 Channel on which to see some b&w films
2 Fleece
3 Noted Deco designer
4 1975 Wimbledon champ
5 New Age author Chopra
6 Apt name for a cook?
7 Lulu
8 Used Gchat, e.g.
9 Went back through a passage
10 Hockey infraction
11 "Yer darn ___!"
12 Clear soda
13 Lit ___
14 Farm setter
15 Story
16 Stereo quality: B
17 Blake who wrote "Memories of You"
18 Roast rotators
20 Fantasy author Canavan, author of the "Black Magician" trilogy
24 Whirl
28 Producers of the most Mideast oil
31 Actress Samantha
32 Rides since 2011
34 Burned rubber
35 Designer Bill
36 U. S. Grant adversary
37 Trouble terribly
38 Learns to live with
39 Set a price of
41 Malodorous
45 Metro areas, informally
46 Sticks together?
48 Luxury car pioneer Henry
49 One may exert pressure
50 Significant advances
51 The other guys
52 Diver Louganis
53 Porgy and bass
56 F.D.R. program
58 Dangerous structure
60 Combat zone
61 Anglican headwear
63 Strong brew
64 "Movin' ___"
65 Call attention to, as a potential problem
66 Small power source
67 Classic shoe name
68 Starting job in Washington, say
69 Fashion sense: A
72 Lead-in to fare
73 Part of a TV transmission
74 ___ Garson, Oscar winner for "Mrs. Miniver"
76 Solomonlike
77 One-eighth part
78 Funeral stands
79 Mushroom that might be served in ramen
81 Uncivil greetings
82 Sign of a smash hit
85 ___ de Vil, Disney villain
89 Patch (together)
90 Way to get to Harlem, per Duke Ellington
91 Desire a piece of the action
92 Conception
93 Chutzpah
94 Mourn
95 Snooker shot
96 Flu symptoms
98 Full
101 Clinton's attorney general for all eight years
102 Rat Pack nickname
104 Quod ___ faciendum
105 Stationer's stock
106 "Let Us Now Praise Famous Men" writer
108 Kid-___ (TV for tots)
110 Tiny criticism
111 Pioneer cellphone co.
112 Fancy-looking name appendage

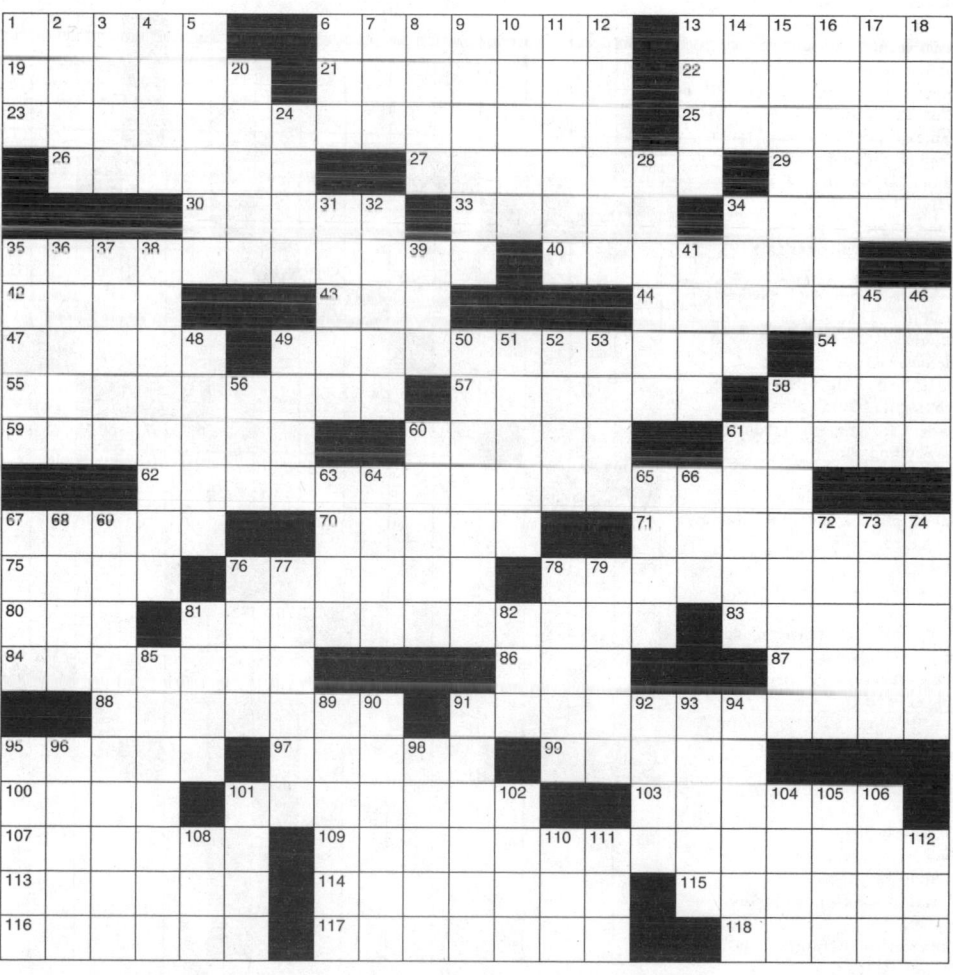

by Randolph Ross

ACROSS

1 Bondsman, of late?
12 Unfold
21 It has some miles on it
22 Not yet in the database
23 A.P. courses, e.g.
24 Summer camp activity
25 Emily Dickinson's "I heard ___ buzz - when I died"
26 Wonder-working biblical prophet
28 Creator of Mike Hammer
29 Cross
31 In the mood for love
33 Main theme of "Othello"
37 Climax of "The Shawshank Redemption"
42 Picnic, e.g.
43 Bumming, as cigarettes
44 Rotting evidence
45 Clicking counters
46 Lacking
48 Imprint permanently
50 Means of communication without interference
52 Insulation and sealing material
54 Thrice due
55 Not generics
59 Went skiing
60 Hit 1997 film condemned by the Chinese government
63 Fixture in a chocolate factory
66 Least normal
67 Like some arts
69 James who starred in 1970s TV's "How the West Was Won"
70 Name originally proposed (but not adopted) for Utah
73 Paint a false picture of
74 Weigh station lineup
75 Fuel-carrying ships
77 Event that usually has gate crashers?
78 Methods of studying pooled data
81 Peak in 1980 headlines
83 Representation of the real world in literature and art
84 NASA's spacecraft Dawn began orbiting it in 2015
85 Clowns sometimes put them on
89 List-ending phrase
91 Big to-do
95 Given a heads-up about
97 Subscription service with an arrow in its logo
100 Free
101 Something that's not contracted very often
102 Partly sheltered area near land in which vessels ride at anchor
103 Petty officers on police duty while a ship is in port

DOWN

1 Nobleman above un conte
2 From
3 Dickens orphan
4 One way to stand by
5 Anticipatory time
6 Certain Thanksgiving turkey serving
7 "Nice and rosy" things in the song "Sleigh Ride"
8 Founder of New York's Odditorium in 1939
9 Like burning rubber
10 Les Aléoutiennes, e.g.
11 House minority leader before Pelosi (1995–2003)
12 Half of a reproach
13 Sitcom/film star who was named People's "Most Beautiful Woman" twice
14 Staying fresh
15 Chicory variety
16 Topics for fashion magazines
17 Elevator near an arch?
18 Something that can be performed da capo
19 Campus abutting Drexel, informally
20 Beat by a whisker
27 Pal
29 What all NaCl molecules have
30 Persian, e.g.
32 "Yeah, right!"
33 Steinbeck family
34 Blake who composed "I'm Just Wild About Harry"
35 Early employer of Steve Jobs
36 Head residents?
37 Many T-ball coaches
38 Spherical bacterium
39 Not regularly standing
40 Something to drive home
41 Cousins of kites
43 Bird on California's state quarter
46 Satisfies
47 Suggest
48 Running mate?
49 Standard features of almanacs
51 Department capital SE of Paris
52 Get married, in slang
53 2004 sci-fi thriller inspired by a classic 1950 book
56 Bigeye, on some menus
57 Some sewers
58 Wine components
59 Mother ___
60 Buzzy body?
61 Like some coincidences
62 French for "twenty"
63 End of many town names
64 Par ___
65 Is thick (with)
68 Shade akin to turquoise
70 Word after old or dog
71 Longtime dairy aisle mascot
72 What a big sock might make you do
75 Reached maturity
76 Onetime Procter & Gamble product on Time magazine's list of "The 50 Worst Inventions"
77 "___ Said," 2019 best seller on the #MeToo movement
79 Rare and valuable instruments
80 Like restaurants with three Michelin stars
81 Usurper
82 Amplifier of radio signals
84 Mild, light-colored cigar
85 German industrial region
86 Dolly in "Hello, Dolly!," e.g.
87 Paris's Place ___ Bastille
88 Neighbor of Lucy and Ricky on "I Love Lucy"
90 Nanny, in Nanjing
91 Lose sleep, so to speak
92 "Not true!"
93 Schoolyard retort
94 Spa offering
96 Publication whose first ed. took more than 70 years to complete
98 Beat by a whisker
99 "Don't text and drive" ad, e.g., in brief

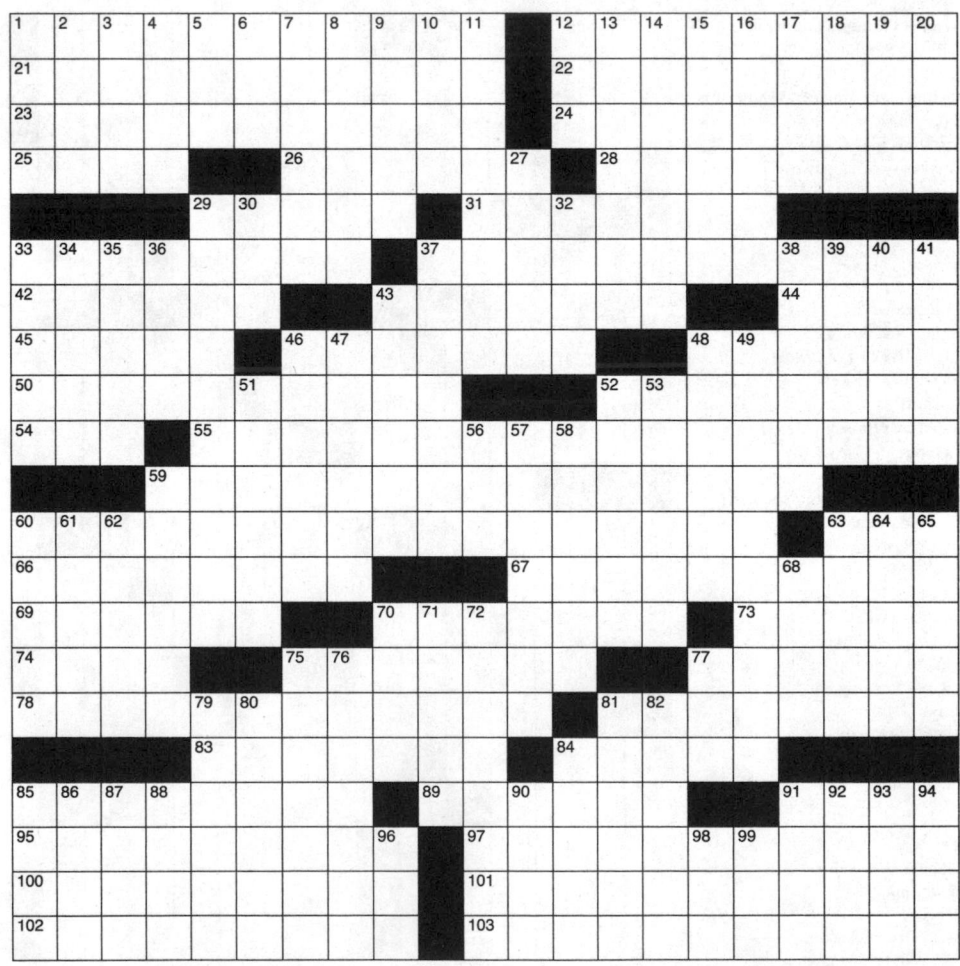

by Frank Longo

ACROSS

1 Unpleasantly surprise
4 Music-licensing org.
9 Big brother?
14 Some Pac-12 athletes
18 Three or four, say
20 Ashton Kutcher's role on "That '70s Show"
21 "Cross my heart"
22 Ingredient in spanakopita
23 Carefree quality
25 Synopsis
26 Saudi king before Abdullah
27 Popular Asian honeymoon destination
29 Ready for publication
31 Comes into view
32 Was given no other option
35 Online publication
36 Funny Foxx
37 Rant
41 Top musical group of the 1990s, per Billboard
43 51 past
44 Patronize, in a way
45 Slow start?
46 Momentarily
50 Supporting, with "up"
52 "I messed up," in slang
54 Comaneci of gymnastics
55 One shouting "Get off my lawn!"
56 PC port
58 Clothing designer Marc
62 "S.N.L." alum who co-starred in 2016's "Ghostbusters"
64 Classic soft drink
65 Response to a funny meme
66 Stopping point
67 Lead-in to meter
68 Manage
70 Follower of Sam or will.
72 Pince-___ glasses
73 Iranian currency with a 75-Across on its bills
75 See 73-Across
77 Game console introduced in 2006
80 It's often included with an R.S.V.P. card
81 Like most Italian singular nouns finishing in -a: Abbr.
82 Scatters about
83 United way?
84 The most recent Pope Benedict
86 Like some "#@&!" language
88 "Actually, I do"
89 Photo ___
92 "Buddy Holly" band, 1994
94 Braced (oneself)
96 New York social reformer whose name is on a Manhattan housing project
98 Amenable sort
99 Pet lovers' org.
103 Phrase on a candy heart
104 Impertinent sorts
106 Birds or wasps
108 Caviar source
110 Good-looking . . . or a phonetic hint to a feature found five times in this puzzle
114 What may follow fire or stone
115 Pulmonologist's expertise
118 Give too much light
119 One way to turn a ship
120 Members of une sororité
121 National currency which, if you drop its second letter and read the result backward, spells another national currency
122 Memo header
123 Knights' titles in "A Game of Thrones"
124 Heart topper, in bridge
125 "Someone Like You" hitmaker, 2011
126 Jokey suffix with most

DOWN

1 Prattle
2 Triangular construction
3 Was taken aback
4 Unable to move well
5 Submits
6 Former TV psychic Miss ___
7 The "A" of W.N.B.A.: Abbr.
8 Ask
9 Parts of hearts
10 Wonderful receptacle?
11 Tampa Bay N.F.L.er
12 Rock-___ (jukebox brand)
13 Romantic preference
14 Where to see Botticelli's "The Birth of Venus"
15 Three or four, say
16 Colorless gases
17 Turns blue?
19 "Well, that's quite a coincidence . . ."
24 Sudden turn
28 Ewe or sow
30 One with superhuman powers
33 Spanish or Portuguese
34 "___ Como Va" (Santana hit)
38 Make alterations to
39 State of disbelief
40 Humdinger
42 Lusaka native
43 "Swell!"
44 NNE or SSW
46 Tattoo artists
47 Fictional land of books and film
48 "Impossible Is Nothing" sloganeer
49 Family nickname
51 University officials
53 ___ canto
55 Part of a short race
57 Draws back
59 Washington's Kellyanne or George
60 Little: Ger.
61 Smith and Nelson
63 Teacher
64 Emphatic denial
69 Arduous
71 Degree for a research scientist
74 Latin law
76 New York Mets epithet
78 Quaint contraction
79 West Coast brew, for short
82 France's Boulogne-___-Mer
85 Disney's Herbie, for one
87 Under attack
88 Visitors' announcement
89 "The Song of Hiawatha" tribe
90 Sierra Nevada, e.g.
91 Oar
93 Frozen Wasser
95 Counterpart of dorsal
97 Immature eggs
98 Doofus
99 First part in an instruction manual
100 Hallucinogen sometimes called a "divine messenger"
101 Parts of waves
102 Give the green light
105 No longer in style
107 Reason for a TV-MA rating, perhaps
109 "Say it ain't so!"
111 Jedi guru
112 Poet who wrote "Jupiter from on high laughs at lovers' perjuries"
113 World's rarest goose
116 A count manager
117 Vardalos of "My Big Fat Greek Wedding"

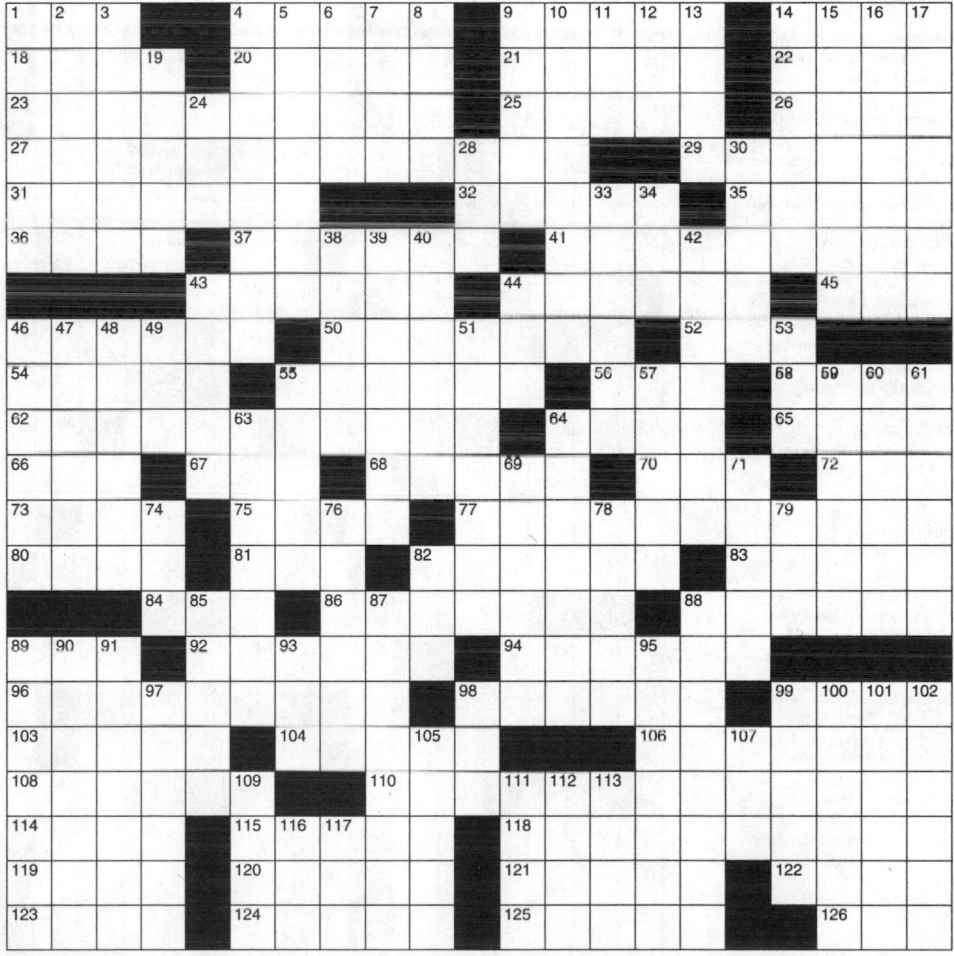

by Emily Carroll

ACROSS

1 Sandwich with an apostrophe in its name
6 Last-minute eBay bidders
13 ___ Speaker
18 Family written about by Margaret Mitchell
20 Laureate
21 California city whose name translates to "the table"
22 Concise and to the point
23 Improvement
24 Desirous
25 Word with coin or ring
26 Enclosure for a slush pile, for short
28 Salsa and guacamole
30 Foe of the Jedi
31 Boor
32 This puzzle's subjects, by another name
36 Beats by ___ (audio brand)
37 For now
41 One of 24
42 Group running a celeb's social media accounts, say
46 "My ___"
47 Fragrant item in a fireplace
49 Doorway
50 What violence might lead to
52 Political figure on whom Snowball is based in "Animal Farm"
54 Hitting close to home?
57 Pattern on a barber pole
61 Shade
62 Word before rip or slip
63 F.D.R.'s last veep
66 Boatload
67 Youngest animal in the Hundred Acre Wood
68 Daily cable show that's covered Hollywood since 1991
71 Part of a parade float on New Year's Day
74 Send over the moon
76 Duties imposed
78 Airer of "Arrow" and "iZombie"
79 Party notifications sent with a click
81 Members of un monastère
82 "Well, golly!"
84 Maximally mannered
85 "None for me, thanks"
87 Brain, slangily
89 Cry just before the birthday guest arrives at a surprise party
92 Juniors, to their fathers
96 Tingling, in a way
100 Tousles, as hair
103 Muscat native
104 Bog growths
107 Bit of off-road equipment
108 Where Orange County is, in brief
109 Something with many variables to consider
110 Chow down on, biblically
112 Judea and Sheba, in the Bible
114 Warehouse stacks
118 Relating to theft on the high seas
122 Some South Africans
127 French schoolteacher
128 Interval known as "the devil in music" on account of its unsettling sound
129 Title role played by Hilary Swank in a 2009 biopic
130 "Alas . . ."
131 Good thing to find on a boat
132 Agreeable response to a parental order

DOWN

1 Can opener
2 Company that introduced Etch A Sketch
3 Takes the plate in place of
4 World of Warcraft enemies
5 "Boo-___!"
6 "Quiet, you!"
7 Admonishment before Christmas morning
8 Dutch banking giant
9 "___ supuesto!" (Spanish "Of course!")
10 Presidential time
11 Contributors to "the front page of the internet"
12 Welcome, as a guest
13 ___ tai
14 Tsps. or tbsps.
15 George W. Bush's nickname for himself, with "the"
16 Where to set your butts down
17 Pandemonium
19 ___ admin
21 Retro-cool music purchases
27 Producer of bills
29 When repeated, "Cheerio!"
33 The Jets, but not the Giants
34 Lead-in to long
35 Drink with a straw
38 Hatcher of "Lois & Clark"
39 Lawman at the O.K. Corral
40 In the slightest
43 What amber comes from
44 Cleaning up the mess, for short?
45 Texter's "ciao"
47 Certain bean or horse
48 "___ run!"
51 Levels
53 Provocative poster
54 Keeper of the books?
55 One who fixes flats?
56 One of Chaucer's pilgrims
58 Hot under the collar
59 Things students take
60 "Whither thou ___ . . ."
63 Mischievous titter
64 Erupt
65 Fortune 500 category, informally
69 Most sinewy
70 Florist's cutting
72 Weather phenomenon whose double lights were said to represent this puzzle's subjects
73 Baseball double play, in slang . . . or a hint to understanding the 12 Across answers that have circles
74 Like a "mwa-ha-ha" laugh
75 Freedom
77 Abbr. on a keyboard key
80 Derrière
82 India's smallest state
83 Orange Sesame Street monster
86 It's a start
88 Founder of the Ottoman Empire
89 "That's odd . . ."
90 Chits inits.
91 Wet firecracker, e.g.
93 Genre akin to goth
94 ___ fly
95 Finish of three U.S. state names
97 Flash drive port
98 The big eau
99 Org. that began welcoming girls in 2019
101 California's ___ National Forest
102 Wiped
105 Seasoning in a yellow-and-blue tin
106 Disgusting, quaintly
111 Picks, with "for"
113 Near impossibilities on par-5 holes
114 Fig. watched by some dieters
115 Bit in a feedbag
116 Some fraternity row letters
117 G.R.E. administrator
119 Coastal inlet
120 "The pond": Abbr.
121 Here's the kicker!
123 Marks out
124 Its seeds whirl to the ground
125 Hit 2011 animated movie
126 Pusher of green eggs and ham

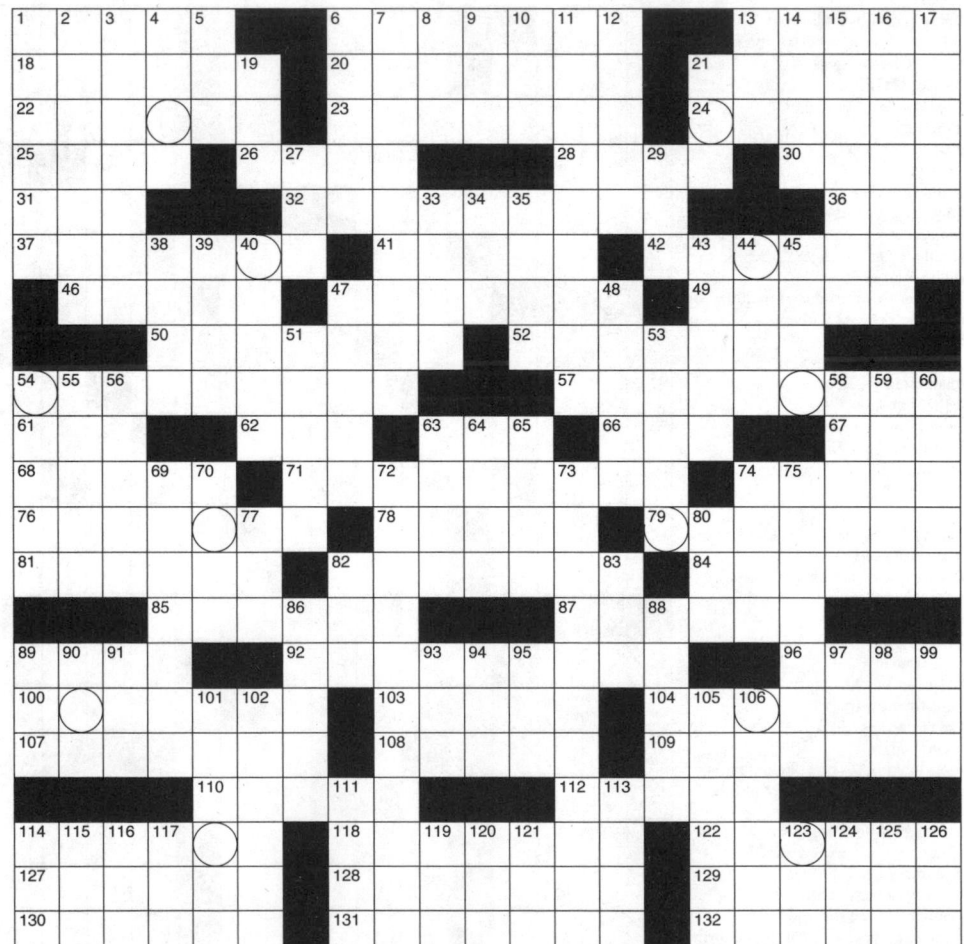

by Christina Iverson and Jeff Chen

ACROSS

1 TV screen inits.
4 Steinful
7 Cut (off)
10 "Nope"
13 Lucky strikes?
15 Massage target
17 Capital of Belarus
19 Spa amenity
20 1/x, for x
24 Top type
25 Hay fever irritant
26 Online payment option
27 Record holder for the most Indianapolis 500 laps led (644)
29 Lowly workers
30 Mythical being depicted in bronze in Copenhagen Harbor
31 Followers of dos
32 Home of the N.C.A.A.'s Rhody the Ram, for short
34 Director DuVernay
36 Govt. org. often impersonated on scam calls
37 Picked a card
39 Abstainers . . . or the central column's answers vis-à-vis 20-, 39-, 74- and 101-Across, respectively
44 One in a pocketful
45 Has finished
47 Speed that would enable a 23-minute D.C.-to-L.A. flight
48 Where fans are often placed on high?
50 Org. whose academy's motto in English is "The sea yields to knowledge"
52 One who might give you a shot
53 Miss
54 Food that Marge Simpson once served with "a whisper of MSG"
58 Big name in denim
59 Collected $200, say
63 "Te ___"
64 Former superstore chain selling diapers and strollers
67 "Egads!"
68 Quite a tale
70 Spirit
71 Charitable offering
73 Film character who says "Kiss me as if it were the last time"
74 It postulates a space-time fabric
80 Congressional budget directives
81 San Francisco's ___ Valley
82 Radio medium
83 Renaissance-themed festival
84 Tears to pieces
86 Who once had all 10 of the top 10 Billboard hits simultaneously
87 "The Gift of the Magi" author
89 "Seriously?"
91 Gobbles (down)
94 Doze (off)
95 Mr. Incredible's actual surname
96 College town of George Washington Carver
98 Hither's partner
99 "Absolutely!"
101 Little Richard hit with "the most inspired rock lyric ever recorded," per Rolling Stone
104 Sea eagle
105 Many-time N.H.L. All-Star Jagr
107 Sheepish
108 Fashionable
110 Nonbinary identity
111 Focus of an egoist's gaze
112 Magazine with annual Women of the Year Awards
113 President Ford and others
114 Traditional, if bulky, presents in Santa's bag
115 Opening words?

DOWN

1 Super Bowl trophy eponym
2 Deep-fried doughy treats
3 Picked nits
4 ___ tear (athlete's injury)
5 Thieves' place
6 Yosemite attraction
7 Hides one's true nature
8 Group with the 2012 chart-topping album "Up All Night," to fans
9 It's pitchfork-shaped
10 "Why do you ask?" response
11 The 1 in (1,2), in math
12 Work times, typically
14 Phaser setting
15 Admiral Graf ___ (German W.W. II ship)
16 Leaf (through)
17 Bearing
18 One might be taken in protest
19 Longtime NPR host Diane
21 Satellite inhabited continuously since 2000: Abbr.
22 Complement of turtledoves in a Christmas song
23 Obsolescent TV companion
28 Paris's ___ La Fayette
30 Disfigure
33 ___ sleep
35 Perturb
38 "The Caine Mutiny" author
39 End of some school names, for short
40 Orbicularis ___ (eyelid-closing muscle)
41 "We ___ Kings"
42 What fools might make of themselves
43 "Je ne ___ quoi"
44 Joint winner of FIFA's Player of the Century award in 2000
46 Top-level foreign policy grp.
49 Monopoly quartet: Abbr.
51 Fold
53 Fuel line
54 Wallop
55 1935 Triple Crown winner
56 Top-ranked professional tennis player for a record 237 consecutive weeks
57 Ark contents
59 ___ fast one
60 Labor day setting?
61 "Beau ___"
62 Signs off on
65 "I tell ya!"
66 Charlotte of "The Facts of Life"
69 Universal self, in Hinduism
70 Preserves something?
72 Houston A.L.'ers
73 Trump who wrote 2017's "Raising Trump"
75 Tiny margin of victory
76 When one usually goes through customs
77 Purple pool ball
78 Brushed up on
79 Lucky ticket holder's cry
84 Famed Chicago steakhouse
85 A couple of Bible books
87 Completely unrestrained
88 Tribute
89 Swollen, as a lip
90 Drain, as blood
92 Swiss dish
93 Derisive expressions
95 Runs smoothly
97 They can't do without does
100 Prefix for a polygon with 140-degree interior angles
101 Headed for overtime
102 A short rest, so to speak
103 He: Lat.
104 Top female baby name of 2014–18
106 Year that Michelangelo's "The Crucifixion of St. Peter" was completed
109 Things the Energizer bunny may need

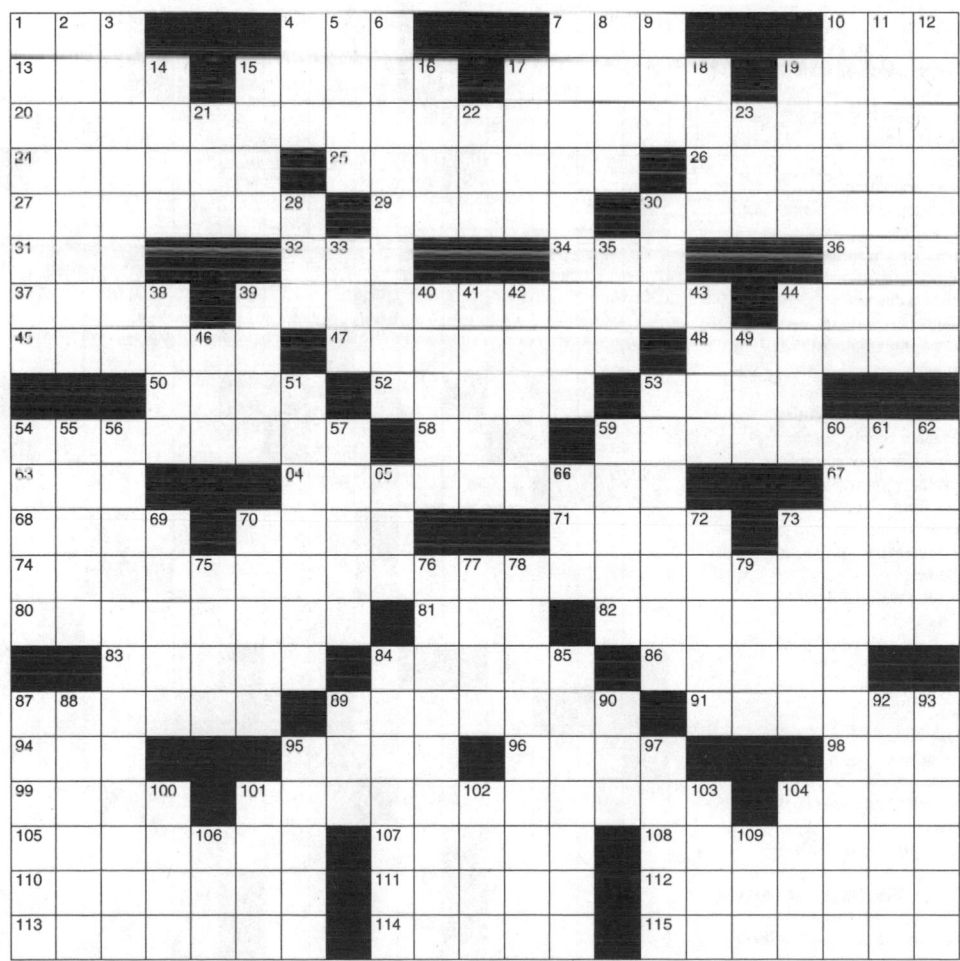

by Laura Taylor Kinnel

ACROSS

1 Reveal, as a plot twist
6 Hit 1980s–'90s show with TV's first lesbian kiss
11 Closed
15 Blemish
19 Groan-inducing, perhaps
20 Pop up
21 The eyes have it
22 Fictional lab assistant
23 Casino gambler's resolution?
26 Reputation
27 Locale of 10 Winter Olympics
28 Match.com, e.g.
29 Helen Mirren or Judi Dench
30 New Age author Chopra
32 Sitcom lover's resolution?
37 Emmy-winning TV producer Klein
38 Morales of "NYPD Blue"
39 Encouraging start?
40 "Wow, awesome!"
42 French, say, to a Brit
44 Georgia, once: Abbr.
46 Sold-out sign
49 Popular Fisher-Price toy for pre-kindergartners
51 Hen's resolution?
56 Round of applause
57 "___-Tiki"
59 Small dam
60 Children's author Beverly
61 Wall St. works on it all summer
62 Simple
63 First of two U.S./U.S.S.R. pacts
64 Locale of New York's Frederick Douglass Blvd.
65 Nun's resolution?
68 ___ Shepherd, former co-host of "The View"
71 Trees used in furniture-making
72 Hub
73 C.E.O.'s deg.
76 Whip, as cream
77 Best Actor winner Malek
78 Junior
79 Many a TikTok user
80 Stalking tiger's resolution?
84 "Arabian Nights" locale
86 Floral wreath by a coral reef
87 Olympic gymnast Raisman
88 Line from the past?
90 Standout star
91 Prominent part of a Mickey Mouse costume
94 Historic plaintiff Scott
96 Ball game
97 Bank robber's resolution?
104 Mideast peace talk?
105 Out of juice
106 Tats
107 Quarreling
109 Cry of woe
110 Union activist's resolution?
115 It usually has a single palm tree, in cartoons
116 Bargaining point that's nonnegotiable
117 Actor/L.G.B.T. rights activist George
118 Saves for later, in a way
119 Word before streak or business
120 Artist Warhol
121 All tuckered out
122 It gets your blood flowing

DOWN

1 Pet cause, for short
2 Takes the lead
3 Megarich group
4 Lickety-split
5 Girl's name ending
6 Actress Metcalf who was nominated for an Oscar for "Lady Bird"
7 Uncultured
8 Blotto
9 Louisville Slugger material
10 Creeping Charlie and Good-King-Henry
11 Many plays are seen in it
12 Actor Rutger of "Blade Runner"
13 Letters naval gazers see
14 What punctual people arrive on
15 They appreciate a nice bouquet
16 Visibly stunned
17 Not italicized
18 Quite a hike
24 Lead-in to "Town" or "Gang"
25 Scenery chewer
31 Direct deposit, for short
33 Verizon offering
34 Da ___, Vietnam
35 Fashionable Christian
36 Pull down
37 Israel's Dayan
41 Feature of many a summer camp cabin
43 Get lost or stolen, in British lingo
44 Metalworker
45 Some of them call Homs home
47 Honest-to-goodness
48 Shrek, e.g.
50 "Auld Lang Syne" time
52 Fuses
53 Spiny anteaters
54 Online magazine since 1996
55 Locale involved in many a New Year's resolution
58 Like Switzerland during World War II
62 Jollity
63 "Same here!"
65 Comic foil of early TV
66 Having the taste of smoke, as some Scotches
67 Nincompoop
68 Toothy tool
69 Get better
70 Famed Deco designer
73 Having deep thoughts
74 Marilyn Monroe or Beyoncé
75 "Consequently . . ."
79 Fly off the handle
81 Treasure chest feature
82 Rock band that Slash really ought to play for?
83 Lip-puckering
85 Kind of monster
89 50 situps a day, say
92 "Feliz ___ Nuevo!" (cry on el 1 de enero)
93 Title heroine of classic 60-Across books
95 P.R. advice for the accused, maybe
97 New moon, e.g.
98 Boxer Ali
99 Beat by a hair
100 "Shall we?"
101 Season ticket holder, e.g.
102 Wields a red pen, perhaps
103 It stops a round and a bout
104 Start a triathlon
108 Trial
111 "Star Wars" villain Kylo
112 Hit with a ray gun
113 Squeeze (out)
114 N.B.A. one-pointers: Abbr.

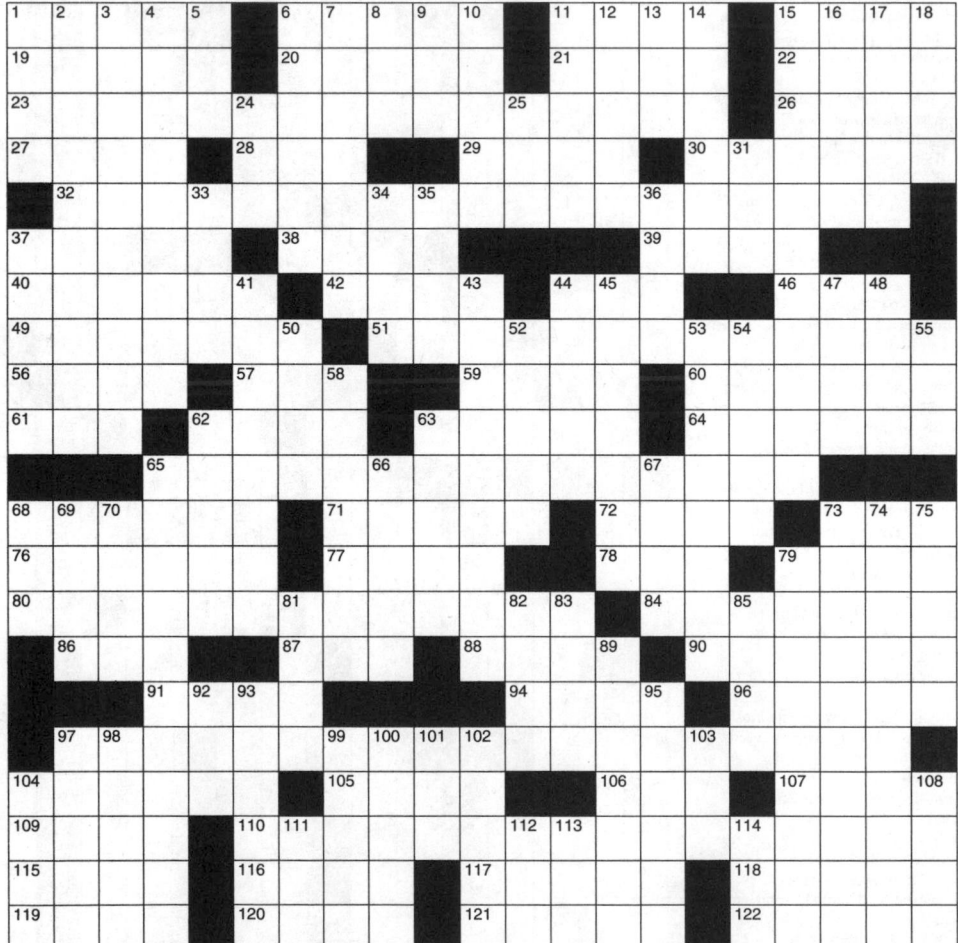

by Andrew Chaikin

ACROSS

1 "Shucks!"
7 They might be covered on your first day of employment
13 Only a second ago
20 Ones with good poker faces?
21 Charm City ballplayer
22 With a leg on either side of
23 Where you can find . . . "jacket" or "yourself"?
25 "Yay!"
26 Lentil or coconut
27 Chinese philosophy
28 Student's saver
29 Plus
31 . . . "go" or "so"?
37 . . . "anybody" or "cooking"?
44 Dog holder
45 A.F.L.-___
46 "Over here!"
47 "Aww"-inspiring
49 Muhammad's birthplace
51 Lover boy
52 Like Fermat's last theorem, eventually
53 Much appreciated
54 They decided what's fair
55 Oteri of "S.N.L."
56 Material in mitochondria
59 Acclaims
60 Issuer of IDs: Abbr.
61 Shade
62 Its material is not hard
64 ___-gritty
65 . . . "got" or "toll"?
69 Result of hitting the bar?
71 "The price we pay for love," per Queen Elizabeth II
72 Goddess who gained immortality for her lover but forgot to ask for eternal youth (whoops!)
73 Flirtatious wife in "Of Mice and Men"
76 They stand up in their bed
77 Kind of gift
78 Sports team bigwig
81 Cash register
82 Like the installments of "A Tale of Two Cities"
83 "Ver-r-ry funny!"
85 Abu ___
86 Obliterate
87 Suspenseful sound
90 ___ Finnigan, friend of Harry Potter
91 Contraction missing a V
92 Kind of verb: Abbr.
93 . . . "two" or "face"?
95 . . . "building" or "hours"?
100 Flames that have gone out?
101 Assist in crime
102 Indian spice mix
107 Things you may dispense with?
110 Take over for
113 . . . "that's" or "special"?
116 "That much is clear"
117 Pays for the meal
118 Stay cheerful despite adversity
119 Back entrance
120 Jellyfish relatives named for a mythological monster
121 Private property?

DOWN

1 Woof
2 "___ your daddy?"
3 River that flows south to north
4 Sets free into the world
5 "Ta-ta!"
6 Directional abbr.
7 "___ Nox" (Mozart title meaning "good night")
8 Greek vessel
9 Enthusiastic Spanish assent
10 Debt docs
11 Scale
12 Collection
13 Chin former
14 "DJ Got Us Fallin' in Love" singer, 2010
15 Women's retro accessory
16 Offensive poster
17 Small bite
18 Part of the classic Chinese work "Shih Ching"
19 Puny
24 "Was ___ hard on them?"
30 "___ Lat" (traditional Polish song)
32 Subside
33 Opposite of -less
34 Paranormal
35 Fine point
36 Provokes
37 Persian Empire founder
38 Impends
39 ___-Loompa (Willy Wonka employee)
40 Fictional braggart
41 The "O" of B.O.
42 Setting for a watch?
43 "We'll teach you to drink deep ___ you depart": Hamlet
48 Et cetera
49 Certain racy magazines
50 Lift
52 "Glad that's done!"
53 Street fair participant
55 "Aww"-inspiring
57 Empire State sch.
58 Org. with an emergency number
61 Razz, as a speaker
63 What the pros say
65 Hesitates
66 Default avatar for a new Twitter user
67 Reconstruction, for one
68 Contraction missing a V
69 From both sides, in a way
70 Songs of praise
73 City whose name looks like it could mean "my friend"
74 Track holder?
75 A Beethoven piece was für her
76 Win every game
79 Exhilarated cry
80 ___ cabbage
81 "End of discussion"
84 Botanist Gray
85 "A man can be destroyed but not ___": Hemingway
87 Age for a quinceañera
88 ". . . ___ quit!"
89 "The Silmarillion" creature
90 Red
94 Newspaper V.I.P. Baquet
96 Pollute
97 Too big for one's britches, say?
98 Hotheadedness?
99 Disposable board
103 Let go
104 Twinkler
105 Lead-in to boy
106 Something to mourn
108 Red giant in Cetus
109 Cozy
110 Rend
111 "The Name of the Rose" novelist
112 "___ Meninas" (Velázquez painting)
113 Highest degree
114 ___-Wan Kenobi
115 Family docs

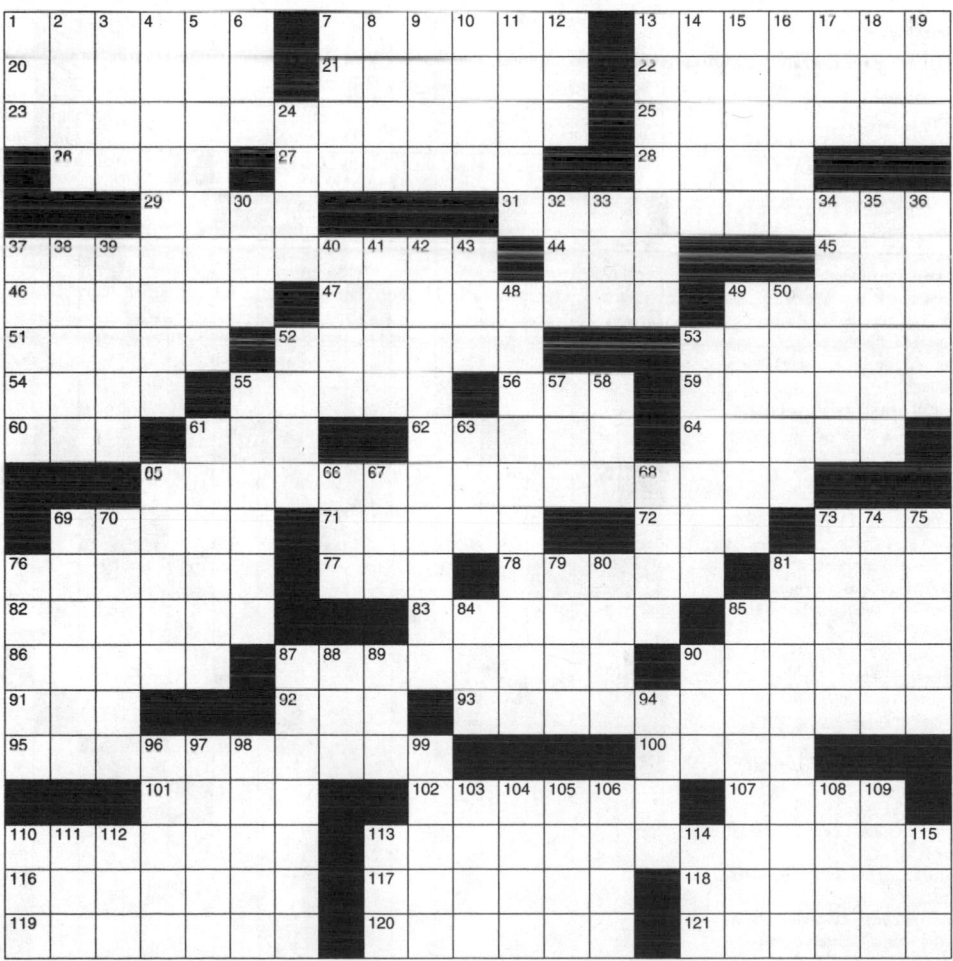

by Tom McCoy

ACROSS

1 Jump to conclusions
7 Off-guard
12 Medium
19 Has reservations
20 It may be waved from the top of a pyramid
22 Olympic group in red, white and blue
23 Result of shaking a soda too hard before opening?
25 Parts of many modern addresses
26 In ___ (gestating)
27 Homecoming giveaways
28 Herbert of the Pink Panther films
30 Limited
31 5 is a high one
32 Busy Apr. workers
34 Noted sexologist, in her infancy?
36 Yahoos
38 Common tidbits in fried rice
40 "Is That All There Is" singer Peggy
41 Any day now
43 Daniel ___ National Forest
44 Stocking stuffer
45 Heroine of "The Rocky Horror Picture Show"
47 Strike caller
48 "The paternity results are in . . . it's the protagonist of a long-running BBC sci-fi show!"?
51 Bury
53 Masseuse's stock
54 Messages you don't want to send to your parents accidentally
55 Nosy person's request
57 Watson's creator
58 Element of one's inheritance
59 Go to ___
60 Cousins of gulls
62 Maiden name of Harry Potter's mother
64 1970s–'80s Sixers star and friends?
68 Take out to dinner
70 Area with R.N.s
72 Disorder that the Ice Bucket Challenge benefited, for short
73 Certain Facebook reaction button
75 Collar
77 One of Spain's Balearic Islands
79 Ones fully agreeing with you, metaphorically
81 Kind of pick
82 "P.U.!"
85 Controversial TV personality's magical sidekick?
88 "I'm not overwhelmed"
89 Overwhelms, as with humor
91 Ironically, small Starbucks size
92 "Two thumbs up!"
93 "Quién ___?" ("Who knows?": Sp.)
95 QB's try: Abbr.
96 "Primal Fear" star, 1996
97 Rimes of country
98 Hurt a Bond villain?
101 A little progress, idiomatically
102 Quick smoke?
105 Loving, as eyes
106 Inits. at Grand Central Terminal
107 Feds
109 Fanny ___, Barbra Streisand role
111 Quickly
113 Sign on Lucy's "Peanuts" booth . . . or a hint to this puzzle's theme
116 Broccoli pieces
117 Four Corners tribe
118 What's played mainly for kicks?
119 Mid-Long Island community
120 Rahm Emanuel's post-White House title
121 Not on board, say

DOWN

1 Make sense
2 "Ish"
3 Sports bigwig every February
4 Alternative to a cab
5 Resort area in northeast Pa.
6 12-Across's skill
7 "___ moi le déluge"
8 Big name in audio equipment
9 Audio equipment
10 Jump-start of sorts, in brief
11 Eucalyptus lovers
12 Our Children magazine org.
13 Release
14 The P.L.O.'s Arafat
15 Just below average
16 Resolve a dispute in a modern way
17 Has the lights off, perhaps
18 Detective's assignment
21 "Butt out!," briefly
24 Certain airline alerts, for short
29 Knight's greeting
33 Continues forward
34 Topless?
35 Plead not guilty
37 ___ and aahs
38 Moue
39 Good listeners
42 "Ask Me Another" airer
43 Suborn
44 Directed the rowers
45 Matchmaking site that asks "Do you keep kosher?"
46 Land in South America
48 "You sure got me pegged!"
49 Strong appetite
50 Latin love
52 Bird so named because of its call
56 Frequent James Franco collaborator
58 Rock whose name sounds good?
59 Certain notebooks
61 Where "The Princess Diaries" is set
63 With 65-Down, technological escalations
65 See 63-Down
66 "The Hunger Games" star, in tabloids
67 Pattern for a forensic scientist
69 Future dealings?
71 Chip material
74 Financial ___
76 Dickens nom de plume
78 Beat
79 Department head
80 In fine shape
81 Yemeni seaport
82 Baseball V.I.P.s
83 Like many uneditable files
84 "Cry me a river!"
86 Tabloid twosome
87 Stereotypically rowdy dudes
90 1961 Michelangelo Antonioni drama
94 Awards won by Stephen King and Agatha Christie
96 Successor to South Carolina's Thurmond in the Senate
97 Time to give up?
99 Kentucky Derby winner's wreath
100 Abbr. on a cover sheet
101 Furnishings
103 More dangerous in the winter, say
104 Comedy, e.g.
105 Loopy little films?
107 Down Under greeting
108 Bad thing to lose
110 Rolling in it
112 Superlative finish
114 Longoria of "Telenovela"
115 She-bear: Sp.

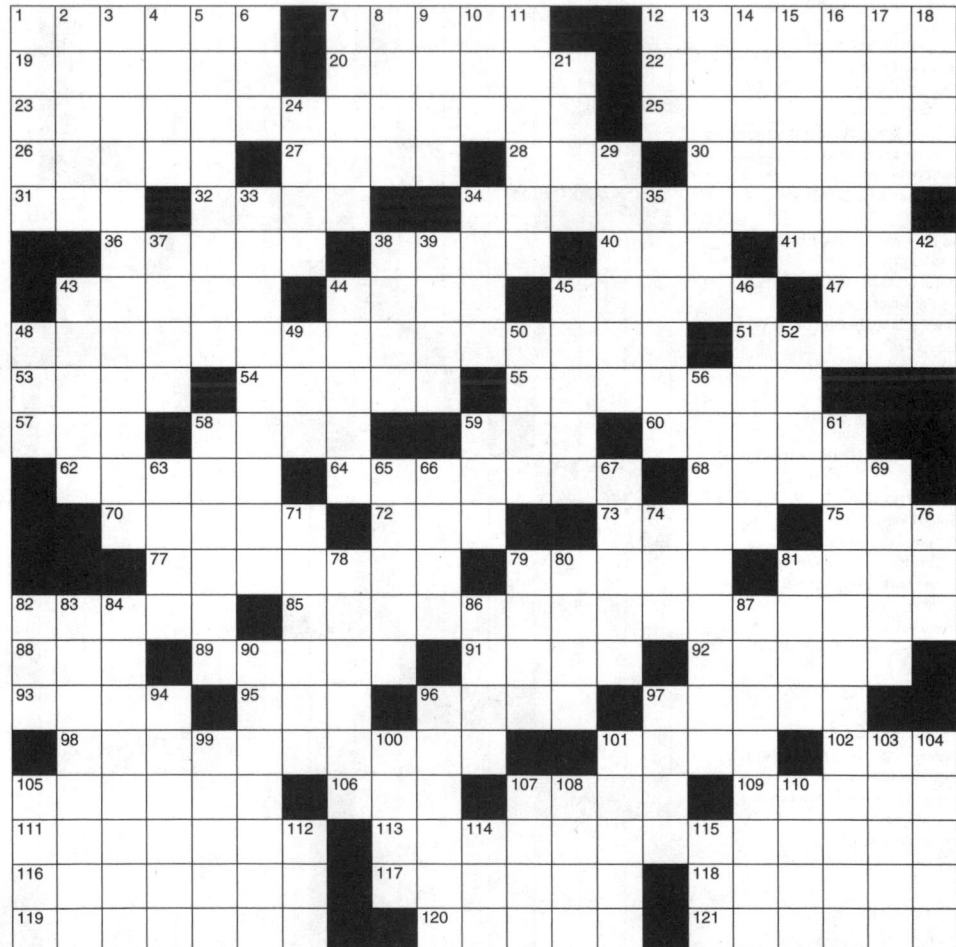

by Finn Vigeland

Note: In the six special squares in this puzzle, the light gray represents green. The dark gray represents red.

ACROSS

1 It's accommodating
6 Comic cries of frustration
10 Grouped for threshing, say
17 Continuing story
18 Busybody
19 Sly one?
20 Many-time Indy 500 pace car
21 Pruritic
22 Goal on a first down
23 Handle letters
24 Boy who challenges stereotypes
26 Ruin
27 Hazel's love in "The Fault in Our Stars"
28 Musical with the songs "Santa Fe" and "I Should Tell You"
30 Blockheaded
31 Showing acute embarrassment, say
32 Anti-Communist fervor
34 1991 film with the tagline "The secret of life? The secret's in the sauce"
36 Symbols of audience disapproval
38 Feller in a forest?
39 ___'easter
41 Spinners
42 Most nail-biting
43 Fill-in-the-blanks diversion
46 The world, idiomatically
47 Soll
48 ___ lane
49 Poet who wrote "Jupiter from on high laughs at lovers' perjuries"
51 Like "E.T." and "Close Encounters of the Third Kind"
53 Finish ahead of
57 Summer, in much of West Africa
58 Former "Live" co-host with Kathie Lee
60 The Rolling Stones' "Get Yer ___ Out"
61 Sidekick in 1990s "S.N.L." skits
62 Trident piece?
64 Clog, with "up"
66 Call before reserving?
67 Stadium store souvenir
68 Stolas : women :: ___ : men
69 Distiller Walker
71 Affix, in a way
73 Bay, e.g.
74 First-year J.D. student
75 Use, as a dish
77 Save, with "away"
78 Top choice
79 Brand with two harnessed horses in its logo
81 Dolls' counterpart
83 Creepazoid
85 Trembling
88 Pilot
90 "Success-s-s!"
91 Meeting around lunchtime
92 Illegal action shown literally in this answer?
94 Not deep, as entertainment
98 Blushes
99 Cinnamon-flavored candy
100 Smarted
102 What spirits may do
103 Workplaces where gloves are worn, for short
104 Ordering option
105 Has a quiet evening, say
107 ___-Caps
108 "For real?"
111 On the double
112 Confront aggressively
114 Incident not worth talking about
115 Its capital is Whitehorse
116 Starting point for Pompeii tourism
117 Busy
118 Idyllic place
119 Part of a kite

DOWN

1 Lab vessel
2 Noted name in suits
3 Long on screen
4 One going for a board position?
5 Like the moon during a total lunar eclipse
6 Designed to clear the air
7 Jerry Siegel or Joe Shuster, for Superman
8 Department store eponym
9 Busybody, maybe
10 Coronary ___
11 Detroit Tiger whose #5 is retired
12 Cambridgeshire city
13 Mobile home: Abbr.
14 Accepted an apology
15 Lusts
16 Calorie counter's temptation
17 Chow (down)
18 Turin title
19 Places to wallow
25 Crossed
26 Is angry
29 Keep, as a garden
31 Youth detention center in England
32 Over the moon
33 Feature of many a reception
35 ___ Umbridge, teacher of Dark Arts at Hogwarts
37 Now
38 Something that might fall off the shelf?
40 1948 John Wayne film
42 Chooses to lead
43 Legal maneuver
44 Requite
45 Cornell athletes
47 Tinder successes, say
48 Strictly follow
50 Limbs' ends
52 Trips in the dark?
54 Fake
55 Dual-channel
56 Stuffing herb
59 Sound heard at a beach
61 Decorous
63 Baltic capital
65 Pages have four of them
67 Frozen aisle icon
69 Ginger feature
70 Miss badly, say
72 Lived
75 Symbol of Washington State
76 "Oops!"
80 Cusps
82 Annual December pub crawl
84 Defects and all
85 Fats Domino's real first name
86 Grows sick of
87 Goofing (around)
88 Kind of body
89 Most common family name in Vietnam
92 Webster shelfmate
93 Key part: Abbr.
95 Break from a band, maybe
96 Crime writer Joseph
97 Brings (out)
99 Harass
101 Fairy tale figure
104 Evolutionary diagram
105 Pre-fries?
106 Org. with Divisions I–III
109 Social gathering
110 Like most children's programming
111 Something said repeatedly on a ship
113 Sgt.'s inferior

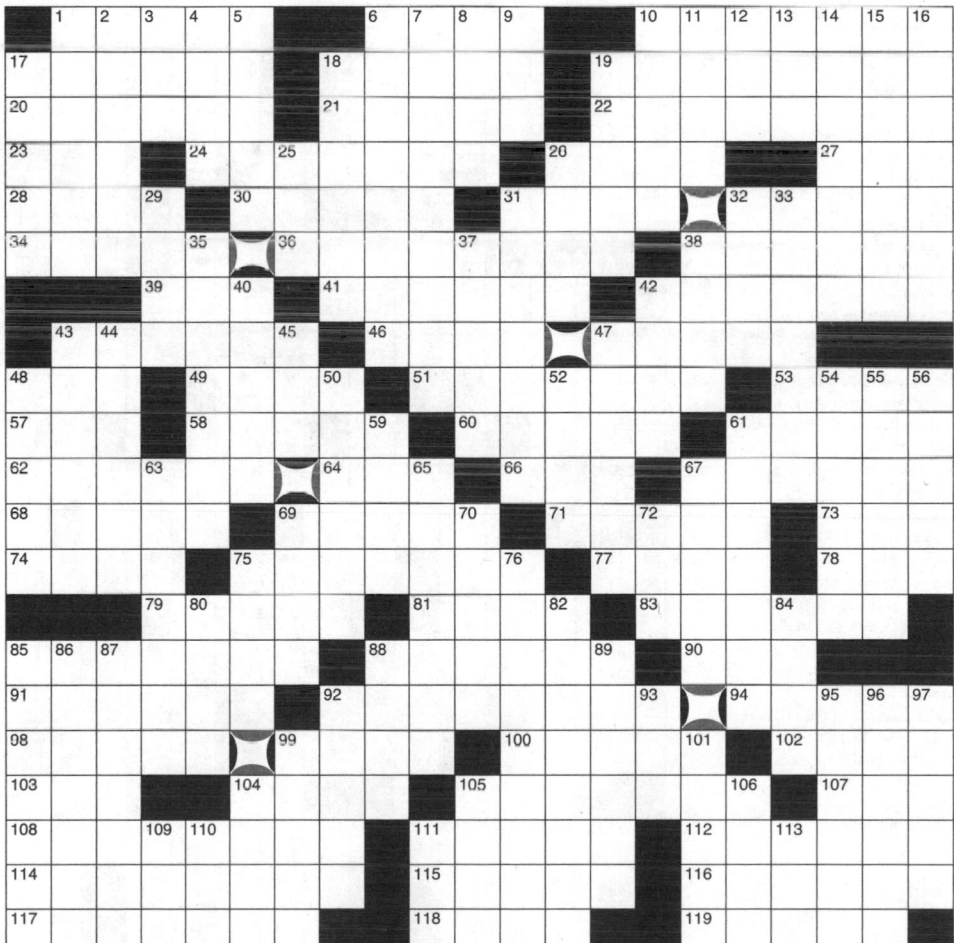

by David Woolf

ACROSS

1 Foyer fixture
9 Paratroopers' gear
15 Building material for an 80-Across (in two different ways?)
20 Unsympathetic response to a complainer
21 Warhol's "Campbell's Tomato Juice Box," e.g.
22 Italian vessel?
23 *Conflict at sea*
26 Asia's ___ Sea
27 Geological flat top
28 Staple at a luau
29 Orange Pixar character
30 Main character in Kafka's "The Metamorphosis"
32 River ___ (tributary of the Thames)
34 Balls or fire preceder
37 Way off
40 Decides, in a way
44 Dura ___ (brain membrane)
46 "That's more than I want to know!"
47 *Parenting problem at a zoo*
52 Luke Skywalker's landspeeder, e.g.
53 Spill one's secrets
54 "The Governator"
55 Focus of study for Niels Bohr
56 Lead-in to dealer or dialer
59 Winter Palace resident
61 Particulars, in slang
62 Logician's word
63 Show weariness
65 Eight days after the nones
67 Choice word?
69 *Cold War synopsis*
74 Rimes with rhymes
75 Othello, for one
76 "Kewl!"
77 Catch
80 See 15-Across
83 It may be recounted
85 Be highly esteemed
87 Not mad
88 Roger Bannister, notably
89 Word repeated in James Brown's "It's a ___ ___ ___ World"
91 "Please show some compassion!"
94 *Show of respect at the Vatican*
99 Wood in Lucius Malfoy's wand
100 Dear one?
101 Rapt
102 Twosome
104 Incapacitate, in a way
105 "Inside the N.B.A." airer
106 Yemen, once
111 Subj. for a radio astronomer
113 One in a gray suit, for short
115 Most-applied-to sch. in the U.S.
119 Split pair
120 *Overthrow of a monarchy*
126 Smart ___
127 Only guest host in the 21 years of Leno's "The Tonight Show"
128 It requires a balancing act
129 City of Light, informally
130 Gives the old heave-ho
131 Faulty connections?

DOWN

1 Food ___ (feelings after big meals)
2 John who wrote "Appointment in Samarra"
3 Hussein : Obama :: ___ : Garfield
4 "Through many dangers, ___ and snares I have already come" ("Amazing Grace" lyric)
5 Burgundy of "Anchorman"
6 "Pardon . . ."
7 Heart
8 Big name in headphones
9 Number cruncher, for short
10 Short shorts
11 Until
12 The Seal of Solomon and others
13 Before, poetically
14 Letters on many a racecar
15 Part of a plot
16 ___ queen
17 Pitched poorly
18 Queen ___
19 SAT org.
24 Raft material
25 Pentium creator
31 Profess
33 Long stretch
35 Supercontinent of 200 million years ago
36 "___ be my pleasure"
38 Scope
39 Climbs
41 World of Warcraft beast
42 Waver of a wand
43 Bathroom tile shade
45 Prepped
47 Cowardly Lion harasser
48 Bathroom bar
49 The Pink Panther, in "The Pink Panther"
50 Takes the place of, in batting
51 Seventh film in the "Rocky" series
52 ___ characters (basic means of writing Chinese)
57 "___ the season . . ."
58 Leftover
60 Hardly original works
63 Curled one's lip
64 Police blotter letters
66 Fair-hiring inits.
68 Org. with the Eddie Eagle safety program
70 Tree with catkins
71 Charms
72 Long stretch
73 Delicacy usually eaten as an appetizer
78 Marching band?
79 Queen ___ (pop music nickname)
80 Stoked
81 Deli roll
82 Rubens or Raphael
84 Gets fitted for a suit?
86 Drive-___
87 Pool site
90 Leave runny on the inside, say
92 Compete
93 Leftovers
95 Once-common campus event
96 Welcome to the fold?
97 Downside
98 Go haywire
103 Clear for takeoff?
107 OutKast chart-topper
108 On the button
109 Southern beauty
110 Low mounts?
112 Take a hit
114 Sein : German :: ___ : French
116 Cotton or country follower
117 Siberian river
118 Dry
120 Time out?
121 ___ russe
122 A card?
123 Deli offering
124 Alternatives to Macs
125 What a constant hand-washer probably has, for short

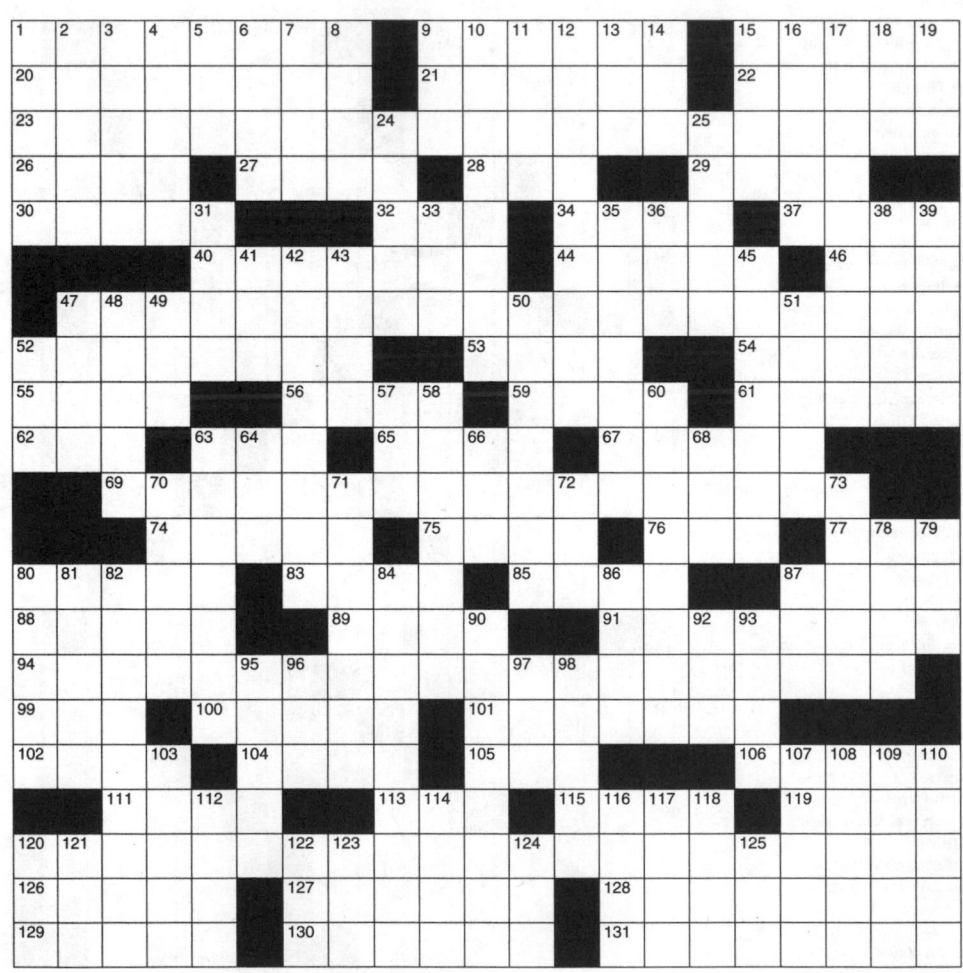

by Priscilla Clark and Jeff Chen

ACROSS

1 Carol opening
7 Unable to make a mess?
11 "Yeah, same here"
19 Crankcase base
20 Rib-eye alternative
21 "S.N.L." cast member, 1985–90
22 Emmerich who directed "Independence Day"
23 Portrayer of Buffett in "Too Big to Fail"
24 Doesn't cool down
25 What's involved in a tongue twister?
28 Alternative to "la"
29 School leader?
30 Good looks or a nice personality
31 Who said "If you even dream of beating me, you'd better wake up and apologize"
32 Very, very top of the earth's crust?
35 Outback baby
37 ___ Na Na
39 Subject of many an internet meme
40 Did some housecleaning
41 Internet annoyances
44 Handler of many trays, for short
45 Unit of bricks, so to speak
47 Beryl and bornite
48 Mary Kay rival
49 First home of the three rich little pigs?
55 Sporty Spice of the Spice Girls
56 We all do it
57 Recently retired Laker great, to fans
58 Green Day drummer
63 Gussying up
66 Wally's bro, '50s–'60s TV
68 Raw footage?
69 Counting rhyme start
70 Bank window letters
72 Donald Duck's nephews, e.g.
74 ___ Barkley, Truman's vice president
75 Sing about?
76 Dixie term of address
78 Curt ___, 2001 World Series M.V.P.
80 Suffragist Elizabeth Cady ___
83 Polish site
85 Entrance requirements, informally
86 The first step
87 Two things the candy lover took to the beach?
90 Going ___
91 Still quite red
95 Abbr. on a copier tray
96 Every leader of North Korea so far
97 Like supermarkets, theaters and planes
99 Sci-fi-inspired toys of the 1980s
101 Suffix with Darwin
103 Point
104 Peer onstage
105 What an overbearing sergeant causes?
108 Green org.
110 Actress Hayek
114 . . . , to Samuel Morse
115 Spirits: Abbr.
116 What improved tire tread produces?
119 Something you might have a handle on
122 New Mexico natives
123 Ruin, as a parade
124 IMAX predecessor
125 Cousin of an impala
126 Seinfeld's "puffy shirt," e.g.
127 Painkillers
128 Spine part
129 Detects

DOWN

1 It helps get the blood flowing
2 Some gowns
3 "American Psycho" author
4 The cantina in "Star Wars," e.g.?
5 Bit of summer wear
6 Onetime Expos/Mets outfielder Chávez
7 X-coordinate
8 Custom
9 New York native
10 "Vive ___!"
11 Response: Abbr.
12 Too tired for the task, say
13 Product that works, and is stored, under the sink
14 Mystery writer Dorothy
15 "___ bodkins!"
16 More run-down
17 Like some soap
18 Shifts to the right
20 Follow
26 Appointment book page
27 Fed. reactor monitor
33 Ink
34 Wee hour
36 Will work
38 Peddle
41 Coddles
42 Have thirds, say
43 Cornmeal dish
44 Hot
46 Winter Olympics powerhouse: Abbr.
50 "Glad the week's almost over!"
51 Pitchfork-wielding group
52 Help illegally
53 Narrows the gap with
54 Only country with a nonrectangular flag
59 Where they sell accessories at a pet shop?
60 Like a satellite's path
61 Unvarying in tone
62 Kind of truck
64 Red Cross setup
65 Humongous
67 Mark
71 Group sharing a tartan
73 Only state with a nonrectangular flag
77 Rap epithet
79 "Nope, huh-uh"
81 Night ___
82 Bottom-line figure
84 Villain in "The Avengers"
88 Historic blocks
89 Internet surfing, often
91 Daphne du Maurier novel made into a Best Picture
92 Flooded with
93 "South Pacific" star ___ Brazzi
94 Squeak (by)
98 Proportionate
100 Like a clear night sky
102 Quill tip
103 Yearly tree growths
104 Long-nosed fish
106 Online finance firm
107 Moved like sap
109 Concern for vets
111 "Peanuts" thumb-sucker
112 North Woods denizen
113 Queen ___ lace
117 Some, to Spaniards
118 Some Wall St. traders
120 "Ideas worth spreading" grp.
121 "Live ___" (Taco Bell slogan)

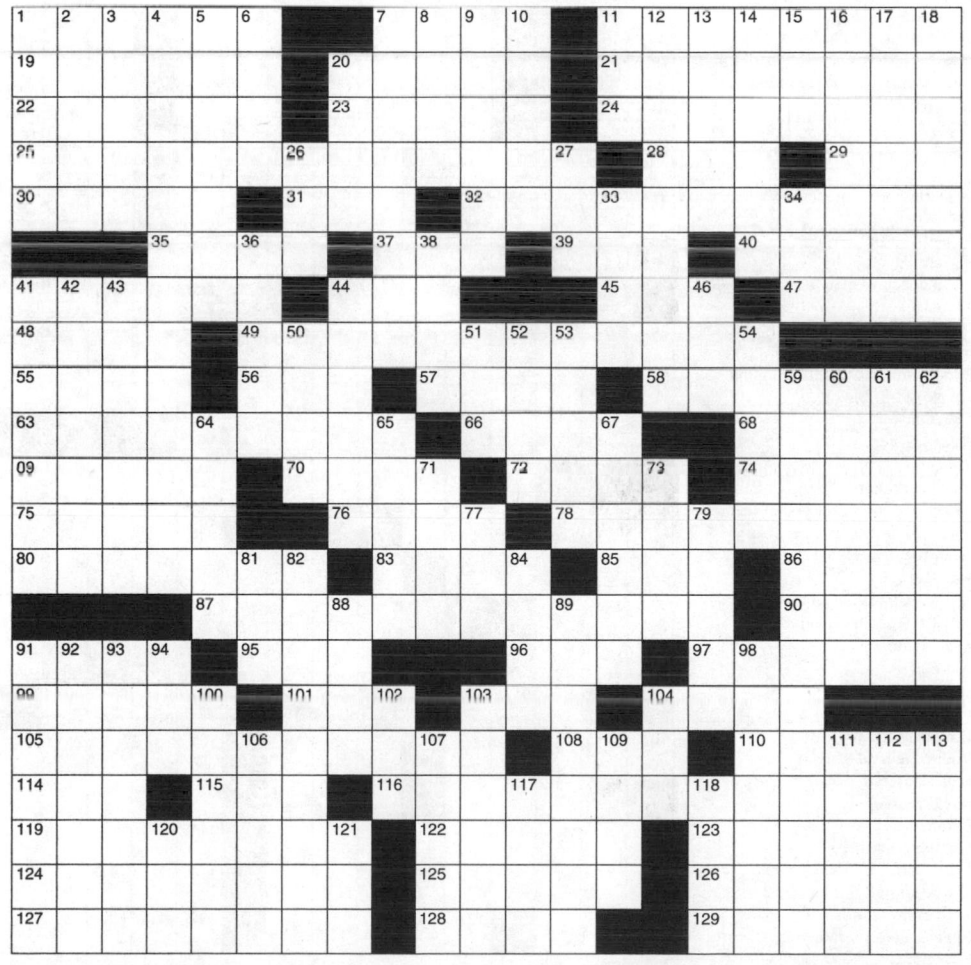

by Samuel A. Donaldson

ACROSS

1 Overawe
4 Things falling out of Vogue?
11 Words to a Spanish sweetheart
16 Mover, but not a shaker (one hopes)
19 Atlantic 10 Conf. school
20 Where techno music originated
21 Belly
23 Camelhair color
24 Surplus
25 Where the Sun shines?
26 Doesn't let it go
28 "Star Wars" name
29 Got into a mess?
30 Pie-eyed
31 Wee bit
32 Call it a day . . . or a career
33 Sunday delivery: Abbr.
34 Woolly ruminant
35 Very lowbrow
37 Fabulous fabulist
39 Achievement
40 Riverboat hazard
42 Linguists' interests
46 Boat that landed on 94-Down
49 Final, countrywide competition
53 ____ tap
54 Go (for)
55 Salary negotiator
56 Alternated
58 Dress down
60 Winner of 11 Grand Slam tennis titles
61 Common seasoning for Italian sausage
62 Elected
63 Sports axiom refuted by this puzzle
69 "The Handmaid's Tale" author
72 Not with it
73 Place in a 1969 western
77 Serious devotee
78 Papal conclave members
82 Ghostly
83 He said "It's not bragging if you can back it up"
84 Group with five members in this puzzle, with "the"
85 Court plea
87 Sleep stage
88 Relief
89 Play the part of
90 Father of Phobos, the god of fear
92 Sound of the South
97 Liability of note?
100 Swagger
102 ____ Minella (Muppet monkey)
105 City ENE of Cleveland, O.
107 Lady's title
108 Anticipate
109 Ball bearer
110 Fruit soda brand
111 Temple of Isis site
112 Where General Mills is headquartered
114 Bank trouble?
116 Dated
117 "Be there in a jiffy!"
118 Encountered
119 Not be straight
120 Cold War-era inits.
121 Eppie's adoptive father, in a George Eliot novel
122 Suffragist Elizabeth Cady ____
123 Not opposin'

DOWN

1 Is up to the task
2 Winston Churchill, notably
3 One concerned with aging?
4 Wedding pair
5 State since 1864: Abbr.
6 McQueen or King
7 Things that corrections correct
8 Tour hiree
9 Aggressive types
10 Typical intro?
11 Heavy winds
12 Maternally related
13 Colleague of Freud
14 Encountered
15 Relatives of bobolinks
16 Only African-American to win an Oscar, Tony and Emmy for acting
17 Relevant, legally
18 With 47-Down, driver's question
22 "Say cheese!"
27 County name in 30 states
32 House speaker after Boehner
36 Sidesplitter
38 ____ platter
39 "Runaway" singer Shannon, 1961
41 "I'm off"
43 "My dear man"
44 Novelist Patchett
45 Fastball, in baseball slang
47 See 18-Down
48 Sharp
49 Pick up
50 Back
51 Unaccompanied
52 Company name ender after "&"
53 First U.S. city to host the Olympics
57 "Baseball" documentarian Burns
58 Half a step?
59 What ballplayers look forward to after playing on the road
61 Sustained
62 Cartoon collectible
64 Mortar carrier
65 Hampton ____
66 Words of confidence
67 Court plea, briefly
68 Opera set in 1800 Rome
69 Not even close?
70 Floor piece
71 German hunting dog
74 1904 Jack London novel
75 Your, to Yves
76 Caste member
78 State with five teams in the 84-Across: Abbr.
79 Double-platinum album for Steely Dan
80 Mythological bird
81 Harriet Beecher Stowe novel subtitled "A Tale of the Great Dismal Swamp"
82 Lining up against
84 Ways of doing things, for short
86 Numerical prefix
88 Parlor pieces
91 Bankrupts
93 Points (to)
94 See 46-Across
95 Actress Ryder
96 Admits
98 Charlotte ____ (Caribbean capital)
99 Proffer
100 Greek island where Pythagoras and Epicurus were born
101 Delivery that's usually expected
102 Prop for a lion tamer
103 Insurance giant
104 Some calls on a police hotline
106 Kind of chips you shouldn't eat
111 Before being outed, for short
113 H.S. study
115 Native Oklahoman

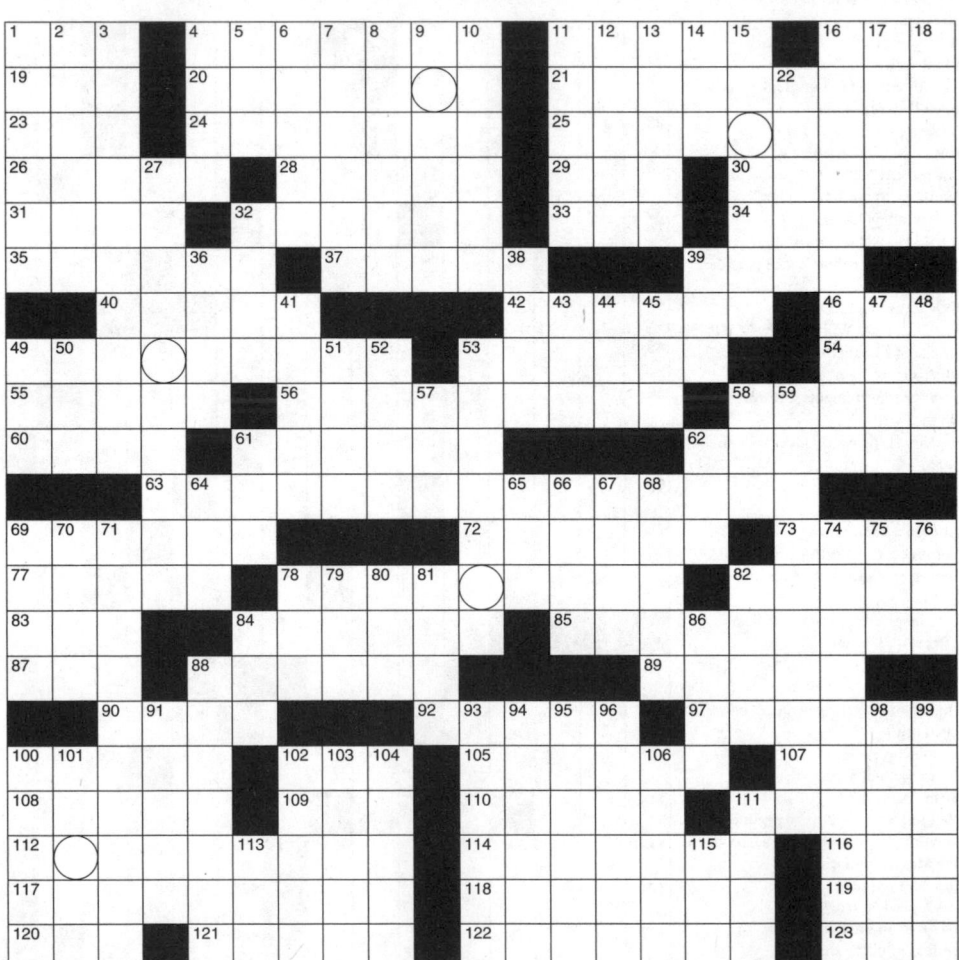

by David J. Kahn

ACROSS

1. "Me too"
6. Expert on jingles
11. U.K. V.I.P.
15. Corp. leadership
19. Baby's woe
20. Nap for a loafer?
21. "Cien ___ de Soledad" (Gabriel García Márquez novel)
22. Bailiwick
23. Lane restricted to allow motorcades through?
26. Ribs
27. Jerry's adversary, in cartoons
28. ___ colada
29. Night vision?
30. Early online forum
32. Honolulu's historic ___ Palace
34. Current
36. Pressing and shoving me as I enter the subway?
41. Sounds before sneezes
42. Word repeated by Romeo in "As mine on ___, so ___ is set on mine"
43. Brown v. Board of Education city
44. Last words of a pep talk, perhaps
48. Not taking a bow?
51. New Haven collegian
52. Mousetrap brand
54. Take a hit
55. Highway obstructed by accidents, detours and construction?
59. Things sometimes stolen in Hollywood
61. East Berlin's land: Abbr.
62. Prosperous period
63. Standing Rock tribe
65. Pays attention to
66. Rope for strangulation
69. Package sender to an enlistee, maybe
71. Kosher
74. Title kitten in a Key and Peele action comedy
76. Not stay in the pail, say
77. Youth org. since 1910
80. They sit in front of a cox
82. Took public transportation while one's wheels were at the shop?
86. City near Provo
87. "Time ___ a premium"
89. Grp. with a co-pay
90. Bit of dangly jewelry
91. "Star-bellied" Seussian creature
93. Net fisher
96. Song lead-in to "di" or "da"
97. Rural turndown
98. "This tollbooth line will make me late!"?
103. Portal in "Alice in Wonderland"
106. Shellac and myrrh
107. Rule against singing
108. Toodle-oos
111. Peddle
112. :-D
115. Where Scarlett got a letter?
116. Split an Uber?
120. Fun-run length, for short
121. Last thing said before eating?
122. Washington, but not Jefferson
123. Any local in "The Music Man"
124. Matter of interest?
125. Spot
126. Like legalized marijuana
127. Alternating-current motor inventor

DOWN

1. ___ no.
2. Home of many Big Apple galleries
3. One with '18 after one's name, say
4. Alma mater of Wm. Hewlett of Hewlett-Packard
5. Colorful summer treat
6. Like the "s" in "aisle"
7. Dodge S.U.V.
8. Brave adversary
9. Condition for some distracted kids, for short
10. Not e'en once
11. Like some oil money
12. Canine coat?
13. "Hmm, the oven was on. Did ___ didn't . . ."
14. Time release
15. Get to Grand Central right at 5:00?
16. Tool for a blacksmith
17. Jason's wife in myth
18. Finger-licking good
24. Thread: Prefix
25. San Francisco : BART :: Philadelphia : ___
31. Sweater damage
32. "No more for me, thanks"
33. Force onward
35. Utah's ___ Canyon (locale of petroglyphs)
36. Kale alternative
37. Fix, as a golf green
38. Pianist Rubinstein
39. Rise above the din, say
40. Somewhere over the rainbow they're blue, in song
45. Carry-___
46. Scraped (out)
47. Cleanup target
49. Tax ___
50. Queen dowager of Jordan
52. ___ Homme (fashion line)
53. Awkward
56. Decision point
57. Simple life?
58. Through
60. "Quantico" actress Priyanka ___
64. Prefix with -phone
66. "I'm scared by the speed you're going in this traffic!"?
67. Not sagging at all
68. No-nonsense quartet?
70. Pout
71. Elton's johns
72. Bring in
73. Special soldier
75. Did some theater work, casually
77. Good ol' boy
78. Certain vodka order, informally
79. Up
81. Neighbor of Hond.
83. Radiate
84. Campaign supporter
85. Expressive facial features
88. ___ Tzu (dog)
92. Doofus
93. Take care of
94. Put on a pedestal
95. Sister of Snow White
99. Delaying response to "Is it time?"
100. Comic Boosler
101. ___ qua non
102. Sends a breakup text, say (tsk!)
103. Helicopter feature
104. Refrigerator handle?
105. Snacks during hora feliz
109. N.Z. neighbor
110. Mlle., in Managua
112. House work?
113. ___ cavity
114. Golden Globe winner Dunham
117. Friend of Francine
118. Kind of paper
119. Help make the bed?

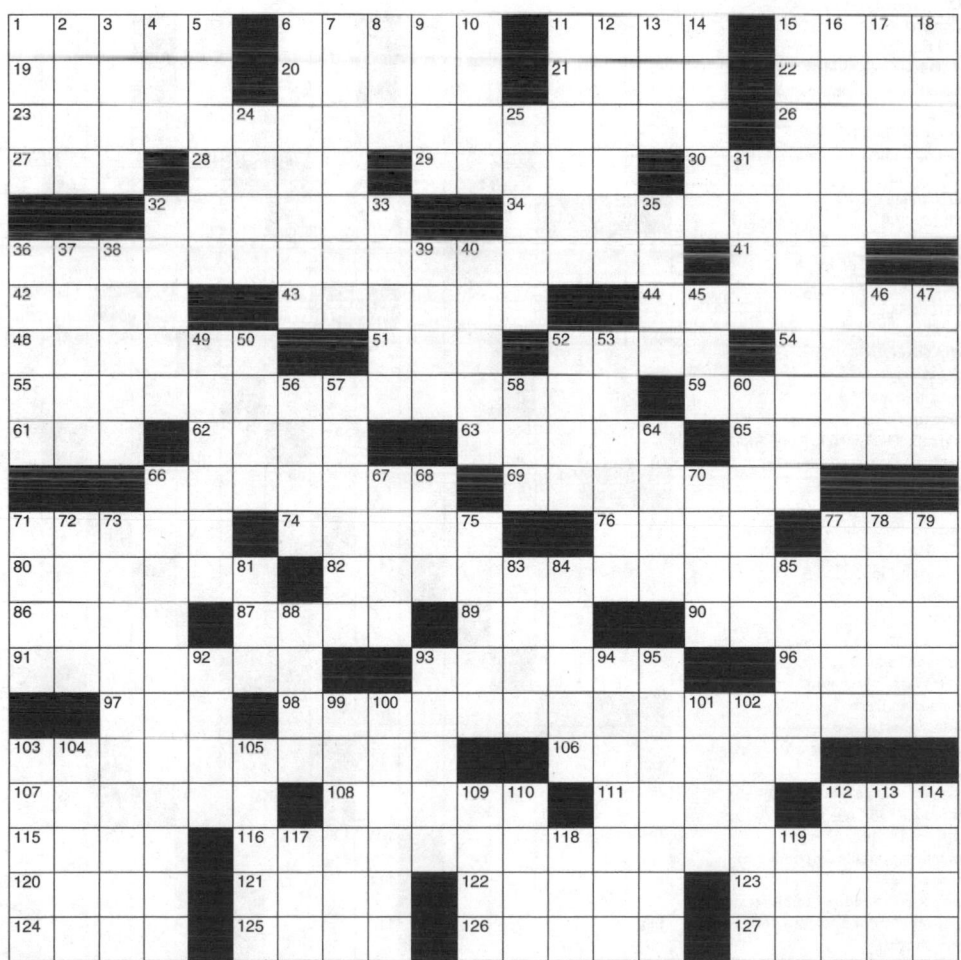

by Ruth Bloomfield Margolin

ACROSS

1 Temporarily stops running
7 Sport-____ (some vehicles)
11 Contain, as a spewing oil well
14 Military bigwigs
19 "Pick me!"
20 Light bite
21 Excitement
22 GPS suggestion
23 Breakfast trio
26 Classic song
27 ____-backwards
28 Smuggler's unit
29 Record label for Pink and Pitbull
30 Lets off the hook?
32 Otello, in "Otello"
33 Even
34 Act as a go-between
35 "You can skip me"
38 Puppet show trio
41 Fall guy?
43 "That's rough!"
44 Some Canadian natives
45 In the tradition of
48 ____ Aldridge, pioneering Shakespearean actor
49 Lost baggage helpers
52 Ad biz awards
54 Producer of public radio's "Radiolab"
55 Spanish seasoning that's a letter short of its English counterpart
56 Youngest daughter on "Black-ish"
57 Hold tightly
58 Dangerous injection
59 Capital city with more than 300 islands
61 Sergey of Google
62 "Nobody's here but me"
64 Sailing trio
67 Surrounded by
69 "Little Latin ____ Lu" (1960s hit)
70 Effervescent citrus beverage
73 Old Ford vehicles, for short
74 Open
76 Skyrockets
77 Open ____
78 Strip pokers?
79 Fumes
80 Some skin art
81 Place for R.N.s
82 Subj. of "The Electric Kool-Aid Acid Test"
83 "lol" alternative
84 Unnecessary extra
85 Gilda of "Saturday Night Live"
87 Folk trio
92 Rap artist Flo ____
93 Dinero
95 Throw
96 State a case
98 Director Taika ____
99 "Star Wars" nickname
100 Pronoun in Dixie
101 Philosopher ____-tzu
104 Fortune 500 company with an avian symbol
105 Survivor of an all-out brawl . . . or a hint to 23-, 38-, 64- and 87-Across
110 Battle of Leningrad, e.g.
111 Something ratable by number of Pinocchios
112 Long transmission of folklore, say
113 Charlotte Motor Speedway org.
114 Underworld
115 Camera with a mirror, in brief
116 Hail on a bridge
117 Trash

DOWN

1 Sammy on a 1998 cover of Newsweek
2 Heaps
3 Good crosswords provide lots of them
4 Chop (off)
5 John who wrote "An Essay Concerning Human Understanding"
6 Arts-and-crafts kit trendy in the 1970s–'80s
7 Open, as a bottle of wine
8 "TiK ____" (Kesha hit)
9 Class for some immigrants, for short
10 Foe of Robin Hood
11 Geographically largest member of NATO
12 Interject
13 In view?
14 Upholsterer's fabric
15 Certain expensive watch, in slang
16 Autobahn autos
17 Michael of R.E.M.
18 Goes with
24 Jesús on the diamond
25 Big name in laptops
31 Digits ending many prices
32 Baking meas.
33 Eponymous New Mexico tribe
35 Do email scamming
36 Radiant emanations
37 "Huh, you know him, too?!"
39 Stadium section
40 Police procedural beginning in 2003
42 News
45 Words before a year
46 City on the Rhône
47 Zenith
50 Flee
51 Have ____ with
52 Ernest who wrote "Ready Player One"
53 Tall and thin
54 Joins
57 Classic horror film locale
58 Actress/singer Hudgens
60 Matches up
61 Makes fuzzy
63 Nursing facility?
65 Huffed and puffed
66 Southern university whose team is the Phoenix
67 ____ Clooney, Barbara Walters's "most fascinating person" of 2014
68 Litter sounds
71 Chopped up
72 BMW competitor
75 Swerve
76 Letter that, surprisingly, is not the end of the Greek alphabet
79 Assail
80 Campus building
83 Spirals
84 Charlize Theron's role in 2015's "Mad Max" reboot
86 Dr. ____
87 Thick soup
88 Sci-fi stunner
89 One who cries "Uncle!"?
90 Contradict
91 "Nuts!"
93 Underworld
94 Three sheets to the wind
97 Things near funny bones
98 Load of laundry
101 Pet peeves?
102 Med. school course
103 Fearsome figure
106 Suffer
107 "Forget about it!"
108 Freudian area of study
109 Cable alternative

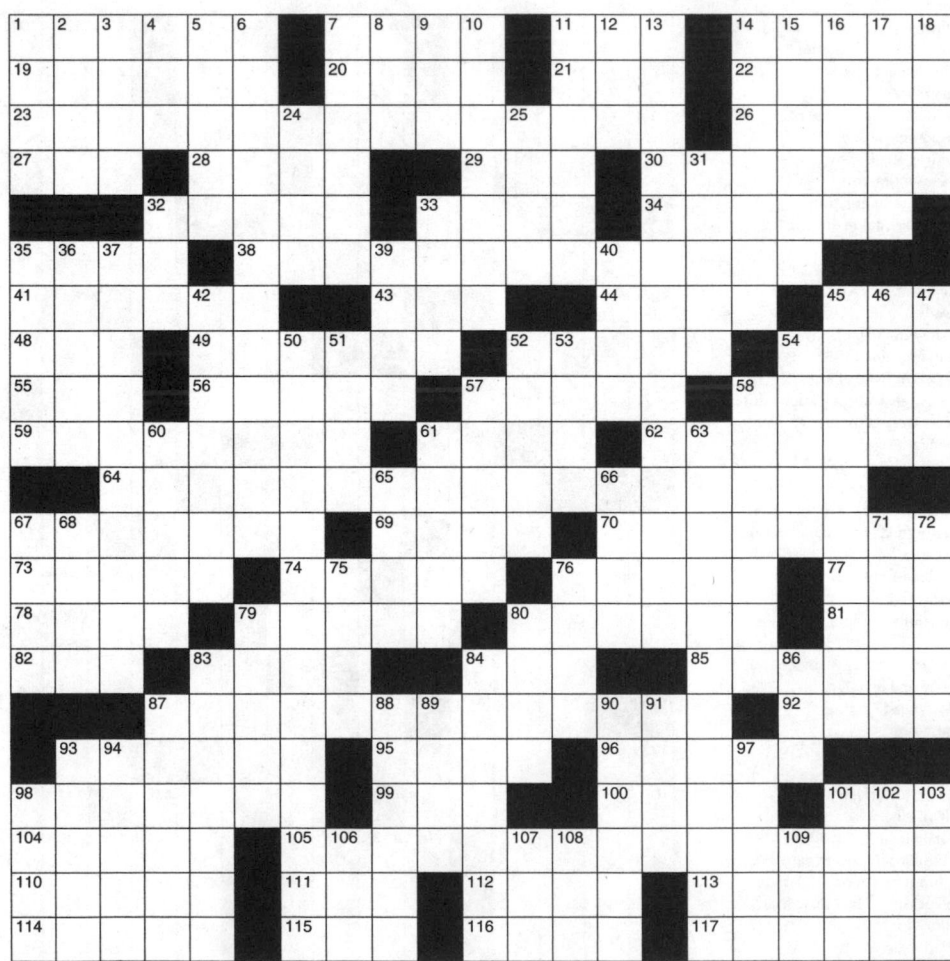

by Amanda Chung, Karl Ni and Erik Agard

Note: After completing this puzzle, draw a line starting at the middle square of 59-Across and connect five appropriate squares in roughly clockwise order to reveal an image suggested by this puzzle's theme.

ACROSS

1 "Friendly" cartoon character
7 Pro
14 Symbols in calculus
20 Simple kind of antenna
21 Expenditures' counterpart
22 Lacking a break
23 Add surreptitiously
24 Worrisome sight for a swimmer
25 With spite
26 Some Houdini feats
28 John of spy fiction
30 Something extraordinary that won't soon be forgotten
32 Some northern Europeans
35 Bit of hydrotherapy
38 Caffeinated drink with tapioca balls
39 Doled (out)
41 Opposite of colorblindness?
42 "___ Jacques"
43 Ones eligible for marathon prizes
45 "Don't bite the hand that feeds you," e.g.
46 Flight board abbr.
47 Sinking feelings
50 Mistrusts
53 Mother or sister
54 Does more than ask
56 Dr. ___ Sattler, "Jurassic Park" paleobotanist
57 Energy giant that fell into ignominy in 2002
58 Elevs.
59 Peevish quality
61 Get a new mortgage
63 [Kiss]
65 Powerful D.C. lobby
68 Scylla or Charybdis
74 Speedy wide receiver, perhaps
80 Skill
81 [Fingers crossed]
82 Buzz out in space
83 And so on: Abbr.
84 Staff leader?
86 & 87 What might cost you an arm and a leg?
88 Silver-tongued
89 2004 also-ran
91 Martin who wrote "The Pregnant Widow"
92 Evening, in ads
93 Southern sandwich
94 Is there in spirit?
96 Zen Buddhist goal
98 Makes fun of
99 Menace in 106-Down
104 Bad-mouth
106 Add spice to
107 Metaphor for deliberate ignorance
109 Gobbled (down)
111 Seriously uptight
112 Fictional setting for 106-Down
115 "A ___ believes no one" (old saying)
116 Pottery
117 Caffè ___
118 Justin Bieber or Justin Timberlake
119 Concerning
120 Conventions: Abbr.
121 "There, there"
122 Disgustingly obsequious
123 Class with drills

DOWN

1 Things investors take an interest in?
2 Suffer
3 106-Down director
4 Pink, e.g.
5 Brought out
6 Christen anew
7 Tidiness
8 Proud, fiery types, they say
9 Save for later, in a way
10 Fathers or brothers
11 Santa ___
12 No longer in force
13 Gives meaning to
14 Horn of Africa native
15 Neon, e.g.
16 Transmission
17 Like the menace in 106-Down
18 Common knee injury site, briefly
19 Locale for a trough
27 Fairy-tale "lump"
29 Hack
30 Hit BBC comedy, briefly
31 Peter of "The Maltese Falcon"
32 Handles deftly
33 Utmost degree
34 Farm machine
36 Something to angle for
37 "In Dulci Jubilo" and others
39 Modest skirts
40 Modern subject of F.A.A. regulation
43 TV show with the season's highest rating, often
44 "___ U.S.A." (1963 hit)
48 Sports arbiter
49 Pixielike
51 Cabaret accessory
52 Country music channel, once
55 Decorative pillowcase
58 Adjudicate, as a case
60 "This is looking bad"
62 Lyricist Sammy
63 Singer Haggard
64 Golfer's obstacle
66 Ska-punk band with the 1997 song "Sell Out"
67 Sunning area
68 Ax
69 Seasonal quaff
70 Small herrings
71 Is a crowd
72 Actor Morales
73 Deteriorates
74 Beginning
75 Precollege, for short
76 Text tweaks
77 Mid-crisis hire, perhaps
78 Word with black or blood
79 Frozen dessert chain
85 Leaves nervously exhausted
88 Thugs
90 Aromatic yellow citrus
93 Preppy wear
95 Himalayan native
97 Cheap and gaudy
98 Charged
99 Scrap
100 Actress Salma
101 Movie org. whose "100 Years . . . 100 Thrills" list has 106-Down at #2
102 Takes a load off
103 Superman, by birth
105 "Coo-oo-ool!"
106 1975 summer blockbuster
107 Morse clicks
108 Indian blueblood
110 Teensy amount
113 Yogi's accessory
114 Oscar ___ (Hollywood honor, informally)

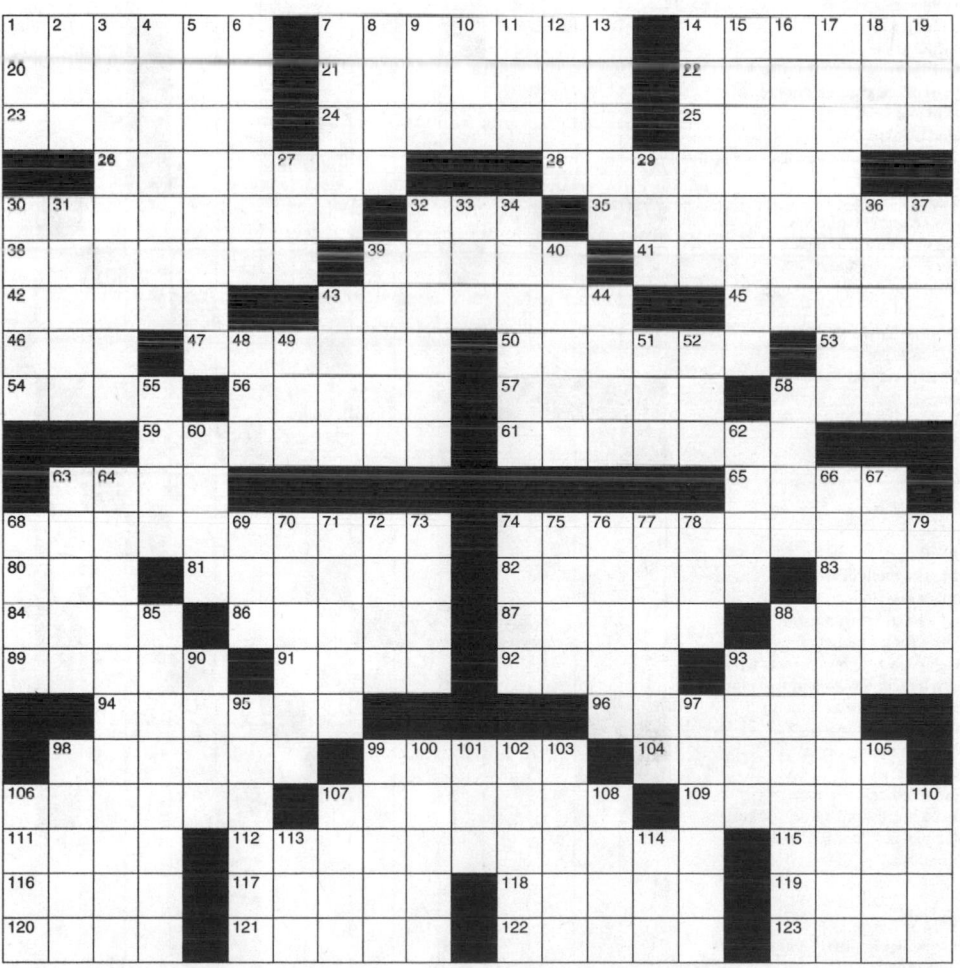

by Timothy Polin

ACROSS

1 Played for a fool
5 Total mess
11 Big piece of cake
15 Buzzed
19 "It's all good"
21 Guido ___, painter of the "Crucifixion of St. Peter"
22 "Do I ___!"
23 Trying to show no signs of life
24 Show out?
26 Metaphorical time in hell
27 Future exec, maybe
28 Began a PC session
29 Seminary study: Abbr.
30 One who "went a-courtin'," in a children's song
32 Hurried along
33 Asian berry marketed as a "superfood"
36 "Darth Vader is Luke's father," e.g.
38 Kind of yoga
39 Lily Potter's maiden name in the Harry Potter books
41 Fair
42 Attention getters
44 Longtime CBS police procedural
48 Voodoo, e.g.
50 Quite a bash, in slang
52 Partner of shock
53 Wrecks, as chances
55 Relating to gaps
59 Norm: Abbr.
62 Burrow
63 Bit of office greenery
65 Dead end sign
67 Kind of state
68 Was forced to turn down an invitation
69 Big character?
71 Take as a bride
72 News commentator Navarro
73 Ball of yarn and others
74 Confession inducers
77 "Jeez, you should keep that private"
78 Get down
79 Go as far down as
84 ___ diagram
86 Green surroundings?
88 Seize
90 Work
91 "You betcha!"
93 Had a leading role?
96 S or M
97 Sam of Watergate hearings
98 Ipecac, e.g.
99 Openly gay
101 Fix, as a mess of wires
103 Singer Garfunkel
104 Big part of an orchestra
108 Bottle for a beachgoer
109 It's left on a highway . . . or a path used by five answers in this puzzle?
111 ___ about (approximately)
112 A little
113 "Yeah, it makes sense"
114 Nota ___
115 Had too much, for short
116 Go on a drinking spree, in slang
117 Nuggets in "Poor Richard's Almanack"

DOWN

1 Not using sensitive language, say
2 Dis-banded?
3 List ender: Abbr.
4 Not wait till evening to crack a bottle
5 Semester's end
6 Rapper ___ Azalea
7 General's assistant: Abbr.
8 Tool for undoing stitches
9 What many runners do before a marathon
10 Senectitude
11 "r u 4 real?"
12 Jared of "Dallas Buyers Club"
13 Nerd's epithet for the president?
14 Lions and tigers
15 Tidbit with rice in Creole cuisine
16 Sidestep
17 It's under helium in the periodic table
18 Dog's warning
20 Endure
25 Per
30 ___ News
31 Annoy, in a way
33 Goal for many a H.S. dropout
34 Donations to certain clinics
35 Pantry item
37 David ___, C.I.A. director under Obama
38 "Watch it!"
40 Took a breather
43 Possess, as thou might
45 Old Testament land
46 "Pick me! Pick me!"
47 Certain Spanish murals
49 Elapse, as years
51 Braided floor covering
54 Where coal miners work
55 Doesn't bother
56 Telly pitch
57 1040 reviewer, for short
58 Humerus connection
59 "How uncool!"
60 "Yer darn ___!"
61 It may bring a tear to one's eye
64 "___ Is Us" (65-Down drama)
65 See 64-Down
66 Bout result, in brief
67 Like a game with equal winners and losers
70 'Vette option
71 Happenin' place
75 Election that's too close to call
76 Peachy
78 "Phooey!"
80 Like many clowns and beachside houses
81 Kennedy Library architect
82 Nickname for a devil
83 Flowery poem
85 Help grow
86 "You agree?"
87 Enjoy consistent, favorable luck, in poker lingo
89 Story line
92 Sort of rooftop unit, familiarly
94 Another name for a porpoise or dolphin
95 Certain domain suffix
97 Subject of a 2001–02 scandal
98 Caught congers
100 Strong desire
101 ___ Reader
102 Shade of green
104 "Absolutely!," to Alejandro
105 Capital of Okinawa
106 Chew (on)
107 Match makers?
108 Get all blubbery
110 Show with Kate McKinnon, for short

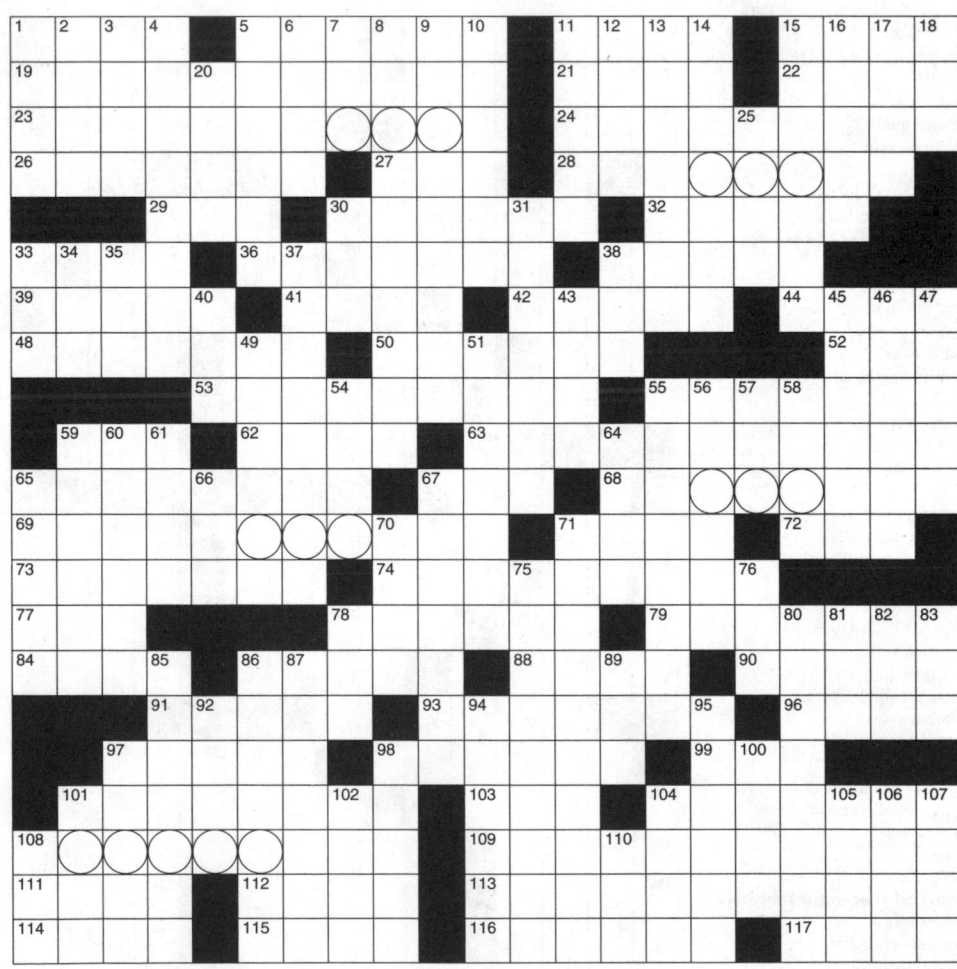

by Sam Trabucco

ACROSS

1 Beguiled
6 Carnival performer
10 Heavy hit
15 Popular self-help website
19 Make a good point?
20 "Three Sisters" sister
21 "The Gold-Bug" author, for short
22 Princess with superpowers
23 Singer / City / Home feature
26 "Safe!," in baseball, or "Safety!," in football
27 Beachgoer's souvenir
28 Leg press target, informally
29 Third-most abundant gas in the atmosphere
30 Emerald or aquamarine
31 "Don't move!"
34 Dog tag?
35 Finished behind
36 Socialite / Resort / Store
41 "Keystone" character of old comedy
42 Sacred symbol of ancient Egypt
43 Word after who, what, when, where, why or how
44 Message in a bottle, maybe
45 Roman orator
48 Gangster tracker
49 How a gangly person might be described
52 Political commentator / Geographical area / Fitness routine
58 World Cup cheer
59 Lots
60 Show extreme instability
61 Alpo alternative
63 NPR's "Planet Money" or "How I Built This"
65 Ceiling
66 Related stuff
69 Texter's sign-off
70 "Shoo!"
72 Cheer with beer
74 ____-Magnon man
75 Actor / Transportation hub / Part of a broadcast
81 Holy terror
82 Unwitting accomplice
83 Suisse peak
84 "Young Sheldon" airer
87 Scott of "Charles in Charge"
88 "With ____ ring . . ."
89 Way cool
91 Comedian / State capital / Record store section
97 "It's a deal!"
98 Some singles
99 Big name in vodka
102 Blockage reliever
103 "Roger that"
105 Upscale hotel chain
107 Father of octuplets on "The Simpsons"
108 Haunted house sound
109 Actress / Mideast area / Crime
113 1960s "It Girl" Sedgwick
114 Longtime "Inside the N.B.A." analyst
115 Primary concern
116 "Speed-the-Plow" playwright
117 RCA competitor
118 Some sports prizes
119 Professor Trelawney in the Harry Potter books, e.g.
120 "Is this really necessary?"

DOWN

1 What some Kaplan guides help prep for
2 Dash
3 Take a few pointers?
4 Three-time N.H.L. M.V.P.
5 Once named
6 Get crazy
7 English actor Idris
8 "Holy moly!"
9 ____ Graham, Meryl Streep's role in 2017's "The Post"
10 Crackpot
11 "Wait just a sec"
12 Many a pageant coif
13 Titan, Triton or Titania
14 Seat at many a wedding
15 "Nothing succeeds like ____": Oscar Wilde
16 Warm, cozy spots
17 Quite, despite expectations
18 Clobbers
24 Plenish
25 Theme park annoyances
30 Barrio grocery
32 ____ Perelman, classic Russian science writer
33 For
34 Lighter igniter
35 Zapped, in a way
37 Words mouthed on a Jumbotron
38 Some girders
39 "That's pretty obvious!"
40 Fashion monthly
45 Take over
46 Divvies up
47 1960s Haight-Ashbury wear
48 Summer swarmer
49 Per unit
50 Myrna of "Love Crazy"
51 Lather
53 Obama ____
54 Hi or lo follower
55 Upscale hotel chain
56 Undo
57 Hip-hop subgenre
62 Add fuel to
64 Part of a crane
65 Try this!
66 What's got ewe covered?
67 Flying Solo
68 Clerical wear
70 Condescending sort
71 "The Situation Room" airer
72 Unflappable
73 Stand-alone business?
76 Kernel
77 Like many a kilt
78 Computer menu option
79 Dumas dueler
80 Contact, in a way
84 Hits the hay
85 Major fuss
86 Like most light bulbs
88 Difficult journeys
89 Cubist of note?
90 Twit
92 Regatta site since 1839
93 Slack
94 Shines
95 Fashion
96 Insurance filings
100 Ticked off
101 All together, in scores
103 Food drive collection
104 Uriah of "David Copperfield"
105 High wind
106 Half of a pair
109 "The Godfather" mobster who was shot in the eye
110 Staples of waiting rooms
111 "I'm thinking . . ."
112 ____ de vie

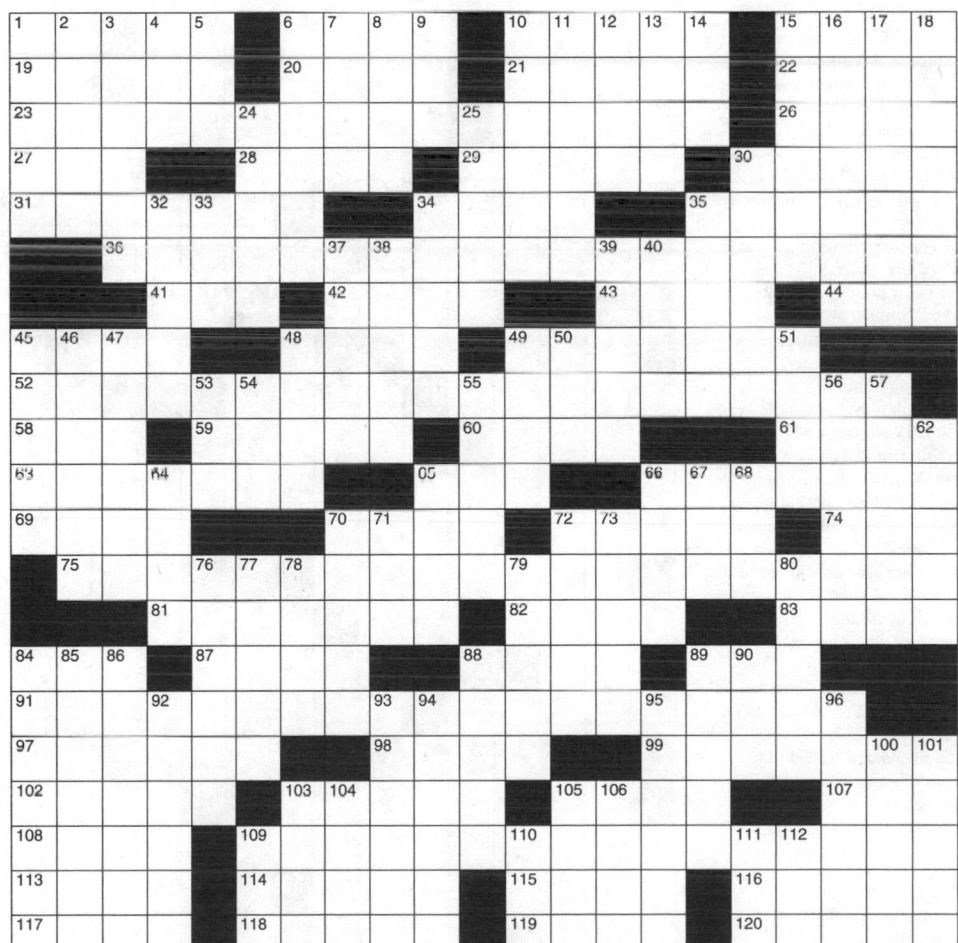

by Bruce Haight

ACROSS

1 Iams competitor
5 Pretend
12 Song sung by Garth Brooks on Jay Leno's last "Tonight Show"
20 Podcast host Maron
21 Fred Flintstone's boss
22 Weathers, as a hurricane
23 "That's me you're looking for"
24 Compliment to a lawmaker?
26 Lesley who played Mrs. Patmore on "Downton Abbey"
28 ___ the sly (be secretive about)
29 Drug used to combat A.D.H.D.
30 Short writing assignment, informally
32 Really like
35 Really like
36 Compliment to a composer?
39 ___ voce
43 Deep, deep hole
44 Crème de ___
46 Lucky strike?
47 Toe, to a tot
50 John, Paul or George, but not Ringo
52 Alternative to first-class
55 Lake vessel
56 Water cooler?
58 Cornbread variety named for where it's baked
59 Film role for the dog Skippy
60 Meditative discipline
62 Compliment to a lecturer?
64 Compliment to a taxonomist?
67 Compliment to a champion speller?
68 Smallville ___
69 2002 Literature Nobelist Kertész
70 Snack with a rock climber on its wrapper
71 Head of communications?
72 Gettysburg general
73 Like many holiday candles
74 Gal of "Wonder Woman"
77 Banned game projectiles
78 [not my mistake]
79 "Why, you little . . ."
81 Word with prayer or paddle
84 Claim in e-cigarette ads
87 Compliment to a charity organizer?
93 Dorm V.I.P.s
95 Major exporter of uranium
96 Hand-to-hand combat weapon
97 Long lines?
100 Athlete honored on Richmond's Monument Avenue
102 Drained of color
103 Compliment to a vegetable gardener?
107 What the "s" stands for in "scuba"
108 Enhanced medium for talk radio
109 Draw upon
110 "___ Enchanted" (2004 film)
111 Result of a computer crash
112 Got back at
113 Difficult situation

DOWN

1 Key of Mozart's "Odense" Symphony
2 Thin layer
3 ___ to sell
4 Color-changing creatures
5 "Yo te ___" (Spanish 101 phrase)
6 How boors behave
7 Some inclement weather, in broadcast shorthand
8 "Oh, by the way . . ."
9 GPS system, e.g.
10 Suffix with señor
11 Bog
12 Weapon resembling the letter psi
13 Posterior
14 Beat after a buzzer beater
15 Rubbish
16 Alternative to Parmesan
17 Chuck ___, four-time Super Bowl-winning coach
18 Pick out
19 Uranians and Neptunians
25 Lack the courage to, for short
27 Musical set in St.-Tropez, familiarly
31 Actress Hoffmann of "Transparent"
33 Half: Prefix
34 What dark clouds might represent
37 Small bone, as in the ear
38 Quai D'Orsay setting
40 Prepared to shoot
41 Beings on TV's "Doctor Who"
42 West Coast beer brand, informally
45 Modern payment option
47 Musical medley
48 Wits
49 Not hold back, to a poker player
51 Ottoman title
53 Twice tetra-
54 More sharply dressed
55 Container for amontillado
56 Easternmost of the Lesser Antilles
57 Kitchen device
58 Meriting only half a star, say
60 French city where D'Artagnan lived in "The Three Musketeers"
61 MSN, for one
62 B on an LP
63 Site for an A.C.L. tear
65 Took off
66 Words said before bed?
72 Peace Nobelist Yousafzai
73 ID card fig.
74 Lose rigidity
75 Not worth ___
76 Florida's Miami-___ County
77 Lightsaber wielder
80 Worlds external to the mind
82 Activity in libraries and movie theaters
83 Diplomatic agreement
85 Record label for Whitney Houston
86 One of the friends on "Friends"
88 Milkshake, in New England
89 Author Gerritsen and actress Harper
90 What one might seek after a computer crash, informally
91 Opera with the aria "Ave Maria"
92 Skim
94 Vice president Agnew
97 Stone that's a star
98 It may be checkered
99 Till section
101 Scrape
103 Crestfallen
104 Tony winner Hagen
105 Dallas hoopster, briefly
106 Roll on a golf course

by Sam Ezersky and Byron Walden

ACROSS

1 Festival of Colors celebrant
6 Mission to remember
11 Whip
15 "Goldarn it!"
19 Orchestra section behind the violas
20 Canon competitor
21 Former QB Tony
22 Treat embossed with its name
23 "Anchorman" = ? (1976) + ? (1980)
25 An "A" in history?
26 Hankering
27 The forest, as opposed to the trees
28 "Rear Window" = ? (2004) + ? (2014)
31 Big, big, big
33 E.-W. line
34 Best in mental competition
35 Like three men of rhyme
39 Big Ten sch. whose mascot is an anthropomorphic nut
41 Foresight
44 "Silence of the Lambs" = ? (1946) + ? (1960)
47 Rockettes motions
52 One-named singer with #1 hits in 1965 and 1999
53 Bikini blast, briefly
54 Yves's yes
56 Smith of Fox News
57 Top dogs
60 Brewing need
63 Split base?
65 Cry of desperation
68 "Transformers" = ? (2000) + ? (1992)
70 Dept. of Justice heads
73 Lofty standards
75 "Me first" sort
76 Uncle with a top hat and tie
77 "Jurassic Park" = ? (1997) + ? (1975)
80 James who played TV's Marshal Dillon
82 Third place
83 City across the Missouri from Council Bluffs
85 Quarantine
89 Scads
90 California's Big ___
92 Maker of the golden calf, in Exodus
95 Shakespeare's stream
96 Keys in
98 "Twister" = ? (2004) + ? (2013)
103 Cracker Jack ingredient
105 One tick, briefly
106 Frederick Forsyth's "The ___ File"
107 Kind of code
111 "Facts First" sloganeer
113 "Sexy" Beatles woman
115 "Dumb and Dumber" = ? (2007) + ? (1979)
119 Passes, as time
123 Bit of physics
124 Manlike monster
125 "The Poseidon Adventure" = ? (1956) + ? (1984)
128 Sylvester's speech feature
129 Villagers victimized by the Grinch
130 Florida tourist attraction
131 Dad who says "D'oh!"
132 Pool event
133 Dupes
134 In position
135 Some beams

DOWN

1 Sweets
2 "___ to differ"
3 Fa or la
4 Mountain ___ (some sodas)
5 Uniform entertainment?
6 Target for an angry Chihuahua
7 Removes from a box, say
8 Alias introducer
9 Choosy ones, in Jif ads
10 N.B.A. great with size 22 shoes
11 Frenzied
12 Only
13 All in front?
14 Bit of baby talk
15 Uncertainty
16 Shower of the way
17 Silents star whose name is an anagram of 112-Down
18 Travel, as thou might
24 Certain wedding officiant
29 Apt radio call letters for a beach town
30 Babe magnet
32 Caesar's "to be"
35 Creep (along)
36 Lower Manhattan area
37 Rates ___ (is perfect)
38 Dangerous juggling prop
40 "___-daisy!"
42 Set one's sights on
43 Slip in lieu of a chip
45 Without a contract
46 Editorial override
48 ". . . but who ___?"
49 Mayhem
50 Mount ___, second-highest peak in Africa
51 Big jerk
55 Birds with long, curved beaks
58 Pittsburgh-based food company
59 Radio format
61 Equal, in math
62 Long tale
64 "Don't ___ surprised"
66 Primarily study
67 Jack of old westerns
69 Alternative to sending to jail
70 No longer on deck
71 Not tomboyish
72 Brownstone hangout
74 Dallas-based carrier: Abbr.
78 Stud fee?
79 Who wrote "All great truths begin as blasphemies"
81 Many a worker in ancient Rome
84 Some small batteries
86 Sister company of Budget
87 Little ones
88 One-named Irish singer
91 1980 Olympics boycotter
93 Some Crown Royal offerings
94 Academy nomination
97 Prep for the ring
99 Title for Meghan Markle
100 Sicily's Mount ___
101 Churns up
102 Long Island university
104 Jabs, in a way
107 Writing attributed to King David
108 Protruding part of the body
109 Presume, informally
110 Lure
112 Niamey's land
114 Daft
116 Ottoman title
117 Tiniest sip
118 Mature
120 Pig
121 "Roll Tide!" school
122 River flooded in W.W. I to thwart the Germans
126 Signature Obama legislation, for short
127 Store door posting: Abbr.

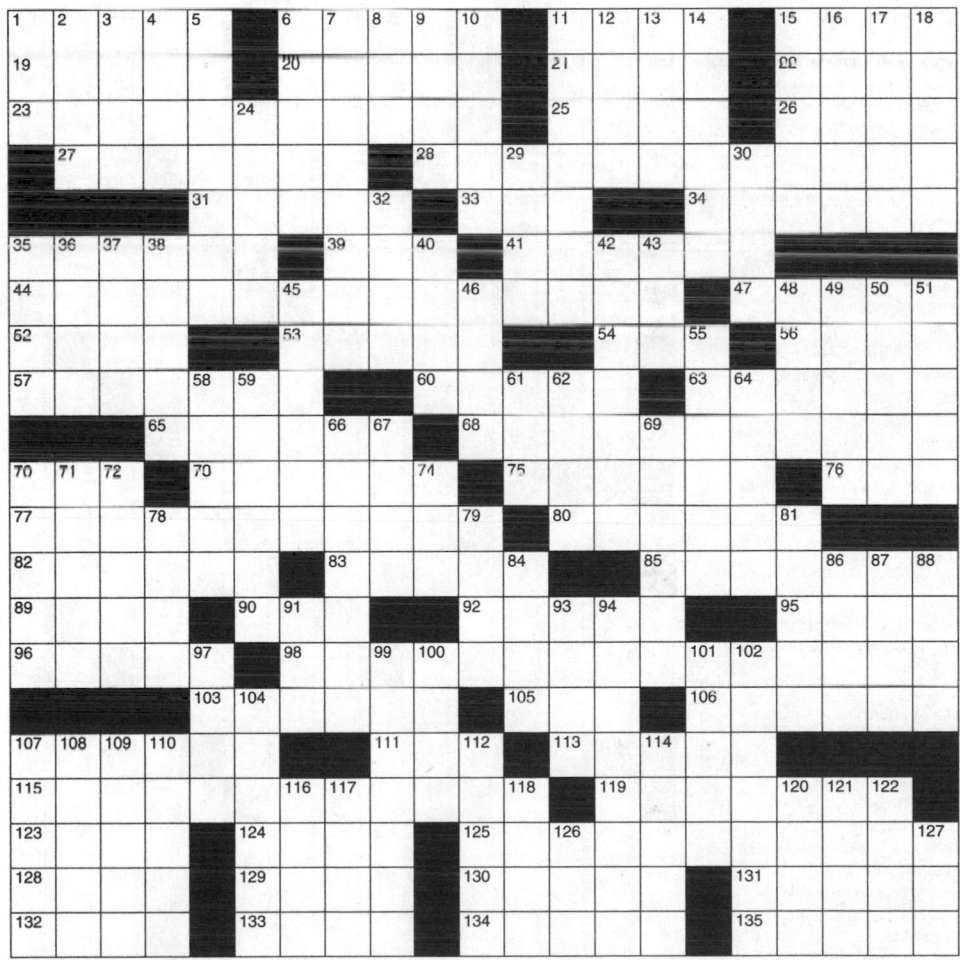

by Patrick Merrell

ACROSS

1 Flaw, metaphorically
5 Antismoking spots, e.g.
9 Cleveland Browns' defense, informally
14 Dress
19 What a line doesn't have
20 Lévesque of Quebec
21 Pelvis-related
22 _____ card (wallet item)
23 _____ Reza shrine (Iranian holy site)
24 *Former supporter of seabirds*
26 Where the frontiersman Bowie died
27 Burdened (with)
29 Snatcher's exclamation
30 Yawn-inducing
32 Postgame shower?
33 The Big Board, briefly
34 Funny Fey
35 Jewelry worn above the elbow
37 What's brewing?
38 *Spray the monarch to keep him cool*
40 *Prosecutor who's sympathetic to the defendants in a witch trial*
42 Play with
43 Winter coat
44 Sound of something rushing by
45 Singer Morissette
47 Not fixed
49 Director Jonathan
50 Agenda starter
51 Hog's home
52 Pontius Pilate's province
53 Liqueur akin to sambuca
54 Place for a browser
55 First character in Genesis
56 T. rex, e.g.
57 Metro _____
58 *Bridle strap utilized only on sidewalk surfaces*
62 When Macbeth delivers the "Tomorrow, and tomorrow, and tomorrow" soliloquy
66 Potential dinner
67 Hitching spot
68 Rating that's on the cusp of NC-17
73 Manitoba, Saskatchewan and Alberta, with "the"
75 Stuck-up person
76 Aplenty
77 Ohio University team
78 Informal expression of gratitude
79 Namesakes of Muhammad's daughter
80 Brilliant debut
81 Ruffian
82 Miss
83 "Who _____?"
84 *What a dog groomer might charge*
86 *Result of wearing a fedora at the beach*
88 Pulled off
89 Make an effort
90 T.S.A. agent's tool
91 Item smashed by the original Luddites
92 Having a crisp picture, say
94 Leave gratified
95 Must, informally
96 "Death of a Salesman" salesman
98 Lead-in to phobia
100 *Result of accidentally throwing a Frisbee into a campground*
103 _____ California
104 Plucked instruments
105 Compound imparting a fruity smell
106 Hence
107 Oodles
108 Shoots out
109 Without much confidence
110 It falls quietly
111 "Swiper, no swiping!" speaker of children's TV

DOWN

1 Sound from a banshee
2 Italian designer menswear since the 1970s
3 Running start?
4 Like kiddie rides among all amusement park rides
5 School opening?
6 Amorous play, in modern lingo
7 _____ Lavoisier a.k.a. the Father of Modern Chemistry
8 Romantically involved with
9 Light tennis shot
10 Reminiscent of
11 Iowa's state flower
12 Move clumsily
13 Charybdis's counterpart, in Greek myth
14 Pharma watchdog
15 Part
16 "This isn't very pleasant, but . . ."
17 Some calls to the police
18 Norwegian money
25 Genetics initials
28 Serving during Prohibition
31 Diplomatic office below an embassy
35 Nose
36 Gathering around a campfire?
38 One target of a childhood vaccine
39 Oven
40 *Apple devoured by an elderly relative*
41 Called
44 United with
46 Look for
48 Car ad no.
49 Carol Ann _____, U.K. poet laureate starting in 2009
50 Not superficial
52 Crave, with "for"
53 Try to hit
55 Stable parents
56 Thoro cleansing
59 "The Great" and "The Terrible"
60 Lookalike
61 "There's nothing else"
62 Blue alerts, in brief
63 Arising
64 Meal with a set menu
65 Certain cleric
69 Foe of Frazier
70 Egg-shaped item from a garden
71 Performer in a campus production, often
72 Sticky stuff
74 Talks hoarsely
75 "On the Beach" novelist Nevil
76 Nasty wound
78 Crime against good taste
79 Dance mentioned in Queen's "Bohemian Rhapsody"
81 Like people who take lifts
82 Camper's light
85 Some winds for seafarers
86 Non-shiny finishes
87 "Sucks to be you"
88 Speedometers, typically
90 Korean money
93 Tied
95 Like a lot of zombie movies
97 Mom's mom
99 Intensifying word add-on
101 Disney collectible
102 Request to Triple A

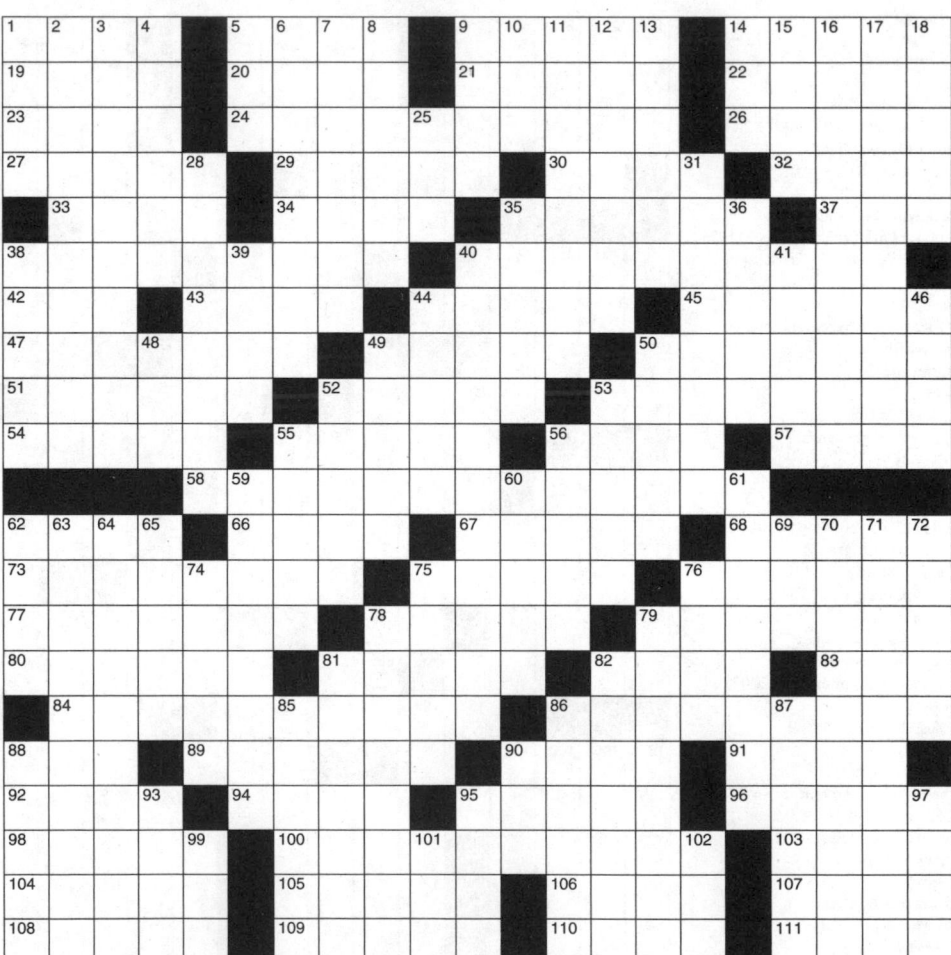

by Will Nediger

ACROSS

1 Word repeated in "Mi ___ es su ___"
5 Skipped town
9 Good name for a botanist?
14 Certain vacuum tube
20 Taiwan-based electronics giant
21 Per item
22 Shred
23 Make airtight
24 Caterer's platter
26 Off
27 Director of "Eat Drink Man Woman," 1994
28 Morticia, to Fester, in 1960s TV
29 Expecting help?
31 Beat generation figure?
33 Tidy
35 ___ Muhammad, mentor to Malcolm X
37 "Mm-hmm"
38 Reagan-era scandal
42 Old Germanic tribe
44 Passes out
48 Oral examination?
50 Initiations have them
52 Dish made from a fermented root
53 Grace's surname on "Will & Grace"
54 Neutron's home
56 Jazz singer who acted in the "Roots" miniseries
59 Whopper maker
60 Hematite, e.g.
62 Like 100% inflation
63 ___ Kippur
64 Sorbet-like dessert originally from Sicily
65 ___ port
68 Wrist watch?
69 Like this puzzle's circled letters vis-à-vis their Across answers
73 Brewer's need
76 Long ___
77 "Nuh-uh!"
78 "Horrible!"
81 Reaches
84 Nearest country to Cape Verde
85 Grammy winner Erykah ___
86 Talkative sort
90 Competitor of Rugby
91 "Li'l" fellow
92 "I'm with ___"
93 Hell, informally
95 It might take only seven digits
97 Sampled
100 Be rumple-free
102 Leaves for baggage claim, say
103 Star followers
105 Vitamin B$_3$
107 Prefix with normal
108 Cause of a tossed joystick, maybe
112 Block from getting close to the basket
115 Gridiron gains
118 Comic ___ Nancherla
119 Stage in getting a Ph.D.
121 Some rustproof rails
123 Chasms
124 Newsroom fixture
125 Frozen breakfast brand
126 "Let's do it!"
127 Risks a ticket
128 "Siddhartha" novelist
129 In case
130 Washington team, familiarly

DOWN

1 ___ Crunch
2 Smoothie flavor
3 Tennis star's feat
4 Place for exhibitions
5 Word with noodle or nurse
6 Viscount's superior
7 Big scholarship awarder, for short
8 Mint family herb
9 "Down goes ___!" (1973 sports line)
10 Mojito ingredient
11 Nail polish brand
12 When jams are produced
13 Place for an altar
14 Long line in Russia
15 Let
16 "Amen to that"
17 Earthen pot
18 What it takes two to do
19 One-on-one Olympics event
25 Chuck in the air
30 Not mainstream, briefly
32 Separations at weddings?
34 Body work, in brief
36 Lead-in to boy or girl
38 Birthplace of the Renaissance
39 RCA component
40 Put claw marks in
41 Sharer of Russia's western border
43 Setting for many G.I. stories

45 Much of Aries' span
46 Postgraduation stressors, for some
47 Lengthy attack
49 Refining, as muscles
51 Lead-in to cone
55 "You only live once," for one
57 Baked beans flavor
58 Mötley ___
60 Schedule-keeping org.
61 Team scream
64 "10-4"
65 Longest American north-south rte.
66 "Fiddler on the Roof" setting
67 In spades
69 Future attorney's hurdle, for short
70 Memphis-to-Nashville dir.
71 2018 World Cup champs
72 Prayer ending?
73 Workplace for a cabin boy
74 Antiquated anesthetic
75 Pong creator
78 All-female group with the 1986 #1 hit "Venus"
79 One-named singer whose last name is Adkins
80 Pitches
82 Albany is its capital: Abbr.
83 Gorsuch's predecessor on the bench
84 Two of diamonds?
85 Trusted news source in the Mideast

87 Friend of Descartes . . . or, in English, question pondered by Descartes?
88 "What chutzpah!"
89 Early record holder
91 Puts to rest
94 Pricey-sounding apparel brand?
96 Tinder, e.g.
98 Surface
99 "Well, I'll be" follower
101 B'way buys
104 It covers a lot of ground
106 Recognition for a scientist
108 Comic's offerings
109 Per item
110 Stud finder?
111 One wearing black eyeliner and ripped jeans, say
113 Desire
114 Makes out?
116 Cause of some insomnia
117 Application figs.
120 Dummkopf
122 Boozehound

by Alison Ohringer and Erik Agard

ACROSS

1 Begin
6 Commercial aunt since 1889
12 Prep to find fingerprints
16 Checkup sounds
19 Deduce
20 Rabid supporters
21 Steel head?
23 Land O'Lakes and Breakstone's?
25 Former Rome-based airline
26 With severity
27 The only way to get respect, so they say
29 Kind of torch
30 Commies
31 Ministering?
35 Giant in direct sales
37 Pro or con
38 Vientiane native
39 Stag's mate
40 Laundry unit
41 "Inside the N.B.A." analyst beginning in 2011
43 Wunderkinds, say
47 "Damn, I can't seem to get a ball into fair territory!"?
53 Fabrication
54 Chicago airport code
55 Wide divide
56 Lose an all-in hand, say
57 Vitriol
58 Aziz of "Master of None"
60 Most susceptible to sunburn
61 Biblioklept's targets
62 Like a trip overland from Venezuela to Bolivia?
67 Musical closings
70 Easy buckets
71 Tiny, multitentacled creatures
75 Operating system since the early '70s
76 Mother ___
77 "Robinson Crusoe" author
80 Fútbol stadium cry
81 Ingredient in a Cuba libre
82 Expensive line of nonsense someone throws you?
85 Novel endings, maybe
87 Informal assertion of authority
88 Indigo source
89 Part of NGO
90 Orders
93 "Feed me!," maybe
94 Tannery stock
95 "What are you hauling in there?" and "How many axles you running?"
100 Course
101 Actress Moreno
102 One putting others down
103 Ivory, e.g.
106 In a state
108 Entering your middle name, then date of birth, then adding a "1," etc.?
112 Missile in a mating ritual
113 Best of all possible worlds
114 Amounts to
115 Amount to
116 ". . . ish"
117 Nitpicky know-it-all
118 Scoring factor at a crossword tournament

DOWN

1 Bros, e.g.
2 Letter-shaped fastener
3 Subsequently
4 Sadly unoriginal works
5 In vogue
6 Box of 12?
7 Manning with two Super Bowl M.V.P. awards
8 "I want my ___" (1980s slogan)
9 Suggestion from a financial adviser, for short
10 Rami ___ of "Mr. Robot"
11 Attack vigorously
12 Title role for Jamie Foxx
13 Like the Statue of Liberty at night
14 Most common U.S. surname
15 Wee one
16 Trattoria option that means "garlic and oil"
17 Poem name whose singular and plural forms are the same
18 Slowness embodied
22 Betrays, in a way
24 "Treasure Island" monogram
28 Genetic messenger
31 Excessive lovers of the grape
32 Classical theater
33 Concrete
34 Temptation location
35 Big name in soda cans and foil
36 Show grief
37 Guest bed, in a pinch
42 Extended writer's blocks?
43 Scrapbooking need
44 Big success
45 Good source of calcium
46 Grasps
48 Hosiery shades
49 This Hebrew letter: ש
50 American Girl products
51 Keep watch for, maybe
52 Overdo it on the praise
57 "The Lord of the Rings" actor Billy
59 He fought alongside Achilles
60 Remote button
61 Aspirin maker
63 Narrow valleys
64 Oreo ingredient until the mid-'90s
65 One ogling
66 "You just blew my mind!"
67 Medical breakthrough
68 "Movin' ___"
69 Tiny
72 Wide-swinging blow
73 CBS's "Kate & ___"
74 Peddles
76 Harbor sight
77 Box of 12, say
78 "Ticklish" toys
79 Raced
82 [The light turned green! Go!]
83 Free trial version
84 Where you might open a whole can of worms?
86 Track down
90 Move in the direction of
91 Jerk
92 Rise to the occasion
94 Comedic duo?
95 Skipping syllables
96 Difficulty
97 2022 World Cup host
98 Alternatives to cabs
99 About to blow one's top
100 3, 4 or 5, usually
103 What a 76-Down pulls
104 Certain buy-in
105 Vet's malady, for short
107 Kerfuffle
109 Turf
110 Luxury hotel amenity
111 Get gold from one's lead?

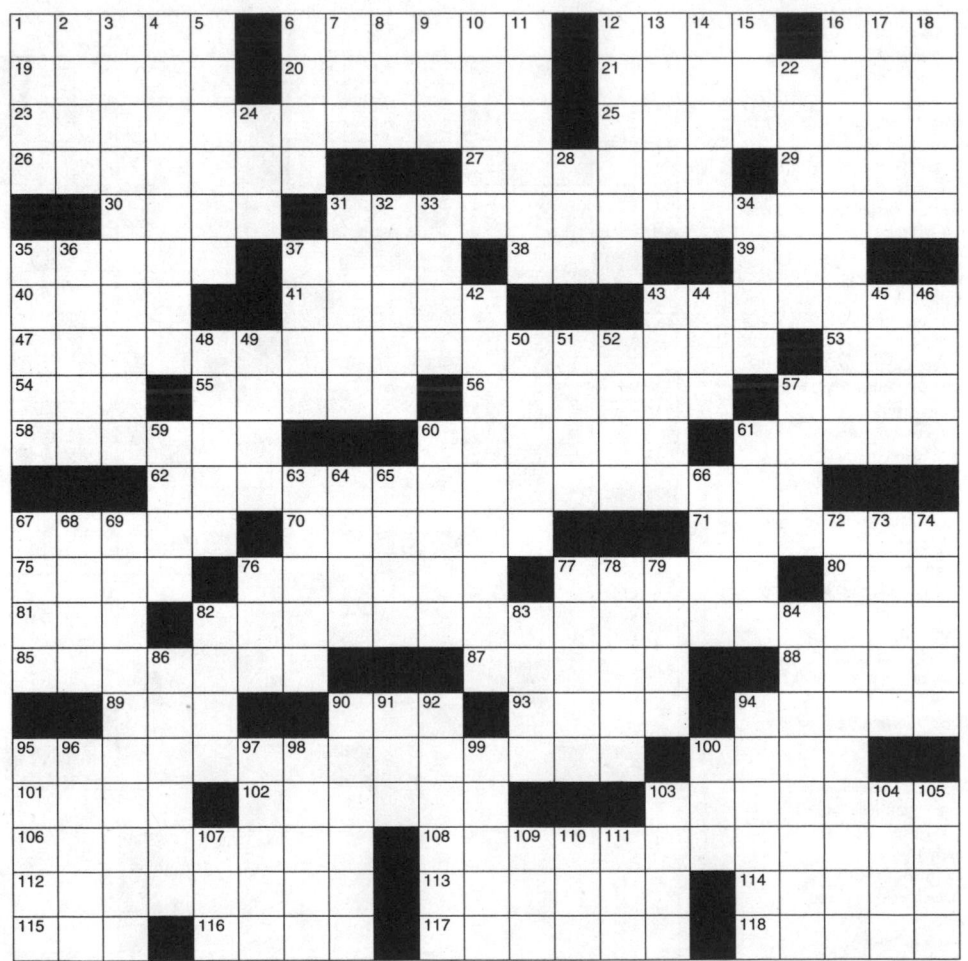

by Ross Trudeau

ACROSS

1 Autumn bloom
6 Ticked off
11 Cast
16 "Madam Secretary" airer
19 Really stood out
20 Bluesman Willie
21 Where the owl and the pussycat went, in poetry
22 ____ provençale
23 Classic film narrated by Spencer Tracy
26 Position
27 "Thanks in old age — thanks ____ I go": Whitman
28 Lead-in to bad news
29 Searched without sight
30 Show what's inside
32 Underscore
34 Early morning setting?
35 The Bears of the Big 12 Conference
36 Remark commonly attributed to Queen Victoria
41 Digs
43 Shaggy grazer
44 Actor O'Shea
45 Third-person form of "être"
46 "Birds in an Aquarium" artist
47 Like some details
49 Handful
52 Fresh
54 Statement at the end of some trailers
61 C neighbors
62 Tool that it takes two to operate
63 Old nuclear agcy.
64 Brewery sight
65 Obeys a sentry, say
66 Skating embarrassment
67 CDs, LPs, etc.
69 Mexican marinade
71 Musician/singer whose name might be shouted in mock horror?
72 Prefix with -pod
74 Frederick III, for one
76 Newspaper section
77 Toy manufacturer's disclaimer
81 Kurosawa who directed "Ran"
82 Hankering
83 Mouse lookalike
84 Tikkanen who won five Stanley Cups
85 Measure of econ. health
87 Top hat go-with
89 Fail to hold
90 Clock setting east of Eastern: Abbr.
91 Non-apology associated with several U.S. presidents
98 Impoverished
99 The Temptations' "Since ____ My Baby"
100 Drake or Future
104 City known for its cheese
105 Up-to-the-minute
107 It's often brown or blue
109 Great ____
110 Zip
111 Protest tactic . . . as suggested by 23-, 36-, 54-, 77- and 91-Across?
115 Continuing education subj., often
116 Operatic baritone Pasquale ____
117 Give up
118 Panegyrize
119 Obituary word
120 Wyoming's ____ Range
121 Corporate department
122 Takes a breather

DOWN

1 Remains in the ground, often
2 Not having quite enough cash
3 Jenga construction
4 Tolkien creature
5 Debate again [sigh]
6 Soviet author Ehrenburg
7 Kerfuffles
8 "Te ____" (Rihanna gold single)
9 Snarl
10 Crowd on a set
11 Carol Brady, to three of her kids
12 Founder of a major appliance chain
13 Kind of bookstore
14 Bygone game console, in brief
15 Bistro dessert
16 Wheedles
17 Cover from view
18 Old-fashioned weaponry
24 "Let It Go" singer, in film
25 "Game over" signal
31 What might follow me?
33 Ticket info, briefly
34 Peachy
35 Cinephile's guilty pleasure, perhaps
37 Model Banks
38 Place to treat yourself
39 Colorist's concern
40 Hilo his
41 Like "@#$!"
42 Ill-fated NASA mission of 1967
46 "You said it!"
47 Catch something
48 Surprised exclamations
49 One singing at the end?
50 Vulcans or Jawas, in brief
51 Becomes grating to
53 The one that got away?
55 Turner who led a slave rebellion
56 "Sonnets to Orpheus" poet
57 Uncool sort
58 Some keys, informally
59 Doctor's order
60 Peak NW of Athens
66 When middle watch ends
68 Fancy neckwear
70 Cannes's Palme ____
73 Like some bologna and golf shots
75 Like Vivaldi's "Spring"
76 Where the Blues play: Abbr.
78 Was out for a bit
79 Fox News commentator Perino
80 "I, Claudius" attire
85 Like Columbus
86 Word hitting two Triple Word Scores in Scrabble
88 First Folio, e.g.
89 Cross-Atlantic flier, once, in brief
90 Egyptian symbol of royalty
91 "Peanuts" character
92 Pursue eagerly
93 Climber's concern: Abbr.
94 Goes at a leisurely pace
95 Peninsula shared by Croatia and Slovenia
96 Humphries of the N.B.A.
97 Egg time
101 Article of apparel never worn by Winnie-the-Pooh
102 Attraction that dropped the word "Center" from its name in 1994
103 Scottish dances
105 Trial for a future atty.
106 Regarding
107 Scotland's Fair ____
108 Empties (of)
112 Black church inits.
113 Jellied British delicacy
114 Hack

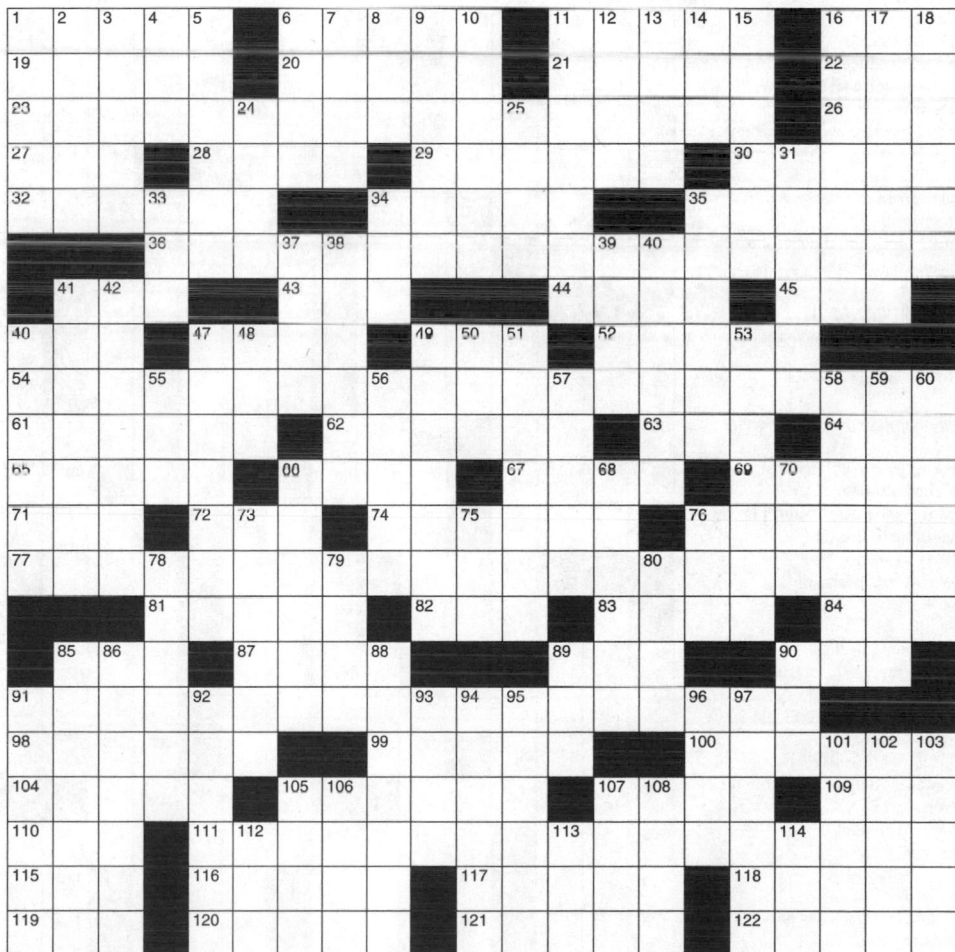

by Jacob Stulberg

ACROSS

1 Lightheaded
6 Underwater workplaces
13 One of four on the annual tennis calendar
18 Navel formation?
19 Not renewed
21 1836 siege setting
22 First name on the high bench
23 Follower of deuce
24 Wordsmith Peter Mark ___
25 Lot of back and forth?
27 Alternative to grass
29 Place for a prize ceremony
30 Nellie who wrote "Ten Days in a Mad-House"
31 Point of no return?
34 Certain corp. takeover
35 It's meant to be
36 NBC hit since '75
37 Ingredient in a Dark 'n' Stormy
38 Muslim holy men
40 Designer inits.
42 "Awesome!"
43 Lead-in to line
44 Rod who was the 1977 A.L. M.V.P.
45 "Bridesmaids" co-star
47 Food with an unfortunate-sounding last two syllables
50 Really fancy
51 Dreams up
55 Sophocles tragedy
56 Get further mileage from
57 Vegetable or pasta, e.g.
58 Drip, drip, drip
59 Annual sporting event that is this puzzle's theme
62 Outside: Prefix
63 Really green
64 Stingy sort?
65 Many a presidential hopeful: Abbr.
66 Treasure map markers
68 Ostracize
69 Lead-in to boy or girl
70 Standard info on stationery nowadays
72 U. of Md. player
73 Spot
74 Conjunction in the Postal Service creed
76 The Eagles, on scoreboards
78 Pérignon, for one
79 "Nature is the ___ of God": Dante
81 Something to live for
83 Chaney of silents
84 One at home, informally
85 Ape
88 "Zip it!"
89 Things found in clogs
90 Bourbon Street's locale, informally
92 Frenzy
94 Stadium name near Citi Field
96 Spectators' area
98 "Harlequin's Carnival" painter
99 James ___, Belgian painter in the movement Les XX
100 Flowchart symbol
101 Saskatchewan native
102 It represents you
104 Old-timey
106 First and last black key on a standard piano
108 Gas type: Abbr.
109 Location of 59-Across
114 Fly-by-night?

115 Canapé topper
116 Computer command
117 Time to vote: Abbr.
118 Italian car, informally
119 Lead-in to "Man," "Woman" or "Fool" in Top 40 hits
120 Further
121 Part of U.S.T.A.: Abbr.
122 City grid: Abbr.
123 Enthusiasm
124 Lion or tiger

DOWN

1 Employs
2 Not for keeps
3 Low soccer score
4 Wittily insults
5 Number on a trophy
6 "Alas . . ."
7 One of a well-known septet
8 Inits. in 2010 news
9 Broadway's Cariou
10 Computer key
11 Utterly uninspiring
12 Oscar-nominated George of "Who's Afraid of Virginia Woolf?"
13 Designer Jacobs
14 Emotionally detached
15 Jungle predator
16 Code you don't want to break
17 Returned to earth?
19 "I can't talk now"
20 Louisville standout
26 Candidate for rehab
28 Square dance maneuver
31 Oscar-winning film of 1984
32 Revel
33 College in Boston
37 Whole host
38 "Why should ___?"
39 Win every game
41 Security agreement
43 One way to answer a server?
46 Winning words
47 Guy
48 Dweller along the Bering Sea
49 The "L" of L.C.D.
52 Genius Bar employees
53 Relish
54 Rugged, as a landscape
60 Impotent
61 Paradigm
64 Submerge

67 Cybertrash
71 Force (into)
72 When the diet starts, perhaps
75 Locale for Charlie Chan
77 Dating profile section
78 Denims
80 Purchases at tire shops
81 Do well with
82 Fit to be tied
86 How the Quran is written
87 Film-related anagram of AMERICAN
88 City in Iraq's Sunni Triangle
89 Clear the air?
91 "I'll take that as ___"
93 Proficient in
95 Much TV fare during the wee hours
97 Towers over
103 Blue hue
105 Metal fastener
107 Three-person card game
110 Vox V.I.P.s
111 Forever and a day
112 Red Sox Hall-of-Famer, to fans
113 "Bravo!"

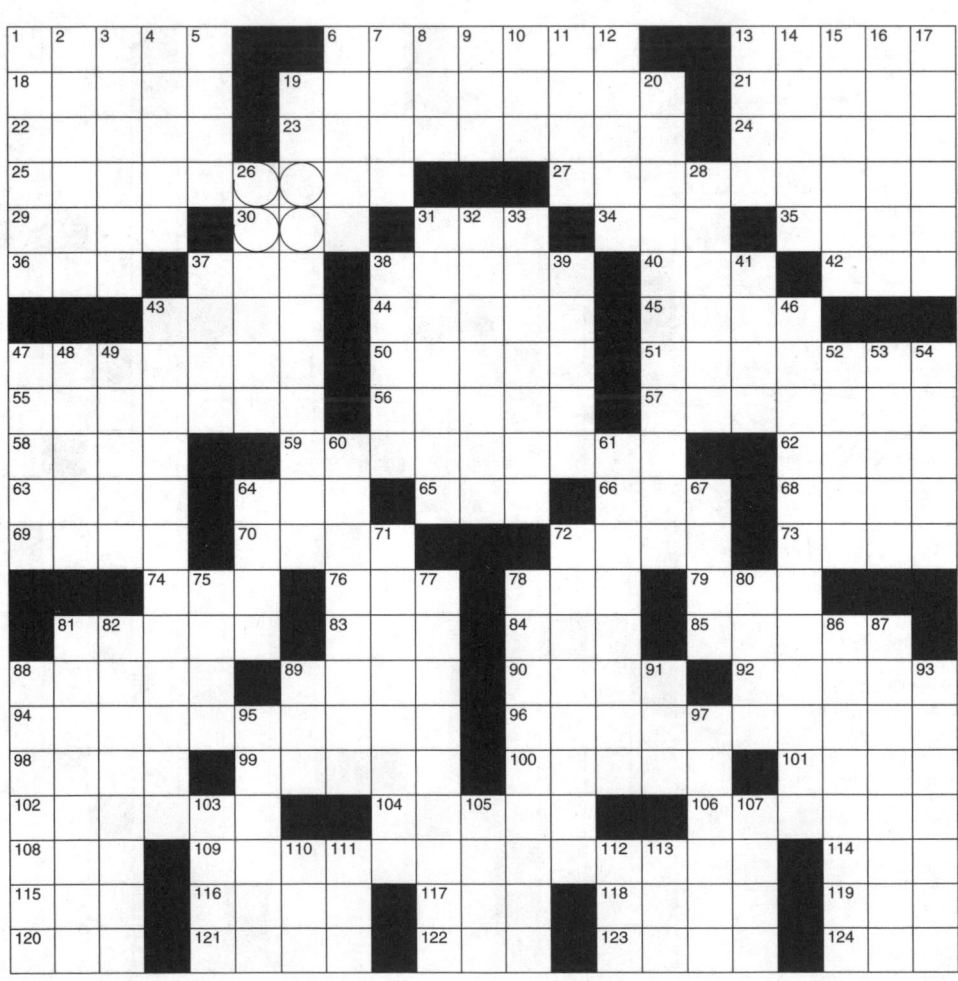

by Olivia Mitra Framke

ACROSS

1 Group of trees
6 Potential queens
11 Word that looks like its meaning when written in lowercase
14 Harmless weapons maker
18 Strong suit?
19 "Continue"
20 "Foucault's Pendulum" author, 1988
21 Like the Gregorian calendar
22 Showdown in Greek mythology
25 A couple of times
26 Word of confirmation on a messaging app
27 Couple
28 Showdown in classic video games
30 Quickened paces
32 Wasn't struck down
33 Realm
34 Tours can be seen on it
35 Triumph
37 Not in any way
39 Showdown in American history
43 Hot ___
44 One of four in a grand slam
47 Univs., e.g.
48 Bent over backward, in a way
50 Bit of P.R.
53 Like baseball's Durham Bulls
54 Speaker of Welsh or Breton
56 Actor Elba
58 One of the o's in "o/o"
59 Rank above maj.
61 Showdown in cinema
65 Mork's planet
66 Brightly colored blazer
67 Obie-winning playwright Will
68 "What is it?"
69 Showdown in the funnies
74 Not use cursive
77 University in Des Moines
78 Greenish-brown hue
79 Neighbor of China
81 What's used to row, row, row your boat
83 Leave fulfilled
85 Less than perfect
88 Geometric prefix
89 Italian "il" or French "le"
90 Prattle
92 Showdown in the Bible
95 Protein shell of a virus
98 Like sauvignon blanc
99 Traditional Christmas decoration
100 Jump to conclusions
103 Some petting zoo animals
106 Word with wonder or world
107 Showdown in comic books
109 Lead-in to boy or girl
111 Simple plant
114 Ostentation
115 Showdown in literature
118 Businesswoman Lauder
119 Apt name for a Braille instructor
120 TD Garden athlete
121 Knock over
122 Cowardly Lion portrayer
123 ___ bit
124 Overjoy
125 Bone: Prefix

DOWN

1 What "Talk to the hand!" is an example of
2 Unswerving
3 "I couldn't agree more!"
4 They're found under a bridge
5 Beats by ___ (headphones brand)
6 Short strokes
7 "Alas!"
8 Sudden impulse
9 Sister
10 "Try me"
11 Be relevant to
12 Country named for its latitude
13 College student's assignment
14 Words after an interruption
15 Stefanik who until 2018 was the youngest woman ever elected to Congress
16 Fast one
17 "___ Jacques"
21 Conductors' announcements
23 "___ where it hurts!"
24 Uncle, in Argentina
29 Under half of 45?
31 Brother of Dori and Nori in "The Hobbit"
32 Surprising lack of Oscar recognition
34 Suitable for a dieter, informally
35 Body of water connected by canal to the Baltic
36 Watson's company
38 Defeat
39 Govt. org. based in Ft. Meade, Md.
40 Word before right or rise
41 Move turbulently
42 Increasingly ripe, say
45 Wedding need . . . or booking
46 Stereotypical therapist's response
49 Pipe cleaner
51 Enthusiasts
52 Go wrong
54 Part of the eye
55 Wapitis
57 British Bulldog : Churchill :: ___ : Thatcher
60 Undistinguished, as many a subdivision house
62 Rapidly spreading vine
63 Get straight
64 Prefix with allergenic
69 Football units: Abbr.
70 Idiot, in Britspeak
71 Vow
72 Relatives of emus
73 Et ___
75 Numbers to avoid
76 Ragged
80 North African land: Abbr.
82 Cry of school spirit
84 Laid-back
86 Data storage items on the decline
87 Organ in the leg of a katydid, bizarrely
88 Frontier lights
91 Unit of explosive power
93 "That sounds awful"
94 Mauna ___
96 Wow
97 Territory name until 1889
100 Brat's opposite
101 Popular dip
102 Skilled laborer
104 Tex-___
105 Bit of corruption
106 Author of the "Fear Street" series for young readers
108 Some saber wielders
109 Bluish-green
110 Ninny
112 TV show set in William McKinley High School
113 Prefix with stratus
116 It's used to cite a site
117 Bonnie and Clyde, e.g.

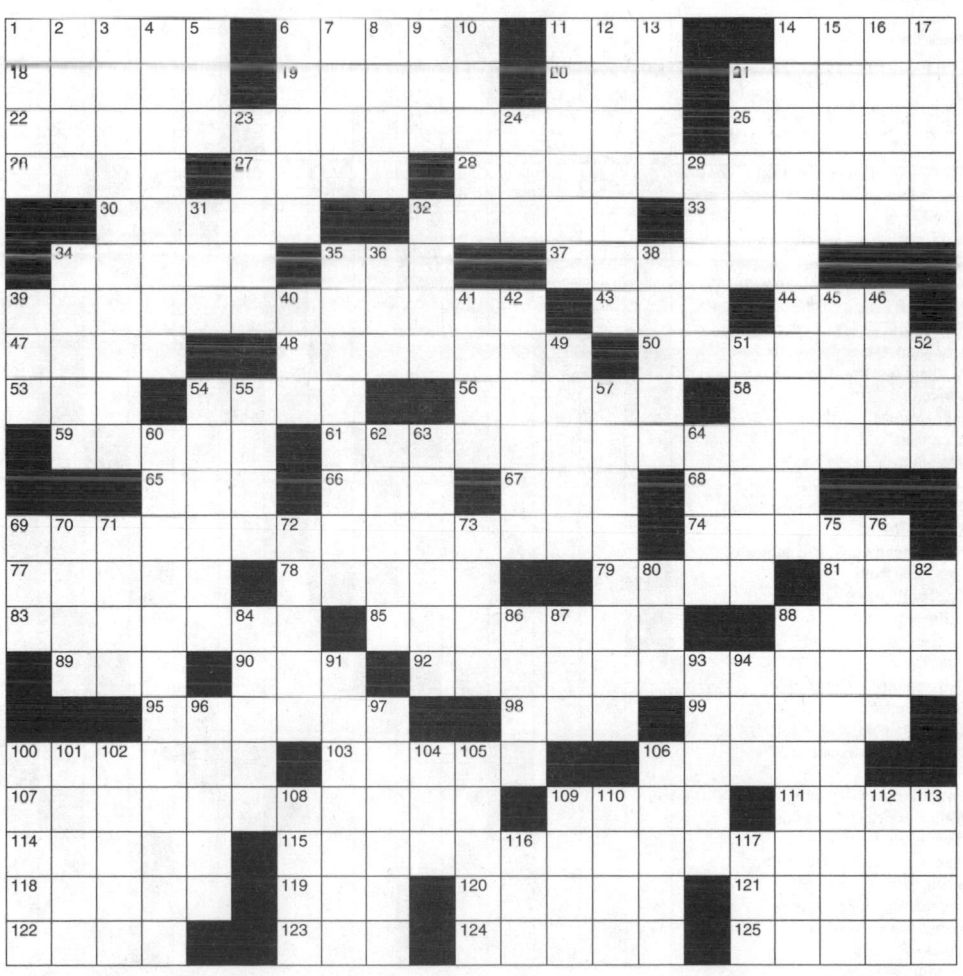

by Tom McCoy

50 MIXED FEELINGS

ACROSS

1 No-goodnik
4 "So long, dear boy"
8 Soap scent
13 Test for purity
18 Bullet ___ (1950s fashion fad)
19 Hiding, with "up"
20 TD Garden, for one
21 Jordan who directed "Get Out"
22 Overwhelm
24 Result of a photographic memory
26 Neighbor of Hungary
27 Harbinger
29 Whopper inventor
30 Tierra ___ Fuego
31 Minor's opposite
33 Where the U.S. won its 1,000th Summer Olympic gold
34 Chooses
35 Id restrainer
36 Sangfroid
37 Pair of diamonds?
41 Swear
42 Robin Williams role in a 1991 blockbuster
44 Reasons to hold one's nose
45 Fan sounds
46 Horror assistant
47 Big name in water filters
48 "I wish!"
50 Black brew
53 Item at the end of a wizard's staff
54 Man just after kneeling?
55 Uncompromisingly direct
56 Classic Chevy
58 Bunker
63 They involve mixed feelings . . . or a hint to four squares in this completed puzzle
67 2008 campaign slogan
68 Major fashion capital
69 Actress Thompson of "Thor: Ragnarok"
70 ___ league (amateur sports group)
71 Efficiency stat
72 Payment to a building board
75 Dance in 3/4 time
78 Set of values
80 "___ bien"
81 One smoothing the way?
82 Leaves in
83 Option for moving an investment
87 Neighborhood
88 Parts of many law firm names
91 Camera setting
92 "___ out!" (ump's cry)
93 Hello or goodbye
94 ___ long way
95 Dukes
96 O'er and o'er
97 Folkie Guthrie
98 Chocolate chip cookie starters?
100 One of the Corleones in "The Godfather"
102 Symbol of luck
105 Public nudity or foul language
109 Place to chat
110 "Princess ___ Theme" (John Williams composition)
111 Chocolatier since 1845
112 Stooge with a bowl cut
113 Checks
114 Certain break point
115 Cries of approval
116 Division in geology

DOWN

1 Small balls
2 Graveside container
3 Attire for the Bond villain Ernst Stavro Blofeld
4 Author Morrison
5 Director of the "M*A*S*H" finale
6 Simple top
7 Skillful
8 Delayed
9 Weights, informally
10 Court do-over
11 Parallels
12 Islamic state
13 Copycats
14 Short time, for short
15 Manta ray, by another name
16 "The Crucible," for McCarthyism
17 Mustard and saffron
19 One living off the land
23 "Why am I not surprised?"
25 "Darn!"
28 Drive
31 ___ Store
32 Mate for Bambi
33 Supervised
37 Milhouse's toon friend
38 Dashboard warnings, informally
39 Imaginary
40 Partner of smash
41 "Kung Fu" actor Philip
43 Fruit juice brand
45 Basically what was said
47 Boxer upset in the biopic "Cinderella Man"
48 Golfer Aoki
49 Nordic native
50 Soothing succulent
51 Explorers and Expeditions
52 Fair
55 Journalist Nellie
57 The Great ___ (Satan)
58 ___-Soviet
59 Cartoon in which one cow says to another "Hey, wait a minute! This is grass! We've been eating grass!"
60 Climb
61 View from a pew
62 Free TV spot, for short
64 Taiwanese computer giant
65 It might be topped with guacamole
66 Tic ___ (mints)
71 Give (out)
73 Modernists, for short
74 Internet connection inits.
75 Sandal-less, say
76 Score starter
77 Shepherd's scene
79 Great Plains tribe
81 Bribes
82 Sent up
83 Nutrition fig.
84 "I'll cover this"
85 Nonsense
86 H.S. courses for college credit
88 Suffix with large numbers
89 17-year-old Peace Nobelist Yousafzai
90 In too curious a manner
93 Composes
98 Fancy French home
99 Once, once
100 The Bravest in the Big Apple, for short
101 N.L. Central squad
103 Ingredient in a Bali Hai cocktail
104 Certain tech exec
106 Actress Long
107 Tender sound
108 Currency with denominations of 1,000, 5,000 and 10,000

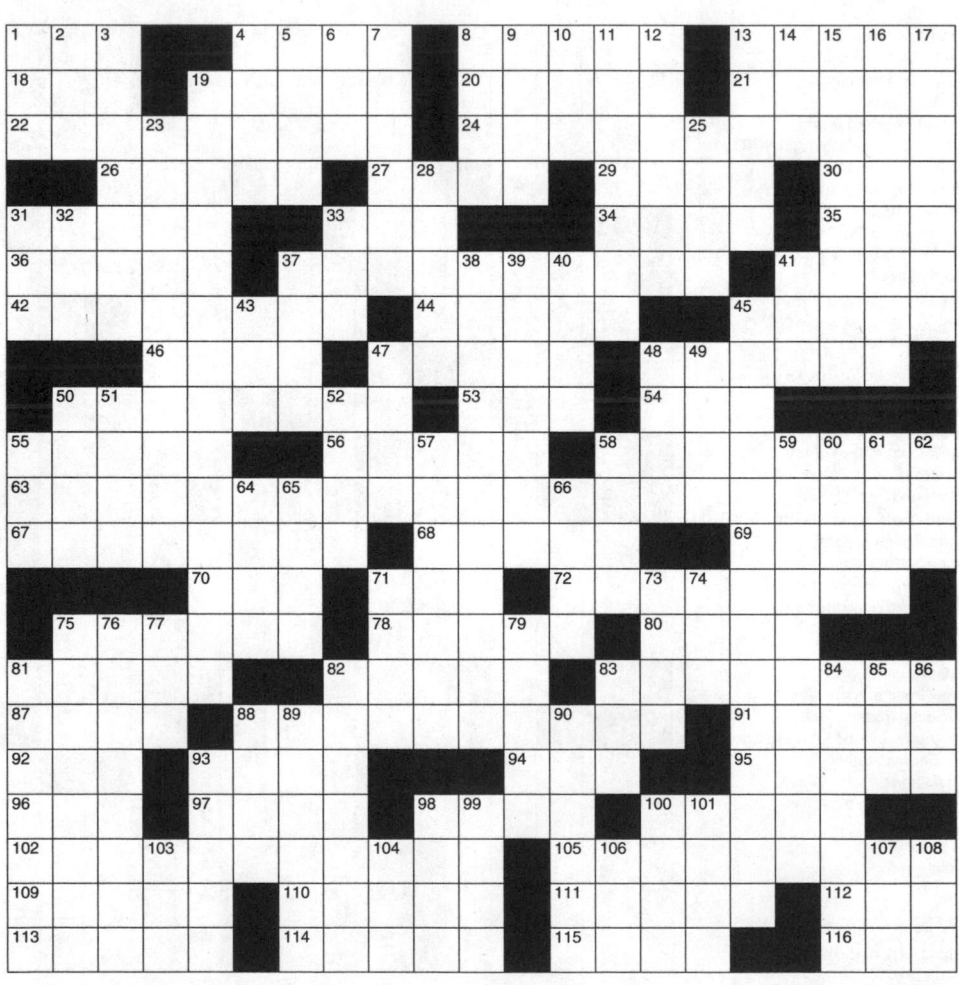

by Hal Moore

ACROSS

1 Like a bull in a china shop
7 Blue
11 Band whose songs are featured in a hit 2001 musical and 2018 movie
15 Tube tops
19 Where Hemingway wrote "The Old Man and the Sea"
20 Instrument whose name sounds like a rebuke of Obama's dog
21 Case load?
22 River that formed an extension of the Mason-Dixon line
23 One who's just moved from Portland?
26 Bit of baseball gear
27 "Jeez, I heard you already!"
28 Number
29 Game played with a dog
30 Peak
31 Tennis great who wrote the 2009 tell-all "Open"
32 Major science journal
33 Satchel for a guy
35 Convert a morgue worker into a spy?
37 Google ___
38 Pre-euro currency
39 Smooch
40 Leave gobsmacked
41 Common plural verb
42 Staple of many a "Real Housewives" episode
44 One of the Leewards
48 LeBron basketball sneaker, e.g.?
51 Foe in "Wonder Woman"
55 – – –
56 Ready for the recycling bin
57 Field trip chaperone
59 Surrender
60 Celebrity chef Oliver
61 Hunger for
62 Will of "Arrested Development"
64 Determined to do
65 Flower said to cover the plains of Hades
68 Brand of 33-Down
69 Intense blowback against a signature Trump policy proposal?
72 Large mobile devices, to use a modern portmanteau
74 Hair net
75 Amazon threat
76 Muppet eagle
79 Highest draft category
80 Garbage barge
81 Tour de France setting
82 Bad person to get paired with for a class assignment?
87 Bender
89 "Present!"
90 Like more
91 Gulf mogul
92 Rulers during the Time of Troubles
93 Jewish mysticism
94 Harmonized
98 Triple-A requests
99 Nickname for a superserious congressman?
101 Trainer of Rey in "The Last Jedi"
102 Eager
103 Fixtures in every Vegas casino
104 Ontario city across the river from Buffalo, for short
105 Craftsy online store
106 Cay
107 For takeout
108 Exemplar of cruelty

DOWN

1 Follower of "ah-ah-ah"
2 Fun adventure
3 Colored layer
4 Hungarians, by another name
5 Noses around
6 Northerner
7 One of the Gilmore Girls
8 Old sports org. with the Kentucky Colonels
9 U.S. food giant
10 Suck-up
11 Red with embarrassment
12 Fad toy of the 1990s
13 Tendency
14 What's better when it's fine?
15 Awaken
16 Yellowfin
17 Workers who are always retiring?
18 "Take that!"
24 Strain
25 Tweet, e.g.
29 Language of Omar Khayyám's "Rubáiyát"
31 Glows
32 Caution on an airplane wing
33 Dip for mozzarella sticks
34 Affecting radically
35 ×
36 Biceps exercise
37 Attack on a big scale
38 Uncool
42 Gig for an aspiring electronic musician
43 Root word?
44 Citation
45 What "..." may represent
46 What "#" means in chess notation
47 Slim
49 Surrendered
50 "Take a hike!"
52 Like an uncorrupted file
53 Academy Awards prop
54 Popular Belgian brews, informally
58 Hurt
60 Ballet jump
63 Music genre at a rave
64 Provider of green juice?
65 Bother
66 Put away
67 Vietnamese broth-and-noodles soup
70 "Yeah, right!"
71 Academy Awards prop
73 Garden toilers
76 Saliva
77 Words from a T.S.A. agent before a pat-down
78 Punk-rock hairstyles
80 Guarantee
81 U.S.P.S. package status
83 Purchase at a sports stadium
84 Sophisticated
85 How whiskey is often served
86 Financially solvent
87 Blue man group?
88 Something made to be destroyed
91 Where soccer was invented: Abbr.
93 Hitchcock triple feature?
94 Should that be the case
95 "Hey ___" (start of a phone voice command)
96 R&B great Redding
97 A bit of disputin' from Putin?
99 Chairlift item
100 Clickable tag on BuzzFeed beside "LOL" and "WTF"

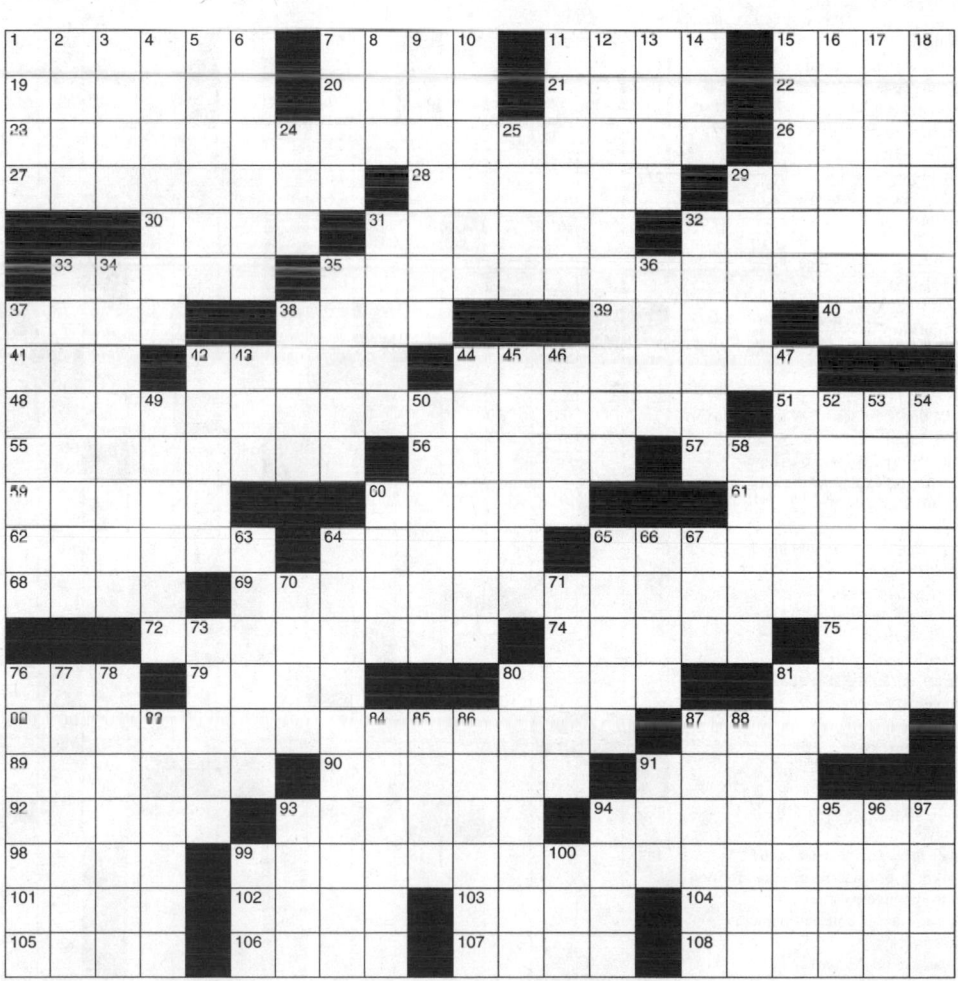

by Joel Fagliano

Note: After completing this puzzle, draw a line connecting the circles, starting and ending at the first circle of 62-Across, to spell a five-word message. The connected circles will reveal a picture related to the puzzle's theme. (Note: Rounded edges look best.) To complete the effect, draw a line between the circle at 36-Across and the circle at the third square of 37-Across.

ACROSS

1 Accents to tuxedos
6 Leader in a robe
10 Stinger
14 Wind-borne seed
19 "Sesame Street" figure
20 "Long live . . . !"
21 Western ski resort
22 N.F.L.'s Kaepernick
23 Where 68-Across is permanently housed
25 How 122-Across is usually described
27 Hoses connect to them
28 Curiosity or Opportunity
29 Imperial ____ (bar orders)
30 Pill alternative, for short
31 Vegas inits.
34 Rug rat
35 Blood parts
36 It may be a shocker
37 Hawaiian for "appetizer"
38 Sum to
39 Sport-____ (off-roaders)
41 Recipe amt.
42 Ones making the grade, for short?
43 Triangular snacks
46 D.J. ____ tha Kyd
48 Time for pampering oneself
51 Lightly bite
52 Dogie catcher
56 Invisible lures
58 Thither
59 Writer with an interest in cryptography
61 Idiot, in slang
62 Not cooped up
64 Sigh of relief
66 Experimental writing?
68 1929 work that is the theme of this puzzle, with "The"
71 Short
73 "Our" side in a sci-fi battle
74 Mild cheeses
77 AAA line: Abbr.
78 California wine city
79 Nickname for the Philadelphia Eagles stadium, with "the"
81 Falsity
82 Lake that's the source of the Mississippi
85 With 96- and 105-Across, how 122-Across explained the subject of this puzzle
89 Tops
92 Bests in a Fourth of July hot dog contest, say
94 Irony or hyperbole
95 MI6 R&D division in 007 novels
96 See 85-Across
99 Certain laundry appliance
101 Three ____ of the Wheel of Dharma (Buddhist concept)
104 Lead-in to cab
105 See 85-Across
109 Spanish greeting
111 Quantity of eggs
115 ____-green
116 Prosy
120 Place for works that are in the works . . . or what the message formed by the connected letters is?
121 Houston-based petroleum giant, informally
122 Creator of 68-Across
123 Established figures?
124 Drying-out woe, for short
125 "Whew!" elicitor

DOWN

1 Modern pic
2 Moving company?
3 Open
4 Set in a cockpit
5 Mailed
6 Tie, as a score
7 Caramel morsel from Hershey
8 Composer of the "Concord" Sonata
9 Dorm V.I.P.s
10 "Time ____ . . ."
11 Grad
12 Cloud type
13 Pirate's pet
14 Lasting reminder
15 Some pullovers
16 Michigan college or its town
17 Choir stands
18 Snare
24 Julius Caesar's first name
26 ____ Park, Colo.
31 Kind of sauce
32 Camera crane operator
33 Something that shouldn't be mixed
37 How to get the permit, say
40 Shot deliverer
42 Circus employees
44 Palindromic musician
45 Palindromic tribe
47 Showed, informally
48 Bub
49 Big stretch
50 Milk-Bone, e.g.
53 Cultural gathering
54 Boot part
55 Scores after deuces, informally
57 Tijuana title: Abbr.
58 Violinist Menuhin
60 Draw out
61 Org. with a June draft
63 Call back?
65 ____ Rand Institute
67 "I agree fully!"
69 Broadcast antennas, e.g.
70 Bit of Queen's "Bohemian Rhapsody"
71 Witches in "Macbeth," e.g.
72 Words upon a shocked realization
75 Form 1099-____
76 Actor Green
78 "See ya!"
80 Plane area
83 Beach house owner
84 ID
86 Graduating grp.
87 Cawfee
88 Channel that aired "Moesha"
90 Half-Betazoid "Star Trek" character
91 German city with a Pennsylvania namesake
93 Dangerous job
95 Play period: Abbr.
97 French queens
98 Fall
99 Figure in the "Arabian Nights"
100 Virtuosic
102 2018 biopic with a 0% rating on Rotten Tomatoes
103 Narrow cuts
104 Boston ____
106 Device outmoded by smartphones
107 Unusual feature of 68-Across
108 Second side to vote
110 Nails
112 Suffix with Motor
113 Unsightly spot
114 Chemical ending
117 Scottish denial
118 Tour grp.
119 Winner of a record eight N.H.L. Norris Trophies

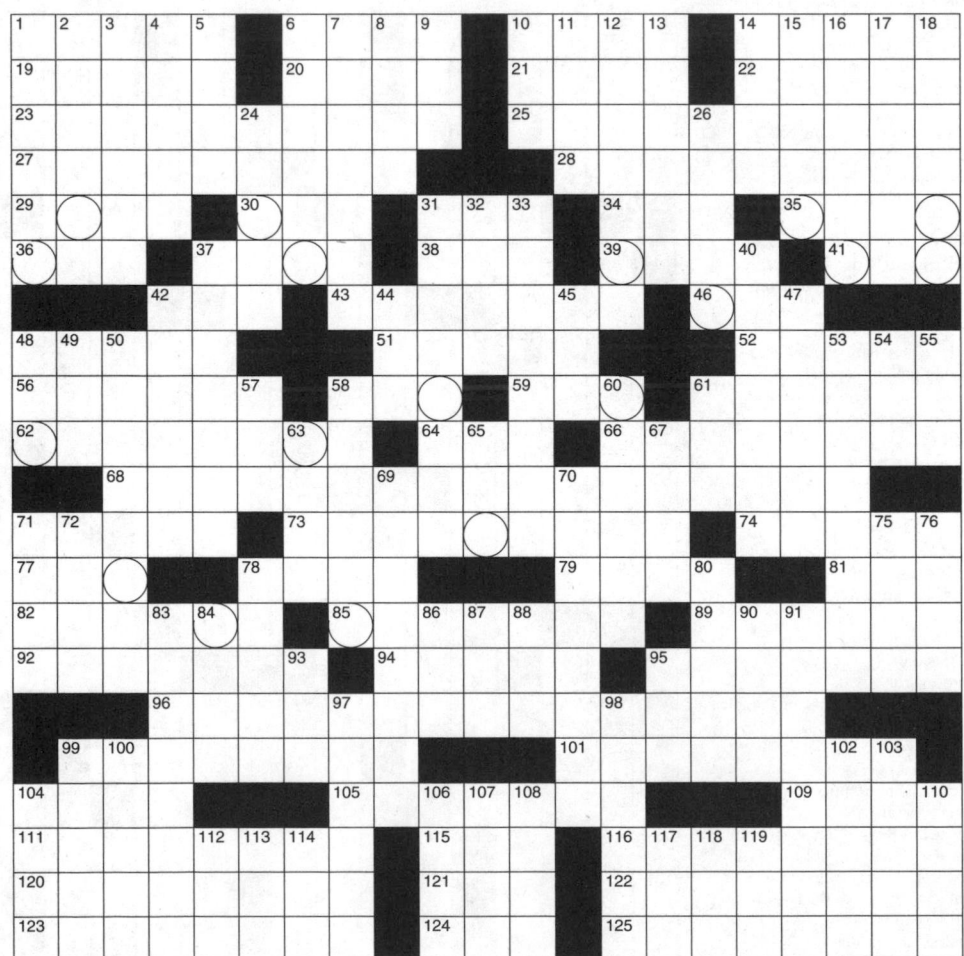

by Andrew Zhou

ACROSS

1 Outlaw
4 Electrical systems
9 2011 N.B.A. champs, for short
13 Bahrain bigwigs
18 Flap
19 Up
20 Jesus, for one
21 Hawaiian island
22 Tease
23 Nissan Leaf, e.g.
25 "C'mon, we'll be fine"
27 1991 Disney heroine
29 Like many Rolex watches sold on the street
30 Establish a mood
31 Epithet for Leona Helmsley
34 Sunbeam
35 Persians, e.g.
36 Fishing tool
37 Fishing tool
38 Lovey
39 100 centavos
40 Took the trophy
43 Ear piece?
45 Admiring words
47 Gave drugs
48 Accra-to-Khartoum dir.
49 Buildup during vacation
51 Fishing tool
52 Troubles
53 Daughter of Anakin and Padmé
55 Right angle
56 Not on terra firma, say
57 Makeup of many a veggie dog
58 Watch chain
61 Like merlot and zinfandel, typically
64 Equal chance
67 Kind of court
68 Back cover?
69 Leather-clad TV warrior
70 In a footnote
71 Test that's done in ink
73 Mary-Kate, to Ashley
75 Fictional creature whose name is Old English for "giant"
76 Up on things
77 Grandiose
80 Command to a dog
81 Heist target
82 Tide detergent capsules
83 New Left org.
84 Basis for a raise
86 Qualifiers
87 Paroxysm
89 Simba's father in a Disney musical
91 Jets can be found in one
92 Allow to
93 Churn
94 "Mamma Mia!" song that begins "Where are those happy days?"
95 British royal
97 It's often served on toasted white bread, for short
99 Cut
100 N.L. Central player
101 Builder of Israel's first temple
106 Website feature resembling an odometer
110 Mate of a colorful bird
111 Hooch
112 Live
113 Western gas brand
115 Popular fruit drink
116 Debunk?
117 Sixth of 24
118 He might provide assistance after a crash

119 French article
120 Bit of salon detritus
121 Collapsed red giant?
122 Marina sights
123 Item that disturbs sleep four times in this puzzle

DOWN

1 Backyard get-together, briefly
2 "So long"
3 Lofty
4 Environmental advocacy group
5 Documentarian Burns who's the brother of Ken
6 Has a vacation day
7 Leave suddenly
8 Bunkum
9 Home to the 72,000-foot volcano Olympus Mons
10 Moisturizer ingredient
11 1980s cartoon robot
12 Islamic sovereign
13 Nobelist Wiesel
14 Item lain upon four times in this puzzle
15 Not farmed out
16 Chaac, to Mayans
17 Places

24 Domain
26 "Who's on First?" left fielder
28 Jazz's McCann
32 Start of the line that includes "wherefore art thou"
33 Approaches
38 Tippled
39 Government study, informally
40 Government aid
41 Beating by a hole, in match play
42 Rock star known for his 360-degree drum set
44 Parts of Mr. Clean and Lex Luthor costumes
46 Antagonist
47 J'adore perfumer
50 Concerning a pelvic bone
52 Certain Far Eastern fruits
54 Shakespeare title starter
56 Suffix with lime
58 Feature of a probability distribution where extreme events are more likely
59 Georgia, in the art world
60 Doctor's orders, often
62 Future plan for many an econ major
63 Home of the ancient Temple of Artemis
65 Flavoring in the Mideast drink arak
66 Cat-meets-dog sound

69 "Skylarking" band
72 Command at a surprise party
74 Popular game with 162 cards
78 Common download
79 "Wicked Game" vocalist Chris
82 Any of the four people disturbed in this puzzle
84 Where Karl Benz debuted the world's first auto
85 16-ounce beers, slangily
87 Grammy winner Meghan
88 "Yes, quite"
89 Unsavory connections
90 Criticize snidely
94 Who wrote "The supreme art of war is to subdue the enemy without fighting"
96 Discharged matter
98 Overly
99 Top
100 ____-de-sac
102 Canoodles, in Britain
103 Clean a spill
104 Air supply
105 Setting of Hercules' first labor
107 Wild ____
108 Grp. with a saving plan?
109 Parent
114 Dead-end job, e.g.

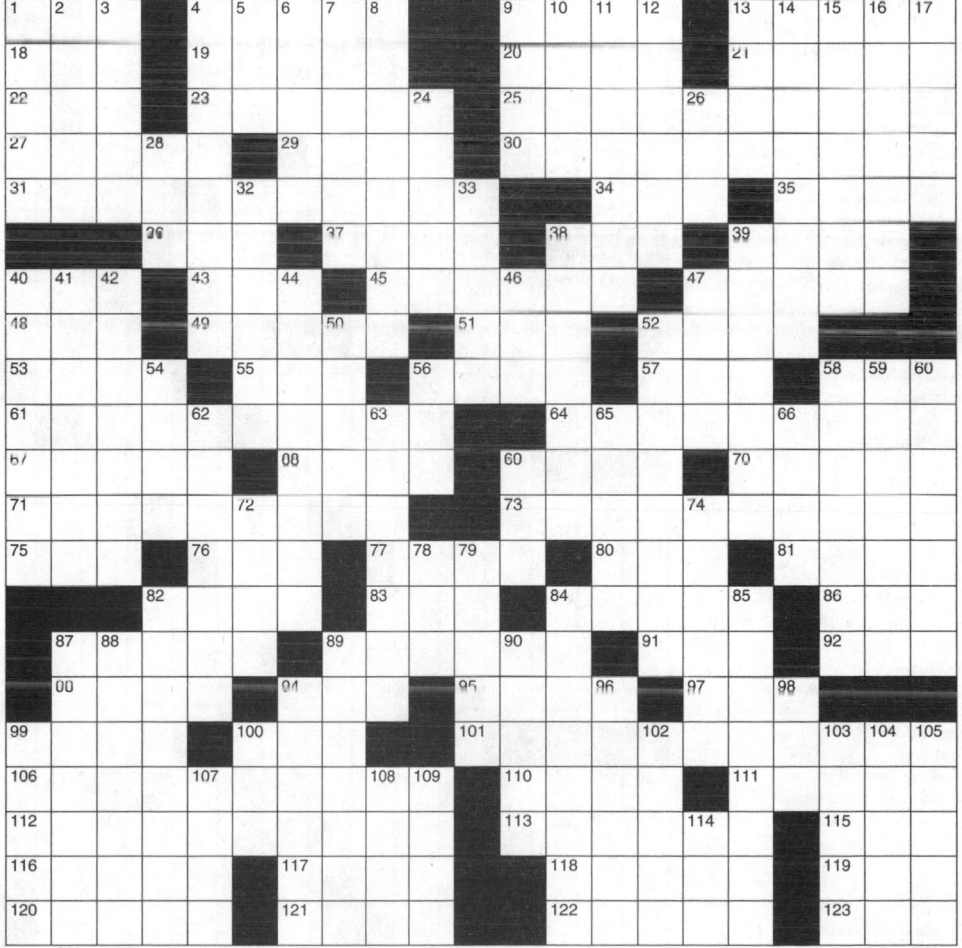

by Natan Last

ACROSS

1 Experts
6 Accord
12 The Harry Potter novels, e.g.
18 External parasites
20 Minuscule, cutesily
21 Not yet packed, say
22 *Another nickname for Old Abe . . . or a description of the circled letter?*
24 Got fit
25 Funny Brooks
26 Eight: Prefix
27 *Astronaut's place . . .*
29 Aves.
30 Let out, as a sigh
33 Venus, but not Serena
34 Truckful
35 A lid usually covers it at night
37 Naval rank: Abbr.
38 Counterpart of Venus
42 *Screen or partition . . .*
47 Kitchen sink attachment
50 Much-disputed part of an airplane
51 *Where decongestant spray goes . . .*
53 Animal with a snout
54 Candidate's goal
57 "___ time"
58 Discontent
59 Alternatively
60 Kind
61 Cellular messenger
62 CBS drama beginning in 2018
63 Negative connector
64 *Cyberexpert's worry . . .*
69 ___ Poke (caramel candy)
72 ___-rock
73 Each "O" of BOGO
74 "___ and the Real Girl" (2007 comedy)
75 "What have I done!"
79 Part of an auto garage's business
81 Hawaiian mash-up?
82 Product much advertised during football games
83 Clutch
84 *Office device . . .*
87 "That's my intention"
89 At the end of the day
90 *Heist figure . . .*
93 General ___ chicken
94 Bear: Sp.
96 Soon
97 Memphis-to-Nashville dir.
98 Coinage during the 2008 presidential election
101 "Spider-Man" baddie
103 ___ drive
106 *Bit of good fortune . . .*
111 Something you might get your mitts on
112 By birth
113 Away from work for a while
114 *Store banner . . .*
118 Early ___
119 Scowling
120 Worry in East Africa
121 Something to chew on
122 Some see-through curtains
123 "Ni-i-i-ice!"

DOWN

1 Common phobia source
2 Overturn
3 Omani money
4 Powerful arm
5 What a "singleton" is, in baseball lingo
6 City from which the U.S. moved its embassy in 2018
7 Big retailer of camping gear
8 Middle-earth denizen
9 About
10 Keep busy
11 Dr. Seuss title animal
12 Be a lousy bedmate, say
13 Physicist Mach
14 Little protestation
15 "Ain't I somethin'?!"
16 Cabinet dept.
17 Kind
19 Is on the up and up?
21 Part of a place setting
23 Mom-and-pop org.
28 Followers of talks
31 "___ tu" (Verdi aria)
32 Chose not to
34 Whigs' opponents
36 "Water, water, everywhere," per Coleridge
38 "You're in my spot!"
39 Like an increasing amount of immigration to the U.S. nowadays
40 Rizzo in "Midnight Cowboy"
41 More cunning
42 The "r" of r = d/t
43 Kind of hygiene
44 Experts in the field?
45 Publisher's announcement
46 Wet
48 Visits a school, maybe
49 Feeling with a deadline approaching
52 Like carbon 12, but not carbon 14
55 Trip up
56 Intrinsically
60 Eyeball layer
61 Calif.'s 101, e.g.
62 Containing iron
65 Gung-ho
66 Quick signatures, quickly
67 Grammy winner Corinne Bailey ___
68 Poet who originated the phrase "harmony in discord"
69 Apostle of Ireland, for short
70 Lounges
71 Have because of
76 Respond to a bumper sticker, maybe
77 Bill
78 Lilac or lavender
80 Section at a zoo
81 Distant source of radio waves
82 "X" isn't really one
83 Void
85 Wallop
86 Org. founded under Nixon
88 General rule
91 "Aw, nuts!"
92 Converts to binary, e.g.
95 Literally, "great O's"
98 "Pretty slick!"
99 Expression of dismay
100 "Gah!"
102 Egg: Prefix
103 Join
104 Have a feeling
105 Bring into the world
106 Truckful
107 Computer command
108 Problem for a plumber
109 Remained fresh
110 ___ chips (trendy snack food)
115 Scot's refusal
116 Scottie's warning
117 ___ Amsterdam (name on colonial maps)

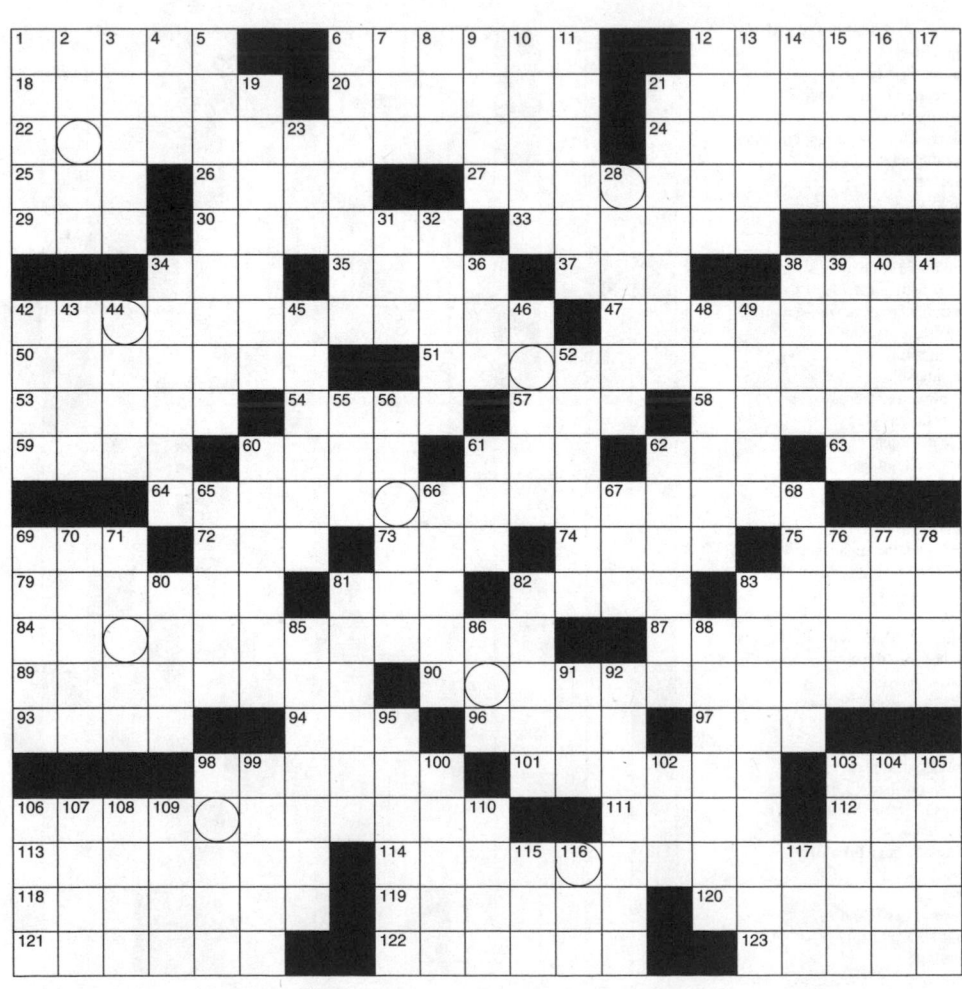

by Tom McCoy

ACROSS

1. _____ Page, the Queen of Pinups
7. Flavorful meat coating
15. End-of-week cry
19. O.K. to play, in a way
20. Obsession with a single subject
22. Country's McEntire
23. "We can't play that game — I can't reach it on our shelf!"
25. Operating system developed at Bell Labs
26. Onetime White House family
27. Corroded
28. Sunken-ship sites
30. Travel option for Birthright trips
31. Natural-gas component
34. Dress (up)
35. Standout
36. Turning point in history
38. "My sincerest apologies, but that game is off the table"
43. Unearth
46. Bills
47. Many a Snapchat posting
48. Suit that's hard to get into
51. Old Buick
53. What's plucked in "she loves me, she loves me not"
54. "We can't play that game unless we borrow someone else's"
56. Laughs and laughs
57. French city grid
58. People vis-à-vis gods
59. It's a trek
60. "It _____" ("Who's there?" reply)
61. Show overuse, as a sofa
62. They may have attachments
63. Strand
65. Hammarskjöld once of the U.N.
68. Provisions
70. _____ school
71. Bone connection with convex and concave fittings
73. _____ Mode, woman in "The Incredibles"
75. Word repeated in the openings of "Star Wars" movies
76. "I'm begging you, let's not play that game!"
77. Antinuclear treaty topic
79. Pop-up site
80. Daniel who wrote "Flowers for Algernon"
81. Island greetings
82. Take over
83. Info in dating profiles
85. "No, that game would be over in a flash"
88. One of 26 for Walt Disney
91. Common filler words
92. Common filler words
93. "If you are always trying to be _____, you will never know how amazing you can be": Maya Angelou
96. Praise for a picador
98. Frida Kahlo, por ejemplo
100. Novelist McEwan
101. Grammy winner Mary J. _____
102. Cosmonaut Gagarin
103. "I've finally decided! I'm . . ."
109. Small matter
110. "Looking to go somewhere?"
111. Densest natural element
112. Bead source
113. Officials in ancient Rome
114. They vary from past to present

DOWN

1. Isolated hill
2. Surround with light
3. 1996 Robert De Niro/Wesley Snipes psychological thriller
4. Bird in a holiday song
5. "Black _____," Georgia O'Keeffe painting at the Met
6. Ewoks or Jawas, in brief
7. One of academia's Seven Sisters
8. Impersonate
9. It might result in a defensive TD
10. Aviary sound
11. Full of broodiness, say
12. Cheerleader's cheer
13. Synchronized states
14. Narcissist's quality
15. Who you really are
16. M→F→M, e.g.
17. One of the first birds released by Noah after the flood, in legend
18. Kind of number not much seen nowadays
21. "Of course!"
24. Krazy _____ of the comics
29. More villainous
31. Hosp. readout
32. Penalties for illegal bowls in cricket
33. Largest active Antarctic volcano
34. Little 'un
37. Vessels seen in 2004's "Troy"
39. Like albino alligators
40. General _____ chicken
41. Work (up)
42. Things needed in passing?
44. Supervillain in DC Comics
45. More smoky, as Scotch
48. Goals
49. Bird named for a Titan
50. Polling calculations
52. Spill coffee on, maybe
53. Blandishment
55. Actor's honor, informally
56. Rigid
59. Attacked
60. They're shared among friends
63. Whiz
64. Classic work whose "shorter" version comes in two vols.
66. Image on the ceiling of la chapelle Sixtine
67. Classic Pontiacs
69. He's often pictured carrying an hourglass
71. Apply haphazardly
72. It comes just before a period
73. List-ending abbr.
74. Scale site
75. Fleet
76. When doubled, dismiss out of hand
78. Low voices
79. Turn's partner
82. Secondary loan signer
84. D.C. insider
86. Get-go
87. Old vacuum tube
89. Suspect statements?
90. Fix, as a model plane
94. _____-nest
95. Aesop's "The _____ and the Grasshopper"
97. Is for all intents and purposes
98. Taurus or Touareg
99. _____ Marino
101. Big name in speakers
102. Go on and on
104. Tyrant Amin
105. Catch
106. "Despicable Me" protagonist
107. Ominous sight at a beach
108. Go bad

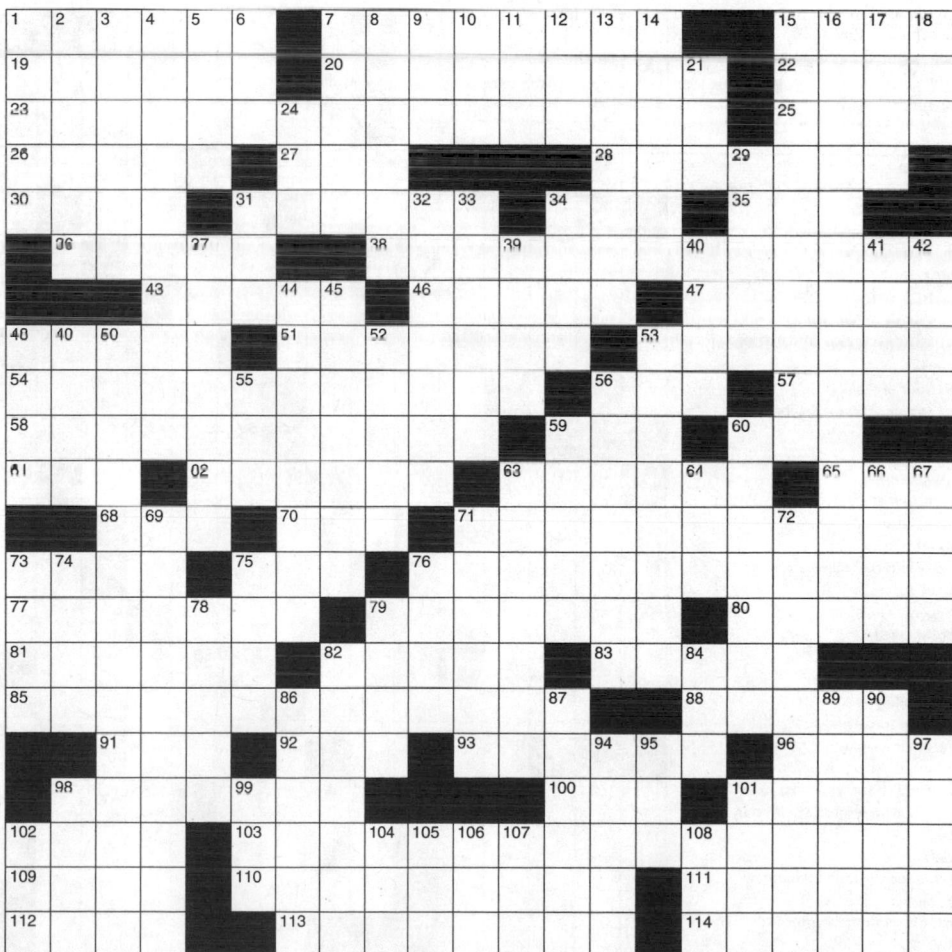

by Ross Trudeau

ACROSS

1 Pinocchio, e.g.
7 Aphrodisiacs boost it
13 Backpack feature
18 Where cuneiform was discovered
19 Superhero outfits, typically
22 Irritate
23 Give unsolicited advice
24 Weapon for William Tell
25 Coming back in
26 Popular singer born in County Donegal
27 Like many wine casks
29 Lie low
30 What starts with a spark of an idea?
31 Snide and sassy
33 Portrayer of TV's Det. Fin Tutuola
35 Jefferson Memorial topper
37 Non-fish aquarium attraction
39 Precalculator calculator
41 Where one might be well-suited
45 Clue weapon
47 "Give it a ___"
48 Street crossing Hollywood in Hollywood
49 Conservative
50 Job for a plastic surgeon, for short
51 Modern name in transportation
53 "Heavens!"
55 Squared building stone
57 Three short, three long, three short
58 Gnocchi ___ Romana
59 Rapper with the 2017 #1 hit "Bodak Yellow"
61 Brought about
62 Kindle download
63 Chant at a political rally
64 First sign
65 Manhattan neighborhood next to the Lower East Side
67 Popular line of dolls with "Kidz" and "Babyz" spinoffs
68 Hole foods?
70 Bundled, as hay
71 1960s–'70s police drama
73 Medicare provision for nonhospital expenses
74 Perch for pigeons
75 Plea to a superhero, maybe
76 Employs
77 Peter Pan rival
80 Trespass upon
82 Seventh-year exam in Harry Potter
83 Lhasa ___
84 "Toodles!"
85 Positive market move
86 Son of Adam
88 Trigger, as an alarm
90 Repossessed
92 Farm measures
94 Kind of humor
96 "Cuz I told you to!"
97 Like rain forests
98 Fourth-down play
99 Spasm
101 Fast-food chain with a hat in its logo
104 Jennifer who wrote "Manhattan Beach"
106 Printer brand
108 Spelunker's helmet attachment
111 Springs
112 Five-time Emmy nominee for "Grey's Anatomy"
114 Key of Dvořák's "New World" Symphony
116 World-weariness
117 "Silly me, rambling again!"
118 The Chainsmokers or Eurythmics
119 Declare
120 TV colleague of Hayes and O'Donnell
121 Didn't sleep well

DOWN

1 Embarrassment for an art curator
2 "Sign me up!"
3 Headline after a toddler C.E.O. resigns, literally?
4 Coiner of the term "generative music"
5 Certain med. specialist
6 It may be cutting things close
7 Car failure only a block from the mechanic, literally?
8 About, on memos
9 Mixture of nature and technology
10 "___ official"
11 Takes off in a hurry
12 Eye socket
13 Takes off in a hurry
14 "For a massage, go that way!," literally?
15 "Darn it all!"
16 Do for Jon Batiste
17 Drudge
20 Its HQ is the Pentagon
21 First country to legalize changing one's gender identity (1972)
28 First African-American sorority
32 Part of a circle
34 Like the dress shirt that's just adorable, literally?
36 Draftable
37 "Wise" ones
38 Chamber music group, often
40 ___ Lingus
41 Calf-length dresses
42 "Not so fast!"
43 Addresses a crowd
44 Firebugs
46 Signature Jacques Tati role
48 Capital of Liechtenstein
52 Puffs up
54 For nothing
56 Perspectives
58 Bore
59 Midnight, maybe
60 Total baller
62 Dissed with flowery language, literally?
65 Hip-hop dance move
66 Classic London theater
67 Angled edge
69 Snacks often paired with milk
70 "Mutiny on the Bounty" captain
72 Underwear brand
73 Punch vs. Judy, literally?
77 One answer to the question "What's your favorite music genre," literally?
78 Agenda entry
79 Music outro effect
81 Prominent parts of goblins
83 Not do so well
84 Haberdashery buys
87 Directive
89 CVS rival
91 "Alea iacta ___": Caesar
93 Barbie attendee
94 About 10% of Russia
95 Afternoon hour
98 Land in "The Hunger Games"
100 Bumbling
101 Orders at the Rose & Crown
102 Quote from a letter
103 Actor Eric
105 Frustrated cry
107 ___ stick
109 Pouty face
110 Urge on
113 Bloody, say
115 Barn greeting

by Finn Vigeland

ACROSS

1 Chunks of land
7 "Be on the lookout" messages, for short
11 Person to take complaints to, informally
14 Polo of "The Fosters"
18 Popular Dominican dance
20 Leave quickly
21 Musical Yoko
22 Get a ___ on someone
23 *Sou'wester*
25 Abbr. in many blood type names
26 "Logic dictates . . ."
27 It's usually put in the middle of a table
28 *Late hours*
31 Messes up
35 Downfall in pinball
37 Music export from Tokyo, for short
38 Sciences' counterpart
39 "Jeez!"
41 Princess who says "I recognized your foul stench when I was brought on board"
43 Campy 1972 vampire film
45 *Peace marches*
48 Grub
51 Part of a preschool day
52 Opinion
53 Nirvana seeker
56 Sorority letter
57 Forbiddance
58 Masthead list, for short
60 More lit, perhaps
62 *"After Earth"*
69 Pothead
70 I am a ___
71 Do the wave?
72 What un desierto lacks
74 Lyrical lament
75 Not able to catch something
77 *Growth ring*
80 Farthest point in an orbit around the moon
82 This woman
83 Closure opening?
84 Vote in France
85 Blue swaths on maps
87 They follow oohs
90 Like the simplest instructions
95 Talk show host Cohen
97 *Trade punches*
100 Hills with gentle slopes on one side and steep slopes on the other
103 Fake
104 Verdi tragedy
105 "Grand Ole" venue
106 Say whether or not you'll attend
108 Blow out
110 Imbroglio
111 *Prostates*
115 French 101 verb
117 Collaborative site
118 Snatch
119 Game suggested by this puzzle's theme
125 Racer Luyendyk
126 Half of dos
127 Taking care of things
128 Nickel-and-diming sort
129 They might break out in hives
130 Cockapoo or cockatoo, maybe
131 Cpls.' superiors
132 Act obsequiously

DOWN

1 Atlanta-based cable inits.
2 Cold and wet
3 Term in tennis, golf and baseball, all with different meanings
4 Hero interred in Santa Clara, Cuba
5 "Later, luv"
6 Rhyming nickname in Cardinals history
7 Midriff muscles, for short
8 "Oh, quit being silly!"
9 Sailor in the Navy
10 Seatbelt, e.g.
11 "C'mon, be serious"
12 ___ Day vitamins
13 Rémy Martin product
14 Bridge-supporting frame
15 Dulles designer
16 Pasta sauce brand
17 Longtime singing talent show, familiarly
19 ___-vaxxers
24 Singer Reese
29 Garment worn by John Roberts that's hidden in his name
30 R&B's ___ Hill
31 Bristol, Conn.-based cable inits.
32 Sister and wife of Cronus, in myth
33 Collect from the soil
34 Result of a religious schism
36 Camping need
40 Japanese dogs with turned-up tails
42 Neighbor of Wyo.
44 Commercial rhyme for "Famous"
46 Transmits
47 Part of a Mario costume
49 Part of a "Which came first?" dilemma
50 Comment before "I missed that"
54 Director Van Sant
55 Cross
59 Maker of the game Zaxxon
61 ___ contendere
62 Pad alternative
63 Chinese New Year treat
64 One of the Castros
65 Shed material
66 Dwarf planet with more mass than Pluto
67 Good throw?
68 "Get outta here!"
70 ___ Taurasi, all-time W.N.B.A. scoring leader
73 Supplementary item
76 Suffix with methyl
78 Gymnastics flip
79 Arizona capital of the Navajo Nation
81 ___ Germany
86 Relatively cool stellar phenomenon
88 "Come again?"
89 Some bathroom installations
91 Brother of Ham
92 Play starter?
93 Sand-burrowing marine creatures
94 Reasons to do something
96 Quaint demographic grouping
98 Number two: Abbr.
99 Revved up
101 Timeline part
102 Align
107 "¡Let's go!"
109 Some flight board info
111 Mop
112 Poop out
113 Over
114 ___ interview
116 Coin in Köln
120 Sci-fi C.G.I. creations
121 Debut, metaphorically
122 Dealership expanse
123 I problem?
124 Hem but not haw?

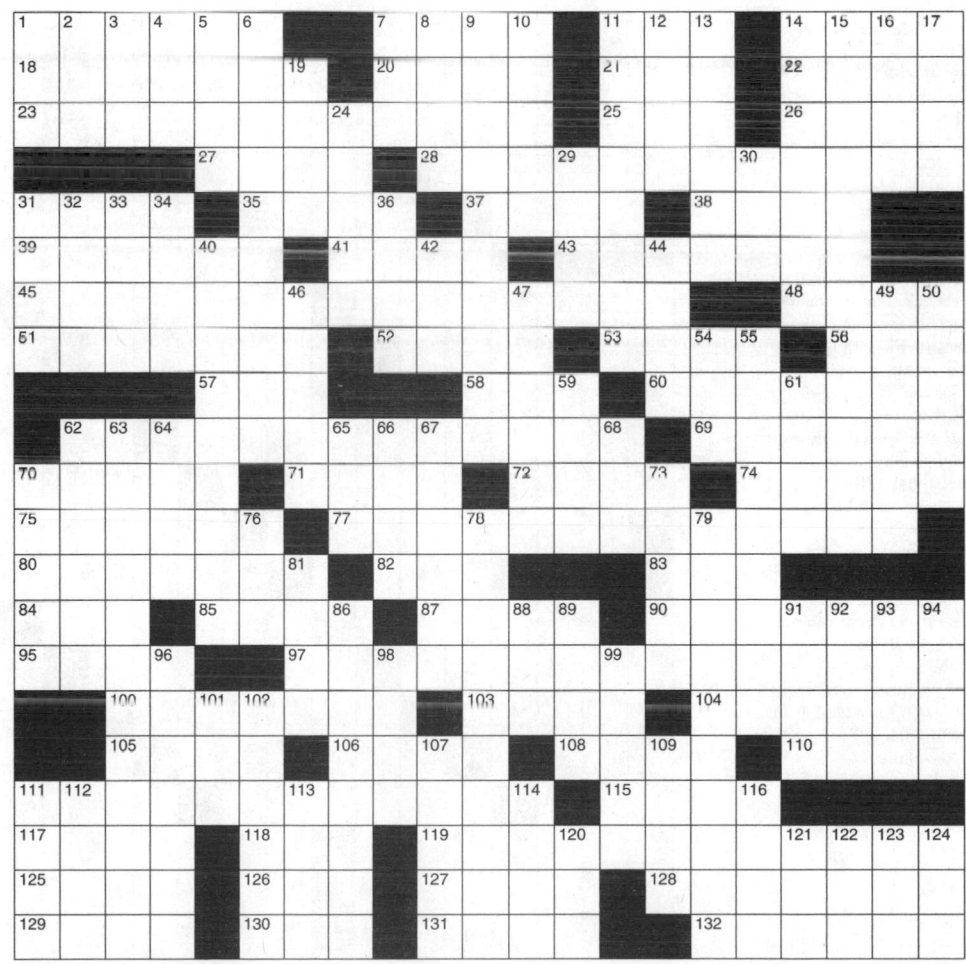

by Erik Agard

ACROSS

1 Goes to grab a bite, say
14 What a crop top exposes
21 "Anything else, or can I go?"
22 "1984" superstate that includes America
23 Early reel-to-reel devices
24 Expired IDs?
25 "Marriage Italian-Style" star
26 Give mouth-to-mouth to?
27 Donny who won "Dancing With the Stars"
29 Construction on Broadway
30 Speak sharply
31 Stockpot addition
32 Stickers forming a patch
33 Keep it under your hat!
34 Petulant expression
35 Leaves mystified
36 Soda brand with more than 90 flavors
37 Ancestry
41 Picks up
42 Tommy or Jimmy of jazz
43 As a whole
44 Two for one?
45 Case workers?
46 Golfing hazards
47 ___ pasta (farfalle)
48 2018's debate over "Yanny or Laurel," e.g.
49 Joey Potter's portrayer on "Dawson's Creek"
51 Travel on-line?
55 Receptive to new ideas
56 Party of 13?
58 Home arena of the Bruins and Celtics
59 Painter's roll
60 Overflow
61 Trunk fastener?
62 Lets out
63 Ringo Starr's real first name
67 Palate cleanser in a multicourse meal
68 Reptiles that can walk on ceilings
69 Casanova's intrigues
70 Ran into in court?
71 Wigs out
72 On the take
73 ___ the Great (ninth-century English king)
74 Cereal ingredient
75 Places to crash on road trips
76 Very
77 Purely academic
78 Striker's replacement
82 Copa América cheer
83 Century in American politics
84 Brewery sights
85 In the ballpark
86 Old "It cleans your breath while it cleans your teeth" sloganeer
88 Awfully large
91 Takes to the sky
92 Paprika lookalike
93 Forerunners of combines
94 You can't go back on them

DOWN

1 Cries loudly
2 Greek hero killed by a giant scorpion
3 Who once said "You wouldn't have won if we'd beaten you"
4 Win every prize in
5 Green housewarming gift
6 Wordsworth wrote one on immortality
7 Crank up the amp to 11 and go wild
8 Name, as a successor
9 Essentially
10 Many faculty members, in brief
11 Stan who co-created Spider-Man
12 Presented perfectly
13 Courtroom periods
14 Travels by car
15 Touchscreen array
16 Document kept in a safe
17 Untrustworthy sort
18 Sort of
19 Shiny beetle disliked by fruit growers
20 You should avoid feeding on them
28 Food & Wine and Field & Stream
31 Rock musician with a knighthood
32 Deadbeat student at TV's Highland High
33 "The Lady Is a Tramp" lyricist
34 Stephen King novel with a misspelling in the title
35 Like some tires
36 Shade in the woods
37 Steve who co-created Spider-Man
38 Absorbed
39 Express
40 Muddling through
41 Wearers of white hats
42 Sphere
44 Game featured in 2006's "Casino Royale"
45 Department of Buildings issuance
47 Became inseparable
48 Selling point?
50 Companies that need help
51 Didn't bid
52 Ancient Mexicas, e.g.
53 Sister of Tiffany
54 It may be open for business
56 Unkind, as criticism
57 German-Swiss author who won the 1946 Nobel in Literature
59 Safer of "60 Minutes"
61 Satine's profession in "Moulin Rouge!"
63 Copper wheels?
64 Torch carrier's announcement
65 Julius Caesar's first wife
66 Calls from quarterbacks
67 Its shell doesn't crack
68 U.S. Naval Academy mascot
70 Small jumper
71 Show's earnings
73 James of TV's "How the West Was Won"
74 Field with lots of growth?
76 Pan resistant to aging
77 Ars ___ (anagram of "anagrams," aptly)
78 Slaloming spot
79 Ford Mustang, for one
80 Valuable possession
81 Round units?
83 Stuff
84 What an essay presents
85 Her 2018 album "Dancing Queen" consists entirely of Abba covers
87 Break
89 Word spoken while waving
90 Well-chosen

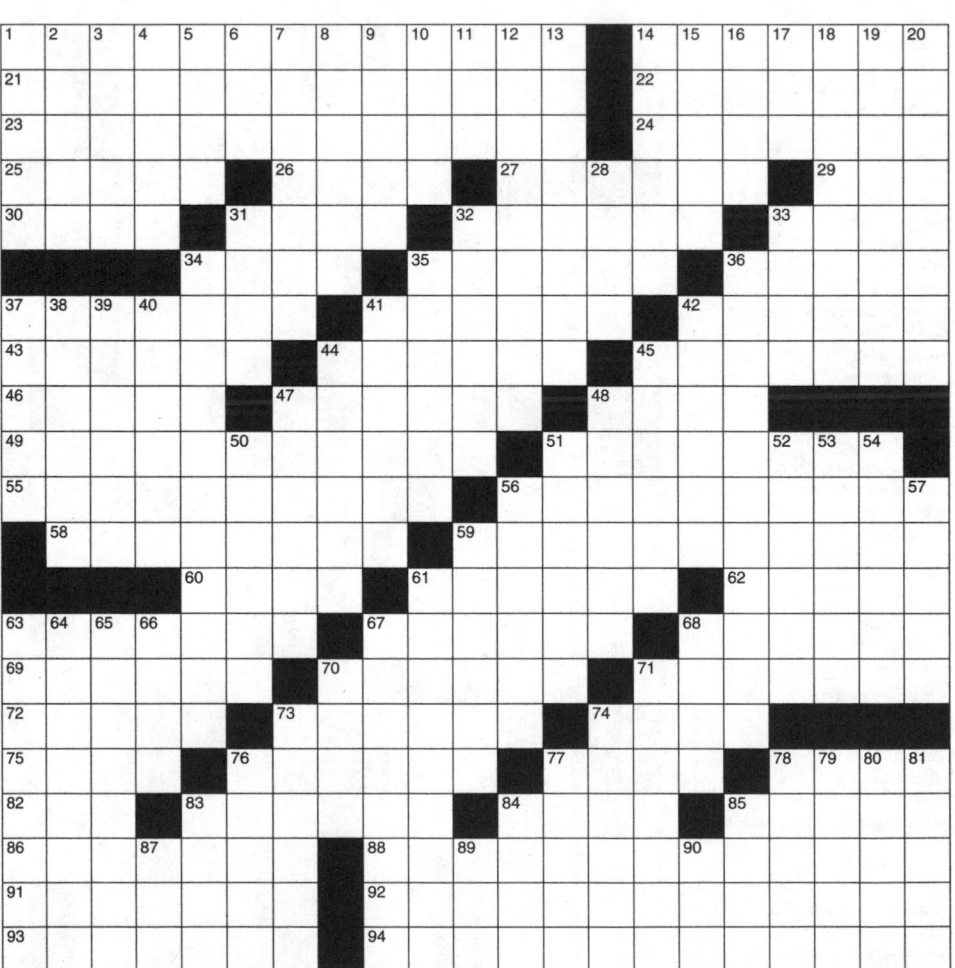

by Patrick Berry

Note: This crossword represents an escape room, with four articles you'll need hidden inside. After you complete the grid, follow the directions at 41-, 70- and 99-Across to find what to do next. Working correctly will lead you to a four-word phrase with a total of 12 letters. That is your answer.

ACROSS

1 Shakespearean father of three
5 "I agree!"
9 Enjoys the sun
14 Pants material
19 Approximately
20 Sycophant
21 Earth tone
22 Movie with a shootout at high noon, maybe
23 _____ Major
24 Band bookings
25 Outside the city
26 Any member of Abba
27 Automotive debut of 1957
29 Some univ. hirees
31 Turkish inn
33 Horror writer Peter
35 Stole, in slang
37 Cold treat
41 What's needed in order to escape this crossword
44 Sandwich loaf
45 Pitcher Hershiser
46 Declares to be true
47 Indie rocker with the 2009 #3 album "Middle Cyclone"
50 Not doing well
52 A snap
53 _____ jure (law phrase)
55 Tobacconist _____ Sherman
56 Virtuous ones
58 N.Y.C. subway org.
59 Words of denial
63 Round fig.
66 A little, musically
67 Charcuterie stock
69 Lycées, e.g.
70 What to do with the items referenced in 41-Across
74 Natural light display
75 Move smoothly to the next thing
76 Great _____
77 Billy _____ Williams
78 Like Russia prior to 1917
80 One of a couple
81 Neon and others
83 Apollo, to Zeus
84 Offshore
86 Possesses, to the Bard
87 Kind of battery
91 Final desperate effort
94 Tickle the _____
97 Prefix on some first-aid products
98 "_____ had it!"
99 After following the instructions at 70-Across, how to escape this puzzle
102 Not as much
105 Ratings pioneer
106 Edmonton athletes
107 "Fine with me"
109 German name component, often
110 Uncool one
111 Unconventional
114 James of the West
116 "Just foolin'"
118 Algerian port
121 Get together
122 "Give it _____!"
123 Verdi soprano
124 Grp. founded by 12 countries
125 Luau, basically
126 Brothers' name in R&B
127 Symbol of fire prevention
128 Vehicle that requires no fuel

DOWN

1 Name one can "skip to"
2 Goof
3 Confidently said
4 Pre-GPS staple
5 Subject with variables
6 Daily _____ (British paper)
7 Part of some physicals: Abbr.
8 Attribute of many political ads
9 Soup with a red color
10 Prefix with pressure
11 React with fear or delight
12 Ralph and Alice, on old TV
13 Actress Ward
14 Trig function
15 Native Iowan
16 Citizen of: Suffix
17 Actor Beatty
18 It's mined, all mined!
28 Common middle name for girls
30 Constantly fidgeting, say
32 Game with 42 territory cards
33 Slovenly type
34 Prefix with byte
35 "Famous _____" (slogan on Idaho license plates)
36 Pause

38 Went on and on
39 Yiddish cries
40 Second of April?
42 Wretched smell
43 "Hey! That hurts!"
48 Kind of Hollywood romance
49 Literary scholars debate what's in it
51 Getting to the point?
54 Solution to a maze
57 Specks
58 They might drop down
60 Almost forever
61 Nothing more than
62 Latin 101 word
63 Petty disagreement
64 Also
65 Beleaguers
67 Horrible headache
68 Anesthesiologist's concern
71 "The Bridge at Narni" painter
72 Internet sensation
73 Nut whose name sounds like a sneeze
79 Shock, in a way
81 Flowering evergreen shrubs
82 Bucks
85 Administrants of corporal punishment

86 "Can you explain that further?"
88 Requiring intellect
89 It might end in a ZIP code: Abbr.
90 Ph.D. requirement: Abbr.
91 Tiny "tiny"
92 Forum greeting
93 Former Yankee nickname
95 Soft and smooth
96 Happy wintertime news for schoolkids
100 Semi fuel
101 Golfer Michelle
103 Kinds
104 "Awesome!"
108 California city north of Ventura
110 Mythical queen of Carthage
111 Your and my
112 It has a big deck
113 Aunt: Sp.
115 Toledo-to-Columbus dir.
117 A Kardashian
119 Dined
120 Silent approval

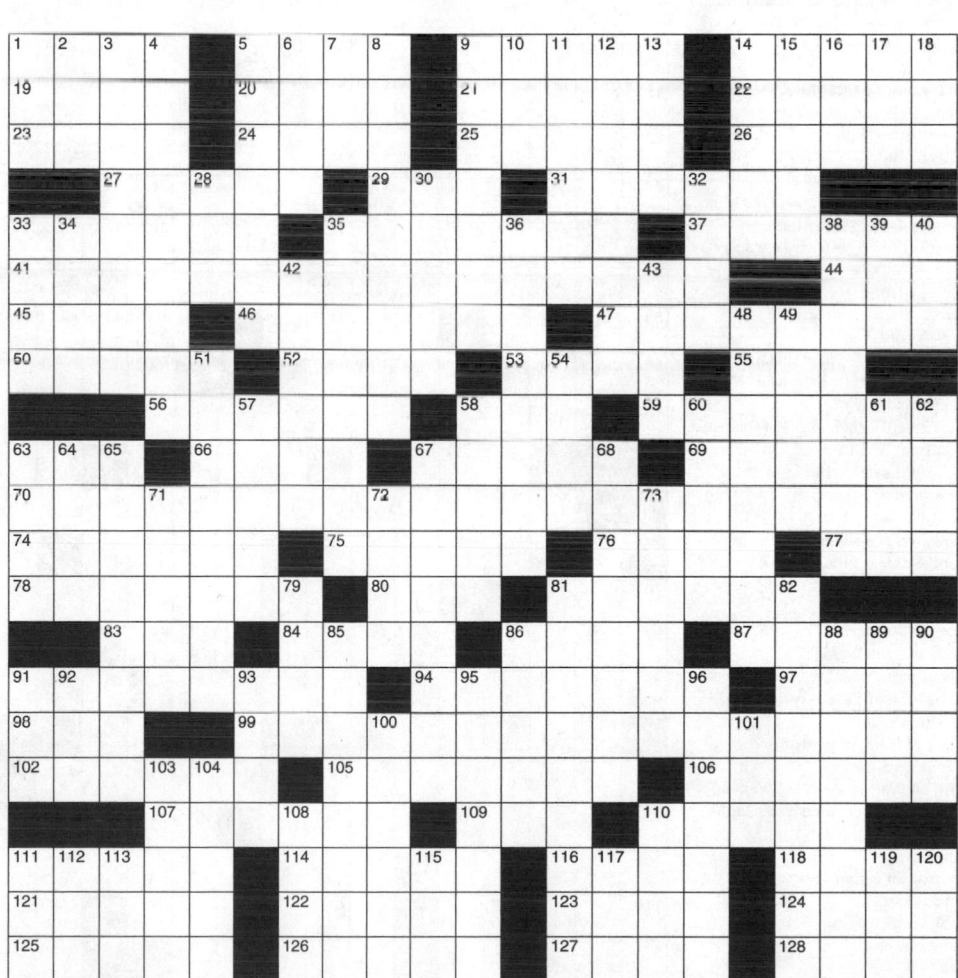

by Eric Berlin

ACROSS

1 Era of ignorance
9 Elevators in an office building?
14 Houston squad, casually
19 Eaglelike
20 Mississippi River bottom feeder
21 "Wouldn't that be nice!"
22 Satchel for a homicide detective?
24 Joe of "GoodFellas"
25 Something found at the top of many a Google search page
26 Manufactured
27 Baking soda has many of these
29 Tush
30 Danny Ocean's ex-wife in "Ocean's Eleven"
31 Unseasonal wear on a winter vacation?
34 Map
36 Parisian waters
37 Jewish mourning period
38 Zoom, e.g.
39 Baseball stats sometimes called 39-Down
42 Jerk
46 Static
48 Swiss canton that was home to William Tell
49 Variety of stud poker, familiarly
50 Berry with two diacritics in its name
51 "Get ___!"
52 Late-morning meal for a TV family?
58 Dorm overseers, for short
59 Sports event with two diacritics in its name
60 Cry after "Company"
61 Who wrote "In the land of the blind, the one-eyed man is king"
64 One way to buy mustard cheaply?
67 Like the number i, mathematically
68 Burns writing
69 Strong bond
70 A pillar of Islam
71 Emails such as "Click this link to become an Apollo astronaut"?
77 Erie Canal city
80 ___ Spiegel, co-founder of Snapchat
81 "Darling, won't you ___ my worried mind" ("Layla" lyric)
82 Peter's chief of staff on "The Good Wife"
83 Down-on-their-luck sorts
84 Hit the hide off the baseball
86 Beauts
87 Backgrounds in theater
88 Tempur-Pedic rival
90 Seawater compound
92 Neophytes
93 Collection of Yule-centric posts?
98 Boxing venue
99 Nagy of Hungarian history
100 Wooded valley
101 Bird on Walden Pond in "Walden"
102 Like services covered by a health insurer
105 Drops
107 Utensil for eating some cured meat?
110 Link with
111 Brainpower
112 See to it
113 When a happy hour might start
114 Haven
115 Seizure cause

DOWN

1 Deaden acoustically
2 Blue shade
3 Kingdom in "The Prisoner of Zenda"
4 Leg-pullers
5 Div. for the Red 106-Down
6 Secures with a band
7 S.A.S.E., e.g.: Abbr.
8 They require stitches
9 What the rotator cuff rotates
10 School extension?
11 Neutral shades
12 Word from the Latin for "noose"
13 One caught by a 12-Down
14 Nurse
15 Can-can dancing?
16 Formula for slope in math
17 Costa Rican president who won the 1987 Nobel Peace Prize
18 Stuffed ___
20 Clay and oil, for artists
23 "For heaven ___"
28 Some ways on Waze: Abbr.
32 Split personality?
33 Branch of Islam
34 Appurtenance for a cartoon Neanderthal
35 Mannheim mister
39 Delmonico steak cuts
40 Document listing technical specifications
41 TV network with a science-y name
43 Prefix with puncture
44 More sensible
45 One is roughly the mass of a speck of dust
47 Festoons with Charmin, for short
49 Charged up
53 Laura of "Big Little Lies"
54 Confucian philosopher ___ Hsi
55 Really trendy
56 Hit just beyond the infield
57 Hightail it, saltily
62 Ocean froth
63 "The Simpsons" bar
64 Asian fruits used in Western alternative medicine
65 Norwegian king near the end of the first millennium
66 Non-___ (food label)
67 Western powwow held every year or so
70 "Come again?"
72 Limit
73 "Fancy that!"
74 People like you
75 Orfeo in Gluck's "Orfeo ed Euridice," e.g.
76 Not catch
78 Crescent-shaped Italian pastries
79 Piedmont wine town
85 Alternatives to gelcaps
86 Semiliquid stuff
87 Neural junction
89 So-so filler?
91 Lunkheads
92 Holiday glitter
93 Flora and fauna
94 Plaster for painting
95 Animal used to guard sheep and goats
96 Spanish crockery
97 Munchkin
98 "___-Tikki-Tavi"
103 Misreckons
104 "It is a riddle, wrapped in a mystery, inside an enigma; but perhaps there is ___": Churchill
106 See 5-Down
108 Numerical prefix
109 Much Top 40 music now

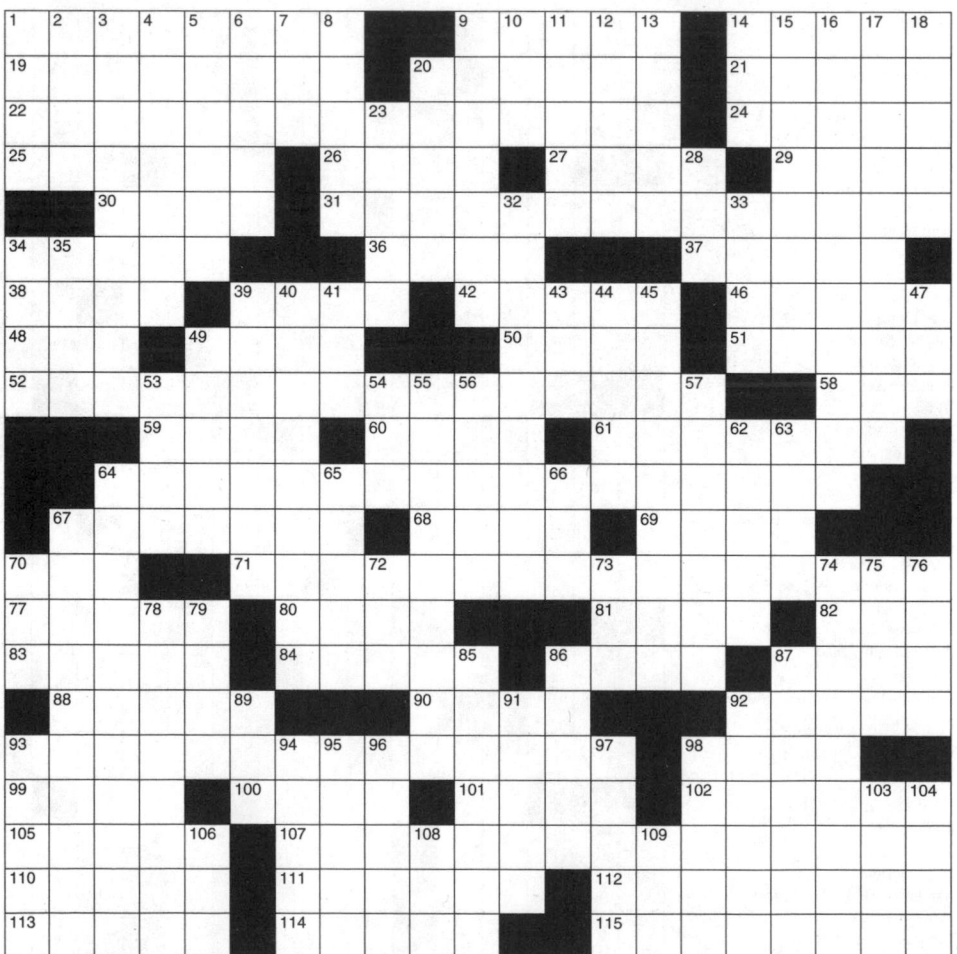

by Byron Walden and Joel Fagliano

ACROSS

1 Late Queen of Soul
7 Places for bears or villains
12 What a recipe may be written on
20 Puts up
21 Veep under Nixon
22 Formal defense
23 Photo caption for the winning team's M.V.P. being carried off the field?
25 Get an F in physics?
26 Bert of "The Wizard of Oz"
27 Powerful swell
28 In the style of
30 First-generation Japanese-American
31 Houdini feat
33 Rey, to Luke, in "The Last Jedi"
36 Place for a stud to go
38 What you're effectively saying when you sign a waiver?
41 Longtime athlete on the U.S. Davis Cup team
45 Line through one's teeth?
47 Torment
48 Full of subtlety
50 Capital of Albania
52 Atlas or Titan, for short
53 Street through the middle of town
54 Energy secretary Chu under Obama
55 ____ neutrality
56 Actress Long
58 Extended diatribe
59 Moon race?
61 Router attachments
63 It's just below 0: Abbr.
64 Medieval poets
67 Piece of writing that's half in verse?
70 Some paid rides, informally
71 First leg of an itinerary
72 Avenging spirits in Greek myth
73 Bad thing to hit with a hammer
75 "Casey at the Bat" poet Ernest
77 Wee bit
78 "I'm f-f-freezing!"
80 Coined money
84 Aids for determining pregnancy, e.g.
86 Pizazz
87 Fellini's "La ____"
88 Inducing forgetfulness
89 Outlook alternative
91 Dollar signs without the bars
92 Word after who or how
93 Dropping the baton in a relay race, e.g.?
98 Bit of ink
99 Optimum
101 Senator Feinstein
103 Blues legend Waters
106 "____ complicated"
107 Area near the shore
109 Publicans' servings
112 Area near the shore
115 Warning not given on a golf course?
118 Something on the rise today
119 Actress Belafonte
120 Start to inhabit
121 Baja California city
122 "The Zoo Story" playwright
123 Movie trailer, e.g.

DOWN

1 Name of what was once the world's second-largest saltwater lake
2 Tabula ____
3 "Hematite, magnetite — take your pick"?
4 Line that ended with Nicholas II
5 "____ Grace" (title of address)
6 "To quote myself . . ."
7 Los Angeles neighborhood next to Beverly Grove
8 Wide-eyed
9 Memo starter
10 Half of a cartoon duo
11 Make official?
12 Super Bowl III M.V.P.
13 Nail polish brand with the colors Teal the Cows Come Home and Berry Fairy Fun
14 Talking-____ (reprimands)
15 Big female role on HBO's "Westworld"
16 Two things you might find in Sherwood Forest?
17 As long as one can remember
18 Work (up)
19 "The Hallucinogenic Toreador" painter
24 Apartment building V.I.P.
29 Mentally sluggish
32 Producer of "60 Minutes"
33 Seniors' big night out
34 European stratovolcano
35 Astronauts' wear
36 Young newts
37 Came down
39 Spike
40 Human Rights Campaign inits.
42 Minor altercation
43 Soccer shot resulting from a corner kick, often
44 Lawn tools
46 Like Tara, several times in "Gone With the Wind"?
49 Singer DiFranco
51 Multi-time music collaborator with Bowie
52 Some magazine perfume ads
53 Conductor
56 Country on the Arctic Circle: Abbr.
57 "Yes for me"
60 The Wildcats of the Big 12 Conf.
61 Brit. legislators
62 [Shrug]
64 Forcibly oppose
65 Following close behind
66 Some celebrity charity events
68 Shirking work, maybe, for short
69 "The Hurt Locker" menace, briefly
70 Scads of
72 Club known for 66-Down
74 Enterprise starter
76 Barely make (out)
78 Two-masted vessel
79 Small stream
81 Places for specific social classes to park?
82 "Any ____?"
83 Heading in the right direction?
85 Fastener with a flange
86 Bête noire
89 Small bother
90 Pageant whose 1986 runner-up was Halle Berry
94 Procedural spinoff starring LL Cool J
95 Antarctic penguin
96 Person who's hard to take
97 Most conservative
100 Page of a movie script?
102 1994 tripartite treaty
103 De bene ____ (legal phrase)
104 In those days
105 Tommy of tennis
107 Temporary cover
108 Hopper
110 Writer ____ Stanley Gardner
111 Tiresias, in "Oedipus Rex"
113 Some gametes
114 Join
116 Capitals' org.
117 Ruby of "A Raisin in the Sun"

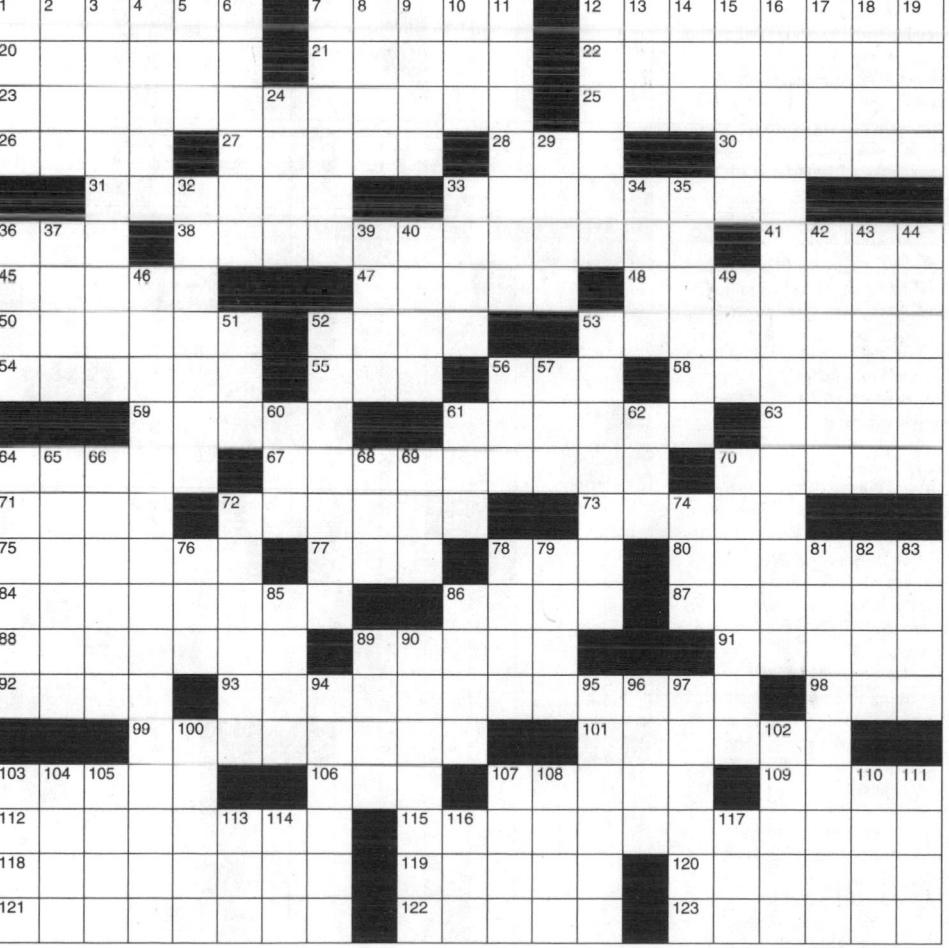

by Joon Pahk

ACROSS

1 Tennis judge's cry
6 Locks in a barn?
10 Icon leading to checkout
14 Traveled in trunks?
18 Large green moths
19 Dateless, say
21 It's frequently in Italian
22 Greek ally in the "Iliad"
23 13579 AZ
25 Hash houses
27 Country on the Red Sea
28 Home sick?
29 Brackish coastal habitat
30 Citrus drink
31 Egyptian god of the universe
33 It often comes before the fall
34 Summer clock setting: Abbr.
36 Large large skip skip
43 Victoria's Secret item
46 Sandra Denton, in hip-hop's "Whatta Man" trio
48 A miner concern?
49 Opening in a battlement
50 Some transitional movie shots
52 Sporting a feathery crest
55 First name on the Supreme Court
56 AT hot dog hot dog RA
58 Tags
60 The Lions or Tigers, on scoreboards
61 Many a fête d'anniversaire attendee
62 Writer Wiesel
63 Invincibility power-up in Mario games
65 Blow away
66 Wound + dis
72 "___ Vickers," Sinclair Lewis novel
74 Doesn't keep
75 Perch for a pie
76 Comment on a blog
78 Dad ___
79 After all deductions
80 P P
   U U
   B B
84 Big name in watches
86 Creator of a draft
88 All you can eat
89 Masters
91 Six-foot runner?
92 Cut, as a log
93 Scratch (out)
94 Per spire
99 Farrokh Bulsara ___ Freddie Mercury
101 ___ Caovilla, Italian shoe designer
102 Part of a buck
104 End of the British alphabet
107 Something studied in toponymy
112 Altar avowal
113 Creator of the detective Adam Dalgliesh
116 Fiery peppers
117 Yearn do
119 Currier's partner
120 Something to take lying down
121 Grassy expanse
122 Certain reunion attendee
123 It's better than never, they say
124 Spanish title: Abbr.
125 Pivot around an axis
126 Less crazy

DOWN

1 White sheet
2 Broadway's McDonald
3 Reversed
4 Kept on going
5 Evictor of the Jews in "Fiddler on the Roof"
6 Palindromic title
7 Pint glass fill
8 "That's all wrong!"
9 Off-road motorcycle race
10 Street fleet
11 What a Mercator projection map notably distorts
12 ___ Bridge (Venice landmark)
13 Like some yoga
14 Explosion fragments
15 Small dam
16 Trojan ally in the "Iliad"
17 Moonshine maker's need
20 Cornerstone abbr.
24 Puts in order
26 Political refugees
32 Announcement over a plane's P.A.
35 Like cleats
37 Minute amount
38 Test for a college sr.
39 "Father ___" (bygone British sitcom)
40 Store event that people may stand in line for
41 Freshen
42 Give a major lift
43 Soul sister, say
44 ___ avis
45 Garden parties?
47 Telepathy term
51 Children's author Blyton
52 Anklebone
53 Abbr. that rhymes with "bill," appropriately
54 Woodworking tool
57 Catbird seat?
58 "At Seventeen" singer Janis ___
59 He wore #6 for the Sixers
63 Like some clean energy
64 Ones place
67 Boiling blood
68 "Ask ___ . . ."
69 Flag
70 Satellite connection
71 Eldest Stark son on "Game of Thrones"
72 Manhattan Project creation
73 Baseball's Garciaparra
77 Long haul
79 Durable yellow cotton cloth
80 Darlings
81 Grassy expanse
82 Boy king in Shakespeare's "Richard III"
83 Atlanta-to-Miami dir.
85 Transmission part
86 Groceries holder
87 Genetic info carrier
90 What all people are, per the Bible
92 Cardinal letters
95 "___, My God, to Thee" (hymn)
96 Sings the blues
97 Funds
98 Discordant
100 Hank who voices Moe and Chief Wiggum
103 Lyric poem
105 German port in Lower Saxony
106 Two in the hand
107 Knight who co-founded Nike
108 What obsidian forms from
109 Partner of aid
110 Lion's share
111 "Cómo ___ usted?"
114 Norwegian P.M. Stoltenberg
115 Sibyl
118 "Despicable Me" supervillain

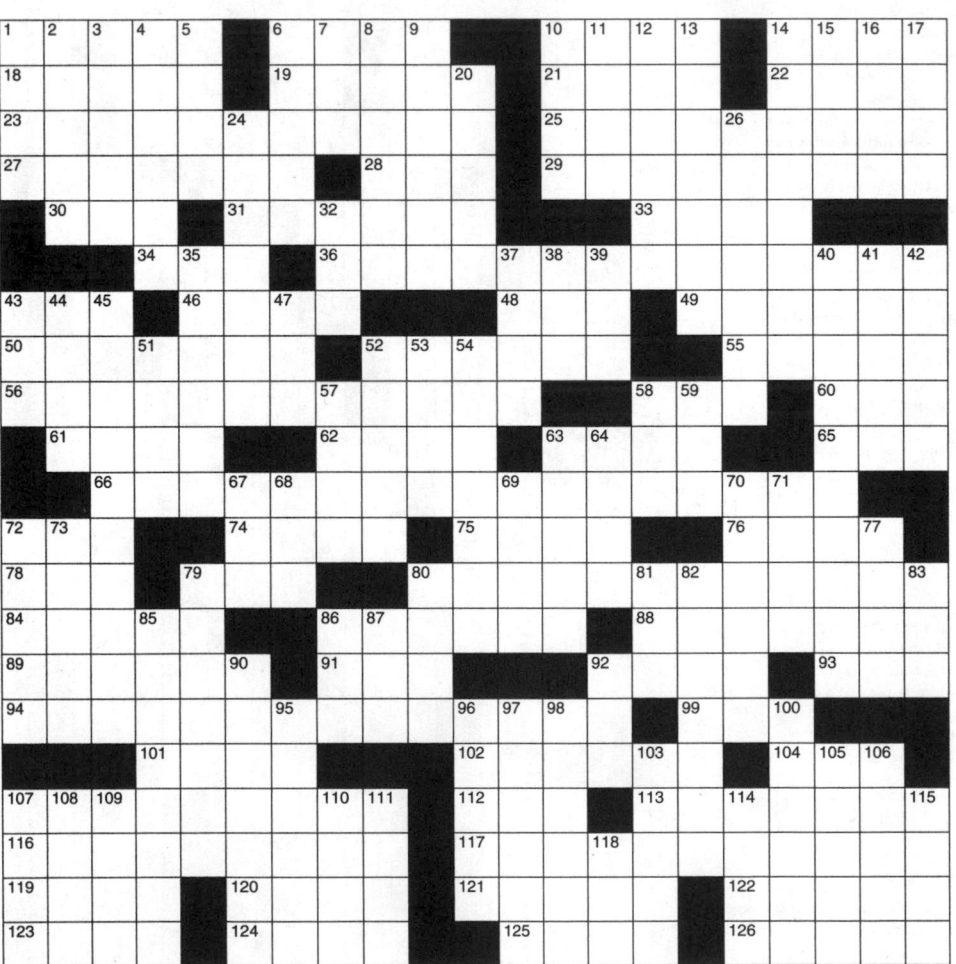

by Paul Coulter

ACROSS

1 Cranky baby's need
4 "Inspector Gadget" antagonist
10 Eschew
15 Starbuck's order giver
19 Brown ___
20 Best seller subtitled "The Grammarphobe's Guide to Better English in Plain English"
21 Pomme de ___ (French for "potato")
22 Part (of)
23 Part of U.C.S.F.
24 Cryptid of the 91-Across
27 Cordial relations
29 Gave two big thumbs down
30 Pluck
31 Cryptid of the 115-Across
36 Kids' TV character who speaks in a falsetto
37 Adler in Sherlock Holmes stories
38 Freshly painted
39 Talk like one smitten
41 Singer Del Rey
43 Cabinet selection?
45 When crepuscular animals are active
48 Cryptid of 105-Across
50 Jersey and others
52 Asian territory in Risk
54 Traitor
55 Surgically remove
56 Inventor Otis
58 "Am not!" rejoinder
60 Smallish batteries
61 P
62 With 68- and 74-Across, J. K. Rowling's first screenplay, with a hint to three pairs of answers in this puzzle
65 Indulges in to an unhealthy degree, briefly
67 Dispense
68 See 62-Across
69 Of service
71 "___ bleu!"
74 See 62-Across
80 Northeast state sch.
81 Meas. in a T.S.A. carry-on rule
83 Failed the class
84 Perfumery oil
85 Barbie's strawberry blond sister
87 Kingston bro
88 Stagger
90 Real Madrid vis-à-vis F.C. Barcelona
91 Creation after the Indian and Eurasian plates collided
93 Total hunk
95 Tape or patch
96 "Happy Birthday" writer, maybe
97 It's not your fault
98 ___ rap (music subgenre)
101 Word before and after "say"
103 Penne ___ vodka
105 It borders Iceland's eastern coast
111 Event not intended to be repeated
113 Bricklayer's tool
114 Weather-controlling "X-Men" character
115 Gaelic's home
120 One with a backstage pass
121 Fast time
122 Sort with a stiff upper lip
123 Capital of Kazakhstan
124 Squeeze (out)
125 ". . . they say"
126 Cupboard with open shelves at the top
127 What old army buddies might discuss
128 "Far out!"

DOWN

1 Like Bob Dylan's voice
2 "Remember the ___!"
3 Medical discovery of 1928
4 ___ Johnson a.k.a. The Rock
5 Burgle
6 Corp. mogul
7 Hobbles
8 2007 #1 Alicia Keys album
9 Narrow down
10 In a perfect world
11 African grassland
12 Cent : U.S. :: ___ : Sweden
13 Return letters?
14 Blue Book value decreaser
15 Also
16 Housewives and househusbands
17 Voice-activated device since 2014
18 Nota ___
25 Mother of the Virgin Mary
26 Be beholden to
28 Like a top-rated Michelin restaurant
32 Demise
33 Junior in the Football Hall of Fame
34 Real: Ger.
35 Shad delicacy
40 Gumbo ingredient
42 Playwright Chekhov
43 Feudal domain
44 Actress Fisher
46 Ghost
47 Person who's happy to go bust?
48 ___ Ski Valley
49 Repair, as a metal joint
51 Certain product of pyrolysis
53 Classic Chrysler
54 Highway gunk
57 Silent communication, for short
59 The golden rule, e.g.
60 Italian wine town
63 Carries away
64 Nursery rhyme seat
66 Harm
70 Motor ___
71 It can come in rolls
72 Like chemotherapy drugs
73 Adaptable sorts
75 Big things for megalomaniacs
76 Telephone buttons that lack letters
77 Acts like a helicopter parent to
78 Panache
79 ___-mannered
82 Enthusiasm
86 Massimo who wrote "The Goodbye Kiss"
87 Adding and subtracting
89 Breather
92 Until now
94 Opus ___
98 Make wealthy
99 Robert who pioneered in electronic music
100 "And if I don't?"
102 Poughkeepsie campus
104 Rearward
106 Value system
107 From Swansea, say
108 Tickle
109 Eleniak of "Baywatch"
110 Psyched
111 Capital on the same parallel as Seward, Alaska
112 Angle
116 Original Beatle Sutcliffe
117 Having many fans . . . or needing a fan?
118 "Fuhgeddaboudit!"
119 Bit of forensic data

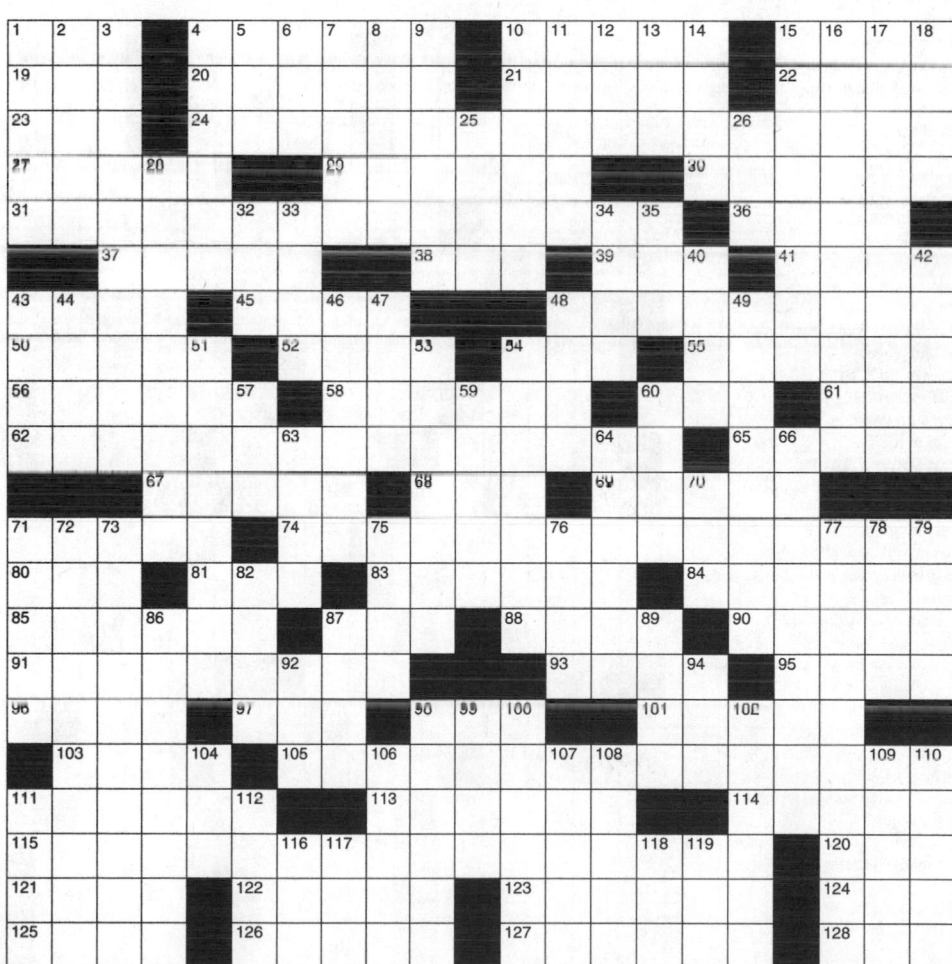

by Ross Trudeau

ACROSS

1 Early wake-up time
7 Title for Iran's Ruhollah Khomeini
11 Herbert of old "Pink Panther" films
14 Penultimate tourney round
19 "Doesn't matter to me"
20 Not yet completed
21 ____ moment
22 Sash go-with
23 Ancient capital of Laconia
24 Brew
25 Letters before single, double or triple
26 Lace tip
27 Casting doubt on
30 Lake Volta's land
31 The best, informally
32 Radio/TV character played in film by Michael Horse (1981) and Johnny Depp (2013)
33 Like some ruins in the Western Hemisphere
35 Lookalike
36 8.5" × 11": Abbr.
37 Scare quote?
38 Words of resignation
40 Topic concerned with hacking and software rights
42 Put on a few layers
44 Three-star mil. rank
45 Pope who supported the House of Borgia
47 Diminishing returns?
50 They're between shoulders
54 Word with shot or suit
55 Rowdydow
56 Not abstaining
57 Much sales
58 "No bid"
60 An end to depend
62 Head honcho
63 "Resume speed," musically
64 Emailing option
65 Riddle-ending query
67 Toward the stern
69 Its first letter stands for "India"
70 Certain tenant
72 Lex, e.g., in N.Y.C.
74 Misfortunes
75 Going for broke
77 Sides in Risk
78 Bette Midler's "Divine" nickname
80 Tense periods, for short
82 Archer of film
83 Dangerous environment
84 Easy-to-swallow pill
85 Food item cracked open before eating
87 Prized duck
89 It comes after II Chronicles
91 "Today was just brutal!"
94 Coiner of the term "Oedipus complex"
96 /
97 Thickheaded
100 Words of denial
101 Lost
103 All-nighter aid
105 Sets of plotted points
106 Shade of pink
108 Immediately . . . or where this puzzle's five shaded squares appear?
111 Floor
112 Japanese symbol of luck
113 Largo or lento
114 Swimming
115 Notable schemer
116 Some dash lengths
117 Rock stars are frequently on this
118 Come out
119 Standard parts of combo meals
120 "I'm good, thanks"
121 E-tail site since 2005
122 King's speech?

DOWN

1 Kind of year
2 Collision
3 Calf raised for its meat
4 Gloucester and Kent in "King Lear"
5 Certain bubbly, informally
6 Final work of Willa Cather's "Prairie Trilogy"
7 Tennis commentator's cry
8 Police officer who's not necessarily on horseback
9 "Play next" command on a music app
10 Shade of green
11 Cowboy's rope
12 "Here we go again . . ."
13 Followers of openers
14 By oneself, in a way
15 It's played for half a beat in 4/4 time
16 Country whose name consists of three consecutive state postal abbreviations
17 Peaceful
18 ____ spawn (hellions)
28 "Ooh, let's do that!"
29 "Eww, that's enough!"
34 MetLife Stadium team, on scoreboards
37 Clear and set, as tables
39 Scanned IDs
41 Italian pistol
42 Gets to
43 One who cracks the whip?
44 Plastic construction piece
45 Serving in a red-and-white striped box
46 Totally out
48 Juice brand
49 Longtime N.B.A. on TNT analyst
51 Who wrote "Some people talk to animals. Not many listen, though. That's the problem."
52 Action of a ladle
53 "Miss ____" (2016 political thriller)
54 Some fall births
57 Heroes of the Battle of Britain, for short
59 Babe
61 Mannerly
66 Freelancers' units: Abbr.
68 Colorful treat that resembles a rocket
71 All-Star Mets catcher of the 1990s–2000s
73 Corner PC key
74 Tow destination
76 Scat snippet
79 "Quién ____?"
81 Sanctuaries
84 Be conned
86 [Shiver]
88 With 93-Down, half of a double helix
90 Skunklike, say
91 Like TV but not radio?
92 "Old MacDonald" farm sounds
93 See 88-Down
94 Purchase at an African market
95 "Yay, team!"
97 Cause damage
98 Volunteer's declaration
99 Snowball fighter's protection
102 Botanical opening
104 Marriage money
105 "Ciao!"
107 Gifts that one usually bows when receiving
109 Certain dirección
110 What stars have

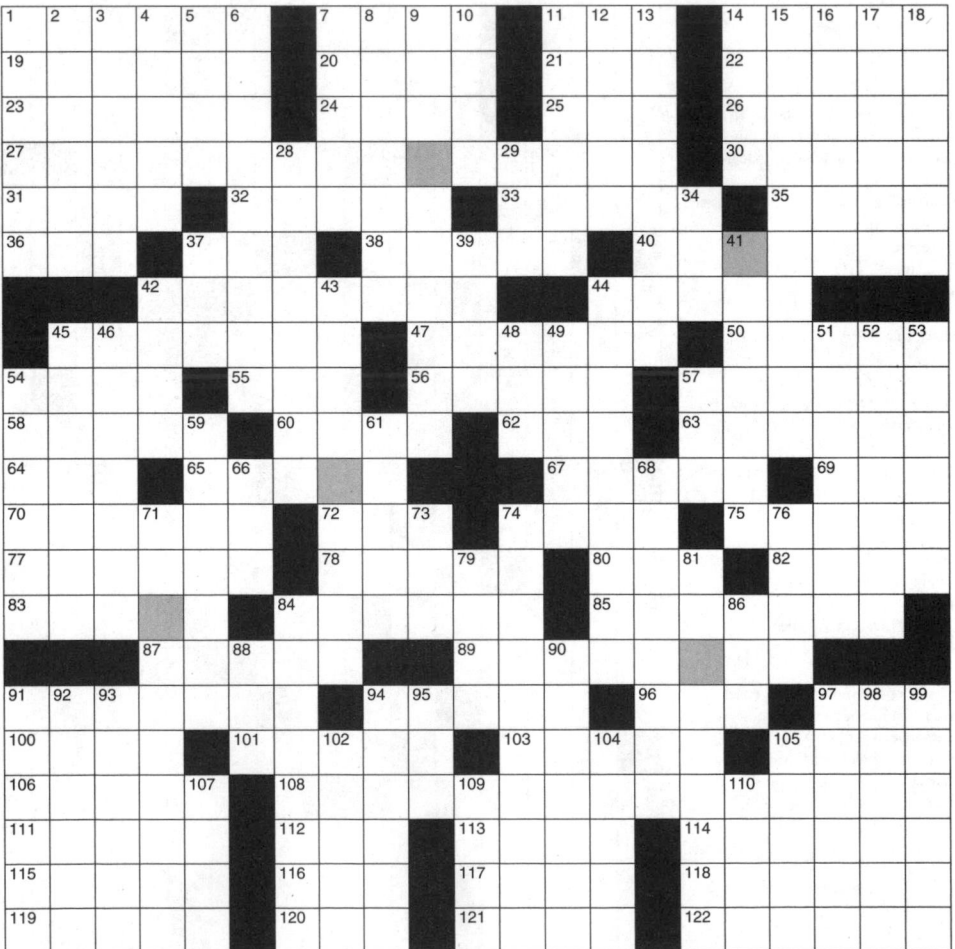

by Sam Ezersky

ACROSS

1 English guy
5 Partner in indecision with 5-Down
8 Alternative to pavement
14 What leads many people to say "Let's face it"?
19 Spanish greeting
20 G.I.'s address
21 California's motto
22 Like a truck descending a steep hill
23 Sources of Manchego cheese
24 How polka bands get their start?
27 Org. with an annual Help a Horse Day
29 Big suit
30 Harvard University Press's ____ Classical Library
31 Hundredths: Abbr.
32 Pontiff's gold treasure?
37 Performed creditably
39 Word with store or sign
40 Value
43 Like powwows
46 Register things
48 Star bursts
49 Summer hat
50 Enthrones
53 Query about the Freedom Caucus or Berniecrats?
56 Noted beauty contest loser
57 Most remote of the Near Islands
59 Irish port, county or bay
60 "Shame!"
61 Sushi eel
63 Improvised
67 Some refuges
69 Figure in Jewish folklore
70 Like some factories . . . or, in a different sense, like 90-, 109- and 119-Across (but not 24-, 32- and 53-Across)?
73 Potentially unhelpful answer to "Who's there?"
77 Speed
79 The 21st Amendment, e.g.
80 Biblical spy
81 Wonder
84 Dutch cheese
87 Pas sans
89 Awestruck
90 Nickname for a hard-to-please girl?
95 Room to maneuver
97 Certifiable, so to speak
98 Bygone office position
99 Unctuousness
101 White part of pearly whites
102 Offshore sight, maybe
104 Vexes
107 Arabic name that sounds like a polite affirmative
109 Data maintained by competitive dentists?
112 Envelope abbr.
114 That's right!
117 Italian article
118 Intentionally lost
119 Speakers' searches for just the right words?
125 Halliburton of the Halliburton Company
126 Buckwheat cereal
127 Restroom sign
128 Antidiscriminatory abbr.
129 Iago or Othello
130 It notably has two bridges
131 Bleachers
132 "x" in $5x = x^2 + 2$
133 Tit for tat?

DOWN

1 Shoddy
2 "Alas!"
3 War-torn Syrian city
4 Philosophical argument for belief in God
5 Partner in indecision with 5-Across
6 Connoisseur of food and drink
7 One might be found near a cloverleaf
8 Modern prefix with tag
9 Series
10 Word with you but not me
11 Main ingredient in Wiener schnitzel
12 Kitchenware brand
13 Like corsets
14 Russian "peace"
15 Terminus
16 Online enticement
17 Codger
18 Botanical bristles
25 Evidence left by a moth
26 Dead reckoning?
28 ____ Alcorn, creator of Pong
33 Wood for a raft
34 "And who ____?"
35 Texter's transition
36 St. Petersburg's river
38 Unduly harsh
41 Has a 42-Down
42 See 41-Down
44 ____ Lee, singer with the 2011 #1 album "Mission Bell"
45 All limbs
47 Audit a class, say
50 Move slowly (along)
51 City near the Sierras
52 What comes before "B"?
54 Islamic mystic
55 Tinker (with)
58 Align
62 Doesn't really see
64 Gift-tag word
65 Lansing-to-Flint dir.
66 Brief swim
68 Protective sorts in showbiz
71 Fervor
72 Some runoff sites
74 BBQ side
75 What can go before watt
76 Rare success story from the dot-com bubble
78 More pulchritudinous
81 Beau's girl
82 ____-Dixie (grocery chain)
83 It's not as simple as a), b), c)
85 "Go ahead!"
86 Italian wine city
88 Trolley sound
91 Bee, e.g.
92 Introvert's focus
93 Cross inscription
94 Seethe
96 Max at the MoMA
100 Sea cow
103 Need for a model
105 Flowering herb also known as devil's nettle
106 Woman's name that means "star"
108 Banisters
110 Not loose, as a diamond
111 4-0 series, say
112 Some refuges
113 Like panang curry
115 "Git!"
116 "I did it!"
120 It fits in a lock
121 Architect Maya
122 Mathematician's 116-Down
123 Inits. before many state names
124 Jesus Christ, with "the"

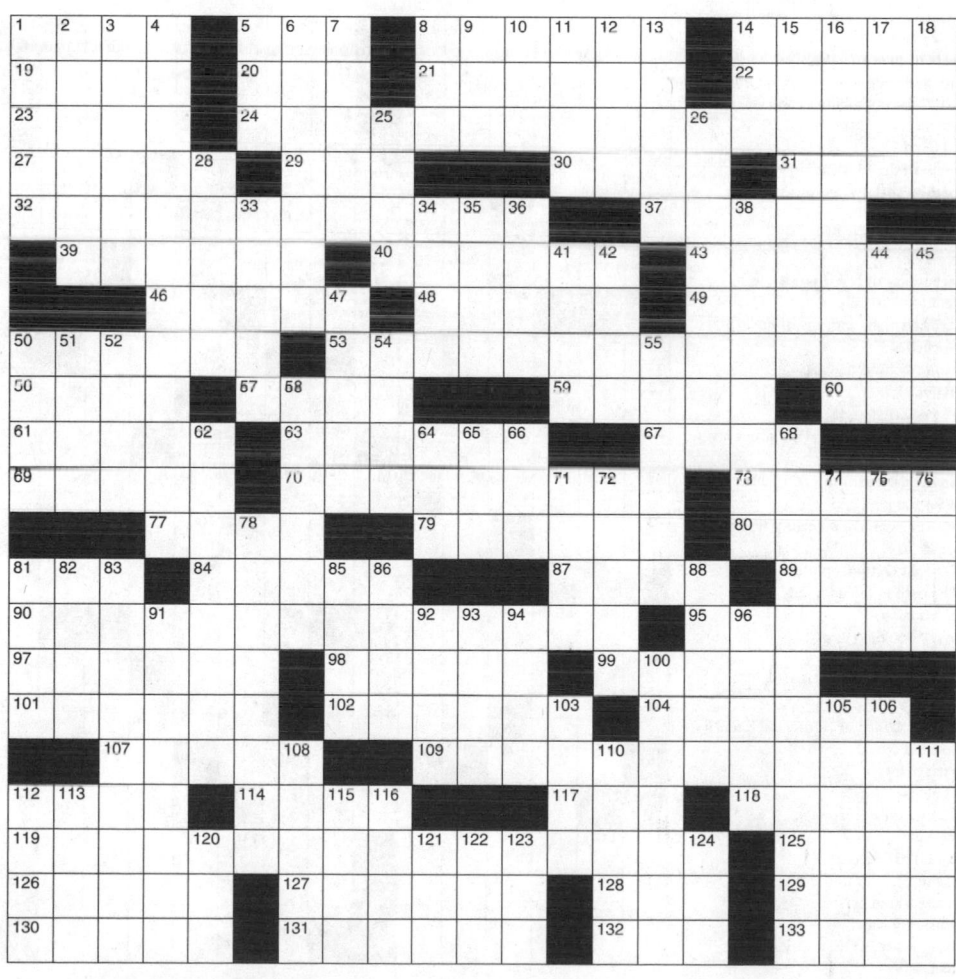

by David Alfred Bywaters

ACROSS

1 Fixture on a ski-lodge deck
7 Sound quality
13 West African capital
19 Like counting your chickens before they've hatched
20 Going great guns, as business
22 Come to terms with
23 "Good golly!," across the pond
24 Close enough
25 Cloaklike garment
26 Nosh
27 Goes around
29 Hardly a right-minded individual?
31 N.C.A.A. rival of Duke
32 To which one might respond "Salud!"
33 Superlative suffix
34 Summer setting in Seattle: Abbr.
36 Reason for an R rating?
39 McGregor who played Obi-Wan Kenobi
42 Gobble
44 Quaint photos
45 Cuban or Zuckerberg?
48 Archie's pal at Riverdale
51 Dry as a bone
52 Largest species of the genus Leopardus
53 Fighting
54 Sprang
57 More ready to go
60 Show stopper?
62 Pure and simple
64 Part of the eye where vision is sharpest
65 Old hand
68 Maker of the MDX luxury S.U.V.
69 Needing certain ink for a color printer?
71 Epitome of laziness
73 Freestyle, e.g.
74 Harbor city of NW France
76 Went to court, say
77 It may be right under your nose, informally
78 Fixture behind the bar
80 IHOP order
82 Billy of infomercial fame
83 Only European capital on both a river and an ocean
86 Kind of vision
88 Fit for the job
90 Impetus behind a paternity test?
93 Not so far
95 "Straight Outta Compton" group
96 "The path to the dark side," per Yoda
97 On a Paleo diet, say?
102 Slow boat
104 ____ Studies (college major)
106 Big Starbucks orders
107 Year the Office of Homeland Security was created
108 Some paints
111 Rumbles
112 "The world's greatest . . . ," e.g.
113 Opposite
115 Capital of Thessaly
117 Washington air hub
119 Post-workout activity
120 Unusually short
121 Start to take off, in a way
122 Shanghai
123 Accents and Sonatas
124 100-meter and 200-meter

DOWN

1 Commotion
2 Connected
3 Reaction to a really bad pun
4 Something you might need to kill
5 Treat like an object
6 Really, really needing some sun?
7 Neighborhood north of the World Trade Center
8 Charges
9 Weasel's relative
10 Beach tops
11 ____ Tin Tin
12 2003 Economics Nobelist Robert
13 One's most ardent supporters
14 Finisher of cakes
15 86
16 Buy one circus animal, get one circus animal free?
17 Most newspapers have one
18 Sport-____
21 Theodor ____ (Dr. Seuss's real name)
28 Live
30 Stealth bomber, familiarly
32 Partner of snick
33 French Alpine river
35 Root of Polynesia
37 Mesopotamian mother goddess
38 Female in a pen
40 In front of, old-style
41 Cowboys' home, for short
43 It's more than a warning: Abbr.
46 Street handout, maybe
47 View from la plage
48 "Aladdin" villain
49 City between Albany and Rochester
50 Stimulate
51 2017 World Series winner, for short
55 Something required
56 Dog or cat transporter
58 Often-smoked cheese
59 First lady
61 Shia of "Transformers"
63 Beginnings of fame and fortune?
65 Some SAT study
66 Kind of alcohol
67 "____ Days" (1990s platinum Bon Jovi album)
69 Anthem contraction
70 On another call
72 Hedy ____, subject of the 2017 documentary "Bombshell"
75 Woman's name meaning "born again"
77 Installment of a women's clothing catalog?
78 Common potato chip flavor, in brief
79 Hybrid tourney style
81 Pure
83 Worker at a hosp.
84 Waterloo's home
85 Something up for grabs on a fishing boat?
87 Director Lee
89 Rules, informally
91 Untagged
92 Quavering sounds
93 Rating somebody?
94 The Supreme Court and the Muses
98 Zoroastrianism's sacred text
99 Author of "The Joy Luck Club"
100 Collision
101 Barbara and Jenna Bush, to Jeb
103 Famous
105 Exams for future J.D.s
109 Traveling from coast to coast, maybe
110 Car sticker fig.
111 "Do you ____?"
112 Robust
113 Part of A.M.A.
114 X
116 Medicinal plant
118 Part of S.A.S.E.: Abbr.

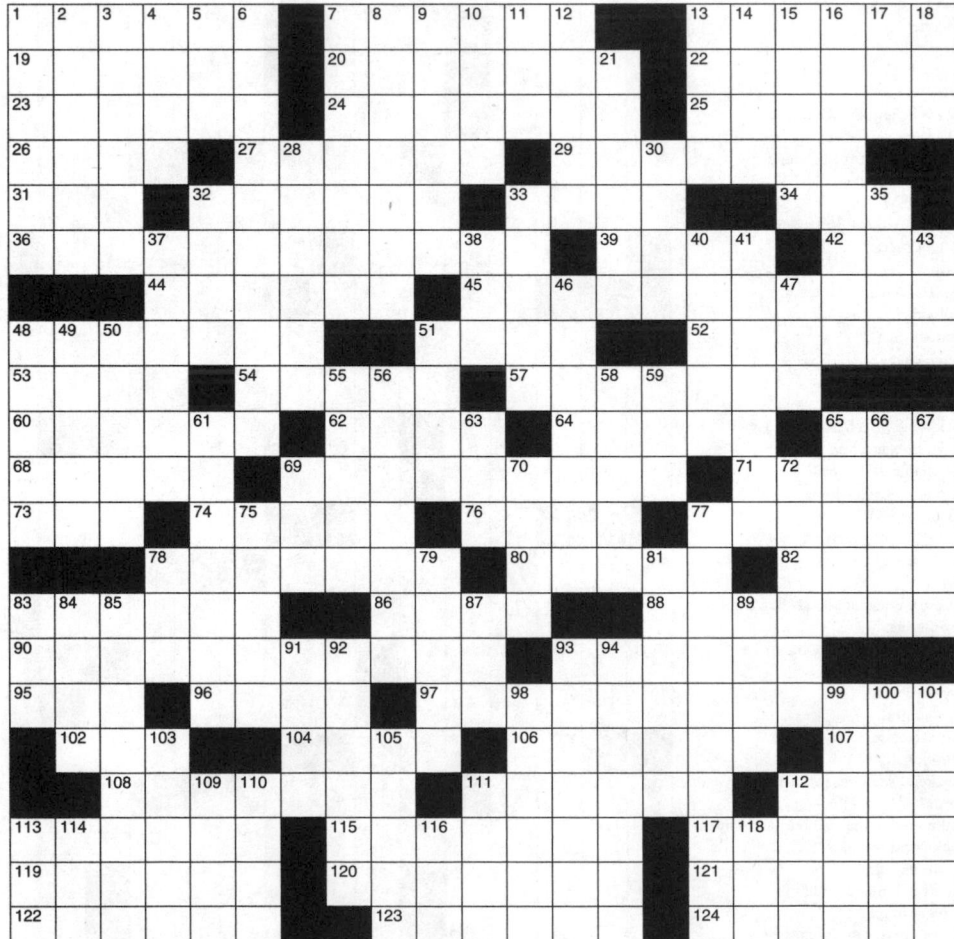

by Luke Vaughn

ACROSS

1 Ocean motion
4 [I expected better from you!]
7 Tracking systems
13 Makes out, in Manchester
18 Stuffed and fried cornmeal pocket, in Mexican cuisine
20 Lizzo or Lorde
21 ____-hole
22 Amazon, e.g.
23 Title for Iran's Ali Khamenei
25 Tailored blouse style
27 Pieces of pentathlon equipment
28 Piece of biathlon equipment
29 Outdoor wedding rental
30 Some reusable bags
32 Give a refill
34 Poet Limón
35 Yearbook sect.
36 Item lugged up a hill
38 Gardener's supply
40 Alphabetically first member of the Baseball Hall of Fame
42 Dull yellowish brown
43 Subject of some teen gossip sessions
47 Sure-footed alpine climber
52 React to, as an online joke
53 "I wish I could ____ that" ("Ick")
54 Document that never lacks a title
55 Divert
57 Solid green ball in un juego de billar
61 It's ground-breaking
62 Way overcharge, so to speak
64 Vape shop inventory
66 Sci-fi's Dr. Zaius, for one
67 Even a bit
68 Bakery item that's often messy
71 Lavishes love (on)
73 Part of R.S.V.P.
74 Business that might hold a blowout sale?
76 Common food drive donation
77 "Julius Caesar" role
78 Lhasa ____
80 Necklace components
82 Parts of volcanoes
85 2007 #1 Alicia Keys album
86 Not keep
88 Caribbean capital
91 Kind of test question
95 Some video-making devices
96 Rod who won four Wimbledons
97 "The very ____!"
99 Yellow bills in Monopoly
100 Lobster-catching aid?
103 Holiday preceder
104 Choose to participate
108 Award won twice by Hammerstein, fittingly
110 Horror director ____ Saul Guerrero
111 Contraction that omits a "v"
112 0 to 60, e.g.
114 Proceeds breezily
117 What a spike goes over
121 Not black and white
122 Early computer
123 "Encore!"
124 "The Life-Changing Magic of Tidying Up" tidying method
125 Take care of
126 "Well, so's your face!," e.g.
127 The antagonist Bellwether from Disney's "Zootopia," e.g.
128 Ask for a treat, say

DOWN

1 Discharges
2 Hassle
3 Genius
4 Not be on the level
5 Anxiously worry
6 Title nickname in a 1984 sports movie
7 Courses
8 WeChat or KakaoTalk
9 Very serious
10 With skill
11 Shakespeare character who cries "Then I defy you, stars!"
12 Power-saving mode
13 "____ Used to Be Mine" (song from "Waitress")
14 Long of Hollywood
15 "My guess is . . ."
16 Realm for comic book fans, say
17 Damascenes, e.g.
19 Gardener's supply
20 "Over here!"
24 "Geaux Tigers!" sch.
26 Liquid in a first-aid kit
31 Noodles sometimes served with tsuyu sauce
33 Onetime sunscreen ingredient
36 Small Jewish communities of old
37 SoCal baseball team, on scoreboards
39 Scintilla
41 Secondary social media accounts, in brief
42 Mournful sound
44 Fiddle with a ukulele?
45 Woman on W.W. II-era posters
46 Cassini who created the so-called "Jackie look"
47 Simba's father in "The Lion King"
48 How detectives may act
49 Orders from regulars
50 Breaking or entering, say
51 Leslie ____ Jr., member of the original "Hamilton" cast
56 Not joke around
58 Enjoys a home-cooked meal
59 Poison-treating plant
60 Bagel choice
63 ____ World Service
65 Digital camera memory holders
68 G-rated, say
69 You might pass on them
70 Apt surname for a mechanic
72 Palm Springs, e.g.
75 Group with the hits "Honey, Honey" and "Money, Money, Money"
79 Big brute
81 Went fast
83 Cocktail with a rhyming name
84 Tinder action that expresses strong interest
87 Other: Sp.
89 Certain pie crust flavor
90 Wok, e.g.
91 Covers of vintage music?
92 "Try it!"
93 Sit on
94 Part of an aircraft that helps reduce drag
98 Put forward
100 H.S. class with dissections
101 Tune out
102 Semi
105 Stick one's nose in
106 Small drum
107 Cockamamie
109 Actress Blanchett
110 Latch (onto)
113 Muppet who sings in the "Try, Try Again" song
115 When it's driving, you might not want to drive
116 Unwanted breakout
118 Back muscle, in brief
119 Prefix with warrior
120 Negative conjunction

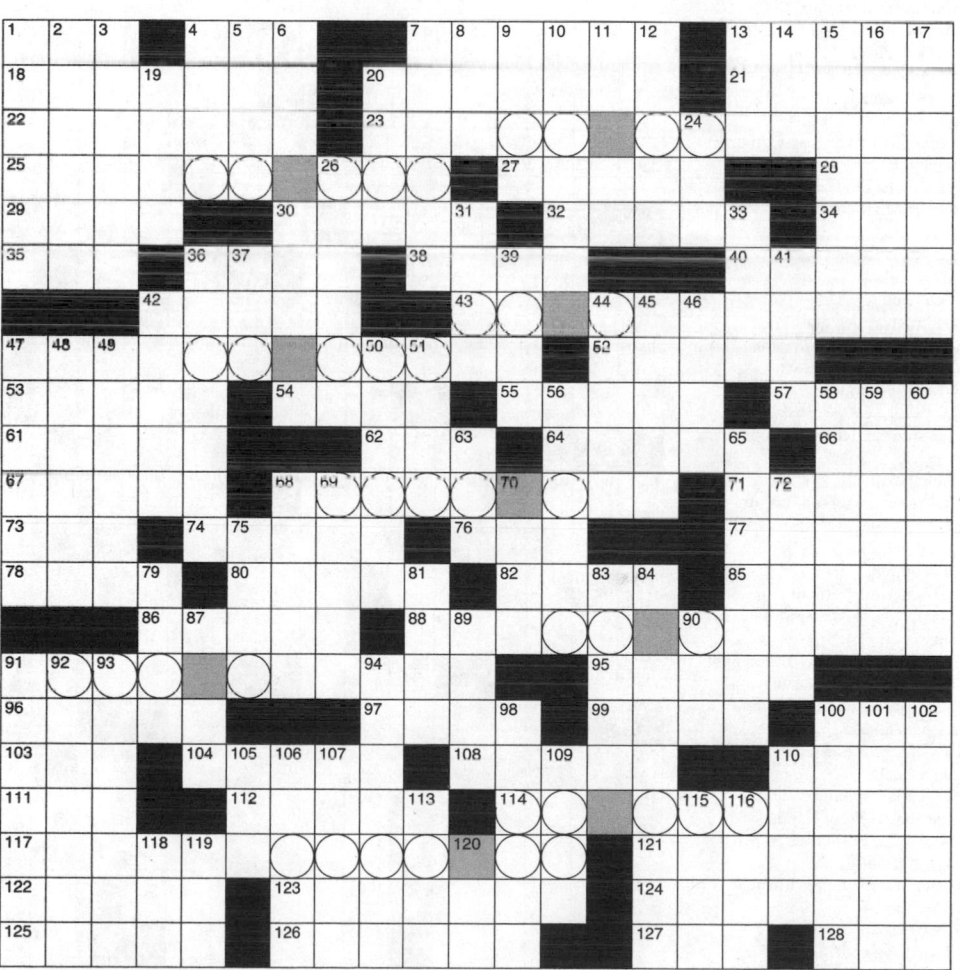

by Paolo Pasco

OH, FOURPEAT'S SAKE!

ACROSS

1 What a deadline increases
9 Dental brand
14 Neaten (up)
19 Jet routes
20 First name in flying history
21 "____ the Doughnut," children's book series
22 Classic saying originated by John Donne
24 Like oxfords, but not slippers
25 Really put one's foot down
26 Shaded
27 ____ O's (breakfast cereal)
28 Love, love, love
29 Population grouping, informally
31 Aid for making a tiki bar cocktail
34 Isn't attending solo, say
38 Bouncer's requests, for short
39 Beethoven title woman (whose identity is unknown)
40 Supreme Egyptian deity
41 Standing on the street
44 Carpenter ____
45 Pin number?
48 "Glad to have you back, dear!"
52 Actor/TV host Joel
55 To take this, paradoxically, might signify taking a stand
56 Wedding exchange
57 The D-backs, on scoreboards
58 Quack doctor's offering
59 London neighborhood west of Covent Garden
62 Most expensive block
64 Kirghizia or Byelorussia: Abbr.
67 Quick hit
69 Word in the Declaration of Independence but not the Constitution
70 ____ Rachel Wood of "Westworld"
71 "Can't you ____?"
72 Post-interruption question
75 Plant used in making biofuel
77 ____ Schomburg, Harlem Renaissance figure
78 Haiti's ____ de la Tortue
79 Like some coffee and sprains
82 Heedless
86 "Fantabulous!"
87 First ruler of a united Hawaii
91 Boot attachment
92 ____ Precheck
94 Loan option, briefly
95 Like a narrow baseball win
96 Fixture whose name translates to "small horse"
99 Result of the '64 Clay/Liston fight
101 Hitting the ground heavily
103 Relatively light foundry product
108 Wash. neighbor
109 Lavishes affection (on)
110 Super-quality
111 "This one's all mine!"
113 Like about 97% of U.S. land
117 Óscar ____, 1987 Peace Nobelist from Costa Rica
118 Potful in some Italian kitchens
121 Given (to)
122 Stock exchange worker
123 Makes Don nod?
124 Things that can be closed with a zip
125 Brains
126 Least spicy

DOWN

1 Trashes
2 ____ shield
3 Bombeck who wrote "At Wit's End"
4 Participates in a mosh pit
5 Los Angeles port district
6 Sea urchin, at a sushi bar
7 Took another take
8 Isaac's firstborn
9 Meditation sounds
10 Click the circular arrow button, say
11 Aids for sleepyheads
12 Top part of an I.R.S. form
13 Red morning sky, to sailors
14 Part of an Italian sub
15 Some pricey handbags
16 Things Wyoming and Nevada lack
17 Guy who hosts "Diners, Drive-Ins and Dives"
18 Overnighting option
20 It's been performed more than 1,000 times at the Met
23 Kan. neighbor
30 Title for a lady
32 Be outta sight?
33 Alice in Chains genre
34 Atlanta hoopster
35 Repeated word in Hozier's 2014 hit "Take Me to Church"
36 Base of an arch
37 Video call annoyance
42 Falling-out
43 Mammal's head and heart?
44 "Pokémon" cartoon genre
46 High-ranking
47 Chutzpah
49 Call to mind
50 Like Parmesan and pecorino
51 "You do it ____ will"
53 Stick (to)
54 That guy
60 Cheri of old "S.N.L."
61 "With what frequency?"
62 "The Masque of the Red Death" writer
63 Duck
64 Tries for a fly
65 Film character who says "That'll do, Donkey. That'll do"
66 Payback
68 Christensen of "Parenthood"
69 Grammy winner Stefani
73 Classic work by Karel Capek
74 Whitney for whom a Connecticut museum is named
76 Certain security officer
79 Prez #34
80 Quick pick-me-up?
81 Send forth
83 Atmospheric prefix
84 Ostracize
85 Be left undecided
88 Watered-down rum
89 Common lecture length
90 Giant in fairy tales?
93 Queen Anne's royal family
97 "Let me clarify . . ."
98 Trashes
99 Yellow brick road traveler
100 Folds and stretches
102 Backpacker's lodging
103 Make lemonade from lemons, so to speak
104 Peter of "Casablanca"
105 "The Dick Van Dyke Show" co-star
106 Wood stain has a strong one
107 Tiny ____
112 Hurtful remark
114 Ploy
115 Pocket rockets, in poker
116 In the event that
119 Symbol on a Junction Ahead sign
120 Future zygotes

by Alex Bajcz

ACROSS

1 Getting warm, so to speak
6 It was established by a 1926 royal charter
9 Ulan ____, Mongolia
14 Be against
18 Send, as payment
19 #1 of 50, alphabetically: Abbr.
20 Former basketball star Gilbert . . . or the places he played
22 Garb in a duck blind, informally
23 Way into a garage, typically
25 California wine region
26 Road trip guessing game
27 Freak (out)
28 Tennis star who won at least one Grand Slam title for a record 13 straight years
29 Initialism that can include an "h" for "humble"
30 Old-timey "OMG!"
32 GPS guess
33 Variables in ϖr^2 and $2\varpi r$
34 Nickelodeon competitor
38 Bagless vacuum maker
40 Savvy couple?
42 ____ the Kid, nickname for N.H.L. star Crosby
43 Party game similar to Catch Phrase
44 Grows increasingly more irksome
47 Starbucks sizes smaller than grandes
49 Dove bar, e.g.
50 Given as a bequest
52 Suffix with mega- or multi-
54 Ones making strong impressions?
56 "Je t'____" (words from a beau)
57 Prince Andrew's younger daughter
60 On the main
61 Prominent women's rights lawyer
63 Member of an Iraqi minority
65 Obscure knowledge
70 Violent, maybe
71 Certain laundry detergent capsule
73 Causing constriction of the pupils
74 Nailed the test
75 007's alma mater
76 Visual phenomenon created by short flashes of light
78 Linguist Chomsky
80 Dense fog, metaphorically
82 When repeated, a Hawaiian fish
83 Major utility pipeline
87 Whimper
88 It has its pros and cons
90 Part of P R
91 Far from wild
93 Pesto ingredient
96 For one purpose only
98 Org. that takes many forms
99 Five-star
100 Quark-antiquark combo
104 Some entertainers at children's birthday parties
107 Europe's longest river
110 Trouble
111 O icon
112 Western Hemisphere grp.
113 Legendary firefighter Red
114 Curler's surface
115 Kind of palm cultivated for its fruit
117 Prove wrong
119 Awards show that airs at night, ironically
121 Part of une éclipse
122 Submits an online return
123 Brown. ender
124 "

125 What's more, it's said
126 Down stream?
127 Easy target
128 Buddy of "The Beverly Hillbillies"

DOWN

1 Sang one's own praises
2 Humor regarding a serious matter
3 "w"-like letters
4 Anthony Hopkins, for one
5 Wi-Fi alternative
6 Complained about getting fleeced?
7 Subject of a Sleeves Up campaign
8 French luxury jeweler
9 ABCs
10 Lead-in to therapy
11 Jazz instrument pitched in the key of B flat
12 Peace activist Yoko
13 Classic dorm room meal
14 Fading process for jeans
15 Deep-toned cousin of an English horn
16 One whose calling is making calls?
17 American Kennel Club designation
21 Stuffing herb
24 Green on the screen
31 QB's passing stat: Abbr.
35 Up to
36 Din from a den
37 Keystone ____
39 Put forward
41 TV channel that owns the website The Undefeated
45 Beer in a green bottle
46 Part of a college visit, typically
47 Prepare to swing, say
48 Unseal furtively, as an envelope
50 Floral fragrance note
51 Behave theatrically
53 Restored to mint condition
55 Lesser Antilles native
56 City that's home to three UNESCO World Heritage Sites
58 "Go ____!" (coach's encouragement)
59 Computer menu with Undo and Redo
60 Expand upon
62 Tony winner Menzel
64 Antarctica's ____ Ice Shelf
66 Nestlé creamer
67 Bothered persistently
68 Not for mass audiences
69 When the Battle of Yorktown occurs in "Hamilton"
72 Took steroids, say
77 Like loud phone conversations in public
79 Designed to deter stealing

81 T-Bonz dog treat brand
83 Word before bag or bar
84 Musical with the opening number "Every Story Is a Love Story"
85 Sallie Mae products
86 Marshmallow-filled snacks
87 University of Montana city
89 Hitchhike
92 Shapiro of NPR
94 Emulates the Mongols
95 Old genre for 12-Down
97 Z4 or Q50
99 Judge
101 Pool competitions
102 Immature egg cell
103 Star of the "Taken" trilogy
105 Like snow leopards and Siberian tigers
106 What tots might go after?
108 Easy two points
109 "Scram!"
115 ____-American
116 Tool for pool
118 Old-timey cry of disgust
120 Will Smith/Tommy Lee Jones film series, for short

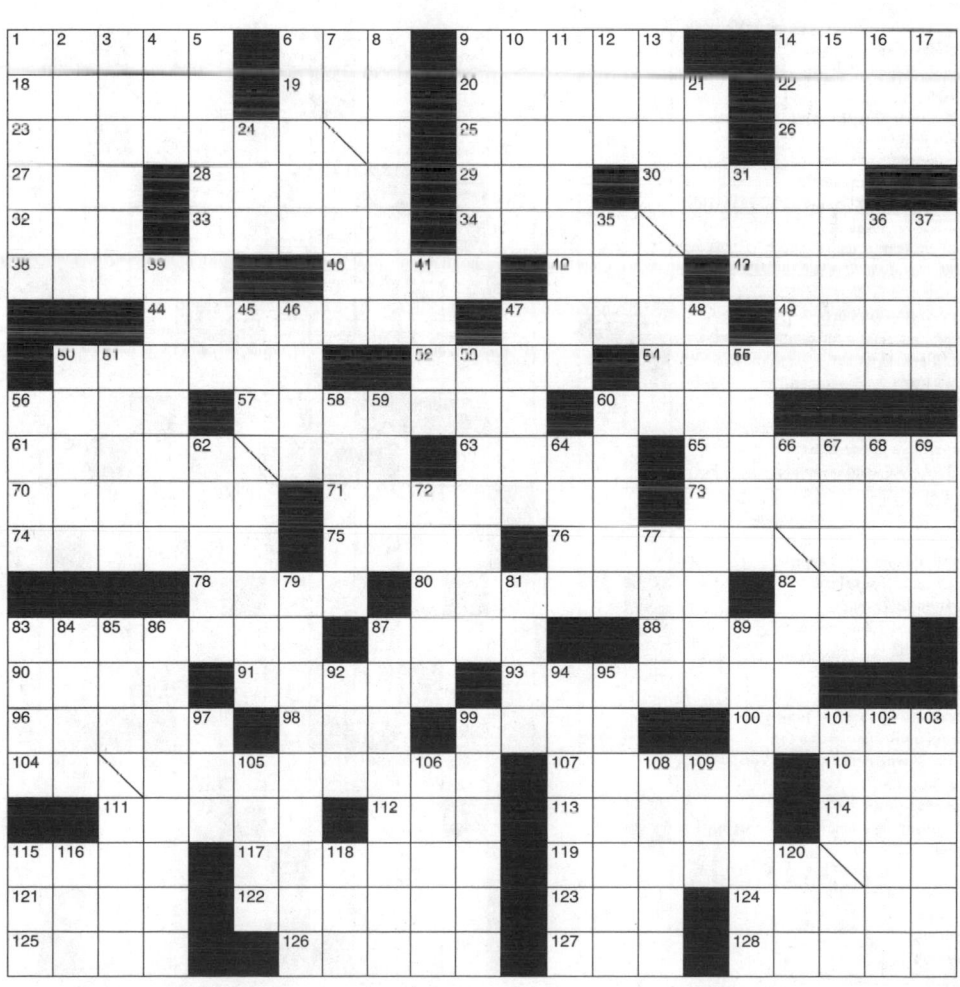

by Tracy Gray and Tom Pepper

ACROSS

1 Onetime Sony rival
8 Off-color
12 Maker of the X6 and Z4
15 Doctors Without Borders, e.g.: Abbr.
18 Deep secret
19 "____ Dead?" (Mark Twain play)
20 Quickly learn one's lesson?
21 Startling sound
22 Bookworms call dad?
24 South Beach and Paleo, for two
26 Swiss painter Paul
27 Company whose business is picking up?
28 Seedy area?
29 Big Apple media inits.
30 Depletes, with "up"
31 A young Justice Ginsburg chuckles?
36 Signature item
37 Singer Watson, a.k.a. Tones and I, with the 2019 hit "Dance Monkey"
38 Apt name for a lawyer
39 False accusation, informally
40 Fancy Feast alternative
43 One "R" in R&R
46 Hoarse
47 Do core exercises all day, every day?
51 "____ Brockovich"
52 Quick drive
53 Elusive legend
54 Business for Sanders supporters?
57 Holiday dish served with sour cream or applesauce
60 Links grp.
62 Hard to handle, in a way
64 Hunky-dory
66 Response to an order
67 Burger King bingefest?
71 Alma mater for Spike Lee and Donald Glover, for short
72 Logical connector
73 With the greatest of ____
74 ____ golf
75 Sloped roof support
77 Govt. org. with a forerunner known as the Black Chamber
79 Race units
81 Dinner table expander
83 Hops-drying oven
84 Supernova in our galaxy?
90 Follower of word or potato
93 "Gimme ____"
94 ____-cat
95 Numerous
97 Symbols in Twitter handles
99 Like ____ of sunshine
100 Anatomical pouch
103 When E.M.T.s bring home the bacon?
108 "I mean . . ."
109 A/C spec
110 Members of the crow family
111 Heavier alternative to a foil
112 Guthrie who performed at Woodstock
113 Cutting edge?
115 Some astronomy Ph.D.s?
119 Longtime Japanese P.M. who stepped down in 2020
120 "Runnin'" team of N.C.A.A. Division I college basketball
121 Comparable (to)
122 Disciple
123 Tarnish
124 Really good time
125 Capital near the North Sea
126 Prepares (for)

DOWN

1 Prepare for a road trip, perhaps
2 End of a threat
3 Nora Ephron and Sofia Coppola, for two
4 The land down under?
5 Walk-____
6 Prickly covering of a seed
7 "____ the only one?"
8 Beatles title woman
9 "____ your request . . ."
10 Feature of a classical Greek drama
11 "You betcha!"
12 "The ____ — is wider than the Sky" (start of an Emily Dickinson poem)
13 Bit of fill-in-the-blanks fun
14 Subject of intl. treaties
15 Compliant sorts
16 Squalid digs
17 Sports team V.I.P.s
20 Corporate money managers, for short
23 Ancient Egyptians
25 Result of a breast pocket mishap, maybe
28 Ally of the Brat Pack
31 Common baking pear
32 Sacred cross in ancient Egypt
33 Chance to go
34 Preserve, in a way
35 Only Stratego piece with a letter on it
37 Sardine container
41 Studmuffin
42 Absorb, as sauce with bread
44 Give extra consideration, with "on"
45 Idaho, e.g., in dialect
47 Color marker
48 Got hip, with "up"
49 How a door might be slammed
50 Subcontractor in a bathroom remodel
51 Gusto
55 One may be nominated for a Hugo Award
56 Least forward
58 Palindromic farm animal
59 "We ____ Overcome"
61 Stubborn sorts
63 It helps in passing
65 Rocker Cobain
68 Japan's street food mecca
69 Diarist who documented the Great Plague of London
70 Gets lost
76 Eponym of the Detroit Lions field
78 Any Olympian, once
80 Drops an f-bomb, say
82 False fronts
85 Promises, promises!
86 Takes steps
87 ____ avis
88 Coarse farm sound
89 Dangerous move on a busy highway
90 "Blueberries for ____" (kid-lit classic)
91 Legendary password stealer
92 Higher, as ambitions
96 Build-your-own Tex-Mex dish
98 Does a dog trick
101 Declare
102 Where hangers hang
104 They go wherever the wind blows
105 They can be batted and rolled
106 When high school seniors often visit the colleges that accepted them
107 Like binary questions
108 Volt-amperes
113 Attention hog, maybe
114 Galoot
115 Portrait seen on renminbi bills
116 Car sticker fig.
117 "Roses ____ red . . ."
118 Nonsense

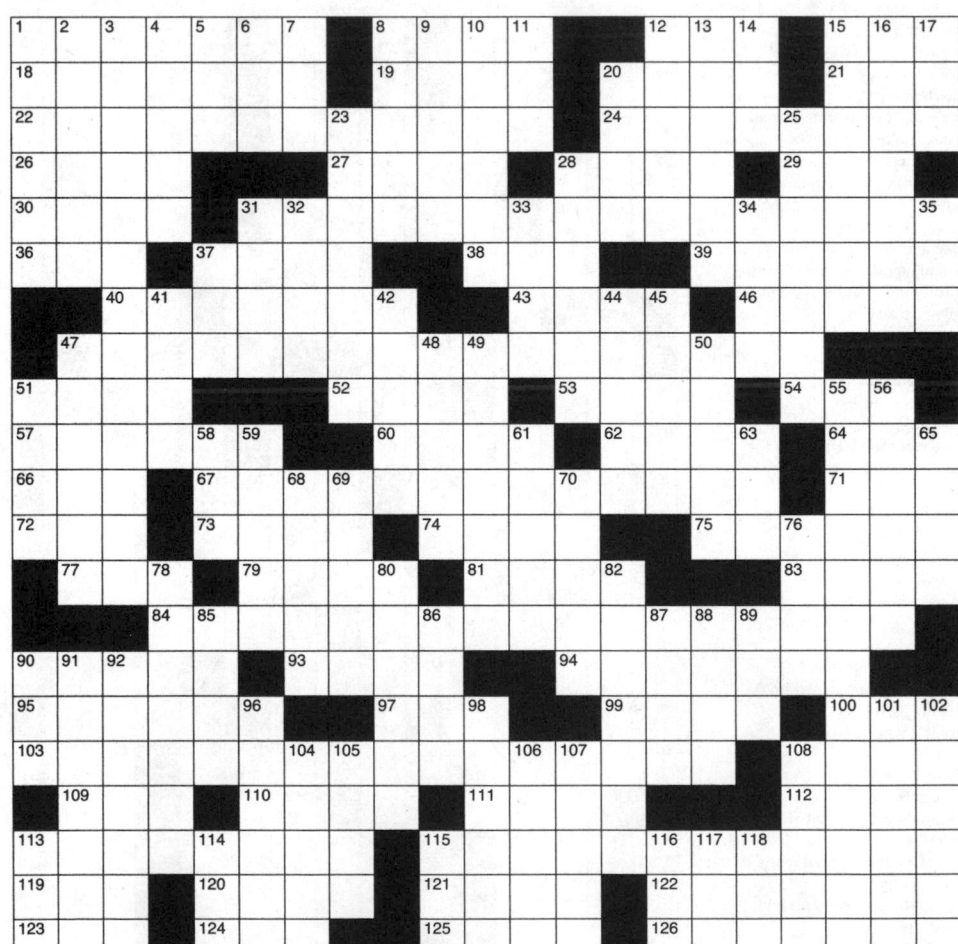

by Lucy Howard and Ross Trudeau

ACROSS

1 Mannerly
6 Philippine currency
10 Just open
14 Second socks, say
19 Offer a judgment
20 Thing with tags
21 Fruit salad fruit
22 Sound of exertion
23 Huge celebration after L.A.'s football team wins the Super Bowl?
26 Nice nicety
27 Great shakes
28 Oldest tech sch. in the U.S., founded in 1824
29 Bygone royalty
31 Oodles and oodles
32 Besmirch
33 Big fuss
35 With 1-Down, address ender
37 Schlep
38 Reason that the prestigious scientific journal refuses articles from President Herbert's relatives?
45 Power symbol?
46 Senate support
47 _____ gras
48 Restorative indulgence
50 Kind of bookstore
51 Oil field sight
53 It's symbolized by an elephant, for short
55 Theater seating option
56 Japanese honorific
57 Apology from a musician to the other band members?
64 Best Picture winner that was banned in Vietnam
66 Lena of "Chocolat"
67 1957 Jimmy Dorsey hit
68 "Lonely Boy" singer, 1959
69 Stiff
71 Morally uncompromised
72 Many a summer position
74 Like writing about how to write
75 Epitome of herd mentality
79 Volunteered at a nursery?
83 General practice?
84 Idle of Monty Python
85 _____ Lou Who of "How the Grinch Stole Christmas"
86 Elton John or Mick Jagger
87 District on Hawaii's west coast
88 Volcanic substance
91 Person fluent in Quechua
94 Et _____ (footnote abbr.)
96 Fool
97 Adding a historic ship as a deal sweetener?
101 Campaign guru
102 Super Bowl played in 2020
103 Past
104 Get hold of
105 Dry
107 Hiker's snack
110 Article from U.C.L.A.?
112 Vatican ambassador
115 Small versions
117 Story about a drinking binge?
121 Frost lines?
122 Awards feat, for short
123 Puccini piece
124 Really lift
125 Ed of "Elf"
126 Movement based on deliberate irrationality
127 Be really impressive, informally
128 Procrastinate

DOWN

1 See 35-Across
2 Uber and Lyft had theirs in 2019, for short
3 Tarzan's transport
4 Didn't just request
5 Is dismissed, as a class
6 On a Seder plate, it represents the arrival of springtime
7 Port. is part of it
8 State symbol
9 Sound from a marching band
10 Pseudonym lead-in
11 Ditch at the last moment
12 Leatherwork tools
13 Largest city on the Arabian peninsula
14 "Lionized" studio
15 Neighborhood
16 Gift in "The 12 Days of Christmas"
17 Push
18 Trap, of a sort
24 Sheik's peer
25 Free from
30 Aussie animals
34 Medal above plata
36 One-up
38 _____ cavity
39 Bowl, e.g.
40 Prefix with nautical
41 One temporarily entrusting property to another
42 Ink
43 Units in the life span of a galaxy
44 Ad _____ tax
45 Brink of transition
49 Folksy possessive
52 Wilt
54 Magazine whose crossword is always accompanied by a photograph
57 Rigged card game
58 Hooked up, as oxen
59 Wolfs (down)
60 Supergiant in Orion
61 Hall-of-Fame quarterback for the Colts
62 More balanced
63 In _____ way
65 Rail container for liquids
70 Bakery buy
72 Cloth woven from flax fibre
73 So last year
76 "You can't make me!"
77 Female goat
78 Gloomy, weatherwise
79 Place to surf
80 Haydn's "The Creation" and others
81 Step on a ladder
82 The Berenstain Bears live in one
87 "A merry old soul," in a nursery rhyme
89 Crack up, in textspeak
90 Bit of kindling
92 U.S. counterpart to Britain's MI6
93 _____-Norman French
95 Common call on a 3rd-and-1
96 Not black-and-white
98 Sticker worn in November
99 How some practical jokes go
100 Burden
101 Prairie east of the Andes
106 Two-fifths of one quarter
108 Sitar selection
109 Move laboriously
111 Houston M.L.B.'er
113 Stressed, in a way: Abbr.
114 Multiple of tetra-
116 Union member of the 20th century, for short
118 Concern for one catching a connection, briefly
119 Sound from a drunk
120 "Stop right there!"

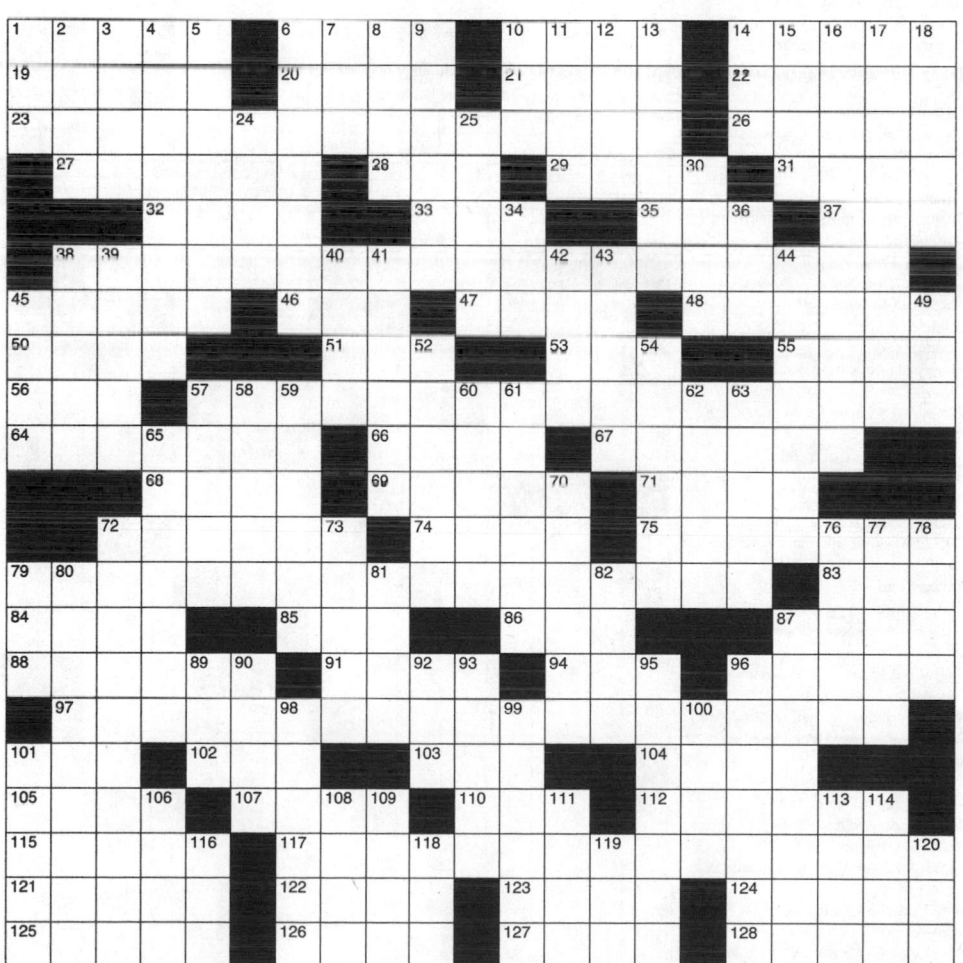

by Jim Hilger

ACROSS

1 Unloading point
5 Trait for a ballerina
10 "Wanna hear a secret?" preceder
14 Not much
18 The "O" of OWN
20 Portrayer of Captain Davies in "Roots"
21 Bind with rope
22 Abacus column
23 Helpful
24 Accept payment from Batman?
27 Eponymous Irish city
29 ____ pickle
30 Counterparts of faunas
31 Cause for celebration at a pachyderm sanctuary?
36 ____ lecithin (chocolate additive)
37 What most pens can't do
38 Jane portrayer in 1981's "Tarzan, the Ape Man"
41 Worry about, informally
45 Flip (out)
46 Rock band that you might think would always be an opening act, with "the"?
48 Ex-Giants QB Manning
49 Finish scooping out a big stir-fry?
54 Signal approval
55 Inexplicably missing, say
56 Brontë who wrote "Agnes Grey"
57 Target of permethrin cream
58 Not very convincing
60 Highly skilled
61 Rare race outcome
63 Unimaginative birthday gift
64 Is stertorous
65 Puritan's goal in 17th-century Salem?
69 Changes topics in a debate, perhaps
73 Scrapes (out)
74 The Rose Bowl, e.g.
79 Czar who co-ruled with Peter I
80 Goes head-to-head
81 Indiana athlete
83 Sunburn soother
84 Specialist publication, for short
85 Monopolize
86 Something a Parmesan vendor might offer?
89 Unflappable state of mind
90 Baron Cohen of film
92 One of all fours?
93 Container words
94 2019 film whose title means "to the stars"
96 A dance and a dip
98 Cartoondom's Olive ____
100 What a stoner actor smoked during rehearsal?
107 Beginning and end of "America"
109 "Ha-ha!"
110 Noise heard during the London Blitz
111 Domain for Jameson and Maker's Mark?
116 Curl target, informally
117 Manual alternative
118 Soul singer Bridges
119 Bank investment?
120 Spanish dagger or Adam's needle is a variety of it
121 New York football team, informally
122 Apt rhyme for "crude" and "rude"
123 It may need to be broken to move
124 Lucretia ____, abolitionist and women's rights advocate

DOWN

1 Childbirth assistant
2 Choose to participate
3 Concern for Superman
4 Superman's birth name
5 Like many a teenage boy's facial hair
6 First Asian tennis player to be ranked #1 in singles
7 Press
8 Bishop's jurisdiction
9 Long period
10 Like some evidence and bulbs
11 Doctor's order
12 I.R.S. ID
13 Live broadcast no-no
14 In
15 One creating draft after draft?
16 Andean empire member
17 Some clicks of the tongue
19 Slice of toast?
25 Comes out ahead
26 Dolts
28 Market launch, for short
32 Amphibians that may have toxic skin
33 Clichéd
34 Shakespeare villain with more lines than the title character
35 Kindle download
39 Skip the big ceremony, say
40 They're found around Scots
41 Bony fish with prized eggs
42 "Bottled poetry," according to Robert Louis Stevenson
43 Active Sicilian volcano
44 Filled with wonder
47 Without concrete evidence
50 "Ad Parnassum" and "Fish Magic," for two
51 Metaphor for a shared experience
52 Be more important than
53 Exaggerated kiss sound
55 Fuss
59 Legal title: Abbr.
60 He wrote lyrics to "My Way" for Sinatra
62 Channel with a lot of house renovation shows
63 Keeps in the loop, in a way
64 Give a start
66 Prez with a rhyming campaign slogan
67 Lab work
68 Cause of some brain freeze
69 It comes in California and New York styles
70 Covered in vines
71 Celebrity who holds the Guinness world record for "Most Frequent Clapper"
72 Half and half?
75 Gallivants
76 On the safe side
77 Ancient kingdom in modern-day Jordan
78 Elusive, in a way
80 Words to learn, briefly
81 In itself: Lat.
82 "Oh, come on!"
85 Aggressive pitch
87 Physically fit
88 Rock song?
90 Big cut of tuna
91 Fill with wonder
95 Attaches, as a button
97 Some shop tools
98 "Now it makes sense!"
99 "____ So Bad" (Tom Petty song)
101 Flying ____ drop (pro wrestling move)
102 Shocks, in a way
103 Hip bone
104 Classic brand of wafers
105 Upright
106 The Apostle of Ireland, familiarly
107 It might come in a branded tote bag
108 Buddy
112 "____-haw!"
113 Laid up
114 Formerly called
115 Perón of politics

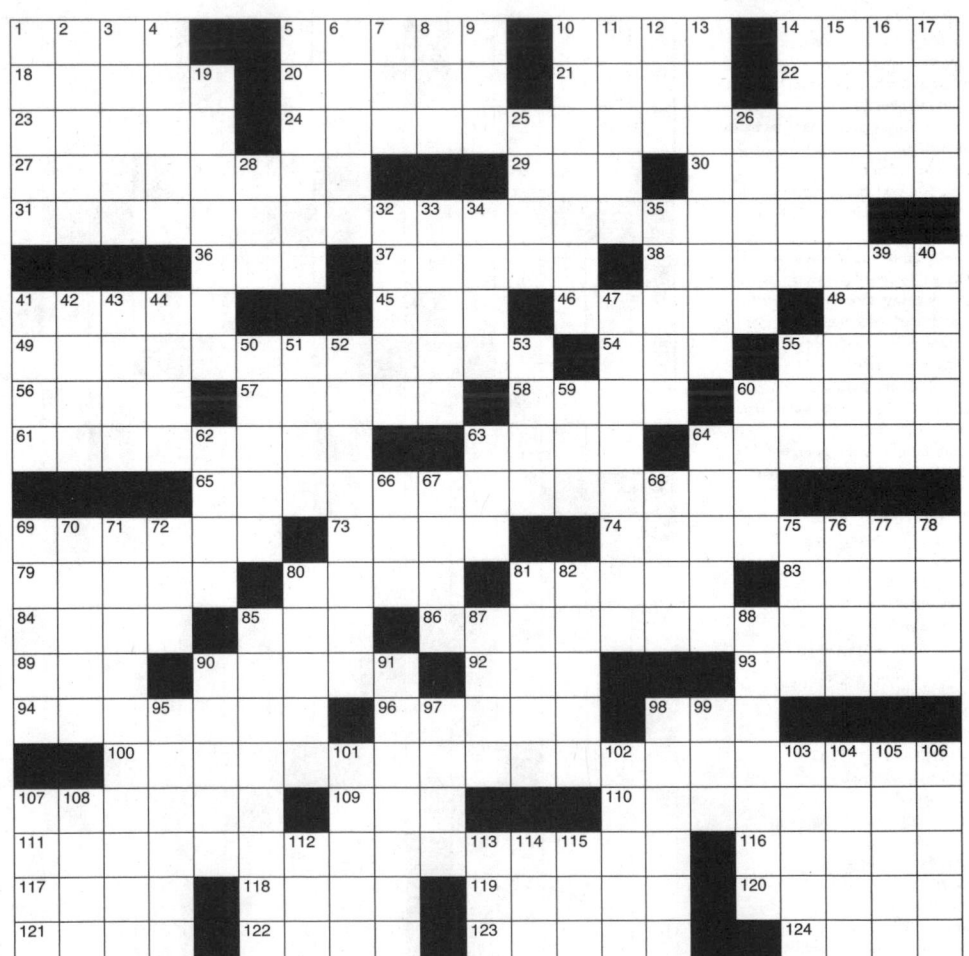

by Katie Hale and Christina Iverson

ACROSS

1 Percussion instrument in a marching band
7 Prefix with sexual
10 Prefix with sexual
14 Animals in a pod
19 Start of a playground taunt
20 Kitchen brand with a palindromic name
21 What an article may come with?
22 Drain, as from soil
23 Fatsis who wrote "Word Freak"
24 Most feathery, as clouds
26 "Thong Song" singer, 2000
27 Sharp, in a way
28 Early tie
30 The ones over here
32 In the capacity of
33 Some Ivy Leaguers
34 Born yesterday, so to speak
36 Calm
38 Comfy slip-on, in brief
39 What an outstretched arm with an open palm can mean
41 Fleet org.
42 It means business
43 Stakes
44 Narrow
46 Group tour vehicle
49 Playground comeback
52 Build up
53 Sci-fi publisher of "Ender's Game" and "The Wheel of Time"
54 Popular beer brand, briefly
57 With 3-Down, one of the Avengers
59 ___ smear
61 Reduced
63 Opposite of a standing order?
64 "Do me this one favor . . ."
67 French vineyards
68 Prats
69 Contrariwise
71 North African capital
72 Nongendered, as language: Abbr.
73 Sui ___
74 Kind of dash
76 Best Supporting Actor winner for "Dallas Buyer's Club"
78 Prefix with friendly
79 Rules out?
80 West Coast beer brand, in brief
81 "___ ruled the world . . ."
83 :
86 Capital of Yemen
87 Kind of modern office plan
89 Smell of a rose
92 Smell of a rosé
95 ___ Fridays
96 Barrister's deg.
97 Bench tool
99 Quibble
101 Student's bonus points
103 Drawn-out campaigns
105 When doubled, another name for dorado
106 Call ___ night
107 Eighth letter
109 British tennis champ who invented the sweatband
111 ___ impasse
112 Guardian spirits
114 Especially
116 Soubise sauce is made from them
118 Greenish-brown
119 ___ cake (dim sum dish)
120 Suffix with social
121 "Wheel of Fortune" freebies
122 Sharp
123 Label for Otis Redding and Isaac Hayes
124 Latin king
125 Sea lion, for one

DOWN

1 Word with sound or solar
2 Few
3 See 57-Across
4 Subsequent versions
5 Thurman of "Kill Bill"
6 Word before and after "a"
7 Turned on
8 Kind of symmetry
9 A pretty capable sort
10 Singer DiFranco
11 Big name in bubbly
12 Small woodland songbird
13 "Town square for the global village of tomorrow," per Bill Gates
14 Jimmy of the Daily Planet
15 L.L. Bean competitor
16 Medieval helmet
17 Exonerate
18 Prime snorkeling spots
25 Like many stuffed animals
29 PX shopper
31 The Quran, for one
35 Mango Madness and Go Bananas, for two
37 Ones initiating handoffs, for short
39 Some mattresses
40 Indulgence
45 Capital of French Polynesia
47 Show again
48 Caterer's container
50 A fine mesh this is!
51 Debussy prelude inspired by a water sprite
54 Outcast
55 Out of focus
56 Surface anew, say
57 Post production
58 Without a doubt
60 Turkish officers
62 Timid sort
63 Instrument in "O! Susannah"
64 They'll be mist
65 Super Bowl of 2022
66 Place with robes and sweaters
70 Seasick sea serpent of old cartoons
71 Bank posting
73 Words after throwing a ball
75 Grams
77 Unbalance
82 Packaging list
84 "L'chaim!"
85 (a, b), e.g.
87 Anthem contraction
88 Suit perfectly
90 France from France
91 Singer who founded Fenty Beauty
92 What ponies express?
93 Field-plowing duo
94 Poem piece
97 Notable point in geometry
98 U.N. member since 1949: Abbr.
100 Glittery decoration
102 Listing
104 Beau ___
105 Ones with plenty of reservations
108 Blade brand
110 Days of old
113 Suffix with court or cash
115 Deli supply
117 Surveillance org.

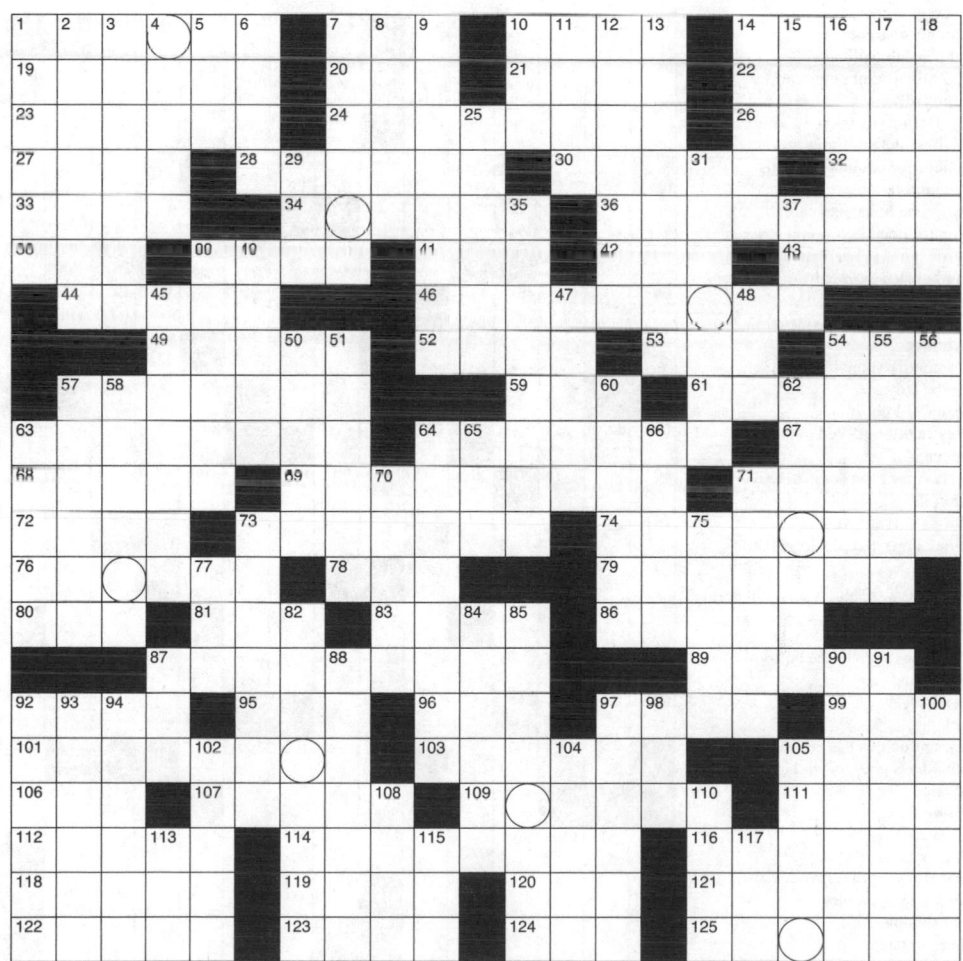

by Lisa Bunker

ACROSS

1 Prayer, e.g.
7 Market index, for short
13 And so on and so forth
19 Actor Ray of "Field of Dreams"
20 Like a certain complex
22 Relative of the mambo
23 High winds
24 Space bars? [Frank Sinatra]
26 Healthy dessert options
28 Overhauled, in a way
29 "____ making a list . . ."
30 Offering in china . . . or from China
31 "Top Chef" chef ____ Hall
32 Geographical name that comes from the Sioux for "sleepy ones"
35 First prize at the Juegos Olímpicos
36 Sink holes
40 Biting
42 Bird whose males incubate the eggs
44 Mathematical proposition
47 Wet bars? [Gene Kelly]
51 Things many people lose as they grow older
53 Big Five studio of Hollywood's Golden Age
54 "Thus . . ."
55 St. Louis symbol
56 Strongly endorse
58 Hot place to chill
59 ____ Adlon, Emmy winner for "King of the Hill"
61 Papal name last taken in 1939
63 Smallest state in India
64 Options for outdoor wedding receptions
67 Like some bread and cereal
68 Director Lee
69 Prison bars? [Elvis Presley]
73 Bamboozled
74 Weight right here!
76 ____ Austin, Biden defense secretary
77 Misidentify something, e.g.
78 For the lady
79 Center of a court
81 They're often parked in parks
82 Relevant
84 Excited cry after scratching a lottery ticket
85 Move a cursor (over)
88 Pride : lions :: ____ : dolphins
89 Hip
92 Cash bars? [Abba]
96 "Same here"
97 "I mean . . ."
98 What goes right to the bottom?
99 Got around
101 "Hoo-boy!"
102 Gist
104 Last option in a list, maybe
107 "That feels goo-oo-ood!"
109 Practice
110 Brainy?
112 A+ earner
116 Singles bars? [Robyn]
120 First House speaker from California
122 Not going anywhere
123 Was snoopy
124 Made square
125 Japanese mat
126 "We got permission!"
127 Makes insulting jokes about

DOWN

1 Sitcom extraterrestrial
2 Did a little lifting
3 Candy bars? [Def Leppard]
4 "You, too?!"
5 Wiped out
6 Stood the test of time
7 Mapo ____ (spicy Sichuan dish)
8 A leg up
9 Häagen-Dazs competitor
10 Low-wattage
11 Where trills provide thrills
12 Something that's well-kept?
13 Comeback
14 It's turned, in a phrase
15 It's a relief!
16 Prefix with conscious
17 Poetic shortening
18 Food pantry donation
21 Broad valley
25 Large expanses
27 2006 film with the tagline "Keep it wheel"
29 Hindu festival of colors
31 Most-watched TV show of 2002–05
33 Gold bars? [Queen]
34 "Do you understand me?"
37 Disappointing court result
38 Black
39 Habitat for Humanity is one, for short
41 Sister restaurant of Applebee's
43 Lets go of
45 Gaping holes
46 Weizenbock or Berliner Weisse
48 Scruffs
49 Ridiculous
50 Seventh avatar of Vishnu
52 It's a long story
57 Muddy
58 Beefcakes
60 Thumbs-up
61 Solving crosswords, e.g.
62 Insect named for the way it moves, not for its length
65 Got hot on Twitter, say
66 Kind
69 ____ Psaki, former Biden press secretary
70 Gymnastics apparatus
71 Oral equivalent of a facepalm
72 Native American tribe of Montana
75 Single
78 Box score column
80 Noted 1815 comedy of manners
82 Actress Chaplin
83 Flag carrier to Karachi and Islamabad
86 Traditional Chinese drink
87 Anointment
88 Perspective, in brief
90 "No more for me, thank you"
91 Minute
93 Element 39
94 Big bleu expanse
95 Alumni grouping
100 Stylish
103 World capital that's home to Kotoka International Airport
105 World capital that's home to Noi Bai International Airport
106 Horror film locale, in brief
108 Egg: Sp.
111 2016 #1 album for Rihanna
112 Pop
113 Really thin type
114 ____ Domini
115 "I beg of you," e.g.
116 Bit of Morse code
117 Actress de Armas
118 D.C. pro
119 "Of course!"
121 They're checked at check-ins

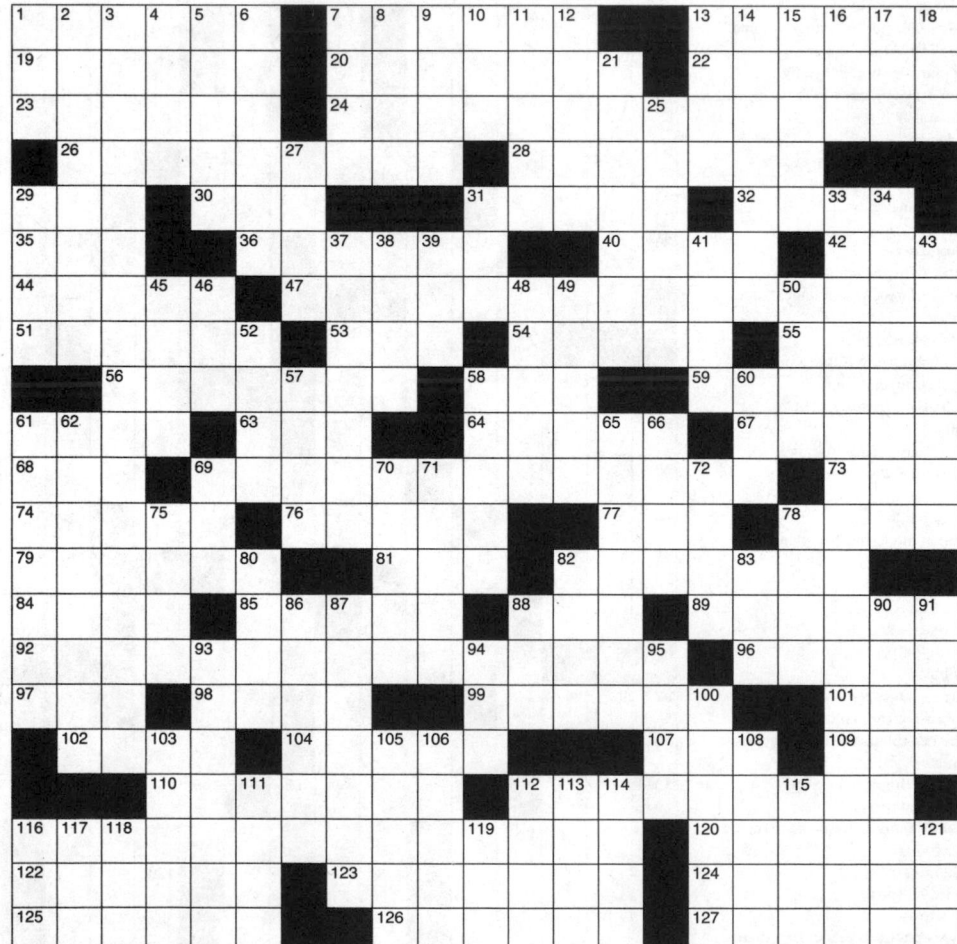

by Matthew Stock

ACROSS

1 Man who had all the answers?
7 Some baggage
14 Fillet, say
20 William Howard Taft or William McKinley
21 "It's just me"
22 First-aid item for allergy sufferers
23 Shared with, for a while
24 Leadership style of the nudist club president?
26 Like a senior year
27 Dates
29 Steamboat Springs alternative
30 Pint-size
31 Like Ahab's pursuit of Moby Dick
35 Winter driving hazard
38 Ascribe to, as fault
41 When the nudist club was founded?
46 They hit the sauce a lot
47 "There's another good point"
49 "Hold on!"
50 Home to the world's three highest capital cities
51 Nicolas who directed "The Man Who Fell to Earth"
52 Puffs
54 Graduation wear for a University of Hawaii student
55 Place for a throne
56 New members of the nudist club?
59 Pans for potstickers
60 Time's Person of the Century
62 Lit into
63 Two are named after Douglas and Fraser
64 Big name in tennis balls
65 Weigh in
67 School with a 15th-century chapel
69 It comes straight from the horse's mouth
71 "Raspberry ___" (Prince hit)
73 Liquor with a double-headed eagle logo
77 Polo course?
78 What happens in the stand-up show at the nudist club?
81 Robert who played A. J. Soprano
82 Pro wrestler Flair
83 John for whom the Voting Rights Advancement Act was named
84 Slangy contraction
85 Rock genre
86 Soon
88 Taco Bell slogan
91 Its size may be measured in liters
92 Hours spent by the pool at the nudist club?
94 Popular hiding spots in hide-and-seek
95 Virtual currency
96 Sensitive subject
99 Mimic
100 "Cómo ___?"
103 Strong desire
104 Not a joke, say
108 How people returned from a week at the nudist club?
113 Mountaineer's tool
115 2006 World Cup champion, to native fans
116 Popping up
117 Follower of high or dry
118 Goal of some workouts
119 Break between workouts
120 Symbolic gestures

DOWN

1 Travel expense
2 Largest South American bird
3 A quarter of vier
4 Where the nudist club orchestra plays its concerts?
5 Graze
6 Site of the Minotaur's Labyrinth
7 Feelings in the room, informally
8 Build up
9 Choreographer Lubovitch
10 Mont-Saint-Michel, e.g.
11 Not in debt
12 One-named Irish singer
13 Final Four game, e.g.
14 Thieves' hideout
15 Cleanup grp.
16 Conference with five University of California schools
17 '60s TV kid
18 Child, in Chile
19 Part of the U.K.: Abbr.
25 "What's more . . ."
28 Poetry night?
32 Humbugs?
33 A negative has a reverse one
34 Acid container
36 Joneses
37 Baseball Hall-of-Famer Slaughter
38 Element of Freddy Krueger's glove
39 Hawaiian house feature
40 Recipe direction
42 "Hey, man!"
43 Balrog's home in "The Lord of the Rings"
44 Techies and Trekkies, stereotypically
45 Elevator innovator
47 You might skip it if you're in trouble
48 Self starter?
51 L.G.B.T. symbol
53 Statistic in football or basketball
56 Kylo ___, "Star Wars" villain
57 Signed i.o.u.'s
58 Published
59 Victory in the annual nudist club 1K?
61 Face card's value in blackjack
63 Supporting
65 Question that introduces doubt
66 Muscle above an ab
68 "___ So Sweet to Trust in Jesus" (hymn)
69 Big name in windshield wipers
70 Need for a jailbreak
72 Nellie's love in "South Pacific"
73 Behaves badly
74 Many a goodie, they say
75 Fighter's fake
76 Releases
77 Lake noted for "lake effect" snow
78 Whale constellation
79 Not as unruly
80 Small inlet
83 Vanderpump of Bravo's "Vanderpump Rules"
85 Privy to
87 Tenor Andrea
89 In relation to
90 Punk cousin
91 Supercilious sort
93 Syngman ___, first South Korean president
94 Sin's counterpart
97 First name on the Supreme Court
98 Like babies' legs, often
99 Thermostat setting
101 Permanent marker?
102 Hightailed it
105 Minimal effort
106 Neural transmitter
107 Common prescription item
108 In shape
109 Dark side
110 Criticize constantly, with "on"
111 Is, in ancient Rome
112 Divest
114 Many a golden parachute recipient, in brief

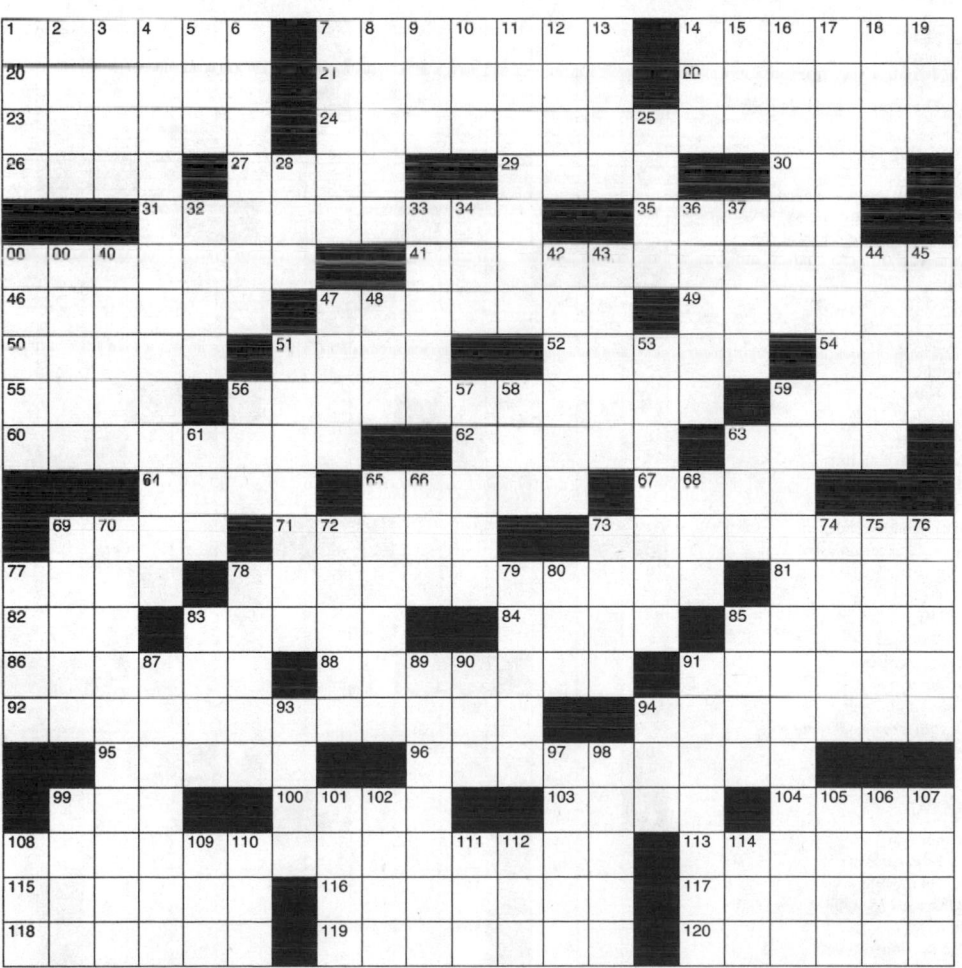

by Brad Wiegmann

ACROSS

1 After the fact, as a justification
8 Co-star of "Golden Girls"
17 Knock over, so to speak
20 Quaker fare
21 Go poof
22 Drop the ball
23 ILLUS_RA_ORS
25 What a third wheel might see, in brief
26 Setting for most of "Life of Pi"
27 Tests the weight of
28 One of the Greats?
30 Oscars of the sporting world
33 Good sign for an angel
34 Intl. org. headquartered in Geneva
37 Some bad sentences
39 ACC_L_RATOR
44 Grapple, in dialect
47 Exercise too much, say
48 A as in Arles
49 LUXUR_ _ACHT
54 "___ Agnus Dei" (Mass phrase)
55 Peak in Turkey mentioned in both the "Iliad" and the "Aeneid"
56 Runner Sebastian who once held the world record for the mile
57 What you might get from a trailer
59 Sport played at British boarding schools
60 Post production?
64 ___ mater, membrane surrounding the brain
65 Popular 90-min. show
66 ENDANGER_EN_
70 Man's name that coincidentally is Latin for "honey"
73 Word with small or fish
74 Weak
75 What may result in a handshake
76 Help to one's destination
82 The Blue Jays, on scoreboards
83 Comeback to a challenge of authority
84 Bitter
85 CONFIG_ _ATION
90 Actor Somerhalder
91 Most in the style of comedian Steven Wright
92 Unfocused
93 POI_T OF _IEW
100 Go all out
101 French fashion inits.
102 "Kinda sorta"
103 Pan-cook, in a way
107 Supermodel Bündchen
109 Pepé ___ (cartoon skunk)
111 Drop off
112 Admit (to)
113 _OTIC_
120 Hit the weed?
121 Have guests over
122 Guest, e.g.
123 Place full of guests
124 Start of a seasonal request
125 Some kitchen utensils

DOWN

1 Entourage
2 Hall's partner in pop
3 Part of a thong
4 "OK, you can stop the story right there"
5 Old-fashioned "cool"
6 One might speak under it
7 Co-star of Kline in "A Fish Called Wanda"
8 Start of a compilation heading
9 Times for some vigils
10 Letters on many towers
11 Busy mo. for C.P.A.s
12 Go bad
13 Three-sport event, for short
14 A chest often has a large one
15 States
16 Recharge
17 Photocopy, e.g.
18 It's the law!
19 Item said to have been burned in protest, once
24 Musical prefix with beat
29 Memphis-to-Nashville dir.
31 Emphatic assent
32 Lively dance genre
34 Hone
35 Contract details
36 Beehive State city
38 Aerodynamic
40 Bishop's jurisdiction
41 Antagonist
42 Hotel room staples
43 Top-notch
44 Booties
45 Playwright Chekhov
46 Garbage
50 Drink similar to a slushie
51 About 460 inches of rain per year, on Kauai's Mt. Waialeale
52 HBO satire starring Julia Louis-Dreyfus
53 ___ bar
54 Org. that takes the lead on lead?
58 Baby fox
60 How a flirt may act
61 Football stat: Abbr.
62 NaOH
63 Radio broadcaster: Abbr.
66 Legislation that was part of F.D.R.'s New Deal
67 Ethnic group of Rwanda and Burundi
68 Two, for four
69 Coin with 12 stars
70 "Zoom-Zoom" sloganeer
71 Hollywood composer Bernstein with 14 Oscar nominations
72 Guarded
73 Like pets and parking meters
75 ___ Slam (tennis feat)
76 Julius Caesar's first name
77 Words of hopelessness
78 Mature naturally, in a way
79 ___ Writers' Workshop
80 Electronic Hasbro toy
81 One side of the coin
83 Arias, typically
86 Scottish folk dance
87 Alternative explanation for a lucky guess, in brief
88 Ear: Prefix
89 Letters on some badges
94 "Stillmatic" rapper
95 Seen
96 Kind of skate
97 Brown shade
98 Kids' observation game
99 Hit musical with an "Emerald City Sequence"
104 Yoke
105 HP product
106 Narrowly beats (out)
108 Singer James
109 Drink for un bébé
110 A full moon will do this
112 Life force, in China
114 ___ Majesty
115 Hosp. areas
116 The Jazz, on scoreboards
117 Brown shade
118 Things for happy campers?
119 Picky person's pick?

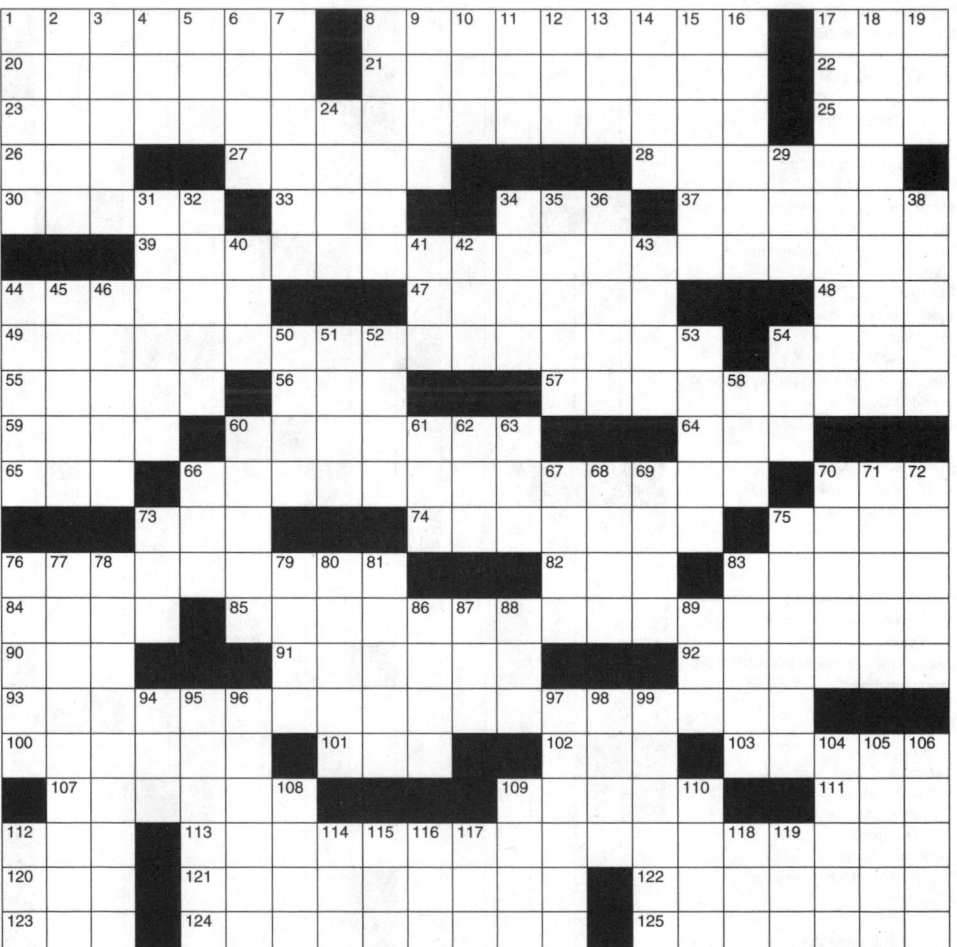

by Celeste Watts and Jeff Chen

ACROSS

1 Some rappers
4 Music genre for Carmen Miranda
9 Pioneer in 35mm cameras
14 Bit of bait
18 His face overlooks Havana's Plaza de la Revolución
19 Fire ___
20 See 67-Across
21 Refurbish
22 Architectural innovation jokingly predicted by 101-Across in 1982
26 Actress Perez
27 Performer's showcase
28 Gave out
29 God of love
30 Goofy images, perhaps?
32 Kitchen brand whose name becomes an animal after adding a "t"
33 Old N.Y.C. subway inits.
36 Wish list items
38 Grooming tool jokingly predicted by 101-Across in 1979
41 "Gotcha"
43 ___ Sea, whose eastern basin has become a desert
44 Either spy to the other in "Spy vs. Spy"
45 Prop in a Shakespeare tragedy
47 Abbr. at the end of a planner
48 Classic board game derived from pachisi
50 Place to order a cassoulet
52 Writing aid jokingly predicted by 101-Across in 1967
55 Therefore
56 ___ block
57 Midnight trip to the fridge, say
58 "Yellow Flicker Beat" singer, 2014
59 Type of headsail
62 Super-duper
63 Shake off
65 Hammer out, say
66 "___ Lisa"
67 With 20-Across, yearly
68 Some sports car options
69 Painter Paul
70 "Them's the breaks!"
72 Butler played by Gable
73 Winter sport jokingly predicted by 101-Across in 1965
75 Treadmill settings
77 They're not known for neatness
78 Word connecting two place names
79 Word connecting two last names
80 Taters
81 Ragamuffin
82 Nominee's place
84 Telephone feature jokingly predicted by 101-Across in 1961
89 Porters, e.g.
92 Stampede member in "The Lion King"
93 Manual readers
94 "___ fun!"
95 Early smartphone model
96 Italian lager
98 Square thing
100 Like some rights and engineers
101 Satirical cartoonist, born 3/13/1921, known for dreaming up ridiculous inventions . . . or are they?
107 Ransacks
108 Peter the Great and others
109 Eponym of an M.L.B. hitting award
110 Jellied British delicacy
111 Goes down
112 Fender product, for short
113 Windows forerunner
114 Droll

DOWN

1 Phil of "Dr. Phil"
2 Intensity of color
3 When the president may make a pitch
4 Ump's call
5 Comedian Wong
6 Gym array
7 Sweet bread
8 Not as scarce
9 Language not traditionally written with spaces between words
10 Ambient musician Brian
11 Like Bach's first two "Brandenburg" Concertos
12 Like dice, shapewise
13 Finding it funny
14 Off the mark
15 Substance that helps a spaceship's fuel burn
16 Direct
17 It's greener the higher it is, for short
21 Glow, in a way
23 Narrow inlet
24 Part
25 ___ of Man
31 Exposed to high heat, in a way
32 Cosmetics brand with "Face anything" ads
34 Ex-QB football analyst Tony
35 Word repeated before "again"
37 Move stealthily
38 Big part of the S&P 500
39 "It's co-o-old!"
40 Toss in a chip, maybe
42 Hid
45 Org. concerned with performance rights
46 Mace, for one
48 Oodles
49 "___ From Muskogee" (Merle Haggard hit)
50 Cartoonist Dave famous for "The Lighter Side of . . ."
51 How anatomy charts are drawn
53 Mormon church, for short
54 Blow
55 "Mountain of God," in Exodus
58 Longtime name in cinemas
59 Hire calling?
60 Like slapstick comedies
61 Feature of a Care Bear's belly
64 Oodles
65 Hazard on an Arctic voyage
66 1960s style
68 Blues ensemble?
69 Slices easily (through)
71 Brush brand
72 Command+Y, on a Mac
73 Swizzle
74 Cartoon speech bubble, often
75 Whirled around
76 Sting, e.g.
77 Egg holders
80 Droop
81 Most sinewy
82 Its coat of arms features a marlin and flamingo, with "the"
83 Baseball's "Big Papi"
85 Since
86 Principles
87 Russian assembly
88 Gutter nuisance in cold climates
90 Apt surname for a hot dog vendor?
91 Alone
97 Gobbles up
99 Suet alternative
100 Survivalist's stockpile
101 It might come in a yard glass
102 High toss
103 Crew's control?
104 ___ diavolo (in a peppery tomato sauce)
105 Year-round Phoenix hrs.
106 Sticky stuff

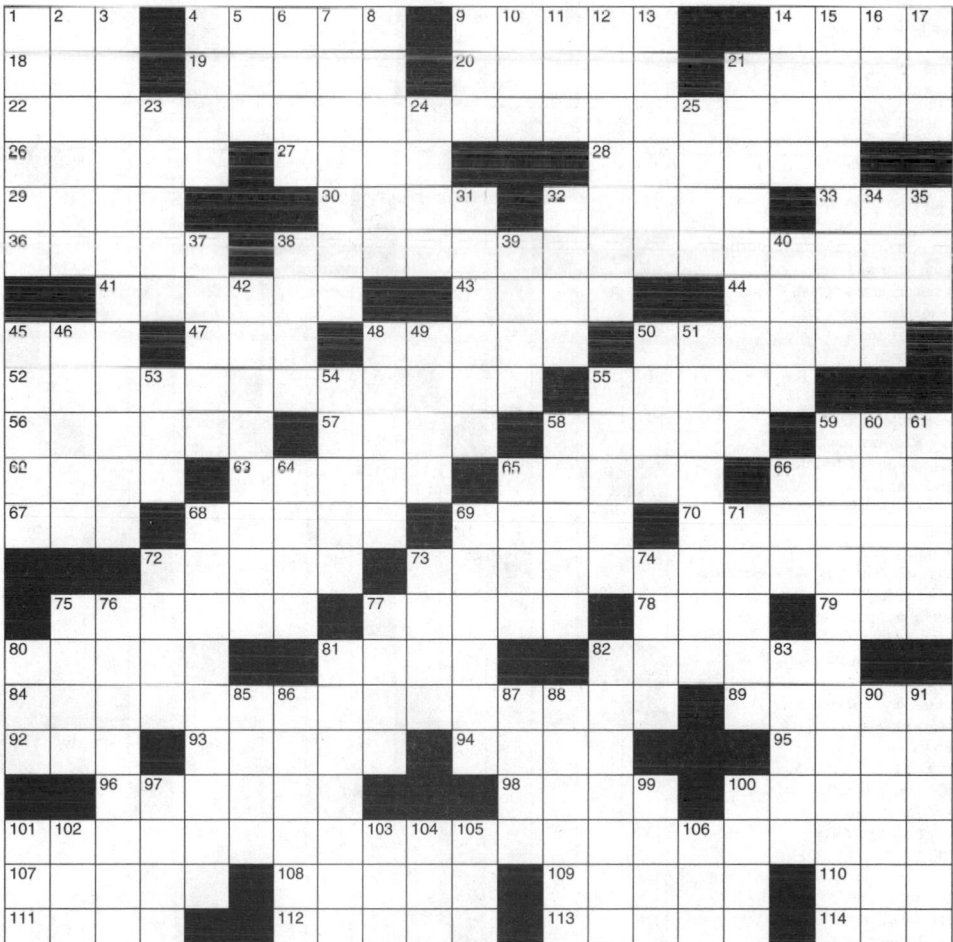

by Jacob Stulberg

ACROSS

1 SAT section eliminated by the College Board in 2021
6 Firth person?
10 Best-selling book of all time
15 Get the attention of
19 Sister-in-law of Prince William
20 Lead-in to pilot
21 Stick on
22 "Goodness gracious!"
23 Nod off at a self-serve restaurant?
26 Jupiter, exempli gratia
27 [Turn the page]
28 Sooner, informally
29 Diamond stat
30 Get down and dirty, in dialect
32 Bovine disease
34 Fancy flooring for an R.V.?
38 Home of Etihad Airways: Abbr.
39 Eyeball creepily
40 Requirement
41 Hoops grp.
44 Like universal blood recipients
48 One layer of a seven-layer dip
50 What the prestigious ice sculptor had?
55 Unable to think clearly
59 Goes nowhere, say
60 Word with holy or heating
61 Grammy-winning singer Cash
63 Certain elite school
64 Appear
65 Back in the U.S.S.?
66 Org. to which Taft was elected president after serving as U.S. president
67 "Yes, that's clear"
69 "Let everyone else get some steak before taking seconds!"
74 Mooches
76 Mate
77 Grand Central info
78 Surreptitious bit of communication
81 "What have we here!"
82 Like many characters in Alison Bechdel cartoons
84 Nintendo release of 2006
85 Show runner
86 2013 Tony winner for Best Revival of a Musical
88 "We should stall!"
91 Long-stemmed mushroom
93 Egyptian god of the afterlife
94 Llama's head?
95 Button clicked to see the rest of an article
97 Not out, say
101 Target of the heckle "What game are you watching?!"
103 Why no one hangs out in actors' dressing rooms these days?
107 Played obnoxiously loudly
111 At 10 or 11 p.m., say
112 Part of lifeguard training
113 Navigation app
115 Lucky charm
116 American ____ (century plant)
117 Bathroom fixture that one never asked for?
122 Their heads get dirty
123 Dirt
124 Typos for exclamation marks if you fail to hit Shift
125 Opposite of neat
126 ____ strategy
127 Fills to the max
128 Set (on)
129 Bathroom door sign

DOWN

1 ____ salt (magnesium sulfate)
2 Mixed martial arts great Anderson
3 What a hiree should be brought up to
4 Brief summary
5 Gab
6 Knocked in a pocket, in pool
7 Handle a job satisfactorily
8 Additional
9 ____ the line
10 Trinket
11 Less certain
12 Many a maid of honor, informally
13 Create an account?
14 Not included
15 Marvel group led by Hercules
16 ____ monkey
17 Lucky charm
18 Plague
24 "My treat next time!"
25 Cheese sometimes paired with fig jam
31 Subject of the Iran-contra affair
33 Requirements for witnesses
35 Jessica of "L.A.'s Finest"
36 Believer in Jah
37 Book fair organizer, maybe, in brief
41 Longtime procedural set in Washington, D.C.
42 Foreshadow
43 Pass up?
45 Declare
46 "All in the Family" mother
47 Tissue that's prone to tearing, for short
49 Italian car since 1907
51 Enemy in the game Doom
52 Sticks in a box?
53 Style of women's leather handbags
54 Isaac and Rebekah's firstborn
56 Piece with a title like "10 Best Places to . . ."
57 First mate?
58 Recolor
62 Comparatively neat
65 Johnson & Johnson skin care brand
68 Moniker after a lifestyle change
70 Initial problem for a storied duckling
71 Man's nickname that sounds like consecutive letters of the alphabet
72 "Phooey!"
73 Japanese "energy healing"
74 Bread for dipping
75 Golden ratio symbol
79 Actress Patricia of "Breakfast at Tiffany's"
80 Phone, wallet, ____ (traveler's mental checklist)
83 Gaudy jewelry
84 Word in obituaries
85 Eponymous member of the Ford family
87 Most cheerful
89 Fictional establishment selling Duff Beer
90 Option for an overnight guest
92 Campsite org.
95 Antacid brand
96 Forms of some mythological sea creatures
98 Turn into
99 Bob hopes?
100 Garment worn with a choli
102 Something Pharaoh's dream foretold in Genesis
103 Make a goat
104 Heavies
105 "Pearls Before ____" (comic strip)
106 Put away
108 Sculptor with a dedicated museum in Philadelphia
109 Throw out
110 Showers attention (on)
114 Lemon bar ingredient
118 Food service industry lobby, for short
119 Command to a dog
120 Male swan
121 Slow (down)

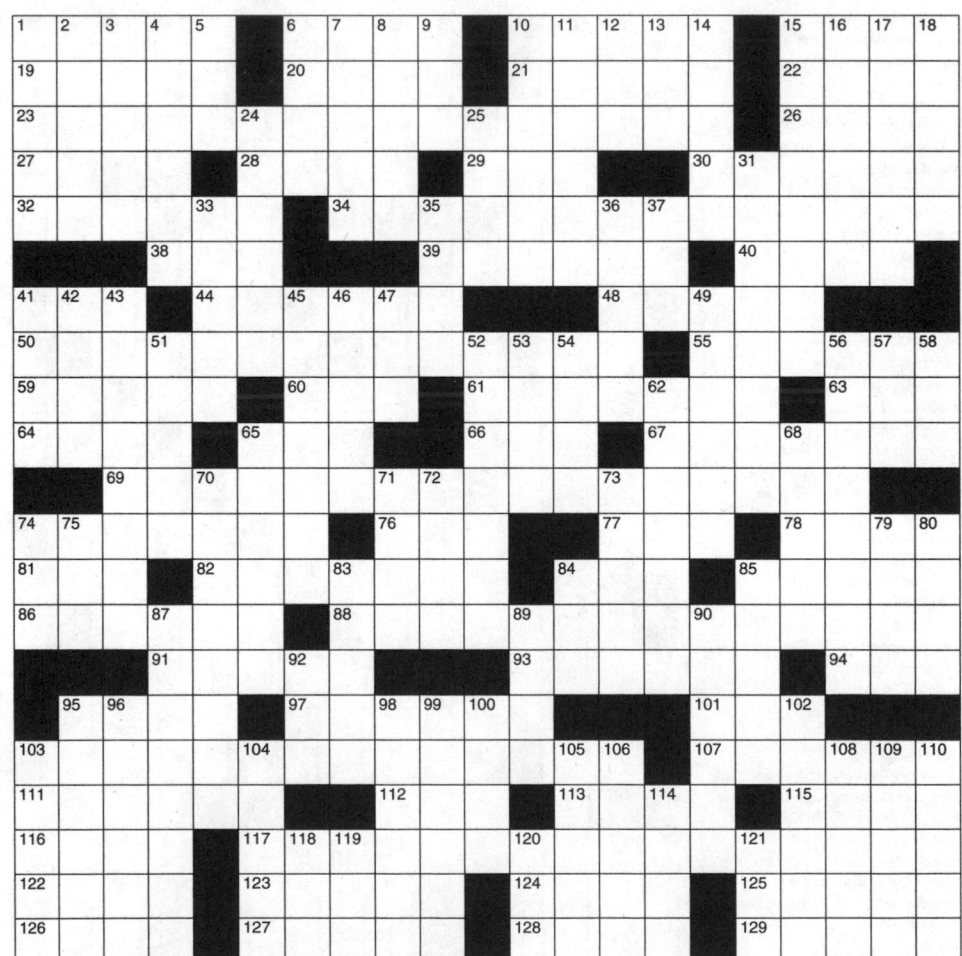

by Julian Kwan

ACROSS

1 Pest control product
5 Luggage label
10 Color effect in graphic design
18 Video game princess of the Kingdom of Hyrule
19 Writer Zora ___ Hurston
20 Take part in a D&D campaign, e.g.
21 Brand of fruity hard candy
23 Personae non gratae
24 URANUS
25 "Arrivederci!"
26 Jerks
27 "___ to differ!"
28 One taking the long view?
31 Tarot deck character
35 Some surgical tools
38 "Unit" of fun
39 All-star duo?
40 Comfort in not knowing, say
47 Request
50 JUPITER
51 Ships passing in the night?
52 Sch. on the Rio Grande
54 Hollers
55 Like some parties and flowers
56 "Back to the Future" antagonist
60 Hit movie released as "Vaselina" in Mexico
62 Husk-wrapped dish
65 Colorful tropical fish
66 Song standard on "Barbra Streisand's Greatest Hits"
71 SATURN
72 With 11-Down, hit 2001 film with an "!" in its title
73 Stirred up
74 Cold shower?
75 Muralist ___ Clemente Orozco
76 2021 Super Bowl champs
80 Boy, in Barcelona
81 Animated character who wears a red shirt and no pants
82 Time before computers, facetiously
85 Fleet runner. Abbr.
86 One feature of a perfect nanny, in a "Mary Poppins" song
91 MARS
92 Hesitate in speaking
93 More inquisitive
98 Jaded sort
99 Solo flier?
105 Prefix meaning "both"
106 Welled (up)
108 Like people who are much looked up to
109 Insurance fraud ploy
110 Determiner of cannabis legality, e.g.
113 Classic carnival ride
116 Cherished family member
117 NEPTUNE
118 Golding of "Crazy Rich Asians"
119 Sporty car
120 Deliver a speech
121 World of Warcraft spellcaster

DOWN

1 Leans (on)
2 Claim
3 Pastoral poem
4 ___ es Salaam
5 Navel type
6 Sticker on the back of a laptop, say
7 Home to the Sugar Bowl and Heavenly ski resorts
8 Draft pick?
9 Neighbor of Belg.
10 Word after focus or Facebook
11 See 72-Across
12 Mountain map figs.
13 Ones getting the message
14 Rio beach of song
15 Hollow center?
16 Turner who led an 1831 slave rebellion
17 Grateful sentiments, in online shorthand
18 "The Greek" of film
21 Corner space in Monopoly
22 Juggling or magic, in a talent show
26 Nobel laureate Morrison
29 Poker variety
30 "This Will Be" singer Natalie
32 Sommelier's métier
33 "Monsters, ___"
34 Be on the level?
36 "Notorious" Supreme Court initials
37 Knocked 'em dead
39 Not spoiled
41 Suffix with serpent
42 One of five in "pronunciation": Abbr.
43 Choice of sizes, briefly
44 Celebratory, quaintly
45 Deception
46 Cowboy or Patriot, for short
47 Zeros
48 Distinct melodic segment
49 Not waver from
53 Fruit also called a custard apple or prairie banana
55 Baby's cry
56 Cue at an audition
57 Land jutting into il Mediterraneo
58 Quaker
59 Community of followers
61 Thesaurus listing: Abbr.
63 Melber of MSNBC
64 Candy featured in a classic "MythBusters" episode
65 Confucian's spiritual path
67 In ___ (peeved)
68 Nintendo dinosaur who eats fruit and throws eggs
69 Bring to court
70 2003 best seller whose title is one letter different from a fantasy creature
75 Pleasures
77 Grammy winner DiFranco
78 Rendezvoused
79 ___ gow (Chinese domino game)
81 Money earned from an event, say
82 Gush
83 Archaeologist's find
84 Brian once of glam rock
86 U.S. health org.
87 "Hands off, that's mine!"
88 Austrian article
89 Sent off
90 Lose a layer
94 Bit of luau wear
95 "No question!"
96 Magazine whose 60th anniversary issue had the cover line "Denzel, Halle & Jamie"
97 What's hard about a melon?
99 Origami shape called "orizuru"
100 Tree surgeon, at times
101 Interior chambers
102 Gem weight
103 Bonnie's partner in crime
104 Quadratic formula subj.
107 Oodles
109 Measurement in plane geometry
110 Camera type, briefly
111 As well
112 DuVernay who directed "Selma"
113 Queue before P
114 Canal locale
115 Piece de resistance?

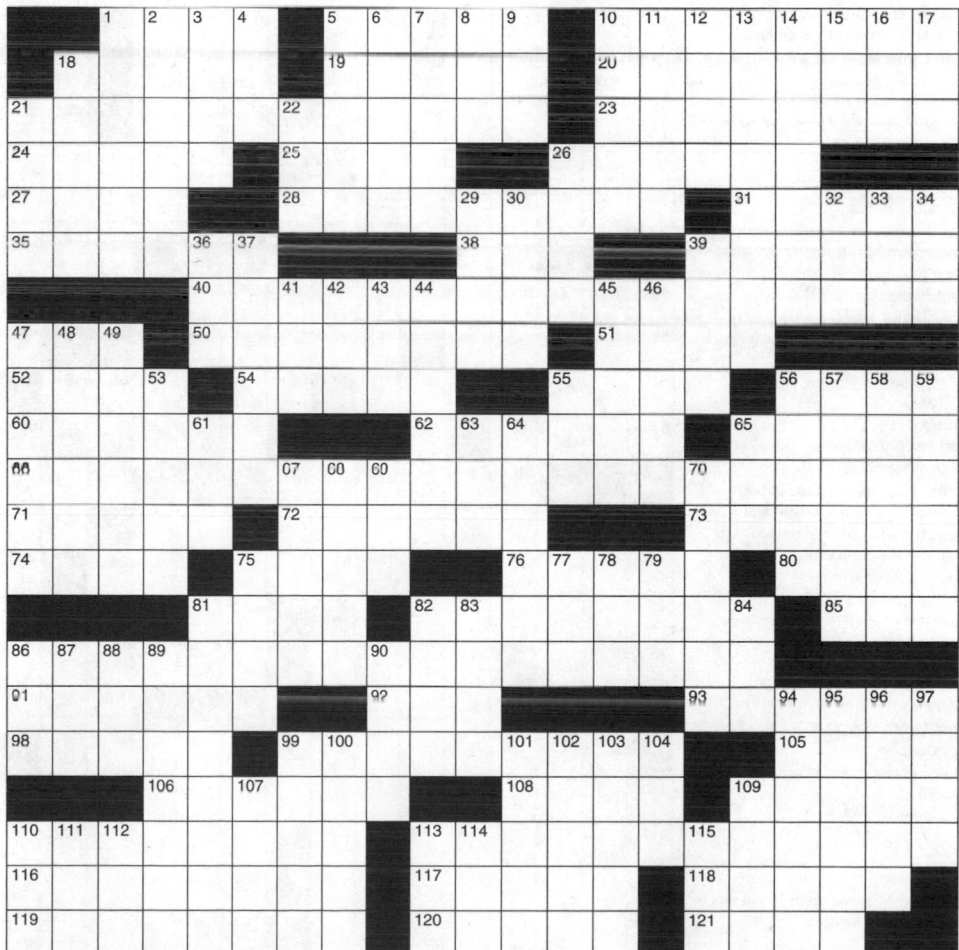

by Olivia Mitra Framke

ACROSS

1 Chow down on
6 "Exactly like this"
12 Word with mild or well
20 Character often found in children's books
21 Emotionally process, in modern lingo
22 Repeated cry in 1931's "Frankenstein"
23 *Perfect curveball?
25 Ivy League city
26 Jam
27 Crucial
28 White coat?
30 Course standards
31 Emergency room concern
33 *Batting coach's instruction to a lackadaisical hitter?
37 Habitual drinkers
39 Opposed (to)
40 *Apprentice groundskeepers?
46 Singer/songwriter Parks with the 2021 album "Collapsed in Sunbeams"
47 It might get pulled in both directions
50 New York's Mount ___ Hospital
51 Dark wine grape
52 Part of a heartbeat
54 Diplomatic official: Abbr.
55 Corn core
57 Cancels
60 Alacrity
61 Afternoon socials
63 Where dreams are made
65 *Overenthusiastic description of a routine base hit?
68 Stand-in for Middle America
71 Pair of socks?
72 *Umpire's aid in judging foul balls?
78 GPS approximation
79 Sgt. and cpl., e.g.
83 Airer of "Nancy Drew"
84 Old salt
86 Fury
88 State where M.L.K. marched: Abbr.
89 Some fins
92 King James on a court
94 Do as Henry VI did
96 Letters on some foundations
97 Jumpy sorts, in brief
99 *Long hours of fielding practice?
101 ___ only
103 Tilting
104 *Imperceptible fastball movement?
109 All over the place
113 Jimmy ___ (luxury shoe brand)
114 Scientist buried in Westminster Abbey
115 Pop artist who sings "Satisfied" on "The Hamilton Mixtape"
116 New ___ (cap brand)
117 Trouble, metaphorically
120 Ballgame extenders . . . and what can literally be found in the answers to the asterisked clues
124 Beekeeper
125 ___ to go
126 Run-D.M.C. and the Jonas Brothers, for example
127 Bands' performance sheets
128 Unruffled
129 ___ Domingo

DOWN

1 Bird that can spend up to 10 months in the air without landing
2 Absolute bottom
3 Digital assistant
4 Food packaging abbr., once
5 What's heard at many a coffeehouse
6 Group sometimes said to be "out"
7 French article
8 Pampering place
9 In use
10 Candle choice
11 Gumbo pods
12 Goddess with a sacred owl
13 Designers' studios
14 Its capital is Sydney: Abbr.
15 "Uh-uh"
16 Go by
17 Compete with
18 Part of EGBDF
19 Places to play cards, often
24 The Daily ___ (online news site)
29 ___ culpa
32 It plays a role in arm-twisting
33 "Venerable" saint
34 Manual readers
35 Air France hub
36 It brought Hope to the world
38 When doubled, a Nabokov protagonist
40 Pre-bar challenge, briefly
41 "Je t'___"
42 Org. with Fire and Sparks
43 It was first won by the N.Y. Mets in 1969
44 Snow blower brand
45 Word on some Oreo packages
47 Nothing special
48 Tina Turner, voicewise
49 Goldenrod, e.g.
53 Append
56 Instrument with a flared end
58 Chinese steamed bun
59 Ratio of an angle's opposite side to the hypotenuse
62 Blueprint details
64 Runs out of juice
66 Eye cream ingredient
67 Symbol on Captain America's shield
69 Villainous English king in "Braveheart"
70 Outstanding pitcher
72 Former Ford models
73 Seller of Belgian waffles and French toast (fittingly, considering the "I" in its name)
74 Super Soaker Soakzooka brand
75 Like some orders
76 Ancient halls
77 Eldest Stark son on "Game of Thrones"
80 G.I.'s garb, at times
81 Speed skater Johann ___ Koss, winner of four Olympic golds
82 One-named Nigerian Grammy winner
85 Pained sound
87 In the Renaissance, they were known as "mala insana" ("mad apples")
90 Baseball's Gehrig and Piniella
91 Most reliable
93 Russian city on the Ural River
95 Butterlike spread
98 French West Indies resort island, familiarly
100 Keep from flying, maybe
101 Profession
102 Camera inits.
104 "With any luck . . ."
105 Tag line?
106 Fancy pourers
107 Paper route hour, maybe
108 Headliner's cue
110 Land between Togo and Nigeria
111 Insider's vocabulary
112 Catch with a throw
113 Alternative to Chuck
115 Wistful sound
118 Man's name that's 123-Down reversed
119 Stanza contraction
121 Home of the world's largest carnival
122 Word with red or army
123 Man's name that's 118-Down reversed

by Angela Olson Halsted and Doug Peterson

ACROSS

1 Men are pigs (after she's through with them, anyway!)
6 The "A" of James A. Garfield
11 Naysayers
20 Lower-cost option on a popular rideshare app
21 Egg: Sp.
22 Frontiersman's headgear
23 Result of a merger between Quaker Oats and Greyhound?
25 Maintaining equilibrium
26 Discourage
27 Soft drink concentrate, e.g.
29 "Night on Bald Mountain" or "Finlandia"
30 With 18-Down, what has four legs and sprints?
32 Musician who was booed in 1965 for playing electric guitar
34 Letters before Gerald R. Ford and Ronald Reagan
35 Luau instrument, for short
37 Zoom
39 Corner
41 Second-longest human bone, after the femur
46 Result of a merger between Kraft and Hershey's?
51 Result of a merger between Google and Planters?
53 Like the wights on "Game of Thrones"
54 Best of the best
56 Spelling ____
57 What Santa checks twice
58 R-rated
59 Rulers' staffs
61 Fire man?
63 On the ____
64 Poet Lazarus
66 Prefix with thermal
67 Bad sound for an engine
68 Result of a merger between Hasbro and Nikon?
72 Bird like the Canada goose or arctic tern
75 Lummox
76 Cheese offered tableside at Italian restaurants, informally
77 Recipe amt.
80 Eagle constellation
81 Passive acquiescence
84 Voice a view
86 Firm decision maker?
87 Revolutionary Guevara
89 Klum of "Project Runway"
90 "My love," in Madrid
91 Result of a merger between Procter & Gamble and Jacuzzi?
94 Result of a merger between Hormel and Instagram?
96 Warehouse
97 10 to 10, say
99 ____ reform, cause for the Marshall Project
100 Middling grade
101 Pub choice
103 Shot across the bow?
106 ____ Waldorf, the so-called "Queen B" on "Gossip Girl"
109 Leaves nothing to the imagination
114 Measured
116 "Been there, done that" feeling
118 Disney's world
120 Result of a merger between Ralph Lauren and Starbucks?
123 "Stop your foolishness outside!"
124 Not on
125 Chops up finely
126 Was uncomfortably hot
127 Basil-based sauce
128 ____ Allen, one of the founders of Vermont

DOWN

1 ____-de-sac
2 Ditto, in scholarly journals
3 Brexit vote, e.g.
4 Home to the Minoan civilization
5 Shine
6 "Now I get it!"
7 2021 Super Bowl champs
8 Drink up during a timeout, say
9 Tex who directed the first Bugs Bunny cartoon
10 Iraqi city on the Tigris
11 Kimono accessory
12 Natural talent
13 ____ Young-White, comedian/correspondent for "The Daily Show"
14 Lead-in to an Indiana "-ville"
15 ____ Ng, author of the 2017 best seller "Little Fires Everywhere"
16 Piehole
17 "Oops!"
18 See 30-Across
19 Part of a musical note
24 Held forth
28 "Two thumbs down" review
31 Answer to "Are you asleep?" that can't be true
33 Drift off to sleep
35 Ordinary
36 "Eh, not really"
38 1981 hit Genesis album whose name resembles a rhyme scheme
40 Balls in the sky
42 Little sounds
43 Muscular
44 "Who's there?" response
45 Nancy who served as the first female member of the British Parliament
47 Come together
48 Like some thinking
49 A.O.C., e.g.
50 Meets
52 Evening prayer
55 Come together
59 Raw material?
60 Quintana ____ (Mexican state that's home to Cancún)
62 Mayhem
65 Land governed by the House of Grimaldi
67 Obedience school command
68 More hackneyed
69 A head
70 A head
71 Best-case scenarios
72 Clipper parts
73 "You can't fire me!"
74 Italian poet Cavalcanti who influenced Dante
77 Procrastinator's problem
78 [Bo-o-o-oring!]
79 In essence
81 Where heroes are made
82 Sass
83 Co-founder of the N.A.A.C.P.
85 Word that, when spelled backward, becomes its own synonym
88 Member of the inn crowd?
90 One of the Canterbury pilgrims
92 One doing the lord's work
93 In which you might do a deep dive
95 Mistruth
98 JAMA contributors
102 Tool in a wood shop
104 Shred
105 ____ hole
107 Battery part
108 Language group related to Yupik
109 Birkin stock?
110 From scratch
111 Quinceañera, e.g.
112 Man's name that spells a fruit backward
113 Passed-down stories
115 "Stop stalling!"
117 "The slightest" or "the foggiest" thing
119 Oscar-winning lyricist Washington
121 Classic Pontiac
122 Phishing target, for short

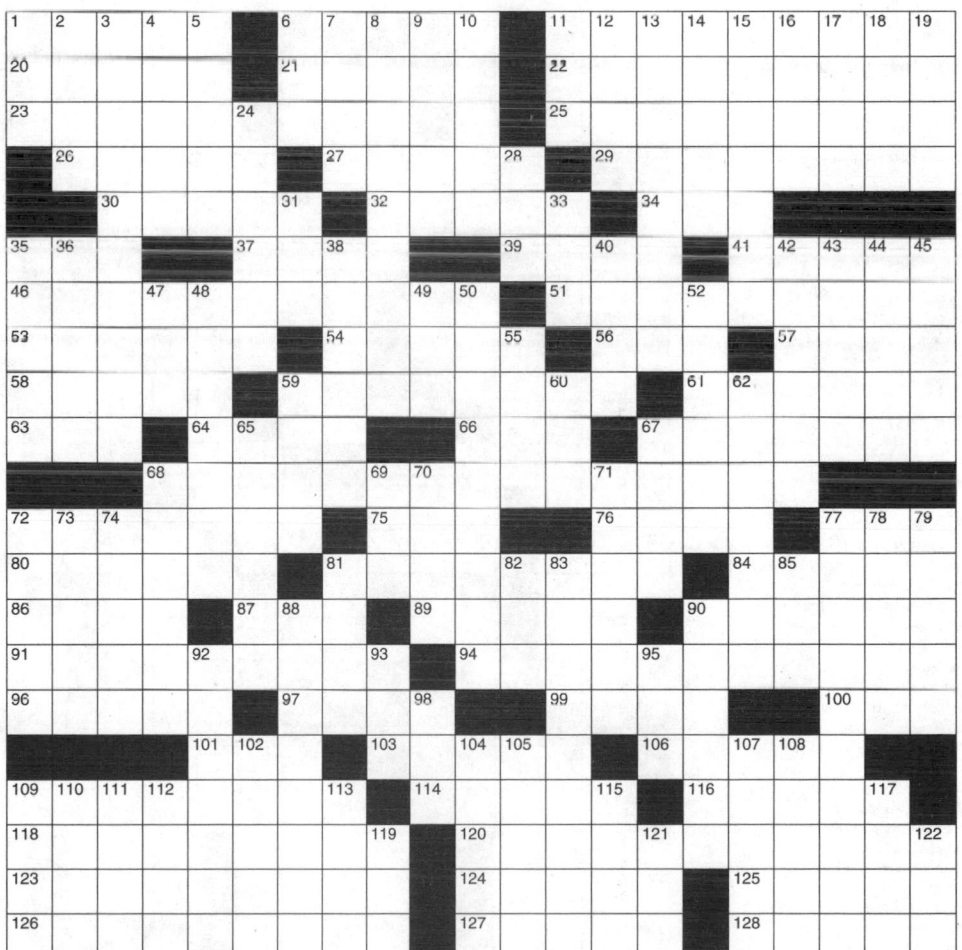

by Dick Shlakman and Will Nediger

ACROSS

1 Not express, in a way
6 Second person in the Bible
10 One of the Blues Brothers
14 "History of the World, ___" (Mel Brooks film that doesn't actually have a sequel)
15 Grp. with Bills and Chargers
18 Bridal adornment at Indian weddings
20 Buckets
21 Goggle
22 Bird that went the way of the dodo (before the dodo)
23 Mr. ___, scheming socialite in "Emma"
24 See 105-Across
25 Popular action film franchise . . . or what trying to find the item in this puzzle can be described as
29 "There's no use" . . . like trying to find the item in this puzzle?
31 "The ___ Holmes Mysteries," young adult series made into a 2020 film
32 Hosp. procedure
33 Keys
34 Architect Maya
35 Foreign correspondent, maybe
38 1976 greatest hits album with a palindromic title
41 Site of Hercules' first labor
45 What's-___-name
46 Experimental offshoot of punk
49 Echidna's prey
50 Service with nearly two billion users
53 ___ reaction
54 Deep cut
55 Liquor store requests
56 Frees (of)
57 Quiet summons
59 Greases
61 What's at the center of some court battles?
62 City of Angels
64 Danger for an exterminator
65 Scratch the surface of
66 Certain customizable computer game character
67 Kick starter?
70 America of "Ugly Betty"
72 [Batman punches a bad guy]
73 Onetime name for China
74 They have big mouths
76 Over
77 More than umbrage
78 Two-wheeled carriage
79 "Anchorman" anchorman
80 Simple earrings
81 Duck Hunt console, for short
82 Walking with flair
84 Odd article of clothing to wear with a tank top
85 Reached
87 Man's name that anagrams to HYENAS
88 Did a Don Corleone impression, maybe
92 Consonantless "yes"
94 Actress Atwell of the "Avengers" movies
96 Product whose sizes have letters
97 Clickable images
99 "As you can imagine . . ."
103 Item hidden somewhere in this puzzle (where is it?)
105 With 24-Across, Emmy winner for "Once and Again"
106 Writer Horatio
107 Word before an explanation
108 Boxer Ali
111 Bookmarked things
112 Vowelless "yes"
113 Personal datum: Abbr.
114 Long-gone
115 Site that competes with Amazon Handmade
116 Affliction also known as a hordeolum
117 Mean

DOWN

1 Collectible records
2 ___ milk
3 Packs tightly
4 Areas in many malls
5 Eldest of the von Trapp children
6 Mnemosyne's daughters
7 Benefits
8 En pointe, in ballet
9 Pizza chain since 1943, familiarly
10 Weapon for Samson against the Philistines
11 Whatsoever
12 "North" or "South" land
13 Undoing
15 Faulty
16 Subway fare
17 Impact equally in the opposite direction
19 Actor Elgort of "The Fault in Our Stars"
26 Taints
27 Sheepish response to "Where did the last cookie go?"
28 How checks are written
29 Hellion
30 "Boyz N the Hood" protagonist
36 Run an online scam
37 Feel rotten
39 Bona fide
40 Big brush maker
42 Starting point on a computer
43 Won over
44 See 50-Down
47 Become rigid and inflexible
48 Slides
50 With 44-Down, making futile attempts . . . and an extra hint to this puzzle's theme
51 Small black-and-white treat
52 Batman portrayer on '60s TV
57 Google Photos precursor
58 Workers in forges
59 Murder weapon in "The Talented Mr. Ripley"
60 What "/" may mean
63 Key used to get out, but not in
64 Man's name that means "king"
68 Palindromic leaders
69 Doctor's order
71 They may be fixed
74 Highland beauty
75 The titular bad guy in "The Good, the Bad and the Ugly"
79 Capital of Saudi Arabia
80 Singer with the 2016 platinum album "This Is Acting"
82 In good shape
83 "Know what I'm talkin' about?"
84 Secret rendezvous
86 Like child's play
89 Block where Sesame Street can be found?
90 Notable period
91 It's constantly breaking around the world
93 "The straight path"
95 German steel city
97 Like neon
98 Bar rooms?
99 It never occurs above the Arctic Circle during the summer solstice
100 One may be sworn
101 Claw
102 Seat of Florida's Marion County
104 Eugene O'Neill's "Desire Under the ___"
105 Go after
109 Word before ride or slide
110 Which card to pick from a magician?

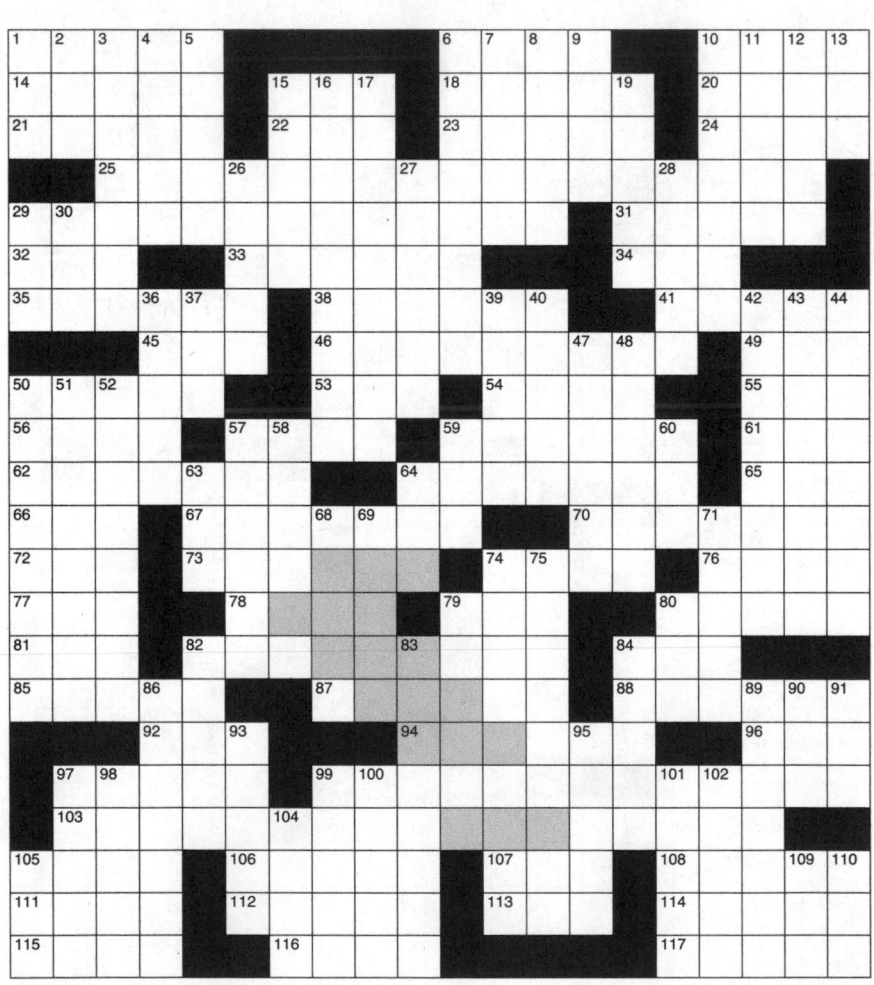

by Johan Vass

ACROSS

1 Muhammad Ali's "Me! Whee!," e.g.
5 "S.N.L." alum Hartman
9 Start off on the wrong foot, maybe?
13 Contaminate
19 What may be in a star's orbit
21 Throw with power
22 Alleviate
23 Sheep's milk product that's often grated
25 Classic name for the land north of England
26 Course taken in shorts, often
27 "Ya don't say!"
28 765-foot-long "water coaster" on Disney cruises
30 Countertenor
31 SWAT team or Navy SEAL group, e.g.
34 Name that sounds like two letters of the alphabet
37 Epitome of smoothness
39 "Roots" author Haley
40 Shocker, at times
41 & 44 It goes around every hour
46 Gaming novice, slangily
48 Secured skates, with "up"
50 Float component
51 Act as a blueprint for, as DNA for proteins
53 Brawled, in the backwoods
55 "Howdy, everybody!"
57 Withstand
58 Fly off the shelves
59 Like bread made from almond flour
61 "Oh, hell yes!"
64 Turn red, say
65 Certain formal duds
66 Nice round number?
67 Bollywood megastar Aishwarya ___
68 "My dear man"
71 Grammy category won multiple times by Kendrick Lamar
77 Racy selfie posted for likes on social media, in modern lingo
80 Not a problem
81 Kennel club category
82 Makeup table
83 "Dead serious!"
85 "And, uh, that about covers it"
86 Supporting role
87 New students at Princeton or Yale in 1969
88 There's a famous "half" one in Yosemite National Park
90 Vessel protected by Hera
91 Uninteresting
92 Encouraging cry
94 Bottom
96 Saves, with "away"
98 "Ain't dead ___!"
99 They often come to professors with excuses
102 Hoodwink
104 Get snake eyes, say
107 Lacking experience
108 Aligns, in a wood shop
112 Set straight
113 Oscar winner for his role as a Mexican narc in "Traffic"
117 Price to pay, informally
118 Major piece
119 Miniature for a World War II buff
120 Were running mates?
121 Quite a jerk
122 Make an appearance
123 Recess for prayer

DOWN

1 Verve
2 It's 50/50
3 "That kinda stuff": Abbr.
4 Buckaroos
5 Mint
6 Fictional pilot with the line "You like me because I'm a scoundrel"
7 "Here ___ again"
8 Milk for un café
9 Onetime MTV reality series filmed near Hollywood
10 Recall regretfully
11 Auditing org.
12 Courtroom statements
13 Bone to pick
14 Lighter than lite
15 Word after soul or solid
16 "You, too?!," playfully
17 Smart
18 Wood that's resistant to warping
20 Mountain chain that stretches from Kazakhstan to the Arctic
24 Do a waving motion by the ocean, say
29 "That proves it"
32 Shade similar to verdigris
33 Distinguish oneself
34 Positioned to win
35 Shared with for quick feedback
36 Cut into
38 Region with a Unification Flag for sporting events
41 Pen pa?
42 Just hanging out
43 It really blows
45 Knucklehead
47 Flinch (at)
49 Ending for a dean's address
50 Cable network with movies like "Sharktopus" and "Mansquito"
52 Least klutzy
54 Made a boo-boo
55 "I won't ___ it!"
56 Pending
58 Risqué communiqué
60 Ancient home to Priam's Treasure
62 Out of practice
63 Quick refresher
68 Visibly scornful
69 Cold that just won't go away?
70 Super-popular
71 Gooey spread
72 Where gymnast Simone Biles won four golds
73 One-celled organism
74 Enter unannounced, in a way
75 Photog's setting
76 Name of the girl on "Game of Thrones" who said "A girl has no name"
77 Spot between programs, e.g.
78 Beehive material
79 Annual May race, informally
84 One of three characters in "M*A*S*H"
85 Ones behind the scenes
87 Consider, with "on"
89 High-priority item
92 Vocalist's asset
93 Directly criticized on Twitter with an "@"
95 Gillette razor name
97 Literature Nobelist Bellow
99 Bit of faulty logic
100 Sandwich supposedly named after low-income New Orleans workers
101 Begins a triathlon
103 Like the clue for 103-Down?
104 Teased incessantly
105 Kind of cavity
106 Hard vehicle to park
109 Telenovela, e.g.
110 Some drink dispensers
111 Extend (out)
114 Org. with lots of money to waste?
115 Order member
116 "Ver-r-ry interesting!"

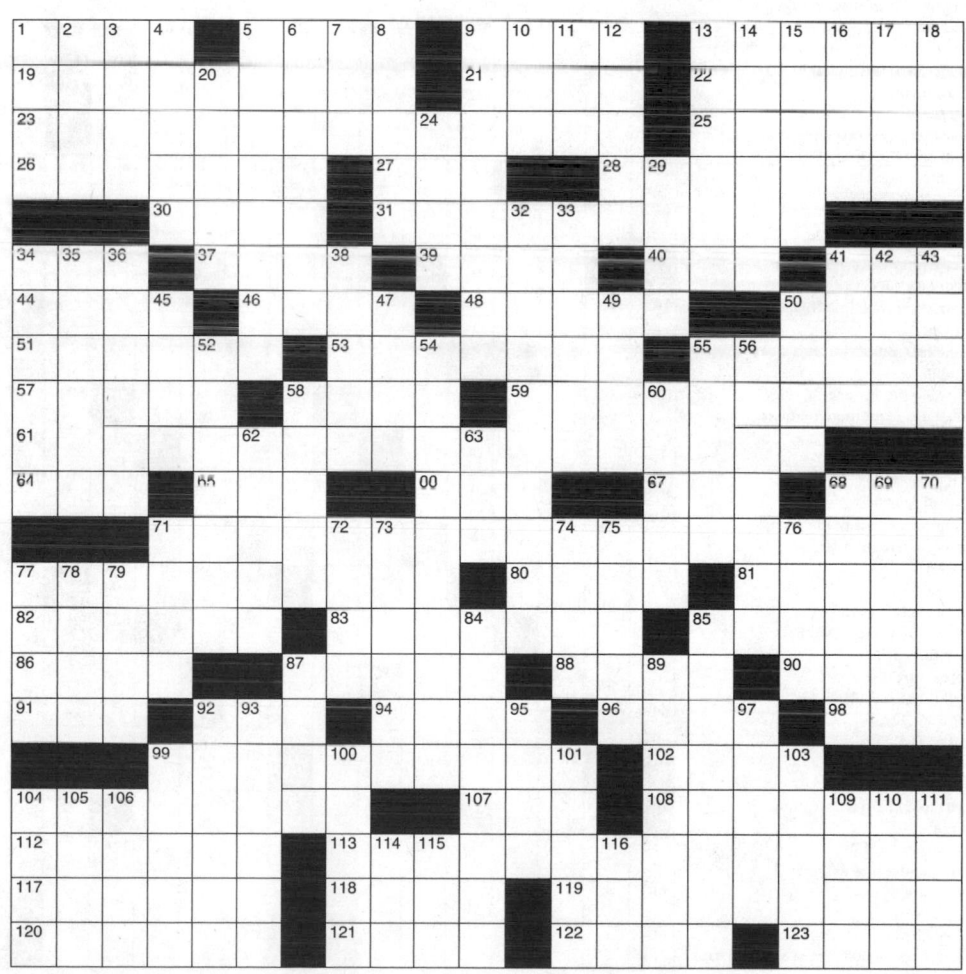

by Jeremy Newton

ACROSS

1 Advantage
6 Tony, e.g.
11 Plunder
18 Weighed in
20 Cow : herd :: ___ : troop
22 One with a discerning palate
23 C-Span?
25 Start brawling
26 Drink name suffix
27 Earth goddess
28 Going from point A to point B
30 Miss piggy?
31 Class acts?
33 Actress Gershon
34 Put back on the market, as real estate
37 Feel bad
38 Champagne name
40 P-trap?
44 G-force?
47 Union concern
48 Setting for C. S. Lewis's "The Lion, the Witch and the Wardrobe"
49 NPR host Shapiro
50 Words said in passing?
51 Deliberate betrayal
53 Butt
54 Father figures?
57 Guam or the U.S. Virgin Islands: Abbr.
59 Surgeons' professional org.
60 2012 Best Picture winner
61 Anastasia ___, protagonist of "Fifty Shades of Grey"
62 Make mention of
63 Top supporter?
64 Susan who portrayed the youngest child on "The Brady Bunch"
65 G-flat?
69 Deodorant type
72 Be short
73 Make music
74 Like Crater Lake, compared to any other U.S. lake
78 LeBron James in his N.B.A. debut, e.g.
79 Anheuser-Busch InBev's stock ticker symbol
80 Avocado pit, for one
81 Cause for revolution, perhaps
82 Escort's offering
83 "Yep, that happened!"
85 [And like magic . . . it's gone!]
87 First of ten?
88 Compete in pursuit of
90 Abbr. on a flight board
91 D-Con?
94 E-bond?
96 Conversely, in brief
97 Worry for a Great Depression bank
98 Ladybug, e.g.
99 Cereal box abbr.
101 Strike-out specialists?
105 See 106-Across
106 Out of 105-Across
108 Son of Zeus
109 Bird of legend
110 Fast-food chain with Famous Star burgers
113 C-sharp?
116 Black-and-white dessert
117 Take care of some personal baggage
118 Word after green or smoke
119 Things consumed for psychedelic trips
120 Men in black, say
121 Deck originally known as "carte da trionfi" ("cards of triumph")

DOWN

1 Kind of news often aired at 6 and 11 p.m.
2 Classical poem form
3 Drives home, say
4 French article
5 Floral archway
6 Pop group with a dedicated museum in Stockholm
7 "___ is mainly a catalog of blunders": Churchill
8 Means
9 "The Burghers of Calais" sculptor
10 Cruella de Vil, for one
11 Beat oneself up over, say
12 Mimic
13 Little beef
14 ___ kicks (ab exercise)
15 Pitch-correcting devices
16 Tribe of southern Montana
17 Range of knowledge
19 School administrator
21 French for "born"
24 Appalls
29 Aesthetically pretentious, informally
32 ___ card
33 Ruby, e.g.
35 Carter who portrayed Wonder Woman
36 Noncommittal response to "You coming?"
39 Load off one's mine?
41 Homonym of 39-Down
42 Trace of color
43 Wore
44 Gallivants (about)
45 Part of Q.E.D.
46 Ralph who founded the American Museum of Tort Law
51 Got ready (for)
52 Mosque leader
55 Launched
56 Product once advertised with the line "The splendor of your skin"
58 Datum for a chauffeur, for short
60 Take in, maybe
62 Supporter of Roosevelt's agenda
63 Actor whose breakout role came as a shirtless cowboy in "Thelma & Louise"
64 Singles
66 Hardly cheery
67 Hoppy request at happy hour
68 Enlighten
69 Wine barrel strip
70 Climate change, e.g.
71 Looked back on
75 Alphabetized, say
76 Wind farm output: Abbr.
77 Stink
79 Split open
80 Lorelei's lure
81 May honorees
83 Mad (at)
84 ___ Hill ('90s R&B group)
86 Decoration at el Palacio Real de Madrid
89 Where livestock eat
91 Mastered
92 Divide into three parts
93 Pattern that's hard to break
95 Nasty looks
100 Lento or allegro
102 Retreats
103 Loggers' competition
104 Track
105 Rap lyrics, in slang
107 Post-O.R. destination, often
108 Doesn't just assume
110 The Rockies, on scoreboards
111 Day ___
112 Sail fixed to a bowsprit
114 "Darn!," in Dortmund
115 Baseball's dead-ball ___ (around 1900–20)

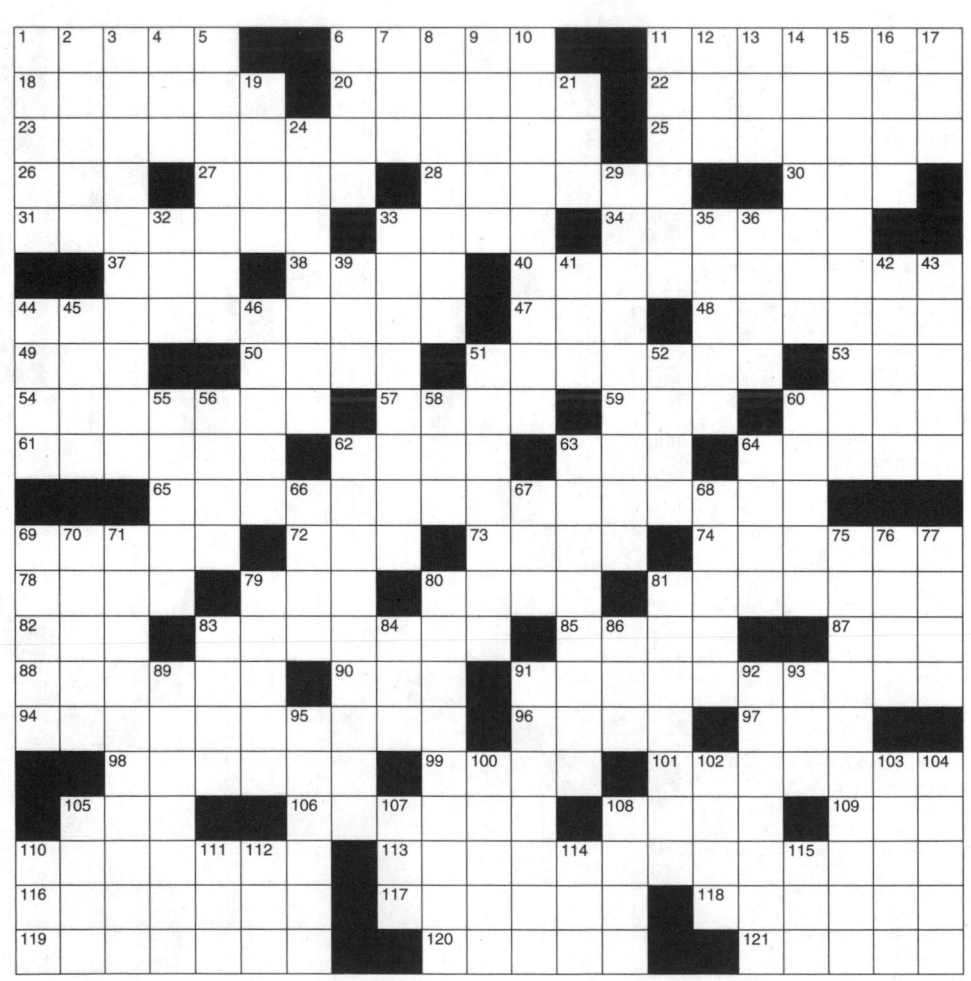

by Dan Schoenholz

ACROSS

1 Computer file, informally
4 Wound up on top?
8 Feels it the next day, say
13 Things served in prison
18 Shout at a Greek wedding
19 Country singer McKenna
20 "Whoa, settle down"
21 More than half of humanity
23 _____ state
24 Mom's comment to her child during prenatal bonding? [Frank Sinatra, 1954]
27 Hot state
28 Bishop's hat
29 They're used mostly on corners
30 What Mom is obligated to do as her due date approaches? [The Beatles, 1969]
36 "_____ the deal . . ."
37 Yes, in Yokohama
38 Bran material
39 Part of a drivetrain
40 The Renaissance, for one
42 Team _____ (late-night host's following)
43 Cancer fighter, for short
44 Henley Royal _____ (annual July event)
49 Mom's reaction to her first mild contractions? [John Cougar, 1982]
54 Midwife's advice to Mom in the delivery room? [Salt-N-Pepa, 1987]
55 Cause of wear and tear
56 Wanna-bees, e.g.?
57 _____ of Maine (toothpaste)
61 Sport whose participants call "Pull!"
62 Pet sound
63 Tennis star with the highest career winning percentage in singles matches (89.97%)
64 Stress test?
65 "Whoa boy, settle down"
66 Mom's remark as contractions grow stronger? [The Ramones, 1978]
70 Org. that delivers
73 Unenthusiastic
74 Went sniggling
75 Vaporize, say
78 Empire
80 Roughly
81 Be crazy about
82 Sappho's "_____ to Aphrodite"
83 Mom's reaction as delivery draws closer? [Usher, 2012]
85 Child's response to Mom's actions? [Diana Ross, 1980]
88 Briskly
90 Actress in eight Bond films
92 Like sea horses that give birth
93 Beast with a humped shoulder
94 Utah ski resort
95 Cable news anchor Cabrera
98 Prey for a formicivorous creature
99 Simple life?
103 Nurse's remark after Mom delivers the first twin? [Britney Spears, 1998]
108 Spanish archipelago, with "the"
110 Touches
111 Witty saying
112 Doctor's comment after Mom delivers the second twin? [The Who, 1965]
117 Director DuVernay
118 Quiet
119 Settle down, say
120 Pacific crop
121 Something you might gloss over
122 Mother's Day delivery
123 Apologetic remark during a breakup
124 Hang it up
125 Consult

DOWN

1 Kind of column
2 Venue for trill seekers?
3 TV reporter's entourage
4 Like snails' trails
5 Beginning that leads to a sum?
6 Singer with the 1968 hit "Think," familiarly
7 Nibble
8 "Oh no!"
9 X
10 Drink with the flavors Poppin' Lemonade and Grabbin' Grape
11 Wyoming's National _____ Refuge
12 Spill clumsily
13 "Bye!"
14 Food delivery route?
15 Piece of equipment for a biathlete
16 Oscar _____
17 Bad thing to do in class
22 Figure (out)
25 Aesthete's interest
26 Complete
31 Hilarious sort
32 U.S. city whose name is composed of two state abbreviations
33 Struck out
34 Poorly
35 Toothpaste option
41 Solicit sales (for)
42 Fishing bait
43 Keeps the beat with one's foot
45 "Who _____ you?"
46 Woman's name meaning "goddess"
47 Relations
48 J.D. holder: Abbr.
50 What a shaken soda bottle will do when uncapped
51 Capital of Fiji
52 Not dismissive of
53 Earn
57 Quaint contraction
58 Rule for trick-or-treaters
59 Improvised
60 Wind down?
64 Janet Yellen's former post, with "the"
66 Site of offshore banks?
67 Life, briefly
68 Garr of "Tootsie"
69 Setting for a scene in the Sistine Chapel
70 Major part of the night sky?
71 It's broken off
72 Olympic athlete category
75 Lions and tigers and bears
76 Raw footage?
77 Davidson of "S.N.L."
79 Stick in the refrigerator?
84 Sun follower?
85 Loving
86 Last name in shoes
87 Exam for some aspiring C.E.O.s
89 Go down the _____
90 Little bit
91 Ron who played Tarzan
95 Boundaries
96 Part of a Milky Way bar
97 Joint: Prefix
99 Book that's the source of the line "It is more blessed to give than to receive"
100 Host of HBO's "Real Time"
101 Año starter
102 Competes on a British cooking show
104 "Same here"
105 Lead-in to trumpet or drum
106 Legally foreclose
107 Tour de France stage
109 The 13th or 15th
113 Mobster's undoing
114 Places to take breaks, for short?
115 Inoculation location
116 Cleaning solution

by Brad Wiegmann

ACROSS

1 Dude, slangily
5 Toaster Swirlz brand
9 Country singer Haggard
14 Lhasa ____ (dog breed)
18 Metallic fabric
19 "____: Legacy" (sci-fi sequel)
20 Hymn of joy
21 Loud thudding sound
23 Shot in the dark
26 Get to the point?
27 Steps up?
28 Court plea, in brief
29 Winner's sign
30 Alternative to a blitz
31 False start?
33 Improved version of an existing product
37 -
38 Skipping syllables?
40 Reward for a big hit, say
41 Two-legged stand
43 Fix for a bald spot
46 -
48 Shock
51 Oscar-winning Hanks role of 1994
54 Tiny bits
56 By-way connection
58 Voice mail prompt
59 Hasbro game requiring increasingly quick reflexes
60 Tiny bit
61 Mensch
63 Meals with Haggadah readings
64 Award to wear
65 Real deal
66 -
68 Like cabernet sauvignon
69 Go over
71 Start of many Portuguese place names
73 Be angry
75 Suffix with age
78 Highly resistant elastomer
81 -
84 Skyscraper support
88 Like some ballots
90 Breakfast drink sans creamer
92 Ill-advised move
93 Intangible qualities
94 Do
95 Anonymous surname
96 Causes of pocket buzzes
97 Loud, sharp sound
98 Like Golden Raspberry-"winning" films
100 Detectives
103 -
104 Whispered sweet nothings
106 It's a sign
108 Unsmiling
110 Like some roller chains and ball bearings
112 -
116 Leaves zip for a tip
119 One given orders around the house
121 Tract of land
122 Nickname for the Wildcats of the Pac-12
124 Smut
126 Collection on Facebook
127 Shot in the dark
131 Three-time American League M.V.P. of the 1950s
132 Varsity
133 Hurt badly
134 Disneyland transport
135 Bill blockers
136 Ta-tas
137 Polishes off
138 Fore-and-aft-rigged sailboat with two masts

DOWN

1 Photo mishap
2 Amassed
3 Congregational chorus
4 Tools for landscapers
5 "You get the idea": Abbr.
6 Food found in some bars
7 Most-often-used
8 Net wt. of many pasta packages
9 Sticker stat
10 It's water under le pont
11 Teller of the third tale in "The Canterbury Tales"
12 Surgical tool
13 Like some casts
14 Makes a scene
15 "Hallelujah!"
16 Marvelous
17 ____-3
22 Slice and dice, say
24 Takes over (from)
25 More than just a talker
32 Indian lentil dish
34 "No info yet," on a schedule
35 Carefully avoid
36 Heating option
39 Composer Bruckner
42 -
43 Unlikely Oscar winners
44 Fighting
45 Tiny bit
47 G
49 Opening for a computer technician?
50 Pro fighter?
52 Swampy stretch
53 V.A. concern, for short
55 -
57 Phenomenon by which electrons radiate from a heated filament, so named for a famous observer
59 "You can't be a real country unless you have a ____ and an airline": Frank Zappa
61 Mil. leader
62 Catch
63 Arc on a music score
65 Investment goal
67 Trucker on a radio
70 Pitchfork-shaped letters
72 -
74 When the first "Peanuts" comic appeared
75 Apple on the teacher's desk?
76 Literature Nobelist Bellow
77 Innovation in push-ups
79 It can represent a folder
80 First offer?
82 "I touched your nose!" sound
83 Coffin frames
85 Squarish
86 A jokester might say "And the pot thickens" after one
87 One of the friends on "Friends"
89 Very easy living
91 -
94 French explorer who founded Detroit
96 Duty
98 According to
99 Bad P.R. for a celeb, maybe
101 Baseball announcer's cry
102 One doing a Spot check?
105 Whom the Secret Service dubbed Renegade and Renaissance
107 Mike who served as a Wyoming senator from 1997 to 2021
109 -
110 Longtime Swedish automaker
111 ____ Johnson Sirleaf, Africa's first elected female head of state
113 Mammal found in the Andean cloud forest
114 Utterly lost
115 "I'm baffled"
117 Botanist's study
118 A sucker for milkshakes, say
120 -
123 ESPNU covers its games
125 Web file format, for short
128 The natural order of the universe
129 Chats over Twitter, briefly
130 Grp. mobilized by a 911 call

by Joe DiPietro

ACROSS

1. Supply for an ultimate Frisbee team
6. 2019 box-office flop described by one critic as "Les Meowsérables"
10. Picks the brain of
14. Extemporizes
19. "Why should ____?"
20. Feeling tender
21. Apartment, in real estate lingo
22. How spring rolls are cooked
23. Oscar-winning actress born Mary Louise
24. One side of a 2015 nuclear agreement
25. It's irreversible
26. University of Florida athlete
27. "That was great!" / "No, it stunk!"
31. Setting for Jo Nesbo's best-selling crime novels
32. They have stems and white heads
33. Mild, light-colored cigars
36. Have because of
38. Drive (from)
39. Recurring pain?
42. Route 70 in {Route 10, Route 95, Route 101, Route 70, Route 25}
45. Snitch
47. Hit film set aboard the spaceship Nostromo
48. Cereal grain
49. Fastener that leaves a flush surface
51. Modern party planning tool
52. Lofty
53. Collector's item
55. Word after combat or cowboy
58. What two Vikings have explored
59. Royal staff
61. Brainy sort
64. Fruits often used in sushi
66. Cattle in [cattle / pigs]
69. Burrito condiment
73. Vodka mixer
74. Hopeless predicament
79. Birthstone for Hillary Clinton, Kamala Harris and Alexandria Ocasio-Cortez
80. Toffee bar brand
82. What the nose knows
84. Major move, for short
85. ". . . unless you disagree"
87. Naturally occurring hexagonal crystals
90. "Dames at ____" (Broadway musical)
91. Was fed up
92. Comics character with the dog Daisy
95. Bear × tiger
98. "Billions" airer, for short
99. Et ____
101. Hamilton, to Burr
102. Green cards, informally
103. Offering to a houseguest
105. Hardly any
106. Car in {plane, car, train, horse, car, car, train}
113. Pong company
114. Shakespeare character who inquires "Are your doors lock'd?"
115. Greet grandly
116. Provide funding for
118. Was accepted
119. ____ mess, English dessert of berries, meringue and whipped cream
120. Its merchandise often comes with pictorial instructions
121. "Set Fire to the Rain" singer
122. Part of a golf club
123. Mathematician Descartes
124. Credit application figs.
125. PC platform popular in the '80s

DOWN

1. Grow faint
2. Coffee order specification
3. Garment whose name sounds like an apology
4. Sign of distress
5. Like many wildflower seeds
6. Boutros Boutros-Ghali's home city
7. Nearly 5,000 square yards
8. Comparative word
9. Matched up
10. What has interest in a car?
11. Sound of disdain
12. Long, loose robe
13. Leave momentarily
14. Brief evocative account
15. Diarist Nin
16. "Hello ____" (old cellphone ad line)
17. Subatomic particle
18. Some nice cameras, for short
28. Wife of Albert Einstein
29. Wipe out, slangily
30. "____ deal"
33. Has a tête-à-tête
34. Pale pinkish purple
35. Light-footed
36. Muhammad's father-in-law
37. Cause of a smudge
39. First work read in Columbia's Literature Humanities course
40. Like some news coverage
41. Squeeze
43. "Nice going!"
44. Crux of the matter
46. Rating for risqué shows
50. ____-in-the-hole (British dish)
53. Whale constellation
54. Massive ref. books
56. Have things in common
57. Like music that uses conventional keys and harmony
60. Org. whose website has a "What Can I Bring?" section
62. Summer Olympics host before Tokyo
63. They may come in a boxed set
65. Summer hrs. in Iowa
67. Co. captains?
68. First line of a Seuss classic
69. Parts of cars and stoves
70. High-profile interviewer of Harry and Meghan
71. Style of "Roxanne" in "Moulin Rouge!"
72. Drawn-out
75. Easterlies
76. Done again
77. Chef Waters who pioneered the organic food movement
78. Mrs. ____, "Beauty and the Beast" character
81. Kind of vaccine used against Covid
83. Slippery
86. Partially
88. Two-person meeting
89. Certain sots
91. Words often replaced when singing "Take Me Out to the Ball Game"
93. Disney character who says "Some people are worth melting for"
94. Less sportsmanlike
96. Where the King lived
97. Tennis's Nadal, familiarly
100. Make sparkling
103. Font flourish
104. Tease
105. Cartographic collection
106. In Touch and Out, for two
107. Texter's "Then again . . ."
108. Cloud contents
109. Trees under which truffles might grow
110. "De ____" (response to "Merci")
111. Took too much, for short
112. ____ contendere
117. ____ Moore, antipoverty entrepreneur of the Robin Hood Foundation

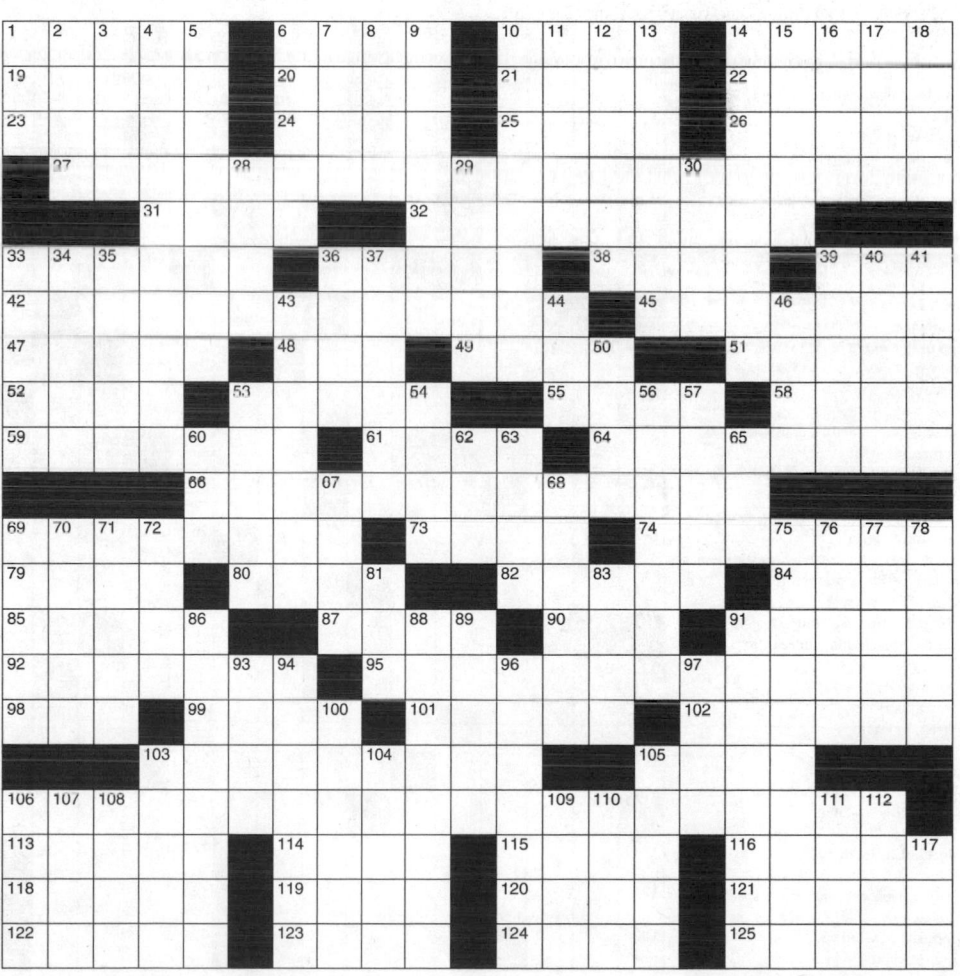

by Jennifer Nebergall

ACROSS

1 Gilda of the original "S.N.L." cast
7 They may need to be cut off
11 Ways of making ends meet?
16 Degree in design, for short
19 Cow's-milk cheese that's often grated
20 Sweet 16 org.
21 Honor named for a Greek goddess
23 Site of a lighthouse that was one of the Seven Wonders of the Ancient World
24 "____ pass"
25 Where snow leopards and blue sheep roam
26 King of a nursery rhyme
27 Went to bat (for)
30 Test versions
31 Good fashion sense, in modern slang
32 Appear
33 Features of some indoor arenas
35 Theater curtain material
37 Fired off, say
38 Grind
40 Money of the Philippines
42 Follow
43 One giving a khutbah sermon
46 Smaller alternative to a Quarter Pounder
48 Chicago team, in old "S.N.L." sketches
50 Ski lodge mugful
54 Fraternity letter
55 King of ancient Israel
56 Comic actress Gasteyer
57 Left, cutesily
60 Great Lakes nation
64 Pickup line?
65 Like the columns of the Lincoln Memorial
66 Cures
68 "____ we good?"
69 King of ancient Egypt
71 Tattoo artist, so to speak
73 Org. with a complex code
74 "Happy Days" network
75 Beach Boys song set to the tune of Chuck Berry's "Sweet Little Sixteen"
78 King of myth
80 4G letters
81 ____ pace
82 Not doing so hot
86 F–, e.g.
87 Discourage
89 Waze way: Abbr.
90 Piece of plastic with a gladiator pictured on it
92 Physics demonstration often done from the roof of a school
95 ____-Briggs Type Indicator (popular personality test)
97 "I will prevent disease whenever I can, for prevention is preferable to cure," e.g.
98 King of Shakespeare
99 "Keep Austin ____" (city slogan)
101 Annual presidential address, for short
103 Partner
107 "No worries"
109 "Bon appétit!"
111 Christ, to Bach
113 Place
114 Chimney channels
116 Warning on presents stashed in the closet
118 King of Skull Island
119 "Huddle up!"
121 Actress Elisabeth
122 When: Sp.
124 Early adolescent years, so to speak
125 Engage
126 Opposite of wind up
127 Infinitesimal
128 Toys with much assembly required
129 Travel brochure listings
130 Named

DOWN

1 Some hip-hop collectibles
2 On dry land
3 Join a conference call, say
4 Quick to fall asleep, in a way
5 Sense of self
6 Día de San Valentín gifts
7 Tearfully complain
8 Tabloid nickname for mother Nadya Suleman
9 Powder in the powder room
10 Course with greens
11 Machiavellian sort
12 Omits
13 Objective
14 Gateway city to Utah's Arches National Park
15 Some after-Christmas announcements
16 Home to about one in five Californians
17 Long-running sitcom set in Seattle
18 Them's the breaks!
22 Spent some time on YouTube, say
28 Nobel Peace Prize recipient who wrote "No Future Without Forgiveness"
29 Sought-after position
34 Pop
36 G.P.s, e.g.
39 City about 25 miles SE of Chicago, IL
41 ____-faire (social adeptness)
44 Level the playing field?
45 Put one past
47 One ending for a classic board game—another of which (when a player resigns) is represented visually six times in this puzzle
49 Tough spots
50 Bother incessantly
51 Scoring win after win
52 Mowry who starred alongside her twin Tia in the '90s sitcom "Sister, Sister"
53 ____ Z
55 Cubs' place to play home games
58 Wilson who wrote the lyrics to 75-Across
59 Play areas
61 The "Bel Paese," to locals
62 Borrower
63 Scale
67 Quintessentially cowardly
69 Mosaic maker
70 Remove from under the seat in front of you, say
72 Ducks known for their soft down feathers
76 Tinker (with)
77 Yes or no follower
79 "I've got it!"
83 Rob ____, British comedian and TV personality
84 Samosa tidbit
85 Part of an office phone no.
88 Tool for a duel
91 Sidewalk drawings
92 One of the Manning brothers
93 Disentangle oneself
94 Main source of energy?
95 Breakout 1993 single for Counting Crows
96 Stay awhile
100 Only color of the rainbow not seen on the L.G.B.T. pride flag
102 Portable dwellings
104 Richie with the #1 hit "All Night Long"
105 Borrower
106 Potato cultivar that was developed in Ontario, despite its name
108 Pelvic exercise
110 Nintendo dino
112 Like diamonds from a mine
115 Father
117 Weak, as a case
119 "Oh, and another thing . . . ," for short
120 Graffiti signature
123 College, to a Brit

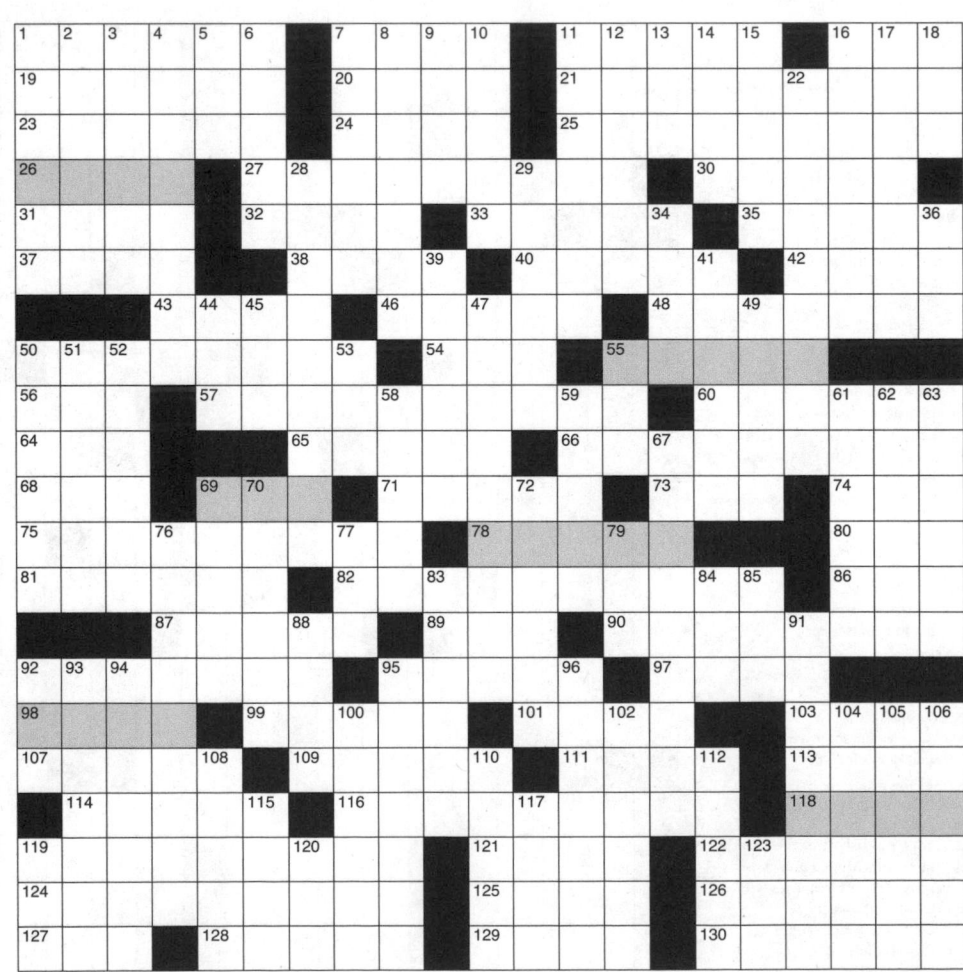

by Adam Wagner

ACROSS

1 Earners of credits
7 One selling airtime, informally
12 Emulates a chipmunk, say
20 Like a beaming smile
22 Go out to get some juice?
23 Pork-cutting option
24 Ingredient in an Alabama slammer
25 Revise
26 Word with "two" or "three" to describe a sloth
27 Small kitchen knife
29 Abstract artist Mondrian
30 Thomas Hardy title character
31 Bottom part
32 Traveled like Charon
34 Schedule keeper: Abbr.
35 One for whom underwear is pants
36 "Wait . . . what did you just say?!"
37 Fuse
39 Three-dimensional
43 "Have You Never Been ____," #1 album for Olivia Newton-John
44 Origami designs thought to bring good fortune
45 One receiving a congratulatory email from eBay
47 Helps secure a loan
48 Recovery center
49 Refused to share
50 Scratch
51 Tablet taken before going to bed, maybe
52 Portrayer of Marvel's Hawkeye
53 Left the harbor
57 Rapper who co-founded Mass Appeal Records
58 Green liqueur
59 Dinosaur of kids' TV
60 It's nothing
61 Host
63 Signaled slyly
64 ____ Top (low-cal ice cream brand)
65 Camaro, for one
66 As one
67 Birth day presence?
68 "All in the Family" subject
71 "Don't dwell on the past"
73 Families-and-friends support group
74 Negotiate
75 Some diners . . . and donors
76 Provide a password
77 Was rife (with)
78 Matthew of "The Americans"
79 Save for later, in a way
80 Skewered
82 Like Queen Anne's lace?
83 Traditional accounts
87 Onetime hair removal brand
89 Let out or take in
90 Stage name for hip-hop's Sandra Denton
91 It's all the rage
92 "What-EVER" reactions
94 Post-distraction segue
97 Light-filled room
98 Way, way off
99 Hitchcock's forte
100 Clearing
101 Like bison vis-à-vis beef

DOWN

1 Key for Chopin's "Heroic" Polonaise
2 It might be organized
3 Foundation options
4 Eclipses and comets, perhaps
5 Joy of MSNBC
6 Parked it, so to speak
7 Maximally
8 Pacific birds?
9 Bit of thatching
10 Take sides?
11 Catapulted, say
12 Bird much seen in cities
13 Reply to a ring
14 Not in the dark
15 Adriatique, e.g.
16 Task for a sous-chef
17 Like sirens
18 Be considered perfect
19 More than just clean
21 Shopping in order to improve one's mood
28 Fire
31 They might be wireless
32 Desktop icon
33 Surname of Harry Potter's adoptive family
35 Pop star nickname, with "the"
36 Bet strategically
38 Mythical nymph
39 Reliquary
40 Inspiration for the Frisbee
41 Floored
42 Longtime Ohio State basketball coach Matta
43 Filet ____
44 Stopped smoking?
46 Half of a notorious outlaw duo
47 Added to the language
50 First little piggy's destination
52 Key hit with a pinkie
53 It helps take the edge off
54 Just going through the motions
55 Complete, as a crossword
56 Creations for Mardi Gras
58 Particles composed of two up quarks and one down quark
59 Did a TV marathon, say
62 Start of some no-frills brand names
63 In a lather, with "up"
64 Happy ____
66 Come back around
67 Bits of hijinks?
68 What Mr. Clean, Captain Picard and Michael Jordan have in common
69 Thought expressed in American Sign Language by extending the pinkie, thumb and index finger
70 Compilations of funny film faux pas
71 Soeur's sibling
72 Warehouse loading areas
74 *shrug*
77 "We want all the juicy details!"
78 Maintain, in a way, as a highway
81 Michael whose initials match those of his famous comedy troupe
82 Cut through
83 "____ and Majnun" (Arabic story that inspired a Clapton hit)
84 One of the "holy trinity" ingredients in Cajun cuisine
85 Advice to one in a lather?
86 Very inclined (to)
88 Sting, perhaps
90 Taverna staple
91 Spice related to nutmeg
93 Argentite, e.g.
95 Fifth of eight
96 Show filmed at Rockefeller Ctr.

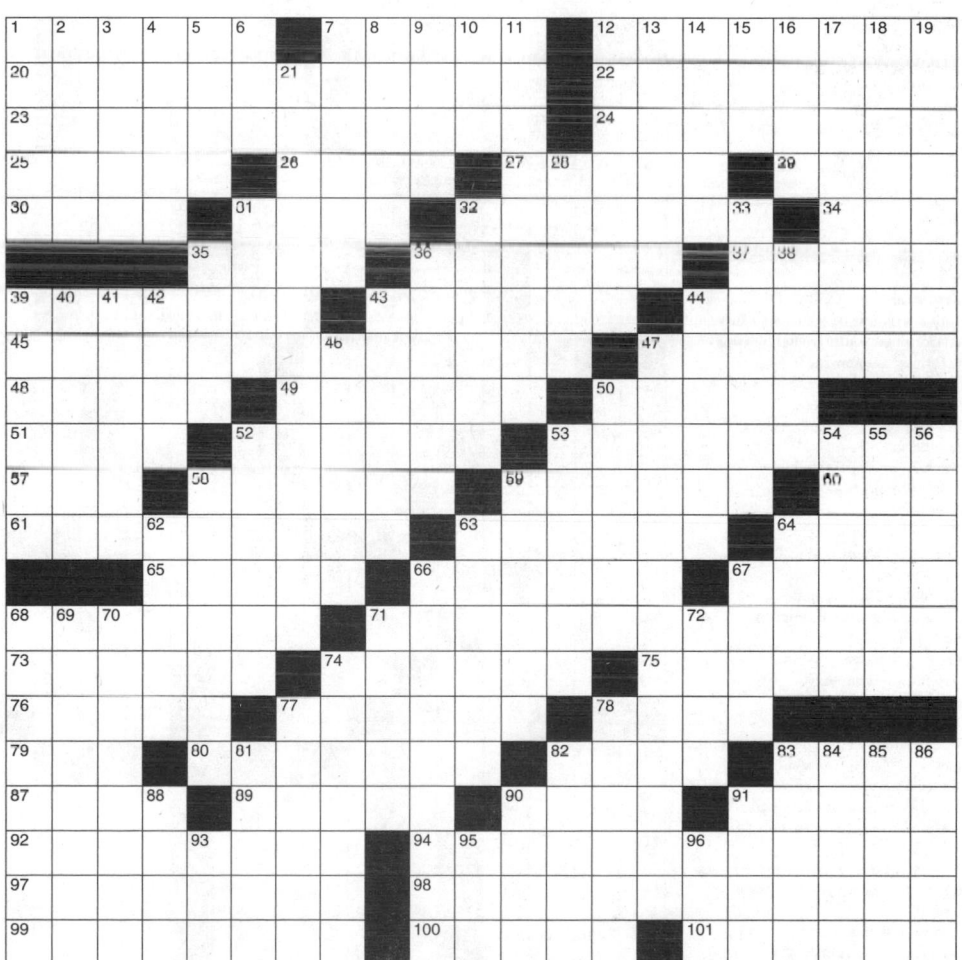

by Robyn Weintraub

ACROSS

1 Writer who created Oz
5 "Obviously," in slang
10 First word of "A Visit From St. Nicholas"
14 ". . . with possibly direr consequences"
17 ___ Berliner, pioneer in phonograph records
18 Lex Luthor, to Superman
22 Raised
23 Bit of asparagus
24 Alternately
25 Lines up
26 Agitated
29 Pricey
30 M.L.B. team with a big "W" in its logo
31 Rx order
32 "Revolution," to "Hey Jude"
34 Space-scanning org.
35 It may be bitter
36 Like bees
37 Not ___ (mediocre)
39 Clear weeds, in a way
40 Part "missing" from p.s.i.
41 Mystery writer Deighton
42 Words cried after "Go"
46 Abbr. after a price in a Craigslist ad
47 Lt.'s inferior
48 Decidedly
51 Québec's ___ St.-Jean
52 Soft drink since 1905
54 Young hombre
56 Biblical verb ending
57 Instruments for Israel Kamakawiwo'ole
60 German auto since 1899
61 "That'll teach you!"
62 Pigeon English?
63 Basketball champions' "trophy"
64 Gillette brand
65 Leader of the house?
67 "Love is love," e.g.
70 Pallid
71 Outlets, e.g.
73 Something that might lengthen a sentence?
74 Moneybags
75 High school hurdle whose first two letters, phonetically, sound like one of its former components
76 Like all the answers with pairs of circled letters, punnily
81 Programming pioneer Lovelace
82 Seasons in Québec
84 15th birthday celebration
85 Tomtit is another name for it
86 Talks up
88 Classical Icelandic literary work
89 Title letters chanted in a 2011 Katy Perry hit
90 Oldsmobile Cutlass model
91 Financial org. once deemed "too big to fail"
93 Newfoundland, e.g.: Abbr.
94 Serpentine swimmer
95 Root beer brand
96 Veterans
100 Range within which you can answer the question "Can you hear me now?"
104 Six-time winner of the N.H.L.'s Art Ross Trophy, born in Saskatchewan
108 "24" and "Suits" actress, born in Halifax
111 Princess who says "Why, you stuck-up, half-witted, scruffy-looking nerf herder!"
112 Dish served on a skewer
113 Congresswoman Omar
114 Actress Lena
115 Suppliers of the milk for Roquefort cheese

116 Singer Mary J. ___
117 Moves quickly and lightly
118 Not only that
119 Rehearsal, e.g., in slang
120 Approvals
121 You can believe it
122 "Likewise"

DOWN

1 Pears with a sweet-spiced flavor
2 Part of B.A.
3 Deploy
4 Alberta city named for an eagle-feather headdress
5 Like some birds or dolls
6 Excite
7 Rank
8 Stops talking, with "up"
9 Mettle that may merit a medal
10 Two-player game invented in Toronto
11 Sardonic
12 ___ of Parliament
13 Stops talking, with "up"
14 "Nice burn!"
15 Battle ___
16 Seasonal destination near Quebec City
19 Program introduced by the Trudeau government in 1984, colloquially
20 Approximate weight of the Liberty Bell
21 Spots
27 Advocacy grp. that filed for bankruptcy in 2021
28 Words at an unveiling?
31 Cry after an award is announced
33 Woman's short hairstyle
36 Portrayer of Senator Vinick on "The West Wing"
38 Level or bevel
43 Like some outlets
44 Desert planet of "Star Wars"
45 Be batty, in a way?
49 Canuck, e.g., for short
50 Capital of Qatar
52 Like bells in carillons
53 Part of L.C.D.
54 Some salon supplies
55 Like Rochester and Syracuse, but not New York City
58 Novel convenience?
59 Band whose 1999 hit "Smooth" spent 12 weeks at #1
66 Sleep stage
68 Overturns
69 "Very high," on a fire danger scale
70 Iowa Cubs baseball classification
72 Et ___ (footnote abbr.)
74 Federal regulatory org.

77 Rose or lilac
78 "Where ___ go wrong?"
79 Novelist Gaiman
80 Pound sound
83 Thrown together
85 They might help with changing your locks
87 One with a phony personality?
90 Snake oil, purportedly
92 Passes
95 Central route thru town
96 Leers at
97 Frederick who composed "Camelot"
98 Helps a dish washer, say
99 One source of oil
100 Cheer
101 Shout, informally
102 ___ Wars, conflicts of 1839–42 and 1856–60
103 It may be perfect or simple, but not both
105 Big elevator maker
106 $15/hour, e.g.
107 What most spiders have eight of
108 Hitchhiker's need
109 International fashion magazine
110 Climb, as a rope

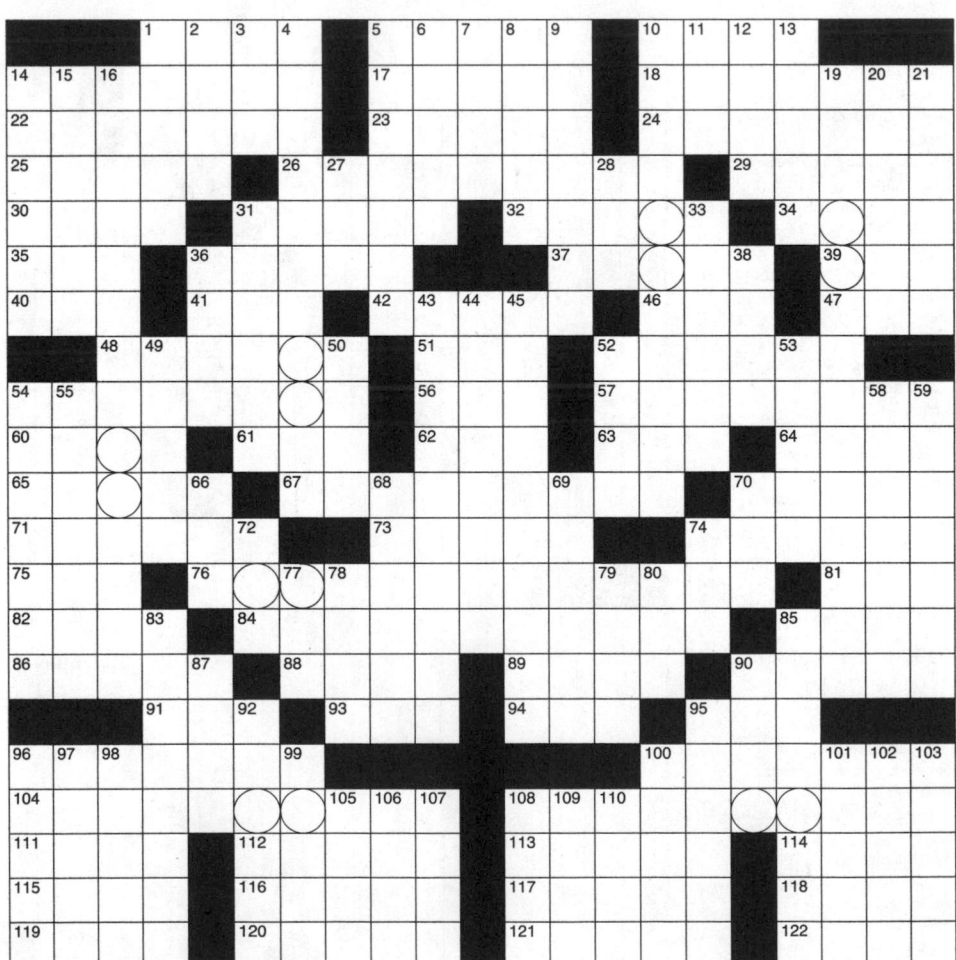

by Stephen McCarthy

ACROSS

1 Home for The Devil
6 Fairy tale villain
10 Ballet-inspired fitness method
15 Web designer's code
19 Dream interrupter, maybe
20 Pitcher Hershiser
21 They might dog a dog
22 "___ there!"
23 Prisoner accidentally causes a power outage?
26 Police unit, informally
27 "Hoo boy!"
28 "Your guess is as good as mine"
29 Small songbirds
30 In a manner of speaking
31 Kind
33 Year, in Brazil
34 Cherokee and Navajo
37 Southern university beefs up campus security?
42 Unlike bread on Passover
45 Pierce-Arrow competitor
46 Popular Hyundai
47 "O mio babbino caro," e.g.
48 Key part: Abbr.
50 Keenness of judgment
53 Chinese zodiac animal
54 Fellow imposes a strict palm fruit regimen?
59 Something that can be tried or cracked
60 Dead giveaway?
61 Put away some groceries?
62 ___ school
63 Convenient transport through urban traffic
64 Go bad
65 One seeing things with a critical eye?
67 ___ cannon (sci-fi weapon)
68 Good spice to add to guacamole (try it!)
71 Wizard of ___ (nickname for a good massage therapist)
72 U.F.C. fighting style
73 Heretics flout them
77 Early Ron Howard role
78 Actress de Armas writes "Mr. Gas" and "Ms. Rag"?
82 World's best-selling musical artists of 2020
83 Target of a pop-up blocker
84 Financial planning option, for short
85 Like the verse "Roses are red, violets are blue . . . ," in brief
86 Body of water that's home to the world's largest marine reserve
88 The Cougars of the N.C.A.A.
91 New York has 28 of them
94 Smartphone advises on poker bets?
98 High-hat attitude
99 "Told you so"
100 Off-road ride, for short
101 Org. whose plans are up in the air?
104 Georgia-based insurance giant
106 Unnamed somebody
109 Ones making you duck down?
111 Kinks song that Weird Al Yankovic parodied as "Yoda"
112 Doctor acquires antibiotics?
115 A short one by Ogden Nash reads "Parsley / is gharsley"
116 Macabre illustrator Edward
117 One kind of plastic
118 Indian wedding adornment
119 Even ___
120 Connecticut-based insurance giant
121 Break
122 Work from Roxane Gay or Jia Tolentino

DOWN

1 Snacks from some trucks
2 Honolulu's ___ Stadium
3 Sought feedback from
4 Willy, in "Free Willy"
5 Telecom with a pink logo
6 Reaction to a stomach punch
7 Chow
8 Add new caulking to
9 Roosevelt credited with saying "No one can make you feel inferior without your consent"
10 Closest of pals, for short
11 Hillary Clinton vis-à-vis Wellesley College
12 Move to a new table, maybe
13 Hip-hop duo ___ Sremmurd
14 What ". . ." may represent
15 José Martí, by birth
16 Social media pic designed to attract sexual attention
17 False
18 Some strong solutions
24 DuPont patent of 1938
25 Skip it
29 Boston airport
32 Work in the kitchen?
35 Abounded (with)
36 St. Kitts, St. Lucia and St. Vincent
37 Saint on the big screen
38 Pulitzer winner ___ St. Vincent Millay
39 Spur
40 Shake an Etch A Sketch, e.g.
41 Full
42 How kids might describe dad jokes
43 Important stretches
44 "___ Too Proud" (hit musical about the Temptations)
49 Visits overnight
51 Ingredient in a Negroni
52 Sporty trucks, in brief
55 Lots
56 Lets hit it!
57 What ". . ." may represent
58 ___ March
59 Word that appears with confetti when texted on an iPhone
63 Big name in synthesizers
65 Cardamom-spiced brew
66 !!!
67 They may be checked at the door
68 Yoga pose with an arched back
69 "High-five!"
70 Like fuschia and turquiose
71 Actor Aziz
74 Spanish hand
75 Spanish love
76 Application figs.
78 Practiced
79 Birds' bills
80 What an integral can be used to calculate
81 One of the Obamas
83 Jellied garnish
87 Low bows
89 Kind of question
90 Old wheels
92 ___ Park, Colo.
93 Raw deal from a restaurant?
95 Categorize
96 "There's no one on me!"
97 Document with two accents
101 Water clover and adder's-tongue
102 Fight setting
103 Purity test
104 Popular dog 105-Down
105 See 104-Down
107 Daughter of Ned Stark on "Game of Thrones"
108 Smelt things?
110 Payment often made around January 1
112 Tour grp.
113 Little eggs
114 Business card abbr.

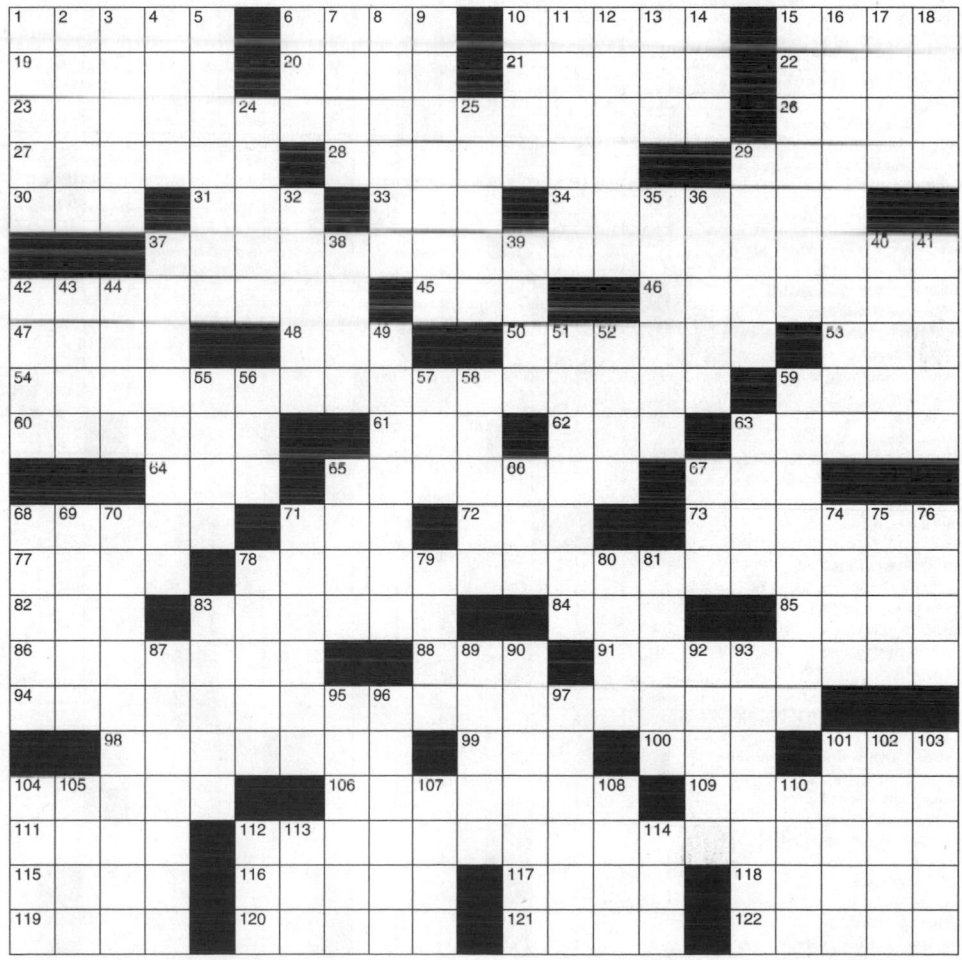

by Michael Lieberman

ACROSS

1 Rackets
6 Spruce or fir
15 Japanese city that shares its name with a dog breed
20 Home to the Ho Chi Minh Mausoleum
21 Homemade headgear for pretend pirates
22 Conducted, as a campaign
23 Undo, legally
24 Highly specialized knowledge
25 Color whose name is derived from "lapis lazuli"
26 Frequent comics collaborator with Jack Kirby
28 Belief
29 Hubbubs
31 "See? I knew what I was talking about!"
32 Gives an edge
33 Indignant denial
34 Bozo
35 "I 30-Down the fool!" speaker
37 GPS suggestion: Abbr.
38 What might follow you
39 1966 Donovan hit
43 Sinatra, to fans
47 Band whose "Gold: Greatest Hits" has sold over 30 million copies
50 Raised a false alarm
52 Tennis's Nadal, informally
56 Fruit with crimson-colored flesh
59 Guest feature?
60 Popular folk rock duo
62 Place for a canal or a kernel
63 1968 self-titled folk album
65 A.L. West team, on scoreboards
66 Rubik with a cube
68 Ice cream holder
69 Cal's game-winning kickoff return against Stanford in 1982, familiarly
71 World's deepest river
73 Little tasks that crop up
75 Wood shop item
77 Investigate, à la Sherlock Holmes
79 Wunderkinder
82 Implement for an Amish driver
86 Features of classic cars
87 It's covered in paint in the Sherwin-Williams logo
89 Oscar-winning song from "Slumdog Millionaire"
90 "Likewise"
91 Media watchdog agcy.
92 "Strange Magic" band, for short
93 Medium for Kehinde Wiley's "President Barack Obama"
94 Took a load off
95 Mars
100 Harmful bits of sunlight
105 Remove calcium deposits from
106 Sharp shooter, for short?
108 Harder to grasp
109 Changes by degrees
111 Whole bunch
112 You might cry if you slice it
115 Word rhymed with "ami" by Lafayette in "Hamilton"
116 Like Merriam-Webster's inclusion of the word "irregardless," originally
119 College admissions fig.
120 Delta hub, on luggage tags
121 Birth control option, briefly
122 In the blink of ___
123 Deli or bar order
124 Stags or bucks
125 Biblical possessive
126 Alcoholic's affliction, briefly
127 Complicated, as a relationship
128 Retired flier, for short
129 Explosive stuff

DOWN

1 California-based soft drink company
2 Divisions of long poems
3 Historical records
4 Place for a pitcher
5 "I'm such a dummy!"
6 Olympic poker?
7 Military hospitals, briefly
8 Period of history
9 Back in
10 Fresh, in a sense
11 A one and a two
12 Bursts in on
13 And the rest, for short
14 Twin in Genesis
15 Prizewinner
16 Instrument often played for comedic effect
17 Tennessee Williams's "The Night of the ___"
18 Babysitter's handful
19 "___ Fideles"
27 ___ Simmons, real name of the late rapper DMX
30 See 35-Across
36 Affectionate attention, briefly
37 One enforcing traveling rules
39 Kind of jacket
40 "Ish"
41 Xbox 360 competitor
42 Chicken
43 Total domination, in gamer-speak
44 Whole bunch
45 Racy
46 Polite form of address similar to "Mr." or "Ms."
47 Criminally aid
48 Yawn-inducing
49 Make yawn
51 Campus leader
53 With the bow, musically
54 Bungle
55 Vipers with upturned snouts
57 Part of a religious title that means "ocean"
58 Southern California county
60 "Mood ___" (Duke Ellington classic)
61 Quit drinking
64 Golf's ___ Ko, youngest golfer to be ranked #1
67 In draft form
70 High degrees, for short
71 Setting for many a Super Mario Bros. level
72 Temporarily out
74 Pesach observers
76 Most peaceful
78 Groups of bees?
79 "You can't expect me to believe that!"
80 Laughable
81 Typical way to take a multivitamin
83 Is legally entitled
84 "It's a possibility for me"
85 Family members that get talked down to?
88 Kind of massage
89 Travels
96 ___ River, part of the Texas/Oklahoma border
97 Even-tempered
98 Skedaddled
99 They might be made after a fight
101 Runs again
102 Without fail
103 State flower of Illinois or New Jersey
104 ___ Faire (event with jousting, for short)
107 Is mad about
109 Source of the milk for chèvre cheese
110 The "R" of R.B.G.
113 Ready for business
114 Condé ___
117 What might make a ewe turn
118 Spanish monarch

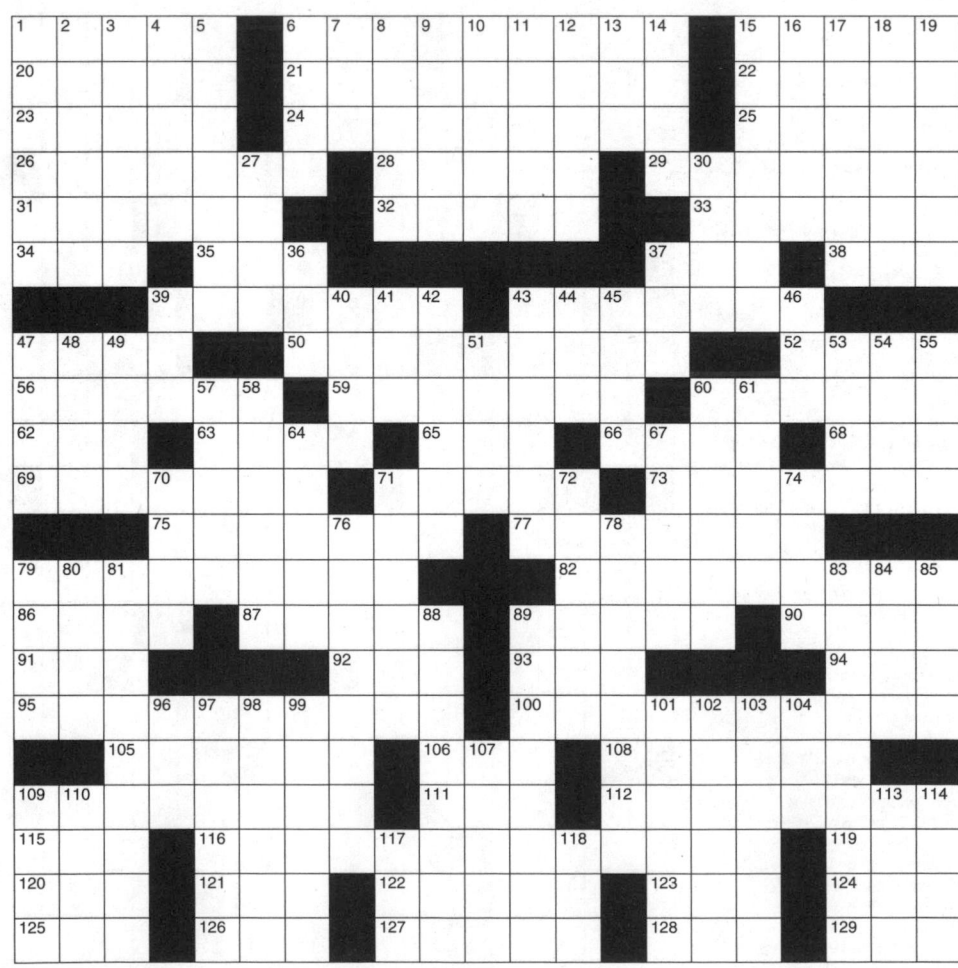

by Ross Trudeau and Lindsey Hobbs

ACROSS

1 Like "American Pie," "American Psycho" and "American Beauty"
7 Proposed portrait for the $20 bill
13 Like sports fans who paint their faces, say
18 Drink with tapioca pearls
19 Peach relative
21 Run off (with)
22 Upbeat sentry's emotion?
24 Many, informally
25 Regarding
26 More, on a music score
27 Auspice
28 King's collaborator on the Grammy-winning blues album "Riding With the King"
30 Take the next step in an online relationship
31 Actress Blanchett
33 Scotland's ___ Lomond
35 Winter Olympics maneuver
36 Some H.S. yearbook staff
37 Bacteriologist's emotion upon a new discovery?
40 Jess's best friend on TV's "New Girl"
43 Glib
44 Maker of Regenerist skin cream
45 Any member of BTS, e.g.
47 Pellet shooter
50 What Kit Kat bars come in
51 "I'm glad to hear it"
53 It's full of hot air
54 Mongolian shelters
55 Novice window-washer's emotion?
58 Scathing review
59 Complete set of showbiz awards, for short
60 Clownish
61 Really play that saxophone
62 Egypt's Sadat
64 Powerhouse in international men's ice hockey
66 Haul away
67 Art gallery tour leader
68 #46
69 Modern reading option . . . or where to read it?
71 ___ Building, Boston's first skyscraper
73 Apt anagram of GIFT
75 Brownish-gray
76 Jester's emotion after the king's laughter?
79 Like Ignatius J. Reilly in "A Confederacy of Dunces"
80 English-speaking
82 A fan of
83 Dionysian ritual
84 Ashleigh ___, 2019 French Open champion
85 Apathetic
87 Duchess of ___ (Goya model)
88 One-named winner of the 2021 Grammy for Song of the Year
89 Notation on a party invite
90 Wild horse's emotion?
94 Huge tub
97 One who's able to rattle off digits of pi, perhaps
99 Wine: Prefix
100 Like Eeyore
101 Hard-to-please type
102 Result of a snow day
105 Eddie Murphy's org. in "48 Hrs."
107 Lifelike video game, for short
108 A mighty long time
109 + symbols, in typography
110 Cat's emotion while sitting in its human's lap?
114 Stuck
115 Brazilian beach made famous in song
116 Coming or going
117 Hits the paper airplane icon, perhaps
118 PC support group
119 Blocks

DOWN

1 Fired up
2 Quiets down
3 Wheel of Fortune's place
4 Airport info, for short
5 Lesser-known song
6 Kind of tire
7 Pay with a chip-based credit card, perhaps
8 As much as
9 Actor Wilford of "The Natural"
10 Old-style copies
11 Easy as pie
12 Column of boxes on a questionnaire
13 "Chill out!"
14 Hair loss
15 Evil genie's emotion?
16 ___ facto
17 "MacGyver" actor Richard ___ Anderson
18 Subpar athletic effort
20 Cable option for film buffs
23 Relentlessly competitive
29 Death Valley was once one
32 The Gettysburg Address, e.g.
34 Massage therapist's substance
37 Some recyclables
38 Jumping the gun
39 Turn over
41 One might take you in
42 Gusto
43 Finished a hole
46 Justin Timberlake's former group
47 When said three times, hit song for 46-Down
48 Famous toon with a Brooklyn accent
49 Farmer's emotion during a dry season?
50 As compared to
51 Eat (at)
52 Commercial lead-in to Clean
56 Responded to the alarm
57 New Mexico art hub
60 One of his paradoxes claims that two objects can never really touch
63 Home mixologist's spot
65 Interior design
66 Big name in lawn care
67 Oppose
69 Silk Road city near the East China Sea
70 What "10" might mean: Abbr.
71 Sleeping spot for a guest, maybe
72 It's way above the recommended amount
74 Youngest recipient of the Mark Twain Prize for American Humor (2010)
75 Apply sloppily
77 St. Cloud State University's state: Abbr.
78 Laze
79 Follow
81 Identified, in Ipswich
86 Birth control options
87 Rescue dog, e.g.
88 Estrogen or testosterone
91 Move from aisle to window, maybe
92 Recent delivery
93 Took steroids, informally
94 Brio, to Brits
95 Staves off
96 Auditory : sound :: gustatory : ___
98 Bursts in on
101 Willem of the "Spider-Man" series
102 Delicious food, in modern slang
103 Theatrical award
104 Nobel pursuit?: Abbr.
106 Putin's parliament
111 N.Y. tech school
112 Castle door destroyer
113 Actor who was once crowned "America's Toughest Bouncer"

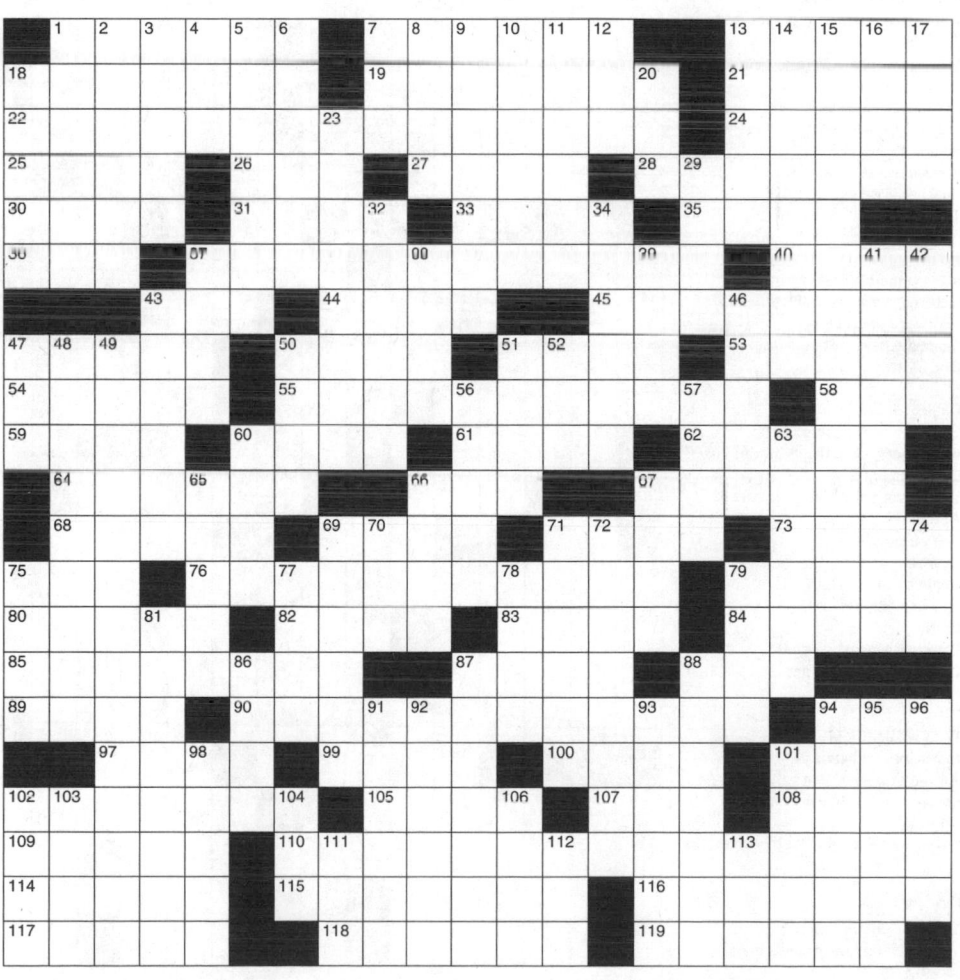

by Howard Barkin

ACROSS

1. Art of riding and training a horse
9. "Mea culpa"
14. Campania's capital
20. Put in other words
21. Bob Marley's "___ You Be Loved"
22. Mark in the World Golf Hall of Fame
23. Lacking self-assurance
24. Onus for a magician's disappearing act?
26. Study of how gels gel?
28. All together
29. Little, to a Scot
30. H
31. Fizzle (out)
33. Miscellaneous task
37. Irish writer Behan
39. Increased, with "up"
44. Actress Polo
45. Pablo Neruda's "___ to Wine"
47. They'll put you head and shoulders above everyone else
49. Constellation almost above the North Pole
50. Autobiography subtitled "The Girl Who Stood Up for Education and Was Shot by the Taliban"
53. Red card
54. ___ Khan, prime minister of Pakistan beginning in 2018
55. Sports broadcast feature
56. Angry Wisconsin sports fans?
59. Fire sign?
61. Like n, where n = 2k (and "k" is a whole number)
62. Unagi, at a sushi bar
63. President Bartlet of "The West Wing"
64. Singer Astley
66. Total-itarian?
69. Law enforcement, slangily
71. Tajikistan, e.g., once: Abbr.
73. "How was ___ know?"
75. Loll
77. Many a marble bust
80. Getting "Amscray!" under control?
85. Like yoga instructors
87. Greet the day
88. One of the Earps
89. –
91. Bathroom cabinet item
92. Certain bridge positions
94. McEachern a.k.a. the "Voice of Poker"
95. Cake topper
96. Wealthiest professional sports org.
98. Abrogates
100. Party animal?
102. Reveals
104. Reply to an oversharer
105. One in a hundred: Abbr.
106. Parrot
110. Power of a cowboy's shoe?
116. Odysseus' wife whispers sweet nothings?
119. Bliss
120. With wisdom
121. In a sense, colloquially
122. Activity for some pen pals
123. Port on the Black Sea
124. Colorful food fish
125. Giveaways during some pledge drives

DOWN

1. What the doctor ordered
2. Where Johnny Cash shot a man, in song
3. Bruins legend Phil, to fans
4. "Cut it out!"
5. Pronounced with authority
6. Twitter handle starter
7. Davis of "Thelma & Louise"
8. Icelandic saga
9. Chicken ___ (discontinued fast-food snack)
10. Dramatic accusation at a dentist's office?
11. Stickers
12. City council representative: Abbr.
13. Onetime White House inits.
14. Lunchtime liaison
15. Bands you might listen to in the car?
16. Salt's musical partner
17. Where "khop jai" means "thank you"
18. God who "loosens the limbs and weakens the mind," per Hesiod
19. Call at home
25. Not gross
27. Île be there?
31. ___ paneer (dish with puréed spinach)
32. Way in
33. "The Adventures of Milo and ___" (1989 film)
34. Cyber Monday offerings
35. She might take care of a kid on a sick day
36. Rock star who wrote the poetry collection "The American Night"
37. Contradict
38. "Mon ___!"
40. 36-Down's anagrammatic nickname
41. "Gay" city in a Cole Porter song
42. Hallmark.com purchase
43. Opposite of "takes off"
46. Something to leave to beavers?
48. Precipitous
51. Grammy-nominated D.J. Steve
52. Thomas ___ Edison
57. Join with rings
58. Smudge
60. Vaper's purchase
65. Neighborhood where you might get kimchi, for short
67. Goddess of the dawn
68. Obama chief of staff Emanuel
70. Campaign pros
71. ___ Gilbert, co-developer of a Covid-19 vaccine
72. Smile with one's eyes, per a modern coinage
74. Long past
76. Some fencing swords
78. Something to play fetch with
79. "Well, golly!"
80. Biting
81. Spongy toys
82. Resets to zero, as a scale
83. ___://
84. John Winston ___ Lennon
86. Professor 'iggins
90. Eaglelike?
93. Appetizers filled with potatoes and peas
97. One of the Jacksons
99. Word following English or green
101. Kind of wonder?
103. Cred
105. Campaign (for)
106. Itself: Lat.
107. World's oldest alcoholic beverage
108. Pulitzer-winning playwright from Independence, Kan.
109. Seriously annoys, with "off"
110. Tora ___, Afghanistan
111. Not overlooked
112. Defendant's plea, for short
113. Determination
114. Fork point
115. Storied cauldron stirrers
117. Spanish "that"
118. Admit (to)

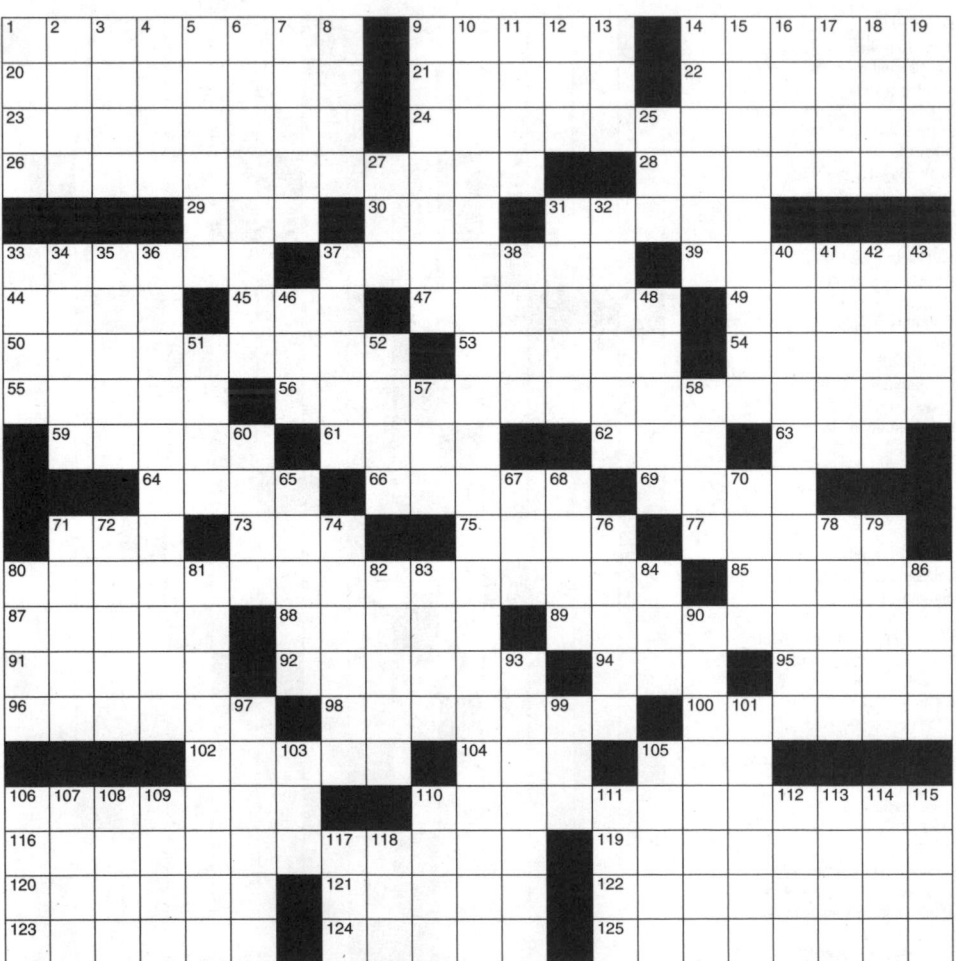

by Ashish Vengsarkar

ACROSS

1 Certain music royalties collector, for short
6 Viva ____ (aloud)
10 Dirty look
15 Even once
19 Part of R.I.
20 Big exporter of saffron
21 Sci-fi intro to "forming"
22 Foul
23 "Enjoy the food!"
25 Sportscaster who memorably asked "Do you believe in miracles?"
27 Crush
28 Emmy-winning FX series created by Donald Glover
29 "Curses!"
30 Challenger astronaut Judith
31 *"With enough butter, ____"
34 Commanded
36 Fuel economy authority, for short
37 Main artery
38 *"A party without cake is ____"
48 Retin-A target
49 Healthful property of a beach town
50 Chicken or veal dish, in brief
51 Merit
55 Boardroom plot?
57 Hangout rooms
58 Pair of quads
59 The Powerpuff Girls, e.g.
60 Filmmaker with a distinctive style
62 Affixes, as a cloth patch
64 Something that's gone bad if it floats when placed in a bowl of water
65 *"If you're alone in the kitchen and you drop the lamb, you can always just pick it up. ____?"
71 Word mistakenly heard at a Springsteen concert
74 Under way
75 Beethoven's Third
79 Reverse
81 Tons
82 Seriously hurt
86 Move quickly, informally
87 ____ o'clock (when happy hour begins)
88 Host's offer at a housewarming
89 Spongelike
91 Focal points
92 *"I enjoy cooking with wine. Sometimes I ____"
96 "Same here"
99 Word with noodle or nap
100 ____ lepton (elementary particle)
101 *"The only time to eat diet food is while you're waiting for ____"
108 Stamps (out)
113 One of Abraham Lincoln's is in the Smithsonian
114 "Welcome to the Jungle" rocker
115 Born with a silver spoon in one's mouth
117 Cause of a smartphone ding, perhaps
119 Chef quoted in this puzzle's starred clues
120 Guitar part
121 Member of la famiglia
122 Letters on an F-22 Raptor
123 One given onboarding
124 1975 Wimbledon champ
125 Like voile and chiffon
126 What may make the grade
127 Direct

DOWN

1 Shady spot
2 Less-than-subtle basketball foul
3 Temporary road markers
4 "I don't give ____!"
5 Pharmaceutical picker-upper
6 Penthouse perk
7 "Coffee ____?"
8 Stone memorial
9 Suffix with exist
10 Actor Jason who was once on Britain's national diving team
11 Four-stringed instruments
12 Financial adviser Suze
13 Dry with a twist
14 Milk: Prefix
15 NASA spacewalk
16 Try to win
17 Page who became the first openly trans man to appear on the cover of Time magazine (2021)
18 L.A. neighborhood referenced in Tom Petty's "Free Fallin'"
24 Coolers
26 Comedian Minhaj
28 How some bonds are sold
32 Himalayan legends
33 Fetch
35 Provided tunes for a party, in brief
38 Backbone of Indian classical music
39 Earth tone
40 Body sci.
41 Toon first introduced in the 1945 short "Odor-able Kitty"
42 Neighbor of Oman: Abbr.
43 Japanese honorific
44 Florida attraction with 11 themed pavilions
45 "His wife could ____ lean"
46 Family name in Steinbeck's "East of Eden"
47 "That's it for me"
52 Exist
53 Outfit
54 Drink garnished with nutmeg
56 Quizzical responses
58 Part of NGO: Abbr.
61 Change from portrait to landscape, say
62 Neither red nor blue: Abbr.
63 Benchmark
66 Locks-up shop?
67 Any set of elements in a column on the periodic table
68 Japanese port near Sapporo
69 War zone danger, for short
70 "A Room of One's Own" novelist
71 Mac
72 Gastric acid, on the pH scale
73 Tribute in verse
76 Classic Langston Hughes poem
77 First name in fashion
78 Saharan
80 Snacks that sometimes come in sleeves
82 Words to live by
83 The Cardinals, on scoreboards
84 Large Hadron Collider bit
85 Many a rescue dog
89 It's not the whole thing
90 Mount ____, California volcano
93 Critical
94 Rank for a rear admiral
95 What the Unsullied warriors are on "Game of Thrones"
96 She turned Arachne into a spider after losing a weaving contest
97 Wags a finger at
98 Separate
102 Tough period of the school year
103 Bayt ____ (destination for a Muslim pilgrim)
104 Krispy ____
105 Crooner Mel
106 Handy
107 Caffeine-rich nuts
109 Still alive, in dodgeball
110 Laissez-____
111 N.J. city on the Hudson
112 Meal at which parsley is dipped in salt water
116 Serious divide
118 Candy aisle name
119 Protrude

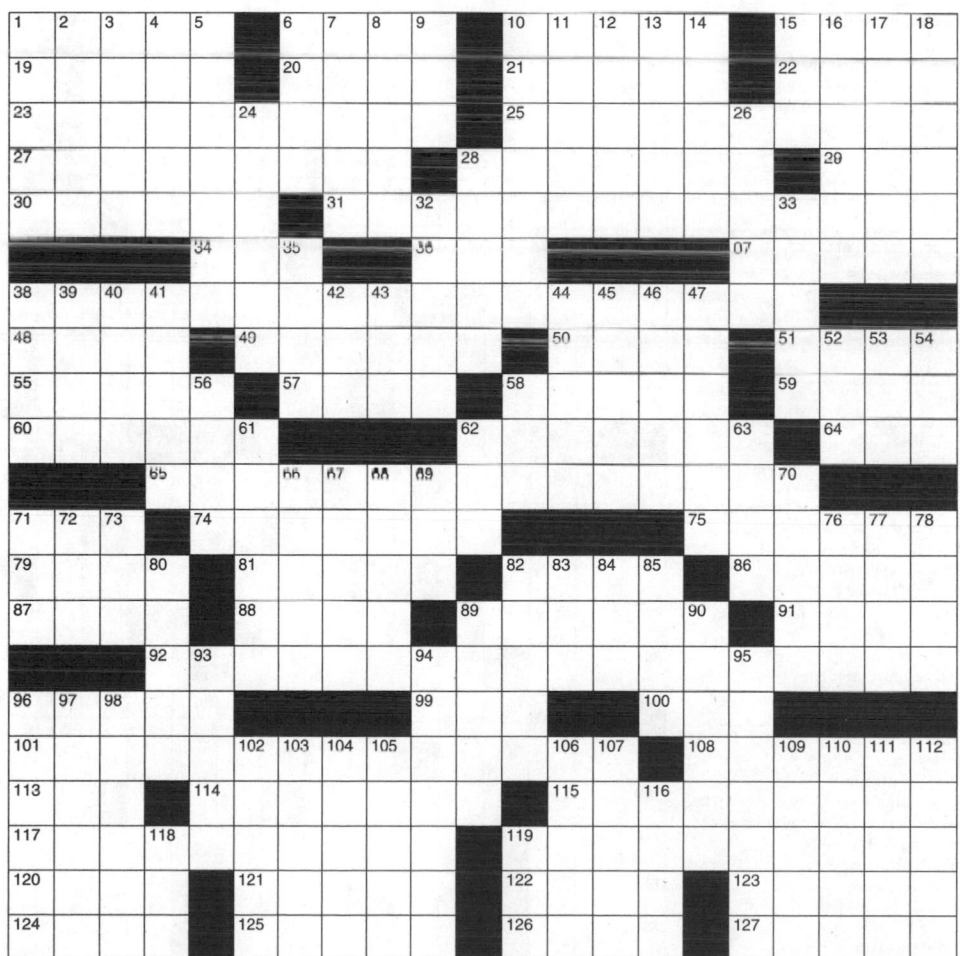

by Jesse Goldberg

ACROSS

1 Symbol of royalty in ancient Egypt
4 Wouldn't stand for it?
7 They have springs in the middle
12 _____ Perez, former Democratic National Committee chair
15 Nutritional fig.
18 Apple tablet option
20 Popular analgesic
21 Belgian city that hosted the 1920 Summer Olympics
23 One of the rooms in Clue
24 N.B.A. superstar Durant
25 Voting "aye"
26 Gilbert and _____ Islands (former colonial names of Kiribati and Tuvalu)
27 Give way
28 Levy of "Schitt's Creek"
29 When the Lascaux caves were painted
32 Furthermore
33 Much of Goya's output
35 Japanese beer brand
36 San Francisco's _____ Valley
37 In which "Stella" means "star"
38 Seaweed used to wrap sushi
41 Descriptor of almost a million and a half Californians
44 Porridge, essentially
48 Real surname for the authors Currer, Ellis and Acton Bell
51 With a yawn, say
52 Less certain
54 Onetime material for tennis racket strings
55 "That much is clear"
56 Symbol of Mexico
57 Country with roughly 6,000 islands
59 Where a pop-up leads
61 Alpha and Beta Ursae _____ (pointers to 68-Across)
64 Noodle soup
68 Guiding light
72 Gentille figure of a French folk song
74 Lord's title
75 Originally from
76 Place to take a suit
77 Executive producer of HBO's "A Black Lady Sketch Show"
80 Risk
81 "_____ Lang Syne"
82 Pesky insect
84 Something to notice in passing?
87 It's between micro- and pico-
88 Horace's "Hymn to Mercury," for one
89 New York political family
91 Fifth-century conqueror defeated in the Battle of the Catalaunian Plains
93 Rap's Lil _____ X
94 Reliable supporters
95 Glazer of "Broad City"
97 Online source for film facts, in brief
99 Repugnance
102 Disguised
105 Author _____ Carol Oates
109 Wine that may be made spumante or frizzante
111 Little
112 Bested
114 Gritty, in a sense
115 Ones committing a party foul . . . or the images depicted in this puzzle's grid?
118 Camping gear brand
119 Letters before an alias
120 Surprising wins
121 Jeu d'_____ (witticism)
122 Little one
123 Female mallard
124 Grommet
125 Black-eyed _____ (flowers)
126 Kind of protein in tempeh

DOWN

1 They get the wheels turning
2 Like proverbial milk
3 Poet Neruda
4 Company that makes recoverable and reusable rocket boosters
5 Overdue amount
6 Content of a Kinder Egg
7 Like many chardonnays
8 Last czarina of Russia
9 Celestial figure depicted in this puzzle's grid, in Roman folklore
10 Unforgivable acts, say
11 iPhone button with an up arrow on it
12 Duty
13 About to enter the stage, say
14 Subject of Hokusai's "Thirty-Six Views"
15 Delight (in)
16 Go on and on
17 Avant's opposite
19 Celestial figure depicted in this puzzle's grid, in African American folklore
22 Celestial figure depicted in this puzzle's grid, in Babylonian folklore
30 Joe and co., e.g.
31 Sharing maternal lines
33 Excoriated
34 Akira Kurosawa film
38 Peacock streaming inits.
39 Italian time unit
40 Utter nonsense
42 Like five-star hotels vis-à-vis three-star ones
43 Gather
45 Rose of rock
46 Nickname on a ranch
47 Spanish title: Abbr.
49 Tower topper
50 Digital writing
52 Buffoon
53 Brawler's memento
58 Is at the Forum?
60 Steamy place
61 _____ Special Administrative Region of the People's Republic of China
62 For all to hear
63 Unit in thermodynamics
65 Chump
66 Unaccounted for, briefly
67 Fumble
69 Went into syndication, e.g.
70 Singer Aguilera's alter ego
71 Star performances, maybe
73 This is a test
75 "Gee, that's swell!"
78 Like Vulcans, typically
79 Central Asia's _____ Mountains
82 "Gloomy" guy
83 "That's just unacceptable"
85 1969–74, politically
86 Tree that lends its name to a programming language
89 Matured, in a way
90 Like the three-toed sloth, among all animals
91 New wings
92 Tweaks
94 Clear, as crystal
96 Like Parmesan, but not mozzarella
98 Bouncy jazz genre
99 Noted book club leader
100 Male mallard
101 Certain caucus voter
103 1938 prize for Pearl S. Buck
104 Big name in trading cards
106 W.W. I Belgian battle locale
107 Green with the 2010 hit "Forget You"
108 Enlighten
110 Roger's cousin?
113 Ireland, poetically
116 Smartphone network std.
117 Home to the Nittany Lions, for short

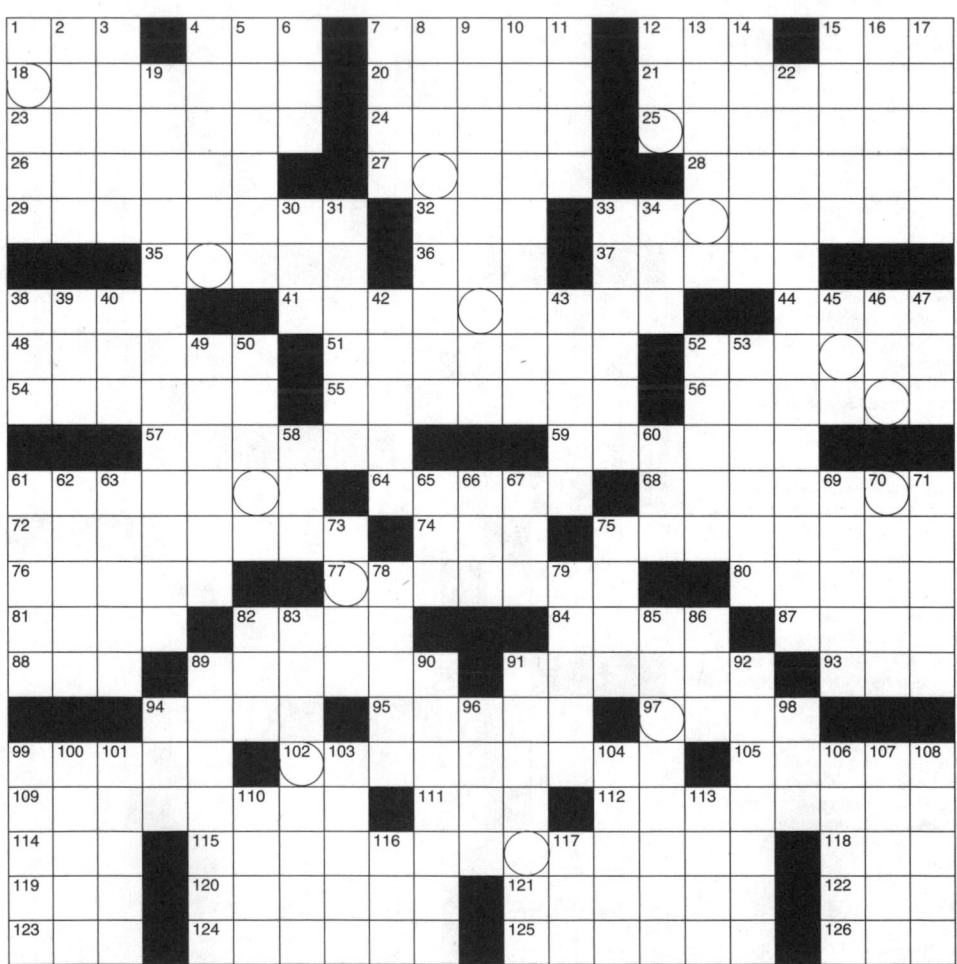

by Chandi Deitmer

ACROSS

1 Hearten
7 "... and it flopped"
11 Attack with snowballs, say
15 Graceful bird
19 Crossword header
20 Clearer in hindsight?
22 _____ Winans, 15-time Grammy-winning gospel singer
23 Apollo 11 landing spot
25 Eligible receiver?
26 Quickly maturing security, for short
27 Helps
28 Flying terrors of myth
29 With 42-Down, Oscars category from 1963 to 2019
30 Misfortunes
31 Semicircular recess
32 Items used by barkeepers, barbecuers and blacksmiths
34 Wackadoodle
35 Enhanced tape format released in 1987
37 Beat poet Cassady
38 Spewed forcefully
40 Take off the board
43 À la _____ (spit-roasted)
47 Spree
48 Black-_____ albatross
49 Knee-jerk response
50 Remove cargo from
53 Describing the 32-Down's image
55 Milk source
56 Impends
57 Inscribed with some ancient characters
58 Whirling toon, familiarly
59 Order, in a way
60 Nonfiction films, informally
61 Metaphor from an hourglass
64 "Come _____!"
65 This: Sp.
66 Sitcom planet of the '70s and '80s
67 Animal life
68 Pondered
69 It's probably over your head
70 One star, typically
73 Relentless go-getters
74 Carl XVI _____ (king of Sweden beginning in 1973)
76 Little bump
77 Eve's third son
78 Soccer chant
79 _____ 3000, half of the hip-hop duo Outkast
80 Persuade with patter
84 A majority
86 Offensive football positions
88 Ruby of "The Jackie Robinson Story"
89 Edgar Rice Burroughs novel, with "The"
94 Talk Like a Pirate Day outbursts
95 Dormer section
96 Turn aside
97 Actress Amanda
98 Taking a bow at the symphony?
99 Waif
100 "A warehouse of facts, with poet and _____ in joint ownership" ("The Devil's Dictionary" definition for "imagination")
101 Its motto is "Agriculture and Commerce"
104 Opposite of exo-
105 Woe for a speeder

106 _____ Blinken, Biden's secretary of state
107 Bit of "kit chat"
108 1974 spoof with the tagline "Would you buy a used secret from these men?"
109 Bits of machinery
110 Latin phrase meaning "based on forecasts"

DOWN

1 Having legs
2 Cool shade
3 Weakness
4 Sledge, wedge, etc.
5 Sports org. with the Pittsburgh Maulers and Philadelphia Stars
6 SFO setting: Abbr.
7 Sang hosannas to
8 Car part the Brits call a "wing"
9 Heading for commonly sought info
10 Capote nickname
11 _____ light
12 Sweeping works
13 Reveals
14 Don't give up
15 Intellectual movement
16 Tyke
17 Performing well on
18 Candy with two flavors in one box
21 Flexible cutters
24 Kid Cudi or Lil Baby, e.g.
29 Fixed look
31 Enveloping atmospheres
32 Pope Pius XII called it "a holy thing perhaps like nothing else"
33 Odor-fighting spray brand
35 Parts of some brackets
36 "Yankee Doodle" has 16 of them
39 Entertainers with bright futures
41 Partner of poivre
42 See 29-Across
44 Juice regimen
45 Like épées vis-à-vis foils
46 Stretches out
48 Curve
50 Experience
51 Music genre for Erykah Badu and D'Angelo
52 Many people find it intolerable
53 About 98% of the human genome
54 Word meaning "desire" in a classic Sanskrit text
57 _____ avis
61 Big tear-jerker

62 Went under
63 Word with fine or signature
68 Hands, in slang
71 1980s White House nickname
72 Dilute something, in a way
73 Battery parts?
75 Up in the air
77 Maker of the Ring in "The Lord of the Rings"
80 Surgical instrument with thumbholes
81 Joy who wrote "Born Free"
82 Forgiving
83 Talent for discernment
85 Mic check noise
87 Cattle ranch identifier
89 "The Crucible" setting
90 Sheepish?
91 "Swell!"
92 "I can do this. Hit me"
93 Some 10-pointers in Greek Scrabble
95 Dish made from durum, say
98 Prefix with futurism
99 Kids of boomers
101 Grads-to-be: Abbr.
102 Not prescription, in brief
103 Scottish negative

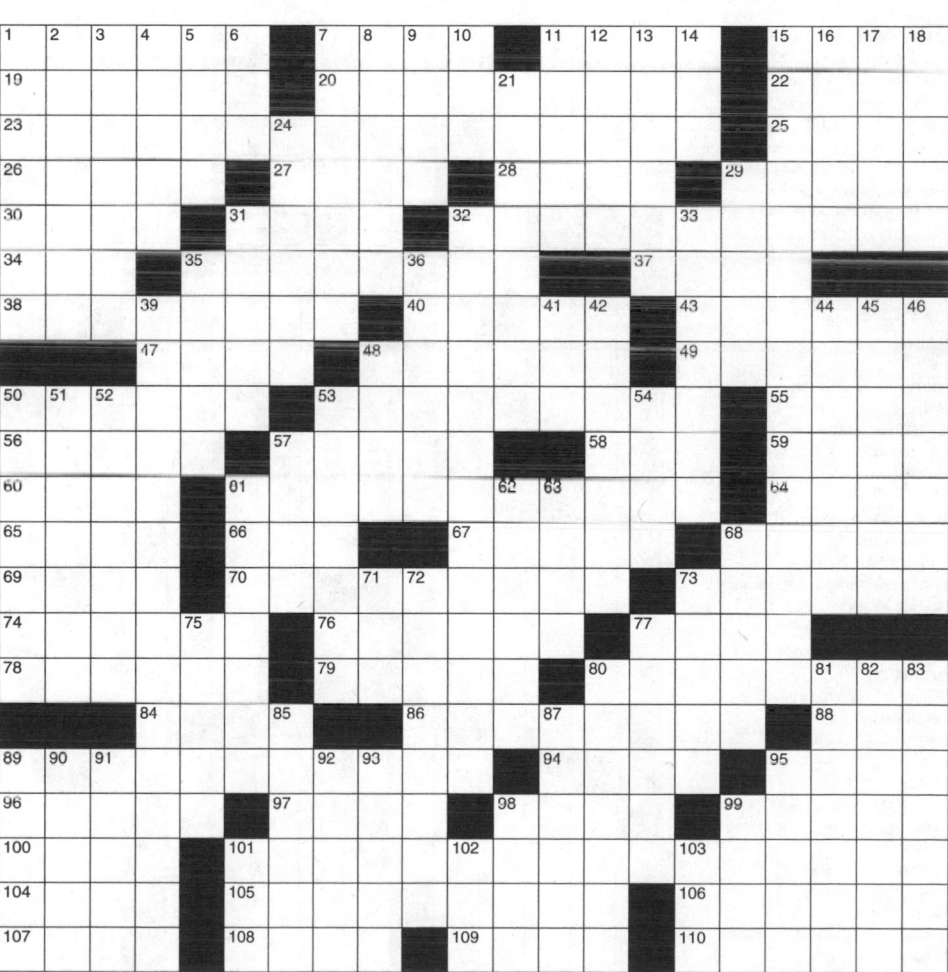

by Byron Walden

ACROSS

1 Sexy one
10 Treat that's dangerous to fillings
15 It has cameras set up around the House
20 Home of the Hittite Empire
21 Novelist Zola
22 Word with box or gloves
23 Unwavering
24 Bit of cinema décor
26 Latin verb that's a letter off from 9-Down
27 Sagelike
28 Get ready for dinner
29 Man-eaters
30 Demeanor
32 Puts the pedal to the metal
34 Outbursts of megalomania
39 Boglike
40 Educator Khan who founded Khan Academy
43 -esque
44 "Ugh, we have so much to sort out"
47 You might come to one suddenly
50 Winston Churchill gesture
52 They're out on their own
54 "Word on the street is . . ."
55 Antiquated source of light
58 Toy brand with colorful rods and gears
59 Partner of dark
60 Starts a course, with "off"
61 Where you might see scrolling credits?
64 Heidi of TV's "Making the Cut"
66 The Arthur Ashe Courage Award and others
67 Spectators taking potshots, collectively
70 Will Smith's actor/rapper son
73 Quickly join hands?
74 G or K
75 "Roll Tide!" school
79 Relishes
80 Eats
82 Feature of a healthy dog
84 Fjord, e.g.
85 Like Hathor, goddess of motherhood
89 Film character who shouts "You are a toy!"
90 Fish with a prehensile tail
92 Primitive time
95 German article
96 Instagram hashtag accompanying a nostalgic photo
97 Two-fifths of a quarter
99 Birthplace of three major world religions
101 What an agoraphobe avoids
105 Uber offering
106 Group email greeting
108 Class
109 "That so?"
111 It's not light reading
115 Advances in a baby's cognitive development
117 Demonology and such
119 Show vanity, in a way
120 Face-planted
121 Cocktail often made with Tennessee whiskey, ironically
122 Looks long and hard
123 Class
124 Not get tense

DOWN

1 March madness figure?
2 Animals in hibernación
3 Twitches
4 "Please, I'll go with you"
5 Friend abroad
6 Home of many schools in the Big Ten Conference
7 Uses chrism on
8 Chuckles online
9 Language that's a letter off from 26-Across
10 Tantalize
11 ". . . that's ____"
12 When many commutes begin
13 Converse
14 "____-haw!"
15 Favorite dog breed of Queen Elizabeth II
16 Where bats and birdies are found
17 ____ the Frog (internet meme)
18 God with a helmet
19 Rapper with the platinum albums "Street's Disciple" and "God's Son"
25 Skater Harding
31 The third of Chekhov's "Three Sisters"
32 Iota
33 Valuable deposits
34 Turning point
35 Actor/activist Davis
36 Stretch
37 Woman's name that's part of the body backward
38 Contacts quickly, in a way
41 Imitation
42 Fertile mixtures
45 Finished the golf hole
46 One might be cold or dry
48 Scatterbrained
49 Shot, so to speak
51 Plot device, in brief?
53 Rejoice (in)
56 Debt holdings
57 Bouts with pay-per-view events, for short
59 Transition
62 Left-leaning organizing grp.
63 Like pronounced muscles
65 Feeling described by this: :|
67 Australia's "City of Light"
68 Covers for campers
69 Spat
70 Former Fed chair Yellen
71 Classroom with cameras, for short
72 Executes perfectly
75 "That's just awful!"
76 One end of a cell
77 ____ circus
78 To now
79 Beyoncé, to Solange, informally
81 Tundra or savanna
83 Fabric in a flat cap
85 Leprechaun's home
86 Idaho, with "the"
87 Nickname in "Star Wars"
88 Country code for Holland in the Olympics
91 N.F.L. star ____ Beckham Jr.
93 Supermodel Lima
94 Like many a beta release
98 Reaction reducer
100 Tackles
102 "I have other ____, sorry"
103 Norse pantheon
104 Birthplace of Zeus
106 Female figure in the "Iliad"
107 Name akin to Agnes
109 Many mainframes
110 Blind sight
112 Number between sette and nove
113 Some petting zoo noises
114 Seaside bird
115 Dash fig.
116 Twitch user's bane
118 Comic Penn

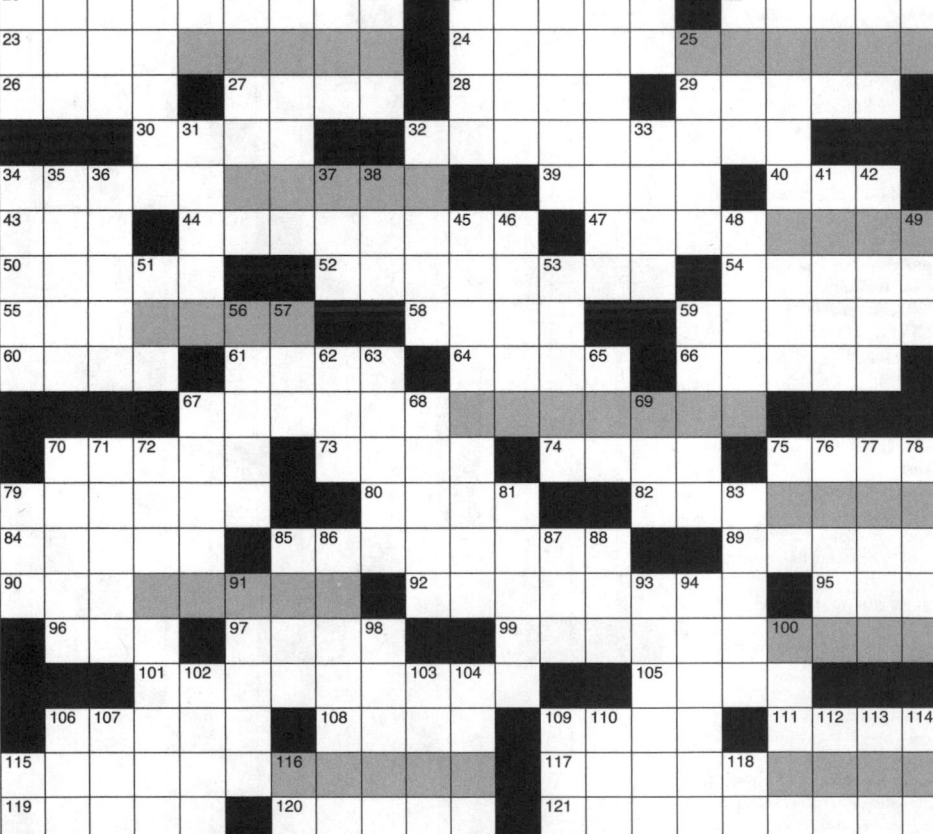

by David W. Tuffs

ACROSS

1 What flowers eventually do
5 Children's character who sings "I Love Trash"
10 Ending with bald or bold
14 Issa of "The Lovebirds"
17 On the drink
18 Must pay back
19 Gross-sounding plant?
20 Toll maker
21 List from 1 to . . .
22 Overhead lights?
23 Spirit of a culture
24 Shoots the breeze
25 One might help with a connection
27 Apt facial hair for a teacher?
30 "Excuse me . . ."
32 Rumrunner, e.g.
33 Lime-A-___ (alcoholic beverage)
34 Daughter of Polonius, in Shakespeare
37 Admitted it, with "up"
38 ¥
39 Bob Marley and the Wailers, for one
41 Passionate (about)
42 Chills
46 Button often denoted by a right arrow
47 China makes up much of it
50 Big brass
51 Like almost all prime numbers
52 Lay down, in a way
54 Word before shot and after hot
55 Spiritual object
56 Words with "with words"
57 It "lifts the veil from the hidden beauty of the world, and makes familiar objects be as if they were not familiar," per Percy Bysshe Shelley
60 Bea Arthur was one before her acting career
61 Church minister
64 Breakfast brand tagline
65 Taking Rx drugs
66 People in a long line, perhaps
67 Covered in long, soft hair
68 Jupiter and Mars
69 It's spineless
70 Private aid grp.
71 "Vital" things
73 Stock paper, for short?
76 Orchestral prelude to an opera
78 Fairy tale sibling
80 Beer ___, drinking/running event
81 Deems right
82 Apt name for a landscaper?
83 "On the other hand, I could be wrong"
86 Crony
87 One of a pair of kitchen tools
90 Like anomalies
91 Chrysler offering of the 1980s
93 Wrestling duos
95 Over-the-counter seller
96 Engaged in some circular reasoning
99 Put on
102 First line in a news story
103 Congas and bongos
104 ___ room
106 Name that rhymes with "edgy"
107 You are: Sp.
108 Essays
109 Attack tactic
110 Dragon roll ingredients
111 Foreign exchange abbr.
112 Big name in skate shoes
113 Cartomancy medium
114 Broadway musical centered around two girls in love, with "The"

DOWN

1 Affable
2 Golfer Aoki
3 Help out
4 Pay attention
5 "How fancy!"
6 Exchange
7 Big star
8 Many, many
9 The "R" of Edward R. Murrow
10 Kicked the ball between the legs of, in soccer slang
11 What Beatles music did at Abbey Road, famously
12 Clean extensively
13 Back talk
14 Undergo a chemical change
15 A Greek letter?
16 Something ___
19 Goes off on
20 Things that might get written down on sticky notes
26 "Scary" Spice Girl
28 Response to "Who's there?"
29 Some purchases for Christmas displays
31 Unaccounted for, for short
34 Ish
35 Identified
36 On edge
38 Safecrackers, in old-fashioned slang
40 Rapper Kool Moe ___
42 Sight at a winery
43 Body feature that approximately 10% of people have
44 Plumbing pipe known as a trap
45 Brings under control
48 Chord whose notes are played in succession
49 Comedian's stage prop
50 Welsh guy
52 Something intricately detailed and impressive
53 Without
54 Expecting, in slang
56 Most valued card in the deck
58 Rock type
59 Big name in chicken
60 Dream idly
61 Chinese qipao, e.g.
62 Jazz pianist Blake who composed "Shuffle Along"
63 Unrivaled
64 The Evian Championship is one of its majors: Abbr.
68 Formal festivities
70 Critic's pick?
72 Absolute beaut
73 Resident of the capital of Manitoba
74 Plod perseveringly
75 Ballet jump
77 Zilch
78 Maker of Ding Dongs and Twinkies
79 Puts up
80 Cooking ahead of time, say
82 Chickpeas and peanuts, for two
84 1/1 'til present: Abbr.
85 "La" place in L.A.
87 Actress Anna of "True Blood"
88 News updates, with "the"
89 "Othello" character who quips "They are all but stomachs, and we all but food"
91 Beer parties
92 Granted through a treaty
93 Land in Rome
94 On the wagon
96 ___ cheese
97 Purchase for the den
98 Mission cancellation
100 Title Disney character from Hawaii
101 Polite agreement
105 What you might get on a log flume ride

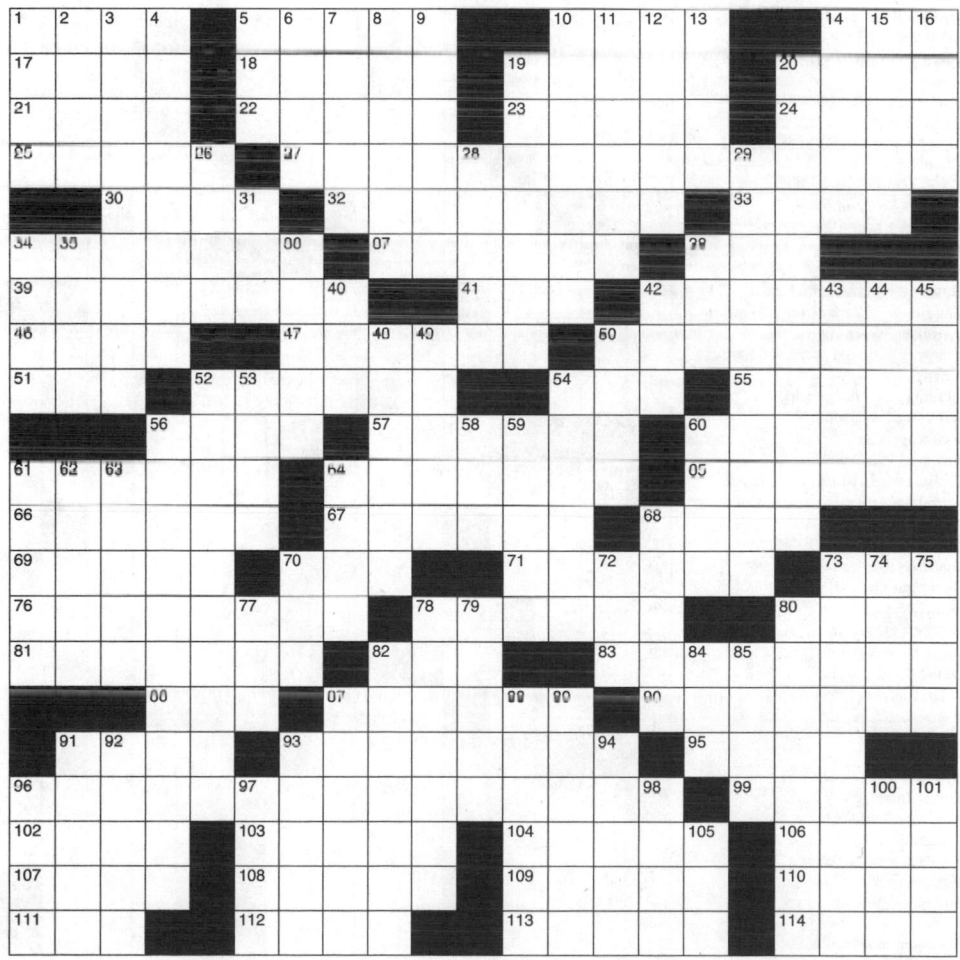

by Emet Ozar

ACROSS

1 Make a bust, say
7 Chew (on)
11 Ointment amounts
15 Modern lead-in to mania
19 "Enough!"
20 Contemporary of Picasso
21 Factory watchdog, in brief
22 Native of the country whose national sport is oil wrestling
23 Bit of company swag for a Genius Bar staffer?
25 With 114-Across, exasperated question to parking enforcement?
27 Awesome time
28 Elements of a Sherlock Holmes sports mystery?
30 A small part of who you are
31 Prefix with medicine
32 "Duck Dynasty" network
33 Irish ____, popular St. Patrick's Day cocktail
36 Like much toothpaste
38 Mountain mammal
42 Plant cultivated by the Incas
43 Program after undergrad, for some
47 "____ rate . . ."
48 Today's plans: watchin' someone's kids?
54 Broadband inits.
55 Overrun
56 "Mr. Mom" actress Teri
57 Data output denoted by "N/A"
59 Super Bowl in 2022
61 Come on down!
63 Name that's a body part in reverse
64 It may be measured in both feet and meters
65 How much Michael Jordan or Wilt Chamberlain could score, hyperbolically?
71 Lead-in to cross
72 Happy companion
73 Focus of the website Brickipedia
74 "The Hangover" character who wakes up with a missing tooth
75 Eschews grains and processed foods, perhaps
78 Common results of penalties
80 Writers such as Sappho
85 Waze way: Abbr.
86 Missile silo's holding?
89 Pie slices might be displayed in one
91 Natural application to waterproof a ship's hull
92 Guacamole go-with?
93 Engine type, informally
94 Playwright Edward
97 Hidden obstacle
100 Transport on a river
102 Transport on a rail
106 "Dope!"
107 Where Sweet'N Low displays its logo?
111 T as in Tartarus
114 See 25-Across
115 Cry following an electrical malfunction?
117 Rufus and Chaka Khan's "____ Nobody"
118 Like garage floors, often
119 Slight amount
120 Old English folklore figure
121 Jumbo
122 When said three times, "What have we here?!"
123 Music score abbr.
124 Jaguar two-seaters starting in 2013

DOWN

1 Catch
2 ____ América (soccer tournament)
3 They call 'em as they see 'em
4 Text back and forth?
5 Like pioneering search engines of the 1980s
6 Polka-influenced music style
7 Yukon and Acadia, for two
8 Canon competitor
9 Sizable urban construction project
10 King of the gods in Wagner's "Der Ring des Nibelungen"
11 Ann of Hulu's "The Handmaid's Tale"
12 Rubbish receptacle
13 Hindi name for India
14 Smooth and glossy
15 ". . . per my understanding"
16 Zap
17 Line on a neck
18 Clears
24 "Resume speed," musically
26 The Golden Arches, on stock tickers
29 One covering plenty of ground
30 Persona non ____
33 Invent
34 When Lady Macbeth cries "Out, damned spot!"
35 Smoke shop purchase
37 Standout in a field
39 Bunch of scoundrels
40 Follows
41 Tissue in a plant stem
42 DNA reviewer, in brief
44 Buy time
45 State of subjugation
46 Male voter stereotype beginning in the mid-2010s
47 Wheels off the road?
49 Run in place
50 In-state attendee of Great Basin College, e.g.
51 Check
52 Brother in the Lemony Snicket books
53 Certain college member
58 Great ____
60 Jokey remark after missing a modern reference
62 Be philanthropic, say
65 Execrate
66 Company computer fixers, informally
67 Big hits?
68 ____ Float (cold treat)
69 Like a situation at the start of an inning
70 Ounce of praise, jocularly
71 Slangy stuff to sell
76 Placed
77 ". . . must all learn to live together as brothers, ____ will all perish together as fools": M.L.K. Jr.
79 Cakewalk
81 Bygone messaging app
82 Cheer for the Vikings
83 Poker giveaway
84 Certain outbuilding
87 Doth proceed
88 Fun plans after work, say
90 Stuff in stuffed pasta shells
94 Aphid that produces honeydew
95 "Ooh, check it out!"
96 Happened to
98 Really miff
99 Tycoon
101 What only one planet, Jupiter, is spelled with
103 ____ Hard Apple (beer brand)
104 Not connected
105 Name that's "all the beautiful sounds of the world in a single word," on Broadway
107 Liver, in Le Havre
108 Like church bells
109 "Bye 4 now!"
110 "Power Lunch" airer
111 Maryland athlete, for short
112 End in ____
113 Doesn't waste
114 Thanksgiving dinner offering
116 Very important

by Sam Ezersky

Note: After you've finished solving, look for an appropriate bonus phrase.

ACROSS

1 You say it when you "get it"
4 Cell connection inits.
7 Dope
12 Sorta
15 Writing tip
18 Film critic with a cameo in 1978's "Superman"
20 Safe bets
22 "Levitating" singer, 2020
24 Stuffed up, in a way
25 Northern New Jersey town
26 Literally, "father of many"
27 2020 #1 hit for Cardi B and Megan Thee Stallion
28 Longtime cooking show hosted by Alton Brown
30 They may be classified
31 Resident of the U.S.'s second-largest city
35 Like some bulls
36 Dangerous part of a tour
41 Fan of the album "Αοxomoxoa," say
43 Dress (up)
44 Flings without strings
45 Yogurt-based Indian drink
46 The Blue Marble
49 "Ditto!"
50 Part of "fwiw"
51 Sit in stir
53 Good people to ask for directions
55 Grok
56 Clothing store sign
58 Owed
59 Parts of many skyscrapers
63 Med. care option
64 South _____
65 Wilson of film
67 Loud and clear, as a call to action
69 First name among billionaires
71 Demean
74 Woolly ma'am
76 Chats over Twitter, for short
77 _____ al-Fitr (holiday)
79 Lump sum?
83 Hawaiian home parts
85 Grabbed the reins
88 The Barber of Seville
89 Singer Grande, to fans
90 Diverse ecosystem
92 Christine of "The Blacklist"
93 French 101 verb
95 Mustangs' sch.
96 Back tracks?
98 Made bubbly
100 Not stop talking about
102 Supreme Court appointee before Thurgood Marshall
104 "Dios _____!"
105 Firm
107 Pin points?
108 Spacecraft's reflective attachment
111 Ominous
112 Flexible spade, say
113 Like werewolves
116 Hairsplitter
120 Late actor Eisenberg
121 In which belts are worn
123 Ideal beta tester
127 Gives a boost, informally
129 Roger _____, first film critic to win a Pulitzer for criticism
131 Boots
132 Algebra I calculation
133 Worries
137 Calendar mo.
138 Captain's log entry, maybe
142 Quinceañera feature
143 2013 Bong Joon Ho thriller
146 Hear out, say
147 N.Y.C. mayor after de Blasio
148 Alien's line of communication?
149 Speedy travel option
150 Precept
151 John, abroad
152 Young 'uns
153 Cares for

DOWN

1 Pioneer in Dadaism
2 "That's amusing"
3 Rose of Guns N' Roses
4 Passport, for one
5 Vegan protein source made from fermented soybeans
6 Big name in ice cream
7 1993 Salt-N-Pepa hit
8 Heart-shaped, as leaves
9 Entree with boiling broth
10 Dash figure
11 #1 N.B.A. draft pick in 1992
12 Journalist _____ B. Wells
13 Outback, e.g.
14 Stereotypical football coach
15 Org. with grants
16 It's got hops, for short
17 Superhero comics sound
19 Ties another knot
20 Bay Area airport code
21 Tennis division
23 Victor _____, role in "Casablanca"
28 Professional saver?
29 Fad accessory of the 1980s
31 It comes off the top of one's head
32 "Cool beans!"
33 Verbose
34 The eighth of eight
37 Feeling bad, in a way
38 "August: _____ County" (Tracy Letts play)
39 Site of Hercules' first labor
40 Ramps up or down?
42 Leave it to beavers
44 _____-Magnon
47 Author Gaiman
48 Plus
52 Pablo Neruda wrote one "to a large tuna in the market"
54 Has online?
57 Slugger with 609 homers
60 Bit of cosmic justice
61 Unlikely feature for competitive swimmers
62 Some trattoria offerings
64 All tucked in
66 Eccentric
67 Top dog, for short
68 Wedding notice word
70 Basket-weaving materials
71 Home of Gulf State Park
72 Behind-the-counter helper
73 Licorice-flavored quaff
75 "_____ With Marc Maron" (popular podcast)
78 Rage
80 Main connection?
81 Some antique furniture
82 Like 100 vis-à-vis 99, say
84 The Trojan priestess Cassandra, e.g.
86 Two-syllable cheer
87 Contest
88 Softened expletive on "Battlestar Galactica"
91 Cutesy ending with most
94 Marijuana compound, for short
97 Some coding statements
98 United
99 Having less vermouth, say
101 Air or Ear ender, in tech
103 "_____ live and breathe!"
106 No longer funny
109 Jay with jokes
110 Does the same as
113 Blood typing, e.g.
114 Runnin' _____ (N.C.A.A. basketball team)
115 In and of itself
117 Shining brightly
118 Former Jordanian queen
119 Formal accessory
122 Text file in a software package
124 Inundate, as with work
125 Runner Bolt
126 Like some parking
128 Attract while exploiting someone's weakness
130 Shades
132 Cuts off the flow of
133 "P.D.Q." in the O.R.
134 Way off the mark
135 Flair
136 Imbibe, old-style
138 Scrooge McDuck, for one
139 Last word of the New Testament
140 "All _____ . . ."
141 Chapters in history
144 "Hunh?"
145 P

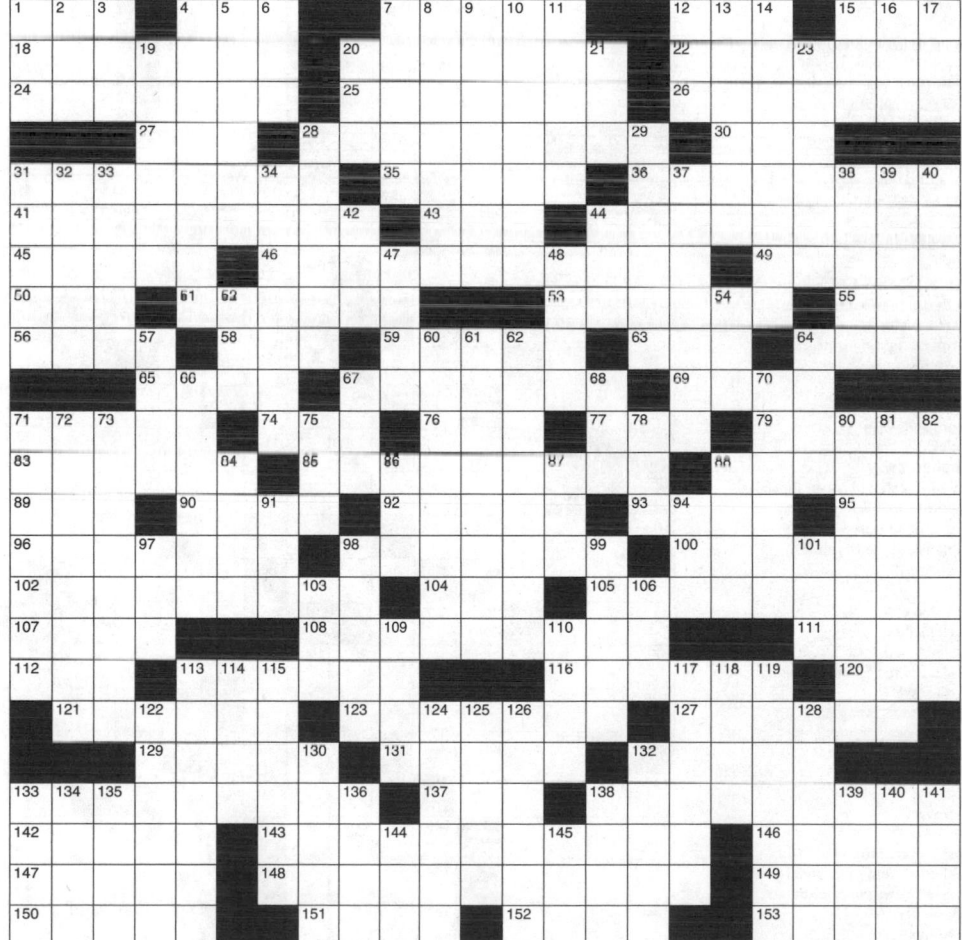

by Brandon Koppy

ACROSS

1 Some old PCs
5 Experience financial ruin
11 Many files in a Downloads folder
15 Talk
19 1990s sitcom starring Tia and Tamera Mowry
22 Beethoven's "Ah! perfido," for one
23 Southwest people known for their dry farming
24 Grand Prix city
25 Fulminate
26 Portent
27 Start a web session
28 Tribute
30 Many zoomers
31 Gush (over)
33 Red lightsaber wielder
36 Singular praise
37 ____ Xtra (soft drink)
38 Soul: Sp.
39 Make it so there's snow way out?
41 1963 hit for the Kingsmen
45 It gets the show on the road
48 Nothing but a number, it's said
49 Call from an old-time paperboy
50 Essayist Susan
51 Attraction, so to speak, with "the"
53 Org. often impersonated by phone scammers
54 Time for a visit from Ong Tao, the "Kitchen God"
55 Slip up
56 Yellowstone sight
58 [Gulp!]
59 House of Commons reps
61 ____ gratia (in all kindness: Lat.)
62 Rush order
64 Like some questions
66 Romanov V.I.P., once
68 Charlotte N.B.A. player
70 ". . . you get the point"
74 "Well, lookie here!"
75 Quaint exclamation of dismay
78 Fee payer, often
79 Thin pancakes in Indian cuisine
80 Laborer of old
84 Dan of "Schitt's Creek"
85 To the ____ power
86 Time for March madness?
88 Ultimate fighting inits.
90 Certain summer baby
91 "There you ____!"
92 Big tower, for short?
94 Years and years
95 Shock
97 Sings, in a way
101 When you should leave, for short
103 Piece of roller derby equipment
104 Classic joke start
105 High five at the Olympics?
107 Unchanged
108 Yea or nay
109 Power source
111 Barfly's flier
112 Added to a thread, say
113 El ____ of the Spanish Renaissance
115 "Amscray!"
117 Egomaniac's thought
119 Noted character with object-subject-verb syntax
120 Dangerous part of a road on which to pass
121 Extroverts
127 Tie down
128 Best Picture winner of 2012
129 Basketball feat suggested by this puzzle's pairs of theme answers, informally
130 1040 figs.
131 Love of languages?
132 In on
133 Add (on)

DOWN

1 Philosophy
2 H.S. class in the same department as chem
3 Yahoo alternative
4 Trusty to the end
5 Pirate's booze
6 One way to learn
7 Like the Six Million Dollar Man
8 "Anchors Aweigh" grp.
9 Amtrak stop: Abbr.
10 Lab worker
11 Logical conundrum
12 Prolong
13 Numismatic grade
14 Plopped (down)
15 Setting for many a diorama
16 Shortcut missing from newer smartphones
17 Lead
18 Affixes
20 Subject of interest, in brief
21 Chess piece whose name is derived from the Persian for "chariot"
29 Cocktails made with ginger beer, informally
30 Pieces in the game Bananagrams
31 Flights connect them
32 All-encompassing Egyptian deity
34 Aromatic beverage
35 Perch for the self-important
37 Gemstone cut named for a fruit
38 Baffled
40 Very bright
42 Eye piece
43 Nobelist Joliot-Curie
44 Really get to
46 Sweetie
47 Weep in an unflattering way, in modern lingo
52 Lugs
57 Hold on to
58 Lunchtime estimate
59 Computer shortcuts
60 Slices and dices, say
61 Scottish hillsides
63 Annoying
65 Walk with swagger
67 It might get swiped in a college dining hall
68 Football trophy name
69 Where some replacements take place, in brief
71 Third column on a calendar: Abbr.
72 Eaglet's hatching spot
73 Certain public transport
75 Sound from a jalopy
76 Played again
77 Words from an ex-lover
81 Go by
82 Put down again
83 Origami steps
85 Bread in Indian cuisine
87 One taking action
89 Certain close relative
92 Invite out for
93 1990s tennis star Huber
94 Off-kilter
96 "Later!"
98 Green vehicles
99 Fried plantain dish of Puerto Rico
100 Country named for its geographic location
102 It makes you you
103 Lobbyists' area in D.C.
106 Radiator cover
110 "Die Hard" squad, in brief
112 Miss ____, famed dial-a-psychic
113 Businesses that see an uptick after New Year's
114 Aussie hoppers
115 Kernel of an idea
116 "Ouch, ouch, ouch!"
118 High style
120 Barnyard bleat
122 "Mais ____!" ("But of course!")
123 "Cyberchase" channel
124 Org. whose members stay in their lanes
125 Business name ender
126 "Yipe!"

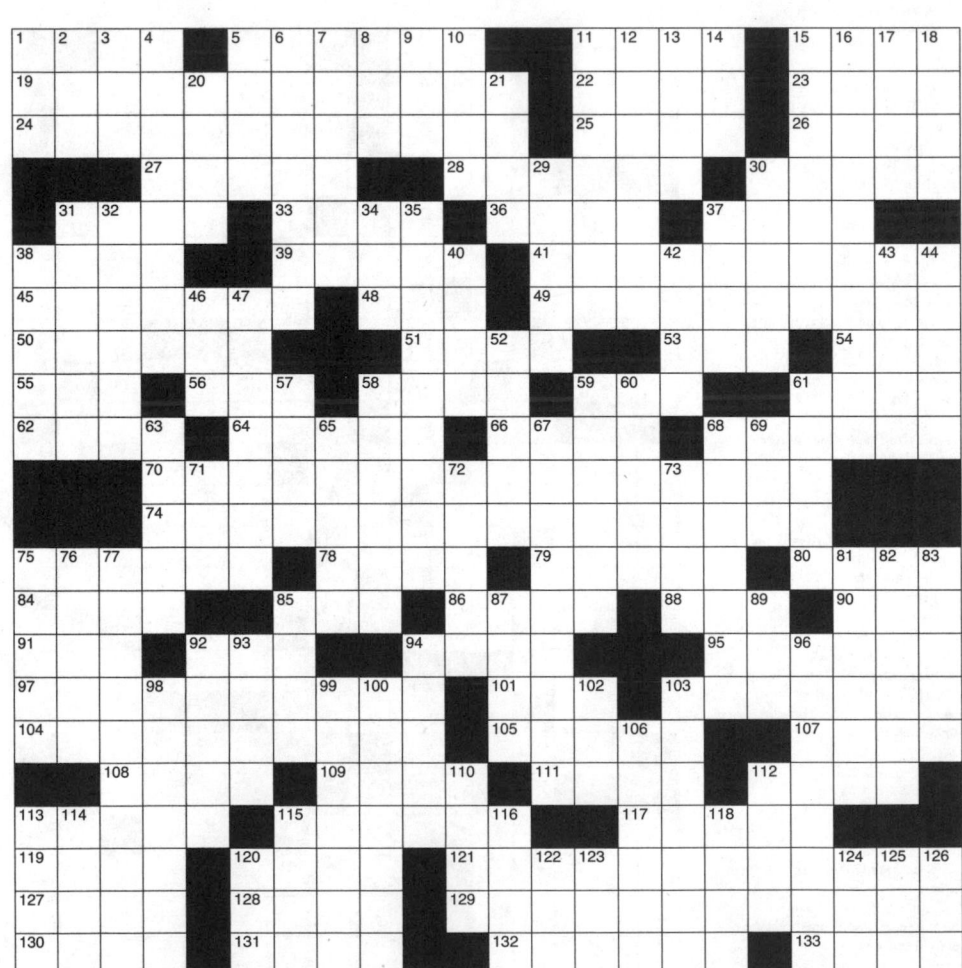

by Matthew Stock and Chandi Deitmer

ACROSS

1 "Meet the ___" (baseball fight song)
5 Pertaining to any of five Italian popes
12 Small rodent
18 To be, in France
19 ___ Jay Hawkins, rock pioneer who wrote "I Put a Spell on You"
20 Hardly a team player?
21 Nickname for 114-Across coined by John Steinbeck
23 Large rodents
24 Corpse ___ No. 2 (morning-after cocktail)
25 German surname part
26 One of the Guccis
28 At the top
29 Skip or drop
31 Down-to-earth
32 Cool
35 Opposite of a breeze
37 Instruction for some Thanksgiving cooking
38 "Downton Abbey" countess
39 Colorful natural attraction along 114-Across
43 An awful state to live in
46 Twitch user, perhaps
47 Spanish : -ando or -iendo :: English : ___
48 Attempt to grasp, as a complicated situation
49 Car-pooling inits.
50 Cuisine that includes gochujang paste
52 "Go ahead and ask"
56 Pastis flavorer
58 Peridot, for one
60 Smart, say
61 Bad stat for a QB: Abbr.
64 Left
65 Tall, curved attraction along 114-Across
69 Gear for gondoliers
71 Trafficker trackers, for short
72 Legend
73 Animal in the genus Bos
74 Following along
75 Roux ingredient?
78 B3, nutritionally
82 Beverage with a "New England" variety
83 Gone to press?
86 Booked it
88 Phrase one might yell at the screen during a horror film
90 What roots are, to powers
92 Graffitied artistic attraction along 114-Across
94 Summers in la cité
95 ___ Austin, Biden's secretary of defense
97 Bugs
98 Jazz bassist Carter, who has appeared on more than 2,200 recordings
99 Being treated, in a way
101 A whole can of worms?
102 Mamas' mamas
106 Bug
107 Bad review
108 Component of lacquer thinner
110 More far out
114 Theme of this puzzle, which winds its way nearly 2,500 miles through all the shaded squares herein
117 Wishy-washy response
118 Captivate
119 The Panthers of the N.C.A.A., familiarly
120 Art in the Television Hall of Fame
121 Dislikes and then some
122 Things sometimes named after presidents

DOWN

1 One of 50,460 in the Chunnel
2 Actress Barrymore, great-aunt of Drew
3 Famed fountain of Rome
4 Half step, in music
5 Character seen on a keyboard
6 Bile
7 Obsequious
8 Sun deck?
9 "That's my cue!"
10 Actress Long
11 Component of a bridge truss
12 Positive results of some strikes
13 TV 6-year-old who attends Little Dipper School
14 Lead-in to "com"
15 Bit of writing on Twitter or Tinder
16 Natural conclusion?
17 Some mil. officers
19 Abbr. on many streets in Quebec
20 "Holy ___!"
22 Pass
27 Not mainstream, for short
30 Sierra ___
31 1990s film with a famous wood chipper scene
32 Word with a wave in Oaxaca
33 Classic Camaro
34 Grant ___, northeast terminus of 114-Across
36 Kind of tape
37 $100 bill, slangily
38 Underwriting?
39 "What malarkey!"
40 Paid penance
41 Site of a U.C. in the O.C.
42 Muscle-bone connector
44 Verb in Poe's "The Raven"
45 Trece menos doce
51 Many a Hollywood worker
53 Brownish-yellow hue
54 Big ___
55 Monogram in the 2016 presidential election
57 Puts away
59 Suffragist and abolitionist Abby ___ Alcott
62 Georgia, e.g.
63 One of two circling the earth
65 Decorates deceptively
66 High part of a deck
67 Bon ___ (fashionable world)
68 One-named New Age musician
70 Mower's trail
74 Means of electronic communication with restricted access
76 Ending with cash or front
77 Self images?
79 Stevenson of 1950s politics
80 They may be ridden to victory
81 Some co. name endings
83 Santa Monica ___, southwest terminus of 114-Across
84 Golden rule preposition
85 Speed skater Kramer with nine Olympic medals
87 Stir in
89 String or integer, in programming
91 Brand with a bull in its logo
92 Critical warning
93 Some scores in horseshoes
96 "My Name Is Asher ___"
99 Offer one's two cents
100 Deprived
101 You usually do this lying down by yourself
103 Naval "Negative"
104 Singer O'Day
105 Bad messages to send to the wrong person
107 Tap-in, e.g.
109 140, in old Rome
110 Covid Data Tracker org.
111 New Deal power agcy.
112 Fools are often seen at its start: Abbr.
113 Peaceful, informally
115 Partner of only
116 Posed for a portrait

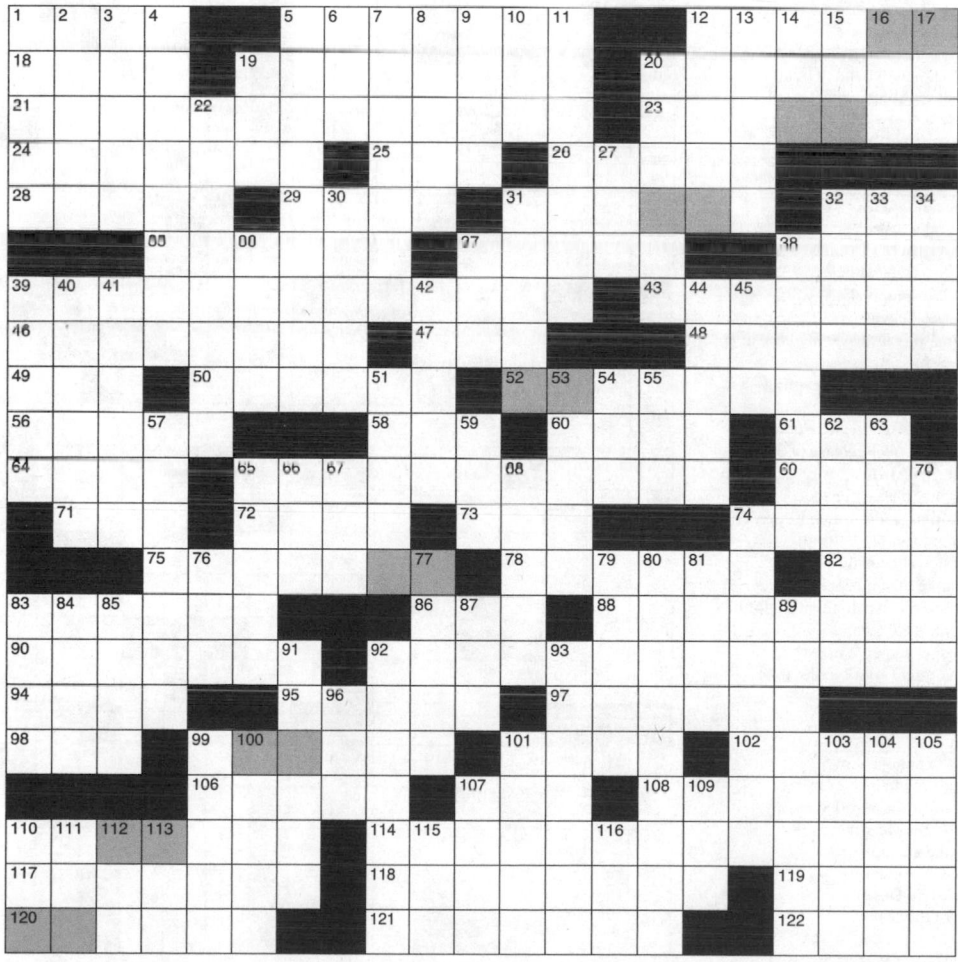

by Daniel Mauer

Note: When this puzzle is done, read the circled letters line by line from top to bottom to get an appropriate word.

ACROSS

1 Dual degree for a physician/scientist
6 "My man!"
9 D.C. figure
12 Impulsive desire
16 An avian abode
17 Janis ___, main role in "Mean Girls"
18 One's time in office, maybe
19 "For ___ is the kingdom . . ."
20 See 5-Down
22 See 12-Down
24 Parts of a machine
25 Creep (along)
26 "Me too"
27 Destroy internally
28 Get rid of
29 Trap
31 They'll give you more of the same
33 Kidney-related
35 Tuckered (out)
36 Straddling
37 Places of refuge
39 "Love ___," Pet Shop Boys dance hit of 2009
41 City between Chicago and Milwaukee
45 Cry while plugging one's ears
46 What cobblers cobble
48 ___ de deux (ballet dance)
49 See 29-Down
53 Like Hitchcock's "Curtain"
54 Passionate feeling in Spain
56 Wall molding
58 Weaken, as support
59 Untrustworthy paper
60 Publication with an annual "Power 100" list
62 See 53-Down
64 Social worker?
65 Olaf Scholz's country: Abbr.
66 Wireless network std.
67 Its life span is short
68 See 61-Down
72 Kind of pear that resembles an apple
74 Exploit
75 It has thousands of openings
76 Laugh at, say
78 Ride in "Calvin and Hobbes"
79 ___ Pro, tech release of 2017
80 See 73-Down
83 Capital player, for short
84 "Rotten" indicator on Rotten Tomatoes
86 Eastern honorific
87 Source of some leaks
90 There was Noah-counting for it
92 Verse's partner
96 Gospel singer Winans
97 You might speak under this
99 Earth, in some sci-fi
100 Works on oneself?
103 Fit
105 Little annoyance
106 Bad way to go
107 Many a summer TV show
109 Title for Mozart
110 Make an oopsie
111 See 84-Down
113 See 104-Down
115 Like the sea
116 Bother
117 European World Cup team, on scoreboards
118 "Beep!" maker
119 Word with tag or tax
120 Parking space
121 Online feed letters
122 Deep, dark hole

DOWN

1 It may run when you cry
2 Cleanses, in a way
3 Offspring
4 They "don't lie," per a Shakira hit
5 Tyrants / Patterns
6 "We're pregnant!," e.g.
7 Southwestern spread
8 No longer at sea
9 In and of itself
10 Snack item that's partly foreordained?
11 Dessert of molten chocolate
12 Anyplace / From which place
13 Turning point
14 Rack up
15 Zooms with, maybe
19 Stumble over
21 Division ___, lowest level of the N.C.A.A.
23 Chews the scenery
29 Made puffier, as cushions / Very desirable job
30 Admits
32 Start-up's announcement, for short
34 Take in, say
38 "O ___ babbino caro" (Puccini aria)
40 Group of vocal people
42 Amounts of sugar, perhaps
43 Person not easily swayed by sentiment
44 Prescription directive
47 Never again
49 Rewards for staying, maybe
50 Point person?
51 It's written with a + or -
52 Take a shot at
53 Tourist, e.g. / Hypnotic state
54 Italian rice balls
55 "Hoo-boy!"
57 Actor Page
58 Uniform
60 Parts of a clutch
61 Tom who hosted "Dancing With the Stars" / Brimless caps
63 Second letter after epsilon
69 Alt-___, PC command to switch between windows
70 Relative of turquoise
71 Capital of Yemen
72 $$$ taker
73 Endurance / Subway map info
77 Fruit with a thick peel
78 Take potshots
81 Sorta
82 Give an address
84 Tryst partner / Discharging, as a liquid
85 Like the motions before a hearing
88 Unfriendly
89 Very much
91 Disputed Asian region
92 River next to Boston's Esplanade
93 "The Divine Comedy," e.g.
94 Weasel family members
95 Eric B, Pimp C and Chuck D
98 Nonbinary possessive
100 Pointed remarks
101 Best ___ Recording (Grammy category)
102 Who may care, so they say
103 Bit of gold reserves
104 Qualifying match, for short / Big name in antifreeze and brake fluid
108 Take back
110 Sudden feeling, as of remorse
112 "Good ___!"
114 Relaxation spot

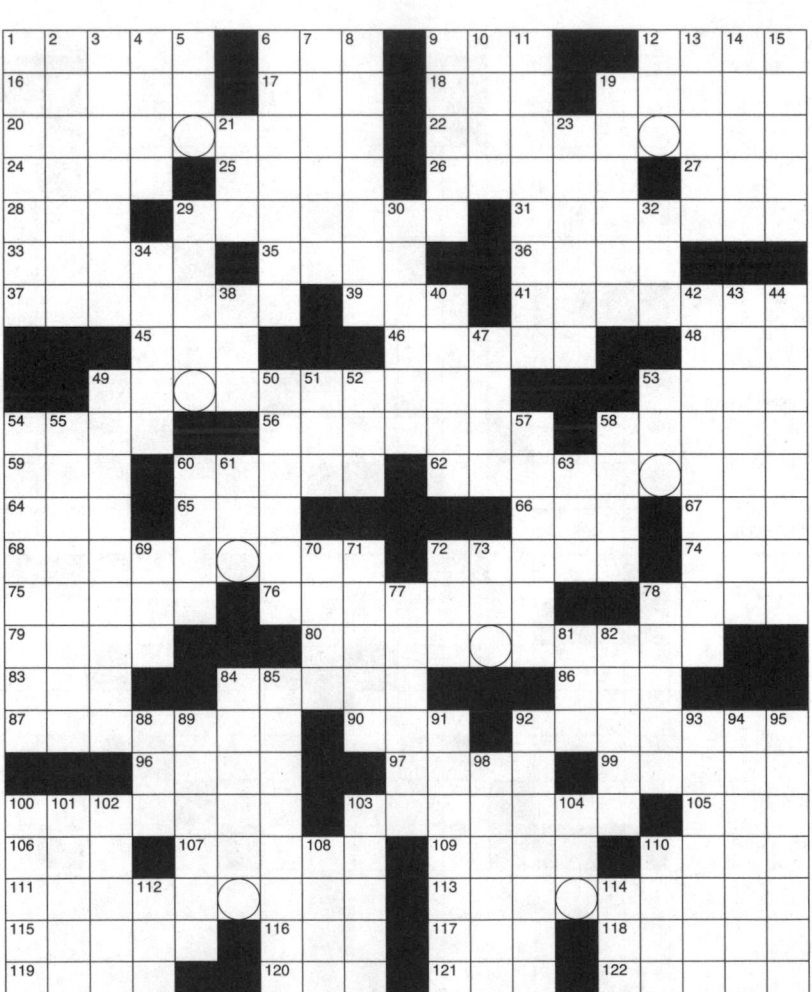

by David and Karen and Paul Steinberg

ACROSS

1 Part of a big media campaign
5 About 200 feet, for a Boeing 777
9 Artist Vincent van ___
13 Tiara go-with
17 Kind of spider commonly found near train tracks
18 Held on to
19 Slacks, say, in slang
20 Apparel in many a Degas painting
21 With 23-Across, what this puzzle's subject promised in his most famous address
23 See 21-Across
25 Premium flight amenity
26 Piercing-free bijouterie
27 Landmark dedicated on 5/30/1922
33 Raymond ___, Best Actor nominee for portraying this puzzle's subject (1940)
36 Hades' collection
37 Rough and uneven
41 Actress Green of "Casino Royale"
42 They watch what you eat, for short
44 Order of doughnuts
45 It's in, then it's out
46 "Norma ___"
47 Pining away
50 Suitcase
51 He played Ferris Bueller's droning economics teacher
53 Something easily snapped
54 Pay-___-click (advertising model)
55 Place for an ace
56 Wish to take back
57 Composer Zimmer
58 N.H.L. great Bobby
60 PDF alternative
62 Get the ___
63 Situated
64 Office
67 Big moneymaker
71 Italicize or underline
74 It's all about me
76 Feature first recommended to this puzzle's subject by an 11-year-old girl
77 Extendable recording device
78 Rivendell resident, in "The Lord of the Rings"
79 Drink (up)
80 "You with me?"
81 ___ Offroad Fury (2000s video game series)
82 Cable news anchor Cabrera
83 Stuffed pockets
85 Nickname for this puzzle's subject
88 Eponymous physicist Mach
90 Have ___ (be able to jump high, in slang)
92 Ulysses S. Grant, e.g.
93 Bit of "deets"
94 Locales in a winery tour, perhaps
96 Bikini's place
99 "Crazy Rich Asians" director Jon M. ___
100 IV site, for short
101 Choose
102 When repeated, cheer accessory
104 Stretches
109 Trattoria staple
111 Takes part in a pilot program?
112 Sanskrit for "great soul"
113 Sent a letter
114 Govt. aid for a mom-and-pop store
115 Some titles with tildes
116 Backs

DOWN

1 Some Asian cuisine
2 Skiing star Lindsey
3 Partner of aid
4 Pieces included with Ikea furniture
5 Barely get wet?
6 Writer Georges whose 300-page novel "A Void" completely avoided the letter E
7 Is ___ (probably will)
8 Utmost
9 Classic Pontiac
10 Title role in a Monteverdi opera
11 Win at life
12 One-eyed giant?
13 McCartney of fashion
14 Maker of the Q7 and Q8
15 Cry from one being tickled, maybe
16 Runs well
22 Snug-fitting underwear
24 Greetings sent with a click
28 Tab inits.
29 Unlikely winners in Fortnite, say
30 Earful in an elevator
31 Dead lines?
32 I.S.P. alternative to 84-Down
33 Diner order
34 Say outright
35 One epithet for this puzzle's subject
38 Another epithet for this puzzle's subject
39 "Buy low, sell high" outcome
40 Aches (for)
43 Nailed
45 Ongoing quarrel
48 Cousin of a bittern
49 Ray of McDonald's fame
51 Arched body part
52 Utility bill unit
59 Campaign nickname that reflected the rustic upbringing of this puzzle's subject
61 Beachside locale
62 Loving turndown
63 Accessory in which this puzzle's subject stashed important documents
64 [Outta my way, slowpoke!]
65 Wrinkly fruit
66 Home to about 75% of the world's tornadoes
68 Rocker Bob
69 More than unpleasant
70 Island whose capital and largest city is Iraklion
71 Habitual drinker
72 Subject of the seven-letter mnemonic PALE GAS
73 "Zip-a-dee-doo-dah," e.g.
75 Fastball stat
77 Hon
84 I.S.P. alternative to 32-Down
86 Biting remarks?
87 ___ on over (go somewhere, in slang)
89 Court figure, informally
91 Perfumed pouches
93 Symbols of rebirth in ancient Egypt
94 Goat's milk cheese
95 Anthony or Joe who directed "Avengers: Endgame"
97 Makeup set?
98 One making a racket?
99 Some arcade machine mechanisms
103 Spooky sounds
105 One chased by un perro
106 Lead-in to historic
107 ___ the Kid, rhyming N.H.L. nickname
108 Otolaryngologist, for short
110 This really blows

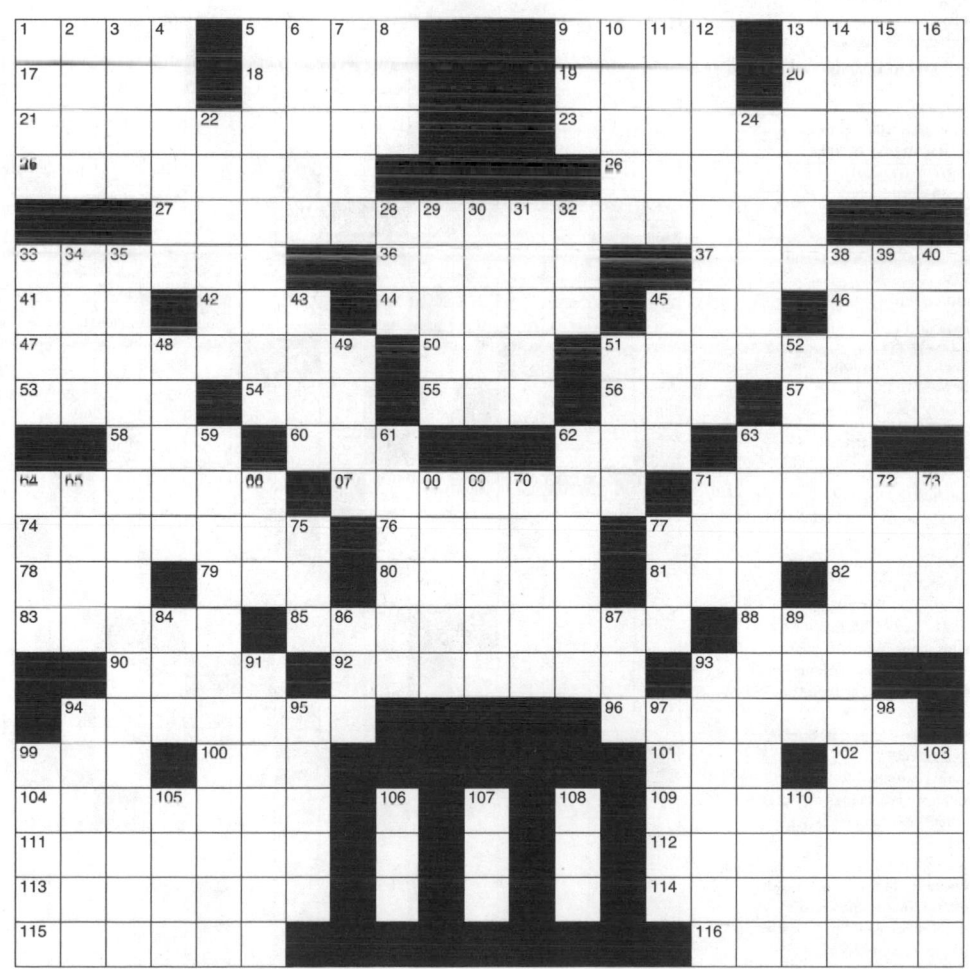

by Daniel Bodily and Jeff Chen

ACROSS

1 Precursor to a circuit breaker
5 ___ bar
10 Pointed remark
14 Common spa descriptor
19 "Hello there, sailor!"
20 Gourmet mushroom with poisonous lookalikes
21 Somewhat
22 Core workout challenge
23 Looks up from reading "Frankenstein"?
27 Moody North Yorkshire setting
28 Handy
29 Restless
30 Split hairs?
31 Words exchanged during an "altar"-cation
32 Revise
33 Reads "Catch-22," "Closing Time" and "Something Happened" — and doesn't stop there?
39 Atmospheric driving hazard
42 Came to
43 Assistant
44 The joy of text?
45 Expression of a grump
47 Cheeky remarks . . . or something near the cheek
48 Kendrick Lamar's 2017 Best Rap Album Grammy winner
50 "Aquaman" actor Jason
52 English indie pop singer Parks
53 Sleek reef swimmers
55 Borrows "The Color Purple" from the library instead of "The Flowers"?
60 1960s activist Bobby
62 Word with play or fight
63 Belgrade resident
64 See 36-Down
65 First in a line of 13 popes
67 Strands
69 Lifewater and Elixir brand
71 "Wow!"
74 Fashion guru Tim
76 "___ the spirit!"
78 D.E.A. target
81 Listens to "Tom Jones" on audiobook?
85 Matterhorn range
87 Wheely good invention?
88 Off
89 ___ tube
91 H
92 Conclude by
94 Dawson in the Pro Football Hall of Fame
95 "Chat another time!" in an I.M.
97 Bolt in a sprint
99 Director Guillermo ___ Toro
100 Reads "Lady Chatterley's Lover" so many times its spine splits?
105 Cryptids on snowy mountains
107 Mars bar with shortbread and chocolate
108 [sigh]
109 Pilot green-lighter, in brief
111 "Ask away!"
113 Iconic scarecrow topper
117 Donates some copies of "King Lear" to the Renaissance Festival?
120 Still
121 Curling locale
122 Musical with the song "Another Suitcase in Another Hall"
123 ___ Rachel Wood of "Westworld"
124 Castles, essentially
125 Chances
126 Not let lapse
127 It can be outstanding

DOWN

1 "Octopuses can use tools," e.g.
2 "This is not good!"
3 Words said while shaking one's head in disgust
4 One might be found next to a neck pillow in an airport shop
5 Suave
6 Decant
7 Painting and filmmaking
8 Person in a head set?
9 Keebler cookie with shortbread and chocolate
10 Send away
11 Biblical analogue of Aron in "East of Eden"
12 High-___ (kind of jeans or apartment building)
13 South Korean "Princes of Pop"
14 Jimmies and corkscrews
15 Debbie of "Fame" and "Grey's Anatomy"
16 Things often next to napkins in place settings
17 Spanish Agnes
18 Absolut alternative
24 Put in order
25 Text-writer's segue
26 Philosopher David
31 Alternative to a diaphragm
32 Like games marked 1→99
33 Strong wind
34 Pains for preschoolers
35 Chivalrous avatar of Vishnu
36 Sounds from a 64-Across
37 Saint associated with a "fire"
38 Birds on Canadian dollars
40 Big-eyed hatchling
41 1989 film for which Denzel Washington won Best Supporting Actor
46 Follower of "So" or "lo"
49 Patronized a restaurant
50 Homes for cattails and bulrushes
51 Childhood friend
54 Blueberry-picking girl of children's literature
56 "Yuck!"
57 "You're right about that!"
58 "You're not right about that!"
59 "Chiquitita" singing group
61 Endurance, so to speak
66 Scarfs down
68 Norm: Abbr.
70 Geological span
71 Chose
72 QB's protection
73 Very rarely
75 Ancient home of a mythical lion
77 Delphic prophet
79 Barbershop specialty
80 Fiber-___
82 "I'm in favor"
83 Rat
84 The Big Easy
86 Sound
90 Fabric made from jute
93 Med. exams with intradermal injections
95 O'er yon
96 "The Muppets" villain Richman
98 Macroalgae
101 Costa ___
102 Baby birds?
103 Deuces
104 Cold War pact city
106 Use, as influence
109 "Here I come, weekend!"
110 In ___ veritas
111 Reported
112 Back
113 Abrade, in a way
114 Head: Fr.
115 Horse with endurance
116 Billowy dress style
118 To's counterpart
119 Broadway, for one: Abbr.

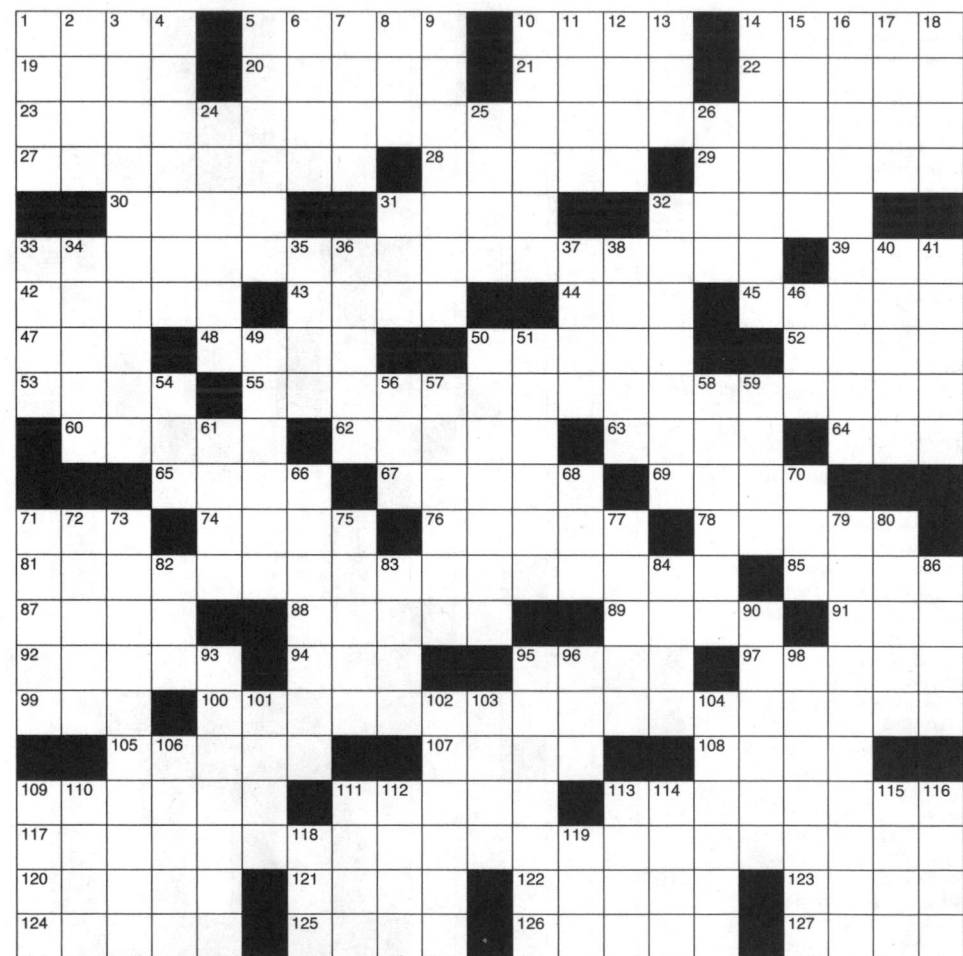

by Christina Iverson and Katie Hale

ACROSS

1 Poses
5 ___ palm (tropical tree)
9 Drive (around)
13 Composer Bernstein who was unrelated to Leonard
18 Doohickey
20 Home to the Dole Plantation
21 Industry show
22 Late singer Judd
23 Contest with lots of "tied" scores
24 In a fight
25 Body part that humans have that other primates don't
26 Term to drop in a serious relationship, informally
27 Argument extender [ref. 18-Across]
30 Tiny amounts
31 Terse denial
32 What seat selection on an airplane often comes with
33 Eerily familiar feeling
35 Scottish refusal
36 Focused on the bull's-eye
39 State fiction as fact
41 Supervise
45 Slowly makes its way through
47 Fun functions
48 With 87-Across, "I've been around the block a few times" [ref. 23-Across]
53 Yoga pose
55 Covering
56 Rock's C.J. or Dee Dee
57 Currency of Qatar
59 Package in Santa's sleigh
61 18+, say
62 Danger
65 Sun block
67 Molecular messenger
70 Classic Yogi Berra quote [ref. 33-Across]
74 Whole bunch
75 Fiber made from cellulose
76 Chemical ingredient in flubber
77 Did some secretarial work
78 The last thing a Mississippi cheerleader wants?
79 Land divided at the 38th parallel
81 Former name for the N.B.A.'s Thunder, informally
82 Crib sheet user
85 Team building
87 See 48-Across
91 Consolidated for easier reading, as a Twitter thread
93 Composer Luigi who pioneered noise music
95 Like some arts
96 Be an agent for
97 Broadway composer Jule
99 Crop that might be insect-resistant, in brief
102 Sleep inducer
104 ___ particle
106 Came next
108 Algonquian people
111 Debut album by Britney Spears [ref. 82-Across]
115 Beginning
116 French pronoun
117 Word implied in "I haven't the foggiest"
118 Crenshaw or casaba
119 "That makes two of us"
120 One with a nose for gnus?
121 A pan might come with just one
122 Elusive giants
123 Tread + riser
124 Becomes less taut
125 Seemingly forever
126 Instrument for Orpheus

DOWN

1 Transport in a Billy Strayhorn standard
2 Showrunner Rhimes
3 ___ pool
4 Sam with 82 P.G.A. Tour wins
5 Lay it on thick
6 Pledge
7 Political unit of ancient Hawaii
8 Highly unconventional
9 Sector for many start-ups
10 Durable leather
11 Give a take
12 Doughnut similar to an éclair
13 Spice up
14 Canadian observance also called Fête du Travail
15 Not worth arguing about
16 Goldman who crusaded for birth control access
17 Barbecue order
19 "Never ___ Give You Up" (Rick Astley song)
28 Useless
29 Prefix with medicine
34 One whose work goes over your head
37 Web portal with a Bing search bar
38 Ambulance pro
40 Monocle-dropping exclamation
42 Be on the bottom?
43 "___-Tripping" (Nikki Giovanni poem)
44 Sixth of five?
46 Home country of the poet Adonis
47 Mouth-watering?
48 Park way
49 Was given no other option
50 "There's no other option"
51 Persuaded
52 Starting position, maybe
54 Relish
58 "Goodness me!"
60 Sojourner Truth or Frances Harper
62 It's illegal for employers to prohibit workers from discussing this
63 Called to mind
64 Talk at length
66 "On the Basis of ___" (2018 legal drama)
67 Swift
68 Goddaughter, often
69 "It therefore follows that . . ."
71 Sport played on a fronton
72 Lazes around
73 Doc who performs Pap smears
78 Black Lives Matter co-founder
80 Valuable to collectors, say
81 High-minded sort?
82 Depress, with "out"
83 Santa ___ winds
84 Comment with a shiver
86 Marks down, maybe
88 Gave officially
89 Deteriorate
90 Guileful
92 Cholesterol-lowering drug
94 ___ and including
96 Share on Tumblr, say
98 "You can learn from anyone — even your ___": Ovid
99 "Yep, you got me"
100 Story of one's life
101 Danish city where Hans Christian Andersen was born
103 ___ al Ghul (on-and-off lover of Batman)
105 Fennel-like flavoring
107 Material for some drums
108 Online forum V.I.P.s
109 Still having a shot at winning
110 "The Thin Man" dog
112 Itches
113 Far from friendly
114 Rest on one's ___

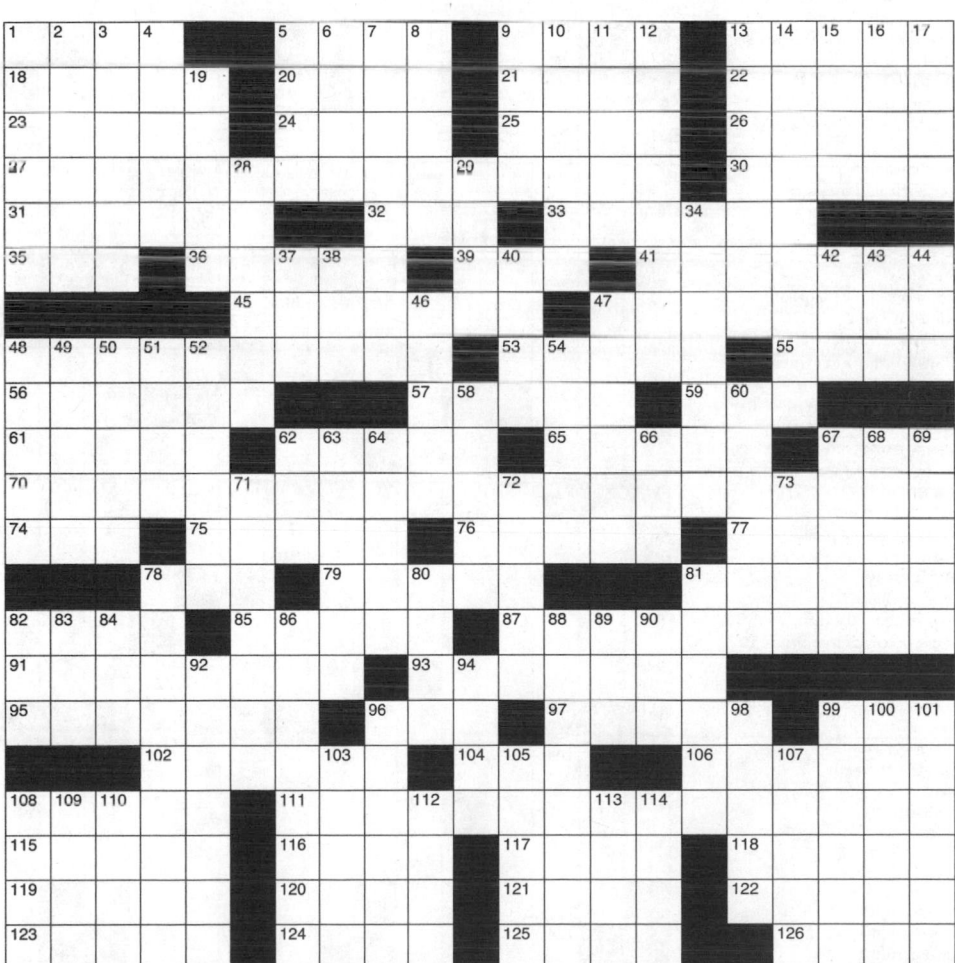

by Will Nediger

Note: When you've finished the puzzle, look for an appropriate hidden word.

ACROSS

1 Partitions between nostrils
6 Place to park a boat
10 Malt-drying kiln
14 Gave a look of "Can you believe that?!"
15 Smaller than small
17 Rub it in
19 What you'll hear after-hours at a sports car sales lot?
23 Cry from a boxing coach
24 Swimmer's assignment
25 RC, for one
26 Fayetteville school, informally
27 City that neighbors Ann Arbor, for short
28 Rodeo Drive uprising?
32 Janelle of "Moonlight"
34 Loire contents
35 Per person
36 Twisted jeans legs?
42 Religion of the Maldives
46 Mission statement's inspiration
47 Expected
48 Bounces around a pool table
51 Antagonist in "Hop-o'-My-Thumb"
52 Drink with crumpets
53 South Asian crepes
55 Thrill
57 Mini manufacturer
58 Chihuahua, por ejemplo
61 Staunch dedication to one's upper leg exercise routine?
65 Country whose name together with its capital city has only eight letters
67 [I'm a cow!]
68 Take for a spin
69 Winter wear for a stegosaurus?
75 "I have my ____"
79 Understand
80 Palestinian political party
81 Some feds
83 "Look, fireworks!"
84 Diver's destination
86 Labor class?
89 Airport code for a Delta hub
90 It's a small world
92 Bracket buster's victory
94 Tire-puncturing way across a river?
97 Region
100 Musician whose name sounds like an exclamation
101 Message written on a Wonderland cake
102 Introduction to a chiropractor's makeshift toolkit?
110 Ankle-length dress
112 First automaker to conduct crash tests (1938)
113 E.R. imperative
114 Pair in an ellipse
115 Capital on the Atlantic
116 Campaign to convince British P.M. Tony to change parties?
121 Like sailors' language, stereotypically
122 Operator of the Valley Flyer and Coast Starlight
123 Urge strongly
124 Wranglers alternative
125 Make
126 Rulers until 1917

DOWN

1 Top of a range?
2 Enter smoothly
3 Proper partner?
4 Number on a bus. card
5 First songwriter to win an Oscar for a James Bond theme
6 One in the driver's seat
7 Head of Eton?
8 Global finance org.
9 Word before or after perfect
10 Tribe whose flag features a circle of tepees on a red background
11 French menu word
12 To such an extent (that)
13 Game with a card that might say "Lawyer: court judge legal crime case"
14 Swabs, say
15 Target for salicylic acid
16 Fourth-most common surname in Korea (after Kim, Lee and Park)
18 Stinky ____ (popular Chinese street food)
19 "Your" of yore
20 ____ system (GPS device)
21 Vogue rival
22 April fool target
28 ____ Paese cheese
29 Secular
30 One-named singer with the 2016 hit "Crush"
31 High school dept.
33 Follower of smart or wise
36 Comic Davidson
37 Big whoop
38 Go over 21, say
39 "What she said"
40 Nonkosher
41 Hindu Festival of Colors
43 Community celebrated in June, in brief
44 Name of BTS's fan base
45 Kitten's sound
49 Anti-D.U.I. org.
50 Mounts
53 Kind of fin
54 One offering intense but unrequited affection, in modern usage
56 Red Muppet
59 4/
60 ____ Studies (Gallaudet University department)
62 Indian state on the Arabian Sea
63 Mellophone, e.g.
64 Debtor's note
66 Arthur Ashe Stadium org.
69 Wrangler maker
70 Great Basin natives
71 "Macbeth," but not "Hamlet"
72 Burn a little
73 Vegetable that's massaged before eating
74 Mythical ship that sailed to Colchis
76 Odds fellows?
77 Specifically
78 "____ All That" (1999 rom-com)
79 "Despicable Me" antihero
82 Half-____
85 Within reach, as a goal
87 Utah's ____ National Park
88 "Hairspray" mom
90 Fig. on a transcript
91 One with a storied education, informally?
93 Race in which one begins in a wetsuit, for short
95 Shade that one might find on the links?
96 "What did I tell you?"
98 Some writing samples
99 Source of Italian bubbles
102 Heart on one's sleeve, for short?
103 Verbal shrugs
104 Perfect
105 Prefix with legal
106 Exclamation while seeing oneself on the Jumbotron, perhaps
107 Tick follower
108 German lament
109 Lab dropper
111 N.Y.C. subway inits.
115 Capital of Qatar
117 Inits. on a cellphone
118 Sports org. founded by Billie Jean King
119 Like the verb "to be": Abbr.
120 Scripts

by Matthew Stock and Finn Vigeland

Note: Seven clues in this puzzle relate to their answers in a manner for you to discover. Standard clues for these answers appear below in mixed order.

- Accounting total
- Communicating (with)
- Leg cramp
- Peyton, to Eli Manning
- Showing gratitude
- Unlikely election winner
- Where golfers practice short strokes

ACROSS

1 Host of the 1952 Winter Olympics
5 Not suited (for)
10 Beatles song with an exclamation mark in its title
14 Wild thing
19 Demeter's mother, in myth
20 Singer/songwriter Jones
21 Abbr. on a "works cited" list
22 Kemper of "The Office"
23 Direct path
25 Lot of land, say
26 Director Frank
27 Sea plea
28 Dole (out)
29 "Sheesh!"
32 Like some cheese . . . or some movies
34 Toothsome
35 "Anything you suggest is fine"
36 Rathskeller decoration
38 Anthropologist's adjective
40 Small bits of dough
41 Color of the Owl and Pussy-cat's boat
44 Connecting words in logic
45 Baby's cry
48 _____ Mysteries (children's series starting with "The Absent Author")
49 Champing at the bit
50 Biologist E. O. Wilson's focus
51 "Alas!"
52 Wimple wearer
53 With 54-Across, commonly believed misconception
54 See 53-Across
56 Panache
57 Go for a spin
59 Symbol of Middle America
60 Emotionally disinvest oneself
61 _____ long-horned beetle
63 Something avoided during awkward situations
66 Firing offense?
67 Isolated hill
68 They're shared between partners, one hopes
69 Extremely mean
71 Theater employee
72 Into pieces
73 Fictional Mr. or real Dr.
75 Popular flooring wood
78 "Ready for _____ . . . ?"
79 Once more
80 Fair part
81 Cocktail made with ginger beer
82 Command to a dog
83 Gets busy
84 Fish with a prehensile tail
87 Symbols of wave functions
88 One of the Furies of Greek myth
89 "Them's fightin' words!"
90 Quickly
93 Suggest, with "of"
94 Excoriate
97 "Oh, that's so nice of you to say!"
99 Disney+ competitor
100 Fool
103 Revise
104 Chill
105 Mad Hatter's social event
108 9 a.m. service
109 Command-Z, on a Mac
110 Falcon's home
111 Harness part
112 Fragrant compound
113 Space heater?
114 Back, in a way
115 Online crafts market

DOWN

1 Suns, e.g.
2 "Scram!"
3 "Enough dillydallying!"
4 Kind of milk
5 Like some expectations
6 Nick of "48 Hrs."
7 The yolk's on them
8 _____ Malcolm, Jeff Goldblum's role in "Jurassic Park"
9 Alternative to this and that
10 Enters
11 "And so on and so forth"
12 Big Bird?
13 Ordinary citizen
14 Looks good on
15 Overjoys
16 A as in Agamemnon
17 Fathers
18 Lachrymose
24 Resident of a Mideast sultanate
30 Thin thoroughfare
31 Melon parts
33 Brand that comes in short sleeves
36 Go across
37 Nobelist Desmond
39 Syntactician's drawing
40 Transitioning phrase
42 Approach
43 Flits here and there
44 Shenanigan
45 Question to someone who looks impossibly young
46 Broseph
47 Animal aptly found in "feather one's nest"
50 Vibe
51 Give a heads-up
53 The _____ things in life
54 Principle
55 Doesn't keep
56 Chemist's container
58 Is really down on
59 Really come down
61 Neighbors
62 Food often served with gari (pickled ginger)
64 Backs of necks
65 Frustrating device in an arcade
70 Hurting
73 Kind
74 Dressage for a horseback rider?
76 Plus
77 Perceptive, as an eye
79 Getting top marks on
80 Betray
81 Wool-gatherer?
83 Into pieces
84 Cacophony
85 Mild expletive
86 Ask for money, informally
87 Pioneer of the Minneapolis sound
88 Poet Gorman who wrote "The Hill We Climb"
90 Banded rock
91 Keeps a watch on?
92 Stave off
93 Quaint contraction
95 Unusual object
96 Last name of the Boxcar Children, in children's literature
98 Consequently
101 Big name in elevators
102 Manhattan address abbr.
106 Part of a giggle
107 "Sweet Dreams (_____ Made of This)" (Eurythmics hit)

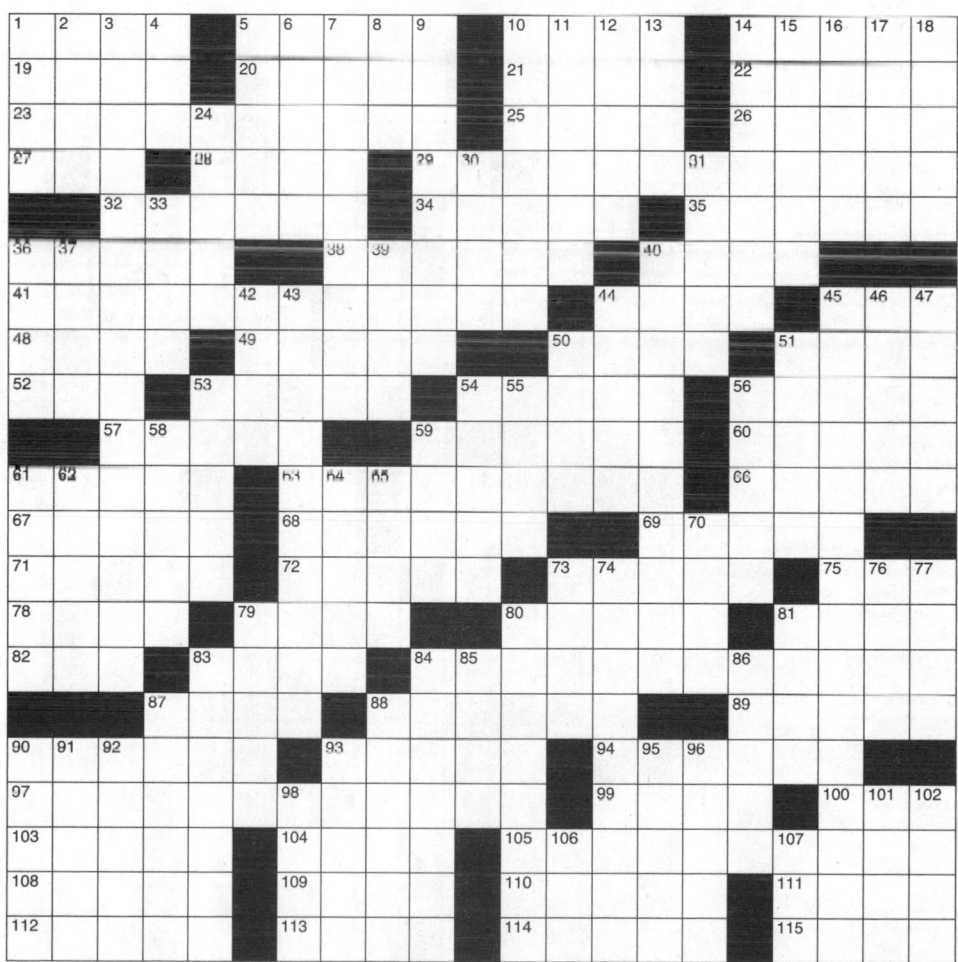

by Tom McCoy

MOVIN' ON UP

ACROSS

1 [omg haha!!]
5 Left speechless
9 Reward for sitting, say
14 Entice
19 Something we share
20 Rocker John whose surname sounds like a leafy vegetable
21 "___ Man Chant," song by Bob Marley and the Wailers
22 Diarist Nin
23 Where some stable relationships form?
25 San Diego State athlete
26 Verge
27 Name that's 98-Across backward
28 The sky, they say
29 "All the Light We Cannot ___" (2015 Pulitzer-winning novel)
30 Certain Chinese teas
32 Roman emperor after Nero and Galba
34 Heep of "David Copperfield"
36 Drop the "Donuts" from "Dunkin' Donuts," e.g.
38 Some four-year degrees: Abbr.
39 Kind of attack with no attacker
40 Michael Jackson hit whose title is heard 88 times in the song
41 What might accompany a grave admission?
44 Claws
47 Cheese with a light, nutty flavor
49 Quite an uproar
52 Design style influenced by Cubism
53 Fabric often dyed with indigo
55 Each of its interior angles measures 135°
56 Swing preventer, of a sort
58 Like some vows
60 Run off together
61 Personal ID
62 Like a sweater that shrank in the dryer, maybe
64 Its alphabet includes delta
65 Some Brothers Grimm villains
66 Artless nickname?
68 Tease
70 Sarcastic punch line
71 That guy's
72 Forty winks
75 Threads
77 Tepid greeting
79 Second word of many a limerick
82 Sans-serif font
83 Thesis writer
85 Meaning of a signal flare
88 2021 Aretha Franklin biopic
90 Strained
92 Greek name meaning "golden one"
93 Something filmed in Broadway's Ed Sullivan Theater, with "The"
95 Journalist Skeeter in the Harry Potter books
96 Train segment
97 Butt end
98 Name that's 27-Across backward
99 "Sweet dreams!"
101 Rapper ___ Rida
102 It's not a good look
106 Family/species go-between
107 The last thing you need?
109 Like the community portrayed in Netflix's "Unorthodox"
111 Piercing tool
113 Tickle
115 Evian, in its native land
117 Cruciverbalist's favorite cookies?
118 "Well, gosh!"
120 Tipsy trips
122 Teatro alla ___
123 Takes a car, in a way
124 Lab assistant in "Young Frankenstein"
125 It may be upper or lower
126 Blue book filler
127 Much of a sponge
128 Mad, with "off"
129 Word of surprise

DOWN

1 Santa ___, Calif.
2 Closing section
3 Banana wielded by a maestro in a pinch?
4 Drug that can be microdosed
5 Berry in a bowl
6 Animated short before a Pixar movie?
7 New York resting place for Mark Twain
8 In the stars
9 Give a scathing review of a major camera brand?
10 Demolish
11 Compound with a fruity smell
12 Had a hero, say
13 Mexican street food mogul?
14 Pair of small hand drums
15 Defunct company of accounting fraud fame
16 Smaug, in "The Hobbit"?
17 Send an e-message to
18 Makes shame-y noises
24 Does a fad 2010s dance
31 Pro using cutting-edge technology?
33 Movie rating that's practically NC-17
35 Political staffers
37 Retreat
42 "Fingers crossed!"
43 Window units
44 Small amounts
45 God whose name sounds almost like the ammunition he uses
46 Starts to go haywire
48 Where 122-Across can be found
50 Places for placentas
51 Surrounding lights
54 Movement championed by the Silence Breakers
57 Get rid of
59 Light-headed sorts?
63 Word after gas or ice, in astronomy
65 Novelist Achebe
66 Wizard's name in books and movies
67 Spun things
69 Kind of patch that may create holes instead of repairing them
72 Otis and ___ (1960s R&B duo)
73 Disciplines
74 Response to "Why art thou queasy?"
76 What Amazon retirees enjoy most?
78 Result of love at first sight?
79 What a dog greets its returning family with?
80 Inter ___
81 Trade jabs
83 Retail takeover scheme?
84 Fix, as laces
86 Nomad
87 Annyeonghaseyo : Korean :: ___ : English
89 Tailgating dish
91 "Tarnation!"
94 Very, colloquially
100 Compassionate
103 Actress Davis who was the first African American to win the Triple Crown of Acting
104 Start of a guesstimate
105 Like a proverbial beaver
108 Model material
109 Place for a run?
110 Rainbows, e.g.
112 "___ saved!"
114 Large amount
116 Bookstore sticker
119 "Euphoria" airer
121 Excellent service?

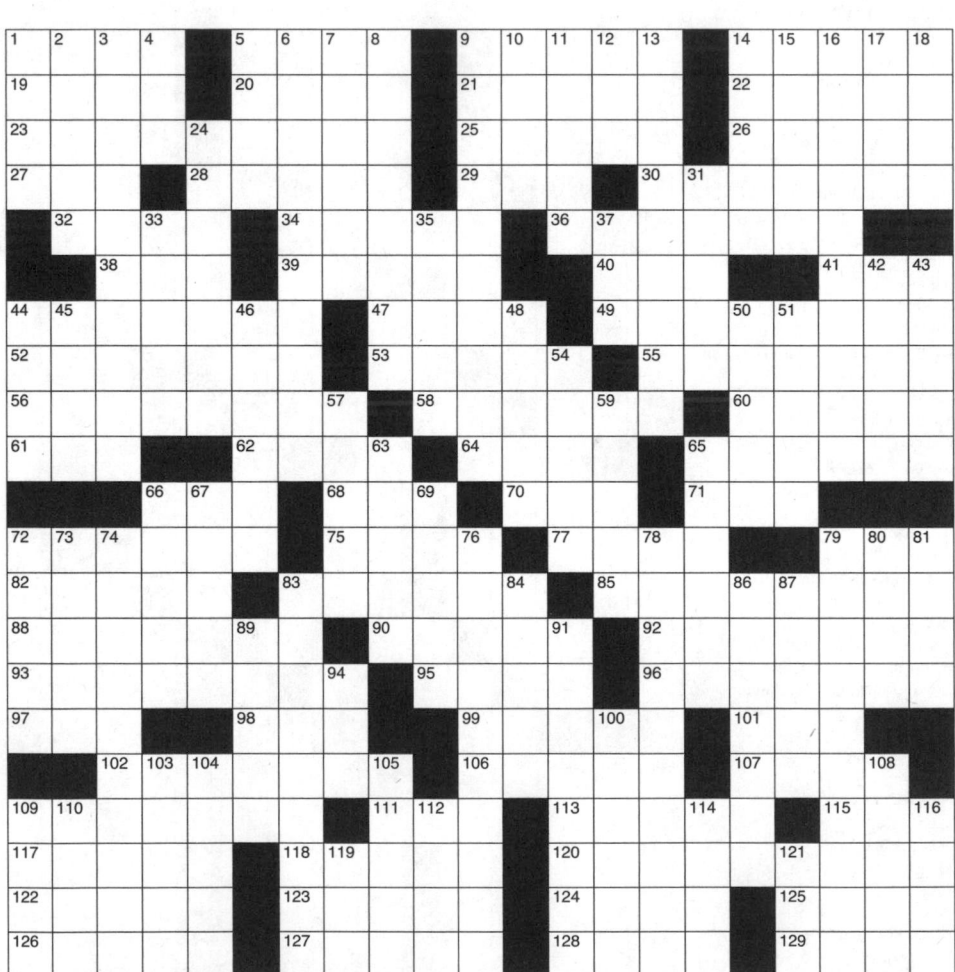

by Christina Iverson and Scott Hogan

A note on Texas hold'em: Players seek to combine one or more of the cards they hold with cards laid out on the table to make the best possible five-card poker hand.

ACROSS

1 Italian almond-flavored cookies
9 Highland boating spot
13 Thick slices
18 Local at St. Mark's Square
19 Put right
21 Bridal path
22 Plant with clusters of tiny white flowers
23 Come forth
24 Do OK, academically
25 Instinctive
26 Source of the phrase "Look before you leap"
28 Opportunity for making professional connections
30 Little cells
31 Traditional Easter entree
33 MGM rival, once
34 Part of a sword
35 Hurriedly
38 More versed in esoterica, maybe
41 Reason one might not go out for a long time?
43 "Forbidden" fragrance
46 Biblical verb with thou
47 One after the other
50 Model Banks
52 Bhutanese bovines
53 Fire-resistant tree
57 Fruit also called blackthorn
58 Works as a mixologist
60 Raid and plunder
62 Taken (with)
65 Water works, e.g.: Abbr.
66 Zip
69 Put on the map, say
71 Control element in medical trials
73 Anger
75 Do some hemming, but not hawing
76 Zip
78 Waters of the world, figuratively
80 From Serbia or Croatia, say
81 Anne Hathaway's role in 2010's "Alice in Wonderland"
83 Actress Perlman of "Cheers"
85 Uses a ride-ordering service
86 Public discussion venues
88 1975 Wimbledon winner
90 Daybreaks
92 Roulette bets with nearly 1:1 odds
94 Old imperial title
96 Steve Martin, Tina Fey and Drew Barrymore, all more than five times
101 Fraser of 1999's "The Mummy"
103 Groups within groups
106 100%
107 Part of U.S.D.A.: Abbr.
108 Original first name of Mickey Mouse
111 It can have a French or pistol grip
112 What can keep a bubble from bursting
115 Trumpeter Armstrong
119 F.D.R. initiative for workers' rights
120 Sci-fi author Asimov
121 "That's cool, man"
123 Some loungewear
126 "Whole ___ Love" (Led Zeppelin hit)
127 Artifacts
128 Held in high regard
129 Scornful look
130 Philosopher Descartes
131 1998 Matt Damon film featuring this puzzle's game

DOWN

1 Pop culture sister site of The Onion
2 "I'm back"
3 Flowers like marigolds and petunias
4 Takes on, as a tenant
5 French summer
6 "___ consummation / Devoutly to be wish'd": Hamlet
7 Yarn
8 Aplenty
9 Apollo vehicle, for short
10 Legislative vacancy
11 Insertion mark
12 Like a geocentric orbit in which the orbital period is more than 24 hours
13 Wise
14 Actor Schreiber
15 Footnote indicator
16 They might be down for a nap
17 Economy part
19 Some tow jobs, for short
20 Aired again
27 Hour, in Italy
29 Resort chain since 1950
30 Tuna type
32 QB stat: Abbr.
35 The Tabard in "The Canterbury Tales," e.g.
36 They're picked by the picky
37 Schleps
39 123-Across's holding that wins this puzzle's game
40 Letter starter
42 Indicator on a clock . . . or one of four in this puzzle?
44 How words may be recited
45 Language in which "khoobsurat" means "beautiful"
48 Frolic
49 "America" singer, 1981
51 Noted sparkling wine region
53 Some gear for a gig
54 Register ring-up
55 Fore, for the H.M.S. Pinafore
56 Consume
59 Recycling receptacles
61 Site of a counter offer?
63 Literature, theater, filmmaking and others
64 Rave attendees, for example
66 ___ the way
67 Title meaning "commander"
68 Benching targets, informally
70 Statistics, e.g.
72 Home of Iolani Palace
74 Place to wear goggles
77 Cardinal point?
79 Good judgment
81 Small songbird
82 Fireplaces
84 Em or Bee, e.g.
86 Missouri site of 2014 civil rights protests
87 Think too highly of
89 Entering gingerly
91 Counterpart of "Thx"
93 Humphrey Bogart role
95 Common component of a tiki bar cocktail
97 Honest and caring
98 Diana Ross, once
99 One picking up the tab
100 Spot
101 "Purple" and "Thai" herbs
102 Polite refusal
104 Big swigs
105 Sign of a full house
109 Public transit customer
110 Patterned fabric
113 Kismet
114 Place to dine on a train
116 Account creator, maybe
117 "___ Excited" (Pointer Sisters song)
118 Yearly January speech to Congress: Abbr.
122 Chill
124 Give new hope to
125 1960s campus activist grp.

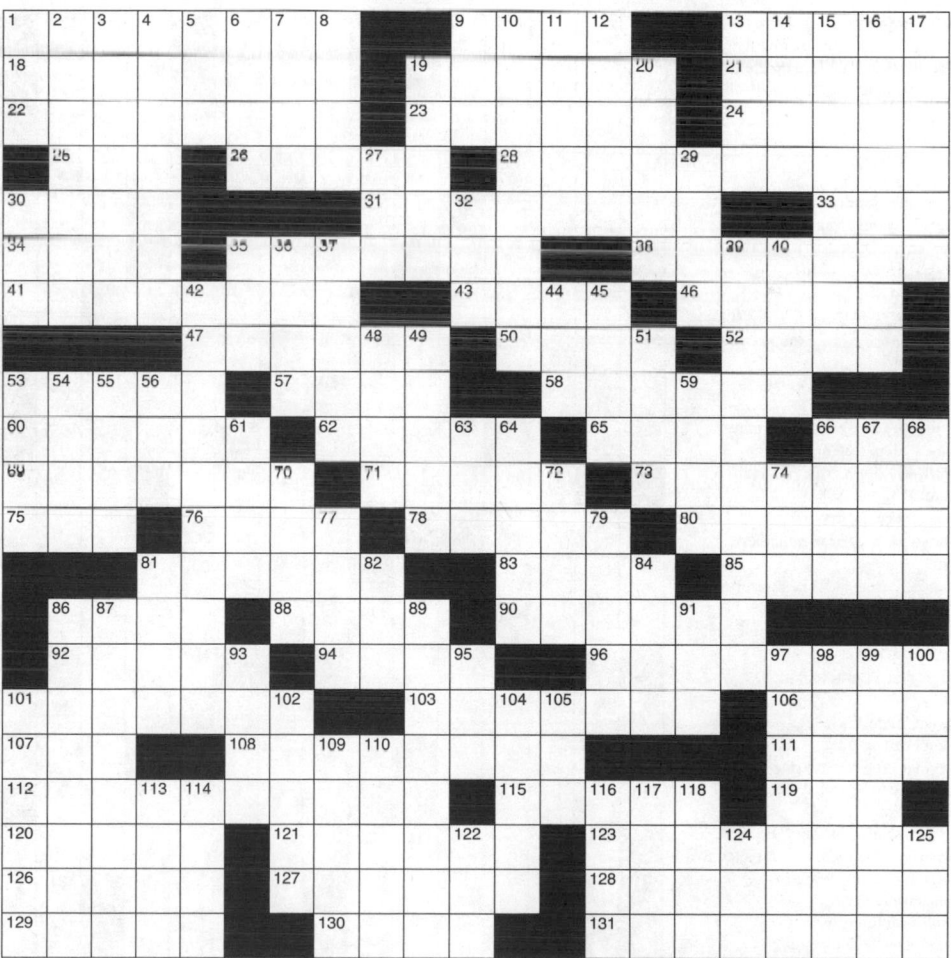

by Greg Slovacek

ACROSS

1 Yankee Stadium has 24 of these
6 In the thick of
10 Org. with X-rays
13 Shape of a heron's neck
16 Bit of publicity
17 Bag for a diamond
18 Yellowfin tuna
19 Cheney and Harris, informally
22 One prone to idol thoughts
25 Marsh birds
27 Clubs often require them, for short
28 Pool locales
29 That: Sp.
30 "Never you worry"
31 Moor
33 Call into question
36 Bouquet
38 Break up clods
40 Bolívar who was known as "the Liberator"
41 Evening, to Yves
42 Reggae-like genre
43 One looking for missing persons
46 Singer White with the 1991 #1 hit "Romantic"
48 Actress de Matteo
50 Inits. on some handbags
51 Two-colored
53 Model world
55 End-of-semester form: Abbr.
57 Flick, as a cigarette, informally
58 Disappearing sculpture medium
59 Big name in jet skis
60 Gumption
62 ___ hall
63 Stylish flair
65 Square type
66 Necessities for drug approvals
68 English landing spot
71 Seat for the Queen?
73 Egyptian symbol of life
74 Stick with it!
76 John Cho's role in "Star Trek" films
77 Level
78 Spill the tea
79 Hits high notes in high places
82 Suit
85 Setting of two Shakespeare plays
87 Some coding statements
88 Edith Wharton's "ruin of a man"
91 Nautical agreement
94 Bearer of roses, maybe
95 Word with American or amber
96 Whiz
97 Aunt ___ (role on "The Fresh Prince of Bel-Air")
98 Habitual fear of being exposed as a fraud
105 N.F.L. star Elliott, to fans
106 Edify
107 Rikishi's sport
108 "Don't be that ___"
109 Part of a skin-care routine
110 First pope to be called "the Great"
111 Dillydallies
114 "In Search of Lost Time" novelist
115 Aphorism that's visually depicted five times in this puzzle's grid
119 Pros with floors
120 Unit of cauliflower
121 Split, then come together?
122 Ultimate needs
123 Parched
124 Apply (to)

DOWN

1 Rosebud ravager
2 Latin for "I believe"
3 Some black-and-white pictures
4 Prone to brooding, say
5 Scatters
6 Stacey of Georgia politics
7 Easternmost leg of I-90, familiarly
8 Suffix with fool or fiend
9 Opus ___
10 Dance shoe attachments
11 Bundles
12 Put on
13 Home of the Simpson and Flanders households
14 Rocker Bob with 10 top 10 albums
15 Casper competitor
20 One side of D.C.'s Federal Triangle
21 iPhone app with a graph in its icon
23 Nail polish brand
24 Where all the people that come and go stop and say "hello," in a 1967 hit
26 It's a huge deal
30 State ___
32 Former N.Y.C. mayor Ed
34 Actress Thurman
35 Locale for a rock climber
37 Noted shopping mecca
39 More like an empty old mansion at night, say
43 Transport on the slopes
44 Stop lying
45 Celebrity chef DiSpirito
47 Point in a network
49 Profess
52 Combines, in a way
54 Fictional documentarian from Kazakhstan
56 Provider of a ball of thread, in myth
59 Like some cars and kisses
61 ___ Club
64 Neighbor of Curaçao
67 Theater rebuke
69 Scratch (out)
70 Botch
72 You might be advised to do this for yourself
74 Memo opener, often
75 "That's rough"
80 Downwind locales for ships
81 "Now!"
83 Home of Nobel Peace Prize winner Shirin Ebadi
84 Spilled the tea
86 "Listen!," in León
89 Cherry and peach
90 Combined
92 "Uh-oh!"
93 Turn inside out
94 Of whom Celine Dion said "If God would have a singing voice, he must sound a lot like . . ."
96 ___ Schneider, winningest woman in "Jeopardy!" history
98 "___ the economy, stupid!"
99 Got together in
100 White as a sheet
101 Paul who was People magazine's 2021 Sexiest Man Alive
102 Tremendous success
103 Squawked in pain
104 Coup result
105 Member of Gen Z, jocularly
109 Busy businesswoman in a rom-com, e.g.
112 Loved
113 Title on Netflix's "Bridgerton"
114 Univ. V.I.P.
116 Any of the Uruk-hai in "The Lord of the Rings"
117 Word with half or hard
118 Fútbol cry

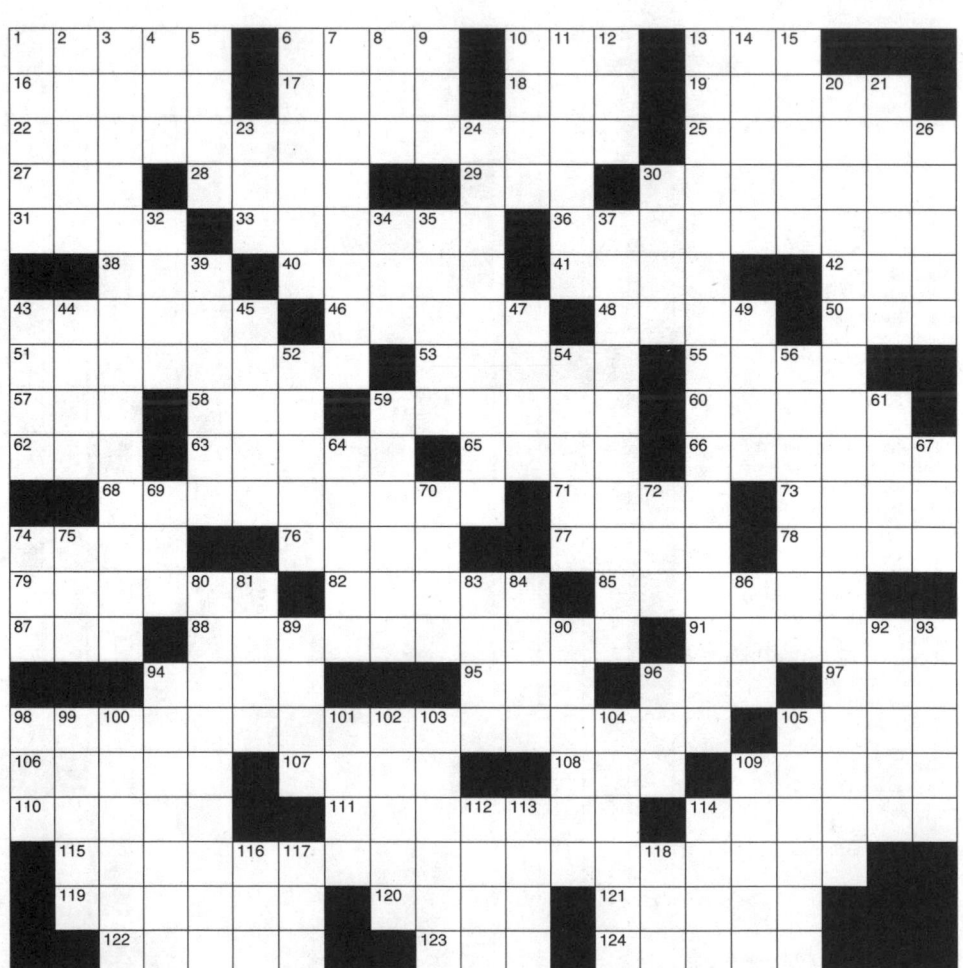

by Jessie Trudeau and Ross Trudeau

ACROSS

1 Homes that may have butlers
7 Singer Dylan of the Wallflowers
12 Supporting beams
18 Bear or boar
19 Bees, e.g.
21 Gleaming
22 The "C" of AMC Theatres
23 The whole package, colloquially
24 Sevastopol is its largest city
25 Not true?
27 Visitor to a website, in analytics lingo
29 "Time _____ . . ."
30 Concedes
33 Santa _____, Calif.
34 m, to Einstein
35 B.C. neighbor: Abbr.
38 Think creatively
40 XL or 11C
42 Beer named for a founding father
45 W-2, for one
47 W.W. I helmet, informally
51 2004 Will Smith sci-fi film
52 D.S.T. starting time . . . or a hint to 42-Across
54 Weightlessness . . . or a hint to 118-Across
56 _____ Compton, first woman to cover the White House for a TV network
57 Rating unit
60 Libya's Gulf of _____
61 Reporter's credit
62 TV tavern
64 Mimic
66 "Royal" bird
67 In
68 Top credit rating . . . or a hint to 25-Across
71 23rd in a series . . . or a hint to 27-Across
73 Trust in
76 Fails to be
78 Keen
79 Google _____
83 Holds in high regard
84 Old lab burners
86 Water bird with a haunting call
88 Bit of HI gear?
89 Cops . . . or a hint to 115-Across
90 Club for farm kids . . . or a hint to 97-Across
91 Pouch on a string
93 Game with L- and T-shaped pieces
96 Locale for a West Coast wine tour
97 Secretive
99 R&R settings
101 Crystal-clear
103 "O, _____ fortune's fool!": Romeo
104 Singer King with the 2014 hit "Ex's & Oh's"
108 Body feature of a mammoth
110 Holy _____
112 It might be taken to the airport
115 Spelling aid?
118 Baseball announcer's call on a home run
121 Nigerian city of 3.5+ million
122 Set on the ground
125 "Jeopardy!" fodder
126 This evenin'
127 Video call glitch
128 "I kid you not!"
129 Rate
130 Like the Xbox One X vis-à-vis the Xbox One
131 Makes some Z's

DOWN

1 Colorful parrot
2 Santa _____
3 Jazz singer born Eunice Kathleen Waymon
4 Warning sign
5 Commercial follower of "-o-"
6 A-game or b-ball, e.g.
7 The "you" of the song lyric "I'm begging of you, please don't take my man"
8 Part of the knee, for short
9 D.I.Y. buy
10 "Magnum, P.I." setting
11 Sauvignon _____
12 Where one might turn on the jets
13 D&D monster
14 Pelvis bone
15 Gregor _____, Kafka protagonist
16 Some genealogical work
17 Pioneering mail-order company
19 Introductory courses
20 Mixes together
26 Not looking good
28 Ctrl+Q
31 First couple of the early 1910s
32 "Shut your trap!"
36 Apply with a Q-tip, say
37 Kerfuffles
39 Wore down
41 RNA polymerase, e.g.
42 Thailand, once
43 River through Tuscany
44 Reaches
46 Bone filler
48 #2 on a table
49 Bone-dry
50 A great deal
53 How-to go-to
55 Obtain
58 YouTube or Gmail
59 "Phew!" feeling
61 They're filled with X's
63 Engraving instrument
65 Lean against
69 Whirlybird whirlers
70 Like some plants and physicals
72 Personal story, informally
73 One calling a "T"
74 Turnoff
75 Wash up
77 Certain fossil preserve
80 The art of music?
81 Vegetables that make a fitting addition to alphabet soup?
82 [Oh, well]
85 "Tsk, tsk!"
87 Classic soda brand
92 "Oh, I see!"
94 Small-screen entertainers?
95 Ibn _____ (former Mideast king)
97 Responsibility of a personnel director
98 Japanese noodle
100 Young salmon
102 Like hawks
104 Hit 1979 musical in which a character's mistress is one of the main roles
105 University of New Mexico team
106 Bank deals
107 _____ Vedder, lead singer of Pearl Jam
109 Garden-variety
111 Some I.R.A.s
113 Licoricelike flavor
114 Rap producers make them
116 The "O's" of Cheerios
117 Old _____, Conn.
119 Spinach is rich in it
120 El _____
123 Drop o' the mornin'
124 Cheer to a matador

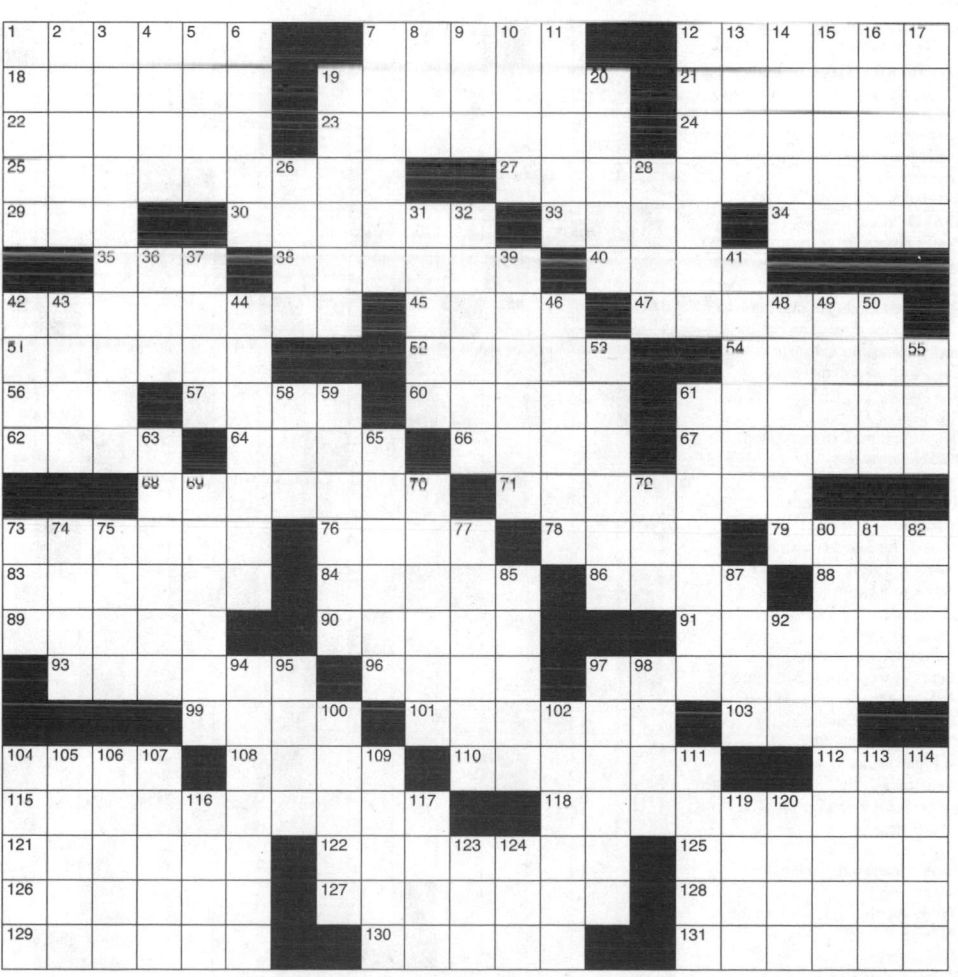

by Tina Labadie

ACROSS

1 Hotel chain operated by Hilton
4 Banned insecticide
7 Big voices with big egos
12 Some users of Cyrillic script
17 Antique furniture expert, perhaps
20 Like bills in arrears
22 Freak out
23 100%
24 Sight at a checkout counter
26 Golfer who won the 1998 Masters (Italy)
28 Attach, as a patch
29 "Baa, baa" ma
30 "Rosy-fingered" Greek goddess
31 Snitch out
34 Zip
35 World's end?
36 Grp. led by Mahmoud Abbas beginning in 2004
39 Apples and pears, botanically
41 Seethe (Norway)
44 Queen Latifah's given first name
46 Playwright ___-Manuel Miranda
47 Benefit
48 Pipsqueaks
49 Give up all at once (Ecuador)
53 Org. with a Summer League
54 Churn
55 Response from a therapist
56 Were, for one?
58 "If we don't end ___, ___ will end us": H. G. Wells
61 Calculus expert?
63 "Inventing ___" (2022 Netflix hit)
66 Die-hard
70 Gate in digital logic
71 Major player in U.S. economic policy (Egypt)
74 Retired jersey number for the 76ers' Moses Malone
75 Post-it notes, e.g.
77 Cousin of a plum
78 It's good for three points
80 Where you might get into hot water
81 ___ Hortons (Canadian chain)
83 Statistician Silver
85 Land with an accent over its first letter
86 Big inits. in TVs
89 Boarding group? (Switzerland)
94 Causes for pauses
97 God: Lat.
98 Stephen of "V for Vendetta"
99 Except for
100 Activity for Santa (Rwanda)
102 Scouts B.S.A. members since 2019
104 Marks, as a ballot
105 "OK, you get it," for short
106 De ___ (freshly)
107 Used room service, e.g.
109 Hamm of women's soccer fame
111 Nickname that's three consecutive letters of the alphabet
112 Torus-shaped gasket
114 One who walks to work? (Qatar)
119 What this puzzle's circled letters are with respect to the surrounding shaded squares?
123 Quite eccentric
124 Noted underground adventurer
125 Sad ass
126 Burger topping that jacks up the cholesterol
127 Rich sources
128 Kidney-related
129 Asphalt component
130 Daily ___ (news blog)

DOWN

1 Disneyland ride
2 McEntire of country music
3 Old map inits.
4 Certain coding snippet
5 Special collection of musical hits?
6 "Je te plumerai la ___" (line from "Alouette")
7 Old gold coin
8 ___ spot
9 Seconds, in brief
10 Open-mouthed responses
11 Temptresses in the "Odyssey"
12 Create an elaborate series of deceptions
13 Part of L.V.
14 Got in the game, perhaps
15 Watch parties?
16 Focus for 15-Down
18 It's a drag
19 Seats
21 Big name in power tools
25 Fail
27 Monitors at school, for short
32 ___-Eaters
33 Kindle competitor
36 "ASAP!"
37 Sondheim and Bernstein's collaborator on "West Side Story"
38 Pungent party bowlful
40 Ultra-aggressive
42 Freshly
43 Quite a fight
45 Fighting
47 "___ días!"
50 Instantly get along well
51 Rush
52 Home of the David Geffen School of Drama
57 Laundry product
59 Like some 401(k) contributions
60 It's touchy to hit
61 "___ Rheingold"
62 "The Chi" channel, familiarly
64 It has a devoted following on Sundays
65 Expiates, with "for"
67 "___ out!"
68 Formal farewell
69 Modifier in digital logic
72 "Oh, really?"
73 Catch a few waves?
76 Lloyd of women's soccer fame
79 Talk smack about
82 Skirt style
84 Getting bored with
87 Suggests
88 Kind of cat or rabbit
90 Flat top?
91 Target of a joke
92 Region of Croatia associated with a canine breed
93 "Did you ring?"
94 Hybrid farm animal
95 Site acquired by Match.com in 2011
96 London's ___ Row
100 Liquor from Mexico
101 Like em dashes vis-à-vis en dashes
102 Benitez of TV news
103 Fuse by heating below the melting point
108 Bomb produced in the 1950s
110 Ritalin target, for short
113 Marvin who sang "Sexual Healing"
115 Offended
116 Food that's a national emblem of Wales
117 "Thus . . ."
118 Standard operating procedures, for short
120 Clinch
121 Plasma particle
122 Ambrose Burnside was its first president, for short

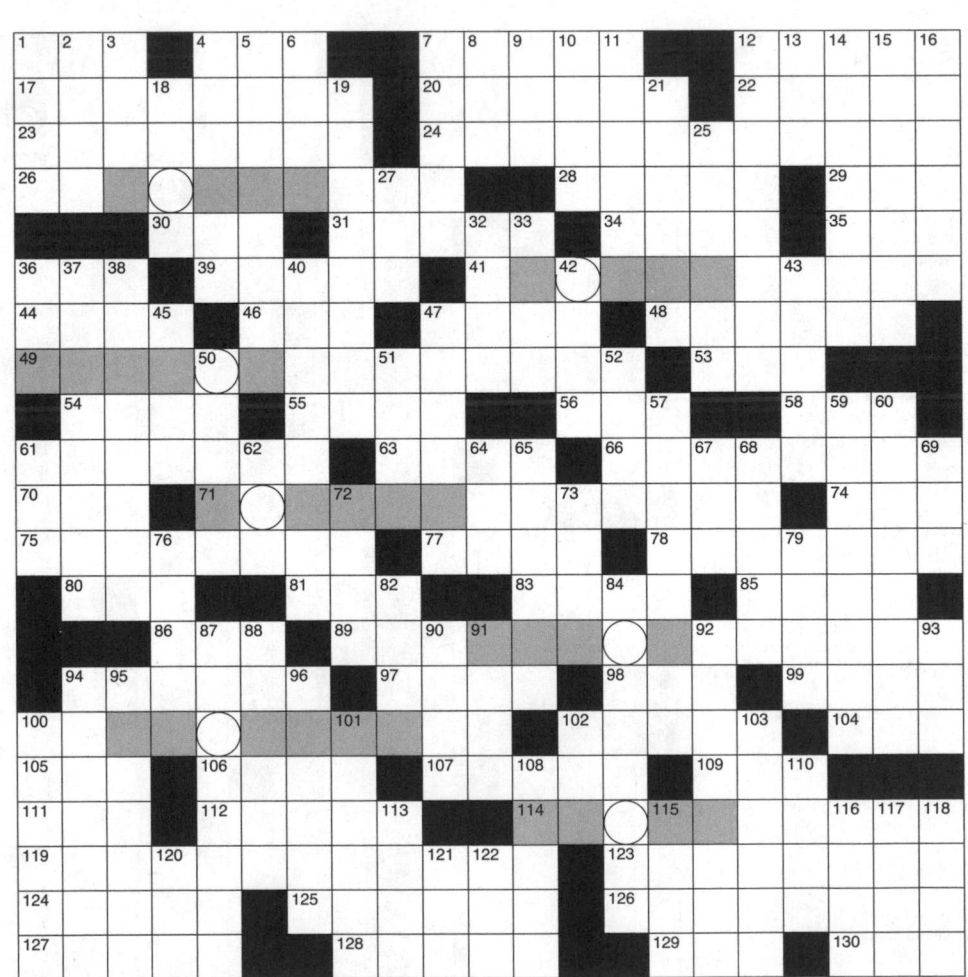

by Jeff Chen and Jim Horne

ACROSS

1 Farm cry
6 Singer Celia Cruz or actress Rosie Perez
16 Second-least populous state capital, after Montpelier
17 Like fire drills and dress rehearsals
19 It may give a bowler a hook
20 "We must wait to see what happens"
22 Pause, in music
23 Legal profession?
25 Embarrassing miss
26 ___ culpa
27 Gently enter
29 Fifth-century nomad of central Asia
31 "___ Te Ching"
32 Needing another dryer cycle, say
33 Org. that regulates pet food and false eyelashes
34 Design, as software
37 Showcase for a first chair in an orchestra
40 Some Minecraft blocks
41 Only sch. to have a gold medal winner in every Summer Olympics since 1912
42 Nuclear model named for a physicist
44 Actress Dennings
45 Symbol of longevity in Chinese numerology
46 "We don't need to hear the details!"
48 Carpentry peg
50 Attack, Quixote-style
52 Specialized vocabularies
53 Indicators of status in Maori culture
55 Disney girl who fosters an alien
56 J.G. Ballard dystopia about a man stranded between motorways
59 Huff
60 Agreement
61 Has an understanding
63 Where many people walk out?
65 Juan ___, baseball star nicknamed "Childish Bambino"
66 Seattle team
67 Pressed (down)
69 Sci. class with dissections
71 E.C. ___, creator of Popeye
72 Pharmaceutical company whose Nasdaq symbol is MRNA
73 Kind of high-fat diet used as an epilepsy therapy
74 "The Marvelous ___ Maisel"
76 Set aside
78 Like Plan B, for short
79 Fromage base
80 Royal house on the Arabian Peninsula
82 It's back on Broadway
83 "Candyman" director DaCosta
84 Online shopping site for handicrafts
85 Vanilla unit
87 Kangaroo ___
88 Mermaid's home, maybe
90 Connections
91 Like many a dinner function
95 Orpheus' instrument
97 They've taken the veil
98 Its falls are quite dramatic
101 Freeway dividers
103 Dillydallying
104 "We're all ___ here"
105 Informal favor request
106 Some bishops

DOWN

1 Response to "Danke"
2 "If we must die, O ___ us nobly die": Claude McKay
3 Like the concept of a flat Earth
4 Side-by-side calculation
5 Certain chew toy
6 Fitting
7 Cold, as agua
8 Word on an invoice
9 What the musicals "Beggar's Holiday" and "Rent" are based on
10 Compendium of case reports
11 Met highlight
12 Like one on stilts
13 "C'mon, ___ be fun"
14 Small fault
15 Words before "gratia plena, Dominus tecum"
16 Italian dance form from the Spanish for "walk in the street"
18 Erbium, terbium or ytterbium
19 Dance move that resembles a front flip
21 Momentary slip
22 Negative responses
24 Performers wearing pa'us and malos
28 "Seems likely"
30 Having free time
32 "That's enough lip out of you!"
35 Kind of tape
36 "Mighty Morphin" TV character
38 Crystalline structure
39 Useless
43 Utility company professional
47 Descriptor for IHOP's Fresh 'N Fruity pancakes
49 Result of a delay
51 Twitter titter
53 Actress/activist Jane
54 Minds
56 Portuguese city with a historic university founded in 1290
57 They don't express gender
58 After-school activities one wouldn't list on a college app
60 Really wallops
62 Noisemakers dangling below a "Just Married" sign
64 Keystone State airport code
67 Tallied
68 Journalist/screenwriter ___ Rogers St. Johns
69 Bongo-playing 1950s stereotype
70 Introduction to an adage
72 Dirk Nowitzki, for 21 seasons, in brief
73 Designer Anne
75 High-speed races with gates
77 Guide outside a bus station, often
81 Triangular snack chip
86 New Jersey athlete
89 Cloud on a summer day
91 Like suboptimal kite-flying weather
92 Singer with the album "Voyage to India"
93 Ethiopia's Lake ___
94 Kind of bra cup
96 Overhaul
99 Day-___
100 Word with hot or headed
102 Bit of land in la mer

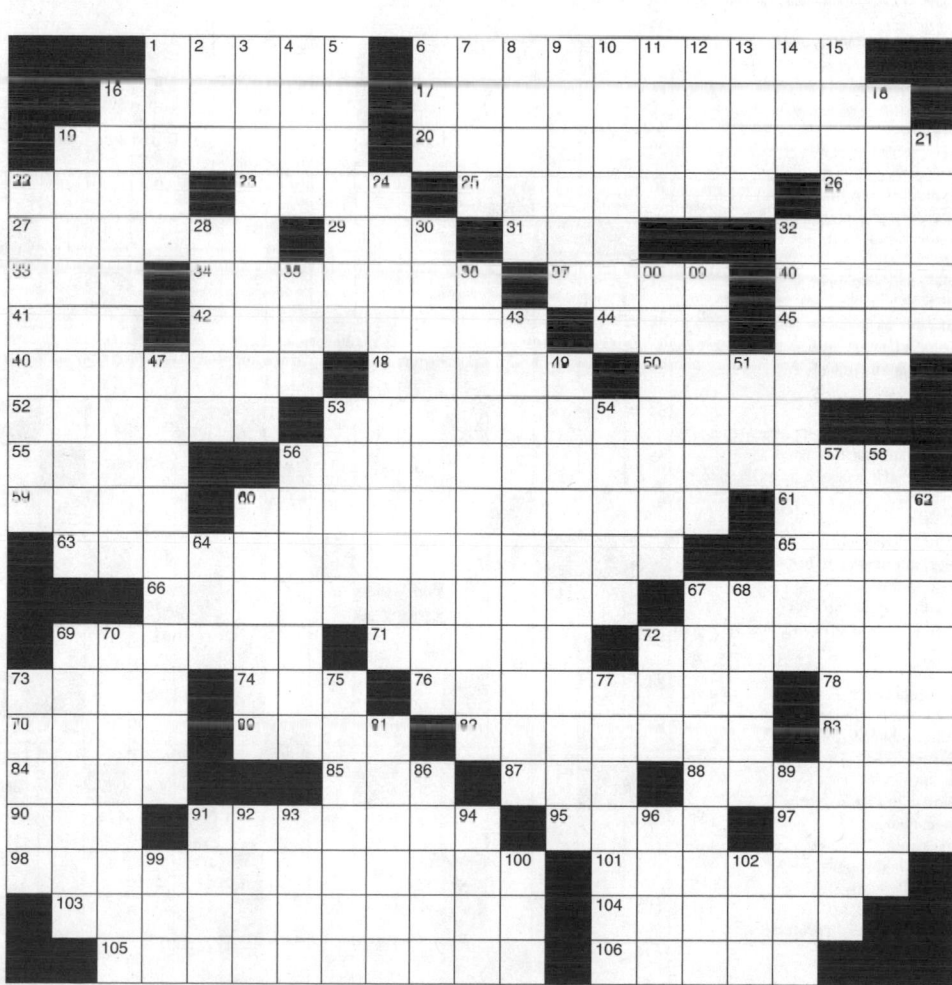

by Brooke Husic and Will Nediger

ACROSS

1 Gaelic garment
7 Creatures described as catarrhine, from the Latin for "downward-nosed"
11 Like Antarctica
15 Spare part?
18 Granada grandpa
19 Cut deeply
20 "Ugh, ___ people!"
21 Go down, in a way
22 Get a party started? [bee, hare, tick]
24 Morning TV host Kotb
25 "Potent Potables for $1,000, ___" (onetime TV request)
26 Crestfallen
27 Actress Seyfried of "The Dropout"
28 Buzzkill [bat, elk, newt]
30 Bias
31 Subjects of some promotions
33 Natural source of glitter
34 A little of a lot? [carp, pig, snake]
38 TV, newspapers, streaming services, etc.
42 How a video game might be played by beginners
43 Ending with orange
44 Best-selling author Hoag
45 Strong connection
46 Pennsylvania school, for short
47 Locale of many vines [cat, elephant, worm]
51 Opposite of une adversaire
52 Fancy flower holders
53 Life preserver?
54 Al-___, family of Syrian leaders
55 Goes wild
57 Glitzy, informally
59 Prankster's offerings
61 Nonmedical org. that uses X-rays
62 Something you might step on by the shower [cobra, moth, seal]
65 Inits. in biotech
68 Legal contract phrase
69 "My bad!"
70 Make dry, as salmon
72 Pain relief pill
75 Placeholder inits.
76 3 ft. × 5 ft., e.g.
77 "So it goes"
78 Long-running soap opera that debuted in 1963 [ant, gorilla, sheep]
83 One might be accessed by a QR code, nowadays
84 Warrant
85 Guard seen around a castle
86 401(k) alternative, in brief
87 Lean toward
89 Certain sports tiebreaker
91 London landmark [beetle, hog, rat]
94 Place
95 ___ song
97 Overnight perch
98 Bridge that's painted International Orange [dog, eel, gnat]
101 Devilish look?
103 Boardroom V.I.P.
106 Drink with a spoon-straw
107 Floor square
108 Mixes animal species . . . as eight answers in this puzzle do?
110 Actress Perlman
111 In good condition
112 Wave to one's math professor?
113 Gets around
114 Part of U.C.L.A.
115 Poetic tributes
116 Fire tablet competitor
117 One of the Williamses

DOWN

1 Things seen in a window
2 Magic trick starter
3 Felt bad about
4 Word with garden or party
5 Lime and soda, e.g.
6 A handful
7 Pros with negotiations
8 Was worthwhile, with "off"
9 Bit of tomfoolery
10 With 47-Down, "That's all" follower
11 Like a vampire's face, stereotypically
12 Rhizome, to a botanist
13 Site to flick through flicks
14 Request for a hand
15 Fashionable spots
16 "Oh, gotcha"
17 Immediately following
21 'N Sync member who later became a gay rights activist
23 Spend time together, in slang
28 "SmackDown" org.
29 Goal
30 Pair in the Winter Olympics
32 Maker of Chromebooks
34 Warhol's "Marilyn Diptych," e.g.
35 Antagonism
36 Target of a modern scan
37 Light touches
39 Medical plan inits.
40 Sapa ___ (ancient emperor's title)
41 Common cause of some impulsive behavior, in brief
44 Details to be negotiated
47 See 10-Down
48 Sacred hieroglyph
49 Sirs' counterparts
50 "Beep!" source
52 Second caliph of Sunni Islam
56 Doubleday who is miscredited with inventing baseball
57 Merchant's stock
58 Cut (off)
59 Auctioneer's aid
60 Name that's a letter off from 25-Across
63 One might develop consciousness in a sci-fi story
64 Nightspot in a Manilow hit, in brief
65 What you can rarely do at a red light
66 Kvetch
67 "Yeah, whatever you say"
68 "Beats me"
71 Tried to fight
72 A long, long time
73 Genesis matriarch
74 Matriculation group
75 "No! Not true!"
76 Wild guess
79 End up being
80 ___ Malnati's, Chicago-style pizza chain
81 Rug thickness
82 Strong hold
87 Gray-brown flycatchers
88 Book
90 Summer top
91 Test for future Ph.D.s
92 Wiped out
93 Sippy cup users
96 Agenda topics
98 Word with power, talk or band
99 Number of planetas en el sistema solar
100 Fasten with a belt
102 Chaplin of "Game of Thrones"
103 Surrender
104 Summit of Mount Purgatory, in Dante's "Divine Comedy"
105 Mount in Greek myth
108 Show with a Miami spinoff
109 Symbol for an audio device

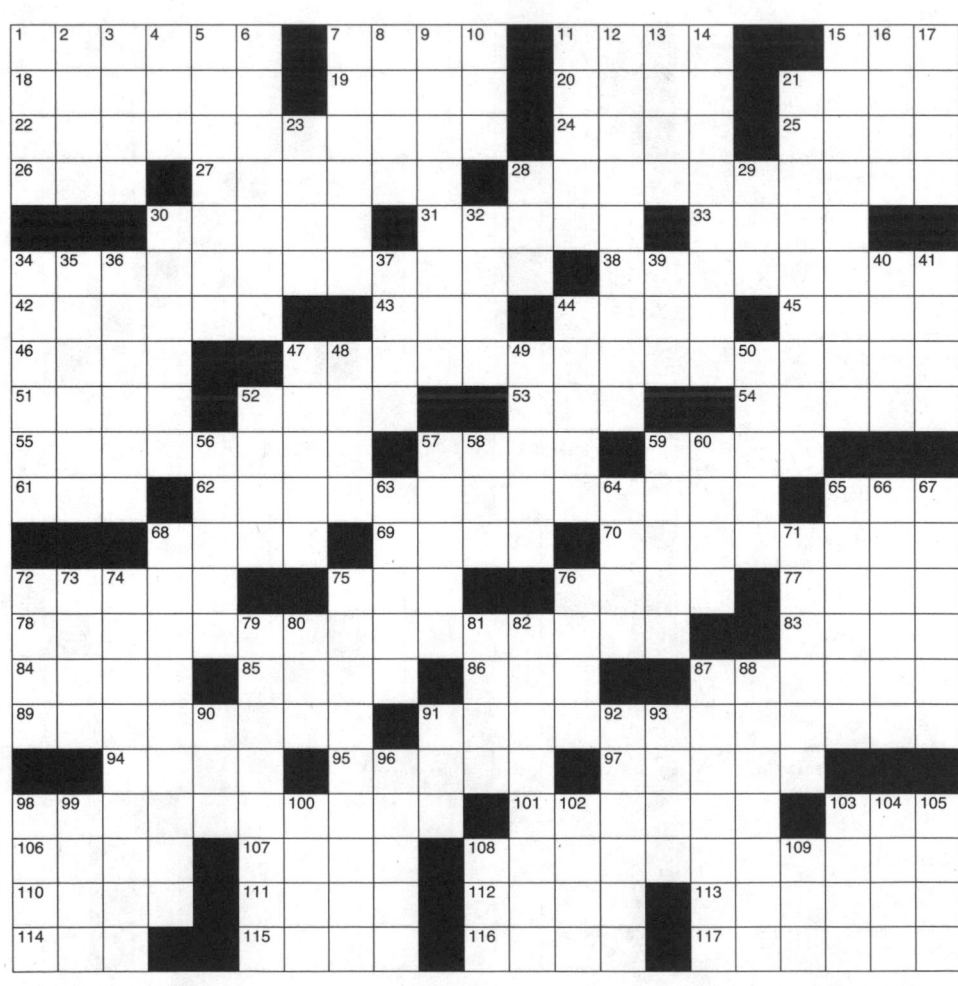

by Ori Brian

ACROSS

1 Exfoliants
7 Foofaraw
10 Cookout chuckouts
14 Thickener used in desserts
18 Like favorite radio stations, perhaps
19 Calico calls
21 Memo starter
22 N.F.L. Hall-of-Famer Yale ___
23 Backpacker's snack
24 Big huff?
25 Have an outsize presence
27 "I didn't need to know that!"
28 What a net might attach to
30 Flying Cloud of old autodom
31 Jazz clarinetist Shaw
32 Soaring shot
33 Some Six Nations members
35 *Mount Everest scaler
37 Hogs
39 *Went out of control
40 A.M.A. members: Abbr.
42 Marketing experiment comparing two variants
44 Some red marks
45 Big lugs
48 Say "Whomever did this . . . ," say
49 Alice who wrote "The Color Purple"
51 Org. with a sizable registry
54 Yellow jacket, for one
55 Syrup brand since 1902
57 Word before Roger or Rancher
58 To a profound degree
60 *"Cinderella" meanie
62 Field trip conveyances
63 Middle van Pelt child in "Peanuts"
64 Use Tinder, say
65 Airs
69 Big exporter of pistachios
70 Features of some bygone muscle cars
71 Give an elbow bump to, say
72 Free of fizz
73 *Lateral-breaking pitches
75 Skulk
76 Maker of the world's first quartz watch
77 Javanese dyeing technique
78 Potala Palace city
79 One of seven represented in the Pleiades
80 *Glide down from above
81 Sleigh driver's need
82 Sound of an ungraceful landing
84 ___ card
85 Fashion house whose logo is two interlocking C's
87 Like the Carolina Reaper pepper
88 Visionary
91 Title for Baltimore
92 Crow language family
95 Sounds of hesitation
96 da-DUM
99 On pins and needles
101 Homebrewer's sugar
103 Cartoonish villains
106 "Little ol' me?"
107 Woodard of "Clemency"
109 Article in Aachen
110 "Where ignorance is bliss, ___ folly to be wise": Thomas Gray
111 "Eh . . . I'll pass"
112 It's a banger in Germany
114 *Portrayer of Scrooge in 1951's "A Christmas Carol"
116 Surgical seam
118 Unagi and anago, for two
119 What parallel lines never do
120 It beats scissors
121 Passionate
122 Secretary, e.g.
123 ___ Noël
124 Place to wallow
125 Butterfly garden bloomers

DOWN

1 Places
2 "Mad Money" host Jim
3 Eye part with rods and cones
4 Kind of port
5 Boot camp exercises performed on all fours
6 Narrow groove
7 One for the roadie
8 Most beloved
9 Dominated, informally
10 Pico de gallo herb
11 Not yet in stock
12 Soup bases
13 Highway heavyweight
14 ___ mode
15 Like toum or agliata sauce
16 Forest between Champagne and Lorraine
17 Cousin of kvass
20 Plant pore
26 "___ Miz"
29 Early computer acronym
34 O.E.D. part: Abbr.
36 Some rideshares
38 They may be hidden behind paintings
41 Knot-tying and lashing, to a sailor
43 Like some short tennis matches
46 Install, as sod
47 Record player annoyances
50 Actor Guinness
51 Improvised comment
52 "Colette" actress Knightley
53 Comedian Wyatt of "Problem Areas"
56 Porter, for one
57 Derby cocktail
59 Bad Brains and Bikini Kill, for two
61 Muckety-mucks
62 Colorful bird named for its diet
64 Not easily moved
65 Ocho menos cinco
66 Buttonholes, basically
67 Actor/activist George
68 Seattle's W.N.B.A. team
70 Absolutely wrecks
71 K
74 Reason to do a "stupid human trick"
75 X
76 Tangential topics
78 Allow to access
79 "I am," in Latin
80 Incomplete dentures
81 Ball game that all players might lose
83 Lacks
85 Place to wear muck boots
86 One roasted or toasted
87 More raspy
89 Dramatize, as a historical event
90 Teller, maybe
93 "That time is fine for me"
94 Lack of musicality
97 Teeny-tiny
98 Word after ring or water
100 Side-to-side movement
102 Pastoral skyline features
104 Tyler of "Whose Line Is It Anyway?"
105 Places for hoses and hoes
108 Oatmeal glob
113 Judgy sound
115 Jupiter's realm, in myth
117 Pic on a pec, say

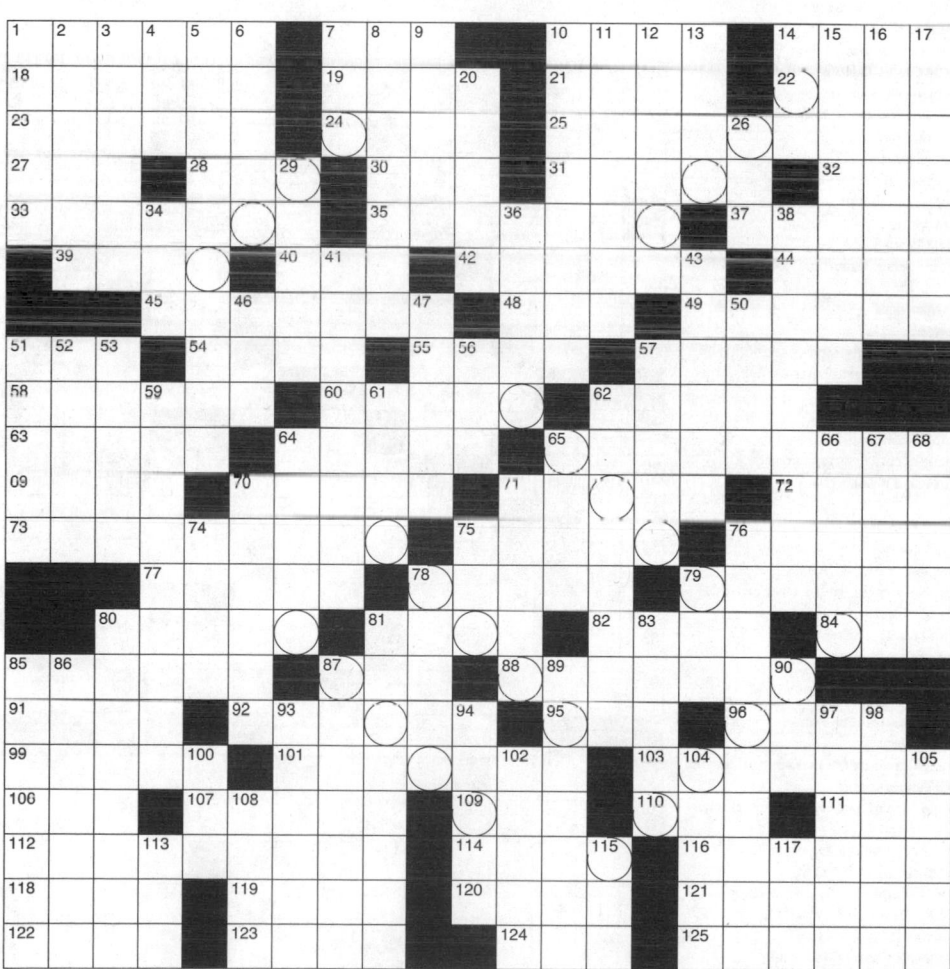

by Tracy Gray

ACROSS

1 Try to hit
7 Numbskull
11 With 108-Down, hot stretch of summer
14 Moment of inspiration
19 "He's" this, in a 1963 hit for the Chiffons
20 Woes
21 "I know, I know!"
23 What this might mean: "
24 English poet who wrote "The Highwayman"
26 World Cup org.
27 Digs in the ice?
28 Persian ___ (rugmaker's deliberate mistake)
29 Humorist Bombeck
30 Early American pseudonym
32 Within
33 Prop that enabled Houdini to "walk through" a brick wall
35 Napoleonic
36 Sounds of disapproval
37 Accept imminent punishment
39 Republic toppled in 1933
41 Red block in Minecraft
42 Sopranos' highlights
43 Rapper Fiasco
45 Curse out
49 Word with open or pigeon
50 I, personally
52 Bird associated with bats
53 Place side by side
56 Doctrine of East Asia
58 Six-Day War combatant: Abbr.
59 Natural fertilizer
60 Jack of old TV
61 Neighbor of Jammu and Kashmir
64 Instrument that makes a "tsst" sound
66 "Mazel ___!"
67 Wrestler's goal
68 Caesar salad ingredient
71 Clanton at the O.K. Corral
72 It's over here
73 Ground
74 Works a wedding, perhaps
75 Flying ___ (martial arts strike)
76 Spots for snorkeling
78 Women's ___
80 Helpful connections
81 Friendly conversation ender
83 Wrap on a rancho
84 Opts
87 Horse-drawn carriage
88 "In Praise of Folly" essayist
90 Norman or English king?
91 With 93-Across, young river critter
93 See 91-Across
96 Tribal circle, perhaps
98 Scramble some eggs, say
101 Smile . . . or shine
104 Burden
105 Large electromotive unit
106 Strong cleaners
107 Branch of dentistry that specializes in root canals
110 Name hidden backward in "excellent"
111 Actress Teri
112 Davis of "Thelma & Louise"
113 Go to sleep, with "out"
114 Noted songwriter behind Wynonna Judd's "Tell Me Why" and Linda Ronstadt's "All My Life"
117 You can't run on this for long
118 ___ Martell, "Game of Thrones" princess
119 Goods for sale: Abbr.
120 Taiwan-born filmmaker
121 George Washington chopping down a cherry tree, and others
122 Total mess
123 Sought redress, in a way
124 Heeded an owner's order

DOWN

1 Org. created under F.D.R.
2 Howler of a movie?
3 Beset
4 Rant
5 "So let us begin ___ . . .": J.F.K.
6 Talk acronym
7 Model for a grade schooler
8 Mountain residence
9 Argues
10 What three dots might mean
11 Accomplish on behalf of
12 Home of Kenyon College
13 Walk, so to speak
14 Org. created under F.D.R.
15 Shower
16 Eponym for one of the earth's five oceans
17 Baby bearer, maybe
18 Stove toppers
22 Vice president after Pence
25 One of Neptune's moons
30 Second half of an incantation
31 Helen Reddy's signature hit
32 Rearward, to a rear admiral
33 It shares space with #
34 Like dipsticks
38 Southwestern art hub
39 Tom Jones and Anthony Hopkins, by birth
40 Make bubbly
44 Suzhou Museum architect
46 Same old, same old
47 He set a Guinness World Record in 2014, reporting for 34 consecutive hours
48 Boob tubes
49 Northernmost N.B.A. city, on scoreboards
50 Magic power
51 Brotherly figures
53 Placate
54 Job with numerous applications?
55 Her name is Greek for "all-gifted"
56 One always having a place to hide
57 Mounds of activity
61 The standard
62 Pro Bowl side, for short
63 Item with straps
65 ___ Master's Voice
68 "I'm in trouble!"
69 Approach gradually
70 One who gave us all a lift?
75 Development in cryptography
77 A few weeks ago, probably
79 Worker with a comb
81 Mountebank
82 "Listen!"
85 Some hangouts for remote workers
86 It has its ratios, for short
87 Popular beer brand, casually
89 Meeting with a dead line?
91 One side of the coin
92 Baited online
93 What all companies try to make
94 Service charge
95 Scoring figs.
97 Lifts up
99 Literary utopia
100 Projecting edge
101 Deck out with spangles
102 The other side
103 Crackerjack
105 Longtime sports journalist Jim
108 See 11-Across
109 Still competing
111 Sold out
114 Tour de France distance units: Abbr.
115 "___, humbug!"
116 Added paper to, as a printer

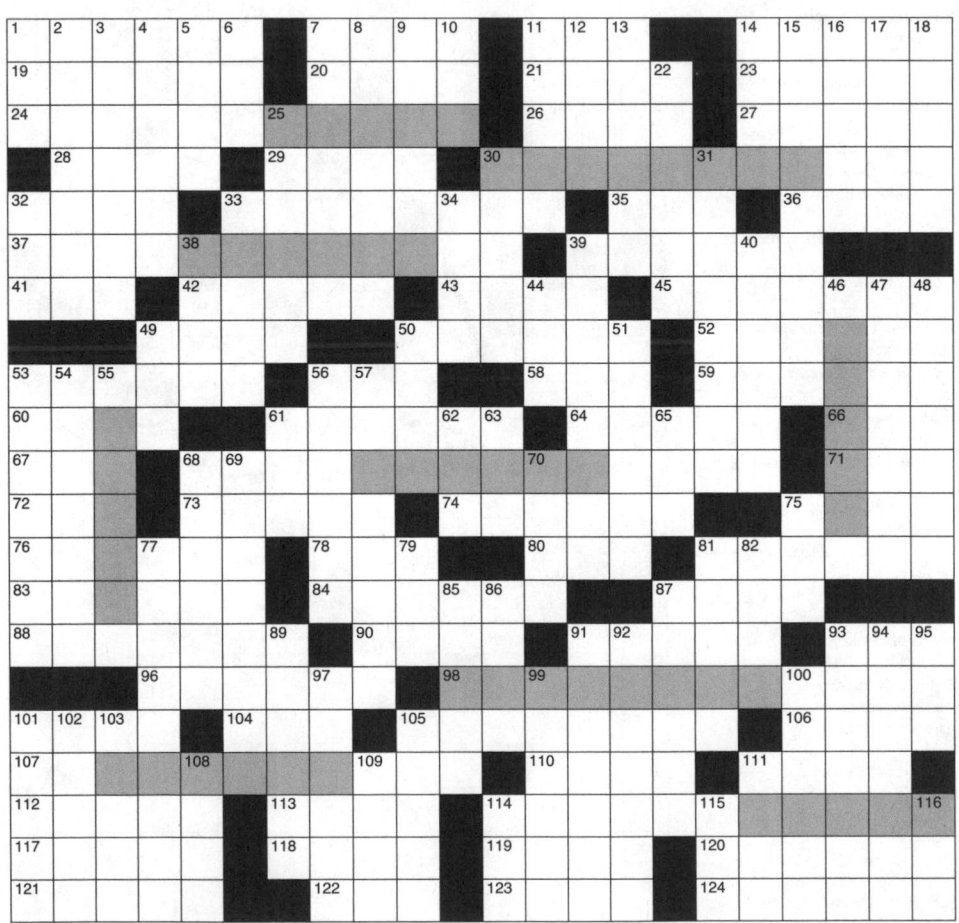

by Derrick Niederman

ACROSS

1 Fish tank buildup
6 Bog product
10 P.M. times
14 Suisse peak
18 Disney film with a titular heroine
19 Pricing word
20 Christmas color for Elvis
21 Pork cut
22 Mechanic's go-to parenting phrase?
26 Painter whose motifs include ants and eggs
27 Give the nod
28 "Check it out for yourself"
29 Mauna ___
31 French liver
33 Some remote power sources
35 Up to 11 meters for a pterodactyl
37 Personal trainer's go-to parenting phrase?
43 Like some restrictions
44 Stephen King's first published novel
45 Your and my relative?
46 Roof overhang
48 Horror star Chaney
49 In the past
50 Affectionate greeting
51 Arid
52 Small building block
55 Conductor's go-to parenting phrase?
63 Liquor in tiramisu
64 TV drama with spinoffs set in Hawaii and New Orleans
65 Cornerstone abbr.
66 Eightfold
69 Animal working in the D.M.V. in "Zootopia"
72 Texas politician Beto
74 It's a drag
75 Singer James
77 Share accommodations
79 Mathematician's go-to parenting phrase?
86 Emmy-winning Ward
87 Lemon ___
88 Insult
89 Hosp. area
90 Clean Air Act org.
92 "Star Wars" order
93 Word seen at the end of many Jean-Luc Godard movies
94 From where
97 From the get-go
100 Air traffic controller's go-to parenting phrase?
103 Accepts the facts
105 Her pronoun partner
106 Farmyard mamas
107 2003 Will Ferrell movie
108 Spooky
110 Lacking the resources
113 Not out of the running
117 Librarian's go-to parenting phrase?
121 Google ___ (Zoom alternative)
122 Chemical suffixes
123 Backless shoe
124 Maybe one, maybe both
125 GPS calculations, in brief
126 "I did it!"
127 Jabbers
128 Jen ___, 2021-22 White House press secretary

DOWN

1 Surrounded by
2 Tragic showgirl of song
3 Chutzpah
4 Like PETA
5 ___ de vie
6 Gift for writing
7 Noshes
8 Feel that gym session
9 What something might appear out of or disappear into
10 Epitome of simplicity
11 Guam's features a sailboat and palm tree
12 "The Burden of Proof" author
13 Like many resorts
14 Ingredient in homemade hand sanitizer
15 Reed of the Velvet Underground
16 Sellers franchise, with "The"
17 Charm
23 Poker option
24 Solo
25 Baroque painter Guido
30 ___ port in a storm
32 Nail polish brand with a "Tickle My France-y" shade
34 Part of a homemade Halloween costume
36 Animal that turns white in the winter
37 Large number
38 "I am not what I am" speaker
39 Pioneering sci-fi film that was snubbed for the Best Visual Effects Oscar for its use of computers
40 Road trip determination
41 Decade in which many in Gen Z were born
42 Main ingredient in poi
47 Kind of diagram
50 In this matter
51 Arose
53 City on the Irtysh River
54 Parcel (out)
56 Elementary particle named for a Greek letter
57 Called a strike, say
58 Like some potato chips and language
59 Part of NATO: Abbr.
60 Jardins d'enfants, par exemple
61 Tech and culture magazine since 1993
62 Has left the office, e.g.
66 Jay-Z and Kanye West song that samples "Try a Little Tenderness"
67 Pigeon coop
68 What a bad dancer is said to have
70 Large number
71 ___ Ledbetter, a.k.a. Lead Belly
73 Newswire co.
76 A4 automaker
78 "___ it!" (informal challenge)
80 Rock used to make ultramarine
81 Pretentious
82 Snack cakes with creamy swirls
83 It might be changed or made up
84 "Look!," in Latin
85 Took to court
91 Miscreant's record, maybe
92 Like a clear night
93 Rival you kind of like
94 "That's amazing!"
95 Color classification
96 Naval Academy grads
97 Basic personal information
98 "Spill it!"
99 Flow slowly
101 "Not gonna happen!"
102 Counts (on)
104 Tropical vine
109 "Brown ___ Girl"
111 Pool shade
112 Kind of discount
114 Nothin'
115 Words of reassurance
116 Actress Garr
118 Hot spot in England?
119 Airport inits.
120 Dance with a paradiddle step

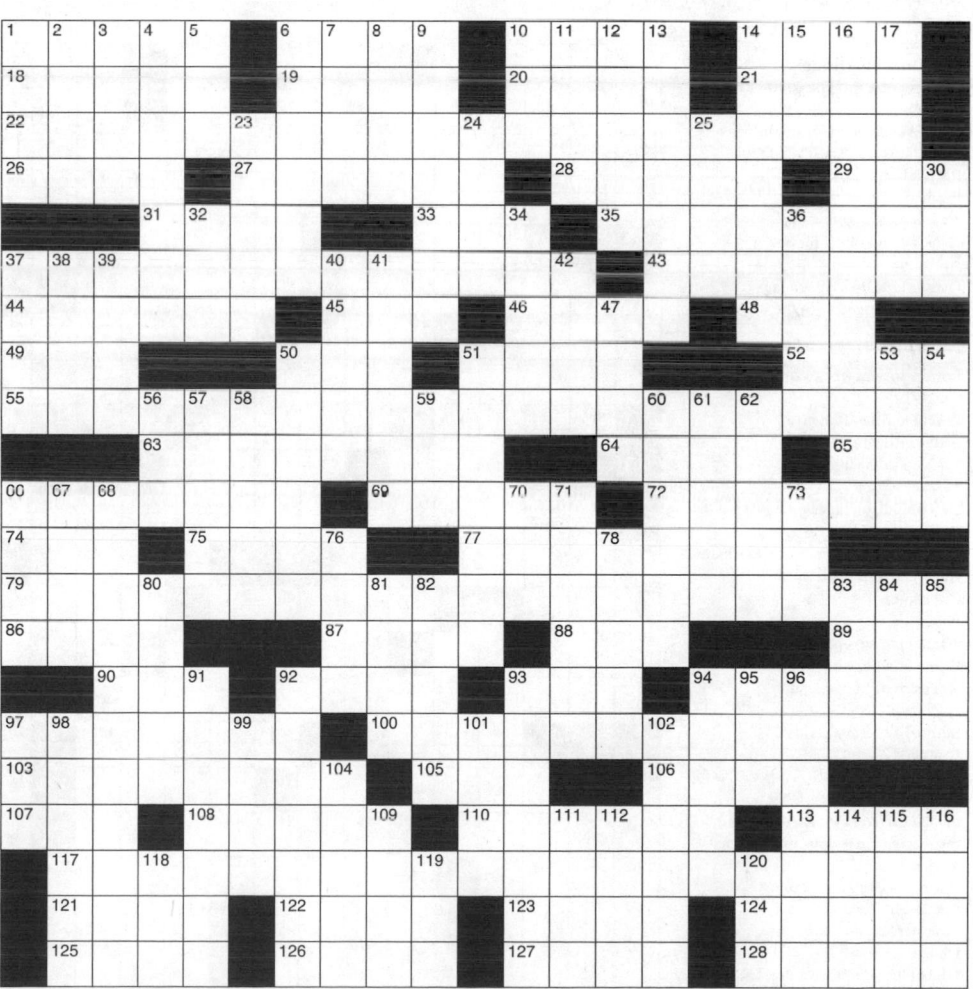

by Katie Hale

ACROSS

1 Do some backup dancing?
6 Things with wires, often
10 Sweets
14 Musical whose name is an anagram of the members of a musical
18 "Here, take this"
20 Hit hard
21 Many a donor, for short
22 "You may disagree, but . . . ," to a texter
23 *What's in your wallet
26 Actress ____ Flynn Boyle
27 Confidence-building mantra
28 Burdens with
29 Trimmer
30 Dash dial
31 Stretches of time
32 *Press junket
34 Country whose capital is named after an early U.S. president
37 Odd-numbered page, typically
39 Take in
40 Buzzing about
41 Bird watcher's org., once
43 *Barbershop quartet
49 *Rocket scientist
53 Lines on which music is written
54 Opera whose title character is a singer
55 Complete
56 Hermanos de la madre
58 Like Legolas in "The Lord of the Rings"
60 Muscle used in a pull-up, informally
61 Word between "what" and "that"
63 R&B's India.____
65 Profit
68 *Security blankets
74 "Black Jeopardy!," for one
75 Apocalypse
76 Qantas hub, on luggage tags
77 Org. that merged with the 41-Across in the 1970s
78 Off-limits
82 Letters to ____ (rock group)
84 Cargo
87 Likely to offend, in brief
90 Author Ellison
92 *A drop in the bucket
95 *Ticketmaster
98 United hub, on luggage tags
99 Expected
100 League designation for the Durham Bulls and Salt Lake Bees
101 Cut choice
103 Power
106 *Ballet movements
111 Game of who, what and where
112 Ancestor of Methuselah
113 Is grating
114 Start of a literary series
116 Cottoned on (to)
120 ____ mater
121 Has no plan B . . . or, when parsed differently, what each of the starred clues does vis-à-vis its answer?
123 Having South Asian roots
124 Small table fare?
125 Summers on the Seine
126 Chorus section
127 Global brand of men's dress shirts
128 Pair
129 Laura of "Big Little Lies"
130 Consulted for feedback about

DOWN

1 Designation on some pronoun pins
2 Rapper with the 2011 hit album "Ambition"
3 The before-times?
4 Reel off
5 Auto hobbyist's project, maybe
6 Airer of the crime drama "Luther"
7 Circulation unit
8 Draws
9 Stands
10 Steps up to the plate
11 John Legend's "____ Me"
12 ____ Park, city west of Anaheim
13 Lifesaver, for short
14 Pico de gallo ingredient
15 Leave slack-jawed
16 Confuse
17 Doesn't just increase
19 Faint pattern
24 Occupy
25 Weekend destination for an N.Y.C. getaway, maybe
29 Twitch, for instance
33 Fountain of youth?
34 Twitch problem
35 "The very ____!"
36 Power (up)
38 Like the head of a badminton racket
42 How you should "take me," in a phrase
44 Modern reproductive tech inits.
45 Some votes in the Bundestag
46 Spanish 101 verb
47 Bitter
48 Major water source
50 Tool chain
51 Missouri county on the Arkansas border
52 Moved fast
57 "Chandelier" singer, 2014
59 Suffix with bad, mad, sad and glad
62 Huff
64 Period in curling
66 "Schitt's Creek" role for Sarah Levy
67 Title play character who never shows up
68 Open, as a gift
69 Bias
70 Maker of the E.T. the Extra-Terrestrial video game
71 "What's up, ____?"
72 ____ sci
73 They're heard in a chorus
74 Reasonable
79 Focus of many a law
80 German chancellor Scholz
81 Sir Isaac Newton work on the fundamentals of light
83 "Let's begin our adventure!"
85 Opera that aptly premiered in Egypt
86 Good name for an archaeologist?
88 Idiot
89 Grumps
91 Excavated, with "out"
93 Give for a time
94 Jennifer Affleck ____ Lopez
96 It's bad overseas
97 What the Beatles never did
102 With 104-Down, playground fixture
104 See 102-Down
105 One of South Africa's official languages
106 Longtime Miami Heat great, to fans
107 Subleased
108 Playground comeback
109 Wood that sinks in water
110 "More or less"
115 Green-lit
117 Zero
118 Tesla, for one
119 Website with a Home Favorites page
121 Crumple (up)
122 QVC alternative

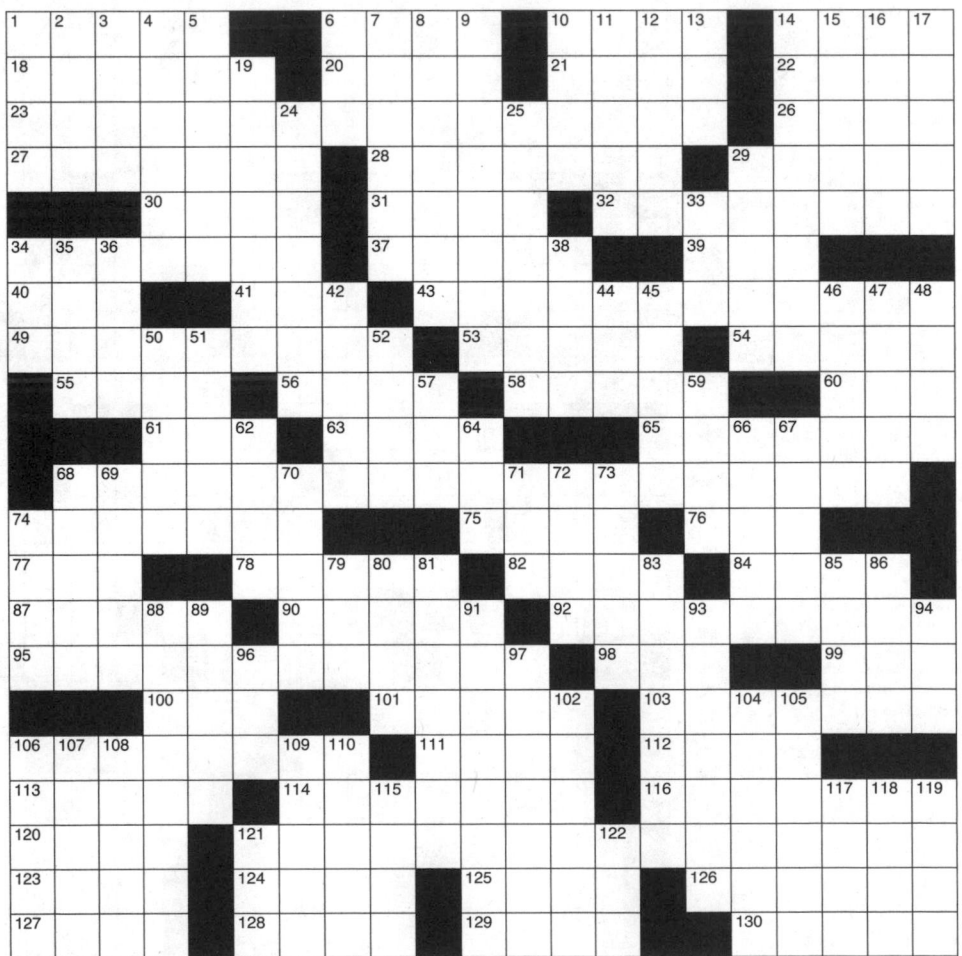

by Meghan Morris

ACROSS

1 Complete jerk
7 Experience equanimity
15 Word with ghost or pirate
19 Inventor Tesla
20 Champion
21 Old-fashioned trial transcriber
22 "When will the leaky faucet get fixed?," e.g.?
24 "___ Speaks!" (Marx brother autobiography)
25 Equinox mo.
26 PC key
27 Actor Astin
28 Spam generator
29 Gridiron gains: Abbr.
30 Bygone theater chain
33 Lithe
36 Spam containers
37 Opposed to, in dialect
39 Song from back in the day
41 German physicist with an eponymous law
42 Focal points
43 Worldly
45 Hoot
46 Part of a how-to manual
47 Oklahoma city named for a character in a Tennyson poem
48 Curt summons
49 Remarks further
50 It may be unlimited in a phone plan
51 One-named singer whose last name is Adkins
52 Faulkner's "As ___ Dying"
53 Setting for a classic Agatha Christie novel
54 Opt for "deluxe," say
56 Baby louse
57 The brother in 24-Across, for one
58 Harvester of the future
59 Potentially offensive, say
62 Easy pill to swallow?
64 Candy bar whose name is an exclamation
66 2015 inductee into the World Golf Hall of Fame
68 Bloke
69 Covers, as the bill
70 Labneh go-with
72 Most popular dog breed in the U.S., familiarly
73 Gives a whirl
75 Without: Lat.
76 A bunch of
77 Common stain on a baseball uniform
80 Adversaries
81 Bit of spice, figuratively
82 Writers not likely to win literary prizes
83 Floppy features of basset hounds
84 Asset
85 Possible cause for road rage
86 Boos
87 Editorial override
88 Word before crow or dirt
89 Prop for a painter
90 Former attorney general Holder
91 Salty droplet
92 Home to the University of Georgia
94 Begins giving solid food, say
96 Green-lights
99 Floating
101 Whip
103 Imitate
104 Country bordering Oman, for short
105 Versatile neutral shade
106 Where you'd find sap for syrup?

111 Sam the ___ (patriotic Muppet)
112 Condition treated with insulin
113 Rang
114 Wedding invitation enclosure, in brief
115 The other you
116 Protests, in a way

DOWN

1 Fidgety
2 Spawned
3 Says "John, Paul . . . and Ringo"?
4 Post ___ (occurring after the event)
5 Basic
6 Brewski
7 Help page initialism
8 URL ender
9 Times outside office hours, in personals
10 Goes berserk
11 About 6.5 inches, on a standard piano
12 Virginia senator Tim
13 From ___ Z
14 Currency that features "The Tale of Genji" on one of its bank notes
15 Show up naked, perhaps?
16 Emma Watson's role in the Harry Potter films
17 Not marked permanently, say
18 Lounge chair location
21 "Yellowjackets" airer, for short
23 Summer abroad
28 Plant fiber used to make some jewelry
31 M ___ U ___ H?
32 It's a slippery slope
34 Loss of the winning ticket?
35 A layoff, crudely
38 Like venison
40 Salon specialties
43 Exploiting
44 Kind of map
46 Leo with the 1977 #1 hit "You Make Me Feel Like Dancing"
49 Asset when playing cornhole
50 New beginnings
51 It may be vegetal or fruity
53 Lightly bite, as a pup might
54 Sappho and Mirabai
55 Certain fed. security
57 Alternatives to shakes
58 Drinks that are "slammed"
60 King and queen?
61 Exhibiting the effects of too little sleep, say
63 The three R's?
65 Stays optimistic
67 Bottomless void
71 Quill go-with

74 Note in the C minor scale
75 Raw power
76 Salon job, informally
77 Develops, as an idea
78 Like some high-quality bonds
79 They might tie the room together
81 Bout enders, for short
82 Caballero, e.g.
84 Bog contents
85 Hosts
86 Nag
89 Dress for graduation
93 Razzle-dazzle
95 Contented sigh
97 Superman's birth name
98 A pomegranate can contain a few hundred of these
100 Corkage ___
102 Name of either brother in a classic Nickelodeon sitcom
106 Computing pioneer Lovelace
107 Teeny
108 Rule, informally
109 Menu eponym
110 Pint contents

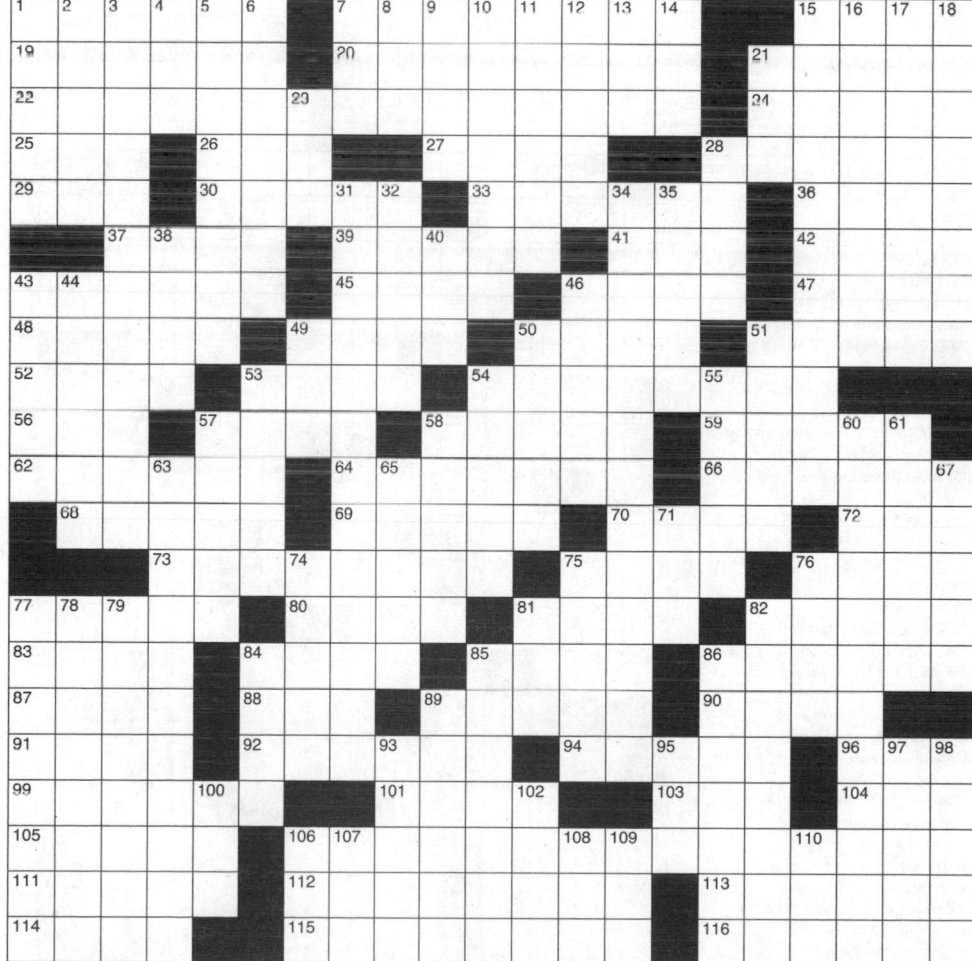

by Kathy Bloomer

ACROSS

1 Like the protagonist at the start of "28 Days Later"
8 –
14 Lady Macduff, e.g.
18 Group of fighters
19 One way to recoil
21 Male deer
22 "My ___" (#1 hit for the Knack)
23 One of the two main branches of Buddhism
24 N.B.A. All-Star Gobert
25 *Worker with a brush [three rungs]
27 Fuel option
29 "Ciao!"
32 Completely pooped
33 –
38 A.C.C. school
39 Place with counselors
40 Maker of Pilots and Passports
41 Team ___
42 "___ Canto" (2001 Ann Patchett novel)
43 Structure resembling a pergola
45 –
47 Airport with a BART station
50 Mail, e.g.
52 Otis who founded the Otis Elevator Company
54 Expelled from the body
56 *Captain with a periscope [four rungs]
58 Some military wear, informally
60 Carpet specification
61 Former make of Ford
62 [I'm frustrated!]
63 Lab eggs
64 Animation and sculpting, for two
65 Advances through corporate ranks . . . and what the answer to each starred clue in this puzzle does
71 "Mon ___!"
74 Singer Grande, to fans
75 Center
76 Celebrity gossip show with an exclamation point in its title
79 Map inits. until 1991
80 Pest control brand
81 –
84 "Really good work!"
86 Sung by a group
87 Writer known for his anthropomorphic animal characters
89 "When r u coming?"
90 *Seasonal orchard worker [eight rungs]
93 Staple of Dutch Golden Age art
95 Feeling while watching a volcanic eruption, perhaps
96 According to
98 Narwhal's tusk
99 Pleasant speech cadence
100 Pen that aptly rhymes with "click"
101 *Worker for AT&T or Verizon [four rungs]
103 Common wall mirror shape
104 Sound on Old MacDonald's farm
105 Chicken scratch
106 –
109 Worker who probably isn't paid enough
110 Really, really spicy
115 1/100 of a franc
119 Dirt clump
120 Googles, e.g.
121 Like people in crowds, whether intentionally or not
122 Donations for the needy
123 *One putting a coat on outside [three rungs]
124 Surreptitious assents

DOWN

1 Communications on Slack, e.g.
2 Org. funding Covid-19 research
3 In the manner of
4 Roughly
5 "Then again . . . ," in a tweet
6 Upscale hotel room fixture
7 One calling for a tow, maybe
8 Visual depiction of the apparatus used by the starred professionals
9 "___ wise guy, eh?"
10 Like some humor
11 Important stretch
12 Stretch longer than an 11-Down
13 Mario who founded a fashion empire
14 Snowboards well, informally
15 Rabble-rouse
16 Something taken by a waiter
17 "Cya!"
19 "How ___ Your Mother"
20 Con's vote
26 Mafia : Sicilia :: Camorra : ___
28 Harden
29 Latin for "trumpet"
30 Disinclined
31 Temple text
34 Beach in Rio de Janeiro, informally
35 "From now ___ won't be hanging around" (bluegrass lyric)
36 1600, in ancient Rome
37 Tick off
39 ___-by-the-Sea, Calif.
44 Welcomes, as the new year
46 Narcissist's treasure
48 Perceived
49 Output from Sappho
51 Cloud
53 Adjustable bike part
55 "I don't wanna hear it"
57 Boxer Laila
58 Stephen who said "Think books aren't scary? Well, think about this: You can't spell 'Book' without 'Boo!'"
59 Director DuVernay
66 Play title that superstitious actors avoid saying aloud in theaters
67 Certain sib
68 Currency to which the Maltese scudo is pegged
69 Opus ___
70 Hypnotized, say
71 Sci-fi novel made into films in 1984 and 2021
72 Skeptical reply to "That's true"
73 Activity one tries to get out of?
77 Sushi condiment
78 Strand, perhaps
80 "Silly me!"
82 Pope of 1963-78
83 Government bonds?
85 Preppy clothing brand
86 Ending with leuko- or oo-
88 Quick kiss
91 One with a marsupium, affectionately
92 Bacardi, e.g., in México
94 Threat from a squealer
97 Antelopes with twisty horns
101 Immune system agent
102 Like luxurious pillows
103 Breakfast that may be prepared overnight
104 Former N.F.L. QB Kyle
105 Pet rescue org.
107 "The Black Cat" author
108 Genderqueer identity
111 Soccer star Messi, familiarly
112 Delta ___ Chi, house in "Animal House"
113 B&O and Reading: Abbr.
114 Either half of pocket rockets, in poker slang
116 ___ Jima
117 Rx from a doc, e.g.
118 Newsroom heads, for short

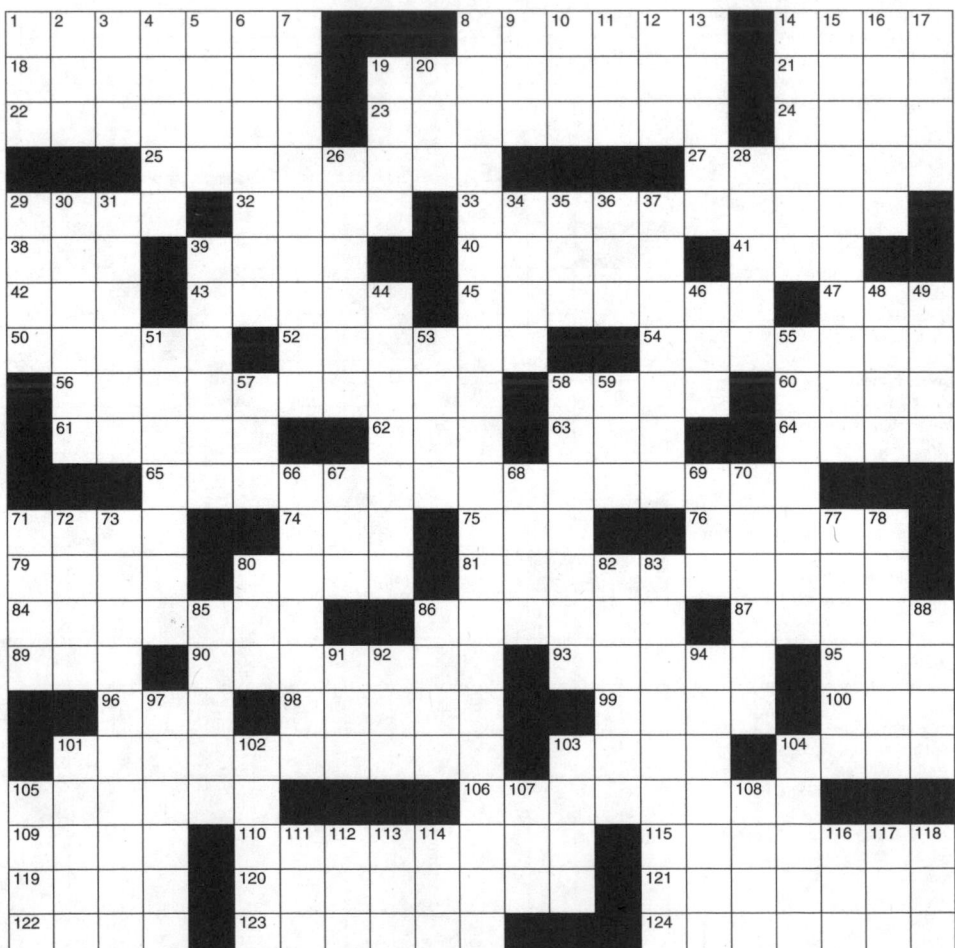

by Jessie Trudeau and Ross Trudeau

ACROSS

1 "Te quiero ____" (Spanish words of endearment)
6 ____ axis, half of an ellipse's shorter diameter
15 See-worthy?
20 Volume on an iPad, say
21 Singer of "Fame" fame
22 "____: Game Over" (2014 video game documentary)
23 Grown-up efts
24 Old-fashioned letter opener
25 Turn into confetti
26 12/25, e.g.
28 ____ Lewis, singer of the 2007 #1 hit "Bleeding Love"
29 Tennis star Naomi, who was born in 29-Across
30 "I'm gonna tell you something huge"
33 Mossy growths
36 River with a "White" counterpart
38 Lil ____ Howery ("Get Out" actor)
41 Stuffs into a hole, say
44 F-, for one
45 Ritual with bamboo utensils
48 God, in Italy
49 Repeated word in an "Animal House" chant
51 Pastry with the same shape as an Argentine medialuna
52 Attorney general before Garland
53 Online promotions, collectively
56 What businesses go by
59 Cut down
60 "Eureka!"
61 Word with easy or stop
64 Provide change in quarters?
68 Long, tragic stories
72 Up to this point
74 Best Supporting Actress nominee for "The Power of the Dog," 2021
75 Letter opener, pencil cup, inbox tray, etc.
76 Phanerozoic ____ (what we live in)
77 Classroom aides, for short
79 British term of address
80 Currency for the prize on "Squid Game"
81 Reddit Q&A session, in brief
82 Most unpleasantly old and mildewy
85 Letters before Constitution or Enterprise
86 Popular subcompact hatchback from Japan
89 Rock commonly used in asphalt
91 Part of a hotel with décor fitting a certain motif
93 Video game series with settings in Liberty City and San Andreas, for short
94 Gobsmack
95 Scottish interjection
96 "Everything Everywhere ____ at Once" (Michelle Yeoh movie)
97 R&B artist whose name sounds like a pronoun
99 Eats
101 Travis of country music
105 One of 2,297 for Hank Aaron, for short
107 Annoyance for a Twitch streamer
110 Figure with equal angles
112 Sunday ____ (end-of-week anxiety, casually)
114 Country whose flag depicts a machete
116 With 121-Across, company that sells scuba gear
117 Certain furniture store purchases
120 Missing
121 See 116-Across
122 "Be My Baby" group, 1963
123 Bygone Microsoft media player
124 The lights in fairy lights
125 Some travel considerations, in brief
126 Tarnish
127 Donkey Kong and others

DOWN

1 Bachelors, e.g.
2 ____ Eats
3 Ninja Turtle's catchphrase
4 One who's super-good-looking
5 Affirmative gesture
6 *Baseball pitching style . . . or a weapon
7 Afore
8 Dining hall offerings
9 About, on a 10-Down
10 See 9-Down
11 Volunteer's words
12 Tennis's "King of Clay"
13 Hour, in Italy
14 *Big name in hotels
15 Access providers
16 Within reach
17 Actress who played "Jessica" in "Parasite"
18 No-go ____
19 Something to pry or twist off
27 Volunteer's words
29 [Gasp!]
31 Chooses
32 More run-down
34 Period in ancient history
35 Like a defeatist's attitude
36 *Indentation on a chew toy
37 Textile-making device
38 *Light again
39 "I mean . . ." sounds
40 *Whom Holmes tells "You do find it very hard to tackle the facts"
42 Telegram
43 *Many a Viking
46 Pulled a fast one on
47 College near Vassar
50 Where van Gogh and Gauguin briefly lived together
52 Dyeing method using wax
54 Chief ____ (rapper with a rhyming name)
55 Where feudal workers worked
57 French equivalent of "Stephen"
58 ____ van der Poel, Olympic speed skater
61 Academic acronym
62 *Grand
63 Hits shore unintentionally
65 *Early French Protestants
66 Burden
67 *Basic rivalry
69 "Continuing where we left off last time . . ."
70 *"G.I. Jane" star, 1997
71 Field goal avg., e.g.
73 Believers in Jah, informally
75 Fatalistic sort, in slang
78 Place in an overhead bin
80 No ____! (punnily named dairy-free chocolate brand)
83 Explosive stuff
84 U.S. ID?
87 Bad place to pour grease
88 "Have ____ make my email stop" (Destiny's Child lyric)
90 Cable in the middle of a tennis court
92 Would really rather not
97 "What's up, everyone!"
98 -ish
100 *"Encore!"
102 Fidel ____, 1990s Philippine leader
103 Tehran's home
104 Fork prongs
106 *Actress Angela
108 How to play solitaire
109 They have high ratings on the Beaufort scale
111 Jokester's arsenal
112 "Leave it," on paper
113 Alien-seeking org.
115 Strip near Tel Aviv
118 Beverage at un café
119 Business card abbr.

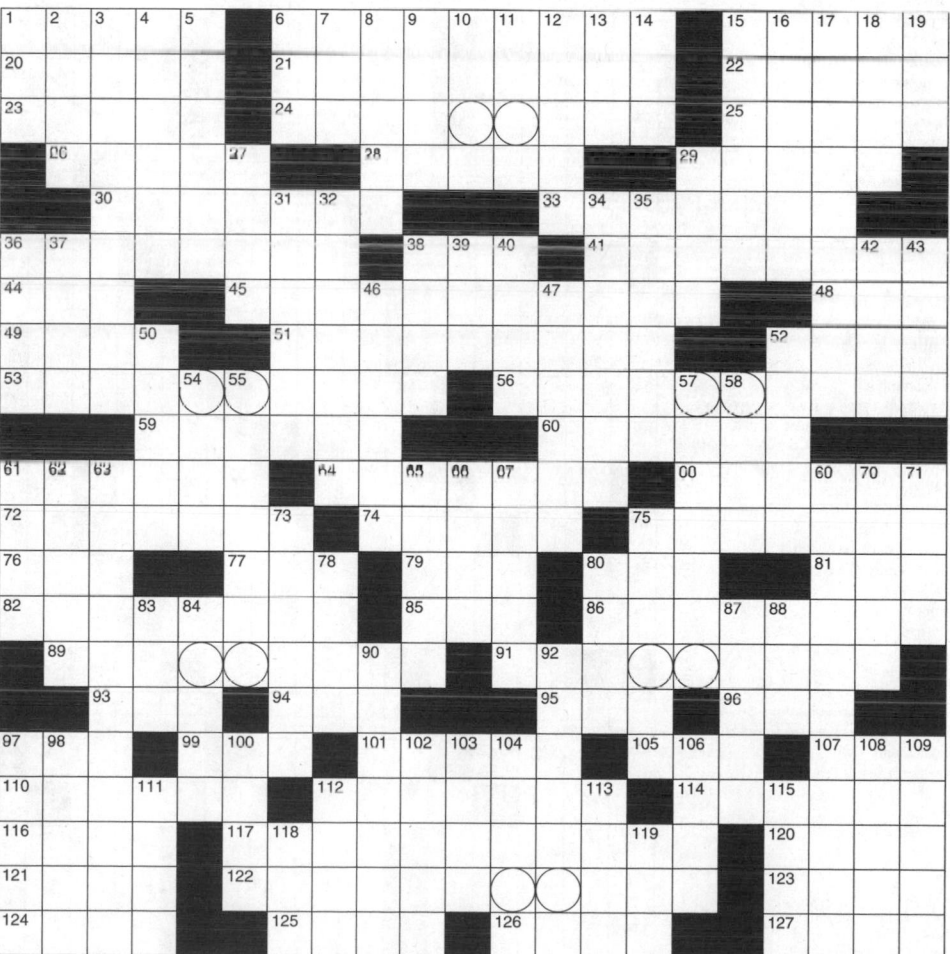

by Paolo Pasco

ACROSS

1 Shops
5 Peddling
10 Collectibles
14 A kitchen might have a good one
19 Instrument for Arachne, in mythology
20 Natural instincts
21 Word on the street, perhaps?
22 Like Superman, but not Spider-Man
23 Symbol of bravery
24 Nephew of Abel
25 One-eyed war god
26 African animal that may be spotted or striped
27 Armed force at sea?
29 "Person of the Year" magazine
31 Big froyo franchiser
33 When said three times, "Get off my case!"
34 White terrier, informally
35 Historic
36 Hockey
37 Upset
38 _____ Toy Barn (where Emperor Zurg chases Buzz Lightyear)
39 "I," in the "Iliad"
40 You'll have to pull some strings to play this
41 Low-scoring Yahtzee category
42 Lower back bones
45 Downsides
46 How many U.N. members have names starting with "W"
47 Lionel Messi's homeland: Abbr.
48 Standoffish
49 Whiz
50 Promotional overkill
51 Capital on the Arabian Peninsula
54 Waste
55 Disposal
56 Locations
57 Things believers believe
58 The "A" in A.D.
59 Racket
60 Children's book series akin to "Where's Waldo?"
61 Word with nursing or training
62 N.I.H. standard
63 Read
64 Here
65 To
66 Understand
67 23 answers in today's puzzle that don't seem to match their clues
68 The "P" of E.P.S. ratio, on Wall Street
69 Adverb repeated in the "Star Wars" prologue
70 Calvin and Hobbes, e.g.
71 Head, in slang
72 Onetime radio host Don
74 "Mad" figure of fiction
76 Dazzling
77 Pattern
78 Generator
79 Like some care services
80 Purplish blue
81 1998 film "Waking _____ Devine"
82 Al _____ (pasta specification)
83 Initialism aptly found in "timetable"
84 Thief's haul
85 Xmas, for Justin Trudeau
86 Synthetic fiber
87 Tiptop
89 City east of Phoenix
90 D-worthy
91 Sweetie pie
92 Classes
93 For
94 Actors
95 Get off berth control?
99 Tarnish, e.g.
100 Crossed out
101 Apt rhyme for "pyre"
102 Revitalize
103 Finalized, as a contract
105 Safe harbor
107 "Let me repeat . . ."
109 Put cargo on
110 She might cry "Uncle!"
111 Last "O" in YOLO
112 Rough rug fiber
113 Unwritten, say
114 Didn't make public for a while
115 Home
116 Decorating
117 Guru

DOWN

1 "I'll _____ it"
2 "Hold the rocks," at a bar
3 Blows one's horn
4 Captcha confirmation
5 Adds to a playlist, e.g.
6 Sights in a funeral home
7 "I," in the "Aeneid"
8 Partitioned
9 Product launches made during sporting events?
10 Chiwere-speaking tribe
11 "Stellar!"
12 They can help you get out of jams
13 Real
14 Having overexercised, maybe
15 _____ gun (alien zapper)
16 When the lighting of the Olympic cauldron happens
17 Wolf, to a shepherd
18 "A penny saved is a penny earned" and others
28 Rice dish
30 Sound of shear terror?
32 Go lightly, with "along"
35 Epoch when the Mediterranean Sea nearly dried up
36 Like difficult water for boating
37 Like Thor
42 It's a long story
43 Fourth man to walk on the moon
44 Gain exclusive control, business-wise
45 More wary
46 Female nature deities
47 A charismatic person has one
50 Gets a move on
51 Some BBQ-flavored fast-food sandwiches
52 Totals
53 Letters near a conveyor belt
55 Online pop-up generator
60 How perjurers might be caught
61 _____ Mary
66 Makes beloved
67 How Usher wants to take it in a 1998 #1 hit
68 The 76ers, on scoreboards
69 Disaster response org.
70 Arctic coats
73 In the public eye
75 Headset?
76 Popular Korean minivan
77 Country with more than 100 active volcanoes
82 Device providing oversight?
84 Verizon, for one
85 Hardly genteel
87 Website overseers
88 Brain cases
89 1600 for the SAT, informally
90 No. listed on the inside of car doors, often
91 Get over it!
96 Actress Catherine who starred as Kevin's mom in "Home Alone"
97 "Red" or "white" wood
98 Prepared to pray, say
100 Idyllic spot
101 Stocking stuffers
102 Italian automaker
104 _____ mode (fuel-saving feature in newer cars)
106 Tape player of a sort, in brief
108 Dunderhead

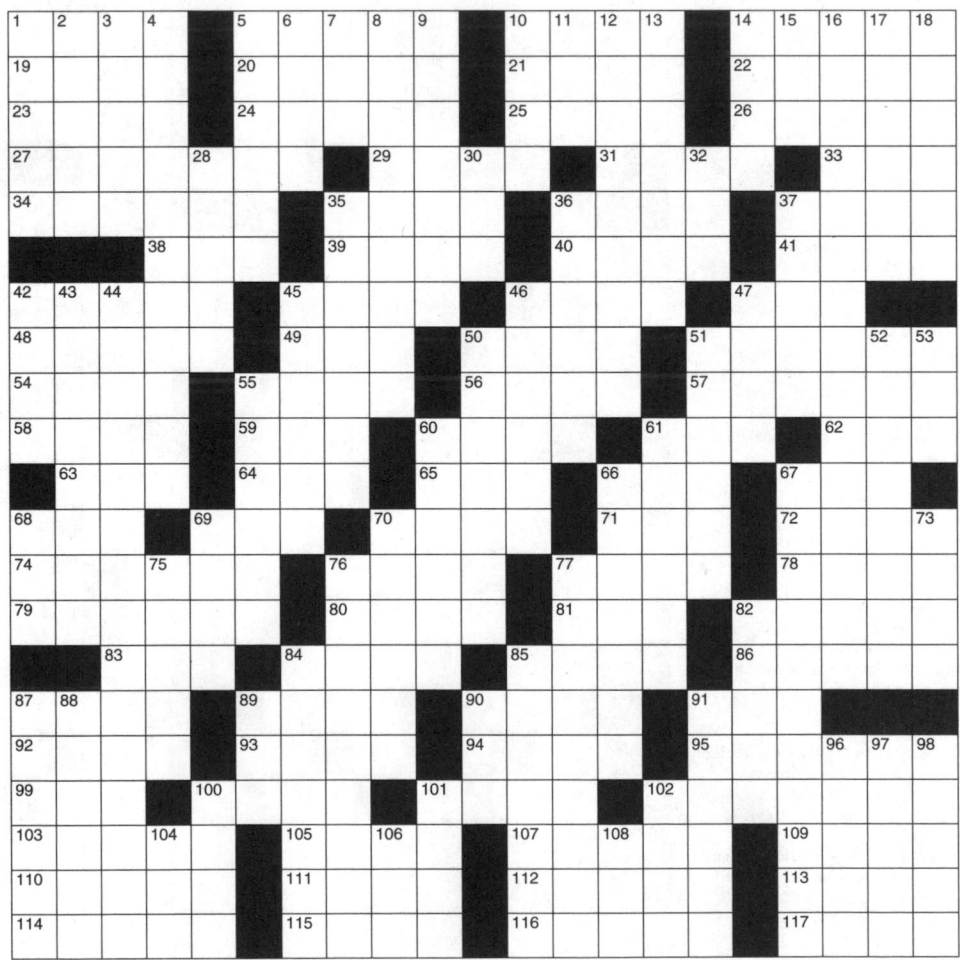

by Daniel Bodily and Jeff Chen

Note: This completed puzzle contains a 114-Across, comprising the eight shaded answers. Put these in order, one after the other. Then use this key to get a line spoken by 25-Across in "The 40-Across": A = R, B = I, C = J, D = P, E = A, G = H, I = O, J = C, K = L, L = U, N = T, O = Z, P = Y, R = M, S = E, T = D, U = S, V = G, X = N, Y = K.

ACROSS

1 Flight path?
7 Pain in the neck?
13 Wish
19 Climbed, as 1-Across
20 TV schedule info
21 Early online forum
22 Pacific harbinger of wet West Coast weather
23 Some tiki bar orders
24 Out in the sun too long, maybe
25 English computer scientist who pioneered the breaking of ciphers generated by the 98-Across
27 Driver of some engines
29 Bind
30 Part of a seat assignment
31 Observed during
33 ____-Seltzer
35 Ready to blow
37 Leaf producer
40 2014 movie portraying the work of 25-Across, with "The"
44 Fission locales
46 Set of clubs
47 "The Merchant of Venice" character who favors wordplay
48 Brazilian jiu-____
50 Prey for a lion
52 Fitting
53 Connect with on social media, maybe
54 How some popcorn is popped
55 Gradually slid (into)
57 Lead-in to dermis
60 Location of the Chair of St. Peter within St. Peter's Basilica
61 Thin porridges
63 Modern prefix with health
64 Appearance
66 "My dear man . . ."
67 Civil rights leader Medgar
69 Troublesome engine sound
71 Hoover, for one
74 One way to segment demographic data
76 Tibia's place
77 Sly plan
80 Space-oriented engineering discipline, informally
82 What ". . ." sometimes means
84 Troublesome engine sounds
86 Arrive at, as an idea
87 Ones without owners
89 What a "Wheel of Fortune" contestant might buy when looking for _NSP_RAT_ON
91 Startled squeal
92 Forthrightly asserts
93 Genghis Khan, notably
94 Herbert Hoover's middle name
96 Many a maid of honor
98 W.W. II-era encoding device
101 Currant-flavored liqueur
103 Itsy-bitsy
104 Santa ____ (desert winds)
105 Wear for a Sufi scholar
107 Hello in São Paulo
109 One with an inside job
111 Takes seemingly forever
114 Sort of encoded message found in this puzzle's grid [SEE NOTE]
117 From long, long ago
119 Express momentary uncertainty over
121 Classified cost?
122 Icon to click for more icons
123 Eeyore's creator
124 Tidy
125 Radial patterns
126 Failed to maintain a poker face, perhaps
127 Figure the worth of

DOWN

1 Curse
2 Rat out
3 Longtime media figure suspected of being the inspiration for "The Devil Wears Prada"
4 Have ____ for
5 Wilbur is one, in "Charlotte's Web"
6 Like some insurance benefits
7 Designer Versace
8 It's for paper shapers
9 Cousin of Gomez Addams
10 Some quinceañera gift-givers
11 Send off
12 Moves from a table to a booth, say
13 Dunderhead
14 Ending with legal or Senegal
15 ____-service
16 Implies
17 Go over, as a cold case
18 When you should be off, in brief
20 Cosette, to Marius, in "Les Misérables"
26 Pull out
28 Comedian Wong
32 Soapbox rant
34 Polar expedition attire
36 Out of juice
38 Frequent victim of Calvin's pranks in "Calvin and Hobbes"
39 Crew vessel
41 Add chocolate sauce and a cherry to, say
42 Pre-deal payment
43 Come to ____
45 Rude way to break up with someone
48 Celebratory dances
49 Letters on a crucifix
51 One accepting the terms and conditions
56 Transports from Midway Airport to the Loop
58 Nose-dives
59 Na+, for one
62 Its in French
65 Rubber-stamps
68 Migration formation
69 Ho ____ Minh
70 Word after party or date
71 Worsen significantly
72 Emotion felt con el corazón
73 ____ Wearhouse (retail chain)
74 Alvin ____, first African American to be elected Manhattan's district attorney
75 Cellist who performed at the Biden/Harris inauguration
76 Attitude
78 Some back-and-forths
79 They generate a lot of buzz
80 Makes right
81 Pulitzer Prize-winning W.W. II correspondent
83 Class for which trig is a prereq
85 Mountain cover
87 Bird of the Baltic
88 Runs down, in a way
90 "I'm good, thanks"
94 Honeydew relatives
95 One of 14 in a fist
97 Carlos in the Rock & Roll Hall of Fame
99 End of Q1, on co. reports
100 Bank run, perhaps
102 Some writing surfaces
106 Memory part
108 Affirmations from the congregation
110 Sci-fi character who was originally a puppet before C.G.I.
112 Rock subgenre associated with David Bowie and Elton John
113 ____ Valley, Calif.
115 Laudatory works
116 French for "fat"
117 O'er and o'er
118 Side in checkers
120 Love of soccer?

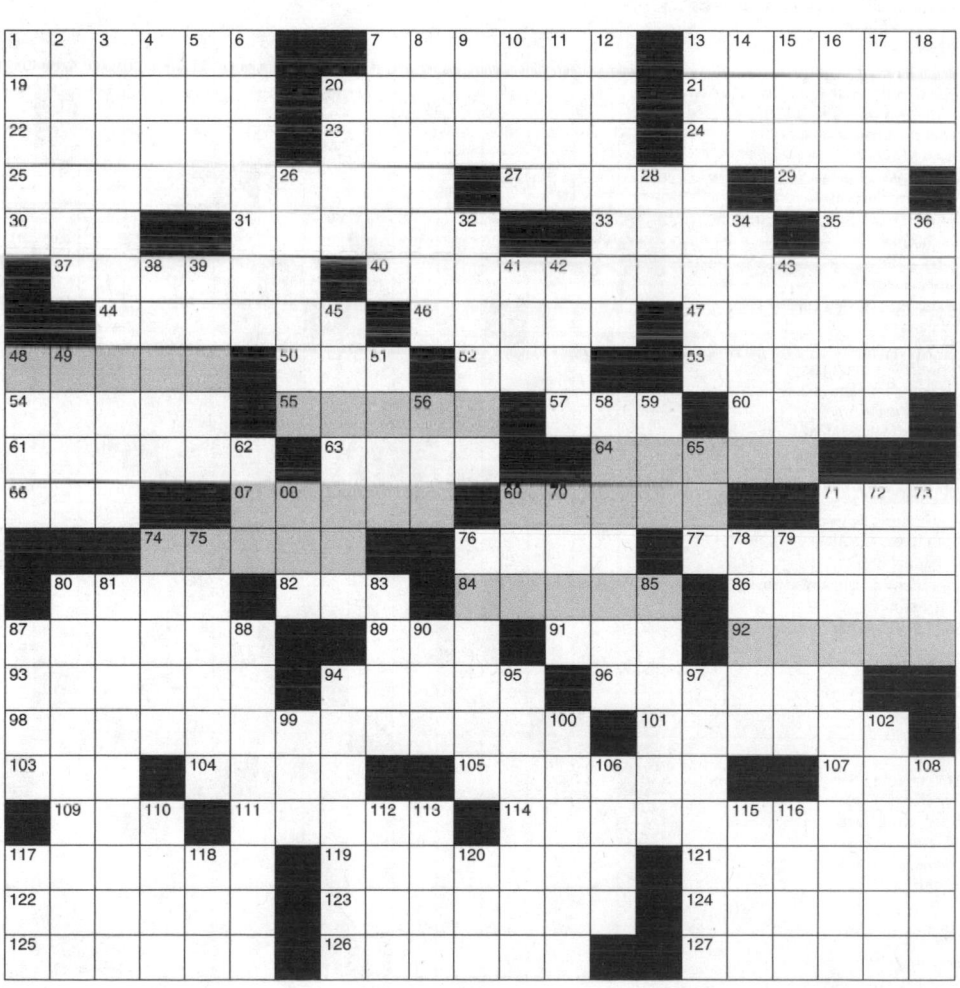

by Addison Snell

ACROSS

1 A is one
8 Ozone-harming compounds, for short
12 Actor Guy
18 "How awesome!"
19 Play with, as a cat might a toy mouse
20 Naysayers
21 *Five guys?*
23 It might have desks and drawers
24 Shade of purple
25 Those: Sp.
26 *Green giant?*
28 Ambulance driver, for short
30 Finished first
32 "___-ching!"
33 Just
34 Like basalt and obsidian
37 Something sent on a Listserv
40 Police broadcast, for short
41 "Special Agent ___" (animated Disney show about a bear)
42 Main character in Larry McMurtry's "Lonesome Dove"
43 Apt name for a Christmas caroler?
44 ___ Clarendon, first openly transgender W.N.B.A. player
48 *Jolly rancher?*
51 Hole
52 Diagnosis characterized by repetitive behavior, in brief
53 Focus of a marathon runner's training
54 Grand opening?
55 Sides (with)
58 ___ school
59 Dessert with some assembly required
61 Grammy recipient Lisa
63 What pro bono lawyers waive
65 *General mills?*
69 The British 20-pence and 50-pence coins, geometrically
71 Member of a South Asian diaspora
72 Photo finish
75 Every last drop
76 Bank, often
78 Exams offered four times a year, for short
81 Grown-up pup
82 "I promise I won't laugh," often
83 Certain guiding principle
84 *Texas instruments?*
87 Meadow grass with brushlike spikes
90 Fermented Baltic drink
91 "Ugh, gross"
92 Stag's date?
93 Doc treating sinus infections
94 X, in linear functions
95 Dolphins' div.
97 Like many a company softball game
99 "That stinks!"
100 Subj. devoting extra time to idioms
102 ___ milk
103 *Band aid?*
107 Truce
109 Litter box emanation
113 Efflux
114 *Old navy?*
117 Like many a grillmaster
118 Supermodel Kate
119 Headache helper
120 Took a little look
121 [Hey, over here!]
122 Rough patch

DOWN

1 Standing on
2 Texter's "Hilarious!"
3 Soy something
4 Ones working block by block?
5 Hoodwink
6 Drift apart
7 Certain Ivy Leaguers
8 Pac-12 school, informally
9 Qualification shorthand
10 "Ple-e-e-ease?"
11 Help when writing a letter
12 Its national drink is the pisco sour
13 State of disorder
14 Some vacation rentals
15 Lube up again
16 Old pal
17 Actress ___ Creed-Miles
19 South American capital
20 Figures
22 Statements of will?
27 "The power of global trade" sloganeer
29 ___ Millions
31 Into crystals and auras, say
34 Its calendar began in A.D. 622
35 Inflated feeling of infallibility
36 Letters on a stamp
38 ___ B or ___ C of the Spice Girls
39 Actor Alan of "Crimes and Misdemeanors"
40 Binghamton Rumble Ponies or Birmingham Barons
41 "My b!"
43 Sign
44 Feudal lord
45 Plots of western films?
46 Brain freeze cause, maybe
47 Does a summer job?
49 Warrant
50 Magic can be seen here
51 Relating to land, old-style
56 They can help you see or taste
57 Like the odds of finding a needle in a haystack
60 Airline based near Tel Aviv
62 Deserving of a timeout, say
64 Big spread
66 "No need to elaborate"
67 Like the Hmong language
68 ___ Ng, author of "Little Fires Everywhere"
69 12/24, e.g.
70 ___ Perlman, role for Timothée Chalamet in "Call Me by Your Name"
73 Means of divination
74 "What ___?"
77 Indicate availability, in a way
79 "Weekend, here I come!"
80 Side dish at a barbecue
85 Upsilon preceder
86 Producer of the world's most widely read consumer catalog
88 Genre for One Direction
89 ". . . finished!"
90 Ties
94 Android alternative
95 Exclamation after a sigh
96 Teeny-tiny
97 Sporty wheels
98 Eccentric
99 Explorer Richard who made the first flight over the South Pole
101 Attempt to control the narrative, in a way
103 Lava, e.g.
104 Took to court
105 Omar of "Love & Basketball"
106 Rolls around while exercising?
108 Quick talk
110 What nyctophobia is the fear of
111 Slobbery cartoon character
112 "___ over" (words after letting off steam)
115 Often-contracted word
116 Tech sch. in Troy, N.Y.

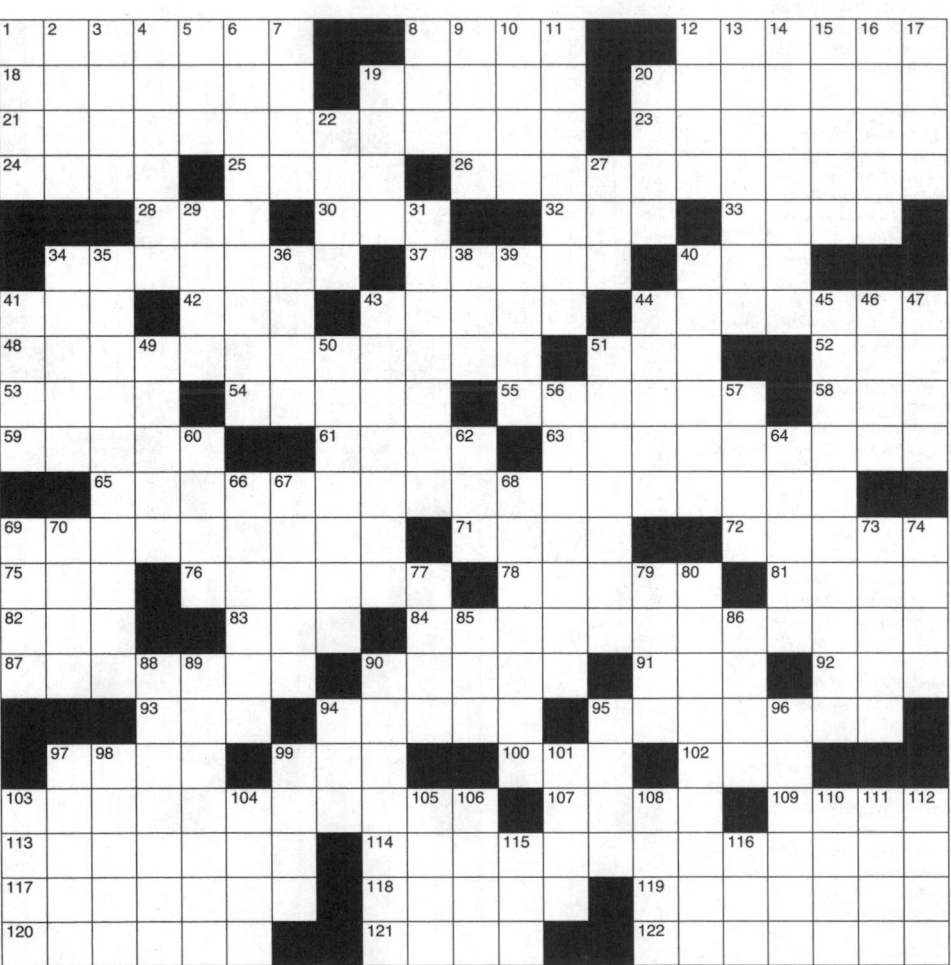

by Matthew Stock

Note: When this puzzle is done, insert the five shaded jigsaw pieces into the box at the bottom to get a three-word phrase, reading across, for what jigsaw puzzles provide.

ACROSS

1 Part of a pie or the earth
6 Style that makes waves
10 Doe in a court case
14 Flubs
19 Keister
20 China holder?
21 Axe target
22 Some Madison Avenue workers
23 End of many a sports broadcast
24 Freestyles, perhaps
25 Barflies
26 Botch
27 *"First, you're going to want to dump out the box and ___"*
31 Francis of old game shows
34 Bounded
35 Capital on a 126-mile-long canal that's used as a skating rink in the winter
39 English breakfast, e.g.
40 *"What's most useful next is to ___"*
45 College app component
46 Role for "Ronny" Howard
48 Joshes
49 State flower of Utah
50 One of the B's in BB&B
51 Field work of note in 1979
54 Rifle, in frontier lingo
57 *"To connect things up you'll have to ___"*
63 Ones getting the crumbs?
66 Bonnie with five Top 40 hits in the 1990s
67 Euphoric feeling
71 Love to bits
72 More like a dive bar or certain bread
74 Beehives, but not hornets' nests
75 Daredevil's hashtag
76 Very in
78 One of the B's in BB&B
79 Good name for an investor?
82 High-end Italian auto, informally
83 *"As you go, make sure you exercise your ___"*
88 At peace
89 Little bouquets
90 "ka-POW!"
93 *"With patience and perseverance you're sure to ___"*
97 Course goal
100 Songs that can be trilling?
102 Castigates
103 Fairy-tale figure
105 Confer, as credibility
106 Gets wild and crazy
108 Legendary
109 Leave skid marks, maybe
111 N.F.L. standout
113 Homes for high fliers
114 Instruction to drivers leaving cars at a garage
115 "C'mon, slowpoke!"
116 Ends, as a mission
117 Mary Poppins, for one
118 Pick up on

DOWN

1 O-line anchor
2 Feel regret
3 Trojans' sch.
4 Distinctive part of a cookie cutter
5 "Tap tap tap . . ." activity
6 Get into a lot
7 Jacob's brother, in the Bible
8 Moved like waves or muscles
9 A certain degree
10 St. ___ University (Philadelphia school)
11 Rescue dog, for one
12 Response to the Little Red Hen
13 Language related to Manx
14 Egg, e.g.
15 Keats, for one
16 Sounds in a yoga studio
17 Government economic org., at any rate?
18 ___-Cat
28 Big suit
29 Derby, e.g.
30 Menial laborer, metaphorically
31 Loads
32 Take back, for short
33 Retreat
36 "Was it ___ I saw?" (classic palindrome)
37 Mists, e.g.
38 Feeling it after a marathon, say
41 Approves
42 Perspective
43 Achievement for Whoopi Goldberg, in brief
44 Like cioccolato or torta
47 Titus and Tiberius
50 Bosom buddies
52 Staple of skin care
53 Sought office
55 UPS competitor
56 Steady, maybe
58 Wrath
59 Exercise program since the 1990s
60 Sharp, on a TV, informally
61 Peak sacred to the goddess Rhea
62 Noshed on
63 "You'll ___ for this!"
64 Words with a ring to them?
65 Letter between foxtrot and hotel in the NATO alphabet
68 How people often scroll through social media
69 "That's gotta hurt!"
70 "The Puzzle Palace" org.
72 More straight-faced
73 Creamy Italian dish
76 Word that becomes its own opposite by putting a "T" at the front
77 Singer whom M.L.K. Jr. called the "queen of American folk music"
80 Play again, as a TV special
81 Companion in Brittany
84 Brain diagnostics, for short
85 Used as a rendezvous point
86 Devote
87 Name suffix meaning "mountain"
90 Fir tree
91 "Is it still a date?"
92 Roman goddess of wisdom
94 Prefix with color or state
95 Sugar ending
96 W.W. II fighters
97 Apps made with jalapeños and cheese
98 "You agree?" (*nudge, nudge*)
99 Gathers some intel
101 Actor Brody
104 Singer Willie
106 Annoying
107 Grannies
110 Blood line
112 Temporal ___

by Christina Iverson and Jeff Chen

ACROSS

1 Confound
6 Sarcastic internet laughter
10 Most Times Square signage
13 Performance check
17 Dark hair and a warm smile, for two
19 Samoan capital
20 To's opposite
21 Full-length
23 Something that bugs criminals?
25 Blabberer
27 Duplicitous
28 Musicianship
30 ____ dress
31 Pasture
32 Signed off on
33 Ukr. or Lith., formerly
34 Places for development
36 Corn kernel, e.g.
38 Actress Merrill
40 Genre for BTS or Blackpink
43 Added to the staff?
45 Alerts
48 ____ of lies
49 Aquafina : PepsiCo :: ____ : Coca-Cola
52 #$%& and @%¢!
55 Practice whose name means, literally, "union"
57 Words before "before"
58 "Deck the Halls" contraction
59 Symbol on the Connecticut state quarter
60 Stop along the highway
61 Quite
64 Finished brushing one's teeth, say
66 Racial justice movement since 2013, in brief
67 "Really, though?"
68 Word in many font names
69 Betray . . . or a hint to four answers in this puzzle
73 ____ the Cat (fictional feline of children's books)
74 Thin incision
75 Some $200 Monopoly properties, in brief
76 Set of 50 on the Argo, in myth
77 Coaxed (out of)
79 Insurance giant bailed out in 2008
80 Word before cap or pop
81 Awesomest bud
82 Spirit in Arabian myth
83 Arizona county or its seat
85 Pushing up daisies
90 Neighbor of Mozambique
92 Nonwriting credentials for Conan Doyle and Chekhov, informally
93 Seller's need
95 Artificial habitat
97 Abolitionist Lucretia
98 The avant-garde "artists" Congo and Pierre Brassau
100 Hedy of the 2017 documentary "Bombshell"
103 Kind of chip
105 Question of perplexion
108 "The Raven" writer's inits.
109 Like
110 Big believer in the freedom of assembly?
112 Press ____
113 What the beleaguered are behind
115 Classic folk story that teaches a lesson of sharing
118 Be up for some biking?
120 Fast runners
121 Advanced math degree?
122 Ninny
123 Sternutation

124 Real cutup
125 Landscaper's supply
126 In the past
127 "As You Like It" forest

DOWN

1 Novelist Margaret
2 Absorb the beauty of, as a scene
3 Lacked the gumption to
4 Gladly, old-style
5 Jazzy James and Jones
6 First law enforcement org. in the U.S. to hire a female officer (1910)
7 Nail polish brand
8 List of performers
9 Star man?
10 Half of a '55 union merger
11 "That's enough arguing out of you!"
12 Lip-puckering
13 Things that may be rubbed after din-din
14 Playwright Will who was a 2005 Pulitzer finalist
15 Crew implement
16 One getting special instruction
18 Ink holders in pens and squid
22 "Just like ____!"
24 Like morning people vis-à-vis night owls, around dawn
26 Response to "How bad was it?"

29 Extends, in a way
35 Lead-in to call
37 Cause for an onslaught of yearly txts
39 "If the pessimists are right . . ."
41 Stroke
42 East: Ger.
44 Wednesday, but not Friday
46 Accelerator particles
47 Overwhelm
48 Some tax breaks
50 Boos and cheers
51 Light
53 Latin list ender
54 Some Hershey candies
56 Bought in
61 Time-consuming assignment to grade
62 Xanax alternative
63 Monthly publication of the National Puzzlers' League, with "The"
64 More convinced
65 "The Magic School Bus" was its first fully animated series
66 Sound at the end of December, appropriately?
67 Beach with a girl who "swings so cool"
70 Part of many a corsage
71 Bite site
72 Job to do
78 High-quality cannabis, in slang
80 "Success!"

81 Decorate
82 "I. Can't. Even."
84 Spain's Duchess of ____
86 Classic novel with the line "You must be the best judge of your own happiness"
87 Environmental opening
88 When repeated, a reproof
89 Overturned
91 Most chiffonlike
94 Figure out
96 Not thinking
97 The Supremes' record label
99 Bad temper
100 Makeup target
101 Where a "Married at First Sight" contestant meets his or her mate
102 Language in which "kia ora" is a greeting
104 Up on
106 Confused responses
107 Fight site
111 Long runs?
113 "A man's character is his ____": Heraclitus
114 "Suds"
116 Prefix with classical
117 Prof's degree
119 Post on Insta

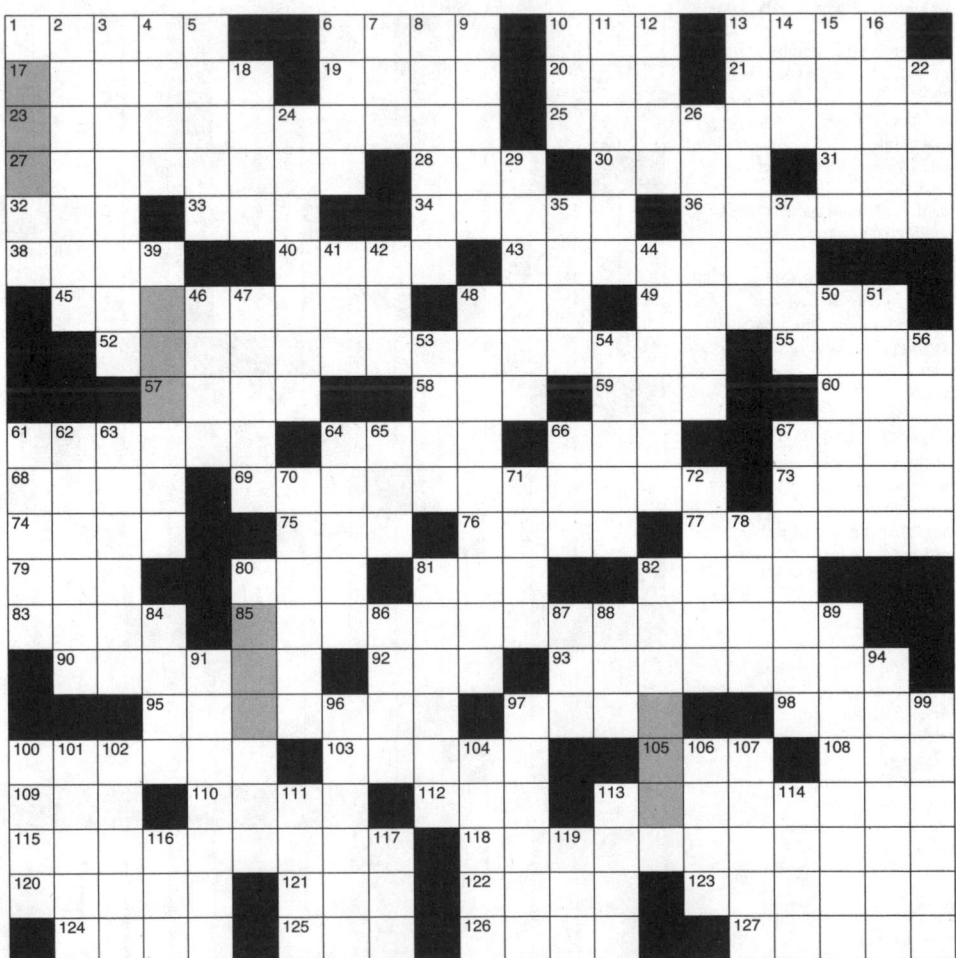

by Aimee Lucido and Ella Dershowitz

ACROSS

1 What a drawbridge may bridge
5 In that case
9 Control tower installation
14 Pass
19 "That one's ___" ("My bad")
20 Amelia Bedelia, e.g.
21 "Go me!"
22 Member of a noble family
23 2004 film about a group of MALIGNERS
25 It might be put on for stage PAGEANTRIES
27 Annual film festival where "Saw" and "Get Out" premiered
28 "___ La La" (1964 hit)
29 Senator, e.g., for short
30 Avoids a bogey, perhaps
31 Being
33 Be hopping mad
34 Cool one
37 W.W. II hero, informally
39 Muletas are waved at them
40 Canon camera
41 Branch of Islam
42 You might be MARVELING AT this as it whizzes by
46 Sort of SCHEMATIC for Christian education
48 Like some casts
49 City nicknamed "The Old Pueblo"
51 French city near the Belgian border
52 Prefix with colonial
53 Tight-fitting
55 Toni Morrison title heroine
56 Annual British acting award
58 Series of questions, maybe
60 Counterpart of elles
62 Opposite of never
64 Many relationships are INSTIGATED on one
68 Healthy eaters may give this A WIDE BERTH
72 Disrupt an online meeting, in a way
74 Mauna ___
75 Grp. that hasn't yet found what it's looking for
76 Wonder Woman and others
79 Valuable load for a mule
81 Influence
84 Pioneering gangsta rap group
85 Burdened
86 Just
88 Preferring one's own company, perhaps
90 They can be NOISELESS while stalking prey
93 Explorers of the UNTRAVERSED
95 Burden
96 Old cable TV inits.
97 Fill in
98 Word repeated in "I ___, I ___, it's off to work I go"
99 Lick, say
100 "___ merci!" (French cry)
101 "On it, captain!"
103 "No need to make me a plate"
106 Five-letter word that replaces a four-letter word?
107 1980s gaming inits.
108 Not even
111 Writing done GRAPHICALLY
115 The Trojans lacked the FORESIGHT to turn this down
116 It's multilayered
117 You should always bring it to a competition
118 Children's author Blyton
119 Be taken aback

DOWN

1 "My Two ___" (2015 Claudia Harrington children's book)
2 Top
3 Appliance brand since 1934
4 Pea shooters?
5 "Sign me up!"
6 Complete travesty
7 Feature of many British accents
8 Binges too much, for short
9 As if orchestrated
10 Indexed data structures
11 Directly
12 Fourth person to walk on the moon
13 Do a double take?
14 Boot
15 Almost
16 What makes Shrek shriek?
17 One side in a debate
18 It may be blown
24 They may be blown
26 House Republican V.I.P. Stefanik
28 Star in Canis Major
32 Just so
34 Hot dog topper
35 Airline passenger request
36 Lion
38 "Dear ___ Hansen" (2017 Tony-winning musical)
41 Responds to br-r-r-isk weather?
42 Like zebras and lions
43 Voice with an Echo
44 Rub it in
45 "It is what it is" and others
46 Mike Krzyzewski, to Duke basketball fans
47 Rise
50 Hot dog topper
54 A little too silky, maybe
56 Justin Trudeau, by birth
57 Don't believe it!
59 Aftmost masts on ships
61 Gives fuel to
63 Gets a move on, quaintly
65 Who can hear you scream in space
66 Ending with poly-
67 Title meaning "commander"
69 "___ Meenie" (2010 hit)
70 Battling
71 Rings up
73 Showing the effects of an all-nighter, say
76 Give one's blessing to
77 It has more coastline than California, surprisingly
78 Score after seven points, maybe
80 Certain radio format
82 Apropos of
83 "Like that'll ever happen!"
86 "Appetizers" or "Desserts," at a diner
87 International cosmetics company ___ Rocher
89 Content people?
91 Larsson who wrote "The Girl With the Dragon Tattoo"
92 Pooh-pooh
94 Common April activity, nowadays
97 Vietnamese sandwich
100 Group trying to sack a QB
102 Make over, as a ship
104 A crowd, they say
105 It has 104-Down legs
106 Obscure, with "out"
109 They may be set by industry grps.
110 Girl in "The Old Curiosity Shop"
111 sin/tan
112 Major Japanese carrier
113 "Kill Bill" co-star
114 You can chew on it
115 Some appliances

by Stephen McCarthy

ACROSS

1 Sliver
4 Politician with the campaign slogan 30-Across
9 Word with poetry or proportions
13 Something you might click to open
16 Elicits a "Whoa" from, say
18 Trimmed (down)
19 Wrestling star John
20 Tailor
22 Beams of one's dreams?
25 Food served in an omakase meal
26 Having very little mental energy left
27 Moonfish
28 Swimmers in kelp forests
30 See 4-Across
33 Visit a museum to see a Rembrandt exhibit?
35 One prone to looking down
36 His tomb is in Red Square
37 Diamondbacks, on scoreboards
38 Face cards?
41 Destination for oenophiles
43 Sicily's Parco dell'___
45 Bug spray ingredient
49 Bird of prey that's gently petted?
53 Popular pops
55 Kind of attack
56 Longtime hockey star Kovalchuk
57 To read: Sp.
59 Gross
60 Error, in totspeak
62 Buys in
65 Look down on
67 Actor Justin sitting poolside?
71 Adds insult to injury
73 Santa-tracking org.
74 River across the New York/New Jersey border
77 Some rideshare info
78 Exploit
81 Award-winning film set in Tehran
83 Bishop's headgear
84 Hang up the cleats, so to speak
86 Make fun of small orange fruits?
90 Something rectangular that might have more than four sides
91 Two-player card game
92 TV character who said "Time to hit the hay . . . oh, I forgot, I ate it!"
93 Old auto with its founder's monogram
94 Storage spot
97 Opposite of "avant"
99 Reason to reschedule
102 Mashed potatoes, on a Thanksgiving plate?
107 Instrument heard in Spanish folk music
111 Vinyl collection
112 Food brand whose sales boomed after the premiere of "Stranger Things"
114 "When We Were Young" singer
115 Sharp
116 Fourth-quarter meltdown at an N.B.A. game in Oklahoma City?
120 Made out
121 Take home
122 Lather gatherer
123 Remained in bed, e.g.
124 Something to shoot for
125 ". . . sting like ___"
126 Clubs
127 ___ Bleus, nickname for France's soccer team

DOWN

1 Boardwalk treat
2 Plugged in, so to speak
3 Actor Leary
4 Missions, for short
5 ___ State, nickname for Massachusetts
6 Basis for an insurance investigation
7 "Build ___ Buttercup" (1969 hit by the Foundations)
8 Spot for a perfume sample in a magazine, maybe
9 Green prefix
10 Staff
11 Lead-in to com or net, but not org
12 Wrinkly-skinned fruit
13 Largest object in the Kuiper belt
14 And the following, in footnotes
15 His birthday is celebrated as "Children's Day" in India
17 Worries anxiously
20 Mounted on
21 Angry reaction
23 Main port of Yemen
24 They're banned in many classrooms nowadays
29 Thing seen in the foreground of "Washington Crossing the Delaware"
31 N.Y. neighbor
32 Calculators of old
34 Partner of starts
36 Speaking part?
38 "In that case . . ."
39 Paul of "Little Miss Sunshine"
40 Didn't hear the alarm, say
42 Where fruit bat soup is eaten as a delicacy
44 Orange follower
46 Widespread
47 Nonstop flight?
48 Maori for "image"
50 Redeems at a casino
51 Sooners, by another name
52 Have a home-cooked meal
53 Like some obligations
54 Dict. listing
58 Setting for Mets games: Abbr.
61 Gradually diminish
63 Residential suffix with Angel
64 High-priced violin, informally
66 All-knowing sort
68 It's represented by a dot in the top-left corner, in Braille
69 Mideast palace parts
70 Son of Gloucester in "King Lear"
71 & 72 A pop
75 ___ Alonso, Mets slugger with the most home runs by a rookie in M.L.B. history (53)
76 ". . . ish"
79 People people, for short
80 Exit
82 "What's ___, Doc?" (old Bugs Bunny short)
85 Grapefruit descriptor
87 Kelly of "Live"
88 Remark after losing
89 Nutritional figs.
95 "___ be an honor!"
96 Snapple competitor
98 "Socialism: Utopian and Scientific" writer, 1880
100 Leaning right: Abbr.
101 Four-time U.S. Open champ
102 Four-time Australian Open champ
103 It has its highlights
104 Maker of the MDX, NSX and TLX
105 Bloc party?
106 Fix up again
107 Brown hue
108 Home of many Sherpas
109 ___ Hughes, name of main roles in "Westworld" and "Downton Abbey"
110 Decade after the aughts
113 Blossom
117 Taipei-to-Seoul dir.
118 Frequently
119 ___ Palmas

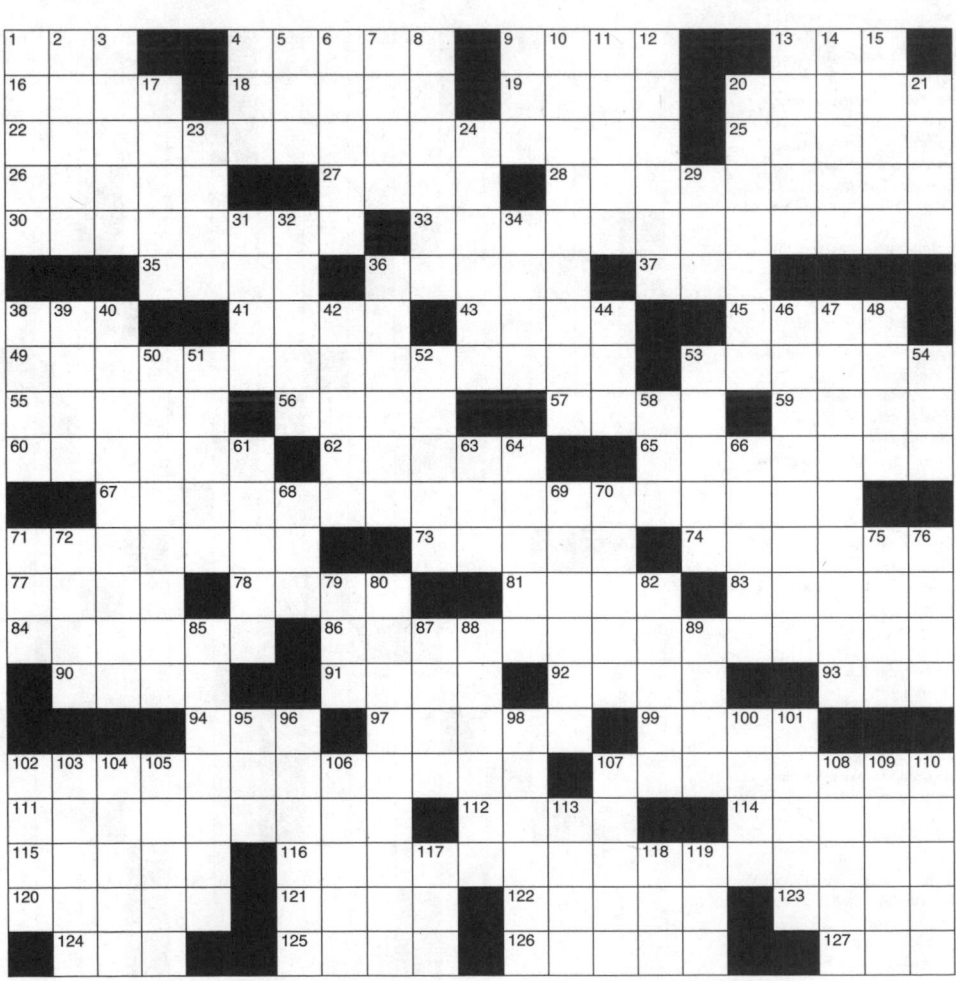

by Dory Mintz

ACROSS

1 Impersonate
6 Bump on a log
11 Get into one's birthday suit
16 Fruit drinks
20 Home of the isle of Tortuga
21 "___ often costs too much": Emerson
22 Word before rock or football
23 Song word repeated after "Que"
24 Charming sort?
26 Olympics projectiles
27 People in charge: Abbr.
28 ___ Lingus
29 Lucy's last name on "I Love Lucy"
31 Like gasoline nowadays
33 30-year host of late-night TV
37 Legal field concerned with long-term care
39 Commotion
40 Televangelist Joel
42 Prima ballerina
46 Some team competitions
49 The "e" in Genoa?
50 With 97-Across, emerge reborn . . . or what the ends of five Across answers in this puzzle do?
52 "Gangsta Lovin'" rapper, 2002
53 Yoga class instruction
55 Food packaging reassurance
56 Good "Wheel of Fortune" buy for REVERSE ENGINEER
57 Sold (for)
59 Toward the back
60 Where dominoes were invented
62 Rule
64 Jazz guitarist Montgomery
66 Some U.N. officers, for short
67 Super Bowl LV champ
68 Took a swing, say
70 Basketball box score column
74 Addiction treatment locale
76 Lead-off selections?
77 Something to file
78 French article
79 Sweet pea
81 Volkswagen model inits.
82 Give wrong information
83 Boring tool
85 Emmy-winning journalist Finch
87 Website with a Seller Handbook
91 "How ___ . . ."
92 Encrypted URL component
94 Red-handed, say
96 Make haste
97 See 50-Across
99 Brand that stylizes its name with a lowercase second letter
100 What a button on an armrest may control
104 Serenade
105 "___ Pal," early episode of "The Jetsons"
108 Shrinks
109 1980 event in Washington
111 Be completely candid
114 Gryffindor, Slytherin, Hufflepuff or Ravenclaw
117 It may be taken in by a traveler
119 Half of sei
120 Treat thought to be stamped with symbols of the Knights Templar
121 "We ___ please"
123 Within arm's reach
128 Something commonly left in an operating room
129 Going by
130 Where the Volta River flows
131 Tea go-with
132 Pull down
133 Those opposite the center and guards, in N.F.L. lingo
134 More teed off
135 Scattered

DOWN

1 Sounds at a sauna
2 Limit
3 20–20, e.g.
4 Hit TV show created by Donald Glover
5 Something close to a colonel's heart?
6 "Today" competitor, for short
7 -
8 Those against
9 Come back again (again . . . again . . .)
10 Harp-shaped constellation
11 Got ready to ride, with "up"
12 Vacuum tube type
13 "Hi" follower
14 Rack up, as charges
15 No-hassle
16 Countless
17 -
18 Slips
19 Holder of merit badges on a scout uniform
25 Jon of "Two and a Half Men"
30 -
32 Gone-but-not-forgotten
33 L.L. Bean competitor
34 Plant family that jasmine and lilac are part of
35 Safe space
36 Announcement maker of yore
38 In early 2001, one of its executives notoriously said "From an accounting standpoint, this will be our easiest year ever"
41 ___ Minella (Muppet)
43 Pot grower's remark?
44 What snakes grow as they age
45 Corrects, as text
47 They used to be a "thing"
48 Floor coverings that feel good on the feet
51 Politician's concern
54 Detective Lupin
55 Present-day saint?
58 Surprise ending
59 Sparkling wine variety
61 Scolded, as in a library
63 Big name in nail polish
65 -
69 Drive
70 Sets aside
71 Popped in for just a moment, perhaps
72 The Ikea logo shares the colors of its flag
73 Lead-in to "of mind" or "of war"
75 Advocate for the better treatment of elves, in Harry Potter
80 Determination from Santa
84 Big tournament news
86 Bare
88 -
89 Spots for window boxes
90 Verbal cringe
93 The St. Lawrence River's misnamed ___ Islands
95 Far from friendly
98 Fatigued over time
99 Set of rules popularized by "How I Met Your Mother"
101 Doctor's orders, maybe
102 Best ___
103 Shaving brand
106 "Let me get this out . . ."
107 Lead-in to -scope
110 Small lab bottle
112 Loud, as a stadium
113 Former second lady Cheney
114 It often has its kinks
115 Sight from a Seattle ferry
116 Bike ride setting
118 Rides
122 Millennium start
124 See 126-Down
125 Take a ___
126 With 124-Down, feature of van Gogh
127 Get hitched to

by Grant Thackray

ACROSS

1 They come with bouquets
6 Away
11 "_____ put our heads together . . ."
15 Singer/drummer Collins
19 Cell component
20 Pal, in Peru
21 Put one's nose where it doesn't belong
22 Tilt-a-Whirl, e.g.
23 One arm held up with bent elbow and wrist, in a children's song
24 Move obliquely
25 Phenomenon such as the tendency to see human forms in inanimate objects
27 Any of the groupings of circled letters in this puzzle
30 Gin product
31 Incredible bargains
32 "Sorry, Charlie!"
33 Fits together
34 Savory Chinese snacks
37 Jump over
41 Smoking and swearing, e.g.
44 They await your return, in brief
45 Have a good cry
46 Syracuse Mets and Worcester Red Sox, for two
50 "Music's most maligned genre," per critic Tom Connick
51 Word with level or lion
52 "Everything happened so fast!"
54 Farm female
55 "_____ Gone Wrong" (2021 film)
57 Brunch beverage
59 One of the brothers on "Malcolm in the Middle"
60 Room in Clue
61 Cause of undue anxiety
63 It may be smoked
64 Hogwash
65 Munch, in modern slang
66 "_____ 17" (W.W. II film)
67 One of two in a jack-o'-lantern?
70 Where charity begins, in a phrase
73 Table part
74 Title for Tussaud: Abbr.
76 "Midsommar" director Aster
77 Digs up
78 Carpenter's wedge
80 Does gentle stretching post-exercise, with "down"
82 Amp knob
84 Die like the Wicked Witch of the West
85 Give zero stars
86 Ne'er-do-wells
88 E.R. inserts
89 By birth
90 Plant said to repel bugs
93 _____ Ryerson, insurance salesman in "Groundhog Day"
94 French pronoun
95 Quarter _____ (when the big hand is at three)
97 No-longer-current source for current events
99 Hot, mulled punch traditionally drunk around Christmas
101 Bacteria destroyer
104 French port on the English Channel
106 Like the Minotaur legend
110 University of Oregon site
112 How to see the image formed by this puzzle's circled letters
115 What's formed by the circled letters in this puzzle
117 "We're live!" studio sign
118 Ancient land in Asia Minor
119 Domino, e.g.
120 Martinez with a statue outside the Seattle Mariners' stadium
121 Makes less powerful, in video game slang
122 Domino, e.g.
123 "To . . ." things
124 Dino's tail?
125 Muse of love poetry
126 Arises (from)

DOWN

1 Eastern cicada killers, e.g.
2 Suggestions
3 ". . . said _____ ever"
4 School
5 Resolves out of court
6 Org. that flew a helicopter on Mars in 2021
7 Fail to mention
8 Information, old-style
9 Rounded quarters
10 Without stopping
11 How Alaska ranks first among the states
12 It's often left on the table
13 What "vey" of "Oy, vey!" translates to
14 _____ Games, company behind Fortnite
15 Rey, to Luke Skywalker
16 Sword handles
17 "Einstein," sarcastically
18 Puts pressure (on)
21 What can make men swear from menswear?
26 "_____ pass Go . . ."
28 Leading medal winner at the Tokyo Olympics
29 Forman who directed "One Flew Over the Cuckoo's Nest"
35 Farm refrain
36 Weight of a paper clip, roughly
38 Ancient: Prefix
39 Soul-seller of legend
40 Half-baked?
41 Duck and goose, at times
42 "See ya"
43 Group dance popularized in the U.S. by Desi Arnaz
45 77-Down is on the most collected one in U.S. history
47 Epiphany
48 Voice actor Blanc
49 Show with over 1,000 handwritten cue cards each week, for short
51 City hazard
52 "My word!"
53 Pol in the "I am once again asking . . ." meme
56 City whose police cars are adorned with a witch logo
58 Card game with a PG-rated name
60 Boring
62 Purse
65 High degree
68 Not at all popular
69 Messes up
70 x, y and z
71 Chaotic skirmish
72 Fragrant compound
74 Saturn has more than 80 of them
75 Golf course machine
77 He performed 636 consecutive sold-out shows in Vegas from 1969 to '76
78 Burn prevention meas.
79 The future Henry V, to Falstaff
80 Fight tooth and nail
81 One who consumes a ritual meal to absolve the souls of the dead
83 Bits on book jackets
87 Roc-A-_____ Records
91 Part of U.C.L.A.
92 Fashion designer Geoffrey
94 It may run from an emotional situation
95 [Mwah!]
96 Departed by plane
98 Green vehicle
99 Frank
100 Duke's org.
101 Pasta topper
102 Like the dog days of summer
103 Acrobatic
105 Make restitution
107 Faint color
108 "Take me _____"
109 Approaches
111 Where the lacrimal glands can be found
112 Pasta topper
113 Pump some weights
114 Not exactly
116 Vaccine-approving agcy.

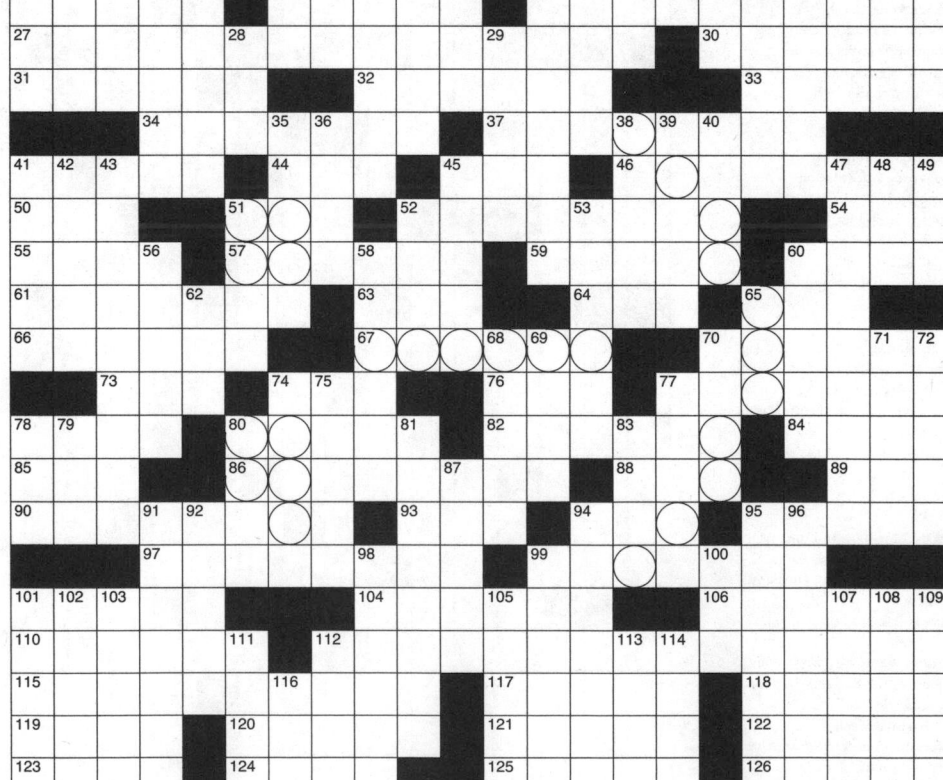

by Alex Rosen

ACROSS

1 Like the Rock vis-à-vis any of the Stones
8 Small doodles, perhaps
15 ____ pants
20 Surpass
21 Candy bar with an exclamation point in its name
22 To love, in Italian
23 Meticulous magical beings?
25 The land down under
26 Sharpen
27 Screams
28 Calendar column: Abbr.
29 Frenzied states
30 High-ranking figures, collectively
32 Like some cross-Caribbean flights?
34 Three-time Pro Bowl wide receiver in the New York Jets Ring of Honor
37 Biblical father of Eliphaz
40 CNN political correspondent Bash
41 Bushy-tailed rodents
43 Postseason tournament pick
46 ____ Reader (quarterly magazine)
50 Journals of a certain stunt performer?
52 Commuting arrangement
54 Body shop fig.
55 Owing
56 Buddy of Buddy, maybe
58 What might whet an appetite
59 Taken down and put up elsewhere
63 Relative of cerulean
66 Scale for some judges
68 Possible reason for refusing to wear a tank top?
71 Worries about something
73 2018 crime biopic
74 "Potatoes done perfect" sloganeer
77 Shape of a doughnut
78 Shape of a canine ID tag, often
80 Fossil suffix
82 "Most miserable hour that ____ time saw": Lady Capulet
83 "Checkmate"
85 Means of learning about Chiang Kai-shek?
91 Massachusetts' College of Our Lady of the ____
92 Some post-pollution efforts
94 Become ticked off
95 Ready
96 Wielder of the hammer Mjölnir
98 Tools used by horologists
99 Inept dancers at Oktoberfest?
105 Express line count
107 Mentor of 50 Cent
108 Valedictorian's pride, in brief
109 Mag space seller
111 Smurf with a white beard
115 Dish at a traditional Bedouin wedding
116 New look provider . . . or a homophonic hint to this puzzle's theme
119 Small hill
120 Poorly lit
121 Series of steps
122 Early R&B group for Missy Elliott
123 Stockpiles
124 Felt on the head?

DOWN

1 "2 Broke Girls" co-star Behrs
2 Bounce off the wall
3 Musk of SpaceX
4 Incendiary explosive
5 Big news to share in the biz world?
6 Company acquired by Allstate in 2011
7 Longtime first name in TV talk
8 Unpartitioned apartment
9 Clicking sounds?
10 Letter two after tau
11 ____ E (skin care brand)
12 Guacamole ingredient
13 Major exporter of nutmeg
14 ____ admin
15 "LOLOL"
16 Big name in microwaves
17 Straight sides of sectors
18 Put up
19 Soccer superstar nicknamed "La Pulga" ("The Flea")
24 Water (down)
29 The National Zoo's Xiao Qi Ji, e.g.
31 Agitate
32 Hungarian herding breed
33 Figure on Italy's 2,000-lira note before euros were introduced
34 Common viper
35 Free
36 People can't lie under it
38 Actor who delivered the line "Nobody puts Baby in a corner"
39 Word with power or brakes
42 GQ V.I.P.s
44 Best
45 "____: Vegas" (TV reboot of 2021)

46 Revolted
47 Treat for Mr. Owl
48 Seward Peninsula city
49 Verve
51 "There was no choice"
53 Person with star power?
57 Triangular piece in a party bowlful
60 Rentals that might come with dolly carts
61 "Wrong!"
62 Nickname for someone whose full name is a calendar month
64 Spur
65 Letter two before tau
67 Obie-winning playwright Will
69 Defamed, in a way
70 "Indeed"
71 Reason to see an ophthalmologist
72 Pea jacket material
75 Caterpillar competitor
76 Thomas Jefferson or John Tyler, by birth
79 Org. that bestows the Community Assist Award
81 Liberal arts sch. major
84 Certain curtain
86 On the ____ (no longer friendly)
87 Overseas speed meas.
88 Go from here to there . . . like *that*

89 Quark's place
90 "It's my hunch . . ."
93 Pithy saying
95 Dish whose yellow color comes from saffron
97 "Rude Boy" singer, to fans
99 Divisions of bushels
100 Like the Mideast exclave of Madha
101 Long rides?
102 Used a prayer rug, say
103 Literally, "works"
104 Pieces of work
106 Traditional rivals of the N.C.A.A.'s 'Hoos
109 Church part
110 There are three of them in a Morse "O"
112 Passing through D.C.?
113 USD : dollar :: MXN : ____
114 Part of 79-Down: Abbr.
116 Frequent C.D.C. collaborator
117 "____ Way" (Kitty Kelley biography of Sinatra)
118 Opponent

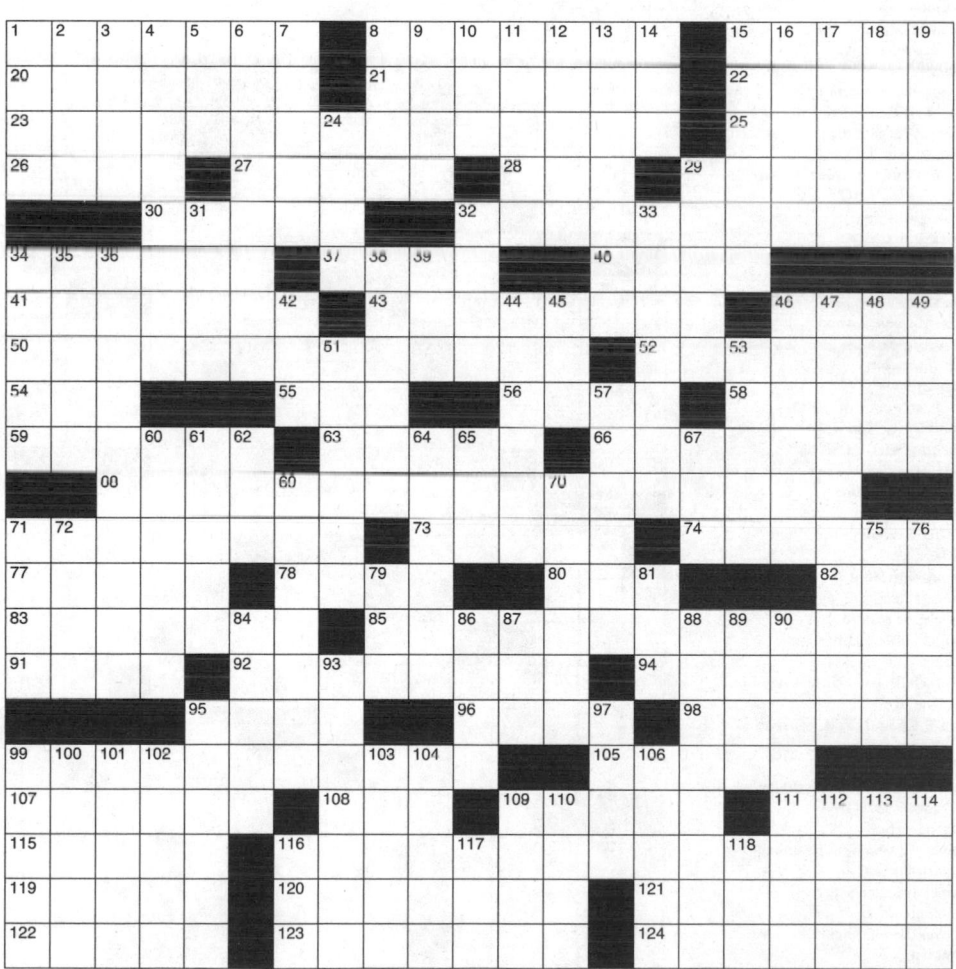

by Peter Gordon

134 SNOOZEFEST

ACROSS

1 Goes wherever the wind blows?
6 Person who likes all your FB posts, perhaps
9 Key with five sharps: Abbr.
13 Western film, in old slang
18 Harriet's partner on 1950s–'60s TV
19 China's Chou En-____
20 Paul Simon's "____ Rock"
21 Tree that Athena gifted to Athens
22 Inaptly named bear of a tongue twister
25 Spanish rice
26 Letter-shaped construction piece
27 Endeavor
28 Winter weather hazard
31 Little black ____
32 Art of verse
33 Jurisdiction of a Catholic church official
37 Get closer and closer
40 Mapmaker's subj.
41 Literary traveler to Lilliput and Brobdingnag
42 Transfixed
43 Former telecom giant that merged into Verizon
45 Ostentatious display
48 Kicked back
49 Singer Lisa
51 Pre-euro currency
52 National tree of the U.S.
53 Paradise lost
54 Scatterbrains
56 Grandma, to Brits
57 Frenzy
59 Rattlesnake's warning
60 Ambrose Bierce defined it as "A minor form of despair, disguised as a virtue"
62 Totally over it all
63 Final creature encountered in "Dr. Seuss's ABC"
68 Far-right state
70 Buckskin, e.g.
71 Something stretched out in a yoga class
74 Has over
75 Go after
78 Like varnished wood
79 "Pretty please?"
80 Sci-fi travelers
81 Pan-fries
84 Violated a code of silence
85 Sportscaster Jim with the classic opening "Hello, friends"
86 Opportunities to win a vacation on "Wheel of Fortune"
90 Stocking stuffer
91 Actress Ana of "Love, Victor"
92 "Alas . . ."
93 Bistro sign word
95 Francis' tenure, e.g.
96 Lively, on a score
97 Collect little by little
99 Makes
101 "Which Disney Princess Are You?" and the like
104 Big Ten powerhouse, for short
107 Eye shade
110 Basic skateboard trick
111 Quick nap . . . or a playful description of the 64-Down here
113 Conflagration
114 Diamond who went platinum
115 Scottish denial
116 Popeye creator Segar
117 Footnote abbr.
118 Icelandic work that influenced Tolkien
119 Key for getting out, not in
120 Like May through August, unlike the other months of the year

DOWN

1 What "piano" can mean
2 Côte d' ____
3 Nickname for Isabelle or Isidore
4 Fashion designer Lange
5 Actress Amanda of 2012's "Les Misérables"
6 What B. B. King was king of
7 Rattles
8 Opposite of flatness
9 Members of bevies and broods
10 Tie the knot
11 Mine: Fr.
12 Many a collaboration between Louis Armstrong and Ella Fitzgerald
13 "C'est magnifique!"
14 Spanish composer Isaac
15 "How to ____ a ____" (popular Google search)
16 One of the Gabor sisters
17 Radiation unit
23 Member in the genus Troglodytes, so named for its tendency to enter dark crevices
24 "Jeepers!"
25 Generational divide
29 Former queen of Jordan
30 Nintendo princess
31 Order of roses
34 Kilt-wearing Greek infantryman
35 Fixed, as tiling
36 Northern California town once home to the palindromic ____ Bakery
37 Chain that sells chains
38 "Jeepers!"
39 Levels
40 Old fogy
41 Quiet valley
43 Partner of glamour
44 Comedian Fields
46 ____ garden
47 When repeated, one of the Gabor sisters
50 Mercedes-____
54 Stupor
55 Multitude
57 Pac-Man navigates through one
58 Wood-shaping tool
60 They're taken out in alleys
61 Six-Day War leader Weizman
62 No-nonsense TV judge
63 Unsightly spot
64 Sleep indicators
65 Counterfeit
66 Spike the Beanie Baby, e.g.
67 Having some pep
68 Alternative to Advil or Aleve
69 Birthplace of the Franciscan order
71 Kind of ray
72 Bit of tomfoolery
73 Nervous state
74 Seven: Prefix
75 Football sideline reporter Kolber
76 Brand of pretzels and chips
77 Electric ____
79 Kvetches
81 Pointy-eared dog
82 Big name in car parts
83 Break away
85 Reason to hang up
87 Victoria Falls river
88 Uniform adornment
89 Center of L.A., once
94 Sufficient, informally
95 Aphids, to ladybugs
97 Beyond cold
98 Woman's name meaning "night" in Hebrew and Arabic
99 Pound and others
100 Worshiper of the rain god Tlaloc
102 Took off
103 One of the Nereids of Greek myth
104 Eleven, en français
105 Parts of snowmobiles
106 Exploits
107 "The White Lotus" airer
108 View from Lake Como
109 Country music's ____ Brown Band
112 In a bad way

by Trenton Charlson

ACROSS

1 Syllables when you forget the words
4 The universe has an estimated 10^{82} of them
9 "A mouse!"
12 Beyoncé chart-topper "Single ___ (Put a Ring on It)"
18 Simile center
19 ___ Lawrence College
20 Magazine co-founded in 1945 by Hélène Gordon Lazareff
22 Similar-sounding phrase, such as "I scream" for "ice cream"
23 Field of Dreams
26 Guys and Dolls
27 Lucrative and undemanding
28 Ingredient in a McDonald's McFlurry
29 Seasonal winds
31 Fictional brand of rocket-powered roller skates
32 "Cross my heart!"
35 Fam girl
36 Sounds of doubt
38 Star Trek
40 Woodworker's tool
42 Some tourist spots in San Francisco
43 Tax pro, for short
45 Ancient work that describes the sacred tree Yggdrasil
46 Trendy home gym purchase
50 Top Gun
55 Baseball family name much seen in crosswords
56 Jerkface
59 Tightly affixed
60 Parrot's sound
61 Insurance department
63 "___ for me, thanks"
64 Big no-nos
66 Letters From Iwo Jima
67 The Imitation Game
69 The Fifth Element
73 Perfectly comfortable
75 1930s migrant to California
76 Spirits
77 Sesh on Reddit
80 Speed reader?
81 Gave, as gossip
83 Trimmed parts of green beans
84 A Man for All Seasons
87 Matricidal figure of Greek myth
89 Golden rule word
90 Spanish "Listen!"
91 Dostoyevsky's Prince Myshkin, so the book title declares
93 Cause for switching positions
97 Scent of a Woman
104 "___ you decent?"
105 ___ Toy Barn ("Toy Story 2" locale)
106 Small things that you pluck
107 Breakout band for Harry Styles and Zayn Malik, familiarly
108 Overlie
111 Mad magazine cartoonist Drucker
112 Get the juices flowing?
113 Wayne's World
114 Space Jam
118 Gene variant
119 Denominator in the velocity formula
120 Beam for train tracks
121 Fragrant ring
122 Candy with the slogan "Not sorry"
123 Skosh
124 Main artery
125 Panic button, of a sort

DOWN

1 Pet that should come with a lint roller?
2 Given that
3 Exasperated parent's retort
4 Flue-like
5 Confucian philosophy
6 Singer Rita
7 "Floating terror" of the sea
8 Many social media users
9 Donkey with a pinned-on tail
10 Two in a million?
11 "The Kiss" painter
12 Successfully uses a password
13 Melodious
14 Place to develop one's chops
15 Innate
16 Part of a makeup test?
17 Texting tech, briefly
21 "___ es!" ("That's right!": Sp.)
24 "Clueless" protagonist
25 Accept eagerly, with "at"
30 Org. with an annual Codebreaker Challenge
32 Double-crossed and half-baked
33 Embarrassing public episode
34 Restless desire
37 Luxurious
39 Product for one who wonders "Am I expecting?"
40 Increased into something much more valuable
41 Spy novelist Deighton
44 Weave off the shoulder?
46 Get ready for vacation
47 Civil rights activist Baker
48 It may be forgiven
49 Mystic's board
50 4x World Series winner Martinez
51 [more info below]
52 Ice cream containers
53 ___ compensation (subject of modern debate)
54 Spanish marinade
57 Drawer of shorts, e.g.
58 Cutthroat mentality
62 Cardinal's hat, in Britain
65 Tender areas
67 Pop in the fridge
68 Hershey's chocolate-and-toffee bar
70 Diatribe
71 Quaint sign word
72 Noun-making suffix
74 Fumble for words
76 Dodos
77 City that replaced Lagos as Nigeria's capital
78 Cameo
79 Predatory insect living in woodpiles
82 French fabric
85 Caramel or hot fudge, basically
86 Euphemistic exclamation
88 Ike's domain in W.W. II
91 Reason the physicist stayed in bed?
92 "The Shape of Water" director
94 Natasha ___, Boris's partner against Rocky and Bullwinkle
95 Some water park rides
96 Olympics symbol for Madrid's country
98 Sang along when you forgot the words
99 Ingredient in healing gel
100 Latte art medium
101 Arch support
102 Bill killers
103 Utopian
106 Like a birthday cake, pre-party
109 "___ All That" (1999 film)
110 Frequently, quaintly
112 Lugosi of horror films
113 Fish with an elongated jaw
115 Singer Sumac
116 Describe in a negative way
117 Toke

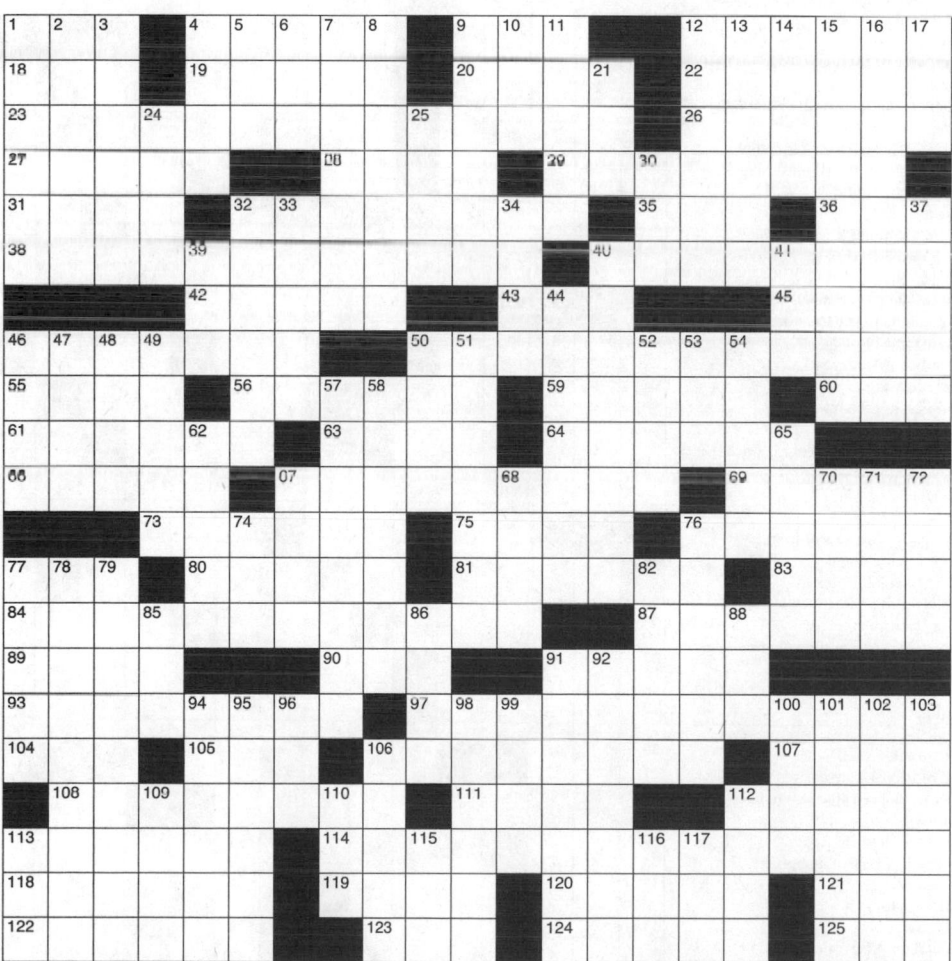

by Brandon Koppy

Note: This puzzle has five Diagonal clues, in addition to Across and Down. Diagonals (in mixed order): 1) Breakfast side dish 2) Compassionate 3) Nickname for Mars 4) Starts drinking 5) Truly magnificent

ACROSS

1 Conveniently forgets to mention, maybe
6 Big name in investing
12 How many writers work
18 Ran out of patience
19 Meghan ___, Grammy's 2015 Best New Artist
21 Get warmed up
22 Word with water or Electric
23 Meaningful work?
25 Rock bottom
26 Special ___
27 Like TV's Niles Crane and Monica Geller
28 Their existence is debatable
30 Conflict in 2017's "Wonder Woman," in brief
32 Source of Supergirl's powers
33 Clothing line
36 Ballet supporter, e.g.
41 N.A.A.C.P. ___ Awards
43 REI competitor
44 Shout of support
45 Gamelan instruments
46 Unflappable
51 Basic point
52 Main squeeze, in modern lingo
53 Texas hold 'em pair nicknamed "ducks"
54 "___ and Fugue in D Minor" (piece used in "Fantasia")
56 Lucifer
58 The "vice of narrow souls," per Balzac
59 Goddess who sprang from her father's head
60 Bibliophile : books :: oenophile : ___
61 "Imperialism, the Highest Stage of Capitalism" author
62 Muck
63 Present without being present
66 Ship for 28-Across
69 Like a space cadet
70 Part of the body named after Dr. Ernst Gräfenberg
71 Accustomed (to)
73 On edibles, say
75 A shore thing
76 Posted one's thoughts
77 Makes a comeback?
78 Souvenir for a Final Four team
79 Ingredient in many balms
81 Hones
82 Lock
83 Company with an iconic yellow Running Man logo
84 "The Lion King" trio
86 Receiver of private instruction
87 Ritzy transports
94 Japanese prime minister before Suga
95 Hosp. diagnostic
96 Where Gal Gadot was born: Abbr.
97 Instigate
98 Once
102 Not worth a ___
105 Pal of Buzz Lightyear
106 You wouldn't want them to have a crush on you
110 Director DeMille
111 Chuck E. Cheeses, in part
112 One way to go
113 Better than
114 Off course
115 One of the Magi, along with Melchior and Balthazar
116 Designated things for bikes and buses

DOWN

1 "Sick burn!"
2 Peace Nobelist Yousafzai
3 Cry of success
4 More orderly
5 Fuel for a camp stove
6 Houston A.L.er
7 Field's yield
8 Macbeth trio
9 Golfer Michelle
10 Sight on an M. C. Escher Möbius strip
11 Balkan region
12 Director Welles
13 Fastidious
14 Feng ___
15 As things might happen
16 Something bottled in Cannes
17 Price abbr.
20 GPS recommendation: Abbr.
21 Look over
24 Get a move on
29 Kenan Thompson is its longest-tenured member, for short
30 Reminiscence about an epic party
31 Ming-Na who starred as Mulan in 1998's "Mulan"
34 Played a Halloween prank on
35 Pickle

37 Olympic gold-medal gymnast Korbut
38 Govt. agency that Jimmy Woo works for on "WandaVision"
39 Santiago of "Scandal"
40 Horse of a different color
41 "Aha!"
42 Sit shiva, e.g.
46 Male deer
47 Completely, after "in"
48 Diez menos dos
49 Most of Greenland
50 Like dim sum
52 One hitting the low notes
53 Name that means "God is my judge"
55 Some Chevy S.U.V.s
57 Present, e.g.
58 She/___
60 Droll
61 Kid ___
64 Denouement
65 One who asks a lot of questions
66 The munchies, e.g.
67 Step two?
68 Nine to five, for example
69 Animal on Ontario's coat of arms
72 "Not this again!"
73 Take out of the game
74 Law that led to a 1773 revolt
75 Actress Ward

76 Abacus piece
77 James who sang "At Last"
78 Nary a trace (of)
80 With 83-Down, puzzle solver's starting point
83 See 80-Down
84 Altitudes: Abbr.
85 It guards against UVB
88 Like the sun at dawn
89 Lite
90 Little blob
91 Critic of the Great Society
92 Radicchio relative
93 Distinctive flairs
95 Real, in Rio
99 Disney villain voiced by Jeremy Irons
100 Bar mixer
101 The Cardinals, on scoreboards
102 Series that might feature a long-lost father-uncle
103 Only known animal to prey on great white sharks
104 Person calling tech support, say
106 Bleat
107 Some conjunctions
108 Summer worker, in brief?
109 French possessive

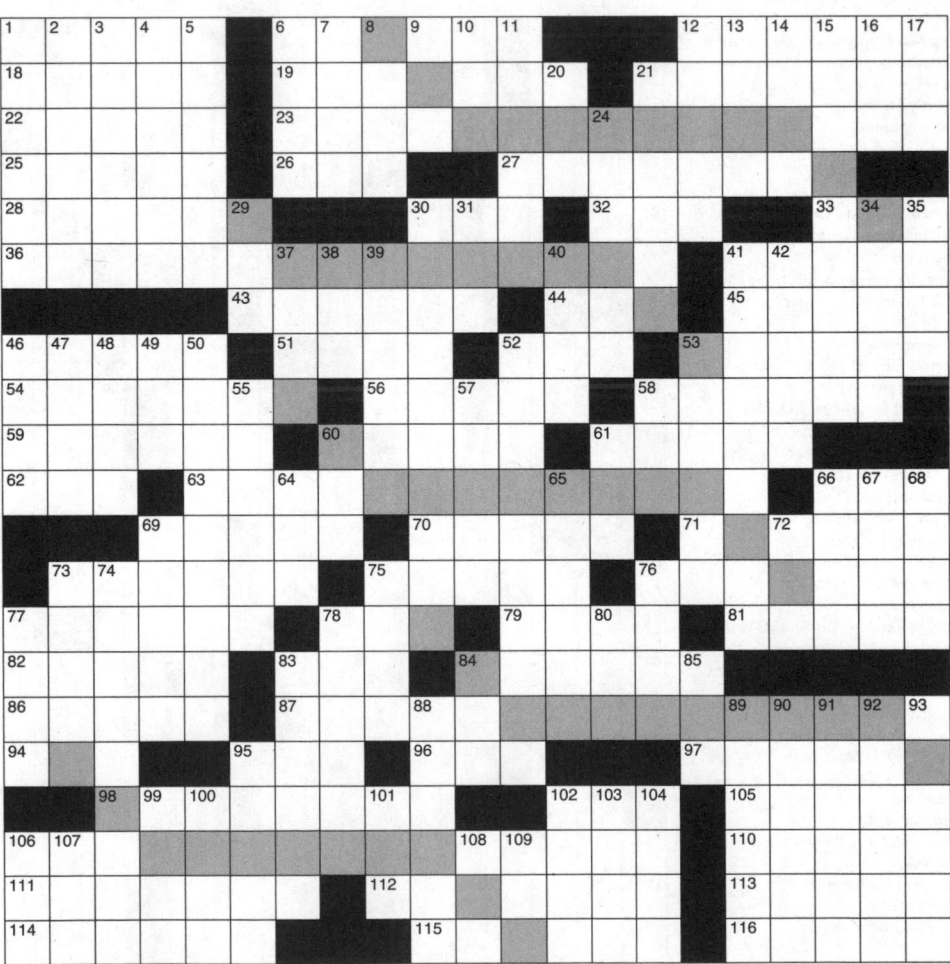

by Jeff Chen

ACROSS

1 One known as "the Alive, the Eternal"
6 Checkout option
11 Org. featured in 2011's "Contagion"
14 Tiff
18 ___ Rose, Catherine O'Hara's character on "Schitt's Creek"
19 Chevron subsidiary
20 Language in the Tai family
21 Kind of skirt
22 Your ex's new date whom you just can't stand?
25 Tabloid twosome
26 Lose sleep (over)
27 Off
28 "Su-u-ure"
29 Half of a legal warning
30 There are 24 in a cuboctahedron
32 Make a big stink
34 Kegels, e.g.?
39 Getting up there
42 Poet Rainer Maria ___
43 "___ yourself"
44 First winner of the Nebula Award for best science fiction novel (1965)
46 It's just passing
47 Therapists' org.
48 Director Craven
51 First square of a crossword?
55 Walking the dog, for instance
58 One might bend over backward
59 Who actually lives in Lapland, some say
60 Accord maker
61 Author of 29 Federalist Papers
64 Laugh and a half
65 Playwright who wrote "Those who cannot change their minds cannot change anything"
68 "I'll be your waiter tonight," e.g.?
70 Raison d' ___
71 Do a certain developer's job
72 Something a mover or a movie might have
73 Threesome
75 The "B" in its name stands for "brush"
77 Oldest independent state in the Arab world
78 Genre for "Booksmart" and "Clueless"
82 Conspiracy theory so wild that it can't be aired?
86 Trident look-alike
87 ___ jam
88 Small bird
89 "I did it!"
90 Southern cooking staple
92 Things you can crack without damaging them
94 Affix with a click
96 Plan to leave at a very specific evening time?
100 Orangish shade
103 Fill with joy
104 Stirs up
106 Doctor Zhivago
107 Where subs are standard
109 Semiaquatic creature
113 Missing
114 Blackjack dealer?
117 Niche mag
118 Stick (out)
119 Product that increases volume
120 "Moonlight" actress Janelle
121 Joie de vivre
122 One doing inside work
123 Chain whose name derives from its founders, the Raffel brothers
124 Orchard products

DOWN

1 Book before Obadiah
2 Converted apartment, perhaps
3 "That's ___"
4 Question after an argument has died down
5 Solo traveling in space
6 Crafts
7 Frequent subjects of Taylor Swift songs
8 Measures, in music
9 Word that can precede or follow pack
10 Actor Menzies who won an Emmy for "The Crown"
11 Fills (in)
12 One hell of a writer?
13 One way for packages to arrive, in brief
14 Protect
15 "Quiet!," rudely
16 Lager alternatives
17 Subdued
19 "It takes a licking and keeps on ticking" brand
23 Herb used in smudging rites
24 Theater award
29 Stars
31 Approached
32 Actress Moreno
33 ___ Kong
34 Melee
35 Abdominal procedure, for short
36 Skin-care brand
37 Dry biscuit used as baby food
38 Op. ___ (footnote abbr.)
40 Any slice of pizza, geometrically
41 Greek goddess associated with witchcraft
44 Archaeologist's workplace
45 Workers' advocate, informally
49 Young partner?
50 Back way, often
52 Winona of "Stranger Things"
53 Work, work, work
54 Texas border city
56 "C'est la vie"
57 "Ay" follower
61 "Now We Are Six" author
62 Crush, as a test
63 German denials
65 Members of a certain den
66 Enter without permission
67 A wood frog's ability to freeze itself in winter and an octopus's ability to change color, for two
69 Vaccine holder
74 In with
76 Props for majorettes
78 Bird with an annual 18,000-mile round-trip migration
79 Instrument that's a homophone of 69-Down
80 Crucifix inscription inits.
81 ___ New York (Brooklyn neighborhood)
83 2020 Democratic also-ran
84 It's nada to Nadal
85 Actor/comedian Barinholtz
91 Dieted
93 Summer shoe style
95 Bed of straw
96 Who's talking on the phone?
97 Personality that's hard to read
98 Pass over, in a way
99 Mathematician John Forbes ___ Jr.
101 Visually evaluate
102 Out of practice
104 Boo-oo-oo, say
105 Boo-boo
107 Smear
108 Site for some creative entrepreneurs
110 What Vulcan's forge lay underneath, in myth
111 Sport
112 "___ chic!"
114 Party people, for short?
115 Repeated word in the U.S. postal creed
116 Rapscallion

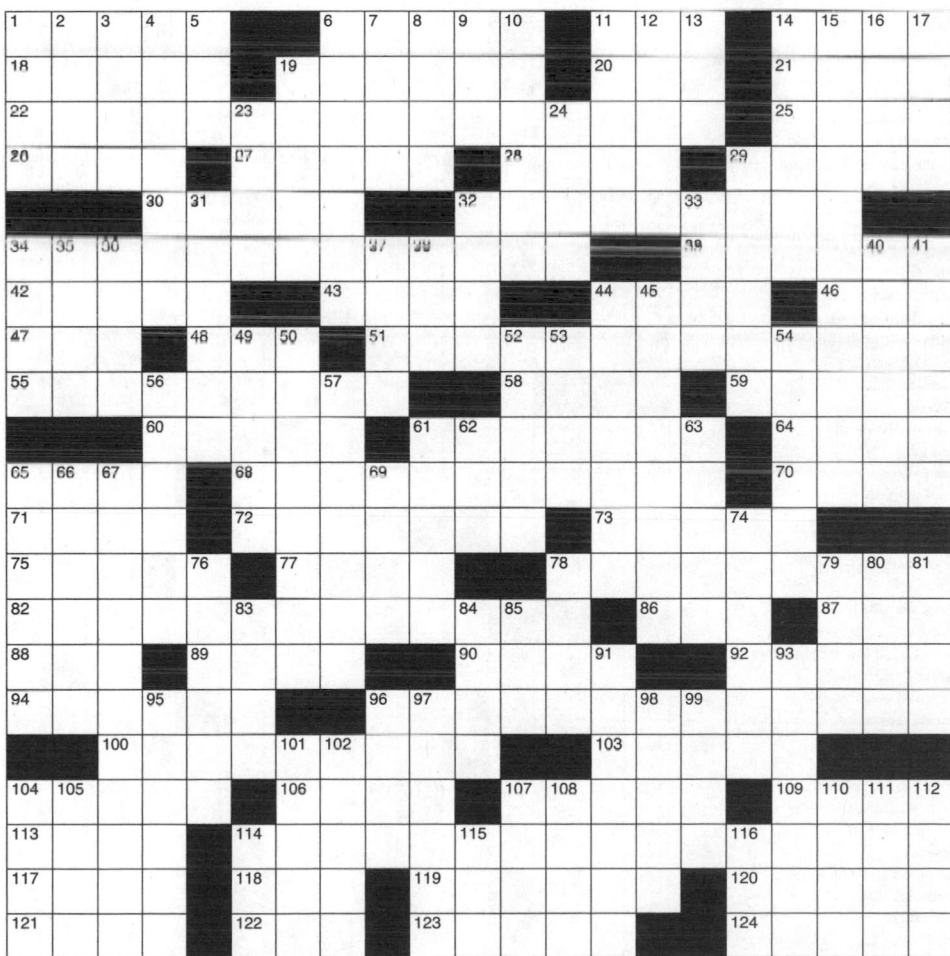

by Katie Hale

ACROSS

1 Action done while saying "Good dog"
4 Mischief-makers
11 It might click for a writer
14 Fall mo.
17 Kind to Mother Nature
18 Harris in the Country Music Hall of Fame
19 Living ___
20 Member of the superfamily Hominoidea
21 Noted Apple release of 1968, to fans
23 Haphazard
25 Some crumbly blocks
26 Inits. for a theatrical hit
27 Send away, in a way
29 Accomplished the task
30 What wiggly lines in comics may represent
32 Cause of boom and bust?
34 Convene for another session
36 Up to it
37 What's frequently used by poets?
38 "To quote yours truly . . ."
41 ___ dish
42 Heath
43 Desperate
45 Traditional British entree
48 Tries for a role
49 S.F. metro
50 "Hey . . . over here!"
51 Derby lengths
53 Equivalent of the Face With Tears of Joy emoji
56 Give a buzz
61 Inconvenience
64 Execute, as a royal of old
67 Classic concert chambers
68 Noted U.S. rock group?
70 Approximately
73 See captain?
74 Studio fixtures
76 "I'm game!"
77 State of equilibrium
80 Code-cracking grp.
81 Match-ending rugby call
82 Bygone sovereign
85 Dance-a-___
87 Build on
90 Military dismissal
96 "You game?"
98 State to be the case
99 ___ Kornfeld, music promoter for Woodstock
100 Daddy-o
102 Great Basin native
103 Stun
104 Heavy weights in Britain
106 "Murder, ___ Wrote"
107 Samuel ___, business partner of Marcus Goldman
109 Gradually wear away
111 Lipton competitor
113 Keypad triplet
115 Critical remark
116 Regardless of the outcome
118 Hectic trip abroad
121 Card in a royal flush
122 Purposes
123 One runs from Me. to Fla.
124 Seminoles' sch.
125 "You betcha!"
126 Northern ___ (curiously named apple variety)
127 Have
128 Boggy expanse

DOWN

1 Fare that's eaten hands-free
2 Wanted badly
3 Mano a mano
4 Negligent
5 Silicon Valley's ___ Research Center
6 Candy bit that comes in a plastic roll
7 "Battlestar Galactica" robots
8 Clerical vestment
9 F, in music
10 Southern region of Mesopotamia
11 Fabric options
12 Sense of self
13 Fluent speaker of Elvish, say
14 Uttered a sound
15 Delta neighbor
16 Bugs
19 Relative of a bug
22 Churchill ___ Rooms (London tourist attraction)
23 Long ball
24 City with a Little Havana
28 Nickname for José
31 Farthest down?
33 Anklebone
35 Least messy
39 Sorority member
40 Yang's counterpart
44 "I Wanna Be Sedated" band
46 Horrid
47 Maximum degree
49 The brainy bunch?
52 Profligate sort
54 Measures of electrical resistance
55 One of the fire signs
57 Alveolar trill, as it's commonly known
58 Concept, in Cannes
59 Just in case
60 Glasgow gal
61 Mischief-makers
62 ___ court
63 Stage between larva and imago
64 Consecrates
65 Act investigated by an insurance company
66 ___ ex machina
69 QVC alternative
71 Journalist Fallaci who wrote "Interview With History"
72 Bindis, e.g.
75 Running behind
78 Kinda
79 Berate blisteringly
81 They can be wrinkled or thumbed
83 Field that deals with fields
84 The newest trend, in slang
86 Inits. at Westminster
88 Trigger
89 Head for the hills?
90 Moved aside (for)
91 Cupidity
92 Changes from commercial to residential, perhaps
93 Words to live by
94 Wash out
95 Popular tick repellent
96 Piercing eye hue
97 Trial
101 ___ of Alexandria (wonder of the ancient world)
105 Clinch
108 Puerto Rico clock setting: Abbr.
110 Ballpark figures, in brief
112 Semiserious "Got it!"
114 Places hangers hang
117 Guff
119 Distributor of CARES Act funds
120 ___ Moines

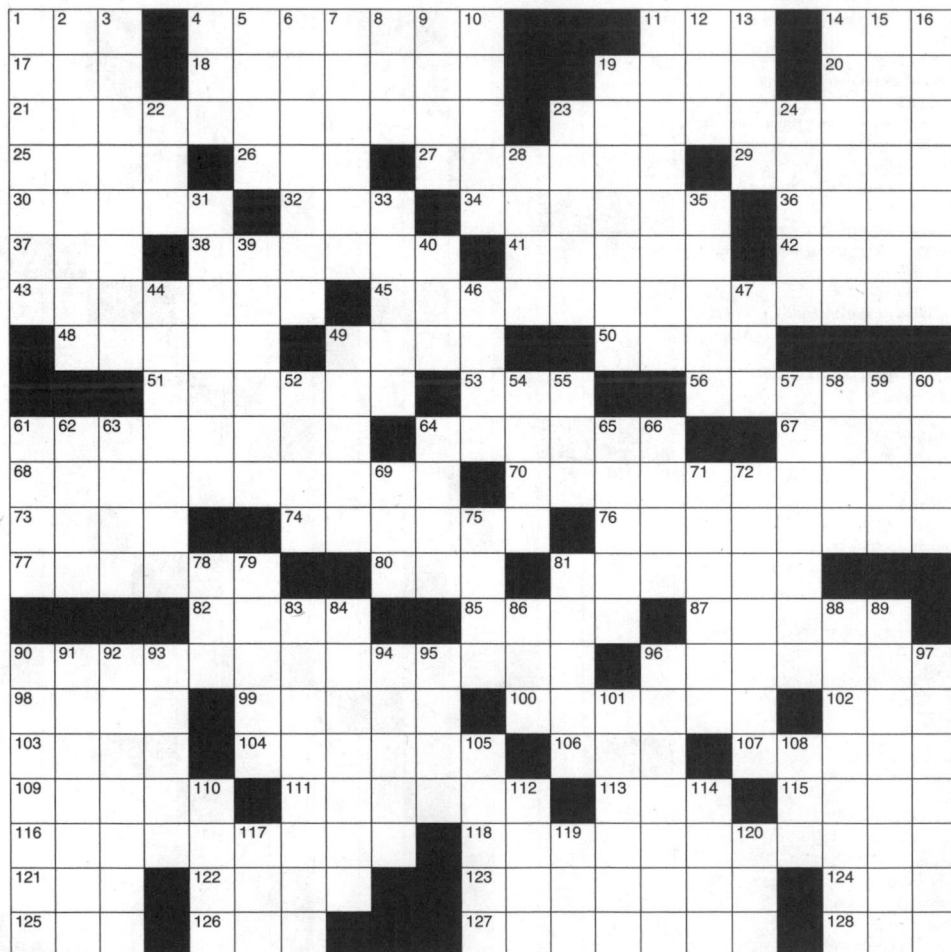

by Alex Eaton-Salners

ACROSS

1 Piles
15 Tablet purchases
19 Setting for Banff National Park
21 Dealer's enemy
22 Disney film with more than a million hand-drawn bubbles
24 Rap's Run-D.M.C., e.g.
25 Ostrich or kangaroo
26 Amtrak service
27 Emulate Ella Fitzgerald
29 Boxer Wolfe who played Artemis in "Wonder Woman"
30 "Yes, indeed"
31 Get-together
33 Rush
35 Clear spirit
36 Seasonal fast-food sandwiches that aren't halal
37 "Star Trek" virtual reality chambers
38 San ___ (European enclave)
39 [stern glare]
40 Italian wine region
41 Certain developer's job
42 Seriously unpleasant
43 Or greater
44 Fall flavoring
45 Some movie theater concession areas
50 Shattered
51 Eateries serving small plates
52 Spoils
53 Up
54 Command center
55 Multiday event, for short
56 2017 CVS Health acquisition
57 Profess
58 Tough bass part?
60 Really grooves with something
61 Quaint locale of first-aid supplies
63 Valorous
64 Bhikkhunis : Buddhist monastery :: ___ : convent
65 The C of C major, e.g.
66 Word with zone or boots
67 Actor Idris
68 Error message?
69 Was completely exhausted
70 Hiking aids
72 Employees who work a lot
73 Bit of reading near a cashier, in brief
76 Grasps at straws?
77 Not at all
78 Big name in pasta sauces
79 N.B.A. coach ___ Unseld Jr.
80 Badly hurt
81 "Capisce?"
82 Rail in a dance studio
83 Images on some Australian silver coins
85 V.I.P. access points
89 Mythos
90 Nutritional plan involving controlled removal of foods
91 Predator frequently appearing in Calvin's daydreams in "Calvin and Hobbes"
92 Special delivery?

DOWN

1 Put on pretensions
2 Island home to Faa'a International Airport
3 It's located in the middle of an alley
4 Drones, e.g.
5 Terse confession
6 Op. ___
7 Bad person to confess bad things to
8 Twisting together
9 Puerto Rico's ___ Telescope, formerly the world's largest single-aperture telescope
10 Impersonate at a Halloween party
11 Immune system component
12 Vegetable in bhindi masala
13 Lens holder
14 Fine crystals used in food preparation
15 Symbol of industry
16 Make a flying jump onto a slope
17 They get left in the dust
18 Treat on a tea trolley tray
20 "___ Mode" (2018 #1 hit for Travis Scott)
23 Labyrinth builder of myth
28 Tarot card said to "radiate" positivity
31 Foretold the future
32 Certain gasket
33 Deterrent to a pickpocket
34 Behaves like a fool, informally
36 Drama linked to the resurgence of the name "Betty" for baby girls
37 Remains tightly secured
38 Acquired family member
39 Actress Meyer of "Beverly Hills 90210"
41 Tested the censor, say
42 Vendors of e-cigs
43 Cruise stop
44 Wet behind the ears
45 Important sales for growing businesses?
46 Argument
47 Totally wipes out
48 Like some very old characters
49 Pallet piece
50 Small drink of whiskey
51 Zap, in a way
54 Items at T.S.A. checkpoints
56 Boeing competitor
58 What the waving of a white flag can indicate
59 Business brass
60 Reduce in rank
62 Style pioneered by Picasso
63 Works at the cutting edge?
66 Hot, in Havana
67 Evidence of a crossword solver's mistake, maybe
68 Dairy-free coffee additive
69 Butcher's offering
70 Quiver
71 Ripply fabric pattern
72 Give a thumbs-down
73 Bespectacled "Peanuts" character
74 Gives a thumbs-up
75 Talk show slate
76 Harped (on)
77 Unfashionable
78 Time off, for short
81 Slightly spoiled, in a way
82 Label signing
84 ___-positive movement
86 Contest
87 Actress Mowry of "Sister, Sister"
88 Authority, metaphorically

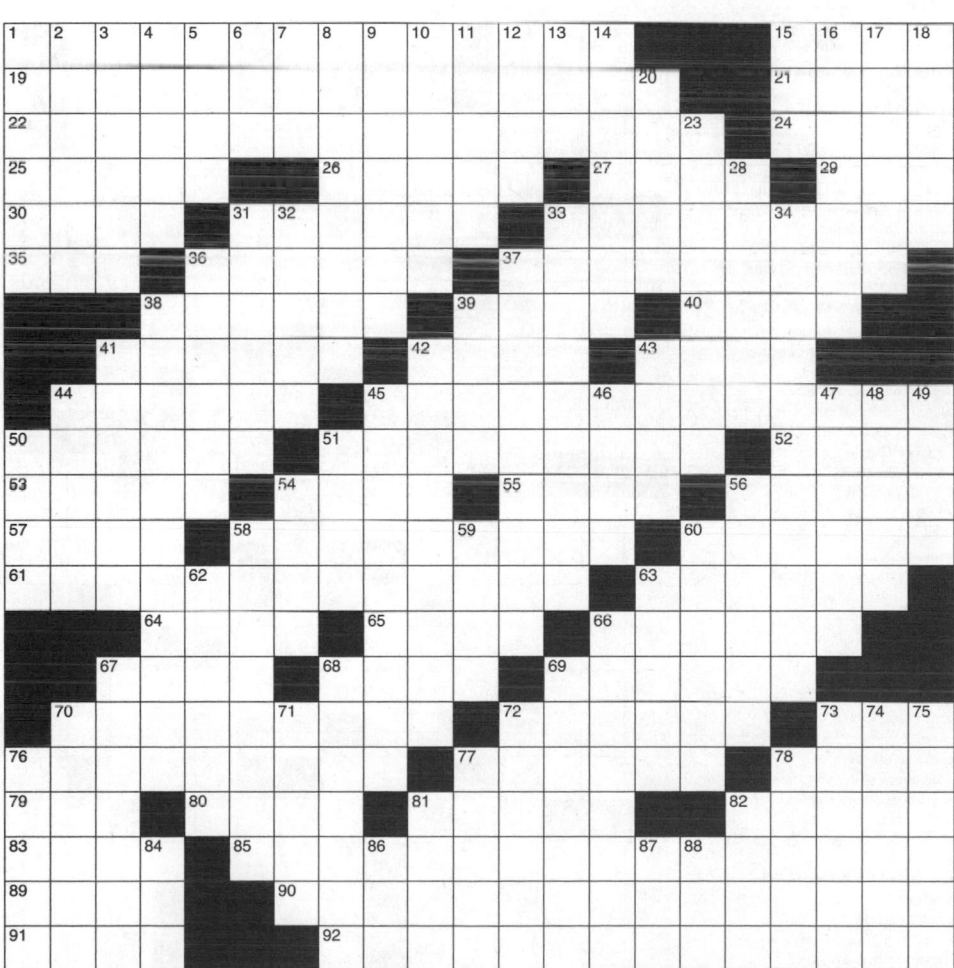

by Sid Sivakumar

ACROSS

1 Miss
5 Fairy tale monster
9 Meat in ragù al cinghiale
13 "Everyone knows the secret now"
19 Lincoln or Ford
20 Purchase in the board game Catan worth one wood and one brick
21 Singer Guthrie
22 Genre for Nirvana and Soundgarden
23 Forgetfulness experienced by soon-to-be moms, informally
26 Final innings, usually
27 Heinie
28 What a baby might start eating at around six months
30 Universal donor's blood type, informally
31 A, in Aachen
32 "Dancing With ___ Hands Tied" (Taylor Swift song)
33 What well-connected people may have
37 Scented plug-in brand
40 "Afternoon, pardner!"
44 "Oh yeah? Give me an example!"
46 Response to a texted joke
47 Worldly wisdom
49 Deg. for a creative type
50 Booting
53 Juice cleanse, essentially
55 Cocktail made from gin, vermouth and Campari
56 Big letters in home security
59 In Latin, it's "stannum"
60 Pound part
61 Church council
62 Succeed in life
64 Portfolio listings
65 Common sense
68 The "gone girl" in "Gone Girl"
70 A negative one might be positive
71 Used colored pencils, say
74 "___ be a real shame . . ."
75 Jovian planets, by another name
78 Changes back to factory defaults, say
80 Way too loud
81 Figure in the iconic "We Can Do It!" poster
85 Quite enough
86 Bit of fiction
89 Suffix with quack and mock
90 National law enforcement, informally
92 Simple flotation device
95 Arranges in random order
96 URL ending
97 TV display option
101 ___ tai
102 Picked up
104 Above
105 Like the bread ideal for bread pudding
107 Theoretical primordial substance
108 Word on an Irish plane
110 Oscar-winning director Lee
111 Obama's birthplace
113 Playing to the crowd
117 Japanese condiment sprinkled on rice
121 Go back to the start, in a way
124 Slogan about willpower . . . or a hint to four pairs of answers in this puzzle
126 Courtroom cry
127 "Something From Nothing: The Art of Rap" director
128 Aptly named bus driver on "The Simpsons"
129 Catering vessels
130 "Whatever you say, sweetheart"
131 Unilever tea brand
132 Bert who played the Cowardly Lion
133 Children's author DiCamillo with two Newbery Medals

DOWN

1 Nordic native
2 Invisible energy field
3 Proofreader's directive
4 Words moaned while eating a cheeseburger, maybe
5 Give one's address
6 Get ready to sleep, cutesily
7 Candidate's focus
8 Ice cream surname
9 British nobleman
10 Like some traditions
11 Et ___ (and others)
12 Sonata movement
13 The uninformed masses, colloquially
14 The Jonas Brothers, e.g.
15 Dish named for a day of the week
16 Toronto's prov.
17 "What a mess!"
18 Your: Fr.
24 Bar ___
25 Queen's "We Will Rock You," e.g.
29 2K, for one
31 She-ep?
34 Award hopeful
35 Passes along to, in a way
36 Like the winner of a handwriting contest
37 Narrow valleys
38 Very affectionate
39 Get on the same page, in corporate-speak
41 URL ending
42 Alternative to fiber or satellite
43 Leave off
45 Early PC software
47 Planting more than one kind of seed in a field, per Deuteronomy
48 Pollution stat
51 Historical subject of Hilary Mantel's 2009 novel "Wolf Hall"
52 Action item
54 Brings back to use
56 Home of Guinea and Guinea-Bissau: Abbr.
57 "Yo ___" (internet meme with rapper Xzibit)
58 Prioritization process
63 It added "essential worker" in March of 2021: Abbr.
64 Author Rand
66 Quaint contraction
67 Title that comes from "Caesar"
68 Assist
69 Day celebrated by "Star Wars" fans
71 Curtains
72 Interior design job
73 Support, as a belief
76 Fellow
77 Like bacon and lobster, in Jewish law
79 Prime-time slot
82 Home of the National Voting Rights Museum
83 Perfect
84 Nail polish brand
86 Like some nachos and questions
87 "Real" ones were first issued in the 2010s
88 Muppet who hosts the "Not-Too-Late Show"
91 Fifth-century invader
93 Poisonous shrub
94 Suffix with Euclid
95 Metric for online traffic, in brief
98 Get ready for action
99 The "C" of D.R.C.
100 World of Warcraft, e.g., for short
103 One who's at home on the job?
105 Branch of Islam
106 Thai taxi with a repetitive name
109 Send, as payment
112 Mail, e.g.
114 Actress Taylor-Joy of "The Queen's Gambit"
115 Costa ___
116 Mother of Don Juan
117 Cheese on a meze platter
118 Gillette razor
119 Daily Planet reporter
120 Gaelic tongue
121 Sorority letter
122 "Yikes!"
123 Pile of cash
125 TV button: Abbr.

by Aimee Lucido and Ella Dershowitz

ACROSS

1 Lets extra light in, in a way
8 Get on the stick?
12 Music genre prefix
15 Arm of the Dept. of Homeland Security
19 Deforestation, for example
20 Not home
21 Pool tester
22 Line through two poles
23 Salma Hayek: 1996, 2002
26 Bop on the head
27 Driven, say
28 "___ Flux" (onetime sci-fi series)
29 Yellow belly?
30 Pair in gossip
31 Dev Patel: 2008, 2016
36 Jerkwad
39 What remains, with "the"
40 Quail :: bevy :: ___ : parliament
41 Liechtensteiner's currency
42 Amount of tips earned by a street performer, maybe
45 Equipment used to play the oldest organized sport in North America
47 Choose
50 Brad Pitt: 2001, 1995
54 Accompanier of smoke
56 Texter's "I think . . ."
57 Catherine of "Schitt's Creek"
58 Outstanding finds
59 Broadband inits.
61 "You mean I'm wrong?!"
64 Utilize a company policy for new parents, say
66 When tripled, playful onomatopoeia for shooting laser beams
67 "Here, have a taste"
68 Owen Wilson: 2005, 2006
71 Baseless rumors
74 The lowest número primo
75 Pickup line?
79 It's at the beginning of this clue
80 Noted fashion monogram
81 Equal
82 "Sunrise" singer Jones
83 Focus of some smartphone updates
84 Before, in poetry
86 Joaquin Phoenix: 2014, 2013
89 Problems with phonograph records
92 Contents of college blue books
94 Early online forum that popularized terms like "FAQ" and "spam"
95 Put on again
97 Some dolls sold in a Universal Studios gift shop
98 When "Alexander Hamilton" is sung in "Hamilton"
101 Mathematician Lovelace
102 Al Pacino and Robert De Niro: 1974, 1995 (twice!)
108 Brother of 99-Down
109 Ramirez of "Grey's Anatomy"
110 Historic trade ally of the Monacan people
111 Dark yellow shade
115 -elect
116 Modern tech feature for watching two programs on one screen . . . or an alternative title for this puzzle
120 Bug-eyed
121 High-value deposit
122 Shore soarer
123 Absolutely devoured
124 Takes from
125 TV's "___ Lasso"
126 Name on a toy truck
127 Places for rubs and scrubs

DOWN

1 Expert
2 Song title shared by hit singles for Ja Rule and Flo Rida
3 In the ___
4 High points
5 Kind of force created by the moon
6 Ending with "brown." or "auburn."
7 What tahini is made from
8 Tush
9 Thanks (to)
10 Actress Gadot
11 Olive ___
12 In any way
13 Sleazeballs
14 Kind of muscle
15 Chess's ___ Caruana, onetime youngest grandmaster in U.S. history (14 years, 11 months)
16 Flowerhorn cichlids and vampire tetras, for example
17 Worker who wants to strike?
18 "Go on, shoot"
24 Sister brand of Saucony and Stride Rite
25 Small valleys
32 Cybersquatters make fake ones
33 What 2 is vis-à-vis 1
34 "Hmm . . ."
35 Badger
36 Barrels of fun
37 Satirist ___ Baron Cohen
38 Entree served with a knife
43 Price jockeying of competing airlines
44 Not paying attention
45 Walgreens competitor
46 ___ Khan of Khan Academy fame
48 Prefix with present
49 Goes to hell
51 "Golly gee!"
52 Stock ticker symbol for a longtime clothing brand
53 Corrects in text
55 Brought on
60 River of old song
62 "Clever ___ are never punished": Voltaire
63 [swoon]
65 Meat Loaf's "Rocky Horror" role
66 Surfaces, e.g.
67 Start of many a limerick
69 Massive adversary
70 Whom you might ask "Where will I be in 10 years?"
71 Forensic pros, in brief
72 Words of eventual understanding
73 "'Fraid not"
76 Supermodel Shayk
77 Went up against
78 Sorority letter
80 Shortest answer from a Magic 8 Ball
81 Measures of acidity
85 Modern joust venue, informally
87 Org. with a noted bell
88 Van Gogh's "La ___ Étoilée"
90 Walking sticks?
91 Packed house inits.
93 Went after
96 Expensive Super Bowl purchase
98 Shower times
99 Brother of 108-Across
100 Timorous
102 Member of a Turkic group
103 Onetime streaming platform of the 2010s
104 Took a bow?
105 Submissions to a casting director
106 Like wool sweaters, often
107 Teensy bits
112 Thick component of orange juice
113 Broca's ___, segment of the brain linked to speech
114 Snoring symbols in Surrey
117 [That smells terrible!]
118 Regret
119 ___ sense

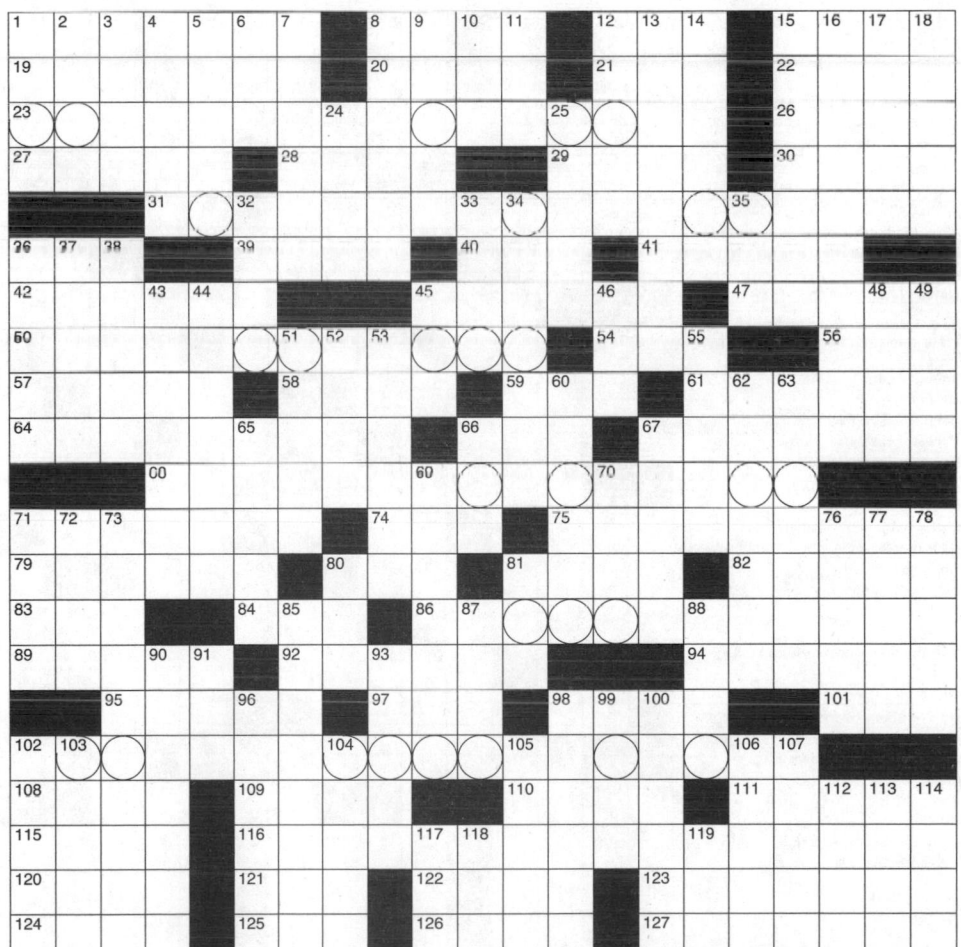

by Adam Wagner

ACROSS

1 Evidence of disorderly conduct?
5 Animated greetings
11 Threads
15 Some words of Wordsworth
19 Mötley ____
20 Fiend
21 Instrument with a solo in Seal's "Kiss From a Rose"
22 "There's no place like ____" (Alaskan's quip)
23 TV, volume knob broken, only $10!
26 A bit
27 "Me too"
28 Food Network host Brown
29 Sandal variety
31 Barbecue side dish
35 Tried one's hand
38 Before, once
39 In large supply
41 What may cover some ground
43 Baseball mitt, has a small hole, just $1!
47 Casual greeting
49 Model featured on many romance novel covers
52 Split personalities?
53 Stretch of time
54 Wipe out
56 "Predictably . . ."
58 Much of Italy's north
60 What the universe may or may not be
62 Huey, Dewey and Louie, e.g.
63 ____ colada
65 She can act as a D.J., nowadays
67 Raised
68 Guitar, never used, $15!
72 Baseball's Matty or Felipe
74 After-tax investment account, informally
75 Award achievement for Audrey Hepburn and Andrew Lloyd Webber
76 Ones coming on board
79 Classic mower brand
81 Loosen
83 Raiser of team spirit
84 Ready for a refill, say
85 Sucker
86 "Voilà!"
89 Running figure
90 Nautilus's locale
91 Textbook, a few pages torn out, $2!
96 Extremely energetic people
98 "Ain't that the truth!"
99 Or rather
102 Least enjoyable parts
105 Super wrong identification?
108 Words that might elicit the response "Prove it!"
110 Goldfinger's first name
112 Blood line
113 Final check?
114 Two fish tanks, accessories included, $5!
120 Started a turn, perhaps
121 Like a tautology, by its nature
122 Name for zinc sulfide that is one letter short of a kitchen appliance
123 Demolish
124 Ingots
125 Source
126 Heir to the throne, as a rule
127 Catch a glimpse of

DOWN

1 Andrew who became the acting F.B.I. director after James Comey was fired
2 It gets the lead out
3 A good dessert to split?
4 Having made up one's mind about
5 Outback sight
6 Stingray or Barracuda, e.g.
7 Taylor of fashion
8 U.S. poet laureate with a 1987 Pulitzer
9 "The BFG" author
10 Disperse
11 "Heaven forbid!"
12 Blood-typing letters
13 Word that can come before or after home
14 Lloyd ____, Dukakis's veep pick in 1988
15 Amenity in G.M. vehicles
16 Prop ax used in "The Shining," a valuable collectors' item, $200!
17 Actress and gender equality activist Watson
18 Trickle
24 "____ but a scratch": Monty Python
25 As well
30 Set up
32 Back
33 Pin point?
34 "A Clockwork Orange" narrator
36 Actress Madeline of "Blazing Saddles"
37 Horror director Aster
40 Started again, as "99 Bottles of Beer"
42 False front
43 Get off one's high horse?
44 Libertines
45 "Sure is"
46 Target with a pass
48 Concern for veterans, for short
49 Not even close
50 Incense residue
51 Wallet, in good condition, plenty of card slots, $5!
55 Person from Calgary or Edmonton
57 Brave's opponent in the 2021 World Series
59 Removes, as a tattoo
60 Stretch of time
61 Special-interest, e.g.
63 Fruit detritus
64 Like a wailing cat
66 TV's Cousin ____
69 Pam's former partner on "The Office"
70 When you're about as smart as a fifth grader
71 Aware of
72 Some beers
73 Hebrew letter between kaf and mem
77 90° bend
78 Kind of blue akin to cerulean
80 Concerns for a homeowners' association
82 Bonobo, e.g.
83 Banh mi toppings
85 Not a "no no"
87 Hooked
88 Regular intake
92 Some beers
93 Cattle call
94 Strip
95 Wash. neighbor
97 It's good, in a saying
99 Netflix crime drama starring Pedro Pascal
100 Take a pot shot?
101 Like the smell of rising dough
103 Bare
104 Ice cream container
106 Course standard
107 Tours can be found on it
108 Website with star ratings
109 ____ mia (Italian term of endearment)
111 "____ all be fine"
115 Wash. neighbor
116 Stick on a table?
117 Only's partner
118 Ward workers, for short
119 Term of endearment

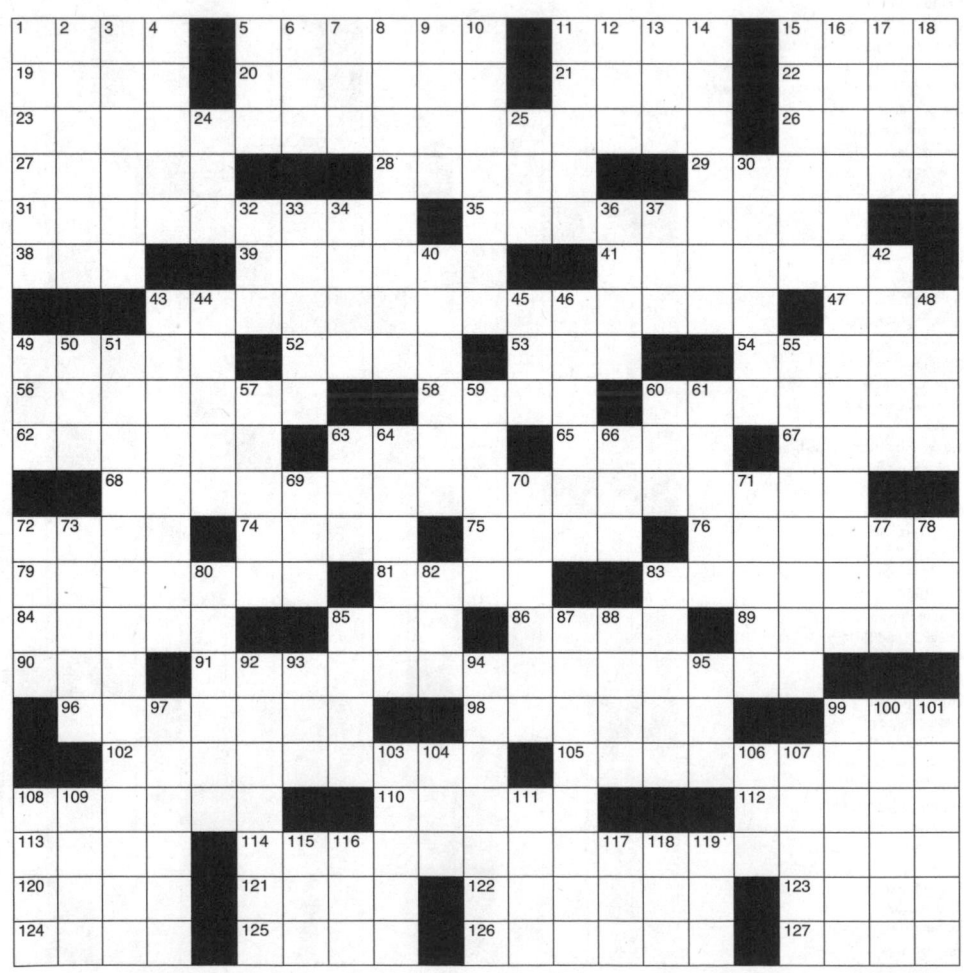

by Jeff Kremer

ACROSS

1 "Bull" airer
4 Out
10 Win for a 10-Down
15 Yukon automaker
18 Set down
20 With 116-Down, artificial intelligence system that mimics the human brain
21 Who is "too small to make a difference," per a Greta Thunberg book title
22 Propel, as a shell
23 "... and to ____ good night!"
24 ... FLOOR FLOOR FLOOR ...
27 It's got some miles on it
29 Home to the Burj Khalifa, for short
30 Singular
31 Stark who was crowned Queen of the North on "Game of Thrones"
32 ... GRIZZLY GRIZZLY GRIZZLY ...
39 First responder, for short
40 Percussion instrument of African origin
43 What some kings and queens dress in
44 Maker of the classic video game Frogger
45 ... PROPOSAL PROPOSAL PROPOSAL ...
49 Kind of milk
50 Rapper with more than 20 Grammys
51 Reps
52 Click ____ (artificial increasers of website hits)
53 Goddess of the dawn
55 Pet lovers' org.
60 James who sang "I Sing the Blues"
61 Grandma, affectionately
65 Roy Lichtenstein's genre
70 Brit's "How shocking!"
71 What many lifeguards have
72 ... COMMERCIAL COMMERCIAL COMMERCIAL ...
74 Steve with eight N.B.A. championship rings
75 Chemical suffixes
76 Like the color of honey
77 "Give me a break, would you?!"
78 Philosopher who wrote "A Treatise of Human Nature"
79 Lead-in to ask or suggest
81 Get hitched
83 They're explained by Newton's law of universal gravitation
84 N.F.L. Hall-of-Famer Shannon
89 Inconveniences
94 Company with a Page Program
97 ... AMBITION AMBITION AMBITION ...
99 Word-of-mouth
101 Actor Spall of "Prometheus"
102 Literally, "I bow to you"
103 Op. ____ (footnote abbr.)
106 ... STAIRS STAIRS STAIRS ...
109 ____ di Pietro, artist better known as Fra Angelico
111 Ta-ta
112 Opposite of down: Abbr.
113 "Let's Stay Together" singer, 1971
115 ... CAUTION CAUTION CAUTION ...
122 Slight problem
123 Pablo Neruda work
124 "Please, I can handle this"
125 Many an informant employed by Sherlock Holmes
126 Org. involved in the Scopes Monkey Trial
127 R.S.V.P. option
128 Way up or way down
129 Pocketful in ring-around-the-rosy
130 Syracuse-to-Albany dir.

DOWN

1 Part of a contract
2 Christmas fir
3 Investor behind the scenes
4 Palindromic feminine name
5 One gifted with the "inner eye"
6 Word on a candy heart
7 Before, poetically
8 Piercing spot
9 ____ cavity (where the lungs are located)
10 Likely loser
11 Hawaiian taro dish
12 Family member inaptly found in "ladies only"
13 High school subj.
14 Vehicle company with a market value over $1 trillion
15 Adventurous kids in a 1985 film
16 Napoleon's famed war horse
17 Shout
19 Some diaper changers
25 Rapper dissed by Jay-Z in "Takeover"
26 Young 'uns
28 Popular Toyotas
32 How a zombie might spread the infection
33 Ostrich relatives
34 Peter out
35 "Symphony in Black" artist
36 Something necessary for gain, they say
37 The "grand slam" of showbiz awards, in brief
38 Like some apparel, in song
41 Mimic
42 Opposite of FF
46 Together
47 Kind of jar
48 Org. that hires cryptanalysts
50 Samurai's sword
52 Awful-smelling
54 Give one's take
56 Religion that emphasizes seva, or "selfless service"
57 Astrology or palmistry
58 Sandiego not usually found in San Diego
59 Lew ____, portrayer of Dr. Kildare
61 Badger
62 Brouhaha
63 When doubled, boring result in the Premier League
64 Word commonly following the Oxford comma
66 Messy sort
67 What seven did to nine, in a joke
68 Lament
69 Celebrity gossip site
73 Like New Jerseyans vis-à-vis New Yorkers
80 Destination for Birthright trips: Abbr.
82 Someone's in the kitchen with her, in song
83 Savory Chinese snack
85 Grinder
86 Put ____ on (limit)
87 Dennis the Menace's appropriately named dog
88 Bishops, e.g.
90 Execs: Abbr.
91 Smartphone predecessors, for short
92 Choice words
93 Card-matching game
94 Prefix with binary
95 Male etiquette, as described by Barney Stinson on "How I Met Your Mother"
96 Eyeteeth
98 Clique
100 Exam with a 35-minute timed essay, in brief
104 What 10s represent
105 Notable chameleon feature
107 Grinds away
108 Not friendly
110 ____ Minor
113 Singer India ____
114 Part of the eye
115 Demure
116 See 20-Across
117 Pac-12 athlete
118 Rapscallion
119 ____-yo
120 They're found below the "To" field
121 Tuna, on a sushi menu

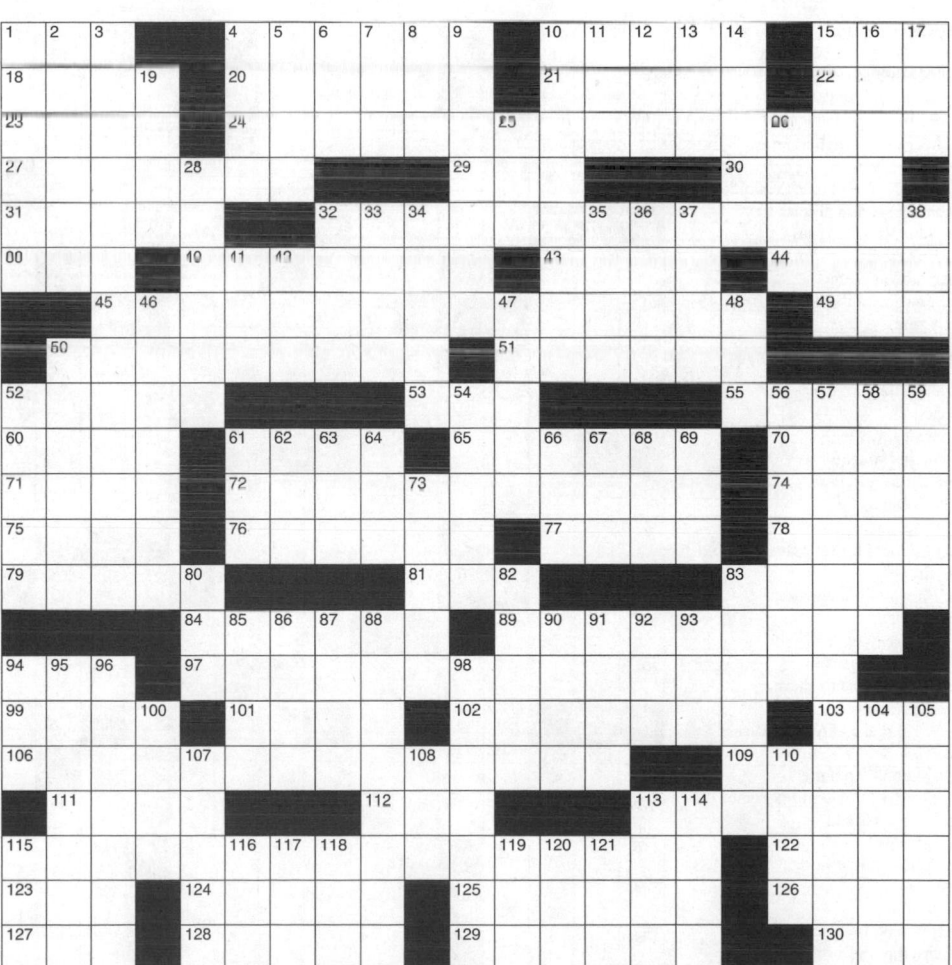

by Chase Dittrich and Jeff Chen

144 JOB SHARING

ACROSS

1 Research subject for which Bohr won a Physics Nobel
5 Grimm account
9 Musical medley
15 Like cranberries
19 Protagonist of Colson Whitehead's "The Underground Railroad"
20 Big-time
21 Tarot deck grouping
22 Trash day reminder, maybe
23 Side hustle for a hairstylist?
25 Rodent-catching feline
26 Maker of Regenerist products
27 Oust
28 French auto pioneer Louis
30 Dan Conner and Danny Tanner, e.g.
32 [Blown kiss]
34 Side hustle for a veterinarian?
36 Manage OK
39 Dangerous crowd
41 Try to lighten up, perhaps?
42 New York Cosmos star of the '70s
43 Metal precioso
44 Polite rejection
46 National gemstone of Mexico
50 Side hustle for a therapist?
56 "A Confederacy of Dunces" author
57 Shed, with "off"
58 Many a Sharon Olds poem
59 Leaf-to-branch angles
62 It may be glossed over
63 Turned
65 Its fleece is hypoallergenic
66 Part of a gig
67 Side hustle for an anesthesiologist?
73 Leon who wrote "Battle Cry"
74 Avid bird-watcher, say
75 URL divider
76 "Mr. Mayor" airer
77 First stroke of the day
78 Holy ones: Abbr.
81 Spanish city north of León
84 Encrusted
87 Side hustle for a carpenter?
90 Netted
93 Give an address
94 Home in the mud
95 Christmas purchase
96 Like Athena
98 Moving ___
100 Record label for Otis Redding and Big Star
101 Side hustle for a marriage counselor?
106 Small sweater?
108 Cold-weather jacket
109 Person with lots to show
111 Kind of license
115 Museum that awards the Turner Prize
116 "Oh yeah? Watch me!"
118 Side hustle for a drill instructor?
120 Tech tutorials site
121 Sub groups?
122 Set of showbiz awards, in brief
123 Hightail it
124 Actress and inventor Lamarr
125 Where the tradition of shaking hands as a greeting originated
126 Clinches, with "up"
127 Show off at the gym

DOWN

1 "Because freedom can't protect itself" org.
2 Animated figure
3 Evil creatures in 7-Down
4 Defiant retort
5 Large orchestral gong
6 Mahershala of "Moonlight"
7 Frodo's film franchise, familiarly
8 Blues great Waters
9 One with a nesting instinct
10 Inflame
11 Shape
12 Something made in a hurry
13 A in French class
14 One getting down, so to speak
15 Cheery "Ciao!"
16 Two-time opponent of Dwight
17 Map lines
18 Guilt-producing meeting, perhaps
24 Maxim
29 Nobel-winning author Gordimer
31 Park supervisor?
33 Refine
35 Economic stat.
36 Male swans
37 Like one Freudian fixation
38 Bouncy toys
40 Thrift-store fashion, informally
45 Blue
46 Order member
47 Hindu, for one
48 Justice beginning in 2006
49 New Testament miracle recipient
51 "Uh-oh" sounds
52 ___ fresca
53 Its etymology may derive from the diminutive of "borough" in Italian
54 "Mission: Impossible" theme composer Schifrin
55 Convention center event
60 Some HDTVs
61 1979 Commodores hit with the lyric "Good times never felt so good"
64 Singer Celine
65 One of two in "Hamilton"
66 Aggressively mainstream, in slang
67 Unit of prevention
68 ___ legend
69 Revise, as text
70 Org. with Divisions I-III
71 Suspense novelist Hoag
72 Pandora native in "Avatar"
78 Side of a block
79 Word after high or weak
80 Classic skit comedy show
82 Sole ingredient in some cookies?
83 Rock with colorful bands
85 Sum total
86 "Buffy the Vampire Slayer" vampire
88 Like a bad outcome for all
89 Great deal
91 Causing quite a stink
92 Opposite of morn
96 Frank
97 "Hold on . . ."
99 Hotel room restriction
100 Drive to the station, say
101 Come down with
102 Nonsensical
103 Checked a box, maybe
104 Accent ___
105 Wizards' wear
107 Giant bird of Arabian myth
110 Blow a fuse
112 Starbucks size
113 Slurpee relative
114 Party mix ingredient
117 Big game show prize
119 Scatter

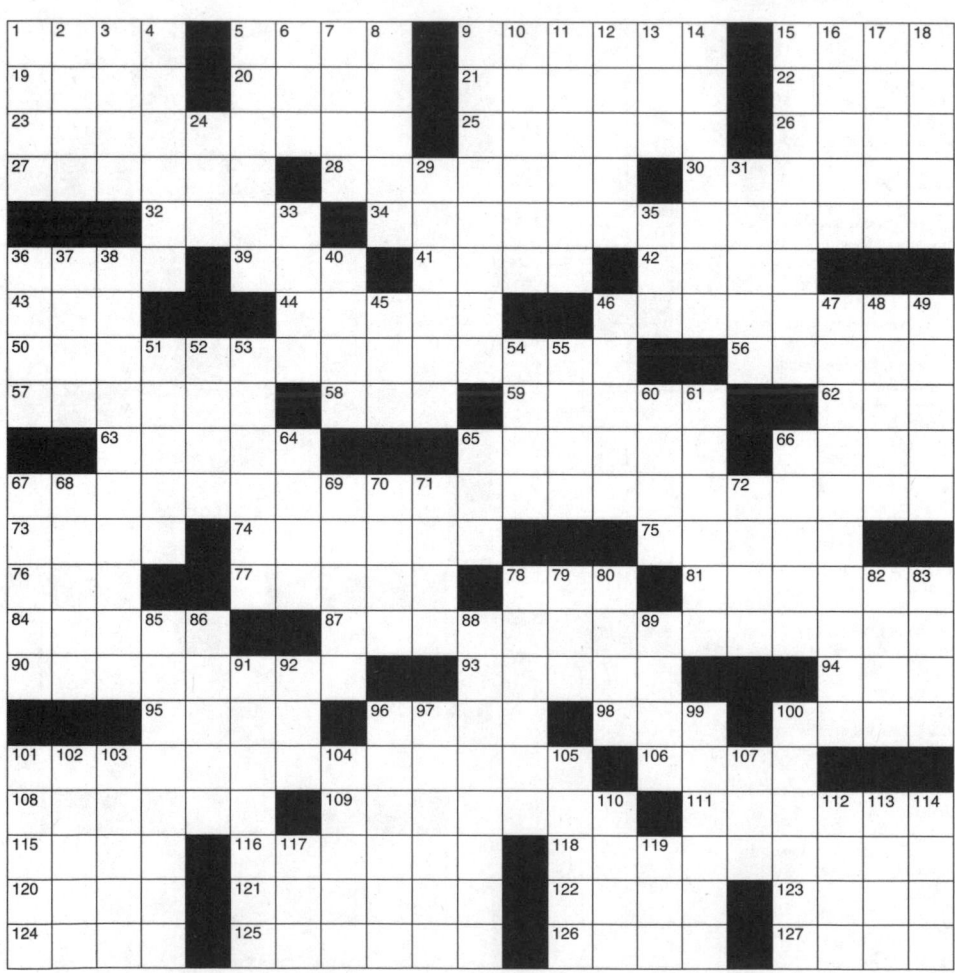

by Daniel Okulitch and Doug Peterson

ACROSS

1 They might be put on
5 Singer Grande, informally
8 Undercover attire?
11 ___ Creole (Caribbean language)
18 Drive-___
19 Certain urban map
22 Demoralize
23 Little tyke / Flatter, with "up"
25 Things bachelors might have
26 Certain Scandinavian
27 "Gimme ___!" (start of a cheer at three Big Ten schools)
28 Noted Dadaist
30 ___ Helmer, Ibsen heroine
31 Scalpel creations
33 Relative of a tee-hee / Bit of marginalia
39 M.L.K. or R.B.G.: Abbr.
41 Stage name of rapper Yasiin Bey
42 Forest spirit
43 Pep / Onesie feature
47 "Sure, I'm game"
49 UNICEF address suffix
50 H.S. subj.
51 Words before point or rate
52 Ring / Hold, as inhabitants
55 Med school subj.
57 Certain Scandinavian
58 "The One I Love" band
59 ___ Hall ("The Wind in the Willows" residence)
60 Loud but friendly growl
61 Bow
62 Adjusts the spacing between, as typed letters
64 No ___ (apartment policy)
67 Big name in cast-iron cookware
69 Reduce in volume / As new
72 It'll knock you out
74 Ogler
75 Chiwere speakers
76 Christmas ornament, often
78 Modern prefix with medicine
79 Becomes less taut
82 Old "Up, up and away" sloganeer
83 Mannheim madame
84 Fivers
85 Kind of leaf / Scientist born on Christmas Day in 1642
89 With 111-Down, cholesterol reducer
90 Musician Brian
91 Paris's ___ Saint-Louis
92 ___ Finch, "ER" doctor
93 Possible result of getting one's wires crossed / Moolah
96 Singer/actress Shore
98 Big block
101 Two-time U.S. Open tennis champion while still a teen
102 Breakfast dish / Fruitcake tidbit
106 Amasses, with "up"
108 Nuclear medicine units
109 "___, Virginia, there is a Santa Claus"
110 ___ culpa
112 Trig function
113 Some laundromat machines
116 This puzzle's images, in two different ways
121 Physician awarded a Presidential Medal of Freedom by G. W. Bush
122 Party staple
123 Prefix with space
124 Chandelier part, often
125 ___-mo
126 Football units: Abbr.
127 Hurdle for a J.D. wannabe

DOWN

1 Court sport grp.
2 Course preparers
3 Becoming faint
4 Solarium activity
5 National dance co.
6 It was eliminated from the U.S. in 2004
7 Library IDs
8 Kitty
9 Project
10 Outback orders
11 Cabinet dept. since 1965
12 Come to ___
13 Fit
14 Nightmare
15 "Got it"
16 "___ Maria"
17 Super Mario Bros. platform
20 Downfall
21 Dropped the ball
24 Remove, as a ribbon
29 Green shampoo
32 Italian thoroughfare
34 Wishy-washy response
35 Get, slangily
36 Genuine
37 Filmmaker von Trier
38 Little lead
40 Some graffiti
43 First and reverse
44 Not learned
45 Proverb-spouting Panza
46 Lancaster-to-Scranton dir.
48 Citrus hybrid
52 Come to ___
53 Present opening?
54 "Gonna Let It Shine" singer
56 Personal essence
58 Where to go on a trip?
62 Not a mystery
63 One keeping others up at night, perhaps
65 Something else
66 Singer Gomez
68 Went in a different direction
70 "What's ___ you?"
71 Pride and prejudice, e.g.
73 Fix, as a lawn
77 Pirate
80 Set
81 Mushroom
83 Woman in Progressive ads
85 Classic dog name
86 Hip bones
87 What some neighborhoods do
88 More than enough
89 Volts/amp
93 Long-tailed monkey
94 Blowout party
95 Piano performance, possibly
97 Some ranges
99 El ___ ("View of Toledo" painter)
100 ___ Cradle (maritime rescue device)
103 Popular adoption agcy.
104 "Sign me up!"
105 High-maintenance
107 Richard famous for large-scale sculptures
111 See 89-Across
113 Agcy. fighting epidemics
114 Bobby of the N.H.L.
115 Part of R.S.V.P.
117 Old-fashioned menorah filler
118 "Kitchy-kitchy-___!"
119 Raises
120 Teetotaler's opposite

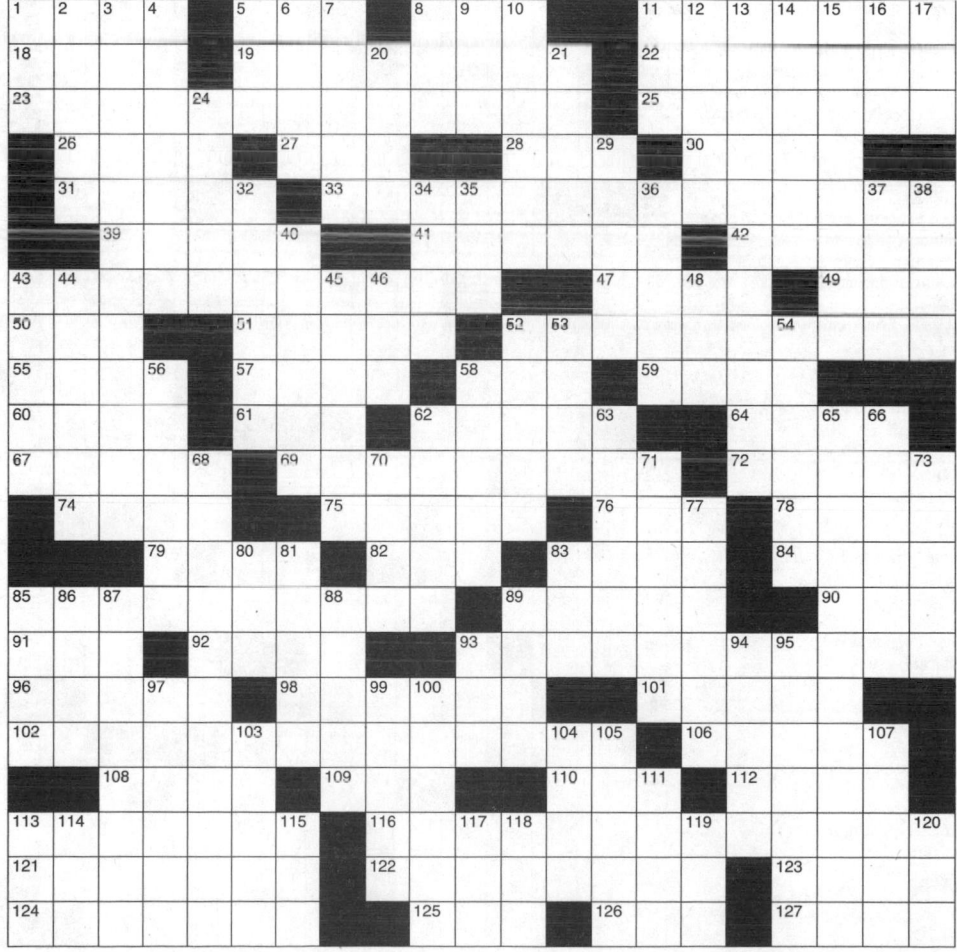

by Laura Taylor Kinnel

ACROSS

1 Appoint
7 People of the Southwest
13 Wishy-washy response
19 Had the opportunity to, casually
20 Entertainment with a private audience?
21 *Malice, more formally*
22 *One wearing chapstick, perhaps*
24 Be up against
25 Poker variety similar to Texas hold 'em
26 Counterpart of "Thx"
27 Saves for later, in a way
29 Ploy
30 Lost
32 *Antarctic coordinate*
35 "A man has cause for ___ only when he sows and no one reaps": Charles Goodyear
38 Bit of tinder
41 First side to vote
42 ___ course
43 New York City transport stopping at Kennedy Airport
46 Beginning stage
47 Prefix with thermal
50 There might be a catch with this
51 *Blouse and broach, perhaps*
54 Wet bar?
55 Form of nepotism, symbolically
57 Herd member
58 Sauce
59 Place, as ceramic tiles
60 Like autumn air
62 Person helping with a delivery
63 Word before film and after clip
65 *It has many beet and beef options*
70 "___ Trois Petits Cochons" (French fable)
71 Sport at the Special Olympics
73 G.I. ___
74 Calling
76 Not be able to stand
77 Ending with invent
78 War and peace, in "War and Peace"
83 Like most dorms nowadays
84 *Tickled*
87 Focus of modern mining
88 "___ be an honor!"
89 They can be graphic
90 Surround, as with light
91 Considerations for N.C.A.A. eligibility
92 ___ Wintour, longtime Vogue editor in chief
93 Spring locales
94 Takes by force
96 *Pop fly*
100 Some family babysitters
102 Match
103 Sarge's boss
105 A-number-one
106 The Venetian way?
110 Alternative to Dropbox
113 Gradually fix something . . . or what to do to understand this puzzle's italicized clues?
116 *Briefly, e.g.*
117 What's used to catch some waves
118 Supreme Egyptian god
119 Bum out
120 Famous cryptid, familiarly
121 Intimates

DOWN

1 Number of sides on a sign reading "ALTO"
2 Space
3 ___ mater (brain cover)
4 Politico-turned-TV host
5 Form thoughts
6 Catch
7 Seeks a favor, say
8 ___ favor
9 Working hard
10 Java activity
11 Product from un ave
12 Boo-boo
13 Texter's qualifier
14 One might be put through the wringer
15 Geek Squad members, e.g.
16 "I can thrill you more than any ___ could ever dare try" ("Thriller" lyric)
17 "The Glass Bead Game" author, 1943
18 Pecan or peach
20 Sch. where a live bear used to take the field during football games
23 Echo, perhaps
28 Pimple lookalikes
31 It usually works in corners
33 "Catch!"
34 Baker's Joy alternative
35 Record speeds, for short
36 Adams of New York City politics
37 *Antelope, say*
38 Parable or allegory
39 Devices with Nunchuks
40 Business news magazine
44 "For shame!"
45 Slugging stat
46 Member of the inn crowd?
47 *Approach for directions*
48 Onetime collaborator with Ice Cube and Dr. Dre
49 Some sports tournaments
52 Big name in women's hair and skin care
53 Boo-boo
54 Word with story or sister
56 Economist/author Emily
58 Screw up
60 Relative of a club, for short
61 Place for boarding
63 You can count on them
64 Member of the modern work force
66 Great Lakes natives
67 Kind of bean
68 Taiwanese electronics giant
69 "I'm about to tell you something shocking"
72 Haddock relative
75 Doesn't put it all on one pony
78 Suvari of "American Beauty"
79 Sounds heard in 93-Across
80 Destructive 2021 hurricane
81 Nouveau-Mexique, e.g.
82 Lip or cheek
84 Put over the moon
85 One hanging around Queen Elizabeth?
86 With it, in old slang
89 "Snowpiercer" airer
92 Sporting a certain natural style
93 Avoids
95 Tortoise's challenge to the hare
96 Nickname for the French Alexandre
97 No longer squeaky (one hopes!)
98 John Wayne, by birth
99 Who ran against George Washington for president
100 "___ chance!"
101 Letters that complete this word: _P_ROPRIA_E
102 Snaps
104 Squeezes (out)
105 Good thing to be in
107 Letters on dreidels
108 Taj Mahal's home
109 Exam that once required fingerprint identification, for short
111 Exercise
112 Animal house
114 Demon of Japanese folklore
115 Folklore villain

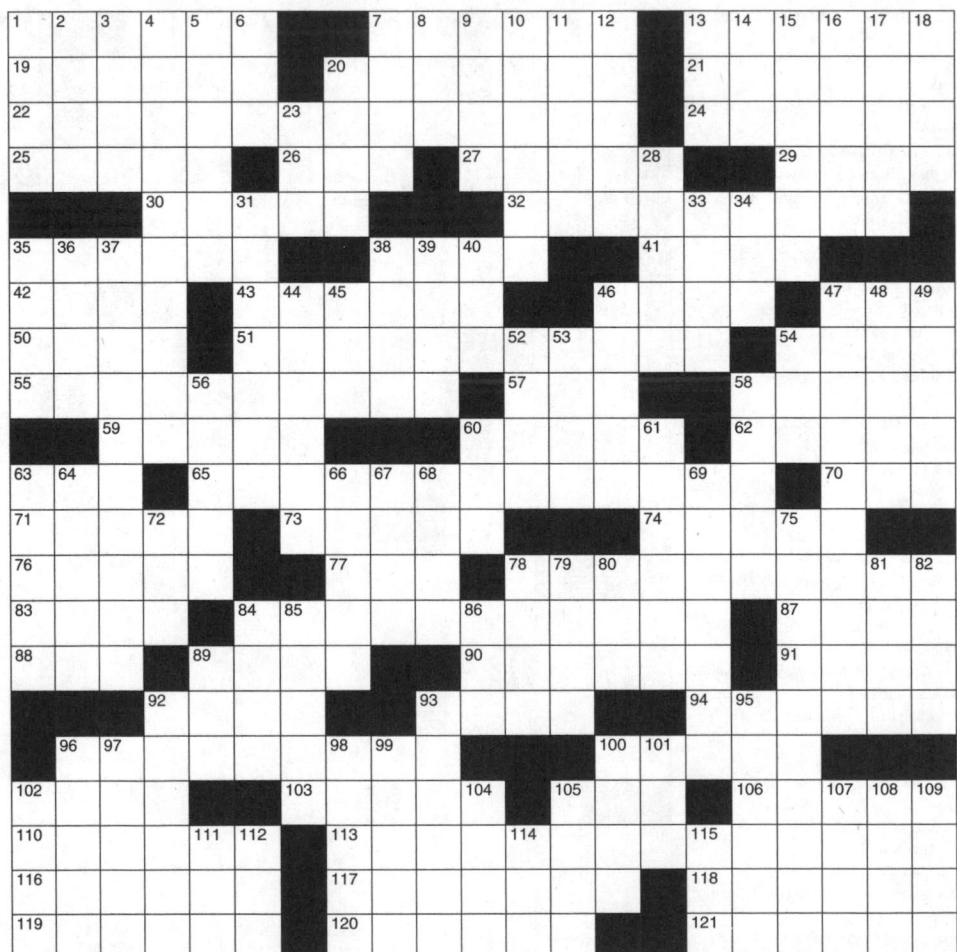

by Christina Iverson

ACROSS

1 Smashing
6 Wide-eyed in wonder
10 Woofer output
14 Casual vodka order
19 Bubbling
20 Pricey
21 Alma mater of Grant and Lee: Abbr.
22 Board game piece
23 Dog's order at a malt shop?
25 The "day" in "seize the day"
26 "Arrival" visitor
27 You can see right through it
28 Part of H.M.S.
29 "Game of Thrones" patriarch has difficulties?
32 Zora Neale Hurston's "___ Eyes Were Watching God"
34 Stand-up comic Kondabolu
35 Drum heard in raga music
36 Creator of Christopher Robin
38 Beat out by a hair
40 Big name in ratings
44 Male sailors
45 Words of affirmation
47 Upscale
48 Android alternative
49 ___ Mahal
51 Kind of diet
53 Chest muscle, informally
54 The "S" of 48-Across
58 Advised a chess player to attack the king?
65 Spanish unit of time with a tilde
66 Yoda, to Luke
67 Shows as an encore presentation
68 A fingerprint can leave one
70 Cell no., say
71 Strips of weapons
72 Coming from two speakers
73 Frequent choice for maid of honor
75 Deg. for an aspiring attorney abroad
76 Part of Disney's advertising budget?
78 How some pranks might go
82 Constellation with a palindromic name
83 Scat syllable for Sinatra
84 Hula loop
86 Academy Award winner for "Moonlight" and "Green Book"
87 Dr. Seuss character who becomes "King of the Mud"
91 Sushi condiment
95 Birds that can recognize themselves in mirrors
99 Beyond sad, or beyond happy
101 Some piercing spots
102 Categorically stated
103 Indubitably
105 Bellybutton fluff
106 Bordeaux wine region
107 Decisively defeat a cabinet department?
111 Musical knack
112 Share on social media
115 Like a zealous fan base
116 School attended by 20 prime ministers
117 Feeling one gets under anesthesia at the dentist?
120 Rat in "Ratatouille"
121 Word before or after run
122 Memo heading
123 Prize for a doc, maybe
124 Stick a fork in
125 Weapon with a bell guard
126 Loathsome person
127 Indira Gandhi's father

DOWN

1 Comedian Mort
2 Instrument from the French for "high wood"
3 Bad shot by Dracula?
4 Affinity
5 Lacking originality
6 Follower
7 Prepare, with "up"
8 Symbol of sturdiness
9 ___ launcher
10 Close pals
11 "Yeah, right!"
12 Process, as ore
13 Language with only 14 native letters
14 He made his final cameo in "Avengers: Endgame"
15 Spilled one's soul
16 '30s migrant
17 Unwelcome look
18 Places to exchange dollars for quarters
24 Stand out from the crowd
30 Little bits of energy
31 Competitor of eBay
33 Tree that lines the Central Park Mall
34 Debut single for both Jimi Hendrix and Patti Smith
36 Flaws and all
37 Shout for 44-Across
39 Put off for another day
41 Building caretakers
42 Higher-ups in a hierarchy
43 Part of a guitar
46 One on the road in "On the Road"
50 Maker of Instant Feathers and Hi-Speed Tonic
52 Laura of "Marriage Story"
55 Does some bronco-busting, e.g.
56 Accustom (to)
57 Broadband device
59 Loosen, in a way
60 Banned display of firepower, informally
61 Conductor Georg with 31 Grammys
62 Passed out in Vegas
63 Gambino crime family patriarch
64 Attractive but vacuous guy, in slang
68 Mary, Queen of Scots, e.g.
69 Prod
71 Prod
72 Philosopher Kierkegaard
73 "Salud!" cousin
74 Heed an army poster
76 "Will you allow me to demonstrate?"
77 Plane ticket info
79 Comfy seating at a carnival?
80 Downwind, at sea
81 New England art inst.
85 "Mind. Blown."
88 Shot served with salt and lime
89 Clean
90 Lexicographer Partridge
92 Singer Knowles with a 2016 #1 album
93 Ever so slightly
94 Perk from work
96 Tex who animated Bugs Bunny
97 Diploma equivalent, in brief
98 Make an engaging offer?
100 British spy Christopher in 2016 news
104 Legally prohibit
107 Parisian equivalent to "molto" or "muy"
108 Increase, with "up"
109 Stage prize since 1956
110 It distinguishes meaning in many East Asian languages
111 Fitch of Abercrombie & Fitch
113 Red carpet interviewee
114 Traffic sign word
118 Card game call
119 Sun follower?

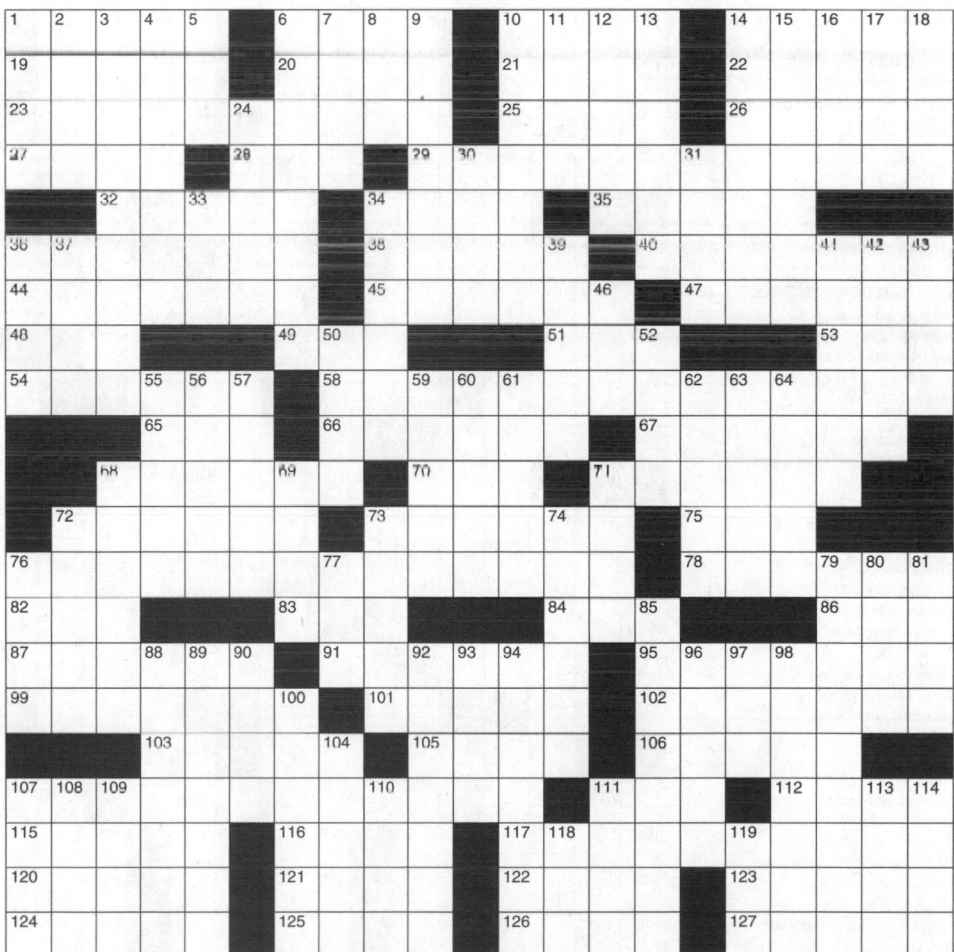

by Ben Zimmer and Brendan Emmett Quigley

ACROSS

1 "For more _____ . . ."
5 Some unwanted mail
9 Terse bit of advice
13 Half of an ice cream brand with a fake Danish name
19 Work up a sweat
20 Rent
21 Like tap water in a restaurant
22 Iris part
23 Wing it [Africa]
25 Blue
26 Chew out
27 Après-ski drink
28 Complete rip-off [Asia]
30 Barrel-flavored, as wine
31 Washington, D.C., legalized it in 2014
32 Wealthy king of legend
33 Recess
36 Charge for admission
37 See 101-Down
38 Quaint contraction
41 Record company [Central America]
45 Two-time third-party presidential candidate
47 "The Walking Dead" channel
48 Beyond great
49 Baking measure
50 Cerebral
51 Take in
53 _____ shoots (salad ingredient)
54 One of five for a dolphin
55 Supple leather
56 Proboscis, informally
58 What subjects and verbs must do [Europe]
62 Ancho pepper, before drying
65 Puzzled
66 Sort by urgency of need [Europe]
70 Misgiving
74 Where meditators look
75 _____ candy
76 Planet where the cry "Shazbot!" is said to have originated
79 Food chain link
80 Treats prepared on an open fire
81 Part of O.E.D.: Abbr.
82 Organic fertilizer
84 Hold up
85 Male 91-Acrosses
86 T-shirt size [South America]
90 Not to mention
91 Forest ranger
92 Shapes made by thumbs and index fingers
93 Glossed over
94 Like some toy cars
97 Sportage maker
98 _____ Cochran, Mississippi senator from 1978 to 2018
99 First month of the year without a U.S. federal holiday [Asia]
102 Dismissed out of hand
106 Want badly
107 Sit at a red light, say
108 Biblical outcast [South America]
109 Exclamation from a cheek pincher
110 Org. behind the New Horizons project
111 One whose job prospects go up in smoke?
112 Responsibility
113 Biggest U.S. union, familiarly
114 Set of two
115 City north of Des Moines
116 Resident of the Palazzo Ducale

DOWN

1 Hankering
2 Manhattan neighborhood west of the East Village
3 Order
4 Cranky codger
5 "Reach for the sky!"
6 Sandwich often served with remoulade sauce
7 Killer of the Night King on "Game of Thrones"
8 "Throw _____ bone"
9 Key of Debussy's "Clair de Lune"
10 Black pie crust component
11 Lead-in to many a joke on "The Daily Show"
12 Senator who once served as an editor of the Harvard Law Review
13 Hurt
14 Many Omanis
15 Group seen in gathering clouds?
16 Discovery that might cause a rush
17 Wellsian race of the future
18 Gram
24 Objects in one of Jesus' miracles
28 Singer Lisa
29 Top of the line
31 Fruit with an obovate shape
33 Media for scientists
34 Unit of brightness
35 Raw material for Cadbury
36 Popular Amazon Prime dramedy from Britain
39 Kind of column seen on the Jefferson Memorial
40 "Funny Girl" composer Jule
42 Copy
43 Vaper's device, informally
44 Nutritional snack from Clif
45 Trig, for calc, e.g.
46 Relaxed
50 Some wetlands
52 Snack with a recommended microwave time of just three seconds
54 Theater impresario Ziegfeld
55 Abbr. in a genealogical tree
57 _____ Strait, separator of Australia and Papua New Guinea
59 What one is in Paris?
60 Kylo _____, "Star Wars" antagonist
61 Candy heart phrase
63 Raises one's paddle, say
64 Each verse of "Deck the Halls" has 32 of them
66 Host Tyler of "Whose Line Is It Anyway?"
67 Dishearten
68 Scottish tradition before battle
69 "We Three Kings" subjects
71 Deodorant brand
72 Sierra _____
73 "Whoops, sorry about that!"
77 Sensationalist newspaper
78 Openings under desks
81 Observance first celebrated in 1970
82 Big to-do
83 Like "Saturday Night Live"
86 Put up with
87 Pull back
88 Mother of 60-Down
89 Item in a toxic internet "challenge"
91 Region around the Beltway, informally
95 Just for laughs
96 Put on a show
97 Work with one's hands
98 Poppycock
99 Classic computer game set on an abandoned island
100 Michelle of "Crouching Tiger, Hidden Dragon"
101 With 37-Across, Ingrid Bergman's role in "Casablanca"
102 Tricky pronoun to use
103 Wine opener?
104 '60s dance craze that evolved from the Chicken
105 Join
108 Helper during taxing times?

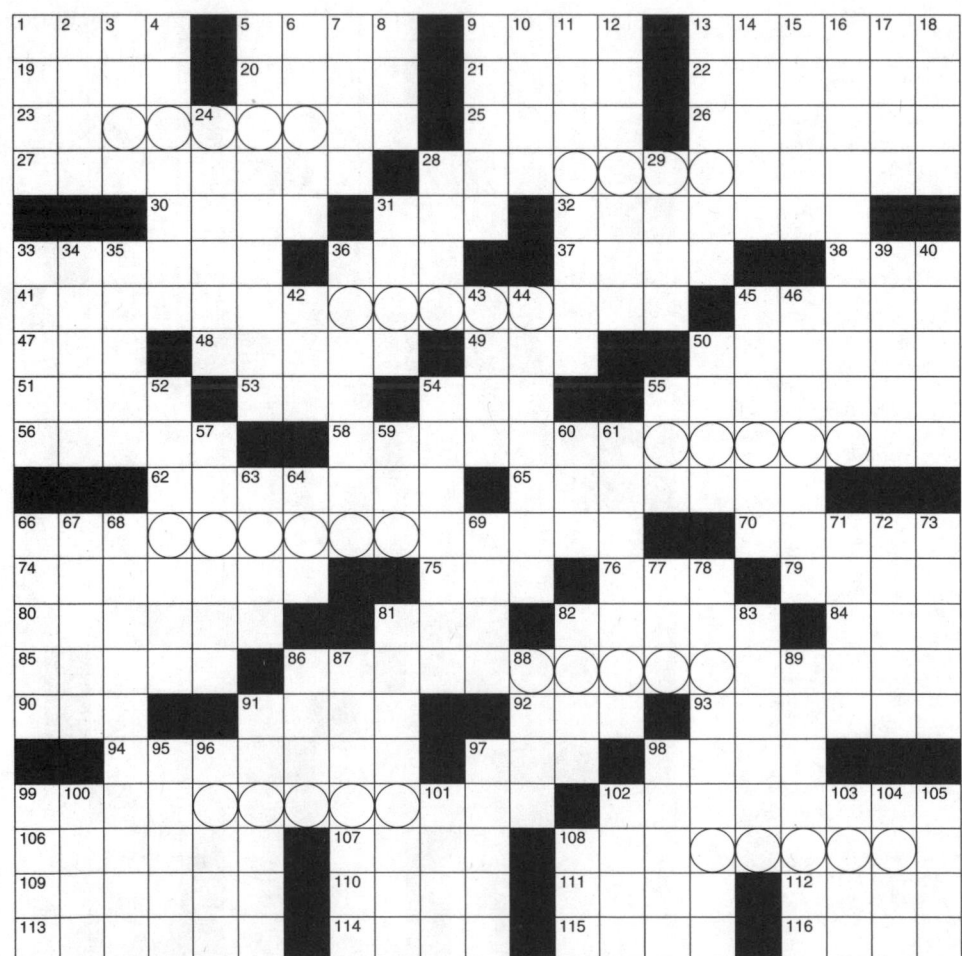

by Adam Fromm

ACROSS

1 How some stock shares are sold
6 Caesar salad ingredient
13 Big name in swimwear
19 African grazer
20 Yalitza ____, Best Actress nominee for 2018's "Roma"
21 Woodworking machine
22 R. J. Reynolds product that once sponsored "The Dick Van Dyke Show"
24 Had legs, so to speak
25 Flying class?
26 Like some leaves and knives
27 Blast
28 "The Confessions of ____ Turner" (1967 Pulitzer-winning novel)
29 Scrapped
30 One who might say "Your money's no good here"?
31 Overwhelming favorite
33 Roofing material
34 Dyes that can be used as pH indicators
35 Echo voice
36 Eponym of Aqaba's airport
38 Editorial reversal
39 Simmering sites
41 On the schedule
45 Chef's creation
47 Crosses one's fingers
49 Sophisticated
50 Subjects of four famous violin concertos by Vivaldi
52 Can't take
54 Body part that's also a Hebrew letter
55 Christ, to Christians
56 Flavorful
57 Colts, maybe
59 Sch. on Chesapeake Bay
60 Interstellar clouds
62 Fundamental dispositions
63 With 55-Down, inning enders
65 Pourable art material
66 Creature seen basking on the shores of the Galápagos
67 Superman co-creator Jerry
69 Sports icon with the autobiography "Faster Than Lightning"
71 Entertainer Minnelli
75 Bitcoin and the like
77 47th U.S. vice president
78 Comic actor whose wife left him to marry their neighbor, Frank Sinatra
81 Airer of the gospel music reality competition "Sunday Best"
82 Classic Chevrolets
84 Eaglelike
85 One with a small but devoted fan base
87 AAA service
88 Restrained from biting
89 Places of intense scrutiny
90 Entertainment on a diner place mat, maybe
91 Alka-Seltzer tablet, for one
92 Early omnivore
94 Returning after curfew, say
95 Substance used to preserve the Declaration of Independence
96 Apt rhyme for "bore"
97 ____ Pieces
98 Has in mind
99 Mary I or Elizabeth I

DOWN

1 Major tributary of the Mississippi
2 Gymnastics event for both men and women
3 The ____ State, nickname for Maine
4 Targets of formicide
5 Mythical flier
6 Isolated
7 Account
8 Popular performance-enhancing supplement for athletes
9 Freaking out
10 Good-sized wedding band
11 Competed
12 Rockyesque interjections
13 Spends extravagantly
14 Some biodiesel sources
15 Victorian home?
16 Whole
17 Judged
18 Things taken while waiting
20 Representative
23 "Capeesh"
27 Whiffs
29 Org. for lightweights
30 End-of-level challenges in video games
32 Items in 18″ × 18″ × 1¾″ boxes
34 Like the hands in the Allstate logo
36 Keystone ____
37 ____ & the Blowfish
39 What sneers express
40 Popular dating app
42 Lake drained by the Truckee River
43 Iniquities
44 Places of iniquity
46 Spanish "that"
48 State capital on the Mississippi
50 Word with roll or bar
51 Muppet wearing a horizontally striped shirt
52 Chinese port city on Korea Bay
53 Occupy, as a booth
55 See 63-Across
56 English county that's home to Brighton
58 Weather map symbol
61 Butter, in Burgundy
62 Doctors Without Borders and others, in brief
64 Having a low neckline, as a dress
66 "Gotta split"
68 Group of 18th-century thinkers that included Voltaire and Rousseau
70 Numbers of concern to showrunners
72 The "Last Great Race on Earth"
73 Love match?
74 Respondent
76 South African money
77 Slo-____ fuse
78 Pan flute musician in iconic commercials of the 1980s
79 Like a jackass
80 Your current occupation?
82 Some skilled workers in "Brave New World"
83 Lead-in to while
85 Party line?
86 Former North Carolina senator Kay ____
89 Let fly
90 Clickable list
92 W.W. II general ____ Arnold
93 Clock setting on the Big Island: Abbr.

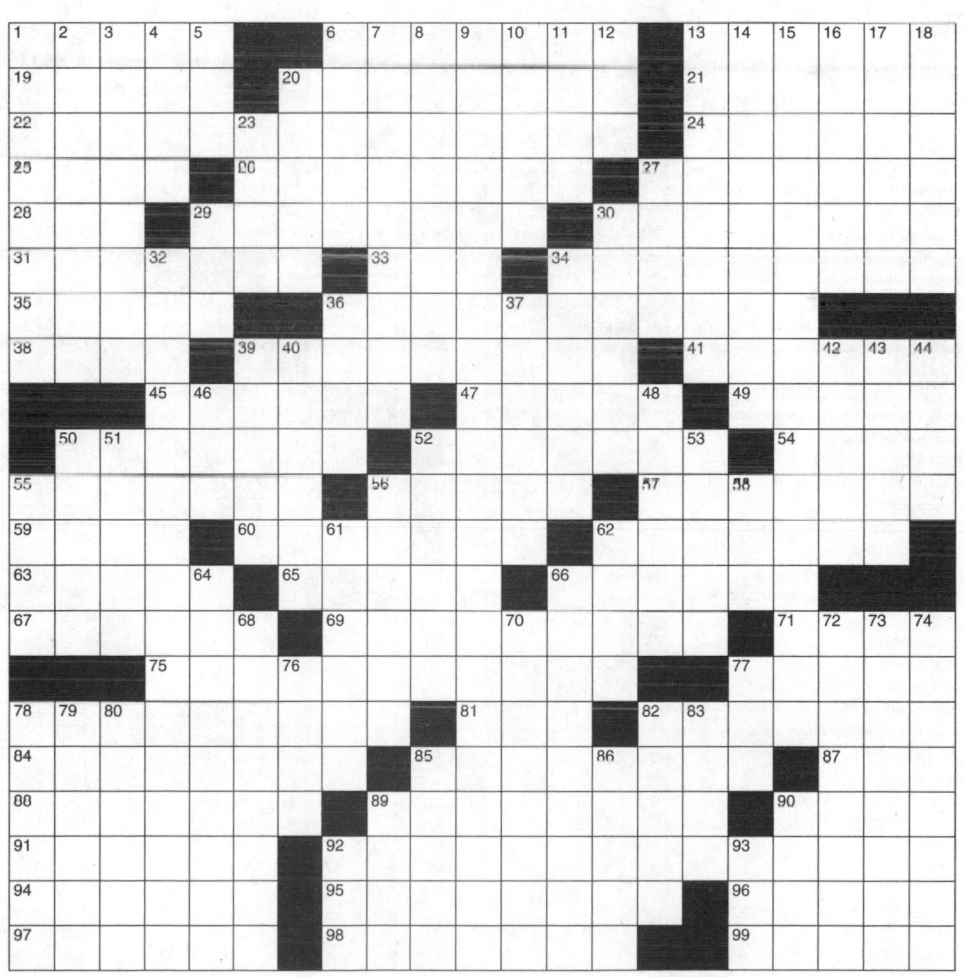

by Byron Walden

150 THE MYSTERY OF McGUFFIN MANOR

Note: This crossword contains a whodunit: "Thank you for coming, Inspector," said Lady McGuffin. "The famed McGuffin Diamond has been stolen from my study! The eight members of the staff had a costume party tonight–it has to be one of them: the butler, driver, cook, baker, page, porter, barber or carpenter. They have all been confined to their respective rooms surrounding the parlor, as shown here." Can you determine who stole the diamond . . . and where it is now?

ACROSS

1 Battlefield cry
7 Sprint competitor
12 Pollen-producing plant part
18 About three miles
19 Excoriates
21 "The Deer Hunter" director Michael
22 An antique might have one
23 What a Venn diagram shows
24 Like
25 As you inspect each room, you find staff members dressed as ____
28 Suspect #1
29 Start of a Christmas refrain
30 "I like it!"
31 Days of old
32 Word that sounds like a number . . . and is a letter backward
33 Russian pancakes
35 Burn slightly
38 Refusals
39 They're all ____, so you can easily identify them
44 Popeye's kid
46 Delta competitor, in brief
47 Woes
50 Suspect #2
51 Have trouble swallowing
53 Like beloved books, often
55 Showers
56 Tech debut of 1998
58 Tucson school, in brief
61 California-based auto company
62 Bristle of grain
63 What it all adds up to
64 A ways away
65 Suspect #3
66 Spawn
69 Music for the masses?
71 Sly and the Family Stone genre
72 Public spat
74 Considered
76 ____ fusion (type of cuisine)
78 Some appliances
79 They catch dust bunnies
82 It might get a licking: Abbr.
83 Musical family with a star on the Hollywood Walk of Fame
85 In the study, you find that the thief accidentally left behind an ____
88 Some sports cars
91 Lots
92 "That's ____"
93 Some modern ones are smart
96 Four-letter word for a four-letter word
98 In ____ (stuck)
100 Hershey toffee bar
101 Suspect #4
102 "You caught me!," says the thief, who then admits: "The diamond isn't here in my room, but it's hidden in ____"
108 "Hungry" game characters
109 What each person gets in an election
110 Spark
111 Ordain
112 Joined at an angle, as two pieces of wood
113 Clothes hanger?
114 Suspect #5
115 Suspect #6
116 "Easy now . . ."

DOWN

1 Source of the robe material for Incan royalty
2 Home brewer
3 Tell
4 Spry
5 Brooklyn Coll. is part of it
6 Thomas who chaired the 9/11 Commission
7 Enjoy deeply
8 Salon brand
9 Magazine audience fig.
10 Suspect #7
11 Style for Edward Hopper and George Bellows
12 What might come with fencing?
13 Suspect #8
14 Goodwill
15 "Despicable Me" character
16 Intestinal: Prefix
17 Some knotted ropes
19 Elie Wiesel's homeland
20 Lowest of the eight major taxonomic ranks
26 Flambé
27 Japanese box lunch
33 Oenology : wines :: zythology : ____
34 Org. in "Die Hard"
36 Teri with a "Tootsie" role
37 It might be snowy
39 Move off the bottle
40 Chip dip, familiarly
41 Badger
42 Diamond family name
43 Like a bad loser
44 Major source of oxygen in the earth's atmosphere
45 Janitor's tool
48 Britain's Broadway
49 City near Monterey Bay
50 Latches (onto)
51 Delta preceder
52 Like a Debbie Downer
54 Women of honour
56 Kinda
57 Very, in Veracruz
59 Swing and completely miss
60 Getaway for two lovebirds?
67 Ireland's best-selling solo artist
68 Home of the original Busch Gardens
70 The compass points
71 Hardy bean
72 Campfire treat
73 "Too busy"
75 Jr.'s junior
77 Suffix with serpent
78 Leader whose name means, literally, "commander"
80 Kilt feature
81 Space to maneuver a ship
83 Seeped (through)
84 Low on dough
86 Big launch of 1957
87 "Time for a break"
88 Fictional city inspired by New York City
89 Sauce put on falafel
90 Squash
93 Springsteen's birthplace, in song
94 Knowledgeable (in)
95 Hard
97 Music to a hitchhiker's ears
99 Thucydides had one
100 Said a 96-Across
101 Went with
103 Anika ____ Rose, 2004 Tony winner
104 Sunrise direction, in Seville
105 "Best. Day. ____!"
106 Stable diet?
107 Rushing group, informally

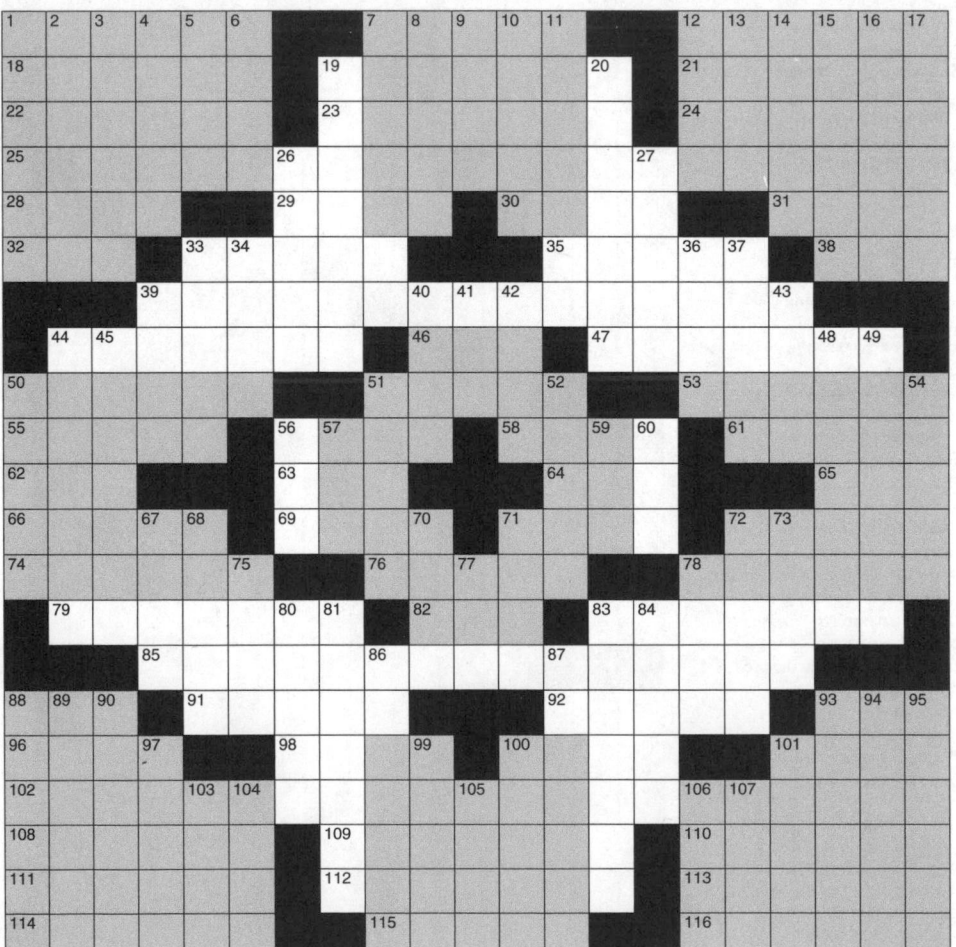

by Andrew Chaikin

ACROSS

1   . . . and the rest: Abbr.
4   Small bit
9   Chilled
13 Feng ——
17 Takes off
19 Word whose rise in popularity coincided with the spread of the telephone
20 It's shorter on land than at sea
21 Bit of change
22 Traditional Hanukkah gift for kids
23 Computing machine displayed in part at the Smithsonian
24 Beachgoer's item
25 Instrument heard in "Eleanor Rigby"
26 Bits of regalia
28 "Git!"
30 Get hammered
32 Providers of books to remote locations
34 Unlawful activity by a minor
36 Land of the Po (not Poland)
37 Special ——
38 ——-cone
39 Home of the world's smallest country: Abbr.
40 Alias letters
41 Demurring words
42 Member of the genus Helix
44 Marcel Duchamp, e.g.
47 Genre for the Spice Girls or Backstreet Boys
49 Passion
51 Bug experts, informally
55 Breathtaking sight in the ocean?
56 Back
58 This and others
59 Downed
62 GPS's guesses
64 Montezuma, for one
65 Assign new functions to, as keyboard keys
66 Some natural remedies
69 Cabinet position once held by Herbert Hoover
72 Give one's take
73 Basic knowledge, with "the"
77 Went after, in a way
78 —— admin
79 Classic brand of candy wafers
80 Magical teen of Archie Comics
82 Give kudos to
84 Pop a wheelie?
86 "I've got that covered"
87 Paid to play
91 Work requiring some intelligence?
93 —— Bahama (clothing label)
95 DNA carrier
96 Word after "so" or "go"
99 Middle of many similes
100 1%-er in D.C.?: Abbr.
102 '60s war zone
103 Not reflective
104 Untimely time
107 Great depth
109 Myth propagated to promote social harmony, in Plato's "Republic"
110 Faux cough
112 "Aw, hell!"
113 Shady outdoor area
114 Collection of stock
116 4 × 100, e.g.
118 Sole
120 Put down
121 Opposite of une adversaire
122 Selfie taker's concern
123 Liberal arts college in Portland, Ore.
124 Just makes, with "out"
125 Recipe amts.
126 Serious-minded
127 Cavity filler's deg.

DOWN

1   Mayonnaise ingredient
2   Directly opposed
3   Like a virgin
4   Cut
5   Good thing to have after work
6   QB Manning
7   Number of concern to a teacher
8   Former New York City mayor with the autobiography "Mayor"
9   Tow truck's destination
10 Org. in "Argo"
11 Jet set
12 Precisely describe
13 It's made up of lines
14 State capital in Lewis and Clark County
15 Crack
16 2017 hit movie about an Olympic skater
18 Songbird with dark, iridescent plumage
25 What A.P. exams grant incoming freshmen
27 Unit of hope
29 IHOP beverages
31 Supply
32 Make, as money
33 Water safety org.
35 U.S. broadcasting service
42 Conductor Georg
43 Long river of Siberia
45 Places for hustlers?
46 "Rent me" sign
48 What marriage merely is, to some
50 Cutting tool
52 Catamounts, by another name
53 1960s counterculture figure
54 Play awards
57 Remote control button
59 A part of
60 Plains structure
61 Order from above
63 Low-hanging clouds
67 Atahualpa's subjects
68 Bawl
70 Sports Illustrated named him "Sportsman of the Century" in 1999
71 Villain
74 Places for strollers
75 German article
76 Something a crab might be found in
80 Coverage in Africa?
81 Penance
83 Shin guards of old
85 Disinfectant brand
88 Held up
89 Like most haikus
90 Source of zest
92 Fighting Tigers' sch.
94 Evil: Fr.
96 Pilot's opposite
97 Heavy winter wear
98 Margot who played the titular role in 16-Down
101 Utmost degree
103 Stage ——
105 Moves like an elephant
106 Bustles (with)
108 Howled like a wolf
111 Museum sections, perhaps
115 Criticize in no uncertain terms
117 JFK alternative
119 Amts. "gained" or "lost"

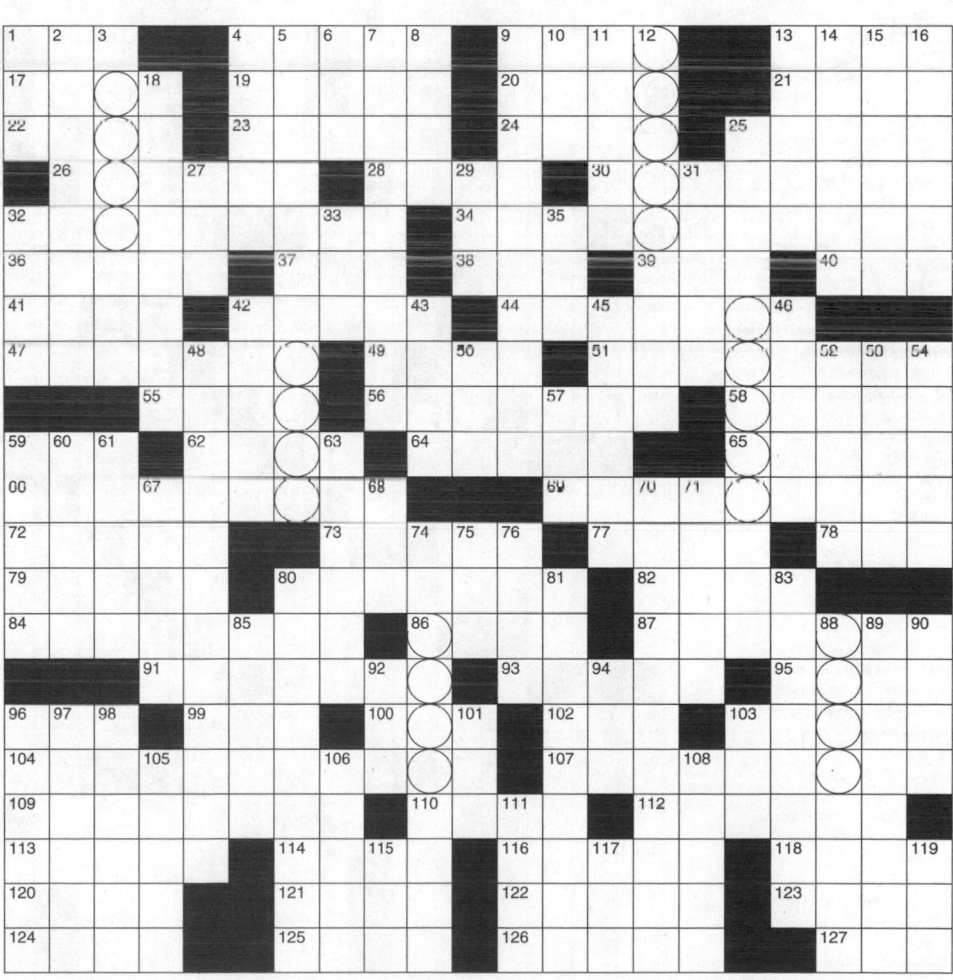

by Lewis Rothlein and Jeff Chen

ACROSS

1 Sadistic feline character in a Scott Adams strip
8 Out
14 Concern for a P.R. team
20 Trembling
21 Land, as a fish
22 The Red Baron, for one
23 "The operation was a success!," e.g.?
25 Unimportant-sounding dessert
26 Novelist/poet Cisneros
27 Posthumous award?
28 Cause of death in many a murder mystery
29 Lampoon
31 Kidney-related
33 Montana, in the 1980s
34 "Let's get going!"
36 People who start arguments out of nowhere?
40 Metal in galvanization
41 Comes after
42 Embedded design
43 Stud fees?
45 Lighthearted movie
46 Painter Velázquez
48 Network that once advertised its prime-time block as "Must See TV"
51 Bygone car company that bore its founder's initials
52 City with views of the Mediterranean and Mount Carmel
54 Officers who woke up on the wrong side of the cot?
57 No longer plagued by
58 The "R" of the Bay Area's BART
59 Material for some suits
60 One who's unfaithful?
63 They're written in chess notation
64 Loose and flowing, as a dress
66 Unit of stamps
67 Felt bad
68 What's the holdup?
69 Soirées where everyone is dressed in their finest board shorts?
72 "Holy guacamole!"
73 Response to a breach of movie theater etiquette
76 Airport monitor, for short
77 Supports
78 Island whose name rhymes with 72-Across
79 Chef's topper
81 ____ kebab
83 Tailors' measurements
85 Be awesome
86 Got 101% on an exam, say?
91 "Don't touch that ____!"
92 Really bothered
93 Stuntwoman Kitty known as "the fastest woman in the world"
94 One of a pair on the table
96 Hotheaded ones?
98 Site of a noted oracle
101 How a tandem bicycle is built
104 "Well, all right then"
105 Why someone might practice deep breathing every five minutes?
107 ____ Mae
108 Multiparagraph blog comment, maybe
109 Nit pick?
110 Celsius with a namesake temperature scale
111 Knit pick?
112 Intrigued by

DOWN

1 Mama ____
2 Shade similar to turquoise
3 Makes aware of
4 March Madness tourney, with "the"
5 Flip inside out
6 Put a bluffer in a tough spot
7 Give a whirl
8 Son of 62-Down
9 Muppet who sings "I Refuse to Sing Along"
10 Humorist David
11 One-percenters and the like
12 ____ Creed
13 Demolition material
14 Like some granola bars
15 Amazon predator
16 Dublin alma mater of Oscar Wilde
17 "Don't worry, that only LOOKED painful!"
18 Early accepter of mobile payments?
19 Haughty looks
24 Doesn't go straight
28 Requiring a lot of attention, say
30 Go on a rampage
32 Off the beaten path
34 Industry magnate
35 "Hands off!"
37 Adidas competitor
38 A.O.C., e.g.
39 Grab (onto)
44 Any member of the Twelver branch of Islam
46 Hornswoggled
47 Author Murdoch played onscreen by Kate Winslet and Judi Dench
48 Faux pas
49 Begin to develop
50 Quartet that performed at Woodstock, for short
53 Revenue sources for podcasts
54 Squirrels away
55 "Good to go!"
56 Stand up at the altar
57 Biodiverse habitat
58 Gets going, so to speak
60 Abbr. that begins some entry-level job titles
61 Start of a conclusion
62 Goddess who cursed Echo to just repeat the words of others
63 Ingredient that turns a Black Russian into a White Russian
64 Entrance
65 Roman triumvirate?
67 German city where Charlemagne was buried
68 Do a favor for a vacationing friend, maybe
70 Four for a grand slam, briefly
71 They often end on a low note
72 Many a Dickensian child
73 Water heater?
74 Polynesian performance
75 Last-eaten part of a loaf, often
78 Women's History Month: Abbr.
80 "Supplies are limited!"
81 Paste used for home repairs
82 Frequent result of wearing a bike helmet
83 Getting three square meals a day
84 Office worker
86 Appetizer often served with mint chutney
87 Pioneer Day celebrant
88 Like urban legends, again and again
89 Figure out
90 Only state capital that shares no letters with the name of its state
95 Animal whose genus name, Phascolarctos, means "pouch bear"
97 What contacts contact
99 Zest
100 Cache
102 Direction for one who's been in Benin to go to Togo
103 Popular name for a black-and-white pet
105 W-2 ID
106 "How ____!"

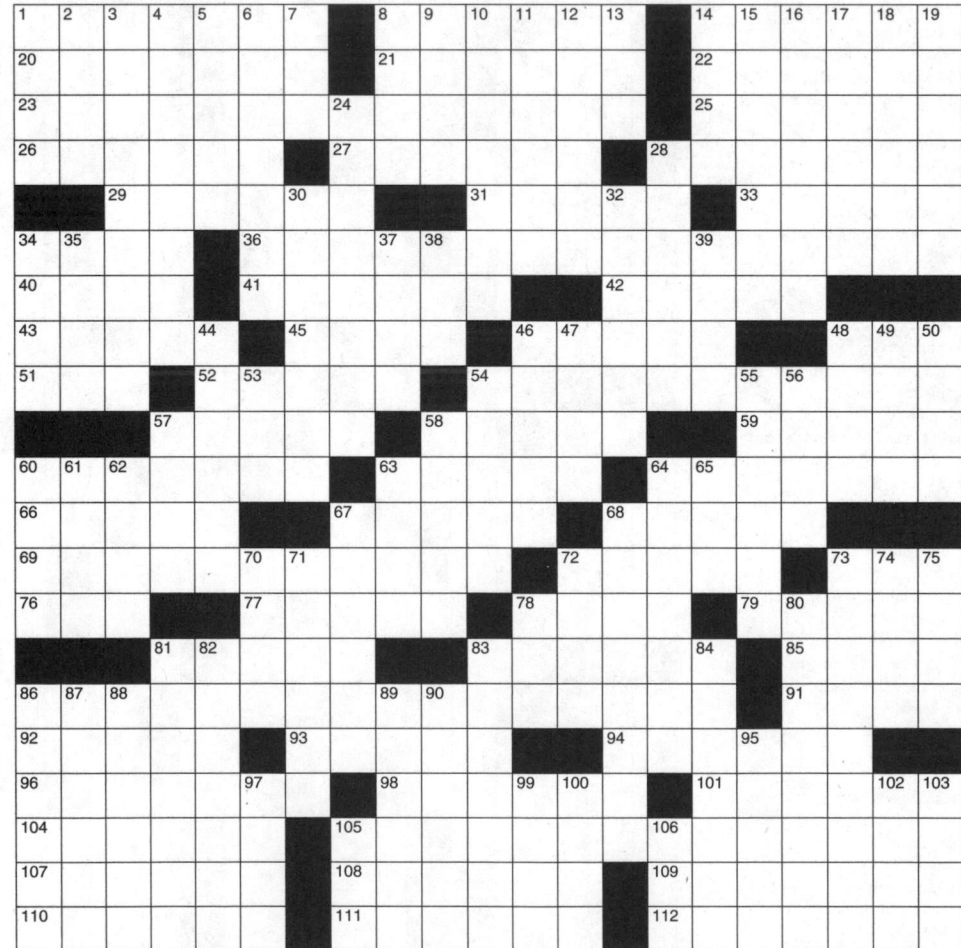

by Andy Kravis

ACROSS

1 Because of
8 "Pet" with green "fur"
12 Illegal thing to grab in football
20 Handkerchief, in British slang
21 Disney+ alternative
22 Turkey piece?
23 Sign at a chemical plant: "This facility is ___ – ___" (with 114-Across)
25 Lists of grievances
26 It ends in Nov.
27 "When pigs fly!"
28 Recess retort
30 Moody who wrote "Coming of Age in Mississippi"
31 Question to an English teacher: "Why did Poe write his poem "___"? Answer: "___?" (with 98-Across)
36 Ingredients in mulled wine
39 "Everything's ready on my end"
40 Idiosyncrasy
41 Rodriguez who starred in "Jane the Virgin"
42 Scheming sergeant of old TV
45 We can tell the boss's assistant is a ___ because he always ___ (with 87-Across)
50 My weight increases when traveling because ___ during ___ (with 84-Across)
54 Scrabble three-pointers
55 Indescribable religious ideal
56 Status for a library book
57 Ice pads?
60 Nick's cousin
61 Dandy, on Downing Street
62 Advantage
63 List makers
64 Someone who is ___ years old now will be ___ in six years (with 68-Across)
68 See 64-Across
71 Small truck maker
72 Agrees (with)
74 Way to go
75 To boot
76 Some cymbals
78 Unlikely candidates for loans
82 What might be broken by doing a flip?
83 Cover some ground
84 See 50-Across
87 See 45-Across
91 Light measurement
92 Scores
93 Prefix with puncture
94 Introducer of the symbol "e" for natural logs
96 "Dallas" family
98 See 31-Across
105 Music played on a sitar
106 Ollie's foil, in old films
107 ___ Marbles (classical Greek sculptures)
108 Opposite of nord
111 Dictatorial leadership
114 See 23-Across
118 Hit (with)
119 One of Zoe's best friends on "Sesame Street"
120 Thistlelike plants
121 Some trolleys
122 Words said in passing
123 "But wait, there's more!," e.g.

DOWN

1 Like some music collections
2 Courts
3 "___ it true . . . ?"
4 The puck stops here
5 Oddly, it's not the biggest size at Starbucks
6 Broncobusters, e.g.
7 Pointed arch
8 Winning quality
9 QB's cry
10 Suffix with percent
11 Open-book examinations?
12 Untruth
13 Bit of negativity?
14 Attendee of the Jellicle Ball, on Broadway
15 In-flight info, for short
16 Jackie Robinson, in his only year in the Negro Leagues
17 Dress with a flare
18 City south of Florence
19 Casey with a countdown
24 Read Across America org.
29 "___ So Unusual," debut album by Cyndi Lauper
31 Opposite of après
32 Collaboratively written page
33 Popular video-making software
34 Things proposed by the Greek philosopher Democritus
35 Business slumps
36 Sci-fi film f/x
37 Mythomaniac
38 "You can count ___"
42 National park with Lake Louise
43 Sit out on a frozen lake, say
44 Old Ford
46 Board hire
47 Troubled
48 One tending to 49-Down
49 See 48-Down
51 "Get ___ here!"
52 Home to Paris
53 Breakfast fare from Kellogg's
58 Valentine candy word
59 Work
60 Absolutely, slangily
62 Best Buy buy
63 Dispatched
64 Kind of acid found in asparagus
65 Get-go
66 Howard Hughes property, once
67 Routing word
69 "The Gates of Hell" sculptor
70 Gambling game
71 "Toodles!"
73 Big Sur home to the human potential movement
76 Blah
77 Promising words
78 Kapow!
79 Part of an escalator
80 Hot spot for a pot
81 Reason for a bad air day?
83 Org. with a pet cause?
85 Product of coagulation
86 Some toy dolls of the 1980s
88 Like the Devil
89 Puts in order
90 Arizona county or its seat
95 Laura of "Love Actually"
96 Put in a good word?
97 Dressed like for Halloween
98 Spot to sample perfume
99 Poker Flat chronicler
100 Lead-in to phobia
101 Key
102 Second takes
103 Major street through Yale's campus
104 Anxiety
108 Snick and ___
109 Sch. with the most N.C.A.A. men's basketball championships (11)
110 Piece of dorm room furniture
112 Elvis's longtime label
113 Europe's second-largest country in area, after Russia: Abbr.
115 Encouraging word
116 Doc bloc
117 Reptile seen in hieroglyphics

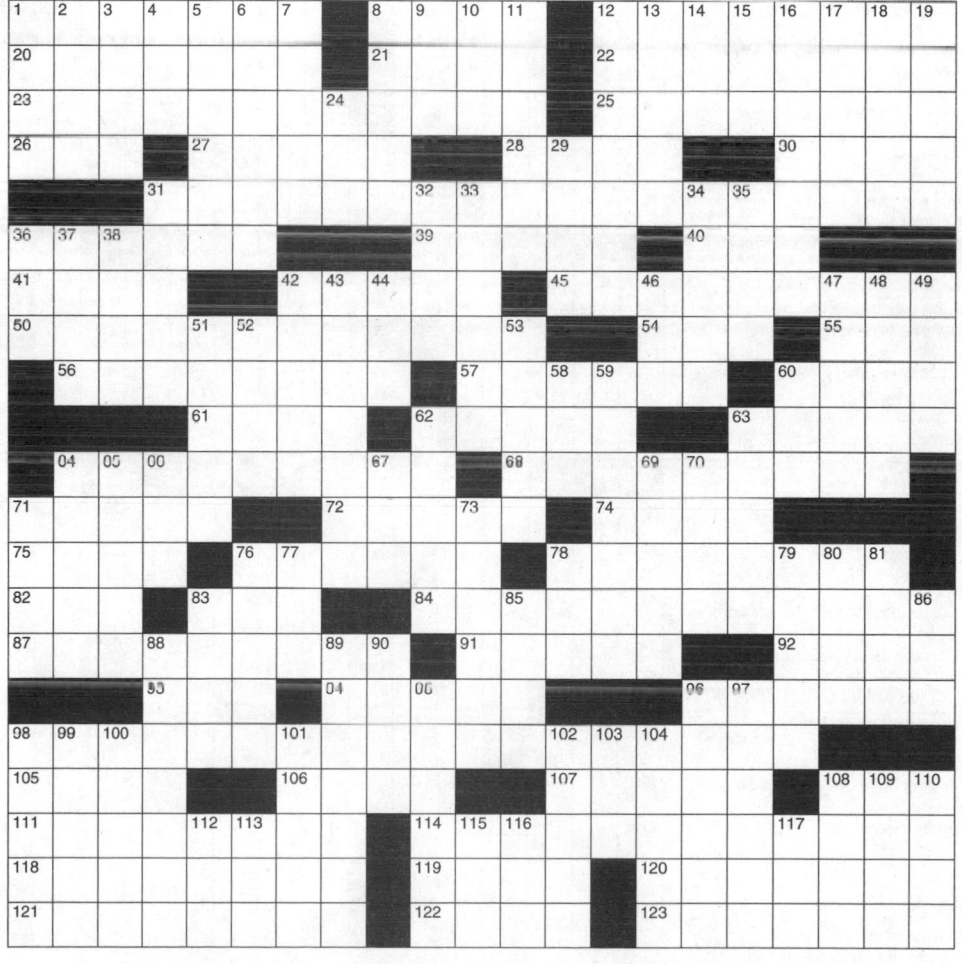

by Randolph Ross

ACROSS

1 Fancy water pitcher
7 Cranks (out)
13 Iranian president Rouhani
19 National park near Bar Harbor
20 Bubble gum brand
22 Go against
23 Put in another light
24 What do you get when you cross 26-Across with a 5-Down?
26 A group of them may be called a memory
28 Bestow
29 Not down so much?
30 Item that can be blown or thrown
31 Coastal environment simulator at an aquarium
34 Onesie protector
36 Some Instagram feed posts
37 Pool unit
38 Tokyo-to-Iwo Jima dir.
39 Iraqi currency
41 Symbols of watchfulness
46 Krispy ____
49 Musical tone below A
53 Rock climber's tool
54 Neighbors of Saudis
56 "Cheese" products?
57 What do you get when you cross 63-Across with a 45-Down?
61 Jungian feminine side
62 Not natural, say
63 Coop group
64 Dazed and confused
66 Went (against)
68 Caper
69 London theater district
72 Flatbread often garnished with rosemary
77 Creatures that can have two sets of jaws and teeth
81 Kind of squash
82 What do you get when you cross 77-Across with a 40-Down?
85 Begin dozing
87 Dandelion look-alike
88 Congregate to rest
89 Fill with love
90 ____ Malfoy, Harry Potter antagonist
91 Logs on to, say
94 Criticizes harshly
96 Tirana's country: Abbr.
98 Cabinet inits. since 1980
99 Abe Lincoln's youngest son
102 ____ de los Muertos
103 Napoleonic symbol
106 "If all ____ fails . . ."
110 Confess
112 Got to work
114 "____ in the Garden" (Robert Frost poem)
116 What do you get when you cross 114-Across with a 93-Down?
120 ____ 101, world's tallest building before the Burj Khalifa
121 Sporty Chevy
122 Picked (up)
123 Shaping wood using a curved blade
124 Get short with
125 Coldly determined
126 Direct

DOWN

1 Wasn't indifferent
2 D.C.-to-Boston transport
3 Nonvenomous, fast-moving snake
4 Get accustomed (to)
5 School group
6 Erode
7 "CSI" broadcaster
8 Spots on ships for anchor cables
9 Weapon used by the Terminator
10 CD-____
11 Aurelius, for Lucius Aurelius Commodus
12 Burrowing lizard
13 Spicy appetizer
14 When National Beer Day is celebrated: Abbr.
15 Tater
16 Gandhi of contemporary Indian politics
17 Queried
18 They might take a few swallows
21 Along with
25 Geographical locale whose name means "waterless place"
27 Back of the neck
32 "For shame!"
33 Make bubbly
35 Rice variety
37 Lex Luthor's sister
39 Classroom assignment
40 What's known for its poker face?
41 Take in the newspaper
42 ____ Stix
43 Suffix with launder
44 Department stores since 1901
45 Ika, at a sushi bar
47 Ireland, poetically
48 Some lapel attachments
50 First letter of the Arabic alphabet
51 Do, ____, fa . . .
52 Exam for college-bound H.S. students
55 "Mad Men" channel
58 Pest control brand founded by Lee Ratner (!) in the 1950s
59 ____ Island
60 Sega mascot
65 Home to Natural Bridges National Monument
67 1,000%
68 Ghana's capital
69 Lessen in power
70 Business class, for short
71 Pop
72 "Never ____!"
73 Prefix with -gon
74 M.R.I. alternative
75 Cactus bump
76 Org. with a classified budget
78 Many stars have big ones
79 ____-majesté
80 Concordes et al.
83 Some HDTVs
84 Father of the Amazons, in Greek myth
86 "Sorry, Charlie"
92 "Moonstruck" Oscar winner
93 Smallest of the big cats
95 Home to the Hana Highway
97 Touchingly?
99 Soothing powders
100 Flighty?
101 Strongly held beliefs
103 Weather forecast figures
104 Inception
105 Hen
106 "My Fair Lady" protagonist
107 Fatty acid, e.g.
108 "____ evil . . ."
109 Endorse online
111 Striking sound
113 Big name in vitamins
115 Lessen in power
117 Singing syllable
118 16th letter
119 Palindromic preposition

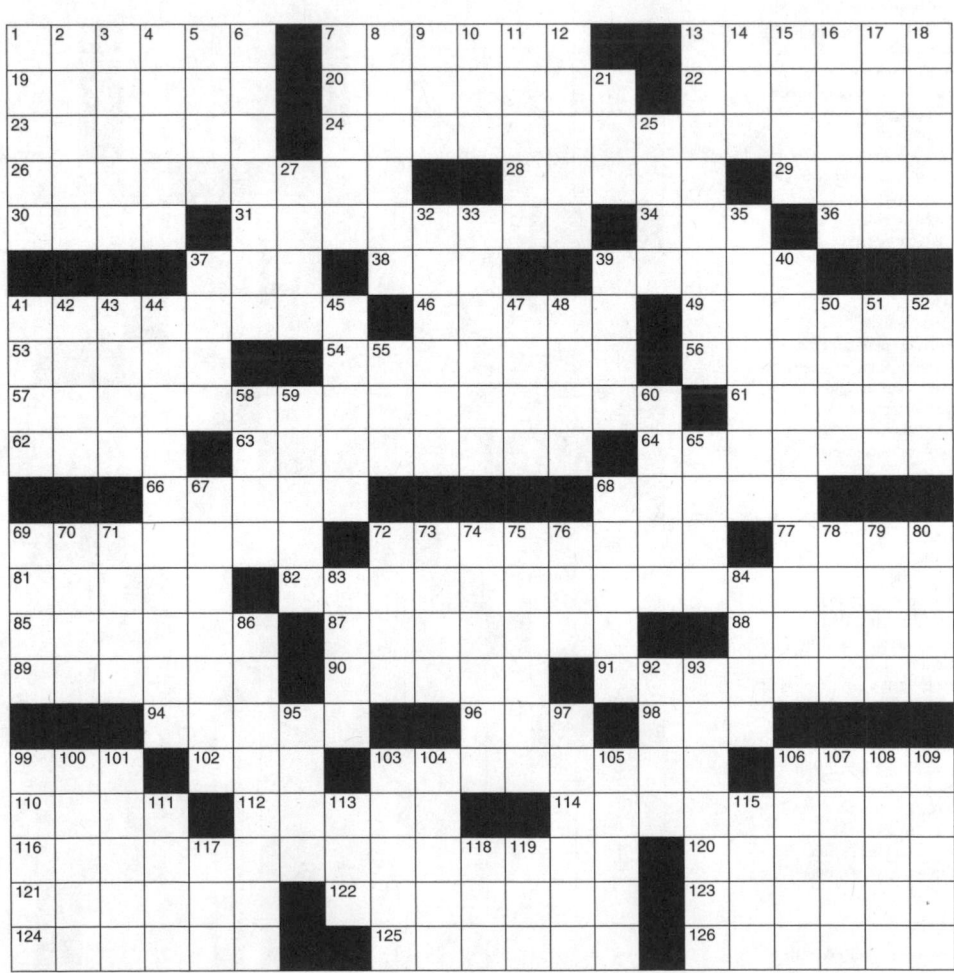

by Byron and Harrison Walden

ACROSS

1 Not fine
7 Expedition
12 Savory jelly
17 Tacks on
19 Mollycoddle
20 Sight on an English farm
21 Slacker role for Jeff Bridges in "The Big Lebowski"
22 Super-enthusiastic
23 Spelman College graduate, e.g.
24 "____ is an emotion in motion": Mae West
25 See 30-Across
27 Morning weather phenomenon
29 See 33-Across
30 With 25-Across, get as much approval from an audience as possible
32 Dalmatians, e.g.
33 With 29-Across, like a deer in headlights
35 N.Y.C.'s first subway line
36 Singer Mann
38 Michelangelo masterpiece
40 Sunset Boulevard sight
42 Utah mountain range
45 What people tend to do when a rush-hour subway train arrives
47 See 50-Across
48 See 53-Across
50 With 47-Across, not change anyone's mind, say
52 Forest of Fangorn resident, in fiction
53 With 48-Across, stops wasting time
57 Dawn
59 Eternally damned
61 Promptness
63 Default consequence
65 Have an influence (on)
69 Iraqi port city
70 Mathematical concepts suggested eight times in this puzzle
74 "I'm telling the truth!"
75 One of the Seven Dwarfs
77 Yeats's "The Lake ____ of Innisfree"
78 Bad place for a fly, in a saying
80 Showy shrub
83 Arch supporter
85 See 90-Across
86 Flat-topped cap
88 See 92-Across
90 With 85-Across, uncomfortably accurate
92 With 88-Across, sacrificed
94 Place that processes ore
96 Eponym of the world's largest church
101 Some team-bonding trips
103 State whose capital is Dispur
105 Drum that can be played with a brush
106 Hypotheticals
107 See 113-Across
109 Cleans, as a deck
112 See 116-Across
113 With 107-Across, bad sort of competition
115 "Freak on a Leash" metal band
116 With 112-Across, "Your misfortune is nothing special"
118 Jocular lead-in to "macation"
119 List ender
121 Abstract artist de Kooning known for her portraits
123 Obsessive cleaner, say
125 Important faculty for school
126 Brought home
127 Lively French dance popular in the Baroque era

128 Big name in nail polish
129 Rug rats
130 Brand whose sales skyrocketed after the release of "E.T."

DOWN

1 Person who's being used
2 Sister of Laertes
3 They're scored from 1 to 5
4 What's found at one end of a rainbow
5 Comfy-cozy
6 Sources of Norse mythology
7 More throaty
8 Pale
9 Ukr., e.g., once
10 Spanish "I love you"
11 Kind of cuisine that's often eaten with one's hands
12 Tied, in scores
13 ____ vide (culinary technique)
14 Do some heavy lifting
15 "Don't pay attention to that"
16 Idle gossip
18 Convince
19 Cracks
20 Actor Dev of "Lion"
26 Lick (up)
28 Stop the flow of

31 House call?
33 Playful growl
34 Run-____ (hip-hop trio)
37 Alternative to an ellipsis
39 Some clickbait articles
41 Potentially risky thing to drop in a relationship
43 ____ Woo-shik, co-star of 2019's "Parasite"
44 ____ cuisine
46 Sanders who played in a World Series and two Super Bowls
49 Charon's domain
51 Lead-in to self
53 They might be caught in the rain
54 ____ Bator
55 Stun, in a way
56 Hard-hit line drive
58 One variety of love
60 Broadway's ____-Fontanne Theater
62 Heckle
64 Part of a hammer
66 Butter alternative
67 "There warn't no home like a raft . . ." speaker
68 Lavish celebration
71 Hard Italian cheese
72 Level, for one
73 Isolated components

76 Deviation in flight
79 Exterminator's target
81 Was bested by
82 Title horror film locale
84 Wrote poorly
86 They have your life hanging by a thread
87 They might involve impersonating a dealer
89 Kingdom east of Babylonia
91 Mini-albums, in brief
92 Ship with three banks of oars
93 Fly catcher
95 Dead Sea Scrolls sect
97 Envelope abbr.
98 Juggling, singing, magic, etc.
99 Scholarly
100 Tells off
102 Just peachy
104 ____ Pro
108 Dental covering similar to a crown
110 Water pipe
111 Dishonest attack
114 Foe of the Morlocks, in sci-fi
116 Major export of Tuscany
117 Place to hang holiday lights
120 Something drawn by a jerk, maybe
122 Sanctuary
124 What a digitigrade stands on

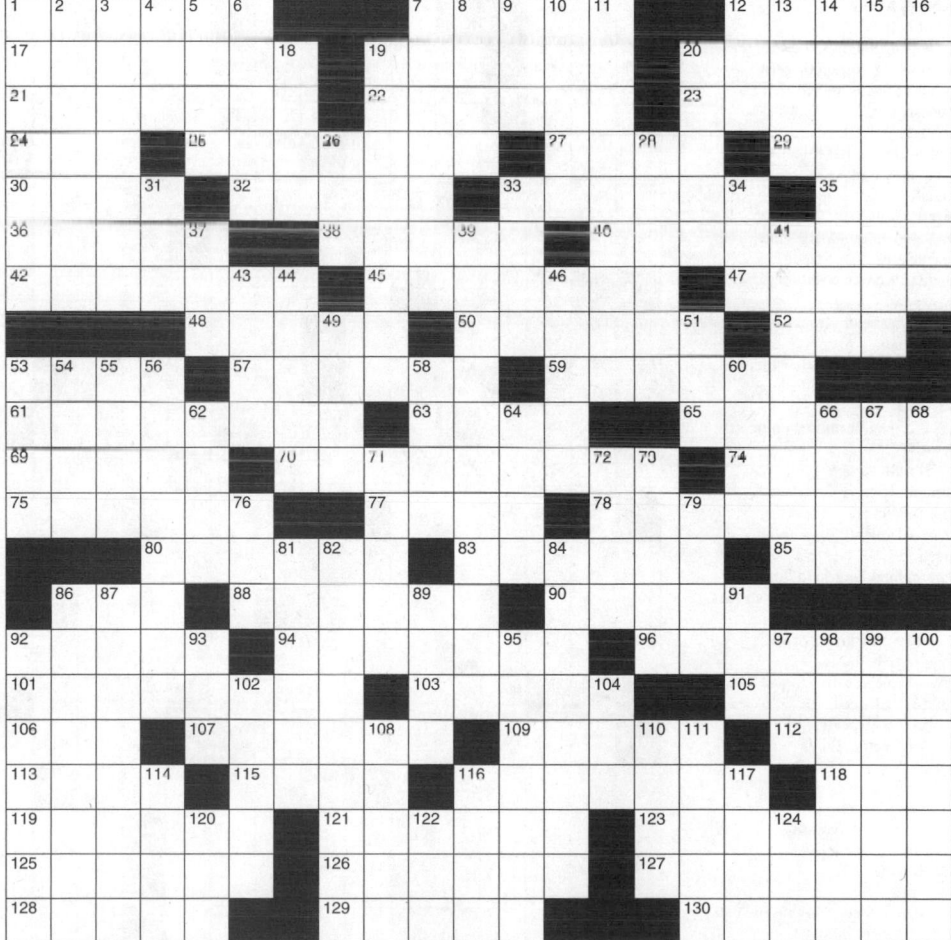

by Jon Schneider and Anderson Wang

ACROSS

1 1/48 of a cup: Abbr.
4 Ad Council offerings, for short
8 Home of the Kaaba
13 Spartan
17 "The Problem With ___" (2017 documentary)
18 Orator's platform
19 "Never meet your ___" (maxim)
20 Less wild
21 Done working: Abbr.
22 About which you might always say "Bee prepared"?
23 They take the form of self-flying paper airplanes in the Harry Potter books
24 Topping for a 25-Across
25 Piece of cake, say
27 Improv class exercises
29 Kids
30 Without aim
31 Mob
33 Fish whose males bear the young
35 Evening gala
37 Note-taking spot?
38 Sustained period of luck, as with dice
39 Litter critter
40 Floor plan unit
42 Restless desire
46 What Franklin famously asked for
49 Floor plan spec
50 Blog feed inits.
52 Debtor's letters
53 Email holder
54 Something lent to a friend
55 Set of skills, metaphorically
57 Father of Scout, in "To Kill a Mockingbird"
59 Declare
61 Best Actor winner Malek
63 Normandy battle site
65 Wads
66 Last dance?
69 Managed an unmanageable group, figuratively
72 Wonder Woman accessory
73 Aware of
75 Playroom chest
76 Downwind
77 They're worn on heads with tails
79 Store
81 Was first
83 Ka ___ (southernmost point on Hawaii)
84 Prefix with -graph
85 Run on
86 Singer Brickell
87 Believed something without question
89 Commercial lead-in to land
91 Elizabeth Warren vis-à-vis former chief justice Earl Warren, e.g.
95 It's frequently under fire
96 Prepare to bathe
98 Olivia Benson's division on TV: Abbr.
99 Conditional word
102 Expressively creative
104 First of the metalloids
106 Border
107 Flight recorder
108 ___ complex
111 A much greater quantity
113 Lead-in to fit or active
114 ___ New Guinea
115 Foreword
117 Org. that kicked off again in 2020 after a 19-year hiatus
118 Studio behind "Platoon" and "Amadeus"
119 Salary negotiator
120 Adversary
121 Embodiment of slipperiness
122 Word before or after short
123 One of the six simple machines
124 State pair: Abbr.
125 Mrs., in Mexico

DOWN

1 Transportation for the Doctor on "Doctor Who"
2 Small suit
3 Tries to make the unappealing attractive
4 Eeyore-ish sentiment
5 Stocking stuffer
6 Donkey Kong, e.g.
7 Imbroglios
8 Play charades
9 Setting for a Sistine Chapel painting
10 Results from
11 Near
12 "Methought I was enamour'd of an ___": Titania
13 Brand of rum
14 Improper
15 Best Actress winner Zellweger
16 Tiny fractions of joules
18 "___ Would Be King," 2018 novel by Wayétu Moore
20 Attach, in a way
26 Stack topper
28 Iconic Chevy
29 "You nailed it!"
32 ___ page
34 Spanish "now"
36 Olympic pentathlete's need
38 Well-being
40 Purse part
41 Flying Clouds and Royales
43 Be fully qualified . . . or a hint to interpreting this puzzle's shaded squares
44 Author of "The Silent World: A Story of Undersea Discovery and Adventure"
45 Czech reformer Jan
46 Coastal inlets
47 It might get a licking
48 Combination meant to change behavior
51 Starter earring
56 Play piano, informally
58 Machu Picchu builder
60 Something frequently made with the eyes shut
62 X-ray alternative, maybe
64 Spanish treasure
67 Anthem starter
68 Businesses with a portmanteau name
70 "It Ain't Me Babe" songwriter
71 Percolate
74 Zip
77 No. in a directory
78 Wimbledon wear, perhaps
80 Chooses not to act
82 Academia figure
88 It follows the Hijri calendar
90 Protruding bit of bedrock
92 Form a new mental picture of
93 Got away
94 Sharing word
97 Canon competitor
99 Leaves weaponless
100 One participating in a new Summer Olympics sport in 2021
101 Fashion designer McCartney
102 Heads-up
103 Two to one, say
105 Time and again
107 Warner ___
109 Like the Liberty Bell in 1846, for the last time
110 Big name in British art
112 Hall-of-Fame catcher Campanella
114 Print maker
116 Tulsa-to-Des Moines dir.

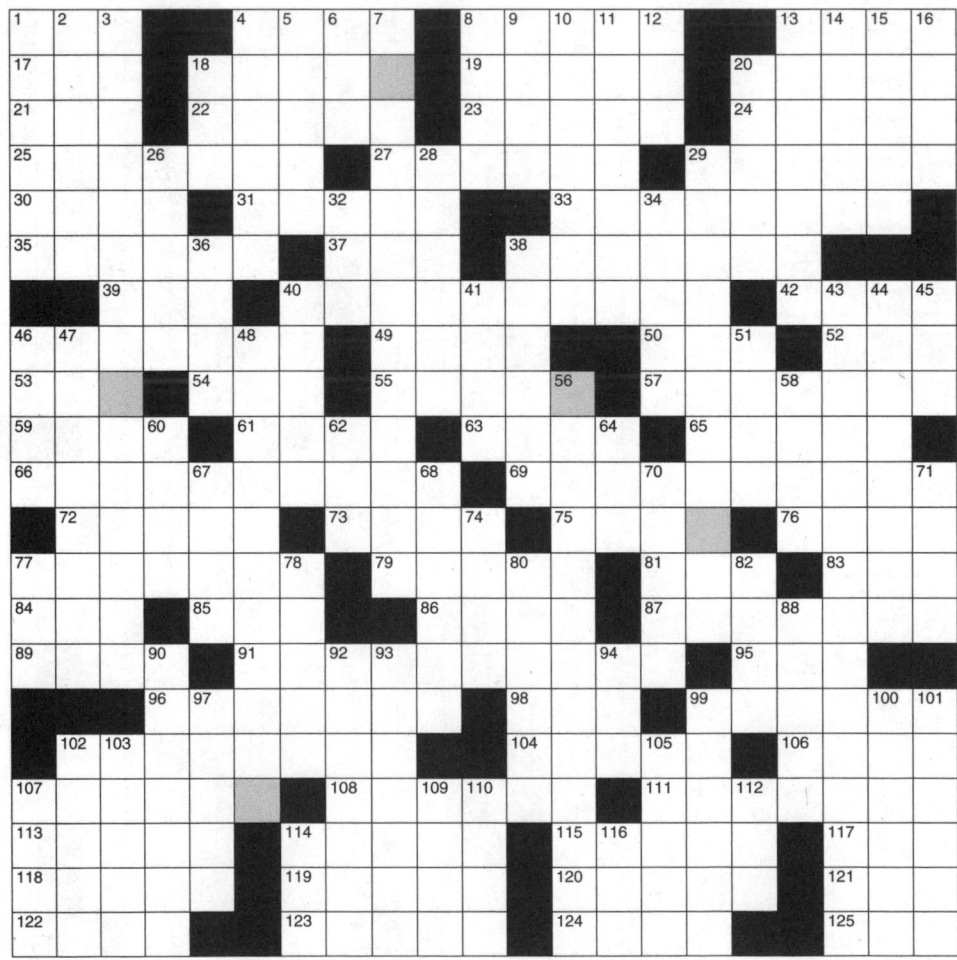

by Laura Taylor Kinnel

ACROSS

1 "The King of Latin Pop"
9 "The Tale of ____ Puddle-Duck" (Beatrix Potter children's book)
15 Give an address
20 Onscreen twins, often
21 Ruler of the afterlife, in Egyptian mythology
22 Benefit of some online purchases
23 Chore for a censor?
25 LaBelle or LuPone
26 With, at a café
27 The Cards, on scoreboards
28 Chore for a satellite TV technician?
30 Wayne's sidekick in old "S.N.L." skits
32 What a digital subscription might end
34 Current location
35 Certify formally, with "to"
36 Scientist who said "I have no special talents. I am only passionately curious"
40 Wet weather wear
42 Chore for a security guard?
47 Notch-like
50 Wildcatter's target
51 ____ Na Na
52 "Othello" setting
54 Like a list of lists of lists
55 Kristen of "Bridesmaids"
57 ____ Verde National Park
60 Having zero talent for
63 Wisconsin senator Johnson
64 Person to look out for
67 Chore for a rower?
69 "Chandelier" singer, 2014
70 "Be honest!"
72 Hoppy medium?
73 Chore for a knight?
77 Eats daintily
82 Japanese vegetable
83 Icy moon of Jupiter
84 Author James
85 Air Force 1 maker
86 Calf-length skirt
88 Bakery enticements
90 "Come to think of it . . ."
93 Proven postulate
94 Zen principle
97 Chore for a dog-walker?
101 More watered down
103 Statement before a demonstration
104 Children's author Richard
106 Insurance giant
109 It's spotted at the craps table
110 Fool, in Canadian slang
114 Chore for an N.F.L. owner?
117 Pro at deductions
119 Daughter of Katie Holmes and Tom Cruise
120 "The Princess Bride" character ____ Montoya
121 Chore for a bowling alley employee?
125 Carrying a key?
126 Forthcoming
127 Goes wild
128 Horse ____
129 Double-black diamond section of a ski mountain, with "the"
130 With a firm grip

DOWN

1 Conference attendee's clip-on
2 Tropical sorbet flavor
3 Magic, once
4 The people's choice
5 B'way posting
6 Kitty paper
7 Utah resort town
8 Fixed charge
9 Average guy
10 Abbr. on a city limits sign
11 Certain Spanish Surrealist paintings
12 Ticked off
13 Cause of a small setback
14 World's largest tennis stadium, familiarly
15 Hitting the right note
16 Common Christmas entree
17 Where Groucho, Chico and Harpo spent a night
18 Crispy cookie brand
19 Live
24 Like most modern TVs, informally
29 Judo levels
31 Coxae, familiarly
33 Most common surname in Brazil
37 Math degree
38 Former SeaWorld attraction
39 San Francisco's ____ Valley
41 Patent
42 Scattered about
43 Nintendo gaming console with a pileup of vowels
44 Tourney format, for short
45 Baked
46 Potential result of social unrest
48 ____ mess (traditional English dessert)
49 Cold and humid
53 "Germ" that's passed from one child to another
56 Heroic exploit
58 Bewitch
59 Redundant name for a drink
61 Captain with a whalebone leg
62 Bad thing for a bluffer
65 Ceremony
66 Home to the landmark Koko Crater
67 Poet ____ Scott-Heron
68 Served as
71 It's due south of Hollywood
73 Shoving match, in a way
74 Thor's father
75 Motel 6 alternative
76 Strike
78 Tops
79 Isolated team of workers, in business-speak
80 "I guess"
81 6:00 broadcast
84 Didn't just assume
87 Noble thing
89 German exclamation
91 "That hits the spot"
92 Michelle of "Crazy Rich Asians"
95 Helmet opening
96 Scottish terrier type
98 Actor Robert of "Spenser: For Hire"
99 Eyes, informally
100 Like the rank of major general
102 Lambaste
104 Barbecue rods
105 Vessel whose name anagrams to where it might be used
107 Woods who voiced Cinderella
108 Open space in a forest
111 Snarky challenge
112 Swashbuckling Flynn
113 Like investing in a start-up
115 Loops in, in a way
116 Small cut
118 Bad fit
122 Six-pt. plays
123 Chapel Hill sch.
124 Houston sch.

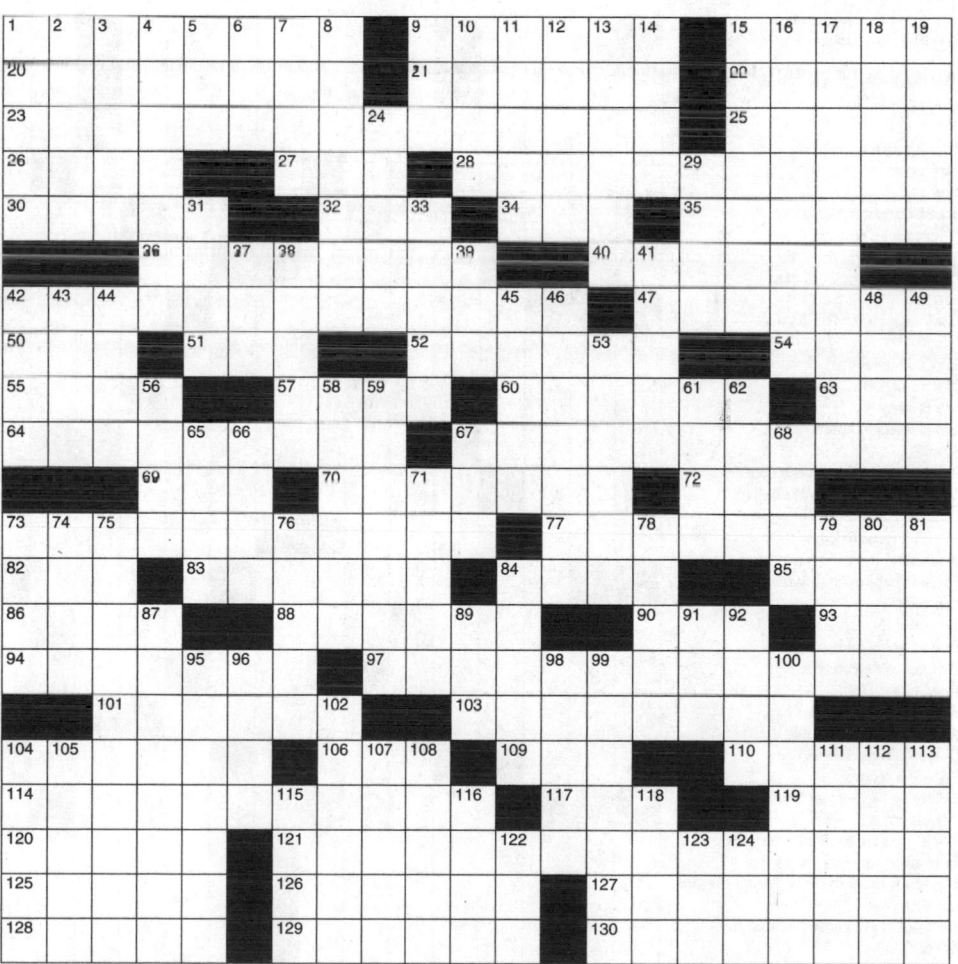

by Samuel A. Donaldson

158 DOUBLES PLAY

ACROSS

1 Ones out of this world, for short
4 Club setting for scenes in "GoodFellas" and "Raging Bull"
11 Something pressed in an emergency
19 ____ Lee (dessert brand)
20 Gets better
21 Oppressive dominance
22 *Performers who set the bar high?
24 *Go-getter's maxim
25 In a way
26 Eves
28 One-named Grammy-winning singer
29 Worried exclamation from Astro on "The Jetsons"
30 Writer and film critic James
31 Platinum-selling rapper-turned-TV cop
33 Sr.'s hurdle
36 English cathedral city
37 Brand with a jingle to the "Dragnet" theme
39 *Public health agency's mission
43 Part of a ventilation system
46 Actress and civil rights activist Ruby ____
47 Boors
48 *Feature of a Chippendales show
51 Fix the colors on, say
54 Boor
55 Special orders on new autos
56 It means well in Italy
57 P.R. event
59 Smooth sailing
60 Gas numbers
63 Bug
66 Stand-up comic Wong
67 *Places for coasters
70 Move in a hurry, quaintly
71 Best horse of the 20th century, per The Associated Press
73 Language spoken on Easter Island
74 Jazz's Jackson
75 Matriarch's title, maybe
78 Chats away
79 Large musical combo
80 Spud
82 Palate cleansers between courses
84 *How to screw in a light bulb
86 Common chords
88 "I didn't need to know that"
89 Tries hard
91 *What keeps up standards in the radio business?
94 Temple cabinets
95 End of many addresses
98 Pioneer of detective fiction
99 Reed in a pit
100 A while back
103 Author/magazine editor Welteroth
105 Singer/activist Horne
107 Half of a record
109 Celebrity . . . but just barely
110 *"Holy moly!"
114 *Occasion for hiding in the dark
116 In trouble, metaphorically
117 Genre for the Smashing Pumpkins and Liz Phair
118 Beat poem allegedly inspired by a peyote vision
119 Carpentry contraption
120 Words of understanding
121 Italian diminutive suffix

DOWN

1 Lengthy reprimand, so to speak
2 Lowbrow
3 Taste
4 "Ouch!"
5 Half of some matching sets
6 Put away
7 Hold tightly
8 National Medal of Arts winner Davis
9 Played miniature golf
10 Altar place
11 Snap
12 Inverse trig function
13 Choking hazard label
14 How TV shows may be shown
15 Some Montanans
16 Plant part
17 ____ king
18 Spanish chess piece
19 Put away for later
23 Expert advice
27 Evaluate, as an opponent
30 Phoenix sch.
32 Like polka
33 What sheep participate in
34 Plant part
35 Alternatively
38 Summer hrs. in Colorado
40 Words of commitment
41 Pyle's portrayer on "Gomer Pyle, U.S.M.C."
42 Pang
43 Love, in Lyon
44 Defeat soundly
45 Couple of fins
48 Head of ____
49 Happy refrain
50 National economic prosperity, metaphorically
52 Adolescent
53 "What's up?," in textspeak
56 A.C. measure
58 First man, in Maori mythology
60 Oil-rich nation that's not in OPEC
61 Sour milk product
62 Cathedral in N.Y.C.
64 "Revelations" choreographer
65 Small, in a way
67 Oscars, e.g.
68 Blue Ribbon brand
69 It's found in a key: Abbr.
72 Mountain nymph of Greek myth
74 Comfy shoes, for short
76 Writing on many a license plate
77 Opposing forces in Risk
79 Preventing spills, say
80 Sporty option
81 Folk singer Guthrie
83 H.S. class
84 Monopoly token
85 Have a serious crush on, informally
87 Less expressive
90 Issa of "Insecure"
92 Puts down
93 Little bump
95 Ancestor of the modern lemon and lime
96 Ring combo
97 She played "the devil" Miranda in "The Devil Wears Prada"
101 "Dagnabbit!"
102 Kind of pants
104 Japanese beer brand
105 Partially landlocked bay
106 Drachma replacement
108 "My word!"
109 Five of these are needed to play Yahtzee
110 Astronaut Grissom
111 Transcript fig.
112 Topic discussed by the bar
113 Barely manage, with "out"
115 Children's author Asquith

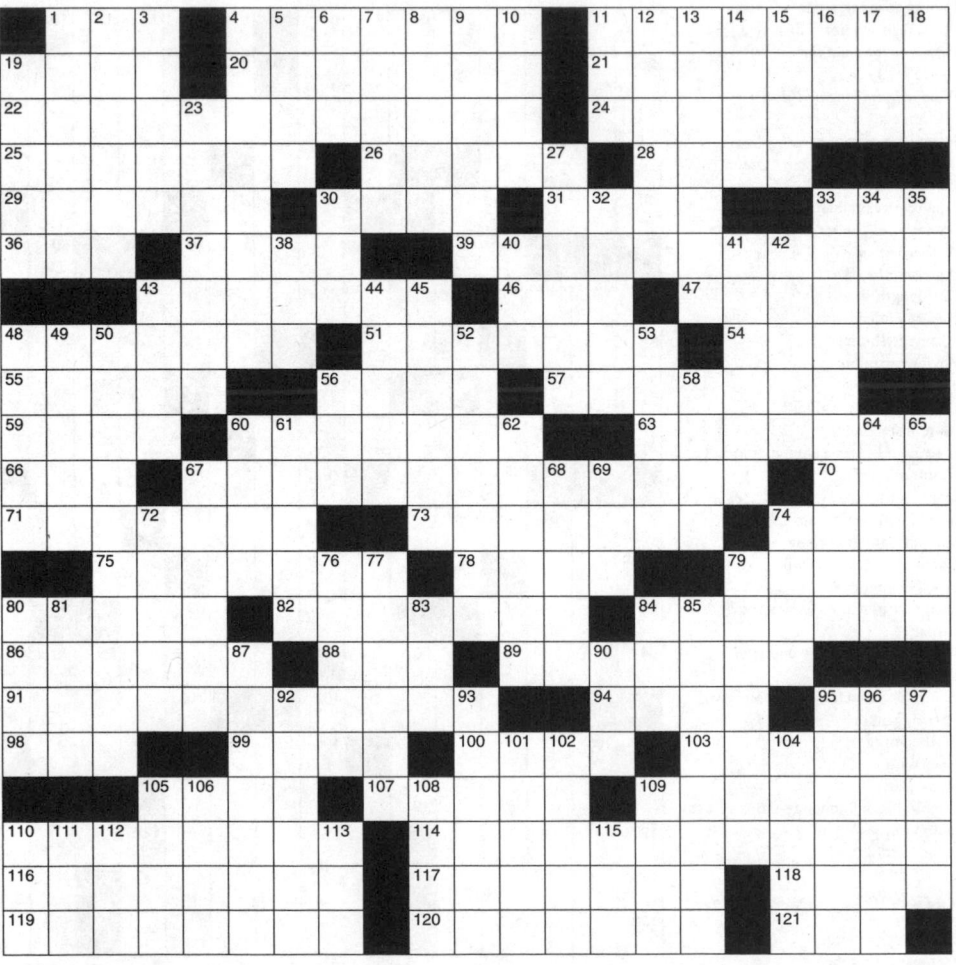

by Wyna Liu

ACROSS

1 Miss
5 More than excited
10 Grub for a grub
14 Elliptical
18 Where a phone might be tapped
19 Last Oldsmobile model
20 Site of the Bocca Nuova crater
21 Regional flora and fauna
22 Facial feature of a Lego man?
24 Sparkling Italian wine
25 With 81-Across, flashy basketball play
26 Completely remove
27 Blew off steam?
29 "Hold your horses"
31 Word before job or joke
33 Emcee during a power outage?
37 Regulus is its brightest star
38 Small change?
40 Most eccentric
41 Formerly
42 What means most in the end?
43 Some somber music
45 "So what?"
46 Tailor's measurement
48 "The elite fighter pilots may skip the rest of the lecture"?
53 New Cub Scout
54 Hairy hunter of Genesis
55 Looney Tunes devil, for short
56 Hostile declaration
59 Decision
60 Expense for a political campaign
62 List of available courses
64 What the abscissa and ordinate are measured from
66 Take in
67 Drive a getaway car through Australia's outback?
72 Cousin _____ ("Jimmy Kimmel Live" regular)
74 Major account
75 Nickname of a 2010s pop idol, with "the"
76 Bird in Liberty Mutual commercials
77 Workmates
79 Answer
81 See 25-Across
84 When Caesar is told to "Beware the ides of March"
87 Give in
89 What you might do after the movie previews are finally over?
93 Yeshiva instructor
94 Civil War side: Abbr.
96 Group who ought to know better?
97 Rx prescribers
98 Pioneering programmer Lovelace
99 Fish whose name means "very strong" in Hawaiian
103 Put away
105 "The devil's lettuce"
106 Where spaghetti and orzo rank in terms of their suitability for making necklaces?
109 Resident of Japan's "second city"
111 _____ Mendeleev, creator of the periodic table
112 Martin _____, star of 1960s TV's "Route 66"
114 Opera singer Fleming
116 Play with, as a toy mouse
118 To boot
120 One who believes exclusively in a sea god?
122 Political columnist Molly
123 Noted Christian
124 Role in the 2005 hit musical "Jersey Boys"
125 Electric flux symbols
126 "Pretty please?"
127 Like child's play
128 County on the Thames
129 Legal postponement

DOWN

1 What Winthrop speaks with in "The Music Man"
2 Give in
3 Musicians' slip-ups
4 Hang-ups
5 Fannie _____
6 Isaac Newton, by hobby
7 Classic soda brand
8 Source of the word "galore"
9 Xbox and GameCube
10 Cause
11 Long-distance travelers, informally
12 Composer Dvorak
13 Passed out
14 De-squeaked
15 Thick cloud above a peak
16 Took in
17 _____ of the land
21 System used in computer code
23 Frist's successor as Senate majority leader
28 That, in Spanish
30 Quizzical utterances
32 Actress Conn of "Grease"
34 Popular tablets
35 Antique shop deal
36 Stove-top item
37 Where a herd might be heard
39 Aretha Franklin's Grammy-nominated sister
44 Thingamajig
47 Kind of order for the circled letters in this puzzle
49 Swedish Air Force supplier
50 Guys
51 Making a clerical error?
52 Exercise in dexterity
53 Grease
57 Cry from a nursery
58 The king of diamonds carries one
61 It might be glassy or icy
63 Ragtime great Blake
65 Shrub that produces a crimson-colored spice
67 Two-time Emmy winner for "30 Rock"
68 Common thing to lie about
69 Rule that ended in 1947
70 Prime cut
71 "_____ is life"
72 Carving in a cartouche
73 Business whose patrons are often fighting
78 Entanglement
80 #44
82 Completely embarrasses, slangily
83 Piece of music that evokes the countryside
85 Certain percussion player
86 Home of the Komodo dragon
88 Knuckleheads
90 *Swoon*
91 Southwestern ski resort
92 Prime meridian std.
94 Absurd pretense
95 20-Across's island, to locals
100 Sum total: Abbr.
101 Storehouse
102 _____ polloi
104 Voting district
107 Like the newspaper Al-Shabiba
108 Ancient empire builders
110 Something to play for
113 Some are shockers
115 Online handicrafts marketplace
116 Part of many a postcard, briefly
117 Gardner of old Hollywood
119 Nine-symbol message
121 Word often spoken in pig Latin

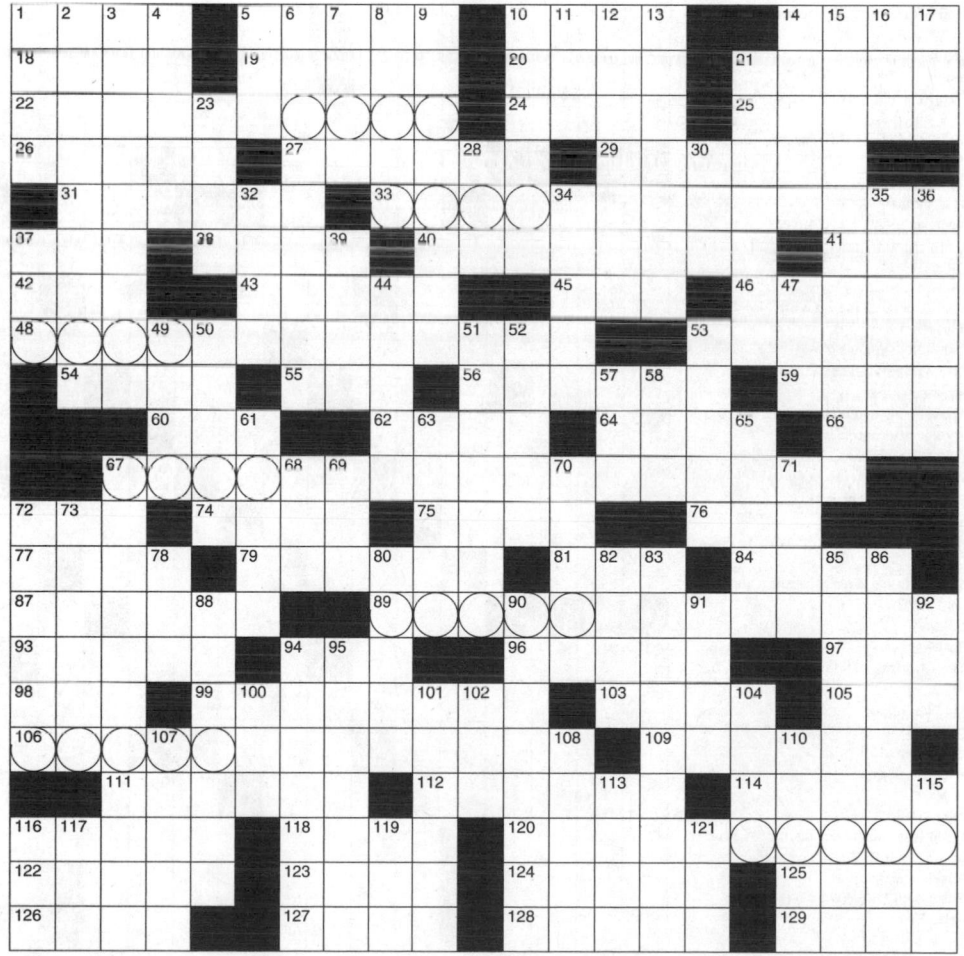

by Trenton Charlson

160 PUZZLIN'

ACROSS

1 What can fall off a shelf
8 Host of MSNBC's "PoliticsNation" beginning in 2011
16 Be profane
20 Something never seen at night
21 Beckoning words
22 For ____ amount of time
23 Nobody but the guy gettin' married on his feet?
25 Put up with
26 Captures
27 House vote
28 Gettysburg general George
29 Like screwball comedies
33 Pig food
34 Gish ____, novelist of "The Resisters" and "Typical American"
35 Sickly-looking
36 Olympic equipment weighing less than 770 grams each
38 Winter item you'll be wearin' for years?
42 Statistic tracked at census.gov/popclock
44 "Mixed Marriage" playwright St. John Greer ____
45 Reduced in rank
46 Receiver of an all-points bulletin
48 Longtime Yankees first baseman Mark
50 Simile's center
51 Row
52 God who becomes a goddess when an "r" is removed
53 Spam sender
54 James of "The Godfather"
58 Danger when walkin' in a silo?
61 One who delivers
62 Mansfield of old Hollywood
63 "Er, uh, that is . . ."
64 Dada pioneer
65 ____ Paulo
66 Rock singers?
67 Hedge fund titan nicknamed "The Palindrome"
68 "Sorry, am ____ your way?"
69 Drivin' around the lot with pop-pop?
71 Overhead expenses?
72 Private Twitter transmissions, for short
73 "Absofruitalicious" cereal, in ads
74 Sponge alternative
75 Slangy possessive
76 What a pro bono lawyer provides
78 Very observant person
80 Shoulder blade
84 Pickup truck capacity, maybe
86 Detects
87 Sayin' "Look, here's the thing about dry land . . ."?
90 To-dos
91 Batting ninth
92 The Children's Defense Fund, e.g., in brief
93 Medical breakthrough
95 "Ish"
96 Boiling mad
97 West Bank grp.
98 Realize
101 Kind
102 What was causin' the doctor to check for joint pain?
108 Very consequential
109 The North Pole vis-à-vis the South Pole, e.g.
110 Go as low as
111 French/Belgian river
112 Apollo and others
113 "Understood"

DOWN

1 Online exchange, in brief
2 Animal feared by an ailurophobe
3 "What's your ____?" (question to a guest en route)
4 Recycling container
5 Michael who wrote "The Neverending Story"
6 Restricts, with "in"
7 Washing machine setting
8 Windshield clearer
9 Certain earring
10 Singer Tori
11 "What's the Frequency, Kenneth?" band
12 Call of the wild?
13 One trading dollars for quarters
14 Paris suburb
15 French marshal in the Napoleonic Wars
16 Camila with the 2018 #1 hit "Havana"
17 Employ with regularity
18 Bird also known as a little auk
19 Scattered (about)
24 Blue Muppet with a pink nose
28 Obsidian, once
29 Aquarium creature with black-and-white stripes
30 Capital in the South Pacific
31 Teasing words when someone starts listing the digits of pi, say
32 Mythical creature seen on old Bhutanese stamps
34 Rock's Joplin
35 Hägar the Horrible's dog
37 Sure winners
39 Cross-country camping expedition, maybe
40 Treat as a bed
41 Hit the nail on the head, e.g.
43 Meager
47 Pope Francis' homeland: Abbr.
49 Modern library borrowing
52 Bring in
54 Longtime media columnist David
55 Mate's reply
56 Basketball Hall-of-Famer who was the first woman to sign an N.B.A. contract
57 Single-serving coffee brand
59 Landlocked Asian country
60 ____ Gorbachev, former first lady of the Soviet Union
61 His tombstone reads "Workers of all lands unite"
62 Moves like Jell-O
65 Told
66 Hiccups
68 Coming-out announcement
69 Buttinsky
70 Certain nest egg, for short
72 Blue-and-white earthenware pottery
73 Dramatic ballroom dance
76 Two-time Best Actress winner Rainer
77 Eva of "Desperate Housewives"
78 Ho-hum feelings
79 Opposite of exo-
80 Soft and wet
81 ____ oxide (red compound)
82 Egg carton spec
83 Special dinner order
85 Boo-boos
88 Home past curfew
89 Like the Met Gala
94 Online notice for a party
97 Phnom ____, Cambodia
98 "____ to tyrants, and my country's friend" (words of Cato in "Julius Caesar")
99 Naval officer: Abbr.
100 Grandson of Eve
102 Budgetary excess
103 Make a decision
104 "There but for the grace of God ____"
105 Intel missions
106 Western native
107 About one inch of a foot

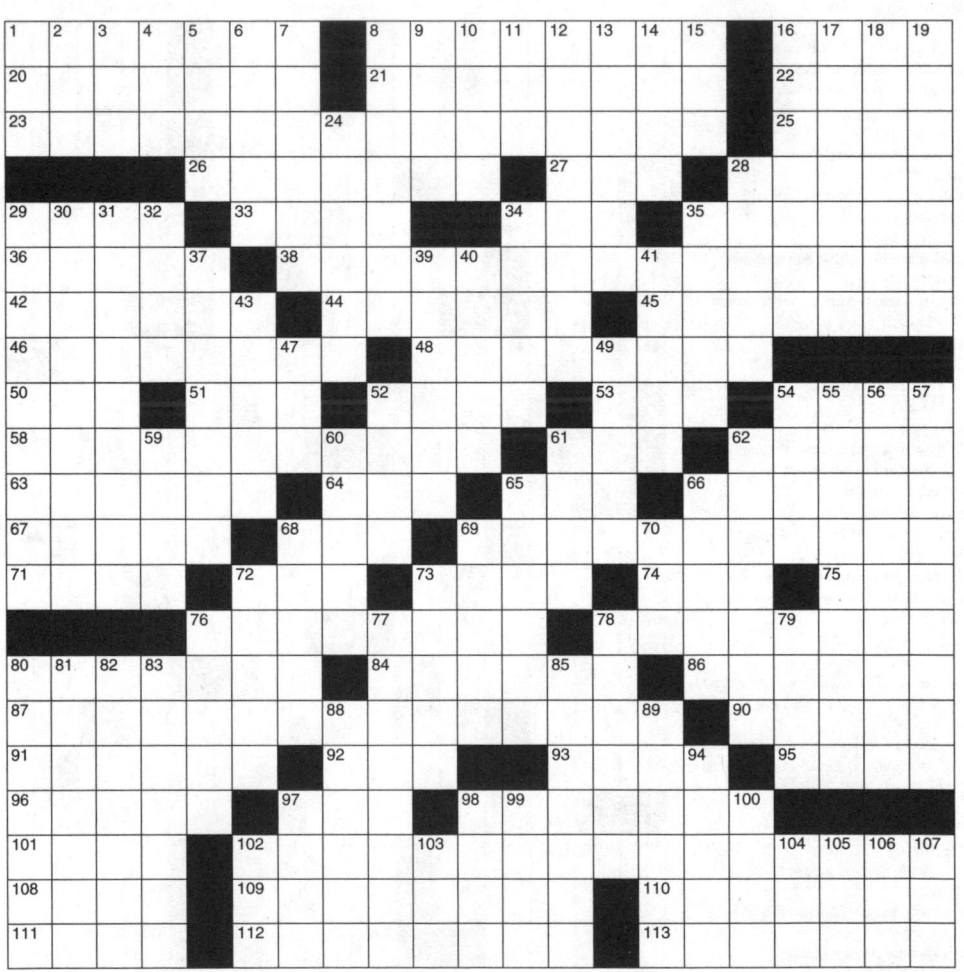

by David Levinson Wilk

ACROSS

1 Front
7 Spanish rice
12 Little sucker?
15 Smallish batteries
18 Like a seacoast after a storm, maybe
19 Ferris Bueller's girlfriend
20 ____ B. Wells, civil rights pioneer
21 ____-mo
22 S as in soup?
23 Kind of drawing
25 Icarus's downfall
26 Skip work for health reasons
28 Words after "Ooh, ooh!"
29 Beau, to Brigitte
30 Verbal stumbles
31 Baseball catcher
32 Ire
34 Boy band with two members who previously starred on "The Mickey Mouse Club"
36 Little suckers
37 Headgear for a tailgater
39 One of the Arnazes
40 ". . . but it's up to you"
43 Famously green shampoo
45 Rap's Shakur
47 Pope after Benedict IV
48 *Winter vacation destination
51 Parades
54 Barely beat
55 Goals
56 Silverback gorilla, e.g.
58 Moreno with an Emmy, Grammy, Oscar and Tony
60 Drag racing vehicles
62 "____ trap!"
63 Meager
65 Tired
66 In perfect order . . . or, as two words, what's formed by applying the answers for the five starred clues to the circled letters
70 Dined at home
71 More skeptical
73 "Hamilton" actor Leslie ____ Jr.
74 Break down, to a Brit
76 Theory
77 Sea ____
79 Prefix with -plasm
80 Piece paid by Pisans for a piece of pizza, previously
82 Safe places
84 *Multi-episode narrative
87 Crucifix inscription
88 Relentlessly question
90 En ____ (as a whole)
91 Having tattoos
92 Event that's a bit off?
94 The butler, stereotypically
97 It gives Ford an "F": Abbr.
99 Buff
100 First Alaskan on a major U.S. party ticket
101 E-4, E-5 and E-6, in the U.S. Navy, in brief
102 Successors to LPs
105 Part of Canada above Alta. and Sask.
106 One of the Gandhis
109 Where to get a mullet trimmed
112 "____ get it now!"
113 *Civic center
115 Colored ring
116 Washington's Sea-____ Airport
117 Non's opposite
118 Ban . . . or bandit
119 By and large
120 College entrance exam org.
121 Hosp. V.I.P.s
122 Author Zora ____ Hurston
123 Son of Aphrodite

DOWN

1 Compete in one leg of a modern pentathlon
2 Loud, as the surf
3 Chills
4 Not incl.
5 Set the boundaries of
6 Perfect
7 Smart ____
8 Painter of the "Four Freedoms" series, 1943
9 Sound from a cheering crowd
10 Even
11 Pinnacle
12 ____ Chemical Company, onetime maker of VapoRub
13 Writer Serwer of The Atlantic
14 Event planner's need
15 Attempts
16 They're listed by degrees
17 ____ boom
19 Struck, old-style
24 Bygone Apple messaging app
27 Members of a blended family
33 Move, in Realtor jargon
35 *Airport logjam
36 *Rick, Ilsa and Victor had one in "Casablanca"
37 First lady between Eleanor and Mamie
38 Fanny
40 Accented cheer
41 Raggedy Ann and Raggedy Andy, for two
42 Restricted zone
44 "Ba-dum-tss"
46 Education support grps.
48 ____ Paulo, Brazil
49 Sea route, e.g.
50 "Frozen" queen
52 Endless YouTube viewing, e.g.
53 French island off the coast of Newfoundland
57 Tropical yellow fruits
59 Writer Rand
61 New York city with a marina
62 Suffix with tour or Tory
64 ____-El (Superman's birth name)
65 Conflict during which the Lusitania was sunk: Abbr.
67 Fateful date
68 What's left at sea
69 Dig in
72 Flat, round bread cooked on a griddle
75 Noted congresswoman from the Bronx, familiarly
78 After-bath application
79 Anatomical sac
81 Hoped-for response to an SOS
83 Lien holder, e.g.
85 Ahab's father in the Bible
86 Desert's lack
89 Hogwarts professor who was secretly a werewolf
91 "Awkward Black Girl" creator and star
92 "Who cares?"
93 Slapstick silliness
95 Gary who created "The Far Side"
96 Award to be hung
98 Start of a playground joke
99 U.S. govt. bond
101 Compass letters
102 Unisex fragrance
103 ____ Street, Perry Mason's secretary
104 Strong ropes used to support masts
107 Verb preceder
108 Bad things on motorists' records, for short
110 "Dies ____" (hymn)
111 Curb, with "in"
114 The Jazz, on scoreboards

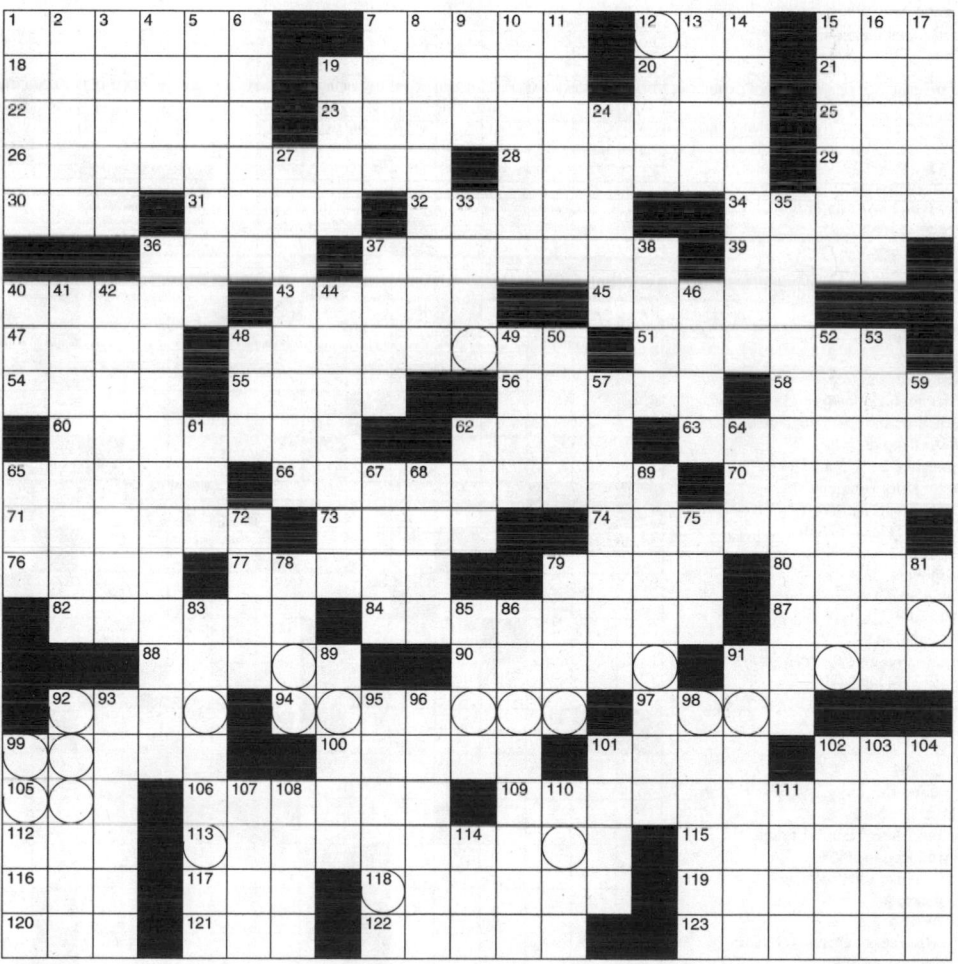

by Ruth Bloomfield Margolin

ACROSS

1 Red Guard members
8 They can get canceled
14 Sticky situation
20 Remove braids from
21 "Likewise!"
22 Way to go
23 Alternative title for "The Dirty Dozen"?
25 Sorted in order
26 Hear here!
27 Complete
28 "Vous êtes ___" (French map notation)
30 Alan with six Emmys
31 Pulled from a raffle drum
33 Alternative title for "Cleopatra"?
38 Words to a betrayer
40 Partner of cut
41 St. ___ Chapel, New York City public building in continuous use since 1766
42 Dessert often topped with caramel sauce
45 Newswire co.
47 Zip
48 Disc brake components
51 Alternative title for "Frankenstein"?
55 Took a load off
56 Monopoly token elected by an internet vote
57 "Sure, that makes sense"
58 Trust
60 "___ Another" (NPR game show)
62 Toyota model since 1966
64 Van ___, Calif.
65 D.C. donor
67 "Hey, pal, over here!"
68 With 70-Across, alternative title for "To Kill a Mockingbird"?
70 See 68-Across
72 Female friend, in France
75 Phillipa who played Eliza in the original cast of "Hamilton"
76 Hook's sidekick
79 "The Hangover" co-star
83 Mortgage co.
85 Just out of the freezer
88 They feature clowns and rope tricks
89 Grp. organizing school dances
90 Make a move
92 Alternative title for "Titanic"?
94 Hello Kitty company
96 Calendar spans: Abbr.
97 Actress Tyler who will be an apt age in 2031
98 Stopovers
99 Gives a hoot
101 "Ella and ___" (1956 jazz album)
104 Sandal brand
106 Alternative title for "Gone Girl"?
110 Sheepskin holders
114 Shankar who taught sitar to George Harrison
115 ASCAP alternative
116 ___-faire
118 "Blueberries for ___" (classic children's book)
119 Nabisco's first cracker brand, introduced in 1899
121 Alternative title for "The Name of the Rose"?
126 Duck dish
127 "Welp, guess I have to try again"
128 Develop over time
129 Lowbrow art
130 Round things?
131 Terry Bradshaw, for his entire career

DOWN

1 Like commercials, often
2 First name of a Peace Nobelist that ends ironically
3 "Einstein on the Beach," e.g.
4 "___ say!"
5 Scholar
6 Seating section
7 Recipients of venture capital
8 Joined a petition
9 What a dental scaler removes
10 Senator Klobuchar
11 Production co. behind "Rhoda" and "Newhart"
12 "Once upon a midnight dreary . . ." penner
13 Ending with ultra- or super-
14 Sauce on chicken Parmesan
15 Parts of zygotes
16 French automaker
17 They don't go much higher than the tongue
18 Soft leather
19 Two-door or four-door
24 Unenthused response to "Wanna?"
29 Upper limit
32 Turned in
34 Charles ___, religious leader known as "The Father of Modern Revivalism"
35 Lengths for rulers
36 Killed time
37 Workload that must be met
39 Pets kept in terrariums
42 Bank-backing grp.
43 Something trademarked
44 Laptop brand
46 "___ be an honor"
49 Head-butts
50 [Actually, don't delete this]
52 Smooth-tongued
53 Painter Magritte
54 "The Simpsons" character with a Ph.D.
55 Catch
59 Nail polish brand
61 Shortcut for a frequent contact
63 Approximately
66 Outmoded part of a laptop
69 Hither and ___
70 What a koozie might keep cool
71 Seller of the Ultimate Waffle Sandwich
72 Nile snakes
73 ___ Hari
74 "Regardless . . ."
76 Stone to cast?
77 Slugger Hideki named the 2009 World Series M.V.P.
78 Pasture parent
80 Nuevo ___ (Mexican state)
81 Like grass you can smell, perhaps
82 IDs assigned at birth: Abbr.
84 Boxer Ali
86 Tharp who choreographed "Hair"
87 Modem letters
91 Soothing summer soak
93 Chart-toppers
95 Raised sculptures
100 Prefix with pathetic
102 Needs medicine, say
103 Humble abodes
105 Italian city NW of Milan
106 Semi, e.g.
107 Ho Chi Minh Mausoleum city
108 Food item
109 "The Loco-Motion" singer Little ___
111 Standard
112 Not glossy
113 More underhanded
117 "A likely story!"
120 O.E.D. part: Abbr.
122 Casablanca's country: Abbr.
123 Ivy League nickname
124 Make a break for it
125 Had

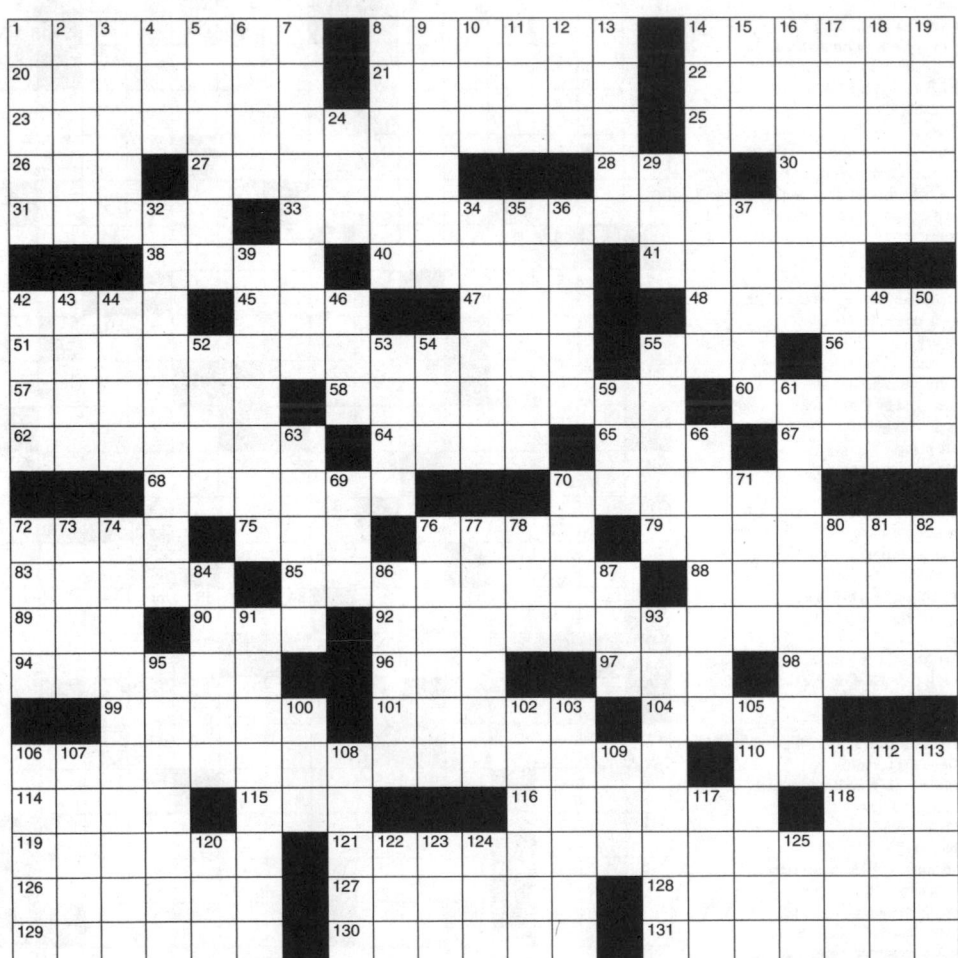

by Francis Heaney

ACROSS

1 Enjoy the sun
5 Completely committed
10 One to whom you tell *everything*
13 Hit show with the series finale "One for the Road"
19 Predator of the Pacific Northwest
20 _____-Grain (breakfast bar brand)
21 Singer Carly _____ Jepsen
22 "Give me a minute"
23 Iditarod, for one?
26 Intertwine
27 Show stoppers?
28 German "please"
29 Bronze that's not winning any awards?
30 Station
31 One driving kids around in a Subaru?
33 B-side to the Beatles' "Ticket to Ride"
36 Ginger, e.g.
37 Turn down
40 Longtime home for Terry Gross
41 Boasts
43 In the same family
47 Letting out all the stops to drown out the other instruments?
52 Set on edge
53 Having the least give
54 Large in scope
55 It's sometimes covered in velvet
56 William who wrote "Shrek!"
57 Not on point
59 Slip of the fingers
61 Angsty genre
62 Cocaine and guns, in a Pacino movie?
67 What Consumer Reports lacks, unlike most other magazines
69 Buzz Lightyear and Woody, e.g.
70 Massive, in poetry
71 Whine connoisseurs?
74 Party symbol since 1870
76 "Is that really necessary?"
78 Jackson known as the "Queen of Gospel"
80 Sidestep
81 Troops who are worried about sun protection?
84 Like this clue
85 Basketball player, in old slang
86 Brain wave chart, for short
87 Like most prime numbers
88 All right
89 New York's iconic _____ Building
93 Give mom's mom the stink eye?
99 Decorative pillowcases
104 Sorry state
105 Juuls and such
106 Bug
108 Quick tennis match
109 "Twelve Days of Christmas" musician who invites sympathy?
111 When 13-Across aired for most of its run
112 Stick in a boat
113 Land in the so-called "Roof of the World"
114 Take into account?
115 Affectionate refusal
116 Fade away
117 Morning _____
118 Where a sloth spends most of its life

DOWN

1 Meals
2 French Foreign Legion, par exemple
3 Scallywag
4 Hummer's instrument
5 Poet Carson
6 Totes
7 Inc., in London
8 Classic Isaac Asimov collection of short stories
9 Ball of vinegared rice topped with raw fish
10 Angels' opposites
11 Side of a diamond
12 Charge
13 Penny pinchers
14 Express displeasure with on the road
15 "Oklahoma!" aunt
16 Excel function that uses a calendar
17 Puerto _____
18 Medical tube
24 Teeny
25 GPS suggestions: Abbr.
29 What a left parenthesis suggests in an emoticon
31 Resolute
32 Suffix with switch
34 Wraps up
35 Big name in music streaming
37 "Fiddlesticks!"
38 "So much for that"
39 Suffix with auto-
41 Middle: Abbr.
42 Where Simone Biles won four golds
43 Creative class
44 Crunchy, green side dish
45 Part of an agenda
46 Infamous emperor
47 Tiebreakers, briefly
48 Canceled out
49 Apple variety
50 A collar might hide it
51 Winters or Somers
52 Italian dumplings
55 Busy time at the I.R.S.: Abbr.
58 "One Mic" rapper
59 Non-U.S. M.L.B. team, on sports tickers
60 More scrumptious
63 Arundhati _____, winner of the 1997 Booker Prize
64 Inner: Prefix
65 What orchids may grow without
66 Lyre player of myth
67 Michelangelo's "The Creation of _____"
68 Peacenik
72 What might come down to the wire?
73 Opinion
75 Sorento or Sedona
76 G.I. fare
77 Former Mideast grp.
79 It helps turn a pond green
81 Word processing command
82 On tenterhooks, maybe
83 The "M" of MHz
85 Bar freebie
88 The A.P.'s Female Athlete of the Decade for the 2010s, familiarly
89 Trim
90 Trim
91 Dutch brewery
92 Car sticker fig.
93 [Not again!]
94 Slowly, in music
95 Correct
96 Perez of "Do the Right Thing"
97 Nurse back to health
98 Mouth-puckering
100 Focus of "Ocean's Eleven"
101 How some bonds are sold
102 Irish novelist _____ Binchy
103 Bender
106 Gradual deterioration
107 Without much thought
109 _____ hook (rock climbing technique)
110 Big step for a start-up, in brief

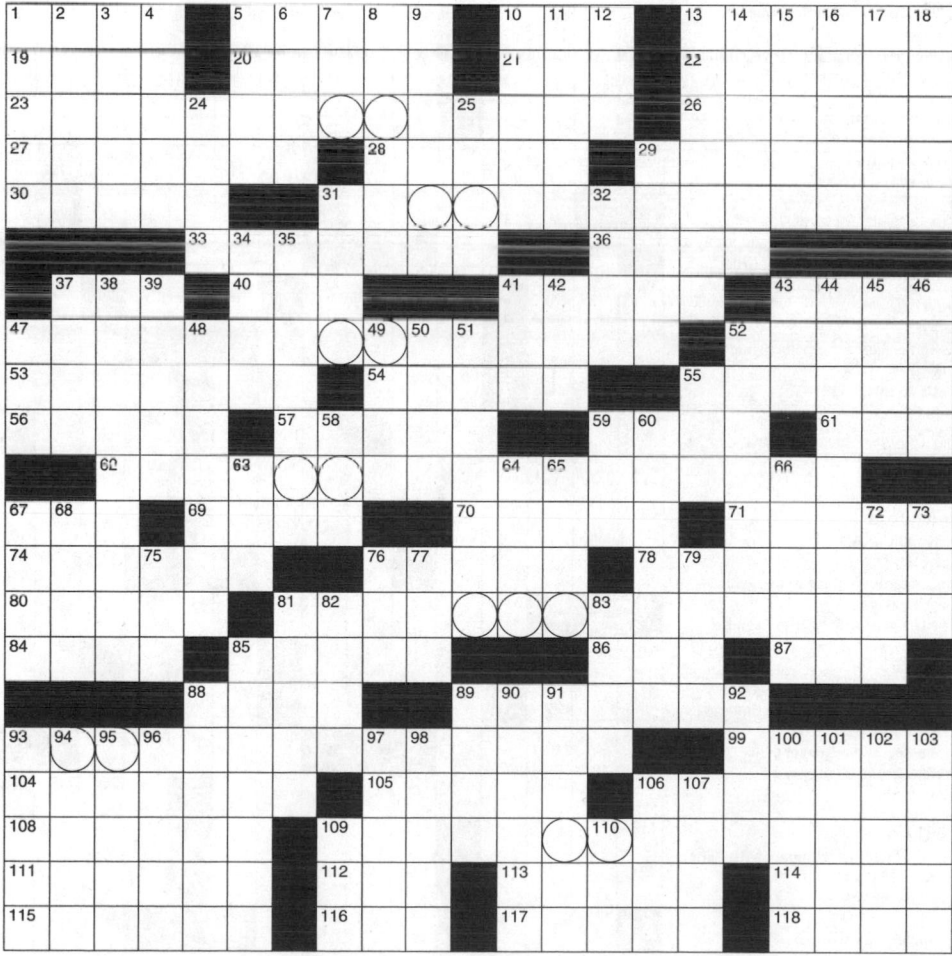

by Barbara Lin

ACROSS

1 Selling point?
5 "___ Catch 'Em All" (Pokémon theme song)
10 Gastric malady
15 Word aptly found in "price control"
19 Nobel laureate Morrison
20 Longtime daily TV show about the rich and famous
21 Mandarin greeting
22 One-named singer with Grammys in 1985 and 2010
23 Protected, in a way
24 Mathematical field that includes the 81-Across
26 Irritated mood
27 Custom-made, as a suit
29 Psychic energy fields
30 The Sims and others
32 Regal home
33 Remains here?
34 "Ciao!"
35 Magical resource in Magic: The Gathering
36 Pianist's pace
37 Sounds of disapproval
39 7/
40 Duds
44 Actress Susan of "The Partridge Family"
45 Soleus muscle locale
48 ". . . you get the idea"
50 Course for a non-Anglophone, for short
51 Keebler crew
53 Worker who might check all the boxes?
54 What may come after you
55 Invitation from a host
56 Scrap, slangily
58 Goddess of witchcraft
59 Hall-of-Fame QB Dawson
60 Split
62 A.L. East team . . . or, after changing a nearby black square, what a little movement by this puzzle's subject might cause
63 Kerfuffle
64 "Pitch Perfect" a cappella group, with "the"
66 "Let's do this!"
67 Bound for
69 Log
71 Prefix with -sphere
72 "You got it!"
74 Goblinlike creatures
75 Practical joke
76 Anesthetic of old
77 Tick off
78 Pop singer known for wearing face-covering wigs
79 When "Laverne & Shirley" ran for most of its run: Abbr.
80 Visionaries
81 Subject of this puzzle, as suggested visually by its central black squares
87 Sports figure
90 First name in the freezer aisle
91 Southeast Asian language
92 Flowed into
93 Table scraps
97 21st Greek letter
98 Famous literary nickname, with "The"
99 "Catch-22" pilot
100 Spanish title: Abbr.
102 Period
103 Computer data structure
105 Up
107 Ready to crash
109 With 113-Across, end of the definition

113 See 109-Across
117 Assessment: Abbr.
118 "Doe, ___ . . ."
119 Exchanges words, say
120 Bit of cunning
121 Repeated word in a Doris Day song
122 They have pointy teeth
123 Ish
124 Words of clarification when spelling
125 Math grouping seen in curly brackets
126 Tolkien race
127 Handles, as an account, in brief
128 Eight-bit gaming console, for short

DOWN

1 Wild guess
2 One of 42 on a Connect Four board
3 Start of a definition of the 81-Across
4 Baker's container
5 Creature that can lick its own eyes
6 Half of O.H.M.S.
7 After-dinner offering
8 Like "Waiting for Godot"
9 Convinced
10 Blue
11 Dupes, in a way
12 Stand-up comic Margaret
13 Wyatt, Morgan and Virgil of the Wild West

14 Rolls-___
15 Some college assignments
16 Middle of the definition
17 Comics dog who walks on two feet
18 N.B.A. team with black-and-white uniforms
25 "I'm listening . . ."
28 Wild Asian equines
31 Break out
35 1957 Broadway hit starring Robert Preston, with "The"
38 Twitch.tv user
39 Rabbit in a red dress
41 Noted 1836 battle site
42 They're parked at national parks
43 Mate for life?
45 Cereal that changes the color of the milk
46 Director DuVernay
47 Clear a path for
49 Bleeps
52 Toy on a grooved track
53 Help to settle
57 Another name for Cupid
58 The last of the Pillars of Islam
61 Seeing red?
65 Not on time for
68 Temporarily adopt, as a pet
70 Pot
73 Tulsa sch.

76 Canceling key
82 Timetable abbr.
83 Traditional Valentine's Day gift
84 Croft of Tomb Raider
85 Tiny terriers
86 N.Y.C. summer hrs.
87 Black suit
88 Does really well
89 Going rate?
94 Return to a theme, as in a symphony
95 Vine support
96 Bring down
98 "Ciao!"
101 Response to a puppy video, maybe
104 Middle black key in a group of three, on a piano
105 Some laptops
106 Sci-fi moon
108 John Wayne, by birth
110 Current fashion
111 Paradise
112 Tidy
114 On an airplane, it's filled with nitrogen rather than air
115 Assumed part of some addresses
116 Those: Sp.

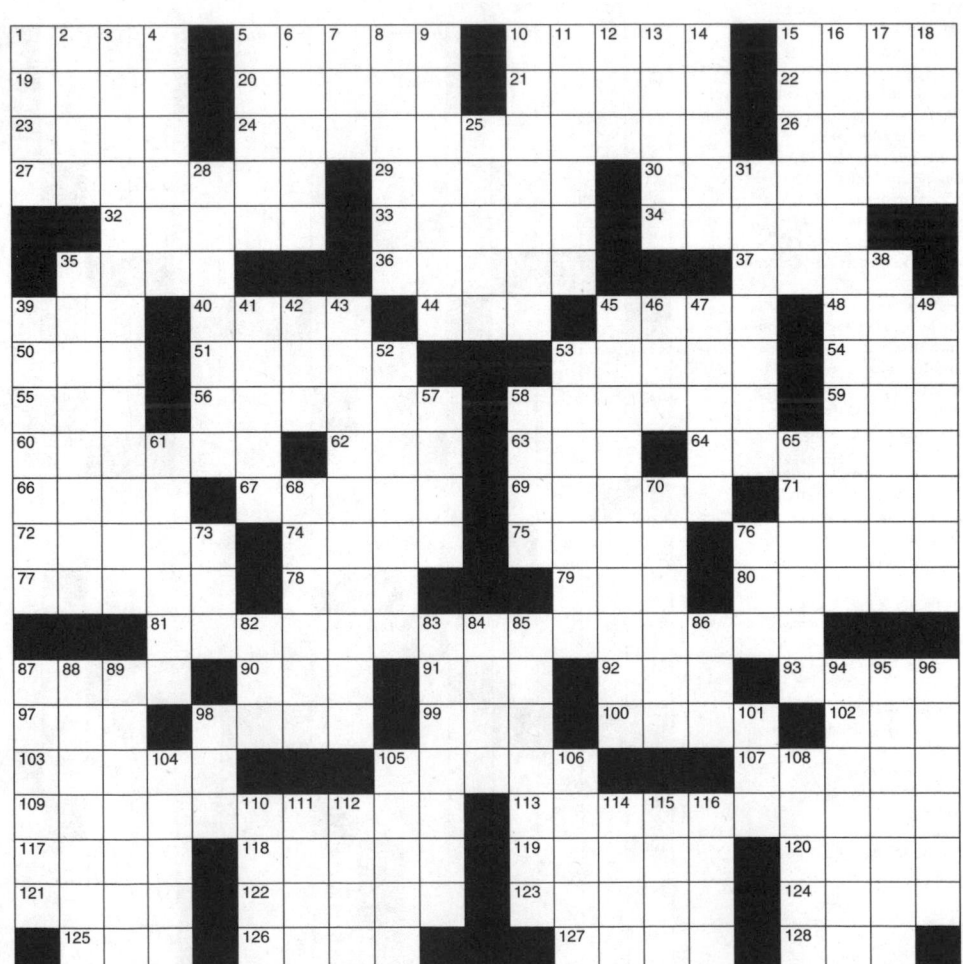

by Olivia Mitra Framke

ACROSS

1 Part of a backpack
6 Pyramids, often
11 Dutch requirements
16 Evan : Welsh :: ____ : Scottish
19 One of Chekhov's "Three Sisters"
20 Hunter of myth
21 Bring to bear
22 Result, maybe, in brief
23 Many apartments in old warehouse districts
24 Japanese comics style
25 Labor Day baby, e.g.
26 Shape formed by an extended thumb and index fingers
27 Good person to believe in
29 Switz. neighbor
30 Writer Tarbell who took on Standard Oil
31 Pins are placed at the end of them
33 07 film
37 Some E.M.T. cases
40 Buying binges
41 Count in music
42 Logical start?
44 U preceder
45 Picked from a lineup, informally
46 Hurt
47 Proverbs
50 Like puppeteers, usually
53 Maven
54 Leafy crown material
55 Day competitor
62 Bailiwicks
63 Legal
64 Chief Chirpa and others, in sci-fi
65 Wastes away
66 "Fantasy" Grammy winner
67 Cool, in old slang
68 "The way things are currently going . . ."
72 Muscle problem
74 Muscular
76 Grammy-winning country singer Black
77 Play combo of old
83 Mark ____, winner of the 1998 Masters
84 George Carlin was its first host, for short
85 State capital on the Colorado River
86 Subject of Newton's first law of motion
88 Dealers do this
89 Have an in-tents experience?
92 QB's pass: Abbr.
93 "____ to My Socks," Pablo Neruda poem
94 Larsson who wrote "The Girl With the Dragon Tattoo"
96 Additionally
98 Deletes, with "out"
99 Tree alternative
103 Kind of salami
105 N.Y.C.'s first subway line
106 Like some gas: Abbr.
107 "Big Sur" novelist, 1962
111 A suggestion
112 World capital whose name comes from the Greek for "wisdom"
114 Humble
116 Jazz composer with an Egyptian-inspired name
117 "____ your call"
118 "Elements of Algebra" author, 1770
119 First lady of the 1950s
120 Kind of pear that resembles an apple
121 Rapper with the 2003 hit "I Can"
122 "Judge ____" (1995 Stallone movie)
123 ____ and curl (salon treatment)
124 Not interfere with

DOWN

1 Tower over the field
2 Sci-fi film with vehicles called "light cycles"
3 Loaded (with)
4 Prone to fidgeting
5 Some 1990s Toyotas
6 American fashion designer who once served as the creative director at Gucci and Yves Saint Laurent
7 ____ pro nobis
8 Mixed together
9 Gets one over on
10 Junkyard warning, maybe
11 Play back?
12 Rust and quartz
13 Equity valuation stat
14 Tiny bit of work
15 Vodka brand, informally
16 She gained fame from her leading role in "Fame"
17 Having the means
18 ____ Lofgren, guitarist for the E Street Band
28 Wolflike
32 Great two-pair poker hand
34 Once called
35 Spanish resort island
36 "Sure, I guess . . ."
37 Relating to egg cells
38 Actor who won a 2016 Presidential Medal of Freedom
39 Six-line verse
43 Wilson of "Meet the Parents"
46 Colloquial contraction
48 Stops up
49 Surreptitious
51 Greek H's
52 Golfer Ernie
53 It ended on Nov. 11, 1918
56 Swell up
57 Laundry soap since 1908
58 "____, all ye faithful"
59 Classic fruity sodas
60 Occupied, with "in"
61 Accept as charged
68 "How sad!"
69 Liquor levy, e.g.
70 Provoke
71 Surgical inserts
72 Painter José María ____
73 Kind words
74 "Va ____" (Italian "All right")
75 Something to bookmark
76 Film director Jon
77 You, to Yves
78 "____ doctor, but . . ."
79 Trait of a clingy romantic partner
80 Lead singer of rock's Yeah Yeah Yeahs (who uses just the initial of her last name)
81 Churchill's trademark gesture
82 Author born Truman Streckfus Persons
87 Not much at all
88 Ballet attire
89 Pig in a poke or pigeon drop
90 "The Simpsons" grandpa
91 "More of the ____" (1967 #1 album)
95 Weepy 1954 Patti Page hit
96 Haberdasher's clasp
97 Of the ankle
100 Stunned, in a way
101 Walk heavily
102 Contemptible sort
103 Toothy smile
104 Jazz's James
108 Condo, e.g.
109 Kaffiyeh wearer
110 Christmas tree hanging
113 Just between us?
115 Family nickname

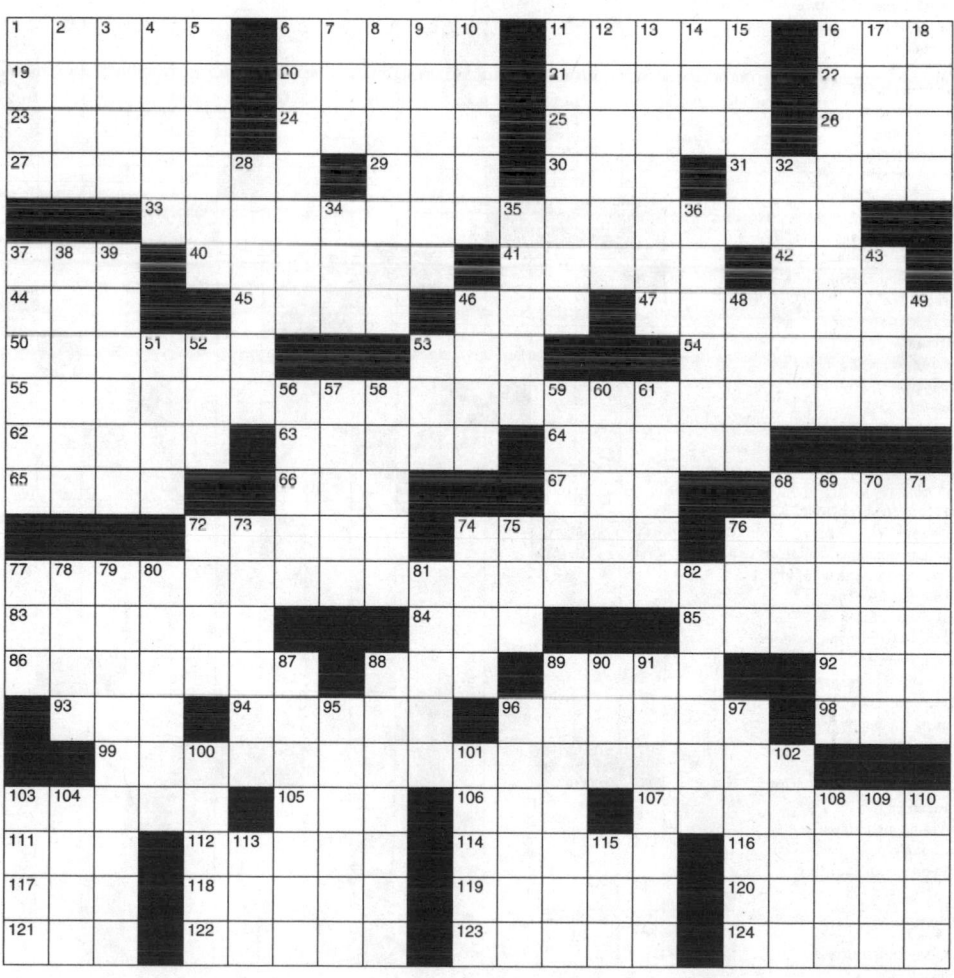

by David Kwong

ACROSS

1 Curse
5 Unit of current
8 Developer of 1982's E.T., a video game so bad that hundreds of thousands of unsold cartridges were secretly buried in a New Mexico landfill
13 Stealing attempts on the diamond?
19 Look extremely stylish, slangily
20 ____ People's Democratic Republic
21 Classic actress Sophia
22 Lacking freshness
23 Always glad to be seated in the back of the boat?
26 Printed cotton fabric
27 Think of together
28 Perfectly placed "Batman" punch?
30 Behind the line of scrimmage
32 Pried, with "in"
33 Look ahead
36 Unfilled spaces
40 Part of New York City's Museum Mile, with "the"
43 Charlatans
46 "Catch you later!"
47 Buddhist temple structure
50 Penny going through the wash once again?
53 Subject of Walter Lord's "A Night to Remember"
54 Epson product
55 Facebook profile feature
56 Soup served at the church social?
58 Persuade by force
61 Sheep's kin
63 Commencement
64 Church officer
65 Grape-Nuts maker
66 Ark groupings
68 Feudal workers
72 In a lively manner
74 What a pointless meeting probably should have been handled by
76 California in San Francisco, e.g.
77 Afternoon gatherings of Mensa?
81 Force at sea
83 Monk's title
84 Withdrew
85 Having no feeling in one's texting hand?
89 Assumed name
90 One of the so-called "Three Crowns of Florence," along with Petrarch and Boccaccio
91 Source of the idioms "fat of the land" and "fire and brimstone"
92 As we speak
93 Small anatomical opening, as in a bone
96 These can go for a lot of bucks
97 Check for mistakes
100 Party tray meat
103 Ad for heartburn medication?
109 Puts forward
114 State you'll never get to
115 "Quit your snickering, Damon!"?
117 Hitting the floppy disk icon, say
118 Islamic rulers
119 Hill resident
120 Soup pod
121 Dangerous fly
122 Dividing membranes
123 ____ flour
124 "No man hath ____ God . . ."

DOWN

1 Labor-regulating org.
2 "Such a pity!"
3 Bugs
4 Doc's needle
5 Without reserve
6 Yucatán natives
7 Fancifully worded
8 Drink rarely drunk with a straw
9 ____ Bora, area of Afghanistan
10 ____ American Heritage Month (April)
11 Foul rulers
12 Says without feeling
13 Start of a magician's phrase
14 Send over the moon
15 Waited at a red light, say
16 FedEx, maybe
17 Order by the border
18 "Please ____ your tray tables" (plane request)
24 World-renowned
25 Sanskrit scripture
29 Part of many California place names
31 Get out of Dodge, so to speak
33 Caustic compound
34 Needing a passcode, maybe
35 Even one
37 Latin clarifier
38 Easy-to-bend metal
39 Greek vowel
40 Lead-in to rail
41 Computer menu with Undo and Redo
42 Dash gauge
43 Word with freeze or fixing
44 Choice word
45 "Don't just ____ there!"
47 Digital passcodes
48 Viewed optimistically
49 ____ snake
51 Japanese city where Lexus is headquartered
52 Classic muscle cars
53 Cards with the most pips
57 Bread
59 Map section
60 Irascible
62 Some Hollywood up-and-comers
65 Responded in court
67 Cowardly sort
69 Turn down
70 Units of distance in physics
71 Sticks a fork in
73 Piece of news
75 Drinks usually drunk with straws
76 Compos mentis
77 Stark who was crowned king in the "Game of Thrones" finale
78 Eight-year member of Clinton's cabinet
79 State
80 Glance at, as headlines
82 Animal for which the Canary Islands are named
86 Opposite of WSW
87 -s or -ed
88 Modern prefix
90 Practices lexicography
93 One vain about his looks
94 "You ____?"
95 Greetings to some mainlanders
97 Ground-dwelling songbird
98 Bit attachments
99 Old enough
101 Kind of acid
102 Like most mouthwashes
103 Brownish shade
104 Greek vowels
105 Classic pop art sculpture with a slanted "O"
106 "Personally . . ."
107 Cut out
108 Male deer
110 Singer/songwriter Lee
111 Appropriate
112 "Suis" is part of its conjugation
113 Comic book publisher Lee
116 Where to find MA and PA

by MaryEllen Uthlaut

ACROSS

1 Something blurred to avoid trademark infringement
5 "Well, that's ridiculous!"
9 One method of coffee-making
13 Fully intends to
18 Reason for people to hide
20 Bit of ancient text
21 Home of Roma
22 Expert on nutrition
23 Bantering remark
24 Feature of Captain Ahab
25 Many M.I.T. grads: Abbr.
26 End of many a name on the periodic table
28 Doctor's hand covering
30 Tokyo, before it was Tokyo
31 Not wanted
34 Pop star Grande, to fans
35 French movie theaters
37 "Ki-i-i-i-nda"
38 "You're on!"
41 Black-market, say
43 Occasion for male bonding, in modern lingo
46 Pressing need when on the go?
48 Part of a media sales team, informally
49 "Agreed"
53 Philosopher who tutored Nero
55 Message made with cut-out letters, stereotypically
57 Chowder ingredient
60 Game in which each player starts with a score of 501
61 West Bank grp.
62 Social media avatar, for short
65 Thing given as a concession
66 Castle defense
67 Nobel winner Morrison
68 One who has a lot to offer?
71 Yellow variety of quartz
73 Norse troublemaker
76 Spotted
77 Fenway team, familiarly
78 "However hard I try . . ."
81 Child-care expert LeShan
82 Parts of ziggurats
85 Twin of Jacob in the Bible
86 Lifetime achievement ceremonies, e.g.
91 Bequeaths
93 Difference between dark and light, in a way
95 Bacterium in some raw meat
96 Center of a cobbler
99 Clorox cleanser
101 Leaves alone
102 Uses a modern engine
106 Kenan's partner on an old sitcom
107 The "L" of B.L.M.
108 "Geaux Tigers!" sch.
110 Love of money, per I Timothy 6:10
113 Brand of nail polish
114 Appeasing
117 School closing?
118 One of the former Big Three information services, along with CompuServe and Prodigy
119 Words from a present giver
121 Sweetheart, in Rome
123 "That one's mine!"
128 Word often confused with "least"
129 Frenzied
130 Sweet Mexican dessert
131 Backsides, to Brits
132 Certain sneak
133 Caesar's accusation
134 Like a fox

DOWN

1 Counterculture drug, for short
2 Geneva accord?
3 Newbie
4 Chose
5 Bit of butter
6 Govt. org. with the motto "Fidelity, Bravery, Integrity"
7 Dramatic touches
8 Comedian Judy
9 Nickname for basketball star Julius Erving
10 Is sorry about
11 Photo-sharing app, familiarly
12 14th-century king of Aragon
13 Written using an outline
14 Witch
15 Basketball star nicknamed "The Answer"
16 Kind of test with unproven accuracy
17 Largest city of Nigeria
19 Word ladder, part 1
21 Big milestone for a start-up
27 Slangy "I messed up"
29 Word ladder, part 2
31 Old food label std.
32 Where an auto racer retires?
33 Enjoyed home cooking, say
36 "I Love It" duo ____ Pop
37 Letter-shaped beam
39 When repeated, king of Siam's refrain in "The King and I"
40 Result of peace talks
42 Some smartphones
44 Oppressive ruler
45 Lacking + or –, electrically
47 "____ and Janis" (comic)
50 Whirlybirds
51 Óscar's "other"
52 Gas that's lighter than air
54 Nile danger
56 Fire in "Jane Eyre," e.g.
58 Like most lions
59 Mrs., abroad
63 Word ladder, part 3
64 Subsided
66 *, *** and *****, say
69 Where to find some cliffhangers?
70 Unpopular legislation of 1773
71 N.F.L. referee, at the start of overtime
72 ____ Valley (San Francisco area)
74 Gem that's also a name
75 New Zealander
77 Start of some Quebec place names: Abbr.
79 French filmmaker Jacques
80 Celebrity chef Eddie
83 Way to go
84 Hot cocoa brand
87 Sublease
88 "Be sharp!"
89 Frequent tabloid cover subject
90 Spot for a houseplant
92 Letters on a Cardinal's cap
94 Greenpeace or the W.W.F., for short
97 Word ladder, part 4
98 Optimistic assertion
100 "____ Beso," Paul Anka hit
103 Prospector's find
104 Start streaming, e.g.
105 Internet meme with grammatically incorrect captions
107 Shower scrubber
109 Eel, on a sushi menu
111 Word ladder, part 5
112 Prospectors' finds
115 Mel of baseball
116 Understand, informally
120 Clarifying word on a school reunion nametag
122 Tinder bio info
124 Amazon worker
125 "Kill Bill" co-star Lucy
126 Jazz composer Beiderbecke
127 Like a fox

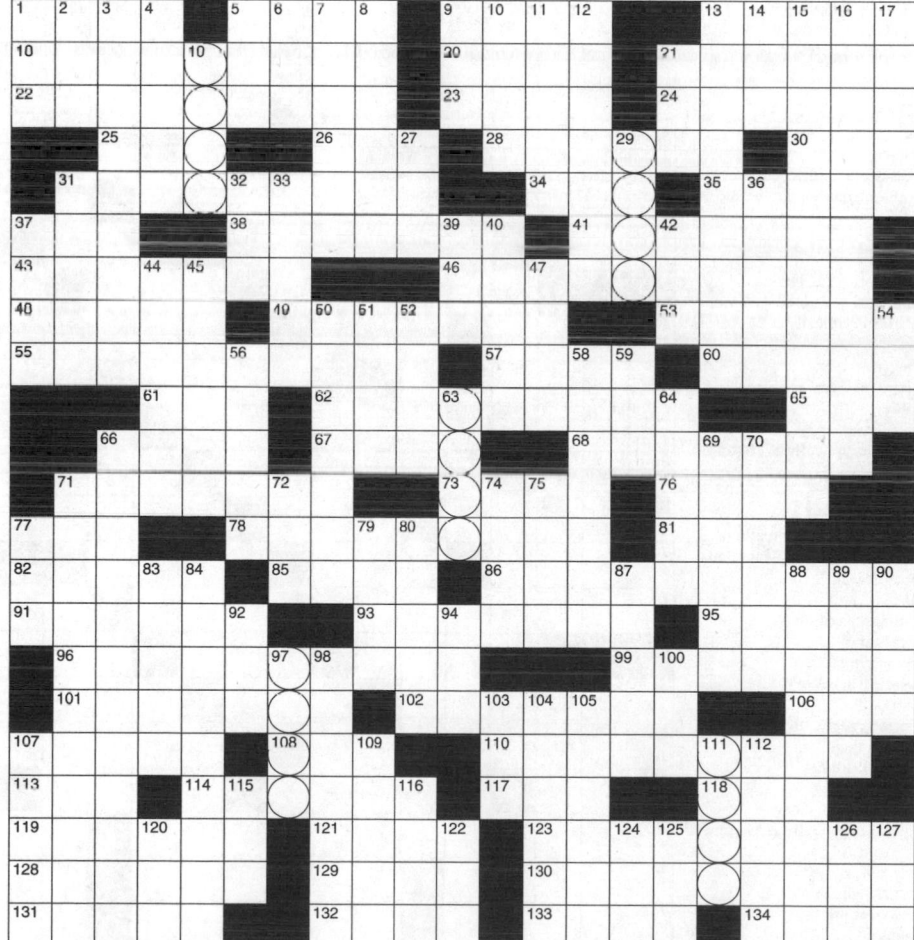

by Sam Trabucco

ACROSS

1 Partly open
5 Drug also known as angel dust
8 "Maybe," informally
14 Window dressing
19 Tyr, in Norse mythology
21 Org. with both left-and right-wingers
22 ____ arteries (what carry blood to the kidneys)
23 "Hmm . . . hard to say"
24 South American financial institution since 1965
26 Reversed
27 Warm up
29 King of Troy in the "Iliad"
30 Currency of Laos
31 1985 thriller with the tagline "A federal agent is dead. A killer is loose. And the City of Angels is about to explode."
35 Firmly establishes: Var.
37 Part of a return address?
38 Experienced network congestion
39 Used to be
41 "I Love You, ____" (book by Nancy Reagan)
42 Twilled fabrics
43 Subject of two squares on a Monopoly board
44 Hip-centric dance
45 It keeps a top up
48 "Good ____!" (shout to a batter)
49 Collectible item with stats
54 Bacchanalias
56 Huge financial loss, so to speak
57 First lady
58 Memo opener
59 Elements of neighborhood watch programs
62 Brewed beverage
63 Single historical record
64 QB stat: Abbr.
65 Fool's gold
66 Lose stiffness
68 Fueled up, in a way
69 California's Point ____ Peninsula
71 Helpful contacts
72 Food depicted cryptically at 24-Across
74 From
75 Notes after sols
76 Consuming Tide Pods, once, inexplicably
77 At peace
78 Food depicted cryptically at 31-Across
81 On, in a way
83 Brain tests, in brief
84 Significant periods
85 ____ Sherman-Palladino, creator of "Gilmore Girls" and "The Marvelous Mrs. Maisel"
86 Overhauls
88 Item creating separation
91 Nail polish brand
92 Viagra competitor
93 Bit of swearing in church?
96 "Pay attention!"
98 Food depicted cryptically at 49-Across
101 Refuge from a flood
102 Youngest Marx brother
104 Skin care brand
105 Love, in Lucca
106 Food depicted cryptically at 59-Across
109 Romps
112 Riverbank romper
113 Book after Nehemiah
114 Places to collect prints
115 Garish signs
116 Adds more lubricant to
117 Good name, informally
118 Jedi who trained Luke

DOWN

1 Central American rodent that resembles a guinea pig
2 TV host with two Peabodys
3 Sports brand with a three-stripe logo
4 Sculptor who said "I invent nothing, I rediscover"
5 Completely defeat, as a noob
6 Deep-six
7 Kirsten Gillibrand, to Hillary Clinton, once
8 Connective tissue that runs along the outer thigh, familiarly
9 Prayer garment
10 Farm enclosure
11 Doing some menial duty, in old army lingo
12 Reinforces, with "up"
13 Puckish
14 Dramatic intro
15 Jedi trained by Luke
16 Jedi related to Luke
17 Grilled sandwich
18 Go by
20 State of drunken confusion
25 Media restriction
28 Goes quickly
32 Venture to state
33 Azalea with the 2014 #1 hit "Fancy"
34 Up to one's ears
36 Caffeinated aspirin brand
40 A tool or a spray
42 Fit of pique
43 Parlor pics
44 Invite to one's home
45 To the extent that
46 Black Lives Matter gathering, e.g.
47 "Let me pay for that"
49 Bundle of hay
50 "Twilight" protagonist
51 Silver-screen actress known as "The British Bombshell"
52 TV-MA's film equivalent
53 Has away with words?
55 Stand-up comedian Mike
56 Spam spewers
60 Many musical chords
61 Classic laundry brand
62 First-class
63 Church recess
66 Feeling amenable (found hidden in this clue!)
67 Bony projection found just behind the ear
70 Cause's partner
72 Gaggle
73 V.I.P. above veep
75 Knowledgeable
76 Parody, say
79 Cold storage facilities
80 Where crumbs might accumulate during a meal
81 Summer Olympics usually take place in one
82 Thumb-twiddling
86 Kelly on the Hollywood Walk of Fame
87 Op-eds, e.g.
88 Hit hard, as brakes
89 Hook, for one
90 Sends an invitation for
91 Be against
92 Sorted laundry load
93 Philippine port with a reduplicative name
94 Euphemistic "extremely"
95 The so-called "Pearl of the Black Sea"
97 Word before hand or jaw
99 Quarters costing dollars?
100 ____ Center, home of the Orlando Magic
103 Father of Anne Frank
107 Layer of farmland?
108 What yellowfin is marketed as
110 "People ____ talking"
111 Indy inits.

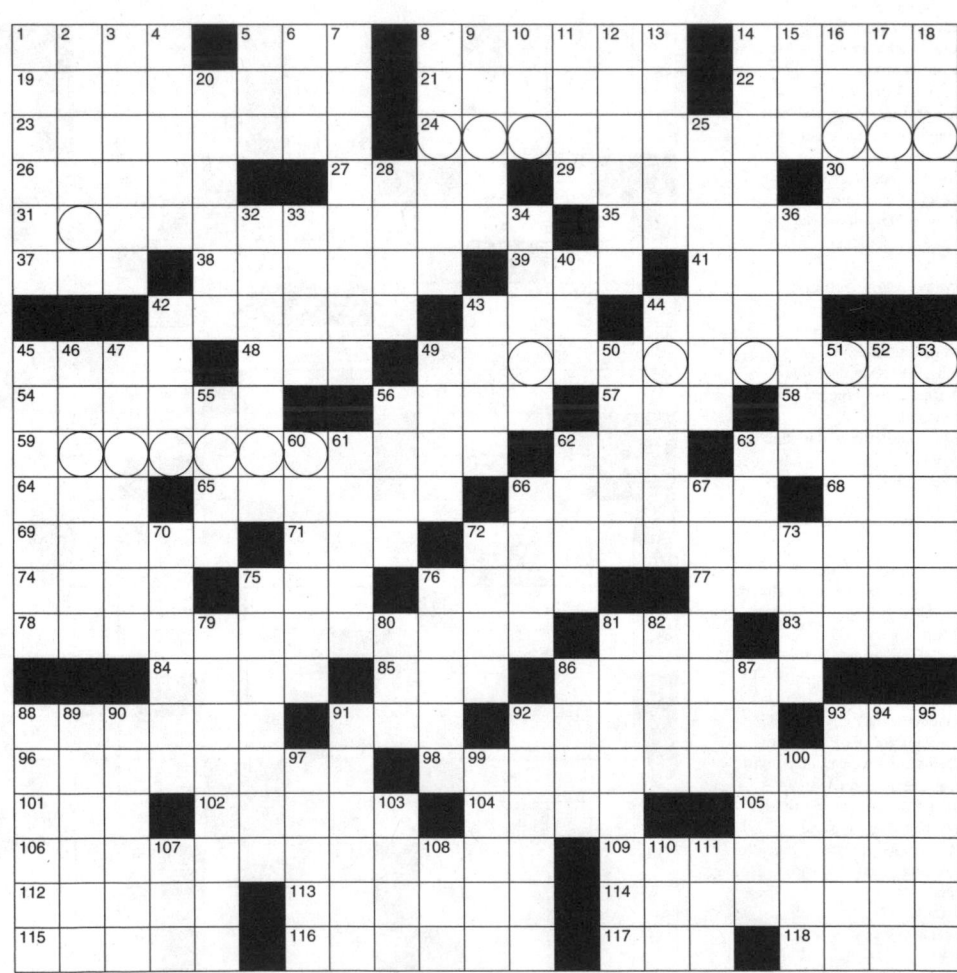

by Alex Eaton-Salners

ACROSS

1 Marvel at
7 L.G.B.T.-aligned advocacy group since 1987
12 Occasion to get all gussied up
19 Stroke of good fortune
21 Newswoman Sawyer
22 "You ain't lyin'!"
23 What the Old English called "Winterfylleth"
24 To a cosmetician: "You're . . ."
26 Home to Antilia, the world's most valuable private residence (27 floors, $2.2 billion)
28 Is
29 Kind of clef
30 To a produce vendor near closing time: "You're . . ."
34 The "B" in GB
35 Fisherman's ____ (San Francisco attraction)
36 Utter nonsense
37 Eyes: Sp.
39 Feature of a batter that needs more whisking
40 Wong of stand-up comedy
41 Drive (away)
42 Laughing matter?
45 Palindromic rulers
47 To a bad free throw shooter: "You're . . ."
52 All ____
54 Ruin, as plans
55 Crowd noise
56 Blubbers
60 The dove's-foot crane's-bill, for instance
62 Big seller of animal supplies
63 To a temp worker: "You're . . ."
65 To a rude driver: "You're ____"
68 Architect Frank
69 Sci-fi classic featuring the Three Laws
71 Taylor Swift's first #1 country hit, 2007
72 Things stuck in clogs
73 Itching to eat and irritable about it, in slang
75 [Leave it]
76 With 98-Across, to an aspiring entrepreneur: "You're . . ."
80 Friendship
85 Vim
86 Parts of Twitter profiles
87 Clicking sound?
88 All over hell's half ____ (everywhere)
89 Item on a president's lapel
90 Placing a call
94 Fishing basket
95 Apt anagram of MY CAR
98 See 76-Across
100 Native speakers of Chiwere
101 Declined
103 Sips
104 To anyone who wasn't addressed above: "You're . . ."
107 Vegan latte option
111 Kings and queens, maybe
112 Large chunk of one's final grade, often
113 Aspen or Alta
114 It's against the rule
115 Move like a peacock
116 Big name in nonprofit journalism

DOWN

1 Adele's "Million Years ____"
2 Medic
3 Spring hrs. in Colorado Springs
4 Organism that structurally resembles another organism
5 Brush off
6 "Never interrupt your ____ when he's making a mistake" (old aphorism)
7 Four-star figures
8 Valerie Plame's org. in 2003's Plame affair
9 Go up against
10 Sui generis
11 Destitution
12 Code edited by a webmaster
13 Many end in "-ite"
14 Ice cream purchase
15 "Expect ____" (road sign)
16 Warranting an "X," say
17 Something to do with your buds?
18 Social climate
20 Physician who co-founded A.A., familiarly
25 Traipse (about)
27 How some like their café
30 Creatures that can have asymmetrical ears, which aid in hunting
31 "Nah"
32 Author Janowitz of literature's "brat pack"
33 Pinot ____
34 Cutesy sound accompanying a poke
37 Greeting when running into someone unexpectedly
38 Book before Amos
41 Texas county on the Mexican border
42 Italian painter known for his frescoes
43 Pain relief brand
44 How some like their coffee
46 Floor
47 One of two on the Titanic
48 "Who wants this?" response
49 Makeover result, maybe
50 Word stylized with extra R's on some cereal boxes
51 Some froyo bar toppings
53 ____ polloi
56 Circus venue
57 A ball and a strike, in a baseball count
58 Useful
59 Toy rocker, in tot-speak
60 Give up
61 What might be "love" or "lesbian" in a TV show title
62 Lead-in to potty
64 El ____ (weather phenomena)
66 It's not a lot to jot
67 Third of seven columns: Abbr.
70 ____ hair
73 Earliest-known Chinese dynasty (dating back to 2000 B.C.)
74 Eagerly excited
75 Villain in 1998's "Mulan"
77 With adroitness
78 División de la casa
79 Like 0.5-millimeter lead, among popular mechanical pencil options
81 Good-looking guy?
82 Cold treat
83 Diagram of relationships
84 App with a Reservations feature
89 Newspaper articles and mentions on social media, in brief
90 Ducks
91 "My turn"
92 Electrically balanced, in chemistry
93 Sandwiches on pita bread
94 Pool chalk target
95 ____ Brava, Spain
96 Georgia's capital, informally
97 Jason who played Khal Drogo on "Game of Thrones"
98 The Reds, on scoreboards
99 2020 U.S. Open tennis champ Naomi
101 ____ Tzu (dog breed)
102 Like sponge cakes
105 Middle of a certain three-in-a-row
106 Lone Star State sch.
108 Wrath
109 Man's nickname that omits the "is" at the end
110 ____ in kangaroo

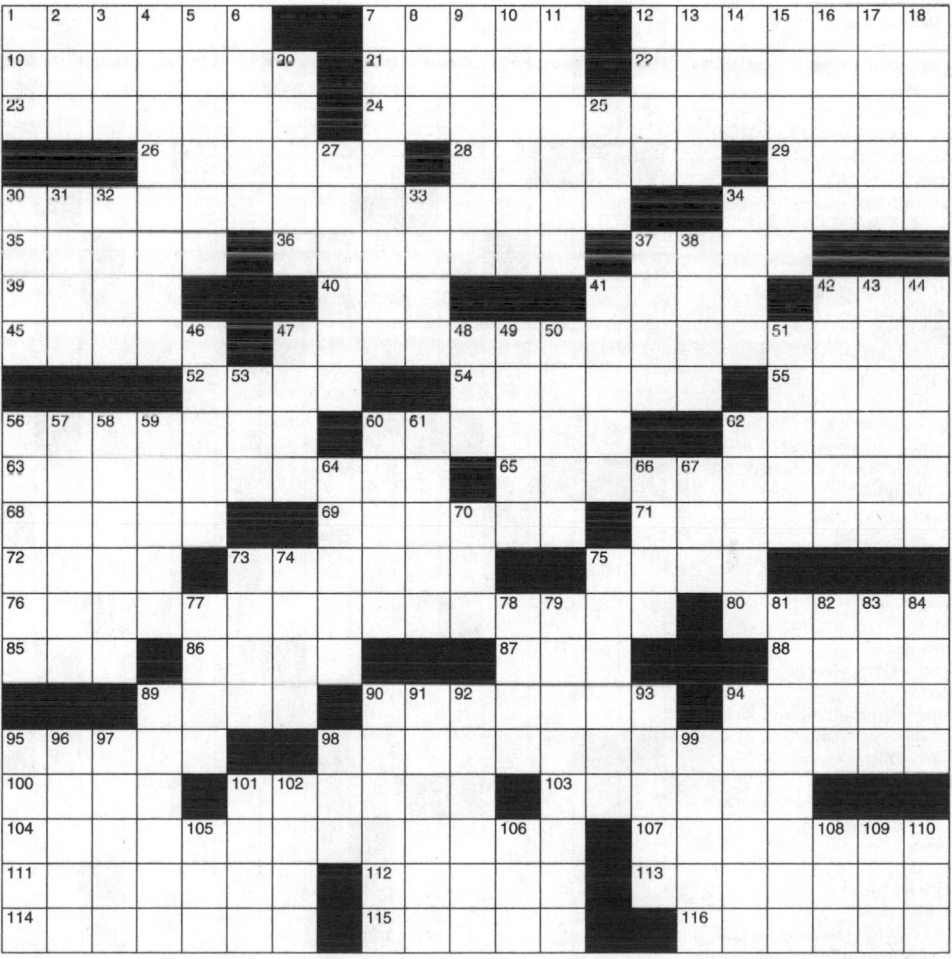

by Sam Ezersky

ACROSS

1 Examples of attention to detail
9 Yearbook award word
13 Lift weights
19 Gingerbread man, often
20 British pop singer Lily
22 In the Caribbean it's known as "the chicken of the trees"
23 "The government has discovered aliens but isn't telling us," e.g.
25 Port on the Loire
26 Missouri site of the Scott Joplin Ragtime Festival
27 Applications
29 Actress Ward
30 Acronym for a North American quintet
33 Intertwine
35 Pains in the neck
38 Spanish article
39 Power of a square
42 Mrs. Addams, to Gomez
43 Nocturnal bloodsucker
46 Steal
48 Stuff
49 It requires no oxygen for growth
50 Pants with baggy legs
52 Task
54 Noodles often eaten cold in the summer
55 Square things
56 Cause of joint pain
59 Relatively new relative, maybe
61 Small songbird
62 Cornmeal bread
63 Wood for violin-making
66 Brian who co-founded Roxy Music
67 "You rang?"
68 Means of breathing
74 Calming retreat
77 Subject of 199 silkscreen paintings by Warhol
78 Present from birth
79 Activist ___ Alamuddin Clooney
83 Hesitating sound
84 Unremarkable
86 Goes out for a bit?
88 Valorous
89 Specialty
91 The continents, e.g.
94 His resignation triggered the first invocation of the 25th Amendment
96 Start up again
98 Wacky
101 Like some flights
102 Triangular flags
103 Aerial maneuver
104 Kiddy litter?
105 Mature
106 Power issue
107 Computer image format
109 More up to it
111 South American mammals with trunks
113 Introductory course?
115 Brand of allergy spray
118 Lime and rust
121 It was known by the Algonquin as the "Father of Waters"
126 Extends
127 Similar
128 Castle in "Hamlet"
129 More out there
130 "May God bless and keep the ___ . . . far away from us!" (line from "Fiddler on the Roof")
131 Return to the fray

DOWN

1 Grumpy co-worker
2 Spanish gold
3 Old country music channel
4 French for "cup"
5 Locale of Kings County and Queens County, fittingly
6 Like some batteries and parties
7 Sapa ___ (title for Atahualpa)
8 Not merely cut
9 Gospel singer Jackson
10 Fútbol cheer
11 Doesn't sit right?
12 Snippy, in a way
13 Spare part?
14 Sch. for Bulldogs
15 '60s sitcom family
16 What "X" marks on a treasure map
17 First-year law student
18 Mission-driven org.
21 "Science Guy" Bill
24 Shades
28 Glittery glue-ons
30 Wheel cover
31 Acting mindlessly
32 "___ Brando: Larger Than Life" (1994 biography)
34 Dog in classic films
36 Flowing forth
37 Steeple feature
40 Cleverness
41 Universal donor's blood type, for short
43 Peacockish
44 Activist Hoffman
45 Milk dispensers
47 Lost cause
51 Only player with three 60+ home run seasons
53 Rest of the afternoon?
57 Slant skyward
58 2010 sci-fi film subtitled "Legacy"
60 Trouble
64 Catering container
65 Color for the right eye of a pair of 3-D glasses
69 Only bird with calf muscles
70 Talking back
71 Graceful spins
72 Informal assents
73 Country singer Price
74 #
75 When doubled, 1934 Cole Porter comedy short
76 Absolutely dazzling
80 Book that's rarely read cover-to-cover
81 Right, as a wrong
82 More N.S.F.W., maybe
85 Mimics
87 Vodka or gin
88 Low-dose pain reliever
90 Mass recitation
92 Symbol meaning "still typing"
93 Tugboat sound
95 Dedicatee of the 1980 song "Woman"
97 Opposite of wide: Abbr.
99 Like slippers versus dress shoes
100 Milky gems
107 Muscly
108 Stumper question
110 Life form
111 Went like the dickens
112 Got rid of
114 German granny
116 Where the infant Moses was found
117 Cathedral recess
119 Maa, in 1995's "Babe"
120 Ukr., e.g., once
122 Genre pioneered in 1950s-'60s Jamaica
123 U.S. overseas broadcaster
124 Unit of work
125 Food writer/TV personality ___ Drummond

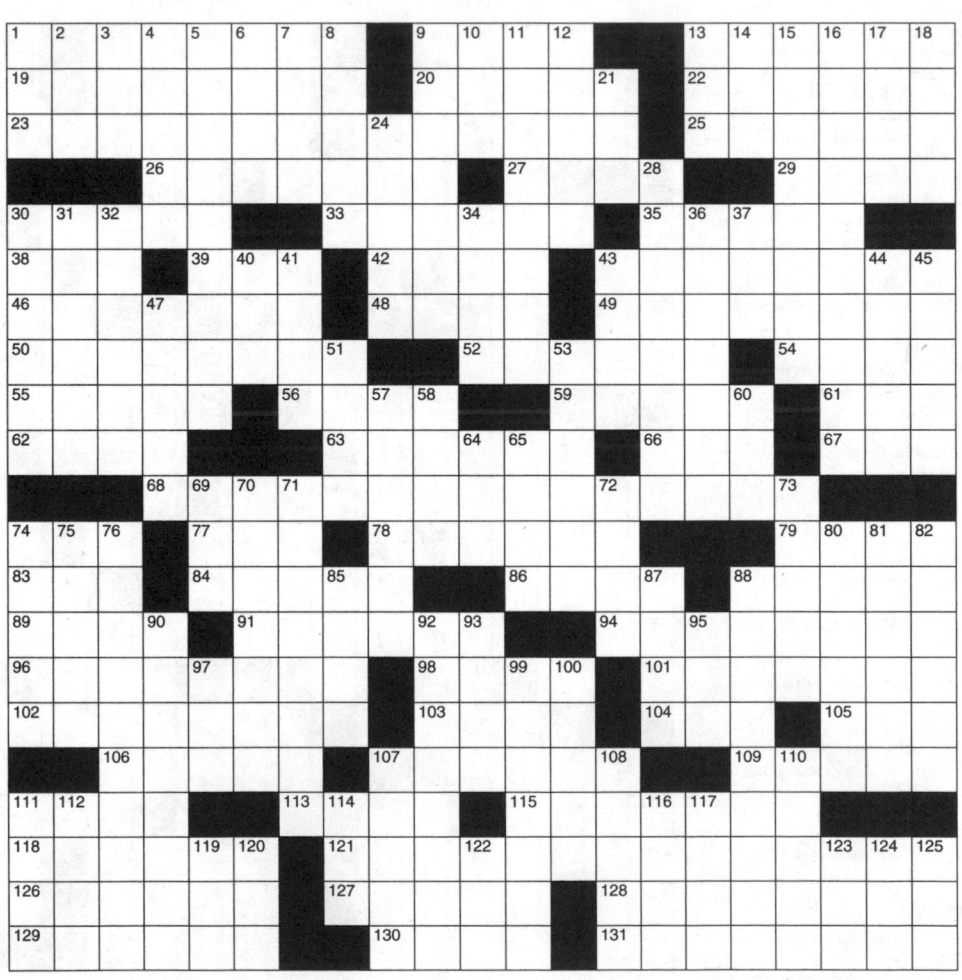

by Gary Larson

ACROSS

1 Dinosaur in the Mario games
6 Titular film character opposite Harold
11 Something offered in tribute
16 ___ Martin DB5 ("Bondmobile")
17 Knock-down-drag-out fights
21 Nudge
22 Barack, Michelle, Hillary and Bill took them, for short
23 Yann Martel's baking memoir?
24 Have heart eyes for
25 Member of Britain's upper house
26 Tone-___
27 Shunned, with "out"
29 "Don't get ___!"
30 F. Scott Fitzgerald's chivalric tale?
36 Just like that
38 Zaps, as leftovers
39 Brainstorms
42 Messes (with)
43 Follower of "Je m'appelle"
44 What a figure skate has that a hockey skate lacks
45 "___ you seeing this?"
46 Voltaire's sweet novel?
50 Scan that excites hydrogen atoms, for short
51 Can't keep one's mouth shut?
54 Alternative to de Gaulle
55 Debussy's "___ d'Étoiles"
57 Prepare to go next
59 "You're making me blush!"
61 Lived (with)
63 Marcel Proust's kitchen mystery?
70 Trouble
71 I
72 "That's ___!" (director's cry)
73 Halloween no. 5 no November 1
74 "Yeesh!"
76 One of six parked on the moon
78 Nasty, in a way
79 Author Ferrante
81 Neutral paint color
82 Break
85 Societal problem
86 "When They See Us" director DuVernay
89 Big e-commerce site
90 Antoine de Saint-Exupéry's pet story?
95 Guarantees
97 [Doh!]
100 Semibiographical source for "Citizen Kane"
101 Small trunks
105 Certain red wine
107 Trap
109 Had a friendly relationship (with)
110 "___ is a wonderful thing if one does not have to earn one's living at it": Einstein
111 "Revenge ___ dish . . ."
112 William Shakespeare's historical romance?
115 Gives one's seal of approval
116 Woman's name that's a piece of furniture backward
117 Classical singing venue
118 Beat
119 Call to reserve?
120 The final installment of "The Godfather"
121 Bit of coffee
122 Sierra Nevadas, e.g.
123 Word that can precede or follow "run"

DOWN

1 "___ ready for this?" (opening of a pump-up jam by 2 Unlimited)
2 Part of an Italian veal dish name
3 Go back to square one
4 Share a workspace, in modern lingo
5 Helpful connections
6 Breakfast order
7 Long period
8 What a weather balloon might be mistaken for
9 Letters on the "3" button
10 Catches a glimpse of
11 What Mrs. Potts and Chip serve in "Beauty and the Beast"
12 Brit's term of affection
13 "Finally!"
14 Resolve, with "out"
15 Precious, to a Brit
17 Goes undercover?
18 Heated accusation
19 Sound effect during a bomb defusing, perhaps
20 "I watched that episode already"
26 Critical time
28 Queen who made Carthage prosper
31 Pittsburgh-to-Buffalo dir.
32 Fair forecast
33 Beat in a boxing match, in a way
34 Corral
35 Command for a right turn, in mushing
36 "It's possible"
37 "You've Got Mail" director Ephron
40 Neutral paint color
41 Sound like a broken record
46 Shoe with holes
47 Top dogs
48 Subject of Rick Steves's travel guides
49 God, in Guadalajara
52 Bullet alternatives: Abbr.
53 Utter
54 Como ningún ___ (unique, in Spanish)
56 Pledge drive gift
57 Giggle
58 Dreyer's ice cream partner
60 ___ Harbor, first official port of entry to the United States
62 Channel that aired "Daria" and "The Hills"
63 Fan mail recipient
64 Exploding star
65 Take pride in something
66 Ruffle
67 What can take a punch?
68 ___ & Chandon (Champagne)
69 Long periods
70 Little bow-wow
75 Wray of "King Kong"
77 Nonresident doctor
80 Lead role on "Parks and Recreation"
82 Writer Stein
83 Green and others
84 Sets (against)
86 The Amazons were the daughter of this god, in myth
87 By way of
88 Director's cry
91 Is employed
92 Movie with the line "I feel the need . . . the need for speed"
93 Dials
94 Some concert tour merchandise
95 Martial arts master
96 Sushi condiment
98 Traitor in the Revolutionary War
99 Warehouse employee
100 "S.N.L." cast member Gardner
102 Lover of Orion, in myth
103 8-Down pilots, in brief
104 Forest grazer
106 Full of spice
108 Where Zeno taught
110 Children's poet Silverstein
113 ___ beam
114 Place for a shvitz

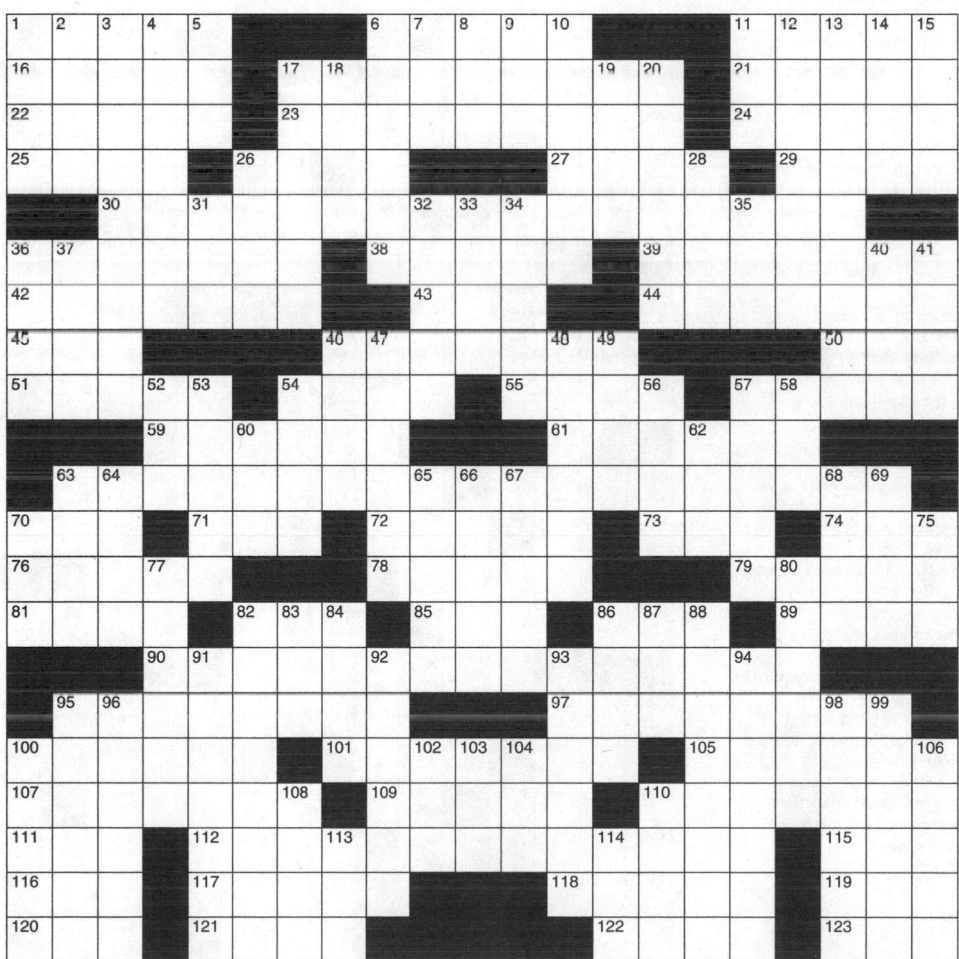

by Miriam Estrin

AT THE HALLOWEEN PLAY . . .

ACROSS

1 Reposed
6 Ruler divisions: Abbr.
9 Objective
12 Source of stress for a returning vacationer
18 Homes staffed with butlers, say
20 Heartburn relief brand
22 Snapple competitor
23 At the Halloween play, when the black cat appeared, the ___
25 Really bother
26 Sound of a candy wrapper
27 Collectibles like ticket stubs and matchbooks
29 Glassy square?
30 "Critique of Pure Reason" philosopher
31 Enemy of Bowser in video games
33 Music producer Gotti
35 Fr. religious title
36 . . . the skeleton gave a ___
43 Belle of a ball
46 Bradley or Patton: Abbr.
47 Citrus fruit with a portmanteau name
48 . . . Frankenstein had ___
53 One of the kids on "Stranger Things"
57 Most common U.S. street name, surprisingly
58 Scarecrow portrayer
59 Blanket that's worn
60 Follow closely, as the curb
61 Pitcher Satchel in the Baseball Hall of Fame
63 Chow
65 "Of course I remember you!," often
66 Glasses, in slang
68 . . . the critics loved the witch's performance, ___
71 Tickled
72 Dragon roll ingredient
73 Friendly
74 Prepare, as mushrooms
75 Vexation
76 Cassandra, for one
78 Vocal critics
81 Hooded jacket
84 Great Lake name
85 . . . the ghost had ___
88 Amazon, for one
90 Old-timey title
91 No-go area, in brief
92 . . . the vampire never ___
99 "Evil Woman" group, for short
100 Most common English letter, in Morse code
101 Joyce Carol with two O. Henry Awards
102 Slumps
106 Send emojis, say
108 Southern shade trees
112 It gained its independence from Ethiopia in 1991
115 Source of some tweets
117 . . . the mummy was a hit ___
119 Try to make out
120 Tot's spot in a lot
121 Certain Bach compositions
122 Fitting anagram of ANGER + E
123 In the style of
124 G.I.'s chow
125 Artoo-___

DOWN

1 Kiss
2 Oscar winner Dern
3 Finish with
4 Final destination, perhaps
5 Long haul
6 Title for Emma Bovary: Abbr.
7 Appreciative cry
8 Arrive unnoticed
9 "As I Lay Dying" father
10 Two of Us?
11 Fashioned
12 Them's fighting words!
13 "It's Raining ___"
14 "This minute!"
15 Formal admission
16 Simple shelter
17 Glossy gown fabric
19 "30 Rock" was inspired by it, for short
21 Apt thing to wear during allergy season?
24 Mortar = sand + water + ___
28 Gymnastics event
32 With skill
34 French towns
37 What you're doing at every moment
38 Bassoon attachment
39 Buck
40 Like royal flushes
41 Beg
42 Museum offering
43 Article of Cologne?
44 She raised Cain
45 Hit ABC dating show, with "The"
49 Component of béchamel sauce
50 Celebration of a life, for short
51 Clouds (up)
52 Tickled
54 Spam filter, of a sort
55 Capital of Samoa
56 Lentil, e.g.
59 Card's place: Abbr.
61 Good thing to make or break
62 One of two for a tee
64 It might be pale or amber
66 Late-night host Meyers
67 Indiana city that's 100 miles west of Lima, Ohio
68 Pale
69 Quaint "not"
70 Tidy up . . . or make less tidy
71 Produce on a farm
73 Poster heading
75 Spy's collection
77 Billy in the Rock and Roll Hall of Fame
79 Not up
80 Fatty tuna, in Japanese cuisine
81 Lead-in to phobia
82 Common sight at a cash-only bar
83 AM radio abbr.
85 Capone contemporary
86 Bone: Prefix
87 Like some Coast Guard rescues
89 Superfan
92 Do another take of
93 Number of sides on a hendecagon
94 More crafty
95 ___ ark
96 ___ Jeffries, chair of the House Democratic Caucus
97 Them's fighting words!
98 Will matter
103 Stop, in France
104 Reach
105 Have the final word
107 "United States of ___," show for which Toni Collette won an Emmy
109 Cow, in Cádiz
110 Bibliography abbr.
111 ___ vez (again, in Spanish)
113 Record speed, for short
114 Gadget that once came with a click wheel
116 Rip (on)
118 It might start with "I-": Abbr.

by Peter A. Collins

ACROSS

1 Amenity in G.M. vehicles
7 R.N.'s workplace
10 "Awake in the Dark" author
15 Down at the bar?
19 Peace and quiet
20 Tease constantly, with "on"
21 Bottom lines?
22 Spanish Steps city
23 What an unsteady tightrope walker may do?
25 Number cruncher, in Wall Street lingo
26 Spelling clarification
27 CPR experts
28 "____ to My Family" (song by the Cranberries)
29 "It's just too $%#@ hot!," e.g.?
31 Fasten again, as documents
34 Dish cooked in an underground oven
35 Bolshoi debut of 1877
36 Thesis defenses, e.g.
37 Thereabouts
39 Me-day destination
40 What a beekeeper receives at work?
45 Pettily punishes
50 Dynamite
51 Explode on Twitter, say
52 "____: Ragnarok" (2017 blockbuster)
54 Catty comments
55 Upstanding person
57 Flood protector
59 Bird that carries Sinbad to safety
61 "Little Fockers" actress Polo
62 Little auk, by another name
65 Japanese audio brand
66 Cousin of a clarinet
67 Why the knight went shopping?
73 Letters no longer seen on most phones
74 Ingredient in une quiche
75 Source of the words "O, beware, my lord, of jealousy; / It is the green-ey'd monster . . ."
76 Bohemian
77 "Hate Me Now" rapper, 1999
78 2019 award for "What the Constitution Means to Me"
79 "Magnifico!"
84 Fully grown fillies
86 Statistician's calculation
88 Cruz known as the Queen of Salsa
91 Regenerist skin-care brand
92 Upfront?
94 Hogs, after being scrubbed clean?
97 Even a little bit
99 Take ____ from (follow)
100 Thrill
101 Resident of the lowest circle of hell, in Dante's "Inferno"
106 Spring setting in San Antonio: Abbr.
107 Border of a lagoon, say
111 What the ecstatic janitor did?
113 Porcine pad
114 Paul of "There Will Be Blood"
115 Actress Taylor
116 "Stop it, I'm blushing"
117 "Michael Jordan's Top 10 Free Throws" and others?
120 Rental units: Abbr.
121 Ballet shoe application
122 Shakespearean prince
123 Cuts off
124 Interlock
125 Choral composition
126 N.F.C. South city: Abbr.
127 Kids' camp crafts project

DOWN

1 Figure skating champ Brian
2 Reinvented self-image
3 Tiffs
4 Spots to shop for tots
5 The Sun Devils' sch.
6 One squat, for example
7 What soap bubbles do
8 Pet shop purchase
9 "Yuck!"
10 Sublime
11 Toto's creator
12 They're full of questions
13 Holds on to one's Essence, say?
14 Fasteners of some heels
15 Go at a glacial pace
16 Book before Joel
17 Boat sometimes built around a whalebone frame
18 Soul, e.g.
24 Give a shout
29 Nothing of the ____
30 Digital sounds?
32 Something up one's sleeve
33 Original site of the Elgin Marbles
34 Beyoncé, for one
38 "How neat!"
40 Uncle ____
41 Heartbreak
42 Martin who wrote the "Baby-Sitters Club" series
43 Conclude (with)
44 Coarse-grained igneous rock
46 Tagging along
47 Martial arts-based workout
48 Trial's partner
49 Went cross-countrying, say
53 Spiked wheel on a boot spur
56 Farm-to-table program, in brief
58 Shish ____
60 Scientist who said "The cosmos is also within us. We're made of star-stuff"
63 First string
64 Puts out
65 How obedient dogs walk
67 Gets a head?
68 Host of an Apple TV+ book club
69 In again
70 More sardonic
71 Paperless airplane reservation
72 Trifling amount
78 Because (of)
80 Sky fall?
81 Whitney of cotton gin fame
82 Headed
83 "Later!"
85 Button on an old video game controller
87 Org. that publishes the journal Emotion
89 Prepare for a guided meditation, perhaps
90 Cavity fillers
93 Homogenous
95 ____ Gobert, 2018 and 2019 N.B.A. Defensive Player of the Year
96 Benchmark: Abbr.
98 "Over here!"
101 Religion symbolized by a moon and star
102 Make a choice on Tinder
103 Isle of Man men, e.g.
104 Gorillalike
105 Suite meet?
108 Made lighter
109 One might begin "Dear Diary . . ."
110 "All That Jazz" director
112 Screenwriter Lee, sister of Spike
113 De-bug?
117 ____ cha beef (Chinese entree)
118 V-J Day prez
119 Ni'ihau necklace

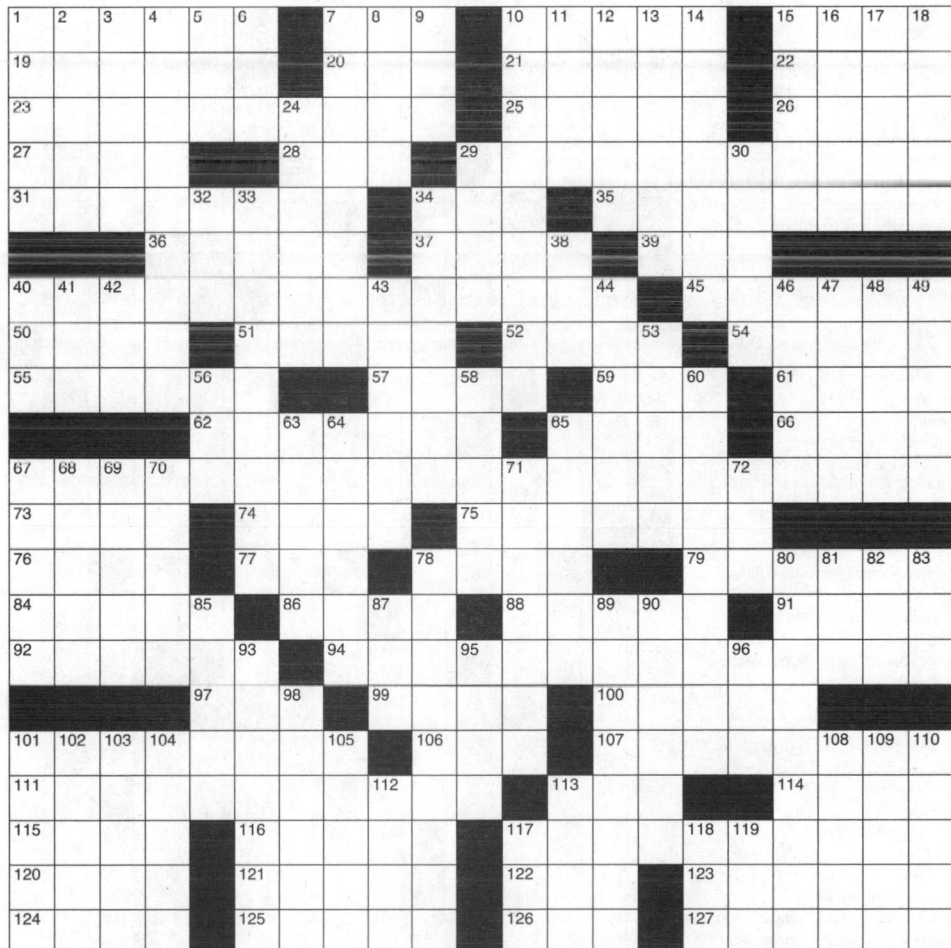

by Julian Lim

ACROSS

1 Aid for a small business
10 Dev of "Slumdog Millionaire"
15 Part of a prairie skyline
19 Strict commitment
20 Sidestep
21 "Way ahead of you"
22 Compliment to a runway model?
24 Low card in Texas hold'em
25 Some donations
26 Stable supply
27 Starting piece on a1 or h8, say
28 ___ Slam (tennis feat)
30 Drain
31 Easily offended by foul language?
34 Kind of high ground
37 Trial
38 Breaks down
39 Spanish "sun"
40 Axel ___, protagonist of "Beverly Hills Cop"
41 X
42 Japanese roadster since 1989
44 Residence that might be named for a donor
45 Question to a tantrum thrower?
49 Costly cuts
51 First two words of "Green Eggs and Ham"
52 ___ fixe
53 Malbec and syrah, e.g.
54 Role model
55 Wet-Nap, for one
57 Friend with a rhyming description
59 Sighting aptly found in "Are you for real?"
61 "Anything you'd like to ___?"
63 Relics proving how Noah steered his boat?
68 Something to do for recovery?
69 Pacific island ring
70 Neil with the hit "Breaking Up Is Hard to Do"
71 Carries out
73 Actor Elwes of "The Princess Bride"
75 Trade blows
77 Mild
79 Driver's org., no matter how you slice it?
80 Relent
83 Prepared for a field trip?
86 Interjections akin to "Yeah, su-u-ure!"
87 Bygone forensic spinoff
89 Android alternative
90 Quits at the last minute
91 Org. that awards the Safer Choice label
92 World capital established in 1535
93 Jackanapes
94 Rap producers' favorite vegetables?
95 Masters of slapstick?
100 Retinal receptor
101 Drink after drink?
102 "To live without ___ is to cease to live": Dostoyevsky
103 Sign of summer
104 Stow cargo
108 Get into gear
109 Title for an oral surgeon's handbook?
113 Certain sexual preferences
114 Italian automotive hub
115 Subject of many an off-season rumor
116 "Young Frankenstein" character played by Teri Garr
117 Tee type
118 4th order?

DOWN

1 ___ Rudolph, portrayer of Kamala Harris on "S.N.L."
2 Role model
3 Amigo
4 Rules' partner, for short
5 El Dorado treasure
6 Like apple seeds, if eaten in huge quantities
7 Fresh from a keg
8 Sore
9 Org. that sponsored the design competition for the Vietnam Veterans Memorial
10 MXN, on a currency chart
11 Adele and Cher, e.g.
12 ___ and Caicos
13 Part of a dean's address
14 "I'd rather pass"
15 Shooting sport
16 All together now
17 Farm-to-table consumer
18 Word that sounds like its first letter
21 Elba who played Macavity in 2019's "Cats"
23 One end of the PolitiFact meter
29 Willing subject
30 "Don't be rude . . . greet our guests!"
31 Loonie or toonie
32 Some are named for kings and queens
33 Stately street liners
34 Coat from a goat
35 High point of Greek civilization?
36 Emeritus: Abbr.
37 "It's me . . . duh!"
40 "Just sayin'," in shorthand
41 Needless to say
42 Mississippi ___ pie
43 Released
44 Thingamabob
46 Brink
47 World No. 1 tennis player between Navratilova and Seles
48 Lived in a blue state?
50 One might be hard to sit for
54 Pipes at some bars
56 Brings out
58 Downfall in many an Agatha Christie novel
60 Buzzed hairstyle
62 Stops harping on something
64 Like a sparsely attended party
65 See 66-Down
66 With 65-Down, "Ditto"
67 Pelvic exercises
72 Give attitude
74 Instruction for a course?
76 Earnings
78 Drew back
80 "Sorry to intrude . . ."
81 Certain monkey . . . or monk
82 "Jackpot!"
83 One needing new, unburned pants?
84 De-lights?
85 Oil-rich state, for short
88 Appliance with apps
92 Yearns (for)
93 Fashionable pair
94 Cover for "little piggies"
96 "Josephine the Singer, or the Mouse Folk" is the last short story he wrote
97 "Take that!"
98 Kind of chemical bond in salts
99 Vivacious quality
100 What a meta clue might do to itself
103 Chicago mayor Lightfoot
104 Brick made of acrylonitrile butadiene styrene
105 New ___
106 Showy basket
107 Lifesavers, for short
108 Piece of equipment for gold medalist Lindsey Vonn
110 Marauder of old
111 Lifelong bud, slangily
112 Partner of hem

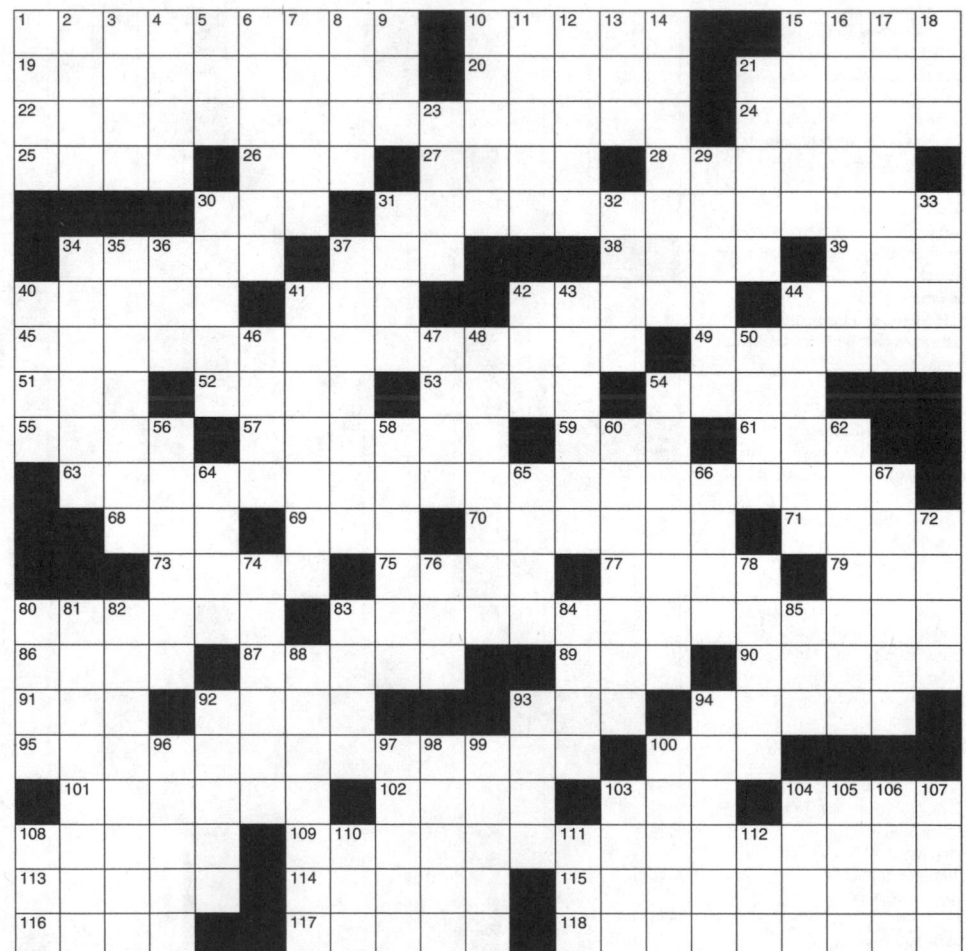

by Evan Kalish and Caitlin Reid

ACROSS

1 Round number?
7 Pick a card, any card
11 Hoops
16 Piano keys
18 Quick study
20 Quick studies
22 Line delivered in costume
23 Source of a trendy health juice
24 Alternative to tarot cards
26 Opportunity to hit
27 Hearing aid?
29 Hole-making tools
30 Hill worker
31 Split
32 Small bird with complex songs
33 He was told to "take a sad song and make it better"
34 "SmackDown" org.
37 Upper limit
38 Olympic figure skater Johnny
39 Make more pleasant
41 First attempt
44 Attire
45 In key
46 "The ___ Locker," 2009 Best Picture winner
47 Declare
48 "Surely you don't think it could be me?!"
49 Bank, at times
51 Hayek of Hollywood
52 Some movie extras
55 Acts like money grows on trees
57 Tool for a difficult crossword, say
58 Added water to, as a sauce
60 Family secret, perhaps
62 In lock step (with)
64 Seasonal song with lyrics in Latin
66 Sacrament of holy matrimony and others
67 Throughway, e.g.
69 Fashion expert Gunn
70 It's sedimentary, my dear
71 Seemingly forever
72 Filmmaker Gerwig
73 Info on an invitation
75 Command, as influence
76 "Don't worry about it"
78 Drown or blacken
79 Hole in the ground
80 ___ card
81 Shaded
82 Went over the limit, say
83 Where to find the radius
84 ___ Lipa, Grammy-winning pop artist
87 "Big Little Lies" co-star of Witherspoon and Kidman
88 Barely afloat?
91 Buzz in the morning
93 Place you may go just for kicks?
94 Mail lady on "Pee-wee's Playhouse"
95 Occasion to stay up late
97 Some surfing destinations
99 You are here
100 Pounds
101 He made a pact with the Devil
102 Makes blue, say
103 One of three for "Mississippi"

DOWN

1 Brand of breath spray
2 Arthurian isle
3 Decay, as wood
4 "___ words were never spoken"
5 Voice, as grievances
6 Potter of children's literature
7 Ambitious
8 Proverbial tortoise or hare, e.g.
9 Poses
10 Branch of the U.N. in 2020 news
11 Soda factory worker
12 1989 Tom Hanks black comedy, with "The"
13 Math measurement
14 Aspiring D.A.'s exam
15 Tennis do-over
17 Result of eating the poisoned apple in "Snow White"
18 Quickly go from success to failure
19 Mudbug, by another name
21 Easy target
22 Many a dare, in hindsight
25 Bring down
28 Part of a high chair
29 Boring things
33 Hera's Roman counterpart
34 "Don't you trust me?"
35 Heat of the moment?
36 First name in jazz
37 Quagmire
38 Mom jeans have a high one
39 Picturesque time for a walk
40 Goes out on a limb
41 Tapered hairstyle
42 Act of omission . . . or of a commission
43 Four for a 4×400, say
44 Pluto, e.g.
45 Pint-size and then some
48 ___ mortal
50 Central
51 Bird feeder bit
53 They're on the case, in slang
54 Garrulous
56 Like a pearl-clutcher
59 Discourage
61 Abbr. on a cornerstone
63 What skies do before a storm
65 Worrisome beach sighting
66 Pro ___
68 Email status
72 Food connoisseur
74 ___ a clue (was lost)
75 Scaredy-cat
77 Frozen dessert
78 Golfer Jordan who won the 2015 U.S. Open
79 Republican politico Reince
82 Hybrid bottoms
83 Spot seller, in brief
84 Keto adherent, e.g.
85 Prepare to deplane
86 Andre who won the 1994 and 1999 U.S. Opens
87 Curses
88 Piece of the pie
89 "That smarts!"
90 De-e-eluxe
91 ___ breve (cut time)
92 Beach ball?
93 Do a veterinarian's job on
95 Beach lotion abbr.
96 Rare color?
98 Texter's "I can't believe this"

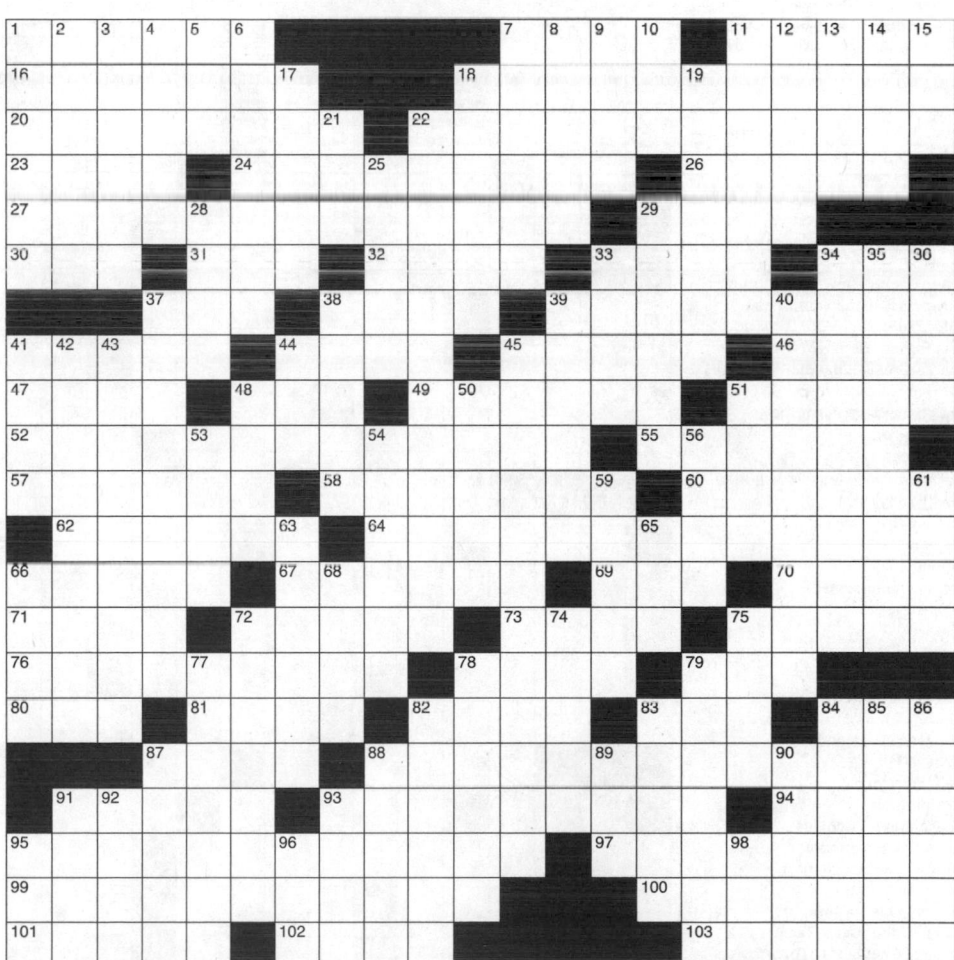

by Caitlin Reid

ACROSS

1 List of courses
5 _____ alla bolognese (meat-based pasta sauce)
9 Don's partner in the underworld
13 Melting point?
19 Condo, e.g.
20 Crowning
21 Crew's control?
22 Wall Street Journal columnist Peggy
23 Bygone office group
25 Final remark in an argument
27 Scratch (out)
28 Like the luck of the draw
30), when it follows :-
31 H
32 "Seems that way"
34 Pieces of gangs
36 Pain reliever containing aspirin and caffeine
38 Golfer Ernie
39 Gave birth
41 Sheltered balcony with abundant natural light
45 Wished
47 Archer's pride
48 "The Dark Knight _____," 2012 superhero movie
50 Bring back on board
51 Actress Jessica
52 No Doubt vocalist Gwen
54 Best-selling self-help book subtitled "Time-Tested Secrets for Capturing the Heart of Mr. Right"
56 Hot spots
58 Moved briskly
60 Council of _____ (Counter-Reformation body)
61 More to the point
62 Part of Q.E.D.
63 Chooses
65 Wanders around the head of a line, briefly?
66 Long-running show whose iconic hourglass is in the Smithsonian collection
70 Rotating engine part
73 Con _____ (with animation, musically)
74 Hot spot
75 It has issues with celebrities
80 See 17-Down
82 Ostensible
84 Had a heaping helping of humility
85 Catchy 1950s slogan
87 Send another way
89 Let go of
90 Serious
91 Runway professional
93 Little louse
94 Purposes
95 Car stereo choices
97 Zoning, so to speak
99 Something that's helpful in a dash?
100 Emotive brass sound
102 Night call
103 Marketer's target
105 Bumbling sort
107 They outrank viscounts
109 Legendary sea monster
111 Floor cleaner, for short
113 Union Pacific vehicle
116 Neither gains nor loses
118 Chant for the Dream Team
119 Eldest of Chekhov's "Three Sisters"
120 Town near Buffalo that sounds like paradise
121 From the start
122 "And now good-_____ to our waking souls": John Donne
123 Desire
124 Digital IDs
125 _____-X (cut)

DOWN

1 Creative inspiration
2 Miso soup mushroom
3 Made the rounds?
4 Native of the Beehive State
5 Knock on, as a window
6 Oodles
7 Words said with a post-match handshake
8 Send to the cloud, say
9 Camp sight
10 Sighing sounds
11 Not custom-tailored
12 Country singer K. T. _____
13 HBO show co-starring Issa Rae
14 Dove's sound
15 Doctor's reassurance before a shot
16 Tech news website
17 With 80-Across, longtime CBS News correspondent
18 Conclusion
24 Smelter's inputs
26 "C'est la vie"
29 Spot from which a dove once notably flew
33 Makes cloudy
35 1943 Pulitzer-winning Thornton Wilder play, with "The"
37 Like the noble gases
39 Singles, e.g.
40 "That so?"
42 Steams up
43 "Garden" or "Center," often
44 Pain in the neck
45 100 satang, in Thailand
46 On the safe side
47 Spiritual retreat
49 Intervene
53 1960s sitcom set at Fort Courage
55 Set in a man cave
57 Bill's time-traveling partner in film
59 "Holy _____!"
62 Favor
64 The deadly sins, e.g.
67 House involved in the Wars of the Roses
68 Scenic vista
69 Holy _____
70 Orange or plum
71 Fleet of foot
72 Qualifies to fight in a certain class
76 "We are the 99%" movement, familiarly
77 Journalists might be invited to it
78 Prospector's find
79 Flock members
80 Misarticulate, in a way
81 Home of a mythological lion
83 Language of Pakistan
84 Working away
86 Au naturel
88 Garments for acrobats
92 "Wow, that's beautiful!"
96 Big bat
98 Ranker of the rich
99 Greasy goo
101 It takes a bow
103 Partner of rice
104 Less well done
105 Thereabouts
106 In the distance
108 + or −
110 Sharp
112 Monk's hood
113 "Fee, fi, fo, _____"
114 Military support grp.
115 D.C. player
117 Designer Posen

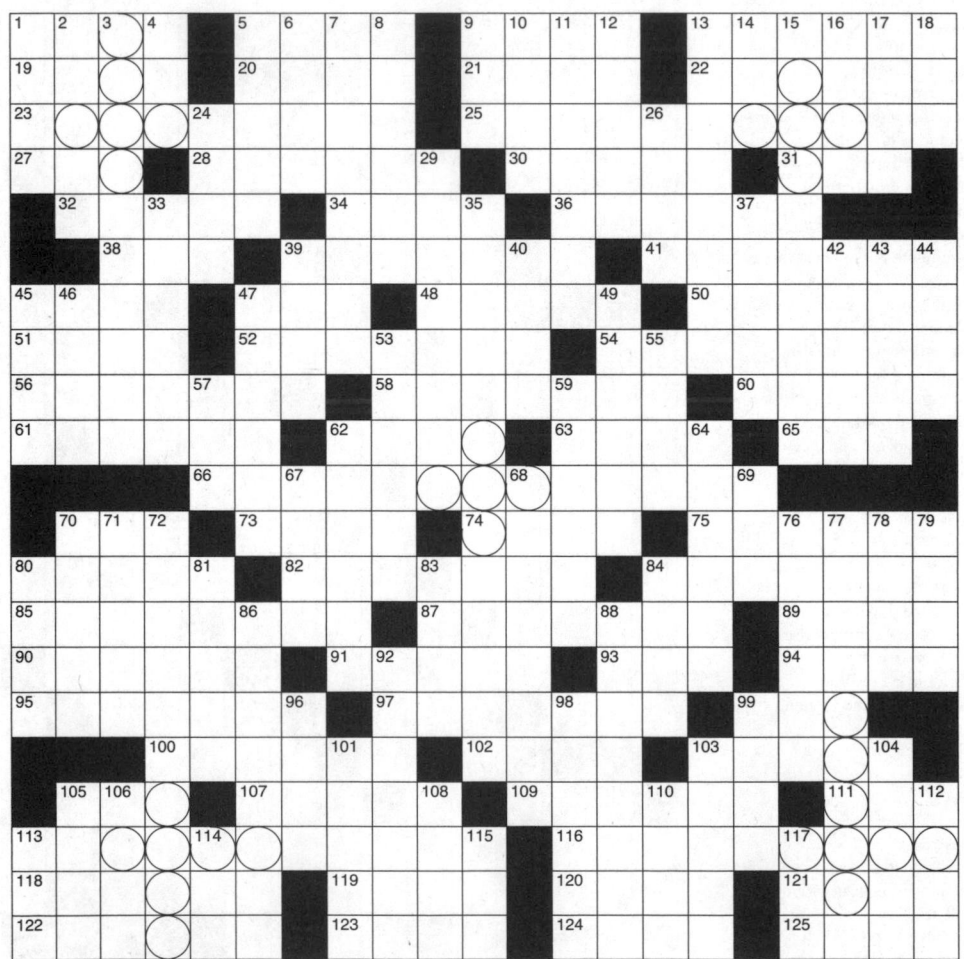

by Alex Eaton-Salners

ACROSS

1 Its logo has a blue, red, orange, yellow and green "M"
6 Win every game
11 Blitzed
17 Beethoven's Third
18 Snoopy sort?
19 You can scratch with it
20 Materials from mollusk shells
21 Tried to respond, as a "Jeopardy!" contestant
22 Gave the latest news
23 Very short-lived gemstones?
25 Nicolas ____, standout player in soccer's Premier League
27 Drake's output
28 Thinly veiled criticism, in modern slang
29 Blow off steam, say
30 Possible fallout of a controversy, informally
31 RR stop
32 Name shouted in "The Chipmunk Song"
34 TV quiz program about an epic poem?
37 Handed a hand
40 Bully's threat
42 World view you might open up to?
43 Suffix with towel
44 NoDoz, for one
46 Help with the dishes
48 Fragment
50 Look back fondly
52 Disney-owned cable channel
56 Ask to be handed a hand?
57 Vereen who won a 1973 Tony for "Pippin"
58 Prefix akin to mal-
59 Haphazardly organized
61 Having four sharps, musically
62 ____ Regal, big name in Scotch
65 "And so on and so forth"
67 Expected
68 General Motors division until 2010
70 Resident: Suffix
72 One-named singer with the 2019 Song of the Year nominee "Hard Place"
73 Some "Babe" characters
75 Designer Gucci
76 Beat box?
79 A brother of 32-Across
81 Zing
83 "Concentration" puzzles
86 Reasonable
87 "The Divine Comedy" poet
89 Brand of cologne with a literary name
91 Jazzed (up)
93 Magnificent plan of action?
95 Bone in the leg
96 Key to get out
97 Maya Angelou's "And Still ____"
98 Nev. neighbor
100 Cloth used in theater backdrops
104 ____ Defense (classic chess opening)
106 Cozy home
107 Dance celebrating 2010 legislation?
109 Glad ____ (good news)
111 Turn up
113 One of 17 in Monopoly
114 Manages, barely
115 Bibliophile
116 Tightfisted sorts
117 Back up again
118 Hip-hop's ____, the Creator
119 First name in cosmetics

DOWN

1 Plot lines?
2 Coffee variety named for a Mideast city
3 Emergency situation caused by a terrier?
4 Pre-snowstorm purchase
5 Hit with a beam, maybe
6 Makes watertight
7 Mascara applicators
8 Dozens of them are sold
9 Actor Wallach
10 Friends you may never have met
11 Salon job named after a comic book hero?
12 Danson of "The Good Place"
13 Building girder
14 Actress Lyonne
15 Compulsive thieves, informally
16 "An apple a day keeps the doctor away," for one
17 Hydrocarbon suffixes
18 The thought is there
19 Serving of tea, to Brits
24 River near Rotterdam
26 Some lawn maintenance tools
30 Who wrote "Undeniable: Evolution and the Science of Creation"
33 Recipient of special treatment, in brief
34 Very cold
35 Klingons, e.g., for short
36 What Hypnos is the Greek god of
37 ____ Plaines, Ill.
38 Liquor component
39 Over
40 Outdoor
41 Part of a glass . . . or glasses
45 Before: Abbr.
47 More dangerous to drive on, in a way
49 Metric prefix
51 Natural bridge
53 Supporting musician in a jazz band
54 Guest's guest
55 Family tree word
57 Chin-up target, informally
60 Leaders of the pack?
61 Bitter brew, for short
63 Pounding on a pie topping?
64 Cloud ____
66 Followers of bees
69 SpongeBob SquarePants and others
71 Opposition
74 Entertainment host Ryan, that smart aleck!?
77 To wit
78 Belt in judo
80 Mustachioed Springfield resident
82 Baseball's Mel
84 One of the Schuyler sisters in "Hamilton"
85 One sharing a bunk bed, briefly
87 Animosity
88 Places to play Skee-Ball
90 Turn off and on again, say
92 With regard to
93 Get worse through neglect
94 "Give it ____!"
95 Need in Boggle
98 Withstand
99 Dancer with glowsticks, often
101 Actress Zellweger
102 Get accustomed (to)
103 Fannie ____ (some securities)
105 Charging option
107 Said aloud
108 Showed up
110 Cyber Monday mo., usually
112 Daisy Ridley's "Star Wars" role

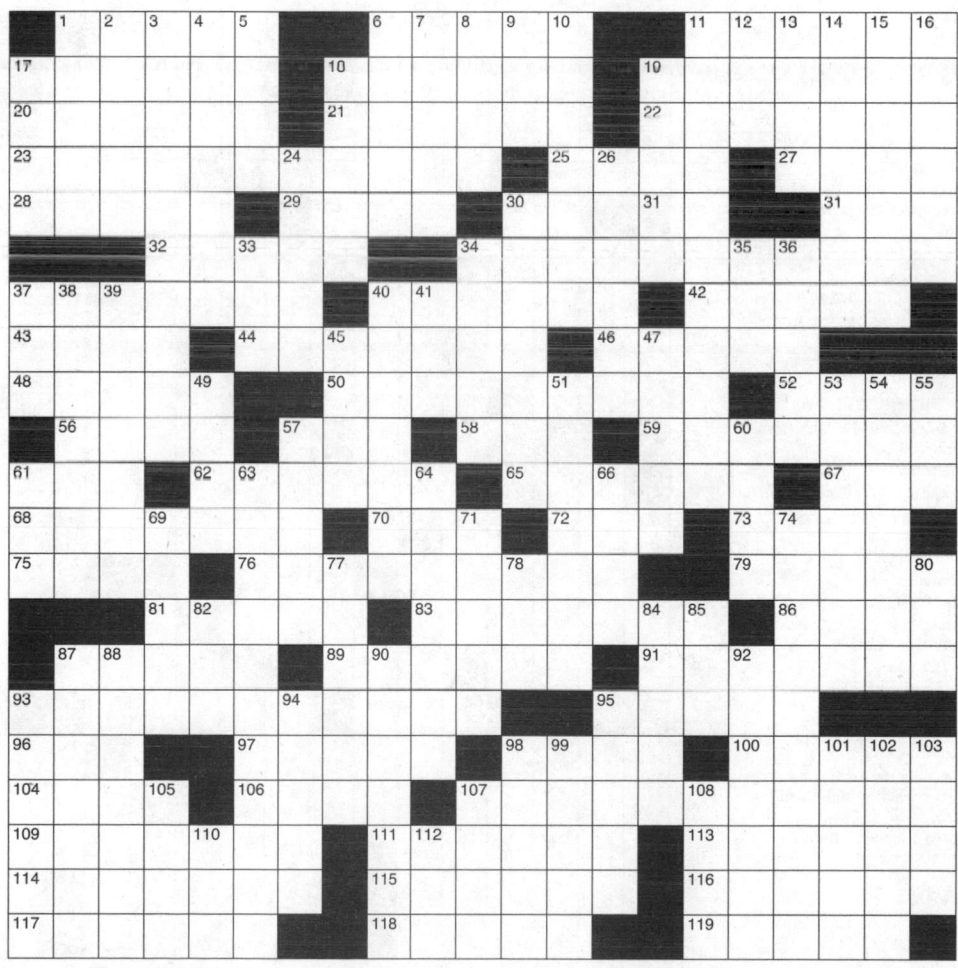

by Eric Berlin

ACROSS

1 Impromptu musical get-together, informally
8 Counting tools
13 Most up to the task
19 Not much
20 Oddball
22 Commotion
23 Archaeologist's assertion about a finding?
25 Jackson not in the Jackson 5
26 Benchmark: Abbr.
27 Members of the genus Lepus
28 Some overseas seasons
30 Common vinaigrette ingredient
31 Russian pancakes
33 Swim team guru?
36 Geri ____, late jazz pianist
38 Authority
39 Used to be
40 Hire Phil Collins's longtime band for a gig?
44 Brand that comes out a head?
45 Explosive sound
49 Curtain call actions
50 One of 32 in the Thai alphabet
51 The Serengeti, e.g.?
54 TV journalist Curry
55 Long
56 Press
57 Covers with goo
58 Speck
59 Quits
62 Shadow during an eclipse
63 Knowing everything that's available to view on Netflix?
67 Look forward to
68 Clay-based
69 Unpleasant
70 Clishmaclaver or bavardage, to use some fancy language
72 Trim
73 A/C measures
74 Hwy. offense
77 Amenity offered at an internet café?
79 Nickname for baseball great Ernie Banks
81 Gets out in dodgeball, say
82 Sticks in
83 Yes, in Brest
84 Bit of reading at a bar mitzvah?
86 Director Lee
87 Entertain
89 Deconstruct for analysis
90 Stand-up's bombs?
95 Keys near G's
98 Actor Rutger of "Blind Fury"
99 Keister
100 Less friendly
101 Assistance
104 Peninsula shared by Italy, Slovenia and Croatia
106 Art shop worker's manual?
110 Urbanize
111 Spit it out!
112 Part of a canopy
113 The plus side
114 Cuisine that specializes in beef barbecue
115 No-parking-zone fixture

DOWN

1 Pokes
2 Bushels
3 "Whoa!"
4 Geneviève, for one: Abbr.
5 Imprinting indelibly
6 M.I.T.'s business school
7 Mathematician Poincaré with a famous conjecture
8 Flabbergasts
9 ____ E. King, singer and co-composer of "Stand by Me"
10 River islet
11 Ye olde news announcers
12 "Same here!"
13 Knee part, for short
14 Fan group?
15 Like "alter ego" and "alma mater"
16 Prayer hands, for one
17 ". . . or ____ think!"
18 Part of L.G.B.T.Q.
21 Short race, for short
24 Your: Fr.
29 "When the country was fallin' apart, Betsy Ross got it all ____ up" ("Maude" theme lyric)
32 Albanian coins
33 Something that's often rigged
34 TV's Burrell and baseball's Cobb
35 Looks longingly
36 Band that won the 1974 Eurovision Song Contest
37 Minnesota's state bird
38 Orlando-to-Miami dir.
41 Role for Patti LuPone and Madonna
42 Brand X
43 Flock member
44 Spotted bean
45 "Well, I'll be," to a Brit
46 Offspring of a 43-Down
47 Taiwanese PCs
48 Big butte
51 A dime a dozen, say?
52 It can help you get a grip
53 Drops (down) heavily
55 Beautifully worded
56 Joe Jackson's "____ Really Going Out With Him?"
58 Van Gogh painting that once fetched a record amount at auction ($53.9 million)
59 Hair pattern protector
60 ____ nous
61 Get in gear?
63 Dubbing need
64 Used a stun gun on
65 ____ pants
66 Take a dive, maybe
67 Digital imaging company that used to make film
71 Apt rhyme for "baloney"
73 Dating notation: Abbr.
74 Start of a seasonal request
75 "Fluff Yeah" slipper sandals, e.g.
76 "Gotcha"
78 Helical bit
79 Be off the mark
80 GPS calculation: Abbr.
81 Exam for H.S. jrs.
84 Original tale of robot rebellion
85 Boxed a bit
86 Untethered
87 Biblical mount
88 Team spirit
90 Spanish term of affection between young women
91 Spring in northern Africa
92 Many rescues
93 Gooseflesh-inducing, maybe
94 Some coin tossers
95 Serve well?
96 Liquor store purchase
97 Suspicious
100 Where Shiraz is located
102 Pic to click
103 Corp. division
105 Exclamations of regret
107 Combine
108 Green of "Miss Peregrine's Home for Peculiar Children"
109 Always, in verse

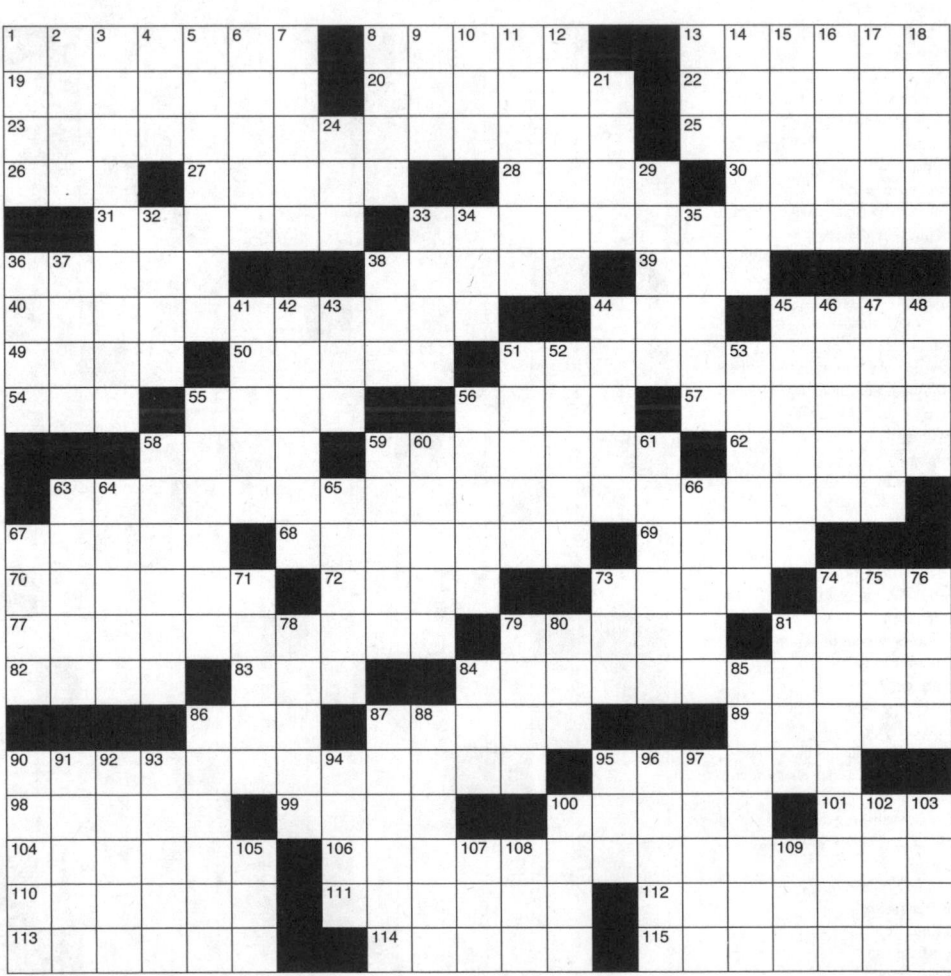

by Tony Orbach

ACROSS

1 Advice columnist Savage
4 Out of tune . . . or bubbles
8 Saturn or Mercury, once
11 ____ fever
16 Prayer leader
18 Opening opening?
20 Yeats or Keats
21 Pliocene, e.g.
22 Something to build on
23 Ancient Aegean land
24 The fly in fly-fishing, e.g.
25 Turn
26 Indy film? (1981)
30 Render unnecessary
31 Female deer
32 Classic sci-fi anthology whose first story is titled "Robbie"
35 Sound from a flock
36 Road movie? (1950)
40 Some M.I.T. grads: Abbr.
41 Bizarre
43 React to a stubbed toe, maybe
44 Confident juggler's props
45 Film director's cry
46 Blood work locales
49 Sound of relief
52 Cannoli ingredient
56 PG movie? (1992)
63 Anthem opening
64 A little bit of work
66 Brush off
67 Draw out
69 One whose range goes from about F3 to F5, musically
70 Hilarious folks
72 World capital with the Gangnam district
74 Challenge
75 Hummingbird feeder filler
77 Blatant
79 N.Y. engineering sch.
80 Actress de Matteo of "Sons of Anarchy"
81 Family film? (1972)
84 Barely contain anger
86 ____ glance
87 Thor : Thursday :: ____ : Wednesday
89 Suffix with hero
90 Oration station
94 Cleverly self-referential
98 Social stratum
100 Common 99¢ purchase
103 Dock-udrama? (1954)
108 Spendthrift's opposite
110 ____ Palace, Indian tourist attraction
111 Perfectly timed
112 Pilot, e.g.
114 Short film? (1989)
118 Where Minos ruled
120 Safe, on board
121 Violet variety
122 Wait in neutral
123 Jack rabbits, but not rabbits
124 Saturnus or Mercurius
125 Part of a sewing kit
126 Nair rival, once
127 Not so moving?
128 Nile reptile
129 Its name is derived from the Greek for "I burn"
130 OB/GYNs, e.g.

DOWN

1 Wear off?
2 Easygoing
3 Hometowners
4 Toy (with), as an idea
5 Least strict
6 ____ mundi
7 Popular ABC programming block of the '90s
8 "Perhaps"
9 Fine spray
10 66 and others: Abbr.
11 One of the Borgias
12 Rubber-stamp, say
13 Kids use it for texts
14 "Vous êtes ____" (French map notation)
15 Grp. with the Vezina Trophy
17 Pastels and charcoal, for two
19 Swear words?
20 More than enough
27 Enjoy some dishes without doing dishes, perhaps
28 Hasten
29 ____ Tuesday (Aimee Mann's band)
33 Dot follower
34 Some ESPN highlights, for short
37 Something often underlined and blue
38 Half-moon tide
39 ____ the crack of dawn
42 Balderdash
45 Trickster of Shoshone mythology
47 Short-legged hound
48 Fuel additive brand
50 17, for an R-rated movie
51 Director Ashby
52 Dappled horse
53 Key
54 Hidden downside
55 Man's name that's another man's name backward
57 In poor condition, as old machinery
58 Choler
59 ____ about (approximately)
60 Undesirable plane seat
61 Often-animated greeting
62 Yes or no follower
65 Flub
68 Eye drop
71 New Deal program, in brief
73 Co. with brown trucks
76 Palindromic title
78 See 118-Down
82 Lady of Spain
83 Anti-mob law, for short
85 Baby shower gift
88 Photographer Goldin
90 ____ Pérignon
91 ____ given Sunday
92 "My package arrived!"
93 Alcoholic drink consumed in one gulp
95 French stars
96 Clench
97 Utah national park
99 Bit of ranch dressing?
100 Got around
101 Street vendor
102 Radio buttons
104 First name of a literary "Papa"
105 Diminutive
106 Cat's pajamas?
107 Extends a tour
109 Invite to enter
113 Parts of kingdoms
115 When repeated, a "Seinfeld" expression
116 Scruff
117 Masseur's target
118 With 78-Down, Greek letters that together sound like a world capital
119 Dashed

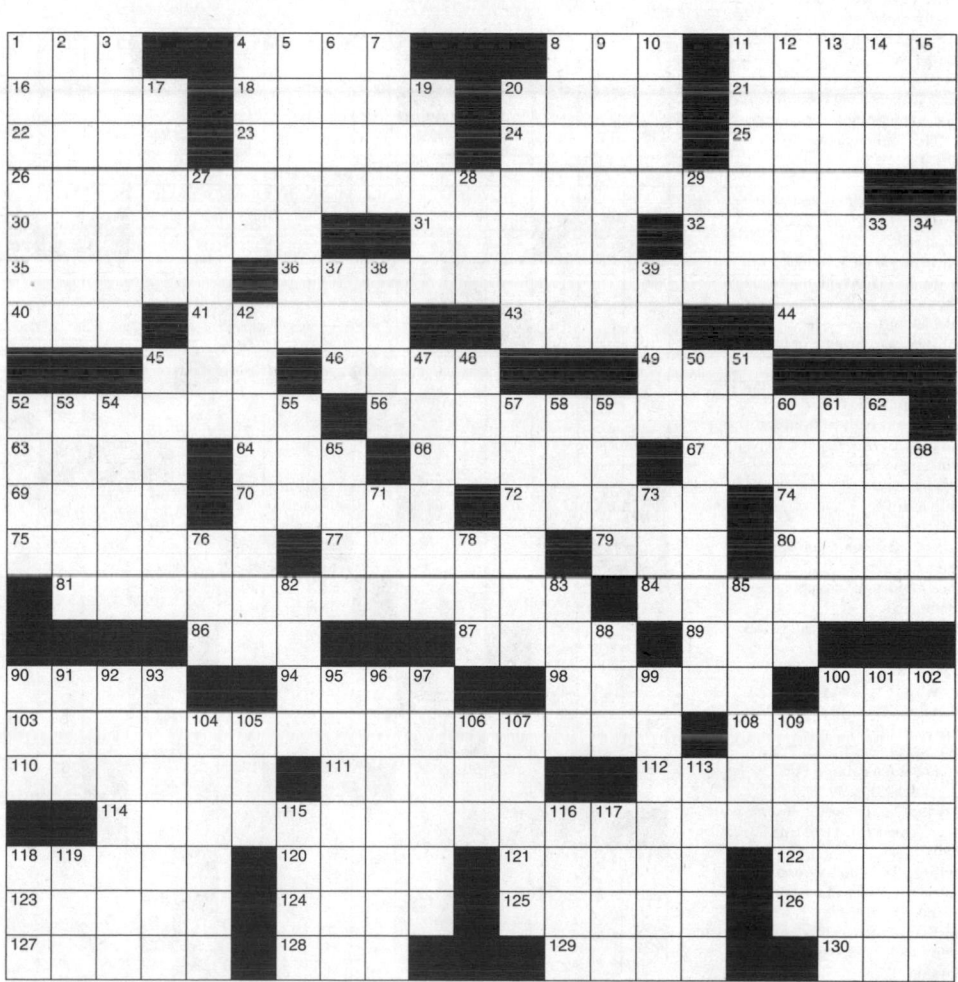

by Dan Margolis

ACROSS

1 Currency of Thailand
5 Kiss
9 U.S. city just south of Timpanogos Cave National Monument
13 Minus
17 Something to shoot for
19 One who hasn't turned pro?
20 Strong adhesive
21 Indiana governor Holcomb
22 She debuted on March 9, 1959, in a black-and-white striped swimsuit
24 Virtual pet simulation game that won an Ig Nobel prize for its Japanese creators
26 [Grrr!]
27 Glenn Miller classic
29 Purchases on 14 de febrero
31 Major talent grp. representing athletes and entertainers
32 Outpourings
36 Overplays, with "up"
39 Toy that was originally called "L'Écran Magique" ("The Magic Screen")
44 "Lost ____ is never found again": Benjamin Franklin
45 Natl. Humor Month
46 Mild, light-colored cigar
47 Things found in wandering souls?
48 Rhodes of the Rhodes scholarship
49 Photo finishes
51 U.S./U.K. divider: Abbr.
53 Loyally following
55 Flag carrier with an alphabetically ordered name
56 Trim
57 Game that got a big boost when Johnny Carson demonstrated it with Eva Gabor on "The Tonight Show"
59 Showy shrub
61 Schlepped
62 City in north-central Florida
63 Writer Arthur Conan ____
64 Umpteen
65 Day to play with new toys
69 Food ____ (Thanksgiving feeling)
71 Like subway walls, often
73 Final authority
74 William ____, founder of Investor's Business Daily
76 ____ area, part of the brain linked to speech production
78 Toy that was derived from a wallpaper cleaner
81 "I'm here to help"
82 Contented sigh
83 Phillies div.
85 ____ treatment
86 Harlem attraction, with "the"
87 Golf great Sam
89 Place for torn-off wrapping paper
91 Combined
93 Most common day to call in sick: Abbr.
94 Right away
95 Toy with 18 spoken phrases, including "I love you" and "May I have a cookie?"
97 Investment firm T. ____ Price
98 A halogen-containing salt
100 ____-Locka, Fla.
101 "My luck has to change at some point"
103 Politician parodied by Dana Carvey on 1990s "S.N.L."
107 Performed a Latin ballroom dance
111 Puzzle toy solved in a record 3.47 seconds in 2018
114 Toy that astronauts brought to space to secure tools in zero gravity
117 Goes off
118 Grannies
119 Not on solid ground, say
120 Piece in the game go
121 Strong criticism
122 Chichi
123 Spring event
124 Rigging pole

DOWN

1 Longest-serving Israeli prime minister, familiarly
2 Driver around Hollywood
3 "And, touching ____, make blessed my rude hand": Romeo
4 Small snare drums
5 Inaccurate information
6 Game with red and yellow cards
7 1904 World's Fair city: Abbr.
8 Flint is a form of it
9 Moonfish
10 Sacking site in A.D. 410
11 Physical, e.g.
12 "Holy cow!"
13 Appointment that may be hard to change
14 Curve
15 Dr. Fauci's former agcy.
16 Poli ____
18 Premiere arrival
20 Classic comics teen with good manners
23 They can elevate art
25 Alley ____
28 Org. with boosters
30 The beginning, in an idiom
33 By the end of 1996, one million of this toy was sold in a shopping frenzy
34 "South Pacific" hero
35 2014 film directed by Ava DuVernay
36 Goes after
37 Simian world
38 First toy to be advertised on TV
40 Open hostilities
41 St. Patrick's home
42 See the sights
43 Feed lines to
46 Its box once read "A sweet little game for sweet little folks"
48 Toy that sold more cars in America in 1991 than the Honda Accord or Ford Taurus
50 Promoting peace
52 Actress Taylor of "Mystic Pizza"
54 "That was Zen, this is ____" (philosophy pun)
58 Smart
60 "The Tempest" king
62 Cleanliness fixation, e.g., in brief
63 Brit. military award
66 Little bits
67 Reason for glasses
68 Singer with a self-titled #1 album in 2002
70 Be less than ambitious
72 Subj. for some aspiring bilinguals
75 Sierra ____
76 Operatic villains, often
77 Totaled
78 Legal assistant, briefly
79 Future J.D.'s hurdle
80 Not just available online
84 Biblical ending
86 Soon
88 With some downside
90 Shot from a doc
92 Statement of resistance
95 Big name in small planes
96 Took care of a tabby, say
97 Counters
99 Tik ____ (app)
102 Ballpark figures
104 Lasting impression
105 Give up (on)
106 Shopping site with a "Toys" section
108 Straddling
109 Sight from the Sicilian town of Taormina
110 Textile worker
111 One whistling while working in the Garden?
112 Address with dots
113 Swimsuit part
115 Suffix suggested by the wiggling of one's hand
116 Calf-eteria?

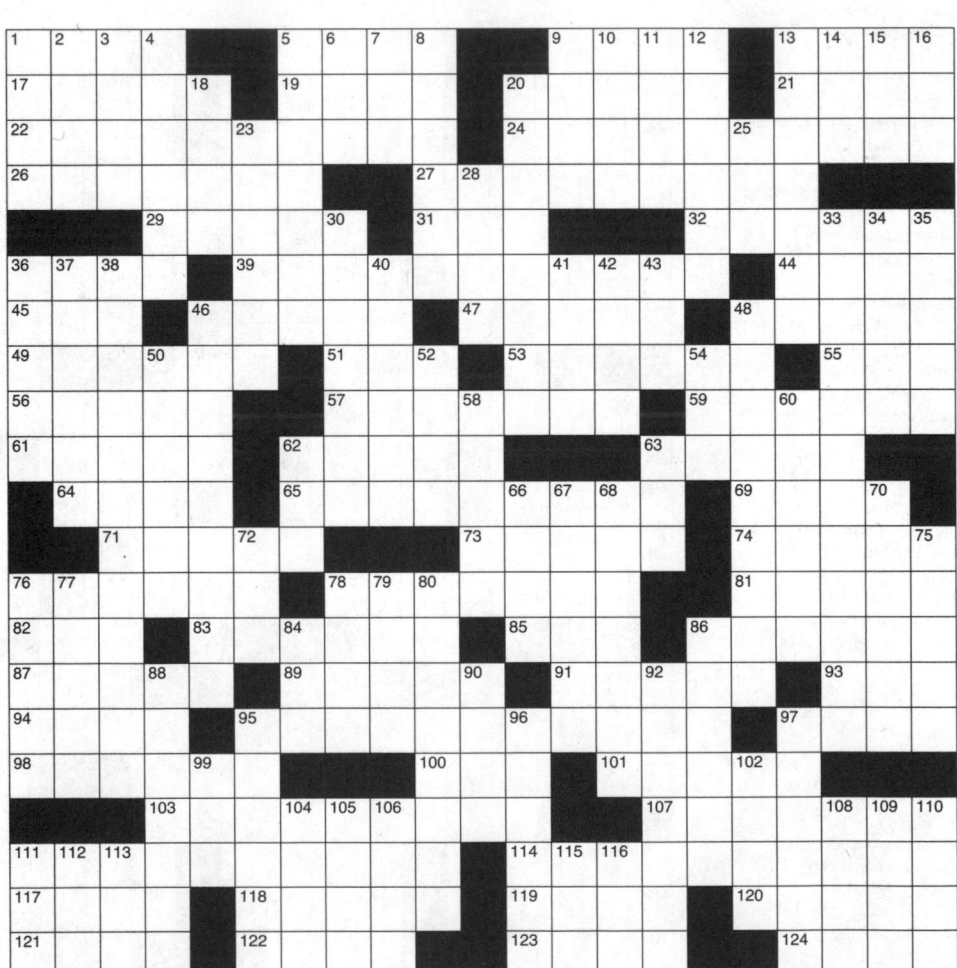

by Randolph Ross

ACROSS

1 Venomous snake
6 "To be honest . . ."
12 "My goodness!"
16 Extinct flightless bird that once grew up to 12 feet
19 Like the water in a whistling teakettle
20 Puzzled remark
21 A student may pass it
22 Kid's refrigerator display
23 Law partners
25 Booty call?
27 How-to manual component
28 ___ learning
29 Richard of "Chicago"
30 Mount ___, workplace of the Cyclopes in Greek myth
31 Having a very high body mass index
33 Singer with the 2020 album "A Holly Dolly Christmas"
35 Problems with streaming
36 Puller of strings?
39 Silent partners
42 Noticeably amazed
43 Leigh who played Scarlett
44 Train ticket info, for short
45 Writing partners
48 Spaceman Spiff and Stupendous Man, for Calvin in "Calvin and Hobbes"
54 Red ___
55 Who "can get in the way of what I feel for you," in a 2007 #1 Alicia Keys hit
56 Business suits?
57 Famous bed-in participant
58 Nest noise
60 For example
63 Salmon and sturgeon delicacies
64 Partners in crime
69 Modern meeting method
70 Some U.S. space launch rockets
71 "See ya"
72 Requests at security lines
73 Chicago mayor Lightfoot
74 Gave up
76 First dynasty of imperial China, 221-206 B.C.
79 Flier trier?
82 Business partners
85 Commotion
86 Fervent believer
88 Walker's need
89 Romantic partners
94 Tight-fitting suits
96 Apartment, in real estate talk
97 Core principles
98 Bake, as an egg
99 Evil Kermit or Grumpy Cat
100 How Phileas Fogg traveled
101 Money in coins rather than bills
104 Earnest request
108 Like some vinaigrette
110 Domestic partners
112 Sponge off of
113 Calendar row
114 Magazine bestowing Best of Beauty awards
115 Not a big studio film
116 Take possession of
117 Makes a typo, say
118 Gave a boost
119 S-shaped moldings

DOWN

1 Officers above capts.
2 What San Diego and Tijuana do
3 Airplane ___
4 "Notorious" rap nickname
5 It may be blond, brown or ginger
6 Of the utmost quality
7 Snapchatter's request
8 1981 Stephen King thriller
9 Certain bolt holder
10 Being fixed, as a car at a garage
11 Vegan milk source
12 Still being debugged
13 Turn against
14 Event organizer's count
15 ___ to come
16 Cocktail with rum, curaçao and fruit juice
17 Like monarch butterflies
18 Debut album for Etta James
24 Apollo's half brother
26 Fool
29 Sweet red dessert wine
32 Representatives' term lengths
34 A thing in poker?
36 Unfortunate events, old-style
37 C.I.A. whistle-blower Philip
38 Encountered by chance
39 Subject of a Magritte work (or not?)
40 Simple palindromic reply to "Madam, I'm Adam"
41 Fiscal year div.
43 Ryder ride
46 Dweeb
47 Rihanna or Mariah Carey
49 Have a preference
50 Deep-fried tortilla dish
51 Group of heavies
52 Universal donor's blood type, in brief
53 Brand of pads
59 Sewing 101 assignment
60 Didn't go anywhere
61 Spanish article
62 Investment options, for short
63 Setting for Hitchcock's "Notorious," informally
64 Portend
65 Emperor who ruled for more than 13 years, dying at age 30
66 More eye-catching
67 Anthony ___, 1950s British P.M.
68 Villain with the "real" name Edward Nigma
69 Teen's woe
73 Big game changer?
74 This is what it sounds like when doves cry
75 P.D. or F.D. worker
77 Kindergarten comeback
78 Indefinite degrees
80 Sweetness and sourness
81 Canoodling in a crowd, for short
82 Prominent feature of the Who's "My Generation"
83 Cheer for Real Madrid
84 Drinking game that requires aim
87 Winter setting in N.Y.C.
89 Deceptive talk
90 Perturbation
91 Small hole-drilling tool
92 Obstinate sort
93 Talents
94 Really stood out
95 Patchy in color
98 Close call
102 Sport with saddles
103 Bevy : quails :: mob : ___
105 Fill with freight
106 Lake largely fed by the Detroit River
107 Lemon or lime drinks, informally
109 Wonder
110 Piano tune
111 Words accompanying a headshot, in brief

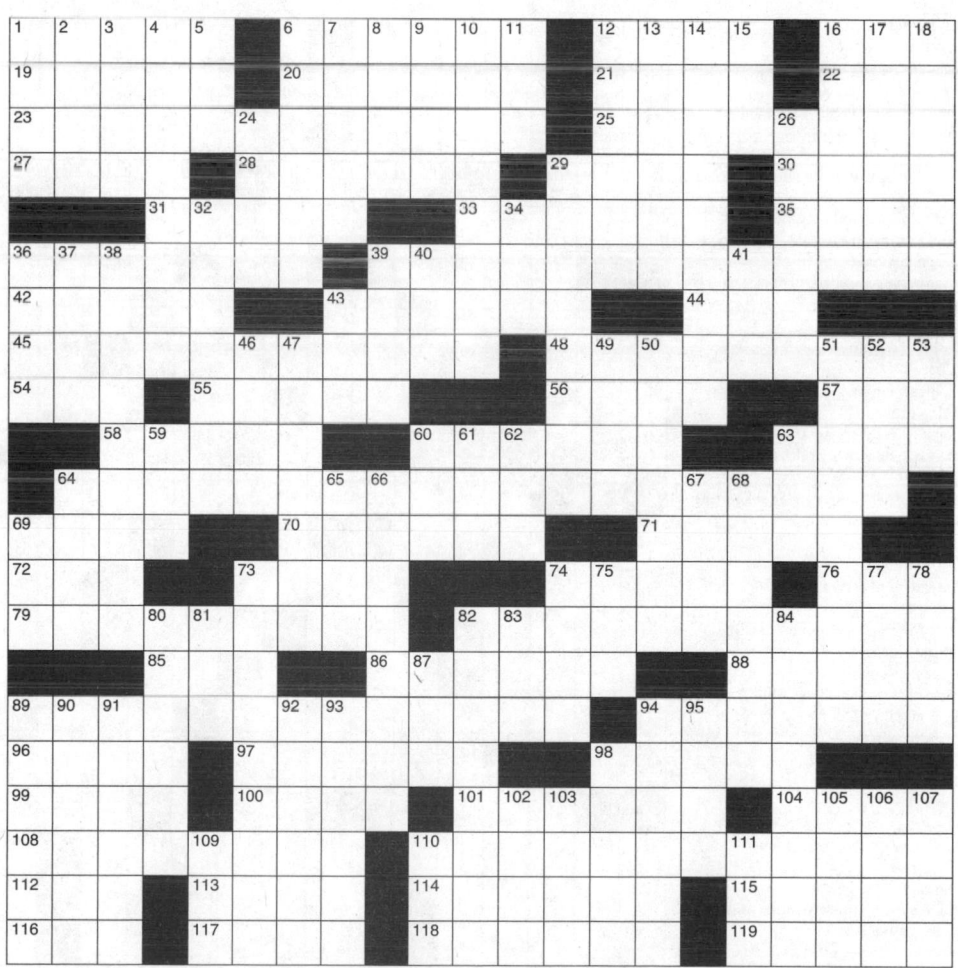

by Daniel Grinberg

ACROSS

1 Kind of kick
8 Product of evaporation
15 Apple product
20 Keep in
21 Brunch menu heading
22 Parts of college courses
23 Sources of stress for many modern workers
24 Utopia?
26 Part of the Dept. of Transportation
27 Channel buildup
29 Packers' grp.?
30 Old tabloid fodder
31 Piece still under consideration for a magazine?
37 Org. concerned with water quality
40 Balsa or balsam
41 Budgetary excess
42 Signal meaning "no disease on this ship"
44 Hurt sharply
46 Workers in some labs, informally
48 Interminable task
49 "____ Must Die" (Claude McKay poem)
50 "Village" newspaper that's namby-pamby?
53 Bull's urging
54 Fashion guru Tim
55 Behave
56 ____ of reality
57 Admitted (to)
59 Jacket material
60 Percolate
62 The "kid" in "Here's looking at you, kid"
64 Kia model
65 Common flower that's poisonous to eat
66 Santa's nieces and nephews?
71 Indiana Jones trademark
74 ____ department
75 Uber-owned company that makes self-driving trucks
76 Agreement
80 Result of a year-end review, maybe
81 "That so?"
84 Also-ran for the golden apple, in myth
86 "I don't reckon"
87 Home to Weber State University
88 Obama's signature health law, for short
89 Like shoppers worrying about getting the right gift?
92 ____ pad
93 Top
95 Scheduled to arrive
96 Like kitsch
97 Fleet for many a commuter airline
100 Doctor's orders, for short
101 Japanese soup
102 Specimen, for example: Abbr.
103 Jailhouse?
108 Prohibitionists
110 Craggy peak
111 Several CBS dramas
112 Short, for short
113 The Prada that one really wants?
118 Part of a postal address for a G.M. plant
121 Thomas of the N.B.A.
122 ____ Aquino, Time's Woman of the Year in 1986
123 With 113-Down, product of flax
124 Miners' aids
125 Women's fashion magazine
126 Warning before lunging

DOWN

1 Genre for TV's "Stranger Things"
2 First name in late-night
3 Unseemly
4 W. Coast air hub
5 When tripled, symbol of evil
6 Toddler garment
7 Amber, e.g.
8 Hand-held dish that doesn't crunch
9 Outback animal
10 Blue Cross competitor
11 Muddy mixture
12 Makes fizzy
13 Network standard for smartphones, for short
14 Recipe abbr.
15 Time to go home
16 Skinny
17 Truck driver?
18 And so on: Abbr.
19 Alphabet string
25 Panegyric
28 Boater's wear
32 Is off
33 Foul-smelling
34 Set of principles
35 "Will ya look at that!"
36 Kind of computing
38 Foe of the Cheyenne
39 Something set in a meeting
43 Insect that spends its larval stage inside a fruit
44 Hot tubs
45 Knight club
46 Car company that owns SolarCity
47 Golfer's need
51 "There it is!"
52 Grand
58 Source for "Book of the Marvels of the World," circa 1300
59 Chinese philosopher Mo-____
61 Part of a club selling clubs
63 Well-ventilated
65 After ____ (to some extent)
67 'Fore
68 HBO political satire
69 Non-prophet group?
70 Sch. in Knoxville
71 Dowdies
72 Cafe
73 Nickname for a Gilded Age businessman with a penchant for jewelry
77 "In Trump We Trust" author, 2016
78 Distillery item
79 Not we
81 "That deep, blue, bottomless soul," per Melville
82 Lacks
83 Part of un jour
85 Ghost story?
88 Most fit
90 Awkward time at family movie night
91 New York City's ____ River
94 Almost falls
98 Amps, with "up"
99 Vehicle at a ski resort
101 Light cotton fabric
104 Wild
105 Long arm
106 Covered in frost
107 Pass over
109 Gather
113 See 123-Across
114 Troop grp.
115 Roll call response in une école
116 Wernher ____ Braun
117 Scale note
119 Dutch financial giant
120 Govt. org. that offers a monthly "Puzzle Periodical"

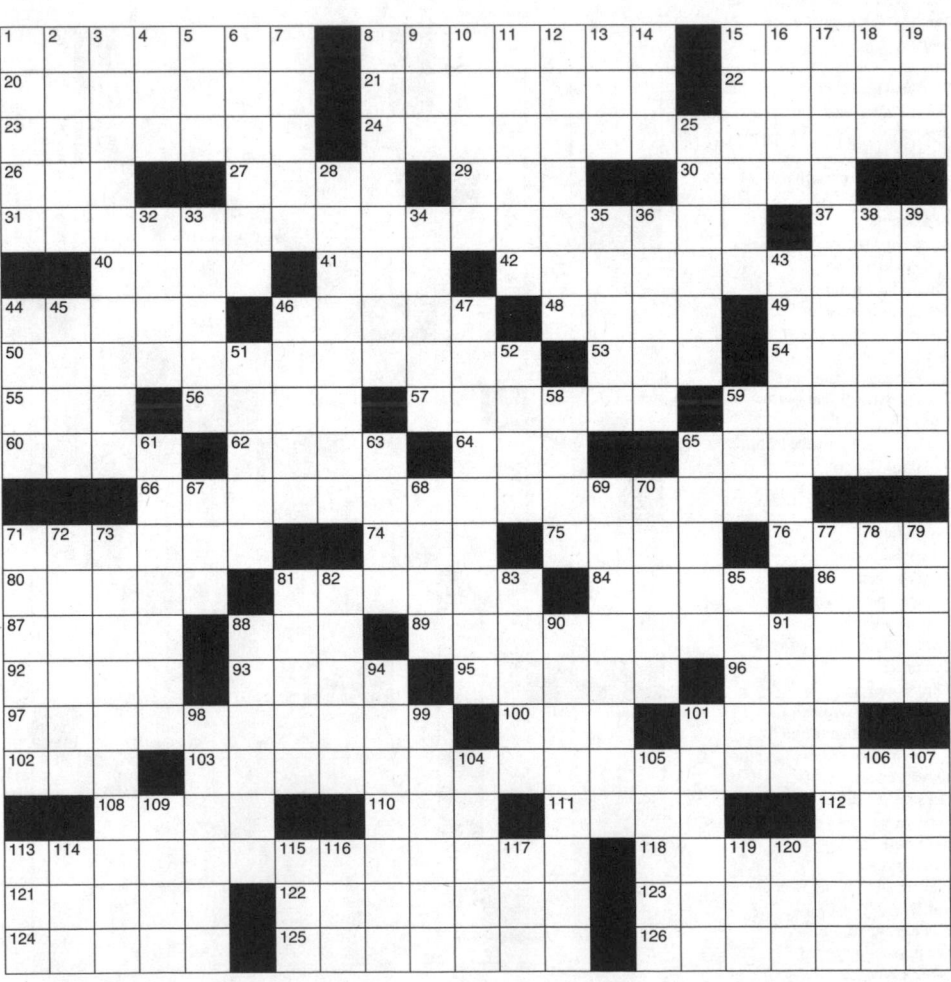

by Joel Fagliano

ACROSS

1 Inconceivably vast
7 Hard looks
13 Stream, as of revenue
19 Baseball-like game
21 Flowery
22 Et ___
23 Witty British judge?
25 Conquistador Cortés
26 Copies, informally
27 It shows who's who or what's what
29 Perform a full-body scan?
30 Pizza, e.g.
32 Quest of 25-Across
33 Ortiz of "Ugly Betty"
34 Site of Spaceship Earth
37 Language akin to Thai
38 Three-legged race, e.g.?
44 School chum, say
46 "Mr. Blue Sky" band, for short
47 World's most voluminous river
48 Chapter in early 20th-century history: Abbr.
49 Property inheritor, legally speaking
51 On point
53 Julie of TV's "Big Brother"
54 "One of the most civilized things in the world," per Hemingway
55 Nail?
58 Consider anew, as a decision
60 Girl with a ball
61 Sound investments, in more ways than one
62 ___ Minor
65 A
66 "America"?
71 Hindi word for "spice mix"
74 Brief second?
75 ___ generis
76 Theological inst.
79 What Cubs fans get carried away by?
81 Grant a girl permission to dis Drake?
86 Fortify
87 Page (through)
90 1990s Indian P.M.
91 Week, on Martinique
92 Alias inits.
93 Game for the goal-oriented?
95 Keeps in the loop, in a way
97 Worn out
98 Ability to score at Madison Square Garden, e.g.?
102 Mouse's resting place
103 Take a timeout
104 French ___
105 Title at Topkapi Palace
106 Egg container
107 Religious image
109 Piano dueler with Donald in 1988's "Who Framed Roger Rabbit"
112 Quiz bowl fodder
114 Like Serbia and Croatia
117 Diving disaster?
122 Maintain
123 Bawdy
124 Gently show the door
125 Give a new tournament ranking
126 Pulls on, as heartstrings
127 Speakers' spots

DOWN

1 Bluecoat
2 Only woman to sing lead vocals on a Beatles song
3 Darn things
4 Sierra ___
5 Drink commonly served with a spoon-straw
6 H.O.V. lane user
7 Farm females
8 Lateral opening?
9 Chest pain
10 Grist for analysts
11 Californie, e.g.
12 Gaming giant
13 I, to Izaak
14 Word for a name-dropper?
15 1960s sitcom set in the 1860s
16 From one side to the other
17 Kind of history
18 Ebb
20 Grammy-winning drummer ___ Lyne Carrington
24 Lorna of literature
28 Codger
30 Opposite of ruddy
31 Thyroid need
33 Embrace
35 Bus. card info
36 N.L. Central squad, on scorecards
37 Don't work too hard
38 Half of a swinging couple?
39 Goes by
40 Alternative to Cinemax
41 "That'll be the day!"
42 Take responsibility for something
43 Atheist's lack
45 Place to hang tools
50 Leave a good impression?
52 One lifting spirits?
54 Jet measure
56 Think tank product
57 Chi follower
59 Diesel in movies
63 Reeling
64 Shivering fit
67 Key locale: Abbr.
68 They'll take your measure
69 Manhattan, e.g.: Abbr.
70 They're dubbed
71 Mullally of "Will & Grace"
72 Hard to tell apart
73 Informal measures of popularity
77 It lies between Cleveland, O., and Buffalo, N.Y.
78 Nut
80 Made out
82 Showy in a cheap way
83 Salmon roe, by another name
84 "Don't worry about me!"
85 Await resolution
88 Relative of "Aargh!"
89 Wetland
93 Measly amount
94 Guitar Hero activity
96 Wolf (down)
99 Mantle, e.g.
100 Some vaults
101 Like cats, typically
106 Secure spots
107 Certain steel beam
108 Racer Yarborough
110 Fig. on a periodic table
111 Mrs., abroad
112 Bedouin shelter
113 ___ facto
115 Common thing to lie about
116 ___ Yost, 2015 World Series-winning manager
118 Mauna ___
119 Poland's main airline
120 Start of the Lord's Prayer
121 Education support grp.

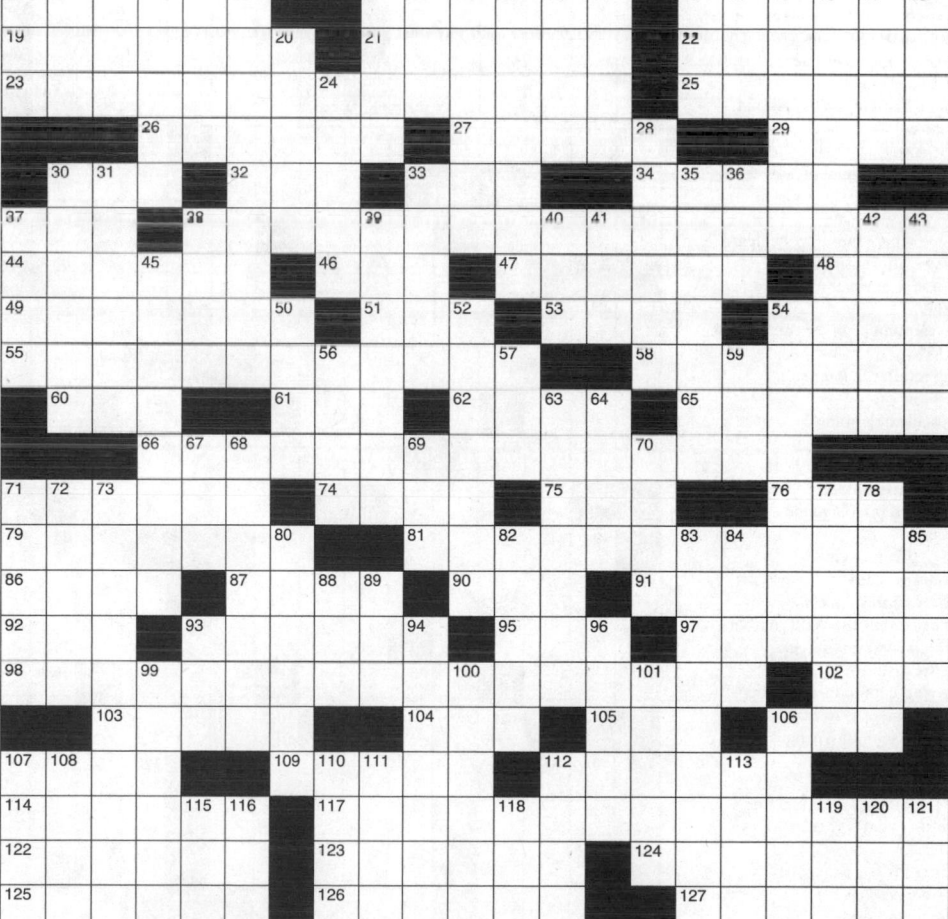

by Dan Schoenholz

ACROSS

1 One side of a 69-Across showdown
7 Strip of buttons
14 Other side of the showdown
20 Collective works
21 "Get lost!"
22 Pinball wizard's hangout
23 Mother ___
24 Entertainment on a Jamaican cruise, perhaps
25 Kind of paper or test
26 Lieutenant, informally
28 It's unreturnable
30 Musicianship
31 Green plant?
33 Path to enlightenment
34 Cannon in movies
36 Developer's purchase
37 Samoan staple
38 Bullets legend Unseld
40 Top-shelf
41 Sushi restaurant wrap?
43 Moxie
45 X-File subject
47 Fairy tale family
52 Celebratory request
58 "Great!"
59 One doesn't hold stock for long
60 "My man"
61 "What ___?"
62 Storied workshop worker
65 Sand wedge, e.g.
66 Sean Lennon's mother
67 Thanksgiving dish
69 Game depicted in the circled squares
72 Carpenters with small jobs?
73 Last mustachioed president
76 See 125-Across
77 Easy-breezy tune
79 Place where taps may be heard
82 Skype alternative
86 Amount of separation, in a party game
88 Investment seminar catchphrase
90 Lost big
91 Big retailer in women's fashion
93 Upscale bag brand
94 "Damn right!"
95 Indy 500 winner A. J.
97 Silly Putty holder
98 Standard poodle name
100 Hound
101 Digital camera mode
102 Countenances
104 Confession subjects
106 "The Call of the Wild" author
110 March Madness stage
115 In the distance
116 Having a lot to lose, maybe
117 "___ Care of Business" (1974 Bachman-Turner Overdrive hit)
118 Eins+zwei
119 Message with a subject line
120 Unlikely partygoer
121 Lieu
122 Bring in
123 1-Across's cry
124 Tel. no. add-ons
125 With 76-Across, like Arial and Helvetica
126 14-Across's result

DOWN

1 Like houseplants
2 Wiggle room
3 Light show
4 The "Y" of Y.S.L.
5 Once, at one time
6 Behind
7 Campaign expense
8 Wine barrel descriptor
9 Linc's portrayer in 1999's "The Mod Squad"
10 One may get smashed
11 Chest-thumping
12 "Up" voice actor
13 Changed, as voting districts
14 Artist who said "I don't do drugs. I am drugs"
15 Speed skater Heiden
16 Entr' ___
17 Delivery instructions?
18 Infers from data
19 Feel bitter about
27 "I think," in texts
29 Neckline shape
32 Word shortened to its last letter in texts
35 Holiday air
36 Tabloid issue
39 Total
40 Citi rival, informally
42 Neuwirth of "Frasier"
43 Some SAT takers: Abbr.
44 Tease
46 Item by many a reception desk
47 Super Fro-Yo seller
48 "Hava Nagila" dance
49 Hotel bill add-ons
50 Right on a map
51 From square one
53 Marked by futility
54 Jane Rochester, nee ___
55 "O.K. by me"
56 Blow off steam
57 Matchmaker of myth
62 Suffix with acetyl
63 Printer paper size: Abbr.
64 BTW
68 Famed Broadway restaurateur
70 Ruhr industrial city
71 Butcher's discards
72 How great minds are said to think
74 Worried
75 Laser ___
77 Maui memento
78 "O.K. by me"
79 Word after snake or sound
80 Container that may have a sharpener
81 Superman, at other times
83 Starting on
84 Like the sign of the fish
85 Marijuana, in modern slang
86 "___ cheese!"
87 Composer Max who was called "the father of film music"
88 Young swans
89 Part of a tour
92 Basis of some discrimination
96 "Lawrence of Arabia" star
99 Maniacs
101 City that's home to the Firestone Country Club
102 Divider in the Bible?
103 Venetian blind parts
105 Bottom of an LP
106 "Twister" actress Gertz
107 Some
108 Intimate garment, for short
109 Bit of progress
111 Company with a noted catalog
112 Dull color, in Düsseldorf
113 Word on a towel
114 Shade

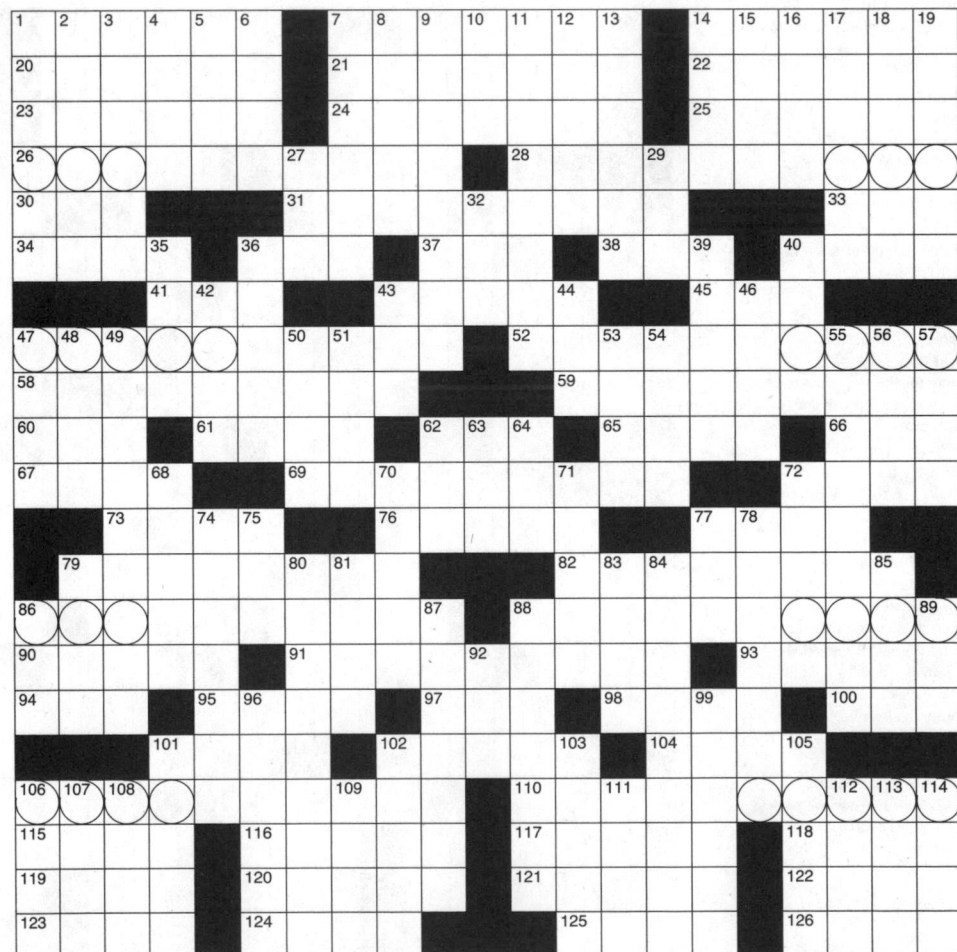

by Jim Hyres and David Steinberg

ACROSS

1 16-ounce container
6 Material commonly used during cathedral construction
14 Primitive timer
19 Pinnacles
20 Sidney Poitier's 1980 autobiography
21 Moretz of "Carrie"
22 Performs, biblically
23 When soap operas first flourished
24 They're measured by pluviometers
25 Geneticist's study
26 Rage
28 Sheena who sang "U Got the Look" with Prince
29 "No worries"
30 It helps you achieve balance
33 Highlighter shades
34 %: Abbr.
35 Reply to "No offense"
37 Aid after a computer crash, say
40 Get
41 Mark
44 Mosaic pieces
46 Question after a photo finish
47 "How's it hangin'?"
48 Click "Going" on a Facebook event, e.g.
49 2013 best seller by Sheryl Sandberg
53 Pennsylvania vacation locale, with "the"
56 Pokey's pal on TV
57 Spanish she-bear
60 Running a bit behind
61 Part of a stock exchange?
64 Overcome a certain career barrier . . . or what the answers to the starred clues do?
68 Heavy weight
69 "Same with me"
70 Move hastily
71 Also-ran in 2000
72 Gray squirrel, in slang
74 Send elsewhere for the night, as a roommate, in modern lingo
75 Easy-to-carry telescope
79 Cubs' home
80 Less safe for a plane landing, in a way
84 Change from black-and-white
86 Classical musician with a Presidential Medal of Freedom
87 Pub vessel
91 Permeates
92 Behind
94 Fix, as an election
95 Cab destination?
100 Geometric toy whose sides change depending on how it's folded
101 Drop a bit
103 Arthurian princess
105 Poetic preposition
106 Scrape (out)
107 Go online
108 Remove fat from, as a soup
110 Caramel candies from Hershey
112 Opposite of standing
113 Getting ready to swing
114 Lake catch
115 White who is the oldest person ever to host "S.N.L."
116 Participate in deciding
117 Took care of

DOWN

1 Superfluous part of an essay
2 *One who 64-Acrossed for Supreme Court justices . . .
3 Emphatic refusal
4 After deductions
5 Gift shop item
6 Hurriedly showed oneself out?
7 "J to ___ L-O!" (Jennifer Lopez album)
8 * . . . for astronauts
9 Like over four billion people
10 "Victory is yours"
11 Former Mexican president Enrique Peña ___
12 Zac of "Neighbors"
13 Professors answer to them
14 Reading material for a Hollywood agent
15 * . . . for British prime ministers
16 Most-wanted invitees
17 Texting while driving, e.g.
18 Anchor's place
27 Enter, as data
31 Cousin of "OMG!"
32 Guido who painted "Massacre of the Innocents"
36 Today
37 "Hmm, guess so"
38 Loo, for short
39 ___ rally
42 What boats shouldn't do
43 ___ Gay (W.W. II plane)
44 Best Foreign Film of 2005 set in South Africa
45 Kennedy who was the mother of Maria Shriver
46 Aid for the handy, informally
49 Letters of "pride"
50 Alternative to a pound
51 Emphatic agreement
52 Org. with a travel ban?
54 Bills, e.g.
55 Hit record?
57 "Yi-i-ikes!"
58 Pacific
59 Ending with teen
61 Certain conservative skirt
62 Hillary Clinton in 1969 or Bill Clinton in 1970
63 Monster
65 Fictional spacecraft created by the Time Lords
66 Like lettuce
67 West Coast air hub
73 Overly
74 Two-___ (smallish car)
75 ___-fi
76 Yapping dog, for short
77 * . . . for secretaries of state
78 "Don't be so dumb!"
81 Rip off, informally
82 Clown (around)
83 [Yawn]
85 Rule by governing board
87 Altar constellation
88 * . . . for Best Directors
89 Ranger's station
90 Che Guevara's real first name
93 Puts forward, as effort
95 Factor in area calculation
96 "___ little silhouetto of a man" (Queen lyric)
97 Desert NE of the Sinai Peninsula
98 * . . . for Nobel laureates
99 1941 chart-topper "Maria ___"
101 Slice for a hearty appetite
102 Miner's strike
104 Catches off base
109 Apologia pro vita ___
111 60 minuti

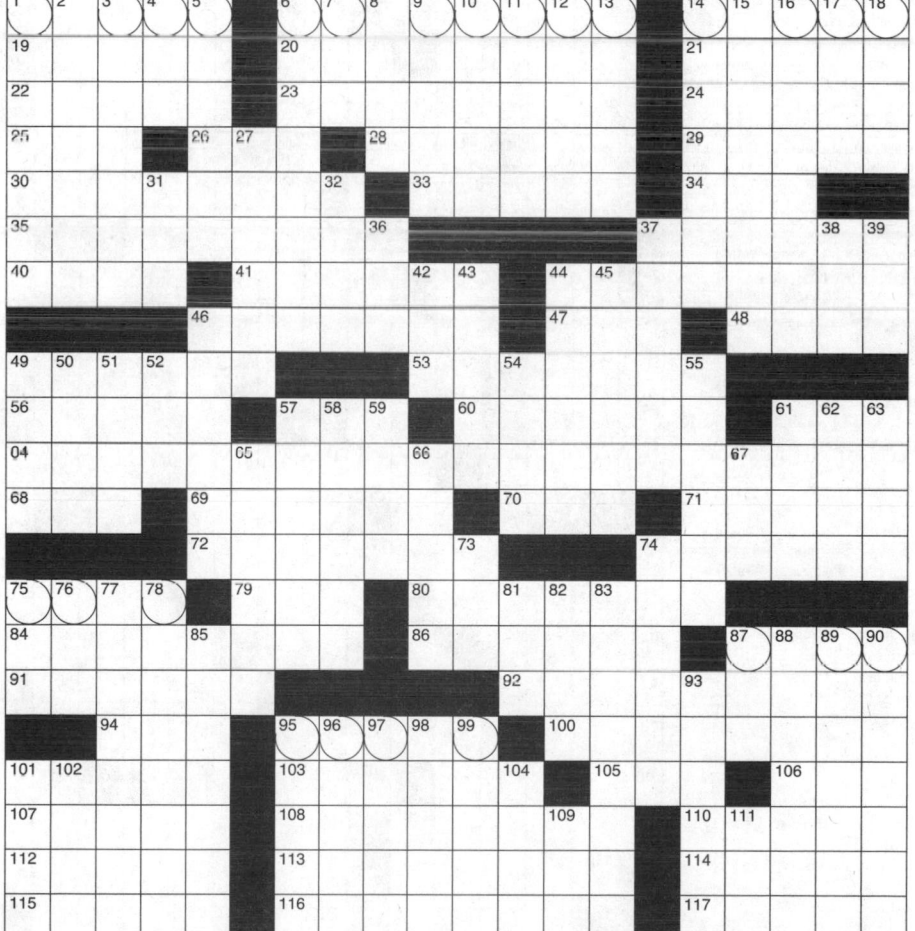

by Sam Trabucco

ACROSS

1 Game option represented by a flat palm
6 Singer with the 2016 #1 album "A Seat at the Table"
13 Disney queen
17 Not clash
18 Front lines?
19 Said without saying
21 CERISE + LAVENDER = certain baby animals
23 God sometimes depicted with green skin
25 State in which "Parks & Recreation" is set: Abbr.
26 Pull some strings, maybe?
27 Clinches
29 Chip away at
30 Employee on an airline or cruise ship
32 CORAL + GOLD = pet store purchase
36 Veto
37 ___ stick
38 Quarterback who holds the N.F.L. record for most consecutive games started (297)
39 "You're on!"
41 Train set
42 Tailor, maybe
43 One-named singer with the album "Lovers Rock"
45 Lipstick choice
46 AMBER + GREEN = imported brew
48 Final Fantasy character who shares his name with a U.S. city
49 Sashay, say
50 ___ B. Wells Society for Investigative Reporting
51 A bunch
52 PEAR + CRIMSON = fighting group
54 Bottle flipping in the mid-2010s, e.g.
55 Hospital settings, briefly
56 Poster board?
57 Max's opposite
58 Bo or bonsai
60 LIME + MAGENTA = visualization
64 ["You're *still* talking?"]
68 Subj. of some collegiate bragging
70 Actor Gallagher
71 Go astray
73 "Herc could stop a show / Point him at a monster and you're talking ___" (lyric in Disney's "Hercules")
74 RUST + SCARLET = celestial group
78 Daughter in the comic strip "FoxTrot"
80 Cha chaan teng serving
81 Plot problems
82 Dis-tressed
83 CREAM + PEACH = nonviolent protest
85 Plantings lining the Literary Walk in Central Park
86 Skier's accessory
87 Many an art print, briefly
88 "No injuries here"
89 2019 space film
91 B's in math?
92 Devotee, informally
93 A ways
94 TEAL + OCHER = breakfast option
97 Absolves
100 Fisher of 2018's "Eighth Grade"
102 One towering over the rest of the field?
103 Actress Rooney
104 ___ Giedroyc, co-host of "The Great British Bake Off"
105 Nappy : U.K. :: ___ : U.S.
107 MAUVE + TANGERINE = restaurant handout
112 African antelope
113 Frenzied
114 Goddess who turned Picus into a woodpecker
115 Throws in
116 Unbelievable rumors
117 Takes the edge off

DOWN

1 2024 Olympics host
2 Deal maker
3 Christopher Street Day celebration
4 Still, for a poet
5 Outlet store come-on
6 Miffed
7 Fantasy creature whose name is an anagram of another fantasy creature
8 Rural setting
9 What's the point of leatherwork?
10 Newcomer
11 Artist El ___
12 "The motor industry's Titanic," per a 1994 book
13 Nwodim of "S.N.L."
14 Ne'er-do-wells
15 Keep from sticking, say
16 "Wait for It" singer in "Hamilton"
18 Stave (off)
20 Got ready for guests, in a way
22 Prefix with centric or vision
24 Volleyball teams, e.g.
28 Lost traction while driving over
31 Sinuous dance that emulates a creature
32 3/4 and 7/8, e.g.
33 Done
34 Hound sound
35 Homophone of the sum of this clue number's digits
38 Took off
40 Who says "That I did love thee, Caesar, O, 'tis true"
41 Wood in some incense
42 Bring down
43 Truth ___
44 "Jung at heart" persona?
46 Talent
47 Par for the course
48 ___ to go
49 Chemistry, for one: Abbr.
52 Grinding tooth
53 Come out
56 High on marijuana, in slang
59 Way to go
61 Twangy, as a singer
62 "Us," "It" or "Her"
63 Progressive alternative
65 Ones doing stellar work
66 Total
67 One arranging for flood insurance?
69 Parts of many gaming rigs
72 Payment sent
74 In a bundle, as documents
75 Wasn't straight
76 Culinary phrase after "pollo" or "scaloppine"
77 Vessels hunted by K-ships
78 Element in many henna designs
79 "I'm in heaven!" sounds
83 Doner kebab bread
84 Latin 101 word
86 For
87 Film director ___ Isaac Chung
90 "That's it"
91 Heavy footwear choice
92 Evening in Italy
95 Car model name made entirely of Roman numerals
96 Novelist Ferrante
97 Of the flock
98 Cross swords
99 Sooty channels
101 Modern checkout device
103 Diagnostic scans, for short
106 Map lines: Abbr.
108 Clean energy grp.
109 Stuff in cigarettes, but not e-cigarettes
110 ". . . is there more?"
111 Rapper known offstage as Mathangi Arulpragasam

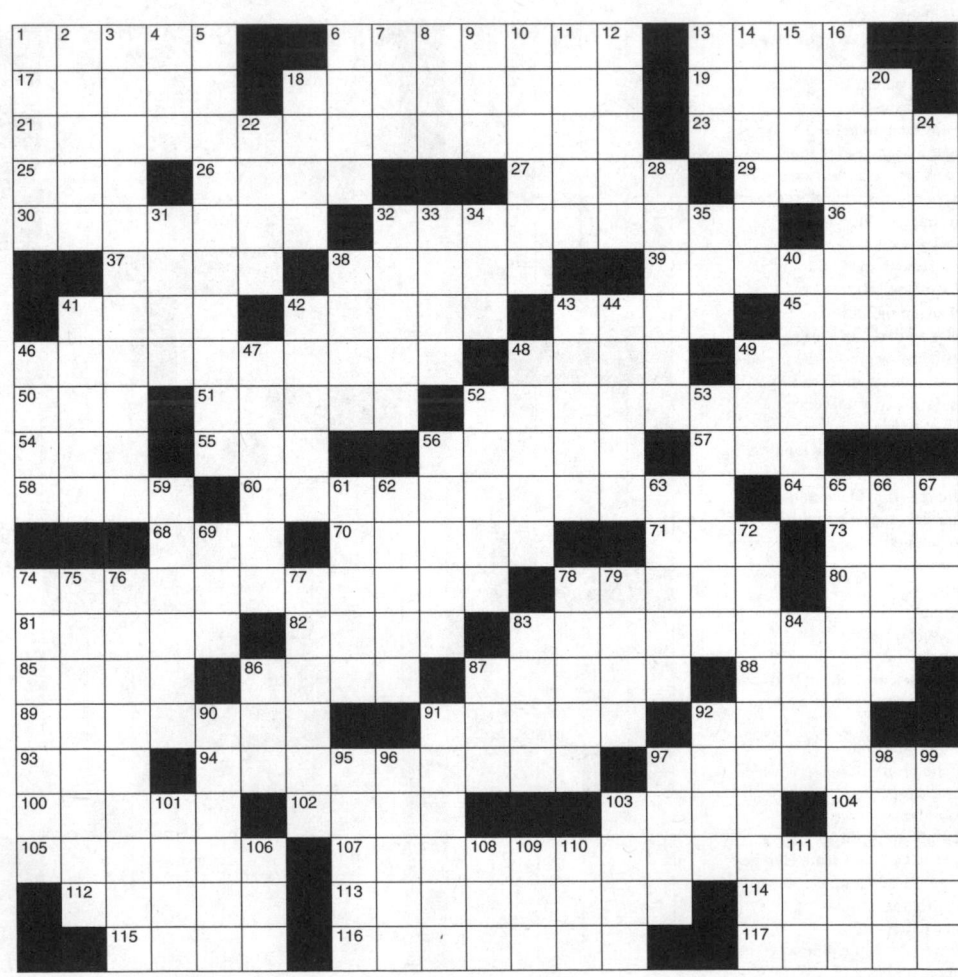

by Paolo Pasco

ACROSS

1 Disseminated
5 JPEG alternative
8 Quick-witted
14 "Forbidden fruit is the sweetest," e.g.
19 Kind of writing
21 Hurting more
22 Mineral used as a flame retardant
23 Aromatic herbal drink
24 Carmen McRae or Anita O'Day, notably
26 Disorganized
27 Sound in the Serengeti
29 Tying words?
30 Horrible boss, say
31 Neighbor of S. Sudan
32 Endpoint of a Shinto pilgrimage
36 What's going up in Chicago?
38 And so forth
40 Munchkin
41 Spade with a short handle?
42 Morse morsel
43 You can have a blast with this
44 "Yes, indeedy!"
47 ___ volente
49 Makes clearer, in a way
51 1997 pop hit with a nonsensical refrain
52 Fete
56 Anago, on a sushi menu
57 In ___ fertilization
58 & 59 Flag bearers, for short?
62 Clap back
63 Many moons
64 Chaired
66 Many, many, many moons
68 Subj. line heading
69 Birthplace of five U.S. presidents, with "the"
73 German title
74 Like discriminatory employers, often
75 Just roll with it!
76 See 88-Across
77 Eliminates, mob-style
79 Driving stick?
81 ___ out a victory
83 Pack (in)
84 Fracases
85 Start of some conventional wisdom
88 With 76-Across, Mexican business magnate who was once the world's richest person
89 Means of a quick recharge
92 "___ funny!"
93 Fab
94 Akin to
95 Rapper ___ Cudi or DJ ___ Loco
97 Comprehension
99 Domain of Mars
100 Boise-to-Spokane dir.
102 Post-default event
104 "Eureka!"
108 "That's the spot"
110 Kinda
111 Lunkhead
113 Court order
114 Red accessory for cartoondom's Huckleberry Hound
116 Scientific contribution from 98-Down, discovered in a manner suggested by this puzzle's theme
120 Crow's-nests, e.g.
122 One living in the rial world?
123 Lingerie fabric
124 Blights
125 More mirthful
126 Defiant refusal
127 ___ Plaines, Ill.
128 Start of a story, in journalese

DOWN

1 Cause of a jolt
2 Really busy, perhaps
3 It's nothing to joke about
4 Artist known for his lampooning cartooning
5 Startin' place
6 "___ moved on"
7 Calming words
8 Holy city near Baghdad
9 Hardly a lover of hot wings?
10 Radio frequency meas.
11 Ad or show follower
12 ___ P. Morton, Benjamin Harrison's vice president
13 Lost deposits, as a bank?
14 Attorney's org.
15 Sorrow
16 Thank you, in Tokyo
17 Stovetop device
18 Breadths
20 Sled dogs, e.g.
25 Word in some cocktail names
28 Baseball's "Master Melvin"
33 Westernmost sch. in Conference USA
34 Actress ___ Pinkett Smith
35 "Er . . . umm . . ."
37 Nonbinary possessive
39 Game show invitation
45 Modern lead-in to "X"
46 Got out fast
48 Exit
50 Tom Petty hit with the opening line "She's a good girl, loves her mama"
51 Rendezvous
52 Nickname for Virginia
53 Declare
54 Is beaten by
55 You might take a lift to one
56 Married mujeres: Abbr.
57 All-in-one purchase from a smoke shop
60 Unforgettable, unstoppable sort
61 They're not to be trusted
65 Julie who played Catwoman on old TV
67 Puzzle (out)
70 Personal bearing
71 Strong pan
72 Hard thing to do?
78 German title
80 Capital of Bangladesh
82 Mushroom in miso soup
86 Afterword
87 Nicolas who directed "The Man Who Fell to Earth"
88 Lab where the Higgs boson particle was discovered
89 Inventory
90 "My Cousin Vinny" setting
91 Airport route
93 Squealed
96 Opposite of a glut
98 Who was famously hit over the head with inspiration?
99 Tech release of 2006
101 Didn't act rashly, say
103 Pit
105 Words before relax or remember
106 Small section of a pit
107 Bowl-shaped cooking vessels
109 German state that includes Frankfurt
112 Manage
115 What's got ewe covered?
117 Hemlock relative
118 Old ___ (London theater)
119 Gag line?
121 Spanish "hey!"

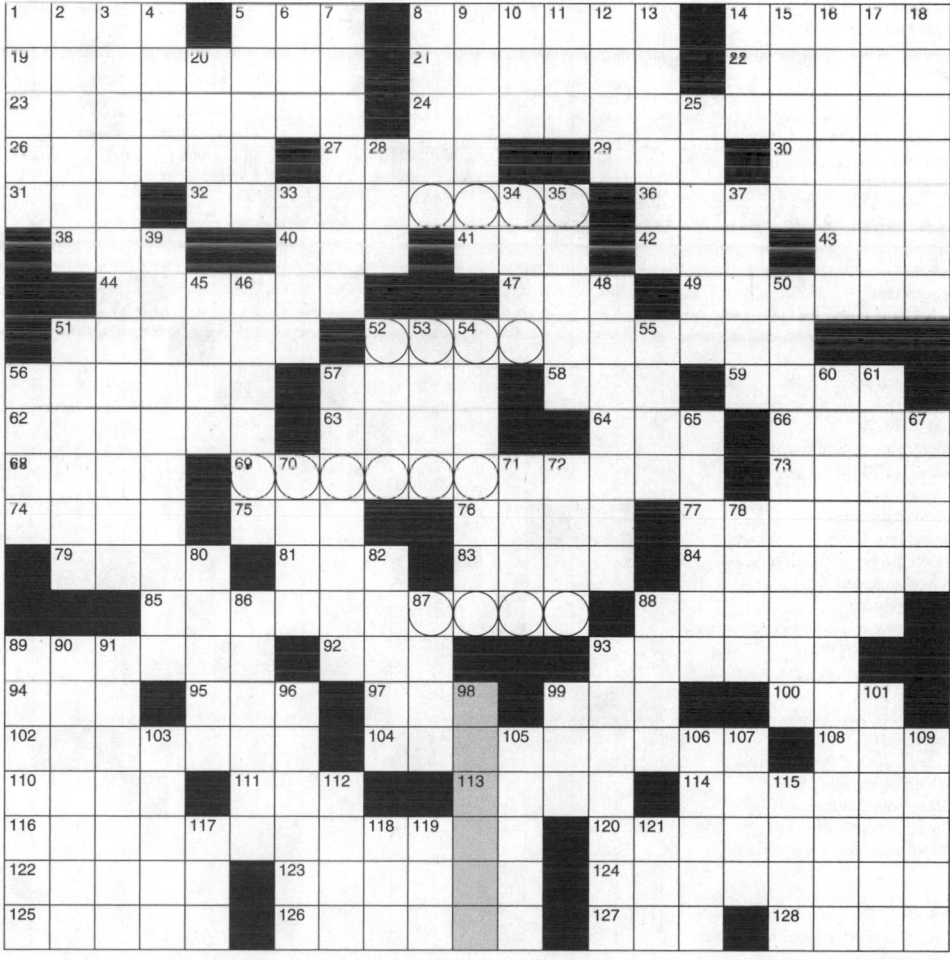

by Timothy Polin

ACROSS

1 Symbol of authority, informally
7 Compañero
12 Delhi issue
16 Reaction to puppy pics
19 Water buffalo, for one
20 French _____ (trick-taking game)
21 Land of blarney
22 Pass during the N.F.L. playoffs
23 THE LADY VANI_____ (#2, 1964)
25 Who infamously boasted "They can't collect legal taxes from illegal money"
27 Luxurious
28 Suffix in some pasta names
29 BILLE (#3, 1972)
31 He gave Starbuck's orders
34 NATO members, e.g.
35 Adorable sort
36 x⁰ (#1, 1985)
41 Barnyard baby
42 Keep one's mouth shut?
43 Porky Pig's girlfriend
44 It cost 5¢ in 1965
47 Home of Iowa State
49 Help with a crime
50 Google web browser
53 Laser pointer chaser
54 Like the Balkans in the 1990s
57 Certain peaceful protest
58 Country singer McEntire
59 Captivate
60 VAUDEVILLIAN (#2, 1988)
65 Become more complicated, say
66 Getting together
67 Sheen
71 LOST, E.G. (#1, 1984)
73 Glacier-scaling tool
74 Yard tool
77 Private student
78 Figure it out
79 _____ Lilly (pharmaceutical giant)
80 "Jeez!"
82 Actress Garr
85 Beach shaper
86 Only player to win the U.S. Chess Championship with no losses or draws
88 Darling
91 Harbor helper
92 _____ story (tale of a car company's bankruptcy?)
93 CHAN_E _PPEA_ANCE TO CONCEA_ _ _D MISLEA_ (#1, 1968)
97 Islamic spirit
99 Brand of insecticide strips
100 Madhouses
101 TITTLE-TATTLE (#16, 2011)
103 Opposite of post-
105 Airline posting
109 Furnace for calcium oxide production
110 ENTICEMENT (#1, 1983)
114 Big club in Las Vegas?
115 The final word
116 Give a lift
117 Know-it-all
118 "_____ Como Va" (Santana hit)
119 Female Olympian of note
120 Palindromic battlers
121 Place of worship whose third, fourth and fifth letters are appropriate

DOWN

1 One of eight in a stick of butter: Abbr.
2 Jolly laugh
3 Dec. 24 and 31, e.g.
4 Minor accident
5 Mary _____ Evans a.k.a. George Eliot
6 Opposite of paleo-
7 Memo abbr.
8 When doubled, Hawaiian food fish
9 Pique
10 Terk in Disney's "Tarzan," e.g.
11 Opera with the aria "Ave Maria"
12 Naval engineer
13 Air traveler's accumulation
14 Quint's boat in "Jaws"
15 Enclosure for a bike chain and sprockets
16 180
17 Arthur who invented the crossword puzzle (1913)
18 Overgrown, say
24 Kind of terrier
26 Young chicken, e.g.
30 Actress Tyler
32 Move barefoot across a scorchingly hot beach, maybe
33 Shock's partner
34 Throw _____ (rant and rave)
36 No longer frozen
37 Kind
38 Crop up
39 Chafe
40 Out of gas, informally
41 Internet ending that's also an ending for inter-
44 Part of the brainstem
45 Chatter
46 Greek letter that might follow "z"
48 Affix, in a way
50 Eyelashes
51 Ketchup brand
52 "One _____-dingy" (Ernestine the operator's catchphrase on "Laugh-In")
55 Arch type
56 Landlord's due
57 Petrol unit
58 Surgically remove
60 Unearthed
61 Mi, in a C major scale
62 Number twos
63 Pelvic bones
64 Air carrier
68 Island where Paul Gauguin painted
69 Book that's the source of the phrase "a land flowing with milk and honey"
70 Go back (on)
72 Instruction in an oatmeal recipe
74 "Zebra"
75 Slugger from Louisville
76 Florida city whose name has three pairs of doubled letters
78 Upscale watch brand
80 Annual eight-day celebration
81 Basketball stat: Abbr.
82 Numbskull
83 Poetic dusk
84 Color of traffic on a GPS
87 Craft carried over a portage
88 Rhythmic part of a heartbeat
89 Same: Prefix
90 Sense of self
93 Protagonist in "The Stepford Wives"
94 FedEx competitor
95 Clears for takeoff?
96 Old Glory
97 1964 Tony Randall title role
98 Like oranges and some gossip
99 Duck or Penguin
102 Frost
103 Davidson of "S.N.L."
104 Richard and Jane in court
106 Commercial prefix with postale
107 Out of office?: Abbr.
108 One-named Irish hitmaker
111 Tops
112 Madrid's country, in the Olympics
113 Song lead-in to "Believer," "Loser" or "Survivor"

by Derrick Niederman

ACROSS

1 Web site?
6 Browser window
9 Streaming service acquired by Fox in 2020
13 Civil rights grp. once led by M.L.K.
17 Fictional character who says "I will take the ring, though I do not know the way"
18 Scorpion, for one
20 Wasn't overturned on appeal
21 Artists sketching pectorals?
23 Stays out all night?
24 Glowing or shining
25 Work rotations
26 French "I like"
27 "Right on!"
28 Spot at a casino
30 Either side of a beaming grin, in a phrase
31 Tony winner McDonald
32 Something to make after you wake
33 Vow to remain mum about hotel guests' secrets?
37 Hoops org.
40 Possibility
41 Scoffing sound
42 Driver of film
43 Nonbinary people, informally
47 Declined
49 Over-poetical?
50 Modern-day "carpe diem"
51 Early times in verse
52 Small distance covered by a naval armada?
56 First sitting prez to fly in an airplane
57 Words after walk or cash
58 Hyperbolic wait time
59 Like climates where cacti thrive
60 Pointy part of a charger?
62 Group of followers
64 Willem who played Jesus in "The Last Temptation of Christ"
66 Some pianos and motorcycles
68 2000s Fox teen drama
69 Playwright Simon
70 "Emotion in motion," per Mae West
71 Thomas ____, British general at Bunker Hill
72 Sweetie
73 Boxer lacking a left hook?
77 One of the boxing Alis
78 Gumbo ingredient
80 :-) alternative
81 Below par
82 Something unleashed in a denial-of-service attack
83 Destination for a return flight
84 Himalayan humanoid
86 ____ eyes
88 "I'm a frayed ____" (punch line of a classic joke)
89 What brass band music has?
92 Court
95 Groups of Greeks, informally
97 Watcher of the skies, for short
98 Old ____ (motherland, affectionately)
99 Announced
100 You can count on them
101 Beat in a race
104 Very productive
106 Not even a little off
107 Tree feature in winter?
109 Quaint bathroom sign
110 Galosh
111 Lumberjack's favorite kind of beer?
112 "What are the ____?"
113 Audience for Cocomelon, the most-viewed YouTube channel in the U.S.
114 Omega's place
115 Columns with angles

DOWN

1 Home with a pointy roof
2 Worked on Wall Street
3 Bring to a repair shop, say
4 Creative springboard
5 Cereal once advertised by Woody Woodpecker
6 Subject for Laozi
7 Sounds from a lab
8 "The Art of Fugue" composer
9 One's kin, casually
10 Loosen, in a way
11 Some zeros and ones
12 Bar necessities, at times
13 It has several steps
14 What a dog walker and a strong-willed pooch might vie for?
15 Run easily
16 Makeup of some music libraries
19 Main
20 Huge quantity
21 Lacking color
22 Brief period of work
26 "Easy . . . everything's going to be OK"
29 Bottle marked with a skull and crossbones
31 Cost for a spot
33 Garden shed items
34 Caramel-filled candy
35 "You can leave this to me"
36 Declaration by one who's done playing
38 Benjamin Franklin famously considered it "a rank coward" with "bad moral character"
39 "Te quiero" sentiment
43 Mideast V.I.P.
44 Response to "No offense"
45 The Bee Gees' Barry, Robin and Maurice Gibb?
46 It might gather lint
48 Somersault
52 Adversary
53 To's opposite
54 Old-timey reproach
55 Scottish cap
58 Aromatic trees
61 Really bother
63 Jacqueline or Jacques
64 For sure, for short
65 Something a snowboarder catches
66 Last word of "Ulysses"
67 Goal in musical chairs
69 Nick of "48 Hrs."
70 Beer brand whose name spells an article of apparel backward
72 Knock on the head
74 Carolers' repertoire
75 ____ dancer
76 Minotaur's foot
77 Bird known in the U.K. as a diver
79 Draws
82 Red-light district establishment
85 Like some vodkas
87 Fly into a rant
90 Spuds
91 Tall tales
92 Dispensed with
93 N.H.L. team with five championship-winning seasons in the 1980s
94 Praising poetry
96 Ballet sections
99 Play station?
100 Got rid of
101 "Duh," in modern slang
102 Pine
103 Like the Radio City Music Hall sign
105 Harvest
106 Something swollen on a pro athlete?
107 Totally fine
108 Alternative to Webster's, in brief

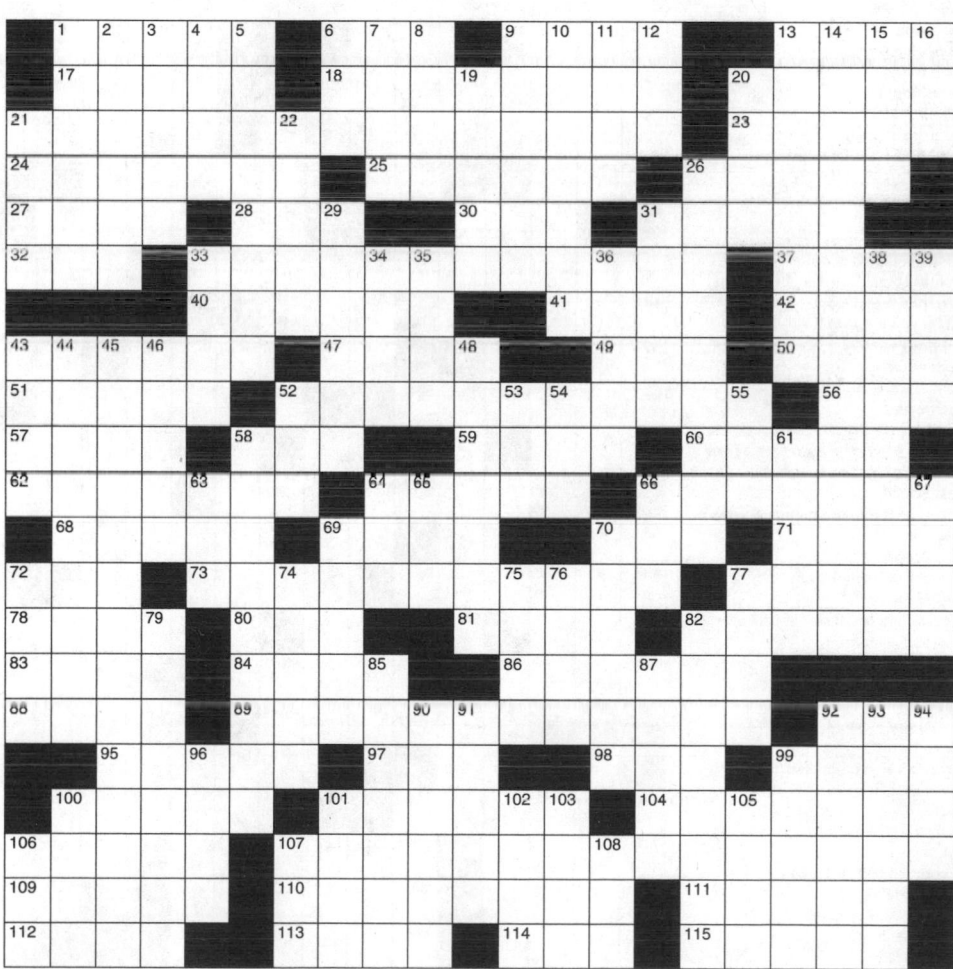

by Nancy Stark and Will Nediger

ACROSS

1 Rock subgenre named for its vocal aesthetic
8 Like some space-saving beds
14 Styles that are picked, informally
18 Amateur
20 Disinclined (to)
21 Royal figure of sci-fi
22 Grammy for Kendrick Lamar's "DAMN." or Cardi B's "Invasion of Privacy"
24 Shuts down
25 American, abroad
26 Apt name for a worrier
27 Moving toward equilibrium, in biology
29 Legerdemain
31 Horse color
34 Prepares for a Ms. Olympia competition, say
36 Tiny foragers
37 "Here's an example . . ."
41 Insect with distinctive pincers
44 Without stop
45 Subj. for some future bilinguals
46 Sources of music in musicals
50 Splinter group
51 Brewing brothers
54 Capital of Japan's Hyogo Prefecture
55 It might be broken in overtime
56 Waits to publish, as an article
59 Second-rate
61 Pronoun pairing
63 Loop trains
64 Hornswoggle
67 De-creased
69 Luxury Hyundai
70 "Still da ___" (Trina title track of 2008)
72 Fluster
74 Kind of squash
77 One using cloves or garlic
79 What gets filled at a shell station?
80 Monthly condition, for short
83 Hairstyle protectors
85 Tabbouleh topping
87 Build, as interest
89 Kind of test
90 Board figure, informally
92 Recipe unit
95 Goddess in a peacock-drawn chariot
96 Marilyn Monroe wore a fuchsia one while singing "Diamonds Are a Girl's Best Friend"
99 Beverage that was a medieval source of nutrition
100 ___ President
101 Literary protagonist raised by wolves
102 "The Sound of Music" household
105 "Horned" creature
107 Turn one's back on
109 Laces (into)
110 Apelike
112 University of Montana city
115 Weasel word?
118 ___ Fielding, co-host of "The Great British Bake Off" beginning in 2017
119 Suffering from a losing streak, in poker slang
122 Secret exits represented five times in this puzzle's grid
125 "Bus Stop" playwright
126 Camping shelter
127 Advocates
128 Romanov ruler
129 Vulnerable
130 Most likely to inspire "thirst"

DOWN

1 Twins, e.g., for short
2 Site with tech tutorials
3 Gets out of a grave situation?
4 Scores for placekickers
5 Mental health org.
6 They're thumped at supermarkets
7 Balls
8 Overly simplistic
9 Bake-off equipment
10 Major-___ (pro ballplayer)
11 OB/GYNs, e.g.
12 Application
13 Royal pain
14 Circus apparatus
15 Laugh or cry, say
16 "Old MacDonald Had a Farm" sounds
17 N.Y.C. retailer with a famed holiday window display
19 Rum ___ Tugger (cat in "Cats")
23 Like a romantic evening stroll, perhaps
28 [someone else's error]
30 Cause chaos
32 –
33 "That's it?"
35 Camping shelter
37 Only person to win an Oscar, Emmy and Tony in the same year (1973)
38 Kitty ___, stunt performer once known as the "fastest woman in the world"
39 Four-limbed animals
40 "Raiders of the Lost Ark" biter
42 Plato's P
43 Halloween decorations that can be made with cotton balls
46 Heavy metal's "Prince of Darkness"
47 "Am ___ only one?"
48 Level
49 Some skin-care products
52 Power up
53 A.L. East squad: Abbr.
57 Slice, for one
58 Give the ___
60 Stopover
62 –
65 –
66 Put on ice
68 Traffic control org.
70 Disco ___ (iconic garment for Lady Gaga)
71 "Chandelier" singer, 2014
73 Longtime record label
74 Annexes
75 Rube Goldberg machines, e.g.
76 Like some vaccines
78 A, in Berlin
80 Incline
81 Expansive work of art, usually
82 Disreputable
84 Annual Austin festival, familiarly
86 "This is too much"
88 One to be dethroned
91 One being coddled, maybe
93 Lacking any adulteration
94 Zing
97 One who may have attachment issues?
98 Small Nintendo console, once
100 Spring month in France
102 ___ 1, Yuri Gagarin's spacecraft
103 Cries in a tattoo parlor
104 Frothy coffee invented in Greece
105 –
106 Sign of resistance
108 Some bank deposits
110 Foul mood
111 Pelicans' home, informally
113 –
114 Girl in a tartan
116 Miner discoveries
117 Relative of "Hey!"
120 March Madness "trophy"
121 Road goo
123 Maliciously reveal personal info about online
124 "Mais ___!"

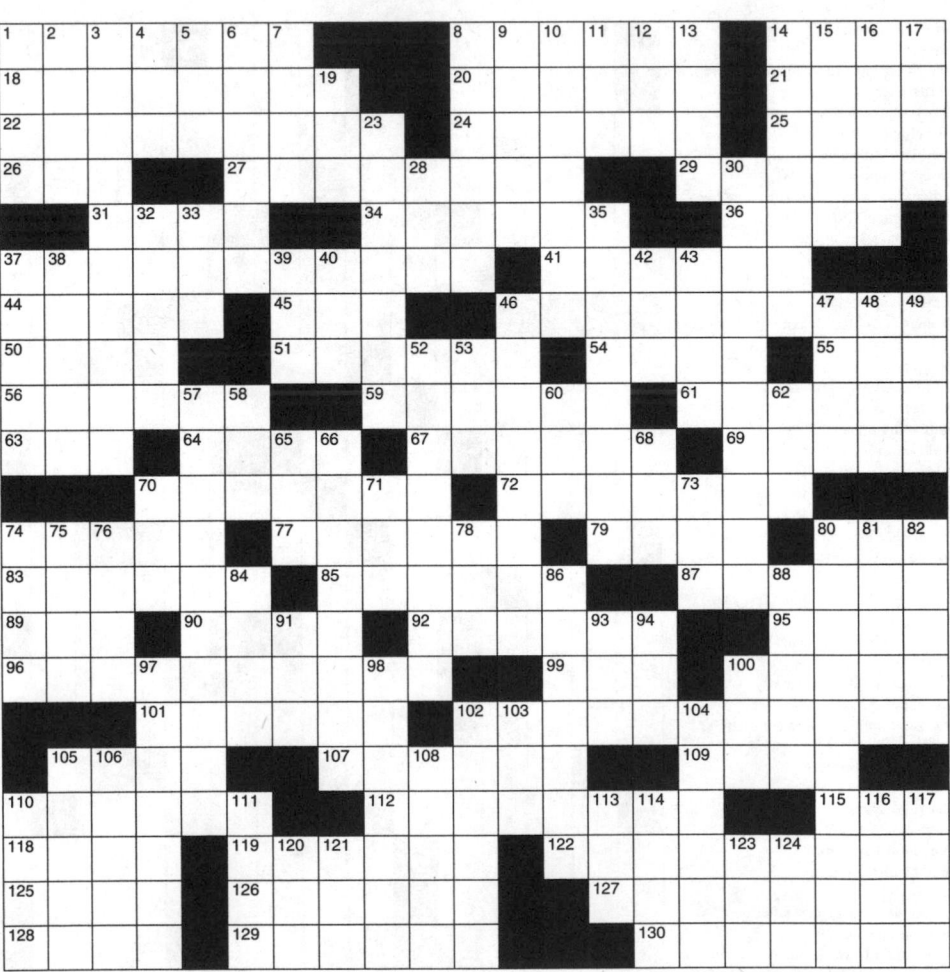

by Ross Trudeau

ACROSS

1 Goal for many a T.A.
4 There's a Winter one in St. Petersburg and a Summer one in Beijing
10 Confront
16 QVC alternative
19 Grande preceder
20 Many a video game player has one
21 Hebrew name of God
22 Major N.Y.S.E. events
24 Vainglory
25 Good side in 70-Across
27 Reid of "Sharknado"
28 Grade school basics
30 Scoundrel
31 Points all around?
32 Celsius of the Celsius scale
33 Director Nicolas
35 Good cheer
37 People to pick from
38 Major role in 70-Across
41 Smartphone forerunners, in brief
42 "___ kingdom come . . ."
43 Big stretch
44 Bluish-gray shade
46 Mobile ___
48 Time might be shown on the side of one
50 Score of 8, in golf slang
52 Events where one person's trash may be another person's treasure
56 Pull back (in)
59 Capital-B Belief
61 Family name on TV's "Succession"
62 Vote in favor
63 Prefix with futurism
64 Outback offering
65 Locale of the 2002 and 2022 World Cups
67 Long-term damage
68 Some copywriting awards
69 The volcano Emi Koussi is its highest point
70 The better of two major sci-fi film franchises?
72 Climb (up)
73 Gives a bad hand?
74 "But ___ counting?"
75 Gentle hill
76 Grams, by another name
77 Voice heard by 500 million people
78 ___ Majesty
79 Not for moi?
80 Pump choice
82 Spot for a patch, perhaps
83 Begins to like
86 Regular at Citi Field
89 Small spot for a castaway
91 Ian McKellen, e.g.
92 Skin-care brand with an accent over its last letter
94 Mens ___
95 Sends a Telegram, in brief?
97 Not looking good
99 Major role in 70-Across
102 Stop at the liquor store?
103 Comforting phrase
106 Newton of the Black Panther Party
107 "___ Darko" (2001 cult film)
109 Distend
110 Who wrote "April is the cruellest month"
113 Scratch-and-sniff page, e.g.
114 Dramatic accusation
115 Good side in 70-Across
118 Misfortune
119 Cousin of a skimmer
120 ___ One

121 "Do you mind?"
122 Brown of HBO Max's "Gossip Girl" reboot
123 WaPo competitor
124 "There's not much hope"
125 Bumper attachments
126 Sazerac cocktail ingredient

DOWN

1 Records in advance
2 Time for a shootout
3 Memorable quote from 70-Across
4 Apple device
5 Affirms
6 Some college classes
7 "Thanks, but I already ___"
8 Diet Coke doesn't have a single one: Abbr.
9 Wipes out
10 "The Clan of the Cave Bear" heroine
11 What's raised in a ruckus
12 Waste of an election?
13 Confesses
14 Bad thing to be stuck in
15 On-line connection?
16 Arrive at, as a solution
17 Memorable quote from 70-Across
18 "Take your time"
23 Audacious
26 A target for Target, say

29 It might be a shocker
31 "The Simpsons" character
33 Social media star Addison
34 Partner of one
36 French skin-care and cosmetics giant
38 ___ teeth (proverbial rarity)
39 Noble title
40 Follower of black or special
44 Slanders
45 Director Waititi
47 Ones involved in a transaction
49 Nutty confections
51 So-called "Breakfast of Champions"
53 They might end on a high note
54 Sound of a jaguar
55 Let out, in a way
57 Some contents of golf bags
58 Needing to butt out
60 Potato or pea preparer
64 Albert who developed a polio vaccine
66 Leaves in a huff, with "off"
67 Body part that precedes "band"
68 Innocent
69 One of the Prairie provinces: Abbr.
71 "It's a ___!"
72 Show of scorn
74 Question of confusion or disgust
79 Sound of a Jaguar
81 Reassuring words
83 "___ Hiring" (business sign)
84 Kind of card

85 The "quail" in Beethoven's "Pastoral" Symphony
87 By plane, say
88 Obvious untruth
90 Q preceder?
93 Aloof
95 "Seems so"
96 Like the inside of a lava cake
98 Devices in atomic clocks
100 Converse, e.g.
101 Rank
102 Common waiting room viewing
104 Jeer
105 Shock treatment, for short
107 Slobber
108 Noises that come from pens
111 "Girls" creator Dunham
112 Carded, informally
113 Tabbouleh go-with
115 "Enough already!"
116 Suffix in organic chemistry
117 Quirk

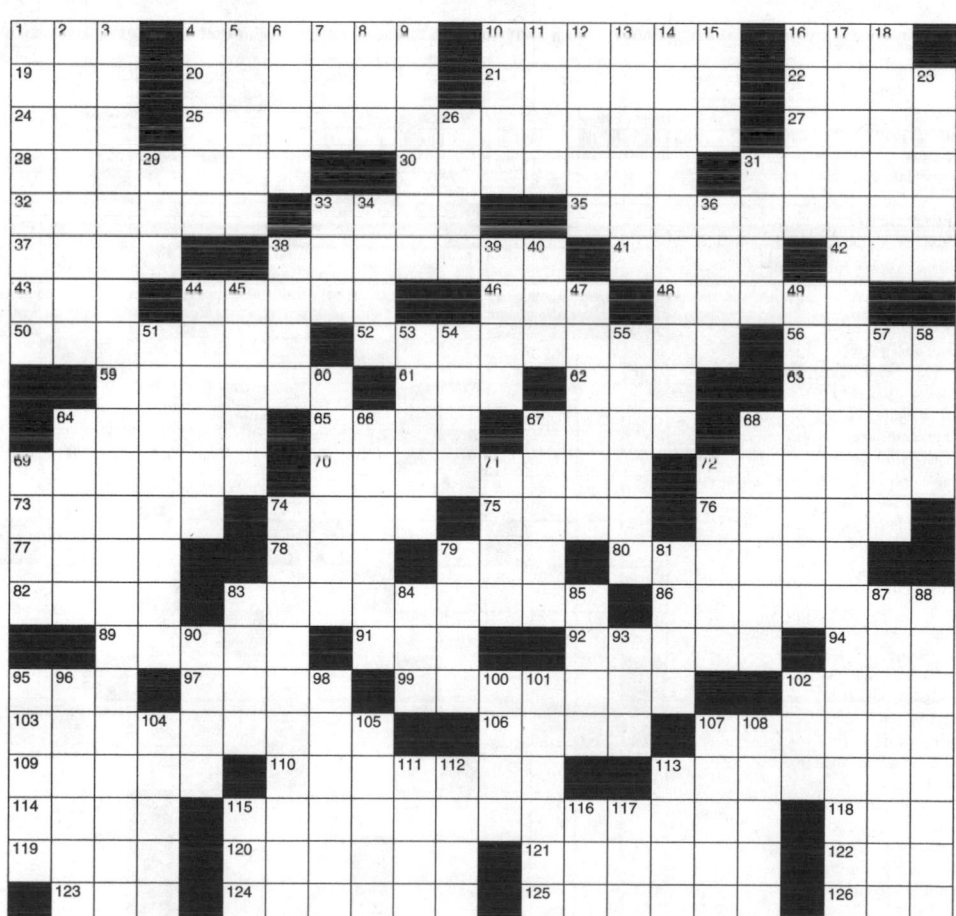

by Stephen McCarthy

Note: The middle letter of the answer to each starred clue can be replaced by a different letter to form two new words across and down. Read the new letters, in order, for a bonus.

ACROSS

1 Bank offerings, in brief
4 Twists
9 Losing roll at dice
13 In itself
19 Piece played with four hands
21 Tart sorbet flavor
22 Kind of bed
23 *Opposite of endearing
24 *Freely expressive
26 Winter eaves dropper
27 Some attacks on castles
29 Día de ___ Muertos (Mexican holiday)
30 Stories that may or may not be true
31 12-year-olds, e.g.
34 Ballerina's bend
35 App whose icon features a camera, in slang
37 Aimee with two Grammys
38 Plank targets
41 Only trisyllabic rainbow color
43 Ferrari of automotive fame
46 *Communicating (with)
49 *Contracting
52 Acceptance principle of improv comedy
53 2-year-old, e.g.
54 What may connect the parts of a school assignment?
55 "Who ___?"
58 Relative of an alpaca
60 "A Christmas Carol" cry
61 Dress in
62 Things people catch and then ride
63 Fifth sign
64 Actress Hepburn
67 Poke
68 Nickname in baseball and gossip columns
69 *Harsh language
71 Up
72 Loses firmness
73 Country with the most archaeological museums in the world (110+)
74 Brand seen at speedways
75 Cut off
76 French menu phrase
77 Sushi chef's eggs
78 Uncle for whom an annual award is supposedly named
80 Not so many
81 When nothing goes right
83 Dutch name starter
85 Frank Robinson or Brooks Robinson of the Baseball Hall of Fame
87 *Watered artificially
89 *Goes well with
94 Turn in a game
95 Canine coat
97 Instant, informally
98 Island with a trisyllabic name
99 Sat around
101 In the thick of
103 Ending remark that's surprising
105 Starting point
108 Suffix with labyrinth
109 Czar known as "the Great"
112 Once called
113 *Noisy disagreement
116 *Ordered
120 Service with a Capitol Corridor route
121 Promote aggressively
122 Without accompaniment
123 Crows
124 Ones in hills or farms
125 Luxury vessel
126 The dark side

DOWN

1 Brains of a tech start-up?
2 Racket
3 Noticeable
4 Roused from a nap
5 Neighbor of Nev.
6 Barely usable pencils
7 ___ sandwich
8 Like some roller coaster drops
9 Task for a crossword constructor
10 Washed quickly
11 Bon ___
12 Instrument used in a medical checkup
13 Out of whack
14 Vessel with a hatch, informally
15 The "teardrop of India"
16 Not exceeding
17 "Dark Lady" hitmaker, 1974
18 ___ Park, N.Y.
20 Christianity's ___ Creed
25 Word with code or card
28 Good witch in Oz
31 "That's enough about your sex life!"
32 Pallid
33 Some have combinations
36 Like J, alphabetically
39 English majors' degs.
40 Having three unequal sides
42 Equal: Prefix
44 Outmoded storage device
45 Witness
47 Some breads
48 Smitten
50 British exclamation
51 One of three for German nouns, or one of four for those in Africa's Zande language
53 Like a tug-of-war rope
55 One may go off in the middle of the night
56 Scientist whose name is associated with a number
57 Wine list section
59 Heavy medieval weapons
60 Robot sound
62 Hot condiment
63 Italian bread that's no longer made
65 Comply with a peace treaty, maybe
66 Some camping excursions
67 "I'm relieved!"
70 H.S. subject
73 "La Tauromaquia" artist
75 Come off as
77 Went ballistic
79 "Easy there!"
80 Small particle
82 Binder inserts with tabs
83 Literally, "revenge"
84 Org. that evaluates toothbrushes
86 Good cheer
88 Singer ___ Marie
89 Joins firmly
90 Epoch when palm trees grew in Alaska
91 In an obvious way
92 All-time connector
93 Big ___
96 Plan in detail
100 Puppy "kisses"
102 Rot
104 Ill-suited
105 9-5 automaker, once
106 Muppet who refers to himself in the third person
107 "At Last" singer James
110 Almond ___ (toffee brand)
111 Computer with a Pro model
114 Ship pest
115 H⁺ or I⁻
117 A ticket may be given for a high one: Abbr.
118 Man's name derived from the Bible
119 Man's name derived from the Bible

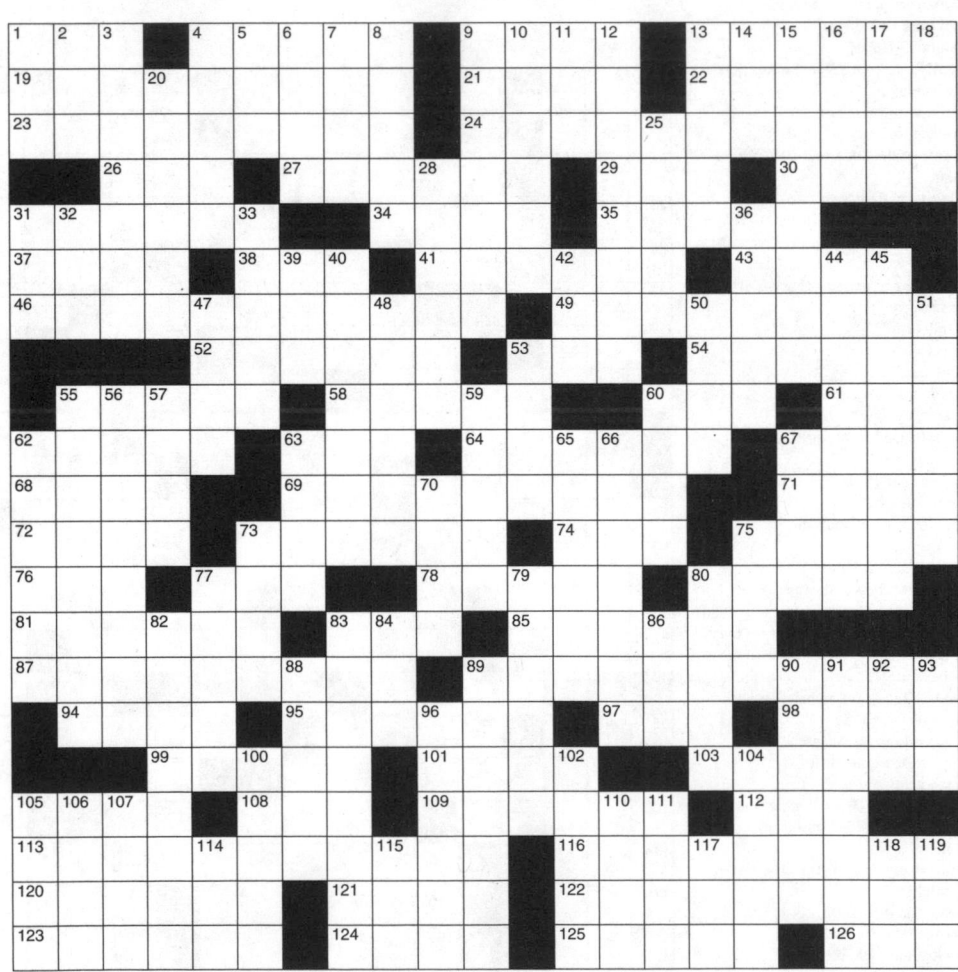

by David Steinberg

ACROSS

1 Tobacco plug
5 Manipulate
10 Graduates of Quantico, informally
14 Taller roommate of 15-Down
18 Showgirl in the 1978 hit "Copacabana"
19 Boomer's kid, maybe
20 Declare
21 Snack item with approximately 53 calories
22 Positive thinker's motto?
25 Textbook section
26 FireWire alternative
27 Letter between November and Papa in the NATO alphabet
28 It might be set at sea
29 When a prime-time drama might air
31 Reason-based belief in God
33 Repeated sound that's hard to get rid of
34 Means of becoming a god?
36 "Call the Midwife" network
38 Had something nice
40 Nonsense
41 Place in danger
45 Ernst and Young, e.g.: Abbr.
46 Peroxide ___
47 It's an affront
51 Where Rapunzel let down her hair?
53 Quarrel
54 It matures quickly, in brief
55 Angled to get attention: Abbr.
56 Suffix with serpent or opal
57 Offed
60 Reach quickly, as a conclusion
61 Perhaps
62 Doc. to ensure secrecy
63 It surrounds a pupil
64 United group, e.g.
65 Holy water?
70 Excites
72 "Salus populi suprema lex ___" (motto of Missouri)
73 Charade
74 One of 17 in Monopoly: Abbr.
77 One with pressing work
78 Feed the guests, maybe
79 Dish that's cooked underground
80 Feb. 14
81 673 parts of the Louvre Pyramid
82 "Old man"
83 Answer to "What is Roquefort or Brie?"?
86 Offed
87 Go the wrong way
88 Green-lit
90 Like drunken speech
91 Announcement on National Coming Out Day
93 Inappropriate
95 Early bird?
96 Spilled milk?
100 Front of a semi
102 Ubiquitous advertiser with an acronymic name
106 Seeing as
107 Weight of an empty container
108 What's clothed in summer and naked in winter, per an old riddle
110 China's largest ethnic group
111 What BankAmericard became in 1976
112 The queen with her pets?
116 School where some of "Shakespeare in Love" was filmed
117 Annual Memorial Day race, informally
118 Red Sox' div.
119 Bit of sports equipment that may be electrified
120 Casino tool
121 Philippine money
122 Fleas and flies
123 What's left on a map?

DOWN

1 Obscure
2 Windsor, e.g.
3 A criminal's may be unbelievable
4 "Time ___ . . ."
5 Big name in jelly
6 Like mosaic tiles
7 Lose possession?
8 One of the books of the Torah: Abbr.
9 Where Wagner's "Tannhäuser" was first performed
10 Prima ___
11 Word that becomes more dramatic when you add an "R" in front
12 Caribbean land, at the Olympics
13 Administer an oath to
14 Echoes
15 Shorter roommate of 14-Across
16 Control, metaphorically
17 Completely, in slang
19 Pedal on the right
23 Man of La Mancha
24 Late-night trips to the fridge, e.g.
30 Shirt or blouse
32 Bit of magic
35 Projecting front
37 Temporarily replace
39 Most likely to win at Trivia Night, maybe
41 Long-billed wader
42 Parent company of Facebook
43 Game starter
44 Home for Holmes
48 One who sees what you're saying?
49 Berliner's "old"
50 Sight on winter roads
52 Sign of overuse
53 "All ___!"
54 Prefix that's mega mega?
58 Not merely annoyed
59 Split
60 BuzzFeed staple
64 Wide ties
66 Netflix series set at Green Gables
67 Manipulates
68 Place to go on a ship
69 Them's the breaks!
70 List in "The Idiot's Guide to . . ."
71 Neighbor of Siberia, in Risk
75 Common still-life prop
76 Looked at
78 Architectural columns in the form of sculpted female figures
80 Threshold
82 Gunslinger's command
84 Schools
85 Held tight
87 A narcissist may go on one
88 Shockingly bizarre
89 What the quadriceps muscle connects to
92 N.Y.C. commuting inits.
94 Bugs
96 Where bile is produced
97 Loos who wrote "Gentlemen Prefer Blondes"
98 Casual response to an apology
99 Panasonic subsidiary
101 Orchestra section
103 "If my luck holds out . . ."
104 Pens
105 Beginning
109 Rhinitis treater, in brief
113 Phoenix-to-Albuquerque dir.
114 Bottle labeled "XXX" in the comics
115 "Do the ___" (soft drink slogan)

by Victor Barocas

ACROSS

1 Items used with PINs
9 There's one for the U.S. Census
15 In a tussle
19 Dismiss
20 Takes it one step at a time
21 Pad Thai garnish
22 *Sea captain: robber, thief (2003)*
25 Photographer's tool, for short
26 Unlike this puzzle, we hope
27 Source of suffering
28 They're hoppy at happy hour
32 Quaint lead-in to while
33 All the kings' men?
34 *True fellow is a find (1946)*
40 With room for interpretation
41 Top
42 Game pieces in Mastermind
46 Word after contact or before cover
47 Chill (out)
49 Bit of deception
50 Unfinished attic space
52 *Re: town fire one night (1974)*
56 "Whoopee!"
59 Origin of the words "club" and "gun"
60 It's a lot in London
61 Tip of the tongue?
62 Best-selling crime novelist Gregg
65 Breed featured in 2009's "Hachi: A Dog's Tale"
67 Miff, with "off"
68 One seeking a new agreement, perhaps
70 Ground-breaking tool
73 "Not interested"
75 *Evil Streep had award (2006)*
80 Be a paragon of
81 Guys that rhyme with "girls"
82 Folder attachment
83 The "Y" of Y.S.L.
87 Beams
88 Wallop
89 One of the Roys on "Succession"
91 *M. Ryan, what's her yell? (1989)*
96 They have massive calves
100 "OK!" in Okayama
101 Puts forth
102 Account
103 Protected creature in the Congo Basin
107 Alternatives to tablets
110 *R.E.M.: alarming to the teens (1984)*
115 ＿＿＿ colada
116 "Louisiana ＿＿＿," music show that helped launch Elvis's career
117 Fried, filled Filipino fare
118 Part of STEM: Abbr.
119 Angry dog sounds
120 Elf at the North Pole, e.g.

DOWN

1 First courses, informally
2 Drudgery
3 First Black woman to win the Nobel Prize in Literature
4 When doubled, a dance
5 Quick to learn
6 Spawn in the sea
7 "＿＿＿ thou love life?": Benjamin Franklin
8 Drove (away)
9 ＿＿＿ Men ("Who Let the Dogs Out" group)
10 One with a password, maybe
11 Document stamp abbr.
12 That: Sp.
13 Blimp, e.g.
14 Humanitarian org. with Halloween fund drives
15 First name in Harry Potter
16 Ranks
17 Would you look at that!
18 Believe in it
20 Onetime dentist's supply
23 Front
24 Company with sound financials?
29 Target with a throw
30 "!!!!!" feeling
31 Crack
33 Held tightly
34 "'Tis an ＿＿＿ cook that cannot lick his own fingers": "Romeo and Juliet"
35 The third of three X's
36 Opposite of da
37 All ＿＿＿ (English card game)
38 Release, in a way
39 Soul singer Bridges
42 School for the college-bound
43 Paper slips?
44 Signs in a bookstore, perhaps
45 Encourages
48 Out of the park
49 Each
50 Airborne irritant
51 Chicken . . . or cowed
53 Addicted
54 Broke the finish line ribbon
55 "＿＿＿ on parle français"
56 Lead-in to day or year
57 Pulmicort targets it
58 Adverb in many legal documents
63 Impose, as a fine
64 ＿＿＿ Lanka
65 Certain banner fodder
66 Didn't ditch
69 Certain partners' exchanges
70 Brand with an iComfort line
71 Less vibrant
72 Harvard dropouts, maybe?
74 Recurrent space in The Game of Life
76 Depends (on)
77 Break-even situation
78 Aid in putting together a fall collection
79 Drives the getaway car for, say
84 Slangy SoCal dialect
85 Sharp turn
86 Designing
88 Rhea with four Emmys
90 Phone-tracking org.
91 Accompanying
92 Shrubby areas
93 Europe's Three Countries Bridge crosses it
94 Big name in locks
95 Grain variety
96 ＿＿＿-Nuts
97 World leader who appeared on a Time magazine cover 40 years after his death
98 Sailing through
99 The world's most expensive one, the Gurkha Royal Courtesan, costs over $1.3 million
103 Angry dog's sound
104 Trompe l'＿＿＿
105 Sticks
106 Some finds in Fortnite
108 Hand over
109 Have the lead (in)
111 Actress Cash of FX's "You're the Worst"
112 Who might bug you?
113 Headwear with a pompom
114 Vaccine molecule

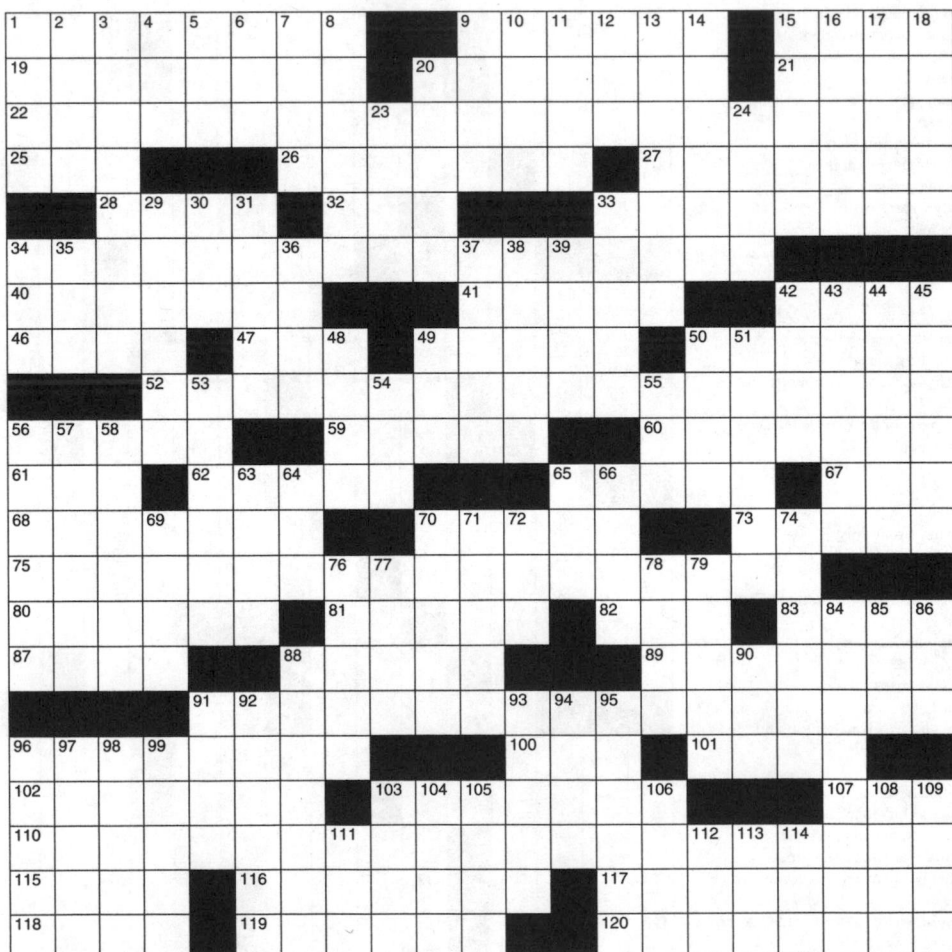

by Sheldon Polonsky

ACROSS

1 "Bon ___!"
8 "See ya later!"
13 It covers more than 30% of the earth's surface
20 Donna ___, member of Bill Clinton's cabinet
21 Klein who wrote the best seller "This Changes Everything: Capitalism vs. the Climate"
22 Desert whose soil has been compared to that of Mars
23 Biting writings
24 Breakfast treat
25 Convinces a customer to pay more
26 "Or so"
27 Much of a delivery person's income
29 Makes a choice
31 Hoppin'
32 Prearranged
33 Suffix with official
34 Nickel found in a pocket, say
35 Actor Barinholtz of "The Mindy Project"
36 Classic Camaro
38 ___ K. Smith, poet who won a Pulitzer for "Life on Mars"
40 Cosmetic that can be applied with a brush
42 Neighbors of exclamation marks
43 "La Dolce ___"
45 Stuffed one's face
47 Bump on a frog
49 Question regarding a mic
51 Hubbub
52 One of the Blues Brothers
55 Above criticism
56 Question from the befuddled
57 Syrian city with a historic citadel
58 What "10" can mean
60 Extra
62 Rolled one's r's, say
63 Linguistic unit
64 Giraffe's closest living relative
65 Deb ___, secretary of the interior starting in 2021
66 Opposite of 'neath
67 Regarding
69 Exams for some future clerks: Abbr.
71 Cold open?
72 Hang out on a line
73 U.K. award bestowed by the queen
74 West Coast news inits.
75 Blunder
76 They cast lots
78 "Love covers a multitude of ___": I Peter 4:8
79 Lawn material
82 Something's essential aspect . . . or what's spelled out by letters in this puzzle's eight "cups"
87 Comedian Margaret
90 2011 film for which Octavia Spencer won a Best Supporting Actress Oscar
92 It takes blades to blades
93 Deal
95 Like the consonants "t" and "d"
97 Eject forcefully
98 Records request inits.
99 ___ history
101 Utah's state flower
102 Org. that sets permissible exposure limits
103 Karaoke instruction . . . or what to do starting at 10-Down
109 P.R. consultant on "Ted Lasso"
110 Start playing for pay
111 Into really small pieces
112 Scott who sued for his freedom
113 Afford, casually
114 Add salt to, say

DOWN

1 Home of St. Clare
2 Starfleet weapon
3 Election night calculation . . . or what's traced by the circled letters
4 Name that's 6-Down backward
5 Save it for a rainy day!
6 La Corse, par exemple
7 Brewery employee
8 Comb through
9 Bubs
10 Worker's "on vacation" inits.
11 "Actually, I disagree"
12 Rococo painter of "Allegory of the Planets and Continents"
13 They might be pregnant
14 Organic energy compound, for short
15 "Mi ___ es su ___"
16 Part of a cold compress
17 Become clear . . . or make like the object represented by the circled letters
18 "So then my response was . . ."
19 Hereditary divisions
28 Physicist Newton
30 Loyalty that's pledged
37 Lemonlike fruit
38 Big rigs
39 "Well, fine then"
40 Age beautifully, informally
41 Cuss out
42 Big Brother's creator
44 Pink pad on a paw, in slang
46 The Lord, in the Hebrew Bible
48 Start of a simple request
49 Roly-poly, scientifically
50 ___ torte (Austrian cake)
53 Warm-up act
54 Move shakily
59 Ross Perot founded it in 1995
60 Lack of engagement
61 More wacky
62 "You're just assuming"
68 It's blown in the winds
70 Showed off one's pipes
77 Airport with a Harvey Milk terminal: Abbr.
78 Harry Styles tune about a woman who "lives in daydreams"
79 Lines of notes
80 Sight line?
81 Cooked with hot seasoning
82 Prefix with -lithic
83 Not against the rules
84 It's under @ on a keyboard
85 ___ lodge
86 Rowing machine, informally
87 Event for moving vehicles
88 Super
89 Actress Tatum
91 Folk medicine practitioner
94 Foolish sort
96 Sports fan's cheer
97 Universal Human Rights Mo.
100 Ability to sustain long-term interest
101 Kiss, in Kent
104 Sports fan's cheer
105 Gift wrapper's final touch
106 Nail polish brand
107 Buffet table item
108 Zoo animal whose name rhymes with "zoo"

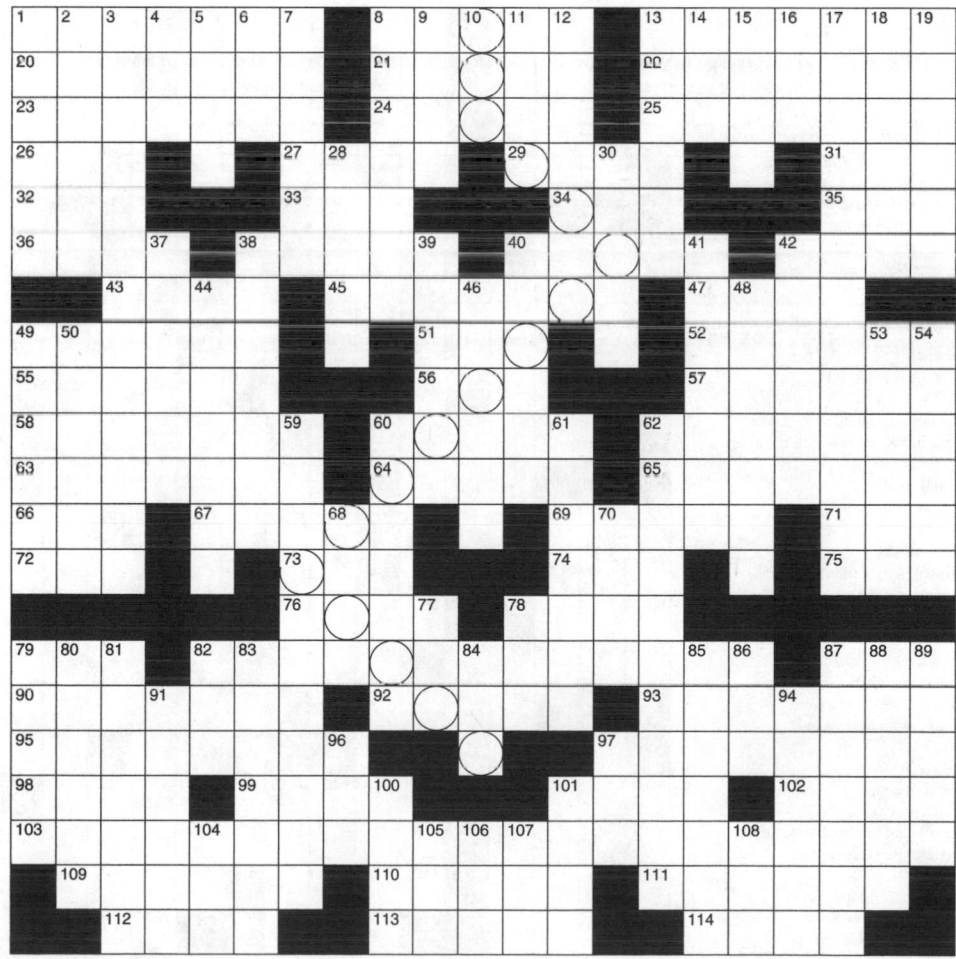

by Matthew Stock and Will Nediger

ACROSS

1 Almost
5 Oven setting
10 Portrayer of the boxer Clubber Lang in "Rocky III"
13 In case
17 When repeated, old-time call to listen
18 Part of a prank
20 Govt. organization with a two-syllable acronym
22 Kind of clarinet
23 Came to know, old-style
24 It empties into the Bay of Bengal
26 Radar spot
27 Bringing in, as income
29 "Keen!"
30 *With 12-Down, spend much more than a fair price*
31 Department store department
32 Lay ___ to
34 Question that's not one of the five W's
35 Big consideration for the expecting
37 Ticket fig.
40 Wisteria and honeysuckle
42 Video game character in a hit 2020 film
43 Educator/writer ___ Johnson McDougald, first African American female principal in New York City public schools
45 Belief of roughly 25% of the world's population
46 Director Craven
47 Downstairs
51 Kept in
53 Lets out
55 Vape's lack
56 Martini & Rossi product, familiarly
57 Emmy-winning Ward
58 Took down, in a way
59 Fly around Africa
62 Doughy dinner item
64 Drug agent's seizure
65 Deseret News reader, typically
66 Did nothing
67 Professor ___
69 *With 74-Across, gesture of approval*
70 On fire
73 Chomping at the bit
74 *See 69-Across*
78 One cutting down, so to speak
79 What babies do faster than college students
80 Feudal land
81 O's, but not P's or Q's
83 *Petty*
84 Some posers
86 Self-titled rock album of 1958
88 Quaint contraction
91 Smoking spot, for short?
92 Former baseball commissioner Bud
93 Sound, e.g.
94 Moves like muck
96 I.T. help center, often
98 Ending with bear or bull
99 "Uncle!"
101 Rocker Rose
102 Heard in court
104 Promotion
105 Letters that might change your mind?
107 Prepare, in a way, as eggs
109 Irritable
112 En voz ___ (aloud: Sp.)
113 *Insincere, as a remark*
116 Kristen of "Bridesmaids"
118 Jaunty
119 Counterpart of "adios"
120 "Yes" or "No" follower
121 Old Icelandic work
122 Fivers
123 Idiosyncrasy
124 Greek performance venue
125 Alternative to Wranglers

DOWN

1 Blues group, for short?
2 *Fully ready to listen*
3 Loretta who sang "You Ain't Woman Enough (To Take My Man)"
4 Cold climate cryptids
5 "The ___ they are . . ."
6 Messenger ___
7 *Walk around at a rest stop, say*
8 "Bus Stop" playwright
9 Be in store
10 "Who, me?"
11 Invitation letters
12 *See 30-Across*
13 Subjects of some tests
14 Actress Burstyn
15 What some insects and insults can do
16 Primo
19 Bit of bad weather, on a weather map
21 Indo-___ languages
25 They're numbered in Microsoft Excel
28 More agreeable
33 Theodor ___ a.k.a. Dr. Seuss
36 Will Smith/Tommy Lee Jones film franchise, for short
37 Flat-earther?
38 Like many a stuffed toy
39 Aware of
41 Word that, fittingly, contains all four different letters of APPEAL
42 Question following a clever trick
44 Shows scorn toward
46 Take by force
48 Wood strip
49 Peak in the "Odyssey"
50 One of the five W's
52 Arcane matters
53 Panache
54 Leave gobsmacked
58 Scatter
60 Sudden sharp pain
61 Have seconds and thirds and fourths and . . .
63 Flatten
64 Lilies with bell-shaped flowers
68 Rachel Zegler's role in 2021's "West Side Story"
70 Allow entry
71 Forehead mark on Hindu women
72 City SW of York
75 Safe bettor
76 Instruments with endpins
77 Some sources of leafy greens
80 F on a gauge
82 It's just not true!
85 Easy opportunity for a basket
86 Vegas venue with an iconic fountain
87 Who might be on the trail
89 Candy bar fillings
90 Emergency request
92 Vikings' foes
95 A goose egg
96 One reporting to an underboss
97 Nauseate
99 *Bankrupt*
100 Bizarre
103 One holding things together, perhaps
104 "___, Can You Hear Me?" (Oscar-nominated song from "Yentl")
106 Sub station?
108 Lemon or cheese product
110 & 111 *In cooperation*
114 Sea-___ Airport
115 Fair-hiring inits.
117 Option for a range

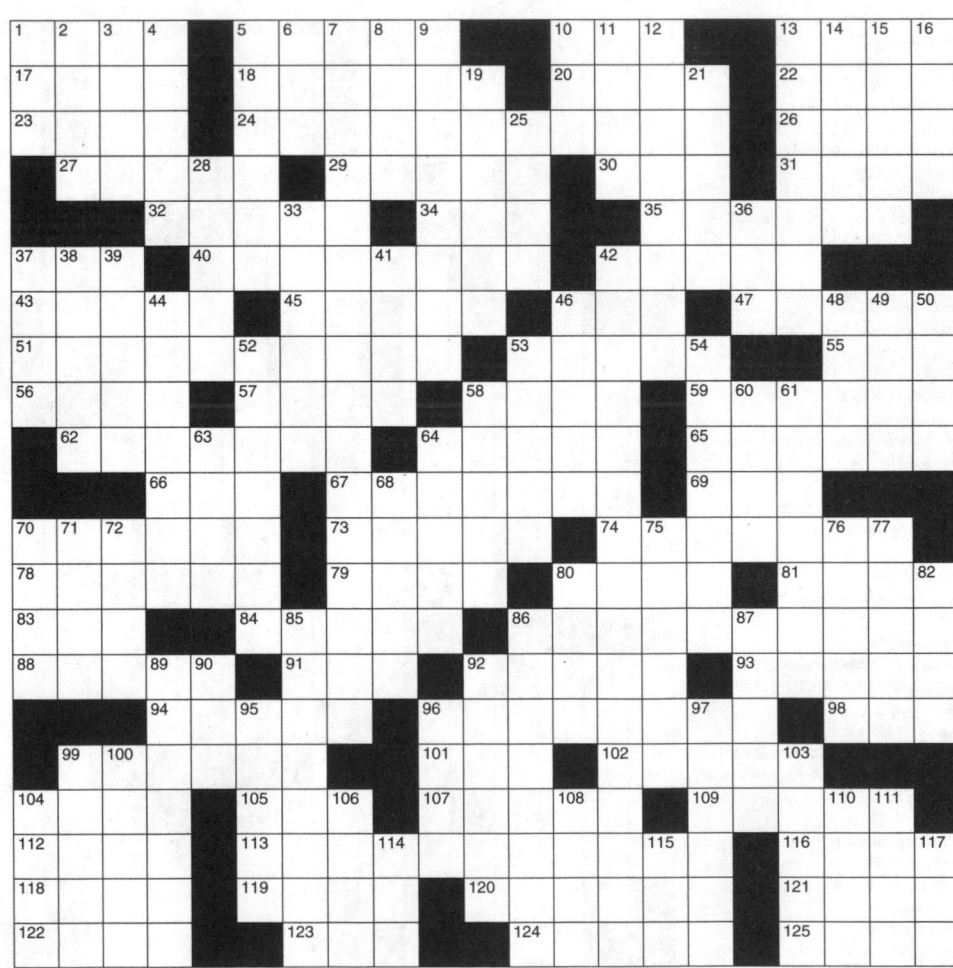

by Christina Iverson and Katie Hale

ACROSS

1 Band of supporters
5 Something absolutely necessary
10 "____ and Janis" (comic strip)
14 Oomph
17 Word from the French for "high wood"
18 Washed out
20 Dock
21 Something a winner may run into
22 *"It's tough finding the right person. My first boyfriend was a perfectly nice atheist, but he . . ."*
24 Tour de France seasons
25 Side dish at a fish fry
26 Main component of Saturn's rings
27 Lena of "Enemies, a Love Story"
28 *"So then I dated a fun couch potato, but he . . ."*
31 Non-starters?
33 Toeing the line
34 Fútbol cheer
35 Italian wine region
36 "30 for 30" airer
39 The 1 in {1,2,3}: Abbr.
40 Lab vessel
42 Camphor, e.g.
45 One getting depressed during exams?
47 They're found near traps
48 *"Then my friend set me up with a recluse, but he . . ."*
52 Comedian Mort
54 Classic Hawaiian folk song
55 Superman and others, for short
56 Book with a notable world premiere?
59 What middlemen do
60 Noisy beachgoer
62 Bun in a bamboo steamer
63 Internet encryption inits.
65 Binary
66 *"I dated my rock climbing instructor for a while, but he just . . ."*
68 ____-Pacific
69 Not sparkling
71 Blast furnace supply
72 Baloney
73 Bad signs for a bank robber
75 Academic journal with a "Breakthrough of the Year" award
77 U.K. track star-turned-politician Sebastian
78 Mishmashes
79 Swindled
80 *"Then I had a fling with a Pittsburgh Penguin, but I knew he . . ."*
83 Cuisine featuring som tam
86 Drill command
88 Feel another's pain
89 Cavalryman of old
91 Big ____ (Olympic snowboarding event)
92 Whimper
93 Starters, for short
97 Outback speedster
98 Keep rhythm, as a conductor might
101 Wisconsin town with a clothing namesake
104 *"I was in a serious relationship with a hippie, but he . . ."*
106 Org. issuing vaccine standards starting in 2021
107 It may be part of a solution
108 Together, in music
109 Fading sea name
110 *"Finally, I started seeing a charming magician, and he . . ."*
113 Pan, in part
114 Fun-size
115 Kind of thesis
116 Weekend warrior's woe
117 Happening offline, to a texter
118 Relaxation
119 Devotee of Haile Selassie, informally
120 Bit of kitchen waste

DOWN

1 Big name in pricey cigars
2 You can't say it doesn't count
3 Lizzie is one, in the "Cars" movies
4 Crossword solving option
5 Watch maker since 2015
6 It lands on the White House's South Lawn
7 ____ Bator, Mongolia
8 On the ____
9 Fastened, in a way
10 Making change
11 Well past the freshness date, say
12 "My Fair Lady" composer
13 Actor/comedian who was a regular on Johnny Carson's "Tonight Show"
14 Meathead
15 Military uniform feature
16 Bluish-gray shades
19 Scintilla
21 "Shameful!"
23 Alley-____
29 Possessive types?
30 Way to go: Abbr.
32 "You're so wrong about that!"
37 Lead-in to Cat
38 Something that all but three U.S. presidents have had while in office
41 "Time out" in the N.B.A.
43 What makes the short list?
44 Total jerk
45 Boxing highlight
46 Apply to
48 Jokesters
49 Some native Alaskans
50 Tile work
51 Leadership position
53 Bit of a chuckle
56 Rubberneck
57 "A house divided against ____ cannot stand"
58 Rubylike gem
60 Richard of "Chicago"
61 Native people for whom a state is named
62 When doubled, a candy
64 Quick with a clapback
66 So-called "Father of Liberalism"
67 Conflict taking a couple of seconds?
70 Soccer star Messi, to fans
73 Capital of Fiji
74 "How ____ Your Mother"
76 Beloved site for the Irish . . . and French
77 Journalist who was the first woman to guest-host "Jeopardy!"
78 Hard stuff that jiggles
80 "We'll be in touch!," often
81 Dr. of 112-Down
82 Counterpart of full, in a way
83 Wise guys?
84 One might be smoke-filled
85 Not surprisingly
87 Big name in hot dogs
90 Face on a penny, familiarly
92 Strong suit
94 Regulate
95 Cupid's love
96 Mideast currency unit
99 Features of some halls
100 Mucky substances
102 Twin sister of He-Man
103 What, in multiple senses, might get tipped
105 Take place?
106 Redding who wrote "Respect"
111 Crispr material
112 See 81-Down

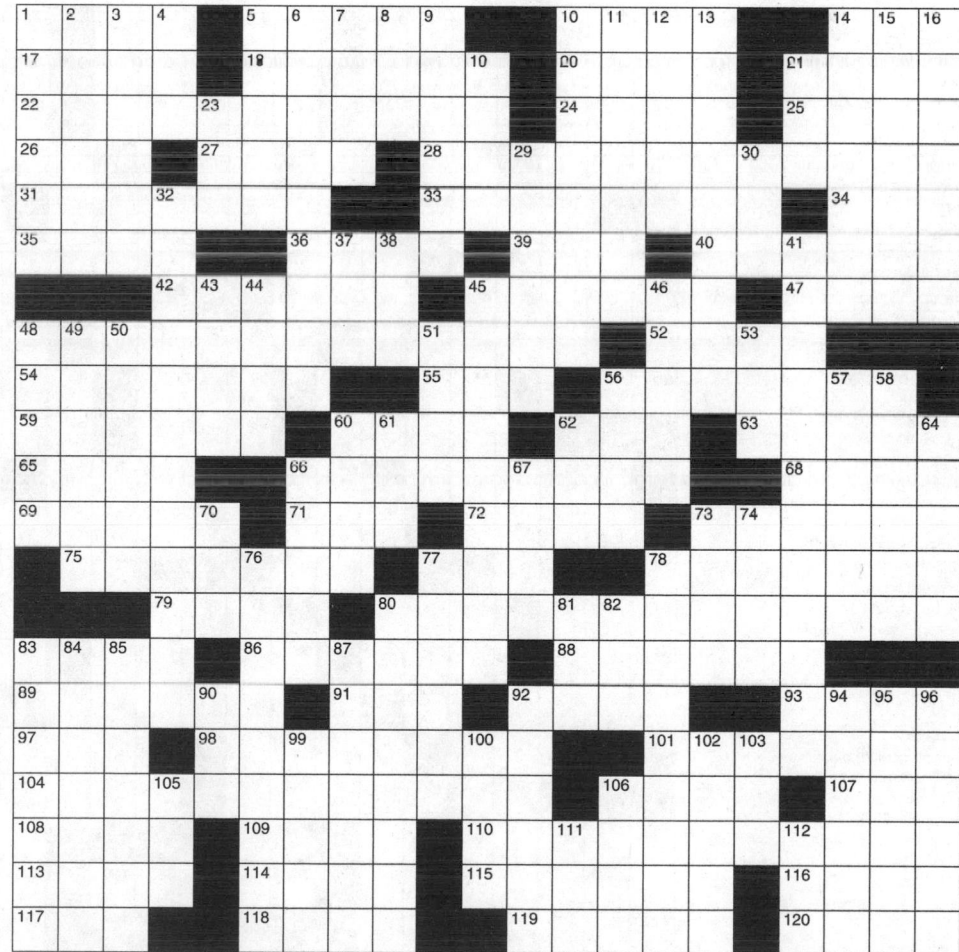

by Brad Wiegmann

ACROSS

1 Swears (to)
8 L.A. region
13 Motto meaning "to the stars"
20 Place with carts
21 Square
22 What oil may do in frigid temperatures
23 1990s–2000s Volkswagen seven-seater
24 Things
25 Overseas land measure
26 Not needing a thing
27 "____ homo"
29 Siri uses it
30 Halliwell a.k.a. Ginger Spice
31 Dino friend of Buzz Lightyear
32 "____ it ironic?"
34 Storm
37 What an up arrow might mean
39 Green-light
41 Approximately 5.5 million tons of it was used to build [see circled letters]
43 Bellini opera that takes place in Gaul
46 A = B, B = C, ergo A = C, e.g.
48 Purchase plan
50 Sneaker, in British lingo
51 See 5-Down
55 Committed to memory
56 Western Hemisphere grp.
57 Gunslinger's cry
59 Former Japanese P.M. Shinzo ____
60 Country between Ghana and Benin
61 Word repeatedly said while plucking petals
62 Clipped
63 Opposing vote from a horse?
64 Blue ribbon or gold star
66 Yarn
68 Make secret, in a way
71 A chance to dream
74 It's often played for
75 Website with an "Everything Else" category
76 Some small batteries
78 C sharp equivalent
80 Mexican poet Juana ____ de la Cruz
81 Sass
82 U.F.C. fighting style
83 Radio host John
84 Head, in slang
85 Play group
87 Frequent victim of an April fool
90 Creep
93 Municipal facility: Abbr.
94 Kind of bar
96 Waterfall feature
98 One forced into a force
100 One-act Oscar Wilde play
101 Burial ____
103 Fútbol cry
104 "You no-good dog," e.g.
105 Spoils
106 ____ bean
108 Some December purchases
109 They're stored in pollen grains
111 Villainous "Star Trek" collective
113 Like some chicken cutlets
116 Element named after a German river
120 "Ugh!"
121 Prehistoric Southwest culture
122 Little squirt
123 Sign of success
124 Trendy
125 Vardalos of "My Big Fat Greek Wedding"

DOWN

1 Periods in history
2 Level
3 They wrap things up
4 Prefix with system
5 With 51-Across and 15-Down, group in which [see circled letters] is the only one still largely intact
6 Egyptian desert, e.g.
7 Harmonize
8 ____ generis (unique)
9 Prompt
10 Greek name for this puzzle's enclosed answer
11 Targets
12 Sleeve fillers
13 Not just smart
14 Active sorts
15 See 5-Down
16 Pepper's rank: Abbr.
17 High-arcing shots, in basketball lingo
18 Like a T206 Honus Wagner baseball card
19 Lion in the "Madagascar" movies
28 Most massive dwarf planet in the solar system
30 Pass it on
33 Singers' star turns
35 Contents of some belts, informally
36 Reason for an R rating
38 It comes before one
39 Regarding
40 Harp-shaped constellation
41 Turkish money
42 Provide resources for
44 [Big kiss, dahling!]
45 Pay (up)
47 ____ and the Pacemakers (1960s pop group)
49 They reflected rank in old Rome
52 "Ooh-la-la!"
53 It gives you a lift
54 2003 #1 Outkast hit
58 Tad
60 Mat made of soft rush
62 You might take them out for a spin
65 Artful
66 Mujeres con esposos
67 Outdoor game for kindergartners
69 Time out?
70 "The Office" role played by Jenna Fischer
72 College voter, perhaps
73 Light shades
74 With 101-Across, where this puzzle's enclosed answer is located
75 Disney's ____ of Arendelle
77 Smooth, in a way
79 Number of 101-Acrosses in [see circled letters]
85 Workmates, e.g.
86 Pale ____
87 Tiffs
88 Sleeve filler
89 Brewer Frederick
91 ____-Magnon
92 Like a book with a bookmark in the middle, say
95 Chewy confection
96 Oxford, e.g.
97 Michelle of "Crazy Rich Asians"
99 Fakes
101 Hotel offering
102 New York town that's home to Playland amusement park
105 Caused
107 The "A" of James A. Garfield
110 So-called "Iron Lady" of Israeli politics
112 "This does not look good!"
113 Fell for it
114 Pi follower
115 "People who love to ____ are always the best people": Julia Child
117 Writer Fleming
118 Weapon in "The Terminator"
119 Actress Farrow

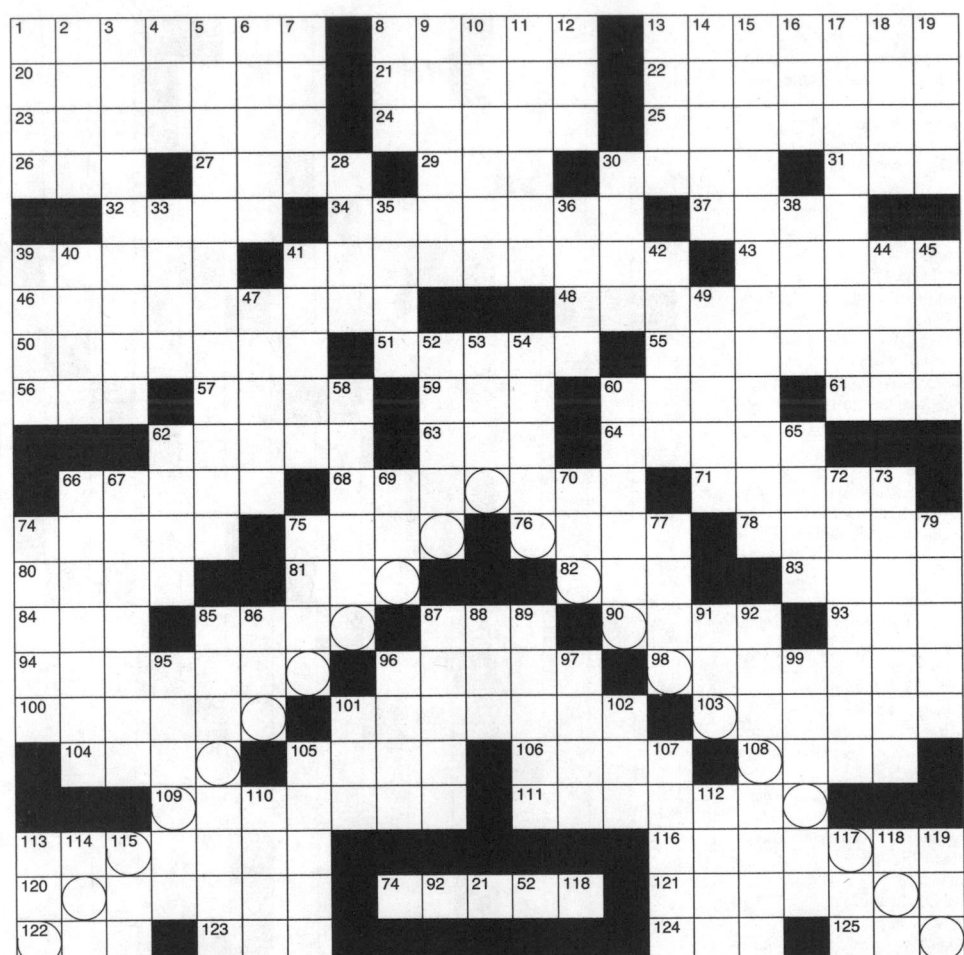

by August Lee-Kovach

ACROSS

1 Pranks with a roll, briefly
4 Casualties of streaming services
7 Updated one's blog
13 Swap (out)
16 Navajo hogan, e.g.
17 Part of NATO
20 Forgo
21 Question from an owl?
22 Austin-to-Houston dir.
23 Chief
24 Actor Joaquin's complete bio?
26 Start of a legalese paragraph
28 Figs. in an author's acknowledgments section
30 "____ Wiedersehen!"
31 Hughes poem that mentions "the darker brother"
32 Troupe of lesser-known actors?
35 Reef-dwelling snapper
38 Unattractive fruit
39 2016 Olympics site
40 What swish shots miss
42 Word repeated in the postal creed
43 W.W. I battle locale
44 Schmaltz in kids' films?
50 "The meaning of life" once sold on it for $3.26
51 Throw together
53 Certainly not wish to repeat
54 Get by
56 "I don't mean to ____ . . ."
57 Like bibs and aprons
58 Sermon topics
59 Muhammad had 13
60 Birthplace of multiple saints
62 Slowly disengages (from)
64 Department store department
65 An airline now serves a Minute Maid beverage?
69 Whined like a baby
72 End of many a toast
73 Touch
76 Popular sans-serif font
77 Schools of thought
78 "Onward!," in Italy
81 Unfiltered
83 U.S. detainment site in Cuba, informally
84 Question posed with feigned shock
85 Ushers in
86 Joint action
87 Some apartments for scaredy-cats?
90 Drank to excess
91 R.V. camper's org.
92 [I'm devastated!]
93 Deli supply
95 Marauding group in Tolkien's "The Two Towers"
96 Game of tag, basically
100 Record half that stirs emotions?
104 Exerciser's target
105 "Shame on you!"
107 Dark force
108 European country slightly larger than Malta
109 Sandwich for a dieter?
113 Appear that way
115 Share
116 Volcano output
117 Slippery sort
118 Size up
119 Letters on some baggage to N.Y.C.
120 Word with sweet or sugar
121 Made damp
122 "Gangnam Style" singer
123 Winter D.C. hrs.

DOWN

1 Channel that aired "Felicity" and "Smallville"
2 Curve-enhancing undergarment
3 Metallic shades
4 Certain Balkanite
5 Not as bright
6 ____ fly
7 Oomph
8 Factory watchdog grp.
9 Search far and wide
10 Home run territory, in lingo
11 Dark time, in poetry
12 Something that gets MADD mad
13 Smacks hard
14 "That is . . . not looking good"
15 Numbskull
17 Argument you may start in school
18 Cops, in slang
19 Sage swamp-dweller of film
25 The witching hour
27 Pat ____, three-time N.B.A. Coach of the Year
29 Discard
33 Inflexible
34 Handy take-along
36 Play-____

37 Modern airport amenity
41 Soft wool source
43 "Sure thing"
45 Parts of airports and fashion shows
46 Actress Kirsten
47 Display clearly
48 Goalie's goal
49 Locale painted on the Sistine Chapel ceiling
51 Caught on, with "up"
52 Junior, often
55 Something starting something?
57 Devices preventing off-hour openings of vaults
58 Image on the Arizona license plate
61 Deli supply
63 Brian of ambient music
64 Offerings to hitchhikers
66 "Challenge accepted!"
67 Common newspaper feature not seen in The New York Times
68 Chill, with "out"
69 E.W. or S.I.
70 One of the Trumps
71 "I'm ____ Her," 2016 political slogan
74 Work of extraterrestrials? - not!
75 Pops some pills, say
77 "No joke!"

79 Shortcuts into clubs
80 Actor Williams of "Happy Days"
82 Put together
85 Guy into hip-hop
86 Where the heart is
88 Colorful pond swimmer
89 ____-pah
90 Kerfuffles
94 Event for snocrossers
96 "You're almost there"
97 "So funny!"
98 "World News Tonight" airer
99 Talk show interviewee
101 Aid for one going places?
102 On edge
103 Worry
104 Kerfuffle
106 Olive or avocado
110 "How precious is that!"
111 Actor ____ J. Cobb of "12 Angry Men"
112 So last month
114 You thinking what I'm thinking?

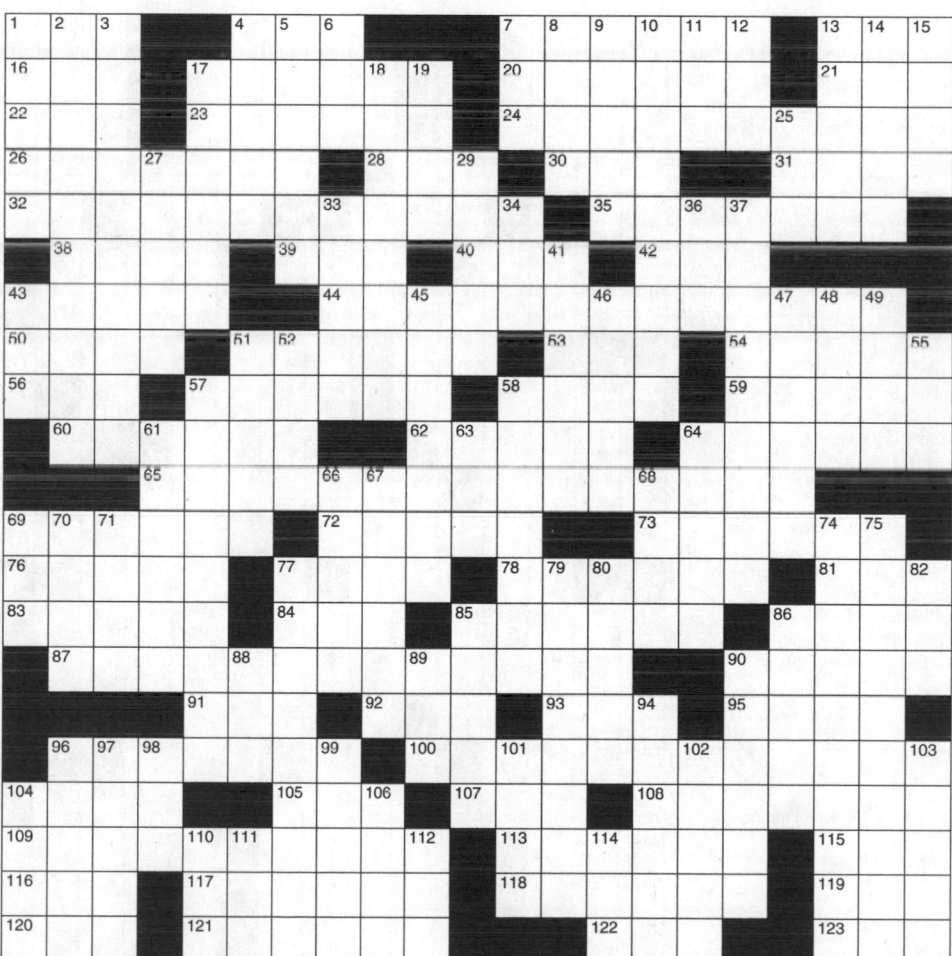

by Jeremy Newton

ACROSS

1 Lament after being backstabbed
5 Crack up
10 Test one's metal?
15 Down
18 Classic word game
20 Dollar competitor
21 Contemptible sort
22 "___ linda!" ("How pretty!," in Spanish)
23 One who's dunzo
24 Glossy fabric
25 Dancer's leader
26 The Bulldogs of the S.E.C.
27 Line at the side of a photo
29 Hoopster observing Ramadan?
32 Electric ___
33 Shepherd's pie bit
35 River through Seoul
36 Bakery buy
37 Nearly dried-up Asian sea
38 Country whose name becomes its language when you drop its last letter
40 Frequent Winter Olympics setting
43 Sign from a third base coach, say
45 Van Susteren formerly of Fox News
46 Gangster Luciano performing a risqué prank?
49 Ankle-exposing pants
50 "___ been thinking . . ."
51 Captains on The Atlantic, briefly?
52 By and large
54 Neighbor of N.Y.
55 Young swan
58 Colleens
60 Uncommon spelling for a common greeting
62 Whole ___
63 I.Q. test name
64 1982 #1 hit with the line "Watch out boy she'll chew you up"
67 Look lecherously
68 Hobo at the wheel?
71 Cunningness
72 Many web advertisements
74 Overly indulge in
75 Movie Hall
76 Bridge words
77 Evil spirits
79 Gently jabbed
80 Enliven, with "up"
82 Build-it-yourself auto
84 Sugar suffix
85 Flatow of NPR's "Science Friday"
86 Drops a line
88 Where to buy certain Christmas decorations?
94 Early PC platform
95 Link with
96 Accident-investigating agcy.
97 Part of STEM, for short
98 Long tale
99 ___-pah
100 Subzero, maybe
102 One whose life is in order?
104 Lament
105 Mild form of corporal punishment?
110 Poor
112 Home of the Pampas: Abbr.
113 "Rumor has it . . ."
114 Partner of live
116 Actress Swinton
117 Golfer Michelle
118 "Scooby-Doo" girl
119 Commercial cow
120 Brownstone feature
121 The Bosporus, e.g.: Abbr.
122 Haven
123 Change with the times
124 Moving well

DOWN

1 Ovum
2 "Walden" writer
3 "Wild Thing" rapper
4 How many college textbooks are bought
5 Lot of fun, informally
6 Saint for whom a Minnesota college is named
7 ___ Hari
8 Powerless group?
9 "It's worse than you can imagine"
10 Org.
11 Party handouts
12 Wicked
13 ___ Chigurh, villain in "No Country for Old Men"
14 It takes months to complete
15 Cheering done in a plaza?
16 Baked with breadcrumbs and cheese
17 Bringing up the rear
19 Set off, as a security alarm
28 China display
30 Under the wire, so to speak
31 ___ speed
34 Cockpit datum: Abbr.
39 Merely superficial
41 Olympics events rarely shown in prime time
42 Carried chairs
44 Nephew of Cain
45 King who's a friend of Oprah
47 First name in fashion
48 Word after liquid or fixed
49 Sword fight sound
53 ___ of Glamis, title in Shakespeare
55 Corp. money pros
56 One holding many positions
57 Big fan of the "Lord of the Flies" author?
59 Mirror buildup, at times
61 Dangerous backyard projectile
63 Pop
64 Erroneously hit "reply all" instead of "reply," say
65 Late author Wiesel
66 Thatching material
68 Underpinning
69 Text on an iPad, say
70 Collars
73 Really feels the heat
75 See 79-Down
77 Hoped-for result of swiping right on Tinder
78 Hot
79 75-Down around a saint
80 Wardens enforce them
81 Emotionally, if not physically
83 TV spinoff of 2002
87 Narrow arm of the sea
89 Part of the inner ear
90 Channel with "Family Feud" reruns
91 Sound of a pebble hitting water
92 Galápagos Islands' country
93 Setting for many New Yorker cartoons
95 They get wetter as they dry
99 Actor Milo
101 Bottom line
103 Beer ___
106 DVR choice
107 Refrain syllables
108 Pluto flyby org.
109 Enthrall
111 They come straight from the horse's mouth
115 Bottom line

by Jim Holland and Jeff Chen

1

```
ALOFT   ATTN   TVPG   WAFTS
SOFIA   TARO   HERO   ELLIE
PUFFPIECES     AXED   BOONE
CITE  LATERON  POTSHOTS
ASH  ELM  GAWK    FRIAR
VERDE  UTES   ALIT   MIA
HIGHDRAMA      SMOKEBOMB
ELROY  GERM   IHAVE  EDIE
ELIS   LANDO  MATE   STENT
LED  SEIS  DUPLE  SCOLDS
JOINTRESOLUTION
CASABA  EASES  RUNT   TCU
LLAMA  KNIT   EMITS  ROOK
ALIA  KENNY  DOSE   GUIDE
ROLLINGIN   THEAISLES
ATM  DISS   AFRO   FLEES
ALIST   PEAR   OLD    TWA
BAKEDHAM  CHICANA  CRIT
AVIAN  NOAH  DIRECTHITS
MONDO  DOPE  ETTA   NIECE
ANGST  STEM  DYED   TASHA
```

2

```
MACHISMO  OSMOSIS    GEDS
ABLATION  TORNADO    RAIN
FLYMYPRETTIESFLY     ERMA
IUD   STAYON   PEES   CLIP
AREAS  ERR   PECS   HOOTS
BEAMMEUPSCOTTY       FRA
SAMOAN    NIH    IDIGIT
EVE  TESS  LEAPS   GEER
MOTT  WICKEDWITCH   DEBS
ICAHN  ERAT  SNOUTS  YAW
NARCO  SIR   OPA   TASTE
ADZ  BITMAP  EAST   LITHE
LOAD  CAPTAINKIRK   LOTT
NOVA  SELMA  TOUR   KOI
SPYCAM   MIC    REDEYE
TAO  SERGEANTFRIDAY
ETUDE  EARS   ION   DEISM
DEJA   APSO  APEXAM  RPI
MRAZ  JUSTTHEFACTSMAAM
ANNE  ATEITUP  NASCENCE
NOES  MERCYME  ENTITIES
```

3

```
FATHERSDAY     COMPACTS
IPHONECASE     INTERRUPT
SPEEDCHESS     VENERATION
COB  ISOMETRIC  LOGONTO
ASIGN  LOREAL  NEWSROOM
LETO  PANTRY  PHDS   SURE
TRESSED   PALOMA    TON
SOPHIST   DARER   FISH
ELLIPTIC  YEAROFTHEPIG
ADIT  OCHO  TRON   HEARME
TISCH  SUBSISTED   DRIPS
ASSHAT  ROAR  SURF   TOUT
CHEESESLICER   PARTERRE
DARK   SHEAF   MOMMIES
ADU  TRYSTS  TABASCO
REPO  OPUS  ATCOST   JOSH
INTHERED  SELENE   FIVEO
ANIONIC   VICEVERSA  ERA
LIGHTSABER  OEDIPUSREX
SHORTLINE   FIREENGINE
THESLOTS   FLYSWATTER
```

4

```
THE   TWIT   ICBM   TUNES
HAND  HAND   MORAL  OMENS
USDA  ORCS   PLACE  PLACE
GIOVANNI  BEIGES   CAPE
STRING   STRING   SCOUT
SEASHORE     PIRATING
MES   ERAT  ALLNET   DEO
AIM  SPASM  OLDAGE  AERO
IDEATED   PERSON   PERSON
WINNIPEG  TROPE    YUM
ASTOR  RATE  RATE   CISCO
RIN   BERRA    SAYHELLO
BANANA  BANANA  TORSION
IMOK  GOESAT  SPINE   DNA
GOV  IAMRFI  STEN    HFF
SKIPANTS     HEDGEHOG
THROB  NATURE    NATURE
BIAS  ACESIT   SMARTIES
CLASS  CLASS  ATEM  UTES
MATEO  KAREN  BASE   BASE
STERN   PSST  ELAL    REX
```

5

```
SEASLUG   IDIDIT   ONBASE
INDIANA   NICOLE   PIANOS
KNEEHIGHHEINIE   UVRAYS
HIES   MOES     ANTLER
SORTA  ERR  BADAREA  TOT
ALF   SIREE  GUN    REAR
MOISTEN   TEATREETREATY
ANN  ONEISH  NERD  ASSES
MPAA  CAB  ADAM   ASHIEST
BOWTIETAEBO    OATERS
ATEAMS  RESULTS   EATRAW
PRISSY    BEEFYPHOEBE
OCARINA  OATH  OVI   RAIL
COMIC  CTRL  MORENO   CDT
TOUCHYCHEETAH   STASHES
ELSE  EAR   RONDA    OSO
TSE  MADISON  ESC   TRIBE
NOHELP    BAIL    TNUT
SCREAM   LOAFERFURLOUGH
IGUANA   ESTEEM   BEGUILE
PIEPAN   DELETE   SCATTER
```

6

```
TIDEPOD   THERANGE   SPRAT
ICONCUR   OOZESOUT   EROSE
KERATIN  KNIGHTTOBEIGHT
IBM  SOREKNEES   ANNUAL
BLACK   ANSELS   MEDICINE
AUNTIEEM    VEX    TESTY
RETOTAL  CHIPSAHOY   HIS
DISHONOUR    ANA
BRAVOS  PERKUP   MAKESIT
OATER  MORN  RESIN  PANIC
ADORE  AKU  TERESA  HUMPH
RINDS  TABLED  PTS  ENOTE
DUCAT  INSET  SPYS  WINOS
SENESCE  CHOPUP   ESTOPS
TSA    CHEROKEES
BTW  NOSFERATU   COWBIRD
IRISH   BIC    GOSSAMER
FANTASIA   CMAJOR   WHITE
OCTANE   PROMINENT   TIS
CHECKMATEINONE   COLLARS
AERIE   FREETOGO   AMPUTEE
LASER   LANDEDON   ABSCESS
```

7

```
RAP  EAGER SCAM  CACAO
APES AGAVE KALE  ATOLL
ISTHISABADTIMER  LEMME
DEPOSITS DUMPS   LIMBS
   RENEE  TERA   HIPPO
ABORTS WORKSFROMHOMER
DEJA THAI  KRONOS  ENO
ELECT  ISLAM EWES  HANG
PICKUPTHEPACER  VALUE
TET  LAMA PULP  THATSIT
    CITADEL  ORPHEUS
RIPOPEN NEAT ORAL  ODE
ETHOS   WATCHYOURTONER
APOP EDAM  LEERS SHIER
CRT STEREO  SETS  GORE
TOOKTHEPLUNGER WARNED
   BERET  TOES  SAVOR
SORER  HELEN  CODEWORD
GIMME FIVESECONDRULER
ORBIT EDIT  VOCAL  PLAN
TESTS EELS  ADORE   SRO
```

8

```
TSA  SCANT RANAT    MAT
RIPS AUDIO ALERT  MAUI
OTOH TRANQUILITY  ANTE
OSLO SAG UMS  GIL  NOOB
PALEO  TELEPATHS OUNCE
ETO  NOOSE  ASTIN   TRA
ROE EAR  APART EVE  HAM
SPLASH ARAMAIC EGRETS
   EDMUND RBG YESIAM
NIVEA COOKIEJAR  ADORE
PRELL ARMSTRONG NIOBE
RENAL ANA   RIO  TONIC
    ISP  ENACTED  ELS
IHADTO DISABLE BEERME
MUDEELS  PBS  NBATEAM
ARM POOLS   GRASP  III
CLIC   FOODCHAIN  GNAT
   THEEAGLEHASLANDED
ITSAGO IDLESSE AENEAS
NOTION NOTATED STEELE
STEP MOMS  NAPES  STRAP
```

9

```
LAMPS  BERG  STOP  THEFT
OZARK  LMAO  CHAR  HELIO
REKEY ATMOSPHERE  ERROL
DREAMON IBERIA NAMEONE
EARMARKS EGOS  RUBAIYAT
    BLASTFROMTHEPAST
CELL TAI  OCT   KISS
COTE MARSH  ISAID SITH
ACH FORTHEMOSTPART NAY
ROYALWE  WOOL  LEOPARD
BALROG SONDHEIM XPRIZE
   MOLTED   APIECE
   CHRISTOPHERMARLOWE
TAHOE KARAOKEBAR ARRAY
SCALDS   XMEN  STANCE
ACME PRIMROSEPATH PICA
RIP  RODEO  GUSTO  ERR
IDA MIXEDMETAPHORS PEZ
NEGRONIS AXED EPIPHYTE
ANNETTE  NATE  SNARLER
STENTS   AMES   GREEDO
```

10

```
 HANGS  CLEAN STEEPEST
CAGIER HOUSE ORDNANCE
BRONTOSAURUS BUDDYCOP
GLUTS TRIO   AREA   ONE
BETH LOIS  ACRID SPREE
MISQUOTESMOSQUITOES
   UGLY  APT  UPTOP
ARIOSI LEAVE  PREAMP
FRONTIERFURNITURE SAL
IMAFAN ELDEST FORSALE
LORE  APU   ADO   CUBA
MISREAD FROLLO ALINES
ERA SCARFACESACRIFICE
DETACH ASKTO  HABITS
   POESY  IAN  AIME
OVERSELLSVERSAILLES
TWIXT TITHE  ASPS EXPO
RED  PLOD   FREE  TAPIR
ASISEEIT BRAINTEASERS
STOUTEST MOUNT STEREO
HOTLANTA WINGS  CASTS
```

11

```
POST   CHARS  TSA   AKA
EULER TAIWAN HILARYSK
SCENE ORGANA AMESIOWA
THEPLOTTHICKENS EATAT
   PIANO  THEY  SALON
OPENTO SPED  ESSO
FARSI VERDI SCOFF  BIO
TAC NEALE POPULARKIDS
EVANGELIZE ROB SIEGEL
NORA LEG MAOTAI  ANDSO
   PSST GERMS  PORN
VESPA SHORTE OHM  ETDS
EXCITE ELI OFFONALARK
SPREADEAGLE RUNIT  KOI
TOY NEWTO SPOSE  EMEND
   NEST CAGE  DAISES
 PLEBS  HEAL   SALSA
PROBE HEADLESSCHICKEN
COCOAMIX GATEAU VANDY
SWANDIVE ATTEND ELENA
SLY  REC  REEDS   LEAD
```

12

```
REGIFTS  ICHECK  QURAN
ICESHEET THESUN USEBY
POTLATCH GOESFORASPIN
ELSE OTERI  DEFCON STY
NIT UNSHORN  KOTB
  HOPS  OOLALA  KIRSCH
UBERS ATM  TENAM CAMEO
RABAT ELBA  TILL OVALS
NILLA SLAP STABS ABLE
SLR RIOT  POLAR  INDUS
   OCTOPI ABO  KAZOOS
 BLAST  MARIO ABET IRE
VOLT AROMA SONY  SONIA
EXITS BRAT ENDS OMENS
GENOA GENES ENS  RISKY
ARGYLE ADAGIO  ARTS
  SETH  CADBURY   OPS
SAW STAKED RAIMI SWAT
TURNTURNTURN TASMANIA
UTICA SENATE EMERGENT
BOTOX HEALER INSERTS
```

13

```
AMIR  MESAS  SWAM  AFAR
RODEO OAKIE  OHHI  DRNO
ANYCOLDTIME  DEADCHEAT
BALANCES ESSAY  SHEESH
   LAHR  DEAL  STARR
HURL  ANTI  WELSH  READS
ATA  TIDAL  SWEARAT  DOE
WINCEMAKER  SALUT  TINE
KLEIN  NEMEA  PAGECRANK
SEEPAGE  MATH  ASARULE
   HBO  BAPTISM  SID
SMELTER  SIGN  NEMESIS
SPARECRIB  CHARO  SAUDI
WIGS  HODAD  CROWHOUSES
ARI  MADEIRA  LAYON  HAS
TEMPE  ESTER  UDON  OILY
   OARED  ASAP  USSR
IAMBIC  HOMER  EDHARRIS
CRESTAREA  NOWYOUSEEME
AINT  SULK  ASHEN  ERNIE
NATS  HEMS  LEAST  YOND
```

14

```
ASH  ARAB  OFF  SKICAP
SIA  MEDE  SLED  CHICAGO
PLINYTHEELDER  RETUNES
COLORWHEELS  LOIS  BLT
ASSAYED  MICCHECK  BEEB
   HAE  COMOROS  LARVA
IMS  NTSB  REI  BOOKREC
DATE  SUE  KEEPSITREAL
CYANS  PREP  POSITED
HITJOBS  MOW  LINT  BARK
IGUANA  APPOLLS  EYEDUP
POEM  SALT  WOO  DREADED
   BASTAYA  TIME  SNAFU
JAMESTAYLOR  ELI  SMUT
JANEROE  SIP  LIRR  SLY
AMINO  GENETIC  OAT
MAST  GLUTENIN  INTEGRA
PIE  ZOOM  SEXCOMEDIES
ACTAEON  JALISCOMEXICO
CATCAFE  LOON  ATAD  NUN
KNEELS  OCT  BANG  GRE
```

15

```
ADVERB  ANGORAS  SUCHAS
BRIDES  GRENADA  ARREST
BURYTHEHATCHET  ONESIE
ENG  DATA  SUR  ADAM
SKID  RNS  HEARTBROKEN
SANE  PATIO  HURRAH  APP
   TWAS  CRT  NAISH  DEA
SHORTSIGHTED  POPINJAY
OOO  RENO  YNEZ  AIRS
SNL  ASLEW  NEAPS  SYMS
   WHATADISGRACE
FIBS  WHIRS  SALON  CTN
IAGO  LAPD  WARD  OHO
DRONEDON  GROUNDNUTMEG
EMT  TIDED  OCT  PEEK
DEN  AVOWAL  KESHA  STIR
ROLLERSKATE  COT  SODA
ESTE  BIL  HORA  PDT
UTHANT  FORTLAUDERDALE
RAISIN  ITALICS  SEEPED
ONNEXT  TBTESTS  TAMARA
```

16

```
TBSP  NSFW  ARES  ALPO
HATE  OHIO  LUMP  SAID
EZRA  TIER  VEIL  ANSE
TAILFIN  DRURY  LIMPETS
OAK  OMEN  APE  SITE  COS
PREMIERE  WPA  GODZILLA
   ZEST  WEDIDIT  ECKO
MOTTO  LENIN  CANSO
FINESSE  PAGED  PILEUPS
ACEN  PAPAL  DUPES  WRAY
MASERATIS  CITIFIELD
   DARENOT  SENTOUT
ALF  NERO  ISE  TENN  AMP
BURP  STEPPROAD  PLEA
CLAIRE  VSIGN  SWILLS
SUMNER  VEINIER  TENETS
   EYES  ANN  OVO  INKY
PAR  IFAPT  QPART  CAP
IMAGE  LIFE  WIIG  MIAMI
NOTER  TNUT  ACNE  ASTIN
TREES  OGLE  REGS  DOSES
```

17

```
DROPCAP  BALSA  IGGY
ACREAGE  BEMOAN  COLAS
BASETAN  REMIND  EWASTE
   KAPPEARANCES  IMMAD
TSO  REALIGN  TROLL  INA
IONIA  LISA  KISSEDANDM
SBENCH  TERSE  OAI  WES
   ETUDE  DURAN  RKO
PURSER  RESIN  VIOLETS
PELT  EVENS  CREDO  POW
ESC  REVERSEPHONEL  ERA
ATE  ALITO  DRONE  MEAT
TORNMCL  SLOES  ENDASH
   ASH  BEAUS  GRIEF
LES  APE  ITSME  TGIRLS
HIGHSPEEDD  PISH  EAVES
UNO  NOTSO  SASSOON  SIN
METOO  STRANSFORMER
PARROT  IMPOSE  SARALEE
RIZZO  NESTED  ENEMIES
POET  GROSS  DISPELS
```

18

```
PUTTS  SLEW  WONT  ERGS
APRIL  EAVE  AARON  LEAP
SHIPOFTHEDESSERT  FIDE
SIB  ETON  OFA  BINGE
GLASSWORK  NOBELMINDED
OLLIE  EEK  RITUAL  ETE
   DECO  EEL  CTRL  ERR
THEMORALEOFTHESTORY
WHO  SUDS  PARE  SHOD
HER  TREKS  DENY  ISAY
ITSNOTROCKETTESCIENCE
MAYA  FUND  SATAN  AHA
LIST  BEDS  RAJA  PER
ICAMEISAWICONCURRED
ENO  REDO  EAU  KNUT
ARM  ITALIA  NTH  SEEME
SEMICOLOGNE  DEATHSTAR
EPOCH  LGA  OARS  HON
DONA  MAJORTHOREAUFARE
USER  ALLOY  URSA  MINIS
PERE  CEOS  ESTS  WREST
```

19

```
WHIR   ODE   BELAS   VASSAR
DOME   REX   REACTIONTIME
SNAP   ABT   ALICEBTOKLAS
 OGOD   TORN   NURSE   SENT
ALOTOF   RUDE   REEDS   NAS
HUNTERSTHOMPSON     HST
ALEE   APER   PIT   TOAST
BURDENED   GAT   BEARPAW
   ACC   ARTHURCCLARKE
FAST   APPHYSICS   LIED
GURUS   IMO   UPS   CENTS
ATOM   OVERTHERE   LEGO
SUSANBANTHONY   SBA
PRETEEN   AHS   SLOWRIDE
AIRES   BRO   OWES   AGES
SAD   STEPHENADOUGLAS
BSA   SPURT   OVUM   MADEDO
EIRE   REARS   ESPY   LOSS
GEORGEMCOHAN   GMC   LIPS
ITSGREEKTOME   ACE   LAIR
NEESON   SHEAR   SAL   SSNS
```

20

```
BRADS   MENORAH   LOWPH
RARER   IMANAGE   SALARY
SOFTBALLPLAYER   URANIA
UNFIT   IOTA   OOPS   GMC
NCIS   MARY   ERMINE   SARI
GOATHERD   SNOOZE   PERON
   UMS   ITSPECIALIST
ONAUTO   ACCRA   DUST   MEH
PALPS   PULSARS   PARKA
TAPS   TADA   NICK   WOMAN
SCHEDULINGCOORDINATOR
PALER   OGRE   TOUT   RHEA
 BLANC   SAMSUNG   STANK
HIE   DELI   NURSE   RESIDE
ORTHODONTIST   CAM
URBAN   SCOTIA   MAGICIAN
SILT   SEATAC   RACE   ONME
EGO   PURR   DORA   TUTUS
CACHED   EPIDEMIOLOGIST
ATKINS   OTTOMAN   AGAME
TESTS   FASTONE   BORED
```

21

```
 AMMAN     BITES
 CLAIRE   LAG   AMECHE
SHALLOW   DIPLO   TINHATS
AIRBEDS   EASEL   ANTONIO
GAMER   REARENDER   SEDER
EPIC   POND   TEAM   DONT
LES   BLOOP   IKNOW   NNE
YTTRIUM   OCCAM   GRANGER
 URNS   ORATE   SIRI
RATEDG   CLIPART   BENICE
ERA   SIGH   BOD   EMUS   MEG
DAMP   NOUN   THAN   SHAG
IGOR   GOTIT   FIEND   POSE
DORIS   DELIVERED   TIMED
 NAVAJO   ELITE   ELATES
 IVANI   TEA   PLUMS
EVILOMENS   MIAMIHEAT
BIGEYE   CAVEMAN   PLINTH
ECIG   SKELETONKEY   NERO
RAVE   OPERATION   EMIR
TRES   ITSY   EAST   DYAN
```

22

```
WMD   BARON   MASSE   SWEAR
HOE   OLINE   ULNAR   UHURU
OVENTIMER   MMIII   GABON
PIPETTE   DEMOCD   LARIAT
PEDAL   STINK   GARTERS
ESOTERIC   CEDE   REDO
REW   CAROM   SORTA   ANDUP
STN   ACTNOW   ISOPOD   RDA
 OPE   URAL   REND   EDY
KELPS   LANAI   CRAZYEYED
ISEE   CANDYSTRIPE   HERA
STARLINGS   LAUDE   HORSY
SAP   INTO   DERN   SOW
ETA   FEELME   ACCOST   MIA
SETHE   RAILS   HAUNT   ACI
 ISON   LIEN   DISASTER
PILLARS   KNEES   MATCH
ENDIVE   EYESUP   ETAGERE
ENOTE   ATWAR   RURALAREA
PIPER   ORATE   EMILE   TAD
SEARS   KEYED   EPEES   OMS
```

23

```
STEWS   THESE   IBIS   TICS
COCOA   WOPAT   NEKO   ASHE
AROOMIEWITHAVIEW   VAIN
MELD   PRICY   LEG   HEALS
 ESCAPEFROMNEWYORKIE
 TOD   AIMAT   EARN
ASCAP   AMICA   DANE   SEA
KIRI   IDOL   RAGINGBULLY
IRONYMAN   BRANDS   NUKE
TEM   GAMERA   CAT   MAIS
ANALOG   YEN   HRH   ASTHMA
 GORE   BOA   ELECTS   PAM
ETNA   RAINON   JOHNWIKI
GOODYFELLAS   POTS   OLES
OWN   ARAL   CARBS   TRESS
 TROD   AGAVE   ZAK
STRANGERONATRAINEE
CHUBS   ETA   TTEST   TALK
URIS   AHARDDAYSNIGHTIE
ZONE   GALA   BRUTE   AIMEE
ZEST   EMMY   ASPER   ICEUP
```

24

```
KTEL   RICCI   DRUMS   MUM
GRAIL   ENRON   VISIT   APU
BASSIINNEEDDOODLE   KEG
 PEAKS   SENIOR   ALAKING
ADM   ELM   GRAF   DANDY
DOESSAABBOOKKEEPING
DONHO   GRASSY   SURCEASE
SRTA   SNARL   ATRIA   STS
 QUEENNOORROOMMATES
STP   TAT   YUGOS   LIRA
HEIDEN   LEAVEON   CHENEY
RARE   ROLFE   WHO   KOS
ISAACCOOLLYYEEHAWS
MET   HARKS   ALVIN   HACK
PRESALES   SILKEN   DELHI
 SWIMMEETTEENNEEDLED
AKBAR   ENOS   YIN   TAD
MOONBOW   SOBBER   RIGHT
ADO   ENROLLEESSEEMMEEK
SAT   DEERE   SLAVS   SERRA
SKY   SANER   TAUPE   NEST
```

25

```
T R E A D   S P I R I T S   C H A S E S
C O R S E T   T I M E C O P   R E C O U P
M O T H E R S U P E R I O R   I N C U B I
  K E E P U P   D E N T I S T   O N I T
      A D I E U   A G I T A   T U D E S
B R E A K I N G B A D   N E U R O N S
L E A D   G E S   D A R T G U N
A L T A R   P A R K I N G F I N E   O R E
S E A P O W E R S   N O R I S K   F O B S
S E T T Y P E   A R T E S   M I D S T
    S C A R B O R O U G H F A I R
M A T T E   O N E A S   L A T E T A G
C I A O   J O C U N D   B E A A R T H U R
A D S   B U C K P A S S I N G   E R O D E
N E T C O S T   R E O   A R I E
  E R O T I C A   W O R K I N G P O O R
M A G U S   L O T S A   S I D E R
A C R E   R E B R A N D   E R I E P A
S H E L V E   B A T T I N G A V E R A G E
S E A L I N   L I E I N I T   E V A D E S
E S T A D O   E N D N O T E   E T S E Q
```

26

```
D A N I E L C R A I G   T A K E S H A P E
U S E D V E H I C L E   U N E N T E R E D
C O L L E G E P R E P   T I E D Y E I N G
A F L Y   E L I S H A   S P I L L A N E
  I R K E D   A M A T I V E
J E A L O U S Y   P R I S O N E S C A P E
O U T I N G   C A D G I N G   O D O R
A B A C I   S H O R T O F   E T C H I N
D I R E C T L I N E   S I L I C O N E
S E I   B R A N D N A M E P R O D U C T S
  T O O K T O T H E S L O P E S
S E V E N Y E A R S I N T I B E T   V A T
W E I R D E S T   D E C O R A T I V E
A R N E S S   D E S E R E T   B E L I E
R I G S   C O A L E R S   S L A L O M
M E T A A N A L Y S E S   S T H E L E N S
  M I M E S I S   C E R E S
S A D F A C E S   E T A L I I   F L A P
A L E R T E D T O   A M A Z O N P R I M E
A T L E I S U R E   R A R E D I S E A S E
R O A D S T E A D   S H O R E P A T R O L
```

27

```
J A R   A S C A P   A B B O T   U T E S
A F E W   K E L S O   T R U L Y   F E T A
B R E E Z I N E S S   R E C A P   F A H D
B A L I I N D O N E S I A   E D I T E D
E M E R G E S   H A D T O   E Z I N E
R E D D   T I R A D E   B O Y Z I I M E N
  N I N E T O   D I N E A T   E S S
I N A S E C   S H O R I N G   M Y B
N A D I A   G E E Z E R   U S B   E C K O
K R I S T E N W I I G   N E H I   L O L Z
E N D   O D O   S E E T O   I A M   N E Z
R I A L   I M A M   N I N T E N D O W I I
S A S E   F E M   S T R E W S   P L A N E
  X V I   A B U S I V E   W H Y Y E S
O P S   W E E Z E R   N E R V E D
J A C O B R I I S   A G R E E R   S P C A
I L U V U   S N I P S   N E S T E R S
B E L U G A   E A S Y O N T H E E Y E S
W A L L   L U N G S   O V E R E X P O S E
A L E E   A M I E S   D I N A R   A T T N
S E R S   S P A D E   A D E L E   E S T
```

28

```
P O B O Y   S N I P E R S   M A D A M
O H A R A S   H O N O R E E   L A M E S A
P I T (C) H Y   U P G R A D E   P I T C H Y
T O S S   S A S E   D I P S   S I T H
O A F   T H E G E M I N I   D R E
P R O T E (A) M   K A R A T   P R O T E A M
  T R E A T   P I N E L O G   E N T R Y
  R R A T I N G   T R O T S K Y
(S) T R I P L I N G   S T R I P L I N (G)
H U E   L E T   H S T   T O N   R O O
E N E W S   R O S E P E T A L   E L A T E
L E V I (T) E S   T H E C W   L E V I T E S
F R E R E S   G E E W H I Z   N I C E S T
  I M C O O L   N O O D L E
H I D E   N A M E S A K E S   N U M B
M (O) U S S E S   O M A N I   M O U S S E S
M U D T I R E   S O C A L   A L G E B R A
  E A T O F   I A N D S
B O X E (R) S   P I R A T I C   B O X E R S
M A I T R E   T R I T O N E   A M E L I A
I T S S A D   S E A L E G S   Y E S M O M
```

29

```
L C D   A L E   L O P   N A W
O R E S   S C A L P   M I N S K   R O B E
M U L T I P L I C A T I V E I N V E R S E
B L O U S E   R A G W E E D   E C H E C K
A L U N S E R   P E O N S   M E R M A I D
R E S   U R I   A V A   S S A
D R E W   T E E T O T A L E R S   P O S Y
I S D O N E   M A C H S I X   A R E N A S
  U S C G   N U R S E   G I R L
P O R K C H O P   L E E   P A S S E D G O
A M O   B A B I E S R U S   E E K
S A G A   B R I O   A L M S   I L S A
T H E T H E O R Y O F R E L A T I V I T Y
E A R M A R K S   N O E   A I R W A V E S
  F A I R E   M A U L S   N O O N E
O H E N R Y   F O R R E A L   S N A R F S
N O D   P A R R   A M E S   Y O N
A M E N   T U T T I F R U T T I   E R N E
J A R O M I R   O V I N E   A L A M O D E
A G E N D E R   N A V E L   G L A M O U R
G E R A L D S   S L E D S   S E S A M E S
```

30

```
S P O I L   L A L A W   S H U T   W A R T
P U N N Y   A R I S E   L A S H   I G O R
C L E A N O U T T H E H O U S E   N A M E
A L P S   U R L   D A M E   D E E P A K
  S E E F R I E N D S M O R E O F T E N
M A R C I   E S A I   A T T A
O H C O O L   S N O G   S S R   S R O
S E E N S A Y   G R O W M Y N E S T E G G
H A N D   K O N   W E I R   C L E A R Y
E D T   M E R E   S A L T I   H A R L E M
  G I V E U P O L D H A B I T S
S H E R R I   T E A K S   N O D E   M B A
A E R A T E   R A M I   S O N   T E E N
W A T C H W H A T I E A T   B A G H D A D
L E I   A L Y   S C A R   S I R I U S
  E A R S   D R E D   L O T T O
P L A N A P E R F E C T G E T A W A Y
S H A L O M   D E A D   I N K   A T I T
W A I L   O R G A N I Z E M Y O F F I C E
I S L E   N E E D   T A K E I   T I V O S
M E A N   A N D Y   S P E N T   S T E N T
```

31

AWNUTS · BASICS · JUSTNOW
RHINOS · ORIOLE · ASTRIDE
FOLLOWINGSUIT · WHOOPEE
SEED · TAOISM · BELL
ALSO · BEFORELONG
CLOSETOHOME · BUN · CIO
YOOHOO · ADORABLE · MECCA
ROMEO · PROVEN · VALUED
UMPS · CHERI · DNA · EXALTS
SSA · HUE · EASYA · NITTY
BETWEENYOUANDME
SPACE · GRIEF · EOS · MAE
STALKS · GAG · OWNER · TILL
WEEKLY · HARHAR · DHABI
ERASE · FOOTSTEP · SEAMUS
EEN · IRR · AHEADOFTIME
POSTOFFICE · EXES
ABET · MASALA · ATMS
RELIEVE · NEXTTONOTHING
ICANSEE · TREATS · BEARUP
POSTERN · HYDRAS · IDTAGS

32

ASSUME · ABACK · PSYCHIC
DOUBTS · POMPOM · TEAMUSA
DRPEPPERSPRAY · ATSIGNS
UTERO · TEES · LOM · FINITE
PAR · CPAS · BABYDRRUTH
BOORS · PEAS · LEE · SOON
BOONE · COAL · JANET · UMP
DRWHOSYOURDADDY · INTER
OILS · SEXTS · MAYISEE
IBM · GENE · POT · TERNS
EVANS · DRJCREW · TREAT
PREOP · ALS · HAHA · NAB
MINORCA · CHOIR · AFRO
GROSS · THEWIZARDOFDROZ
MEH · SLAYS · TALL · GREAT
SABE · ATT · GERE · LEANN
DODRNOHARM · DENT · CIG
GOOGOO · MTA · GMEN · BRICE
INHASTE · THEDOCTORISIN
FLORETS · NAVAJO · SOCCER
SYOSSET · MAYOR · ASHORE

33

BANDB · ACKS · SHEAFED
SERIAL · SNOOP · STALLONE
CAMARO · ITCHY · TENYARDS
AKA · TOMGIRL · SINK · GUS
RENT · DENSE · BEET · SCARE
FRIED · TOMATOES · BEAVER
NOR · ROTORS · TENSEST
MADLIB · GODS · EARTH
HOV · OVID · RATEDPG · BEST
ETE · REGIS · YAYAS · GARTH
WINTER · GUM · LET · JERSEY
TOGAS · HIRAM · SEWON · ARM
ONEL · EATFROM · SALT · TEE
LEVIS · GUYS · SLEAZO
ASHIVER · AIRMAN · YES
NOONER · RUNNINGALIGHT
TURNS · HOTS · STUNG · SOAR
ORS · TOGO · STAYSIN · SNO
ISITTRUE · APACE · ACCOST
NONEVENT · YUKON · NAPLES
ENGAGED · EDEN · TALON

34

COATRACK · CHUTES · ADOBE
OHBOOHOO · POPART · CRUET
MARINERSBATTLEPIRATES
ARAL · MESA · POI · NEMO
SAMSA · LEA · SPIT · AFAR
VOTESON · MATER · TMI
TIGERSCANTHANDLECUBS
HOVERCAR · SING · ARNIE
ATOM · AUTO · TSAR · DEETS
NOR · SAG · IDES · EENIE
YANKEESDEFEATREDS
LEANN · MOOR · RAD · NAB
ABODE · TALE · RATE · SANE
MILER · MANS · HAVEPITY
PADRESBOWTOCARDINALS
ELM · DIARY · FOCUSED
DYAD · TASE · TNT · SHEBA
SETI · REB · UCLA · EXES
NATIONALSTOPPLEROYALS
ALECK · COURIC · UNICYCLE
PAREE · EXPELS · BADDATES

35

ADESTE · AWOL · ANDSODOI
OILPAN · TBONE · NORADUNN
ROLAND · ASNER · STAYSMAD
TRICKYDICTION · UNE · PRE
ASSET · ALI · DIRTPORTION
JOEY · SHA · CAT · SWEPT
POPUPS · TSA · TON · ORES
AVON · STRAWMANSION
MELC · AGE · KOBE · TRECOOL
PRETTYING · BEAV · PORNO
EENIE · FDIC · TRIO · ALBEN
RATON · YALL · SCHILLING
STANTON · NAIL · TIX · ATOB
SWEETNLOTION · RATE
RARE · LTR · KIM · AISLED
EWOKS · IAN · AIM · GYNT
BASETENSION · EPA · SALMA
ESS · ALC · BONUSTRACTION
CHATROOM · ZUNIS · RAINON
CINERAMA · ELAND · BLOUSE
ANODYNES · DISK · SENSES

36

COW · INSERTS · TEAMO · VAN
URI · DETROIT · UNDERSIDE
TAN · OVERAGE · BALTIMORE
STEWS · VADER · ATE · OILED
IOTA · RETIRE · SER · LLAMA
TRASHY · AESOP · DEED
SHOAL · USAGES · ARK
NATIONALS · SPINAL · VIE
AGENT · TOOKTURNS · CHIDE
BORG · FENNEL · CHOSEN
THERESNOIINTEAM
ATWOOD · UNCOOL · ETTA
FIEND · CARDINALS · ASHEN
ALI · MAJORS · NOCONTEST
REM · SOLACE · ACTAS
ARES · DRAWL · TINEAR
STRUT · SAL · ERIEPA · DAME
AWAIT · TEE · FANTA · ASWAN
MINNESOTA · EROSION · OLD
ONESECOND · RANINTO · LIE
SSR · SILAS · STANTON · FER

37

```
A S A M I   A D M A N   Q E I I   M G M T
C O L I C   S U E D E   A N O S   A R E A
C H U T E F O R T H E S T A R S   K I D S
T O M   P I N A   D R E A M   U S E N E T
    I O L A N I   P R E S E N T D A Y
C R A M P I N G M Y S T I L E   A H S
H E R S   T O P E K A   G O G E T E M
A S T E R N   E L I   D C O N   T O K E
R O U T E O F A L L E V I L   S C E N E S
D D R   B O O M   S I O U X   H E E D S
    G A R R O T E   A R M Y M O M
L E G I T   K E A N U   S L O P   B S A
O A R M E N   B U S S E D Y O U R B U T T
O R E M   I S A T   H M O   E A R B O B
S N E E T C H   S E I N E R   O B L A
    N A W   I N E E D T O L O S E W A I T
R A B B I T H O L E   R E S I N S
O M E R T A   T A T A S   V E N D   L O L
T A R A   P A Y Y O U R F A R E S H A R E
O N E K   A M E N   S T A T E   I O W A N
R A T E   S I T E   T A X E D   T E S L A
```

38

```
S T A L L S   U T E S   C A P   B R A S S
O O H O O H   N O S H   A D O   R O U T E
S N A P C R A C K L E A N D P   O L D I E
A S S   K I L O   R C A   U N C L I P S
    T E N O R   T I E D   L I A I S E
P A S S   K U K L A F R A N A N D E
H U M P T Y   O O F   C R E E   A L A
I R A   I D T A G S   C L I O S   W N Y C
S A L   D I A N E   C L A S P   V E N O M
H E L S I N K I   B R I N   I M A L O N E
    W Y N K E N B L Y N K E N A N D D
A M O N G S T   L U P E   L I M E S O D A
M E R C S   O V E R T   Z O O M S   M I C
A W L S   S T E W S   H E N N A S   I C U
L S D   H E H E   F A T   R A D N E R
    P E T E R P A U L A N D Y   R I D A
M O O L A H   H U R L   A R G U E
W A I T I T I   A N I   Y A L L   L A O
A F L A C   L A S T O N E S T A N D I N G
S I E G E   L I E   S A G A   N A S C A R
H A D E S   S L R   A H O Y   D E L E T E
```

39

```
C A S P E R   O L D H A N D   S I G M A S
D I P O L E   R E V E N U E   O N E A C T
S L I P I N   D O R S A L  FIN  M E A N L Y
    E S C A P E S   L E C A R R E
A L L T I M E R  FIN  N S   S A L T B A T H
B O B A T E A   M E T E D   B I G O T R Y
F R E R E  FIN  I S H E R S   A X I O M
A R R   D R E A D S   D O U B T S   N U N
B E G S   E L L I E   E N R O N   H G T S
    H U F  FIN  E S S   R E  FIN  A N C E
  M W A H                   A A R P
S E A M O N S T E R   D E E P T H R E A T
A R T   H O P E S O   A L D R I N   E T C
C L E F   G R E A T   W H I T E   G L I B
K E R R Y   A M I S   N I T E   P O B O Y
    H A U N T S         S A T O R I
R A Z Z E S   S H A R K   M A L I G N
J A Z Z U P   D E A F E A R   W O L F E D
A N A L   A M I T Y I S L A N D   L I A R
W A R E   L A T T E   T E N O R   A S T O
S T D S   I T S O K   S L I M Y   S H O P
```

40

```
U S E D   F I A S C O   S L A B   R A N G
N O T A B I G D E A L   R E N I   E V E R
P L A Y I N G(C A R D)  S T A G E D O O R
C O L D D A Y   M B A   L O G(C A B)I N
    R E L   F R O G G Y   R A C E D
G O J I   S P O I L E R   H A T H A
E V A N S   E X P O   A H E M S   N C I S
D A R K A R T   P A R T A Y   A W E
    T O R P E D O E S   L A C U N A R
S T D   L A I R   P O T T E D P L A N T
N O O U T L E T   Z E N   H A(V A N)A N S
B L O C K(B U S T E R)  W I V E   A N A
C A T T O Y S   T R U T H S E R A
T M I   B O O G I E   S T O O P T O
V E N N   T R A P S   G R A B   K N E A D
    U H H U H   U S H E R E D   S I Z E
  E R V I N   E M E T I C   O U T
U N T A N G L E   A R T   S T R I N G S
(S T R U C K)O I L   P A S S I N G L A N E
O N O R   S O M E   I C A N S E E T H A T
B E N E   O D E D   G E T L I T   S A W S
```

41

```
L E D O N   G E E K   W H U M P   E H O W
S C O R E   O L G A   E A P O E   X E N A
A L G R E E N B A Y W I N D O W   C A L L
T A N   Q U A D   A R G O N   B E R Y L
S T A Y P U T   F I D O   L O S T T O
    P A R I S H I L T O N H E A D S H O P
K O P   I B I S   E L S E   S O S
C A T O   G M A N   A L L L E G S
O L I V E R N O R T H P O L E D A N C E
O L E   R E A M S   Y O Y O   I A M S
P O D C A S T   C A P   W H A T N O T
T T Y L   S C A T   S K O A L   C R O
S E A N P E N N S T A T I O N B R E A K
    W I L D O N E   T O O L   A L P E
C B S   B A I O   T H I S   R A D
R I C H L I T T L E R O C K M U S I C
A G R E E D   E X E S   A B S O L U T
S T E N T   C H E C K   O M N I   A P U
H O W L   M A E W E S T B A N K H E I S T
E D I E   O N E A L   V O T E   M A M E T
S O N Y   E S P Y S   S E E R   M U S T I
```

42

```
A L P O   A C T A S I F   T H E D A N C E
M A R C   M R S L A T E   R I D E S O U T
I M I T   O U T S T A N D I N G B I L L S
N I C O L   D O O N   A D D E R A L L
O N E P A G E R   A D O R E   D I G
R A D I C A L M O V E M E N T   S O T T O
    A B Y S S   M E N T H E   O I L
P I G G Y   S A I N T   E C O N O M Y
C A N O E   B R I G   A S H C A K E
A S T A   T A I C H I   S W E E T T A L K
S T E L L A R C L A S S I F I C A T I O N
K I L L E R B E E   P O D U N K   I M R E
C L I F B A R   T E L E   M E A D E
S C E N T E D   G A D O T   J A R T S
S I C   S O N O F A   W H E E L
N O T A R   S O L I D F O U N D A T I O N
R A S   N I G E R   S T I L E T T O
E P I C P O E M   A S H E   A S H E N
S M A S H I N G P U M P K I N S   S E L F
A M S T E R E O   T A P I N T O   E L L A
D A T A L O S S   A V E N G E D   S P O T
```

43

```
H I N D U . A L A M O . . F L O G . . D A N G
O B O E S . N I K O N . . R O M O . O R E O
N E T W O R K F A M E . A N N O . U R G E
. G E S T A L T . S A W N E I G H B O R S
. . O B E S E . L A T . . O U T W I T
I N A T U B . O S U . V I S I O N
N O T O R I O U S P S Y C H O . K I C K S
C H E R . N T E S T . O U I . S H E P
H O N C H O S . Y E A S T . B A N A N A
. H E L P M E . T R A F F I C T O Y S
A G S . I D E A L S . E G O I S T . S A M
T I T A N I C J A W S . A R N E S S
B R O N Z E . O M A H A . I S O L A T E
A L O T . S U R . A A R O N . A V O N
T Y P E S . S I D E W A Y S G R A V I T Y
. P E A N U T . S E C . O D E S S A
P O S T A L . C N N . S A D I E
S U P E R B A D H A I R . R O L L S B Y
A T O M . O G R E . G I A N T S P L A S H
L I S P . W H O S . E P C O T . H O M E R
M E E T . S A P S . R E A D Y . I B A R S
```

44

```
W A R T . P S A S . D A W G S . F R O C K
A R E A . R E N E . I L I A C . D O N O R
I M A M . E X T E R N A L L Y . A L A M O
L A D E N . Y O I N K . D U L L . E S P N
N Y S E . T I N A . A R M L E T . A L E
M I S T A K I N G . P R O P A G A N D A
U S E . R I M E . W O O S H . A L A N I S
M U T A B L E . D E M M E . I T E M O N E
P I G P E N . J U D E A . A N I S E T T E
S T O R E . S O F T G . D I N O . D E S K
. . R E I N F O R C E M E N T
A C T V . P R E Y . A L T A R . H A R D R
P R A I R I E S . S N O O T . G A L O R E
B O B C A T S . T H A N X . F A T I M A S
S P L A S H . B R U T E . L A S S . A M I
. P E R P E T R A T E . M A N H A T T A N
D I D . S T R I V E . W A N D . L O O M
I N H D . S A T E . G O T T A . L O M A N
A G O R A . D I S C O N T E N T . B A J A
L U T E S . E S T E R . E R G O . A T O N
S P E W S . S H Y L Y . S N O W . D O R A
```

45

```
C A S A . W E N T . F L O R A . T R I O D E
A C E R . E A C H . R I P U P . S E A L U P
P A R T Y T R A Y . A M I S S . A N G L E E
N I E C E . L A M A Z E . H E A R T R A T E
. N E A T . . E L I J A H . I S E E
I R A N G A T E . T E U T O N S . D E A L S
T A S T E T E S T . R I T U A L S . P O I
A D L E R . A T O M . C A R M E N M C R A E
L I A R . I R O N O R E . S O A R I N G
Y O M . G R A N I T A . U S B . P U L S E
. L O S T I N T H E S H U F F L E
Y E A S T . A G O . N O T T R U E . B A H
A T T A I N S . S E N E G A L . B A D U
C H A T T Y C A T H Y . E T O N . A B N E R
H E R . S A M H I L L . L O C A L C A L L
T R I E D . L I E F L A T . D E P L A N E S
. M A G I . N I A C I N . P A R A
G A M E R R A G E . B O X O U T . Y A R D S
A P A R N A . O R A L S . B R A S S B A R S
G O R G E S . T V S E T . E G G O . I M I N
S P E E D S . H E S S E . L E S T . C A P S
```

46

```
S T A R T . J E M I M A . D U S T . A H S
I N F E R . U L T R A S . J P M O R G A N
B U T T E R R I V A L S . A L I T A L I A
S T E R N L Y . . E A R N I T . T I K I
. . R E D S . W O R K I N G T H E S O U L
A M W A Y . S I D E . L A O . D O E
L O A D . O N E A L . P H E N O M S
C U R S E S F O U L E D A G A I N . L I E
O R D . C H A S M . G O B U S T . B I L E
A N S A R I . P A L E S T . B O O K S
. J U N G L E A L L T H E W A Y
C O D A S . L A Y U P S . H Y D R A S
U N I X . T E R E S A . D E F O E . O L E
R U M . H U N D R E D D O L L A R B U L L
E P I L O G S . S E Z M E . A N I L
. N O N . H A S . M E O W . H I D E S
T R U C K Q U E S T I O N S . P A T H
R I T A . A B A S E R . B A R S O A P
A G I T A T E D . P A S S W O R D H U N T
L O V E D A R T . U T O P I A . C O S T S
A R E . O R S O . P E D A N T . S P E E D
```

47

```
A S T E R . I R A T E . S L U N G . C B S
S H O N E . L O M A X . T O S E A . A L A
H O W T H E Y W O N T H E W E S T . J O B
E R E . A L A S . G R O P E D . E M O T E
S T R E S S . A L A R M . B A Y L O R
. T H A T D O E S N O T A M U S E U S
P A D . Y A K . M I L O . E S T
A R P . G O R Y . F E W . N O V E L
N O O N E H A S R A T E D T H I S F I L M
D F L A T S . P I T S A W . A E C . V A T
H A L T S . F A L L . R E C S . A D O B O
O N O . I S O . K A I S E R . S P O R T S
W E I N C L U D E D N O B A T T E R I E S
. A K I R A . Y E N . V O L E . E S A
. G N P . C A N E . S A G . A S T
P E O P L E M A D E M I S T A K E S
I N N E E D . I L O S T . R A P P E R
G O U D A . L A T E S T . I R I S . A P E
P E P . P A S S I V E R E S I S T A N C E
E S L . A M A T O . Y I E L D . E X T O L
N E E . T E T O N . S A L E S . R E S T S
```

48

```
W O O Z Y . S E A L A B S . M A J O R
I N N I E . C A N C E L L E D . A L A M O
E L E N A . A D V A N T A G E . R O G E T
L O N G R A L L Y . H A R D C O U R T
D A I S . B L Y . A C E . L B O . F A T E
S N L . R U M . I M A M S . Y S L . R A D
. B A S E . C A R E W . W I I G
F A L A F E L . A D O R E . I D E A T E S
E L E C T R A . R E U S E . N O N M E A T
L E A K . T H E U S O P E N . E C T O
L U S H . B E E . S E N . X E S . S H U N
A T T A . U R L S . T E R P . E S P Y
. N O R . P H I . D O M . A R T
. T O D A Y . L O N . U M P . M I M I C
S H U S H . F E E T . N O L A . M A N I A
A R T H U R A S H E . G R A N D S T A N D
M I R O . E N S O R . A R R O W . C R E E
A V A T A R . R E T R O . A S H A R P
R E G . Q U E E N S N E W Y O R K . B A T
R O E . U N D O . T U E . A L F A . I M A
A N D . A S S N . S T S . Z E S T . C A T
```

49

50

In the above answer grid an asterisk (*) represents L-O-V-E going Across,
H-A-T-E going Down.

51

52

53

54

55

```
BETTIE  SPICERUB  TGIF
UNHURT  MONOMANIA  REBA
THERISKISTOOHIGH  UNIX
TAFTS  ATE  SEABEDS
ELAL  ETHANE  TOG  ACE
ONEBC  SORRYNOTSORRY
DIGUP  BEAKS  SELFIE
ARMOR  LESABRE  COROLLA
IHAVENTACLUE  HAS  RUES
MEREMORTALS  HAJ  ISI
SAG  EMAILS  MAROON  DAG
IFS  MED  SADDLEJOINT
EDNA  FAR  PLEASEDONTGO
TESTBAN  TOASTER  KEYES
ALOHAS  COOPT  TYPES
LIFESTOOSHORT  OSCAR
ERS  UMS  NORMAL  OLES
ARTISTA  IAN  BLIGE
YURI  ASKINGFORTROUBLE
ATOM  NEEDARIDE  OSMIUM
PORE  TRIBUNES  TENSES
```

56

```
FIBBER  LIBIDO  STRAP
AMARNA  UNITARDS  CHAFE
KIBITZ  CROSSBOW  RETRO
ENYA  OAKEN  HIDE  ARSON
SNARKY  ICET  DOME
OTTER  ABACUS  MENSSHOP
WRENCH  REST  VINE  TORY
LIPO  UBER  EGAD  ASHLAR
SOS  ALLA  CARDIB  LEDTO
EBOOK  USAUSA  ARIES
NOLITA  BRATZ  DONUTS
BALED  THEFBI  PARTB
LEDGE  SAVEUS  USES  JIF
INVADE  NEWT  APSO  TATA
GAIN  ABEL  TRIP  SEIZED
HECTARES  TOILET  SEZME
LUSH  PUNT  TWITCH
ARBYS  EGAN  EPSON  LAMP
LEAPS  SANDRAOH  EMINOR
ENNUI  THEREIGO  POPDUO
STATE  MADDOW  TOSSED
```

57

```
TRACTS  APBS  DOC  TERI
BACHATA  BOLT  ONO  READ
SWEETANDSOUR  NEG  ERGO
ANTE  HEARTANDSOUL
ERRS  TILT  JPOP  ARTS
SHEESH  LEIA  BLACULA
PEACHESANDCREAM  EATS
NAPTIME  TAKE  YOGI  RHO
BAN  EDS  SUNNIER
TARANDFEATHER  STONER
DALAI  SURF  AGUA  ELEGY
IMMUNE  RIGHTANDWRONG
APOLUNE  SHE  DIS
NON  SEAS  AAHS  ONESTEP
ANDY  STANDUPANDCHEER
CUESTAS  SHAM  OTELLO
OPRY  RSVP  SPEW  MESS
STOPANDSTARE  ETRE
WIKI  COP  MIXEDDOUBLES
ARIE  UNO  ONIT  SCROOGE
BEES  PET  SGTS  KOWTOW
```

58

```
BOBSFORAPPLES  MIDRIFF
AREWEDONEHERE  OCEANIA
WIRERECORDERS  TOETAGS
LOREN  KISS  OSMOND  SET
SNAP  BONE  BRIARS  HEAD
POUT  BEFOGS  FANTA
DESCENT  LEARNS  DORSEY
INTOTO  HALVES  PORTERS
TRAPS  BOWTIE  MEME
KATIEHOLMES  PARASAIL
OPENMINDED  BARMITZVAH
TDGARDEN  MASKINGTAPE
TEEM  CORSET  RENTS
RICHARD  SORBET  GECKOS
AMOURS  FOULED  GOESAPE
DIRTY  ALFRED  BRAN
INNS  PRETTY  MOOT  SCAB
OLE  SENATE  VATS  CLOSE
COLGATE  ASBIGASAHOUSE
AVIATES  CAYENNEPEPPER
REAPERS  ONEWAYSTREETS
```

59

```
LEAR  AMEN  BASKS  CHINO
ORSO  LAC(K)  OCHRE  OATER
URSA  GIGS  RURAL  SWEDE
EDSEL  TAS  IMARE(T)
STRAUB  PINCHED  ICEPOP
LETTERSONTHEKEYS  RYE
OREL  ATTESTS  NEKOCASE
BADAT  EASY  IPSO  NAT
SAINTS  MTA  WASNTME
SPH  POCO  MEATS  ECOLES
PLACETHEMINTHECORNERS
AURORA  SEGUE  DANE  DEE
TSARIST  MRS  GASSES
SON  ASEA  HATH  NICAD
LASTGASP  IVORIES  MEDI
IVE  READNEWDOWNWORDS
LESSSO  NIELSEN  OILERS
O(W)DOKE  VON  DWEEB
OUTRE  JESSE  IKID  ORAN
UNITE  AREST  AIDA  NATO
ROAST  ISLEY  SMO(Y)  SLED
```

Four answers in the grid have KEY in one direction and single letters in the other, as shown. LAC(KEY) crosses N(A)STINESS; O(KEY)DOKE crosses S(W)EET; SMO(KEY) crosses SNOW DA(Y); and HAW(KEY)E crosses IMARE(T). The instructions at 41-, 70- and 99-Down say to place the letters on the keys (that is, A, W, Y and T) in the corners of the grid and read the new words formed reading down. When the letters are placed correctly, the new Down words in order—top left, top right, bottom left and bottom right—spell YOU ARE OUT NOW

60

```
DARKAGES  HEELS  STROS
AQUILINE  MUDCAT  IWISH
MURDERCASEMURSE  PESCI
PAIDAD  MADE  USES  REAR
TESS  SKIRESORTSKORT
CHART  EAUX  SHIVA
LENS  RBIS  SPASM  INERT
URI  HILO  ACAI  AGRIP
BRADYBUNCHBRUNCH  RAS
EPEE  HALT  ERASMUS
GREYPOUPONGROUPON
NONREAL  POEM  GLUE
HAJ  SPACEPROGRAMSPAM
UTICA  EVAN  EASE  ELI
HOBOS  RIPIT  GEMS  SETS
SERTA  NACL  TYROS
BURNINGLOGBLOG  RING
IMRE  DELL  LOON  INAREA
OMITS  SALTEDPORKSPORK
TIETO  SMARTS  MAKESURE
ATSIX  OASIS  EPILEPSY
```

61

```
ARETHA   LAIRS   NOTECARD
RAISES   AGNEW   APOLOGIA
ASTARISBORNE     MISSPELL
LAHR  SURGE  ALA    ISSEI
     ESCAPE    PROTEGEE
EAR  BYEALLRIGHTS    ASHE
FLOSS     AGONY   NUANCED
TIRANE  ICBM    MAINDRAG
STEVEN  NET  NIA  TIRADE
     EWOKS    MODEMS  OPER
BARDS   SEMIPROSE   UBERS
ATOB  FURIES      THUMB
THAYER  TAD   BRR  SPECIE
TESTKITS    BRIO  STRADA
LETHEAN   GMAIL    ESSES
ELSE  RUNNINGLAPSE    TAT
     BESTCASE    DIANNE
ETHEL   ITS   SHELF  ALES
SHALLOWS   UNCALLEDFORE
SEALEVEL   SHARI   SETTLE
ENSENADA   ALBEE   TEASER
```

62

```
FAULT   MANE    CART  SWAM
LUNAS  ALONE   ARIA  HERA
ODDSANDENDS    BEANERIES
ERITREA  OUT   SALTMARSH
ADE    AMENRA       TRIP
    DST   TOOBIGTOIGNORE
BRA  PEPA    ORE   CRENEL
FADEINS   TUFTED   ELENA
FRANKSINATRA   IDS   DET
AMIE   ELIE   STAR    AWE
    ADDINSULTTOINJURY
ANN    ROTS   SILL   POST
BOD   NET   PARALLELBARS
OMEGA   BREWER   EDIBLES
MAVENS  ANT    SAWN   EKE
BREAKINGASWEAT     AKA
    RENE    ANTLER   ZED
PLACENAME   IDO   PDJAMES
HABANEROS   LONGOVERDUE
IVES  REST   SWARD  NIECE
LATE  SRTA   SLUE   SANER
```

63

```
NAP   DRCLAW   AVOID  AHAB
ALE   WOEISI   TERRE  SOME
SAN   ABOMINABLESNOWMAN
AMITY   PANNED    TWEEZE
LOCHNESSMONSTER    ELMO
    IRENE    WET   COO  LANA
FILE   DAWN    THEKRAKEN
ISLES  URAL  RAT   RESECT
ELISHA  ARETOO  AAS   RHO
FANTASTICBEASTS   ODSON
    ALIOT   AND   UTILE
SACRE   WHERETOFINDTHEM
UNH  OZS   GOTANF   NEROLI
STACIE  MON   REEL  RIVAL
HIMALAYAS    STUD   MEND
ICER  LET  EMO    NEVER
    ALLA   THENORWEGIANSEA
ONEOFF   TROWEL   STORM
SCOTTISHHIGHLANDS    VIP
LENI   STOIC   ASTANA   EKE
ORSO   HUTCH   THEWAR  RAD
```

64

```
FIVEAM   IMAM   LOM  SEMIS
IMEASY   TODO   AHA  TIARA
SPARTA   SUDS   RBI  AGLET
CALLINGINTSTION    GHANA
ACES   TONTO   MAYAN   TWIN
LTR  BOO   IQUIT  CYBHICS
    BUNDLEUP    ITGEN
PIUSIII   ECHOES    ROADS
LONG  ADO   USING   RETAIL
IPASS  ENCE  CEO   ATEMPO
BCC  WHAII     ABAHI    IPA
ROOMER  AVE   ILLS   ALLIN
ARMIES  MISSM  OTS   ANNE
SNAKT   GELCAP   CRABLEG
    EIDER    BOOKOFRA
IMSPENT   FREUD  PER   DIM
NOTI  ATSEA   NODOZ   LOCI
CORAL  ATTHEDROPOFAHAT
AMAZF  KOI   SIOW   NATANT
PONZI  EMS   TOUR   EMERGE
SODAS  NAH   ETSY   SERMON
```

65

```
CHAP   HEM   GRAVEL   MECCA
HOLA   APO   EUREKA   INLOW
EWES   WITHONEACCORDION
ASPCA  CEO   LOEB    PCTS
PAPALBULLION    DIDOK
DOLLAR   ESTEEM   TRIBAL
    SALES   NOVAE   PANAMA
CROWNS   ISTHATAFACTION
HERA  ATTU    SLIGO   TSK
UNAGI   RIFFED    DENS
GOLEM  UNIONIZED   ITSME
    RACE    REPEAL   CALEB
AWE   GOUDA    AVEC   GAGA
MISSIMPOSSIBLE    LEEWAY
INSANE  STENO   SMARM
ENAMEL  OILRIG   ANNOYS
    YASIR    FILLINGSTATS
ATTN  EAST   UNA   THREW
RHETORICALQUESTS   ERLE
KASHA  LADIES   EEO  ROLE
SITAR  STANDS   TEN  SWAP
```

66

```
HOTTUB   TIMBRE    BISSAU
UNWISE   ROARING   ACCEPT
BLIMEY   INRANGE   SERAPE
BITE   ORBITS    LIBERAL
UNC   SNEEZE   IEST    PDT
BEHINDSCENES    EWAN   EAT
    SEPIAS    WELLOFFMARK
JUGHEAD   SERE    OCELOT
ATIT   LEAPT    EAGERER
FINALE  MERE   FOVEA   VET
ACURA   OUTOFBLUE   SLOTH
RAP   BREST   SUED  STACHE
    BEERTAP   STACK   MAYS
LISBON   XRAY    HIRABLE
POPQUESTION    NEARER
NWA   FEAR   AGAINSTGRAIN
ARK   FILM   VENTIS   MMI
    ENAMELS   MELEES   HYPE
ACROSS   LARISSA   SEATAC
SHOWER   STUNTED   UNLACE
KIDNAP   SEDANS    EVENTS
```

67

```
EBB   TSK   RADARS   SNOGS
GORDITA  POPIDOL  HIDEY
ETAILER  SUPREMELEADER
SHIRTWAIST  EPEES    SKI
TENT   TOTES   TOPUP  ADA
SRS  SLED  SOIL    AARON
  KHAKI    BOYPROBLEMS
MOUNTAINGOAT   LOLAT
UNSEE  DEED  AMUSE  SEIS
FAULT   ROB  ECIGS   APE
ATALL  CRUMBCAKE  DOTES
SIL  SALON  CAN   CASCA
APSO  BEADS  RIMS  ASIAM
   GOBAD  PORTAUPRINCE
SHORTANSWER    IPADS
LAVER   IDEA  TENS   BIB
EVE   OPTIN   OSCAR  GIGI
EER   RANGE  SAILSALONG
VOLLEYBALLNET  INCOLOR
ENIAC  ONEMORE  KONMARI
SEETO  RETORT   EWE  BEG
```

68

```
PRESSURE    ORALB   SPIFF
AIRLANES  AMELIA   ARNIE
NOMANISANISLAND  LACED
STAMP  HUED  OREO  ADORE
   DEMO  BAHAMAMAMAMIX
HASADATE    IDS   ELISE
AMONRA   CRED   ANT   TEN
WELCOMEHOMEHON  MCHALE
KNEE   VOWS  ARI  ELIXIR
   SOHO   PRIMETIMETV
SSR  TOKE  GOD  EVAN  SEE
WHEREWEREWE     ALGA
ARTURO   ILE  ICED  RASH
TERRIF  KINGKAMEHAMEHA
SKI   TSA   REFI   ONERUN
   BIDET  TKO  THUDDING
ALUMINUMINGOT   OREG
DOTES  AONE  DIBS  RURAL
ARIAS  ROMATOMATOSAUCE
PRONE  TRADER  REVERSES
TENTS   SENSE  BLANDEST
```

69

```
CLOSE   BBC   BATOR   ABUT
REMIT   ALA  ARENAS  CAMO
OVERHEARDOG  SONOMA  ISPY
WIG  EVERT   IMO   EGADS
ETA  RADII  CARTCONNETWORK
DYSON   VEES   SID  TABOO
   FESTERS  TALLS  SOAP
LEFTTO   PLEX   ETCHERS
AIME   EUGENIE   ASEA
GLORIAALL  RED  KURD  ARCANA
RATEDR  TIDEPOD  MIOTIC
ACEDIT  ETON  STROBEFFECT
  NOAM  PEASOUP  MAHI
GASMAIN   MEWL   DEBATE
RICO   STAID   PINENUT
ADHOC   IRS  AONE  MESON
BALLOONARTISTS  VOLGA  WOE
OPRAH   OAS  ADAIR   ICE
ACAI  REFUTE  DAYTIMEEMMYS
LUNE  EFILES   EDU  DITTO
LESS    TEARS   SAP  EBSEN
```

70

```
TOSHIBA   RACY   BMW   ORG
ARCANUM  ISHE  CRAM   BAM
NERDSRINGPOP  FADDIETS
KLEE   UBER   SOIL   NYT
USES  BABYRUTHSNICKERS
PEN  TONI   SUE   BUMRAP
WHISKAS   REST   RASPY
CRUNCHNOWANDLATER
ERIN   SPIN  YETI   KFC
LATKES   USGA  EELY   AOK
AYE  WHOPPERSSPREE  NYU
NOR  EASE  DISC  RAFTER
NSA  LAPS  LEAF    OAST
  MILKYWAYSTARBURST
SALAD   ASEC  SCAREDY
ALOTOF  ATS  ARAY   SAC
LIFESAVERSPAYDAY  WELL
BTU  JAYS  EPEE   ARLO
HAIRLINE  MARSSMARTIES
ABE  UTES  AKIN  PROTEGE
MAR  GAS  OSLO  GETSSET
```

71

```
CIVIL   PESO   AJAR  MATES
OPINE   AUTO  KIWI  GRUNT
MONSTERRAMRALLY  MERCI
SEISMS   RPI  TSAR   ATON
   SOIL   ADO   DOT   LUG
NATUREABHORSAHOOVER
CARET   YEA  FOIE  SPADAY
USED   RIG   GOP   LOGE
SAN  MYSOLORUNNETHOVER
PLATOON  OLIN  SORARE
   ANKA  RIGID  PURE
INTERN   META  LEMMING
WORKEDFORPLANTERS  WAR
ERIC   STU   SIR   KONA
BASALT  INCA  SEQ  NINNY
THROWINGINTHEBOUNTY
POL   LIV   AGO   SNAG
ARID  GORP  LOS  NUNCIO
MINIS  TALEOFTHESCOTCH
POEMS  EGOT  ARIA  ELATE
ASNER  DADA  ROCK  DELAY
```

72

```
DOCK   POISE   PSST  ABIT
OPRAH  ASNER  LASH   TENS
UTILE  TAKEAWAYNECHECK
LIMERICK    INA   FLORAS
ANELEPHANTINTHEWOMB
   SOY   ERASE   BODEREK
SWEAT   WIG  DOORS   ELI
HITWOKBOTTOM  NOD  AWOL
ANNE   LOUSE  WEAK  ADEPT
DEADHEAT   CASH  SNORES
   GETWITCHQUICK
PIVOTS   EKES  NCAAGAME
IVANV  VIES  PACER  ALOE
ZINE   HOG  THEWHEELDEAL
ZEN  SACHA  ARM   USEBY
ADASTRA   SALSA   OYL
   WEEDBETWEENTHELINES
SCHWAS   LOL   AIRALERT
WHISKEYBUSINESS  BICEP
AUTO  LEON  LEVEE  YUCCA
GMEN  LEWD  LEASE   MOTT
```

73

```
SNA[REDR]UM  PAN  AMBI  ORCAS
YOMAMA  OXO  NOUN  LEACH
STEFAN  WISPIEST  SISQO
TART  ONEALL  THESE  QUA
ELIS  C[REDU]LOUS  TRANQUIL
MOC  STOP  USN  INC  BETS
TAPER  CHARTE[REDB]US
ARESO  HYPE  TOR  PBR
CAPTAIN  PAP  ONSALE
BESEATED  ALLIASK  CRUS
ARSES  VICEVERSA  CAIRO
NEUT  GENERIS  HUND[REDY]ARD
JA[REDL]ETO  ECO  ANARCHY
OLY  IFI  ISTO  SANAA
OPENFLOOR  ATTAR
NOSE  TGI  LLD  VISE  NIT
EXTRAC[REDI]T  SIEGES  MAHI
ITA  THETA  F[REDP]ERRY  ATAN
GENIL  NOTLEAST  ONIONS
HAZEL  TARO  ITE  RSTLNE
SMART  STAX  REX  EA[REDS]EAL
```

74

```
APPEAL  THEDOW  ETCETC
LIOTTA  OEDIPAL  CHACHA
FLUTES  FLYMETOTHEMOON
FRUITCUPS  REWROTE
HES  TEA  CARLA  IOWA
ORO  DRAINS  ACID  EMU
LEMMA  SINGININTHERAIN
IDEALS  RKO  ANDSO  ARCH
SWEARBY  SPA  PAMELA
PIUS  GOA  TENTS  OATEN
ANG  JAILHOUSEROCK  HAD
SCALE  LLOYD  ERR  HERS
THRONE  RVS  ONTOPIC
IWON  MOUSE  POD  WITHIT
MONEYMONEYMONEY  ASAMI
ERM  TALC  EVADED  MAN
MEAT  OTHER  AAH  PLY
CRANIAL  STARPUPIL
DANCINGONMYOWN  PELOSI
INARUT  NOSEDIN  EVENED
TATAMI  ITSAGO  ROASTS
```

75

```
TREBEK  VALISES  DEBONE
OHIOAN  IMALONE  EPIPEN
LENTTO  BARELYMANAGING
LAST  SEES  VAIL  WEE
OBSESSIVE  SLEET
BLAMEON  MANYMOONSAGO
LADIES  THATTOO  NOTYET
ANDES  ROEG  DRAGS  LEI
DAIS  RAWRECRUITS  WOKS
EINSTEIN  HADAT  FIRS
PENN  ODINE  ETON
REIN  BERET  SMIRNOFF
EASI  COMICSTRIPS  ILER
RIC  LEWIS  AINT  INDIE
INABIT  LIVEMAS  ENGINE
EXPOSURETIME  CLOSETS
ECASH  SOREPOINT
APE  ESTA  LUST  REAL
FULLYRECOVERED  ICEAXE
ITALIA  ARISING  SEASON
TONING  RESTDAY  TOKENS
```

76

```
POSTHOC  BEAARTHUR  ROB
OATMEAL  EVAPORATE  ERR
STRIPTEASEARTISTS  PDA
SEA  HEFTS  PETERI
ESPYS  SRO  WTO  RUNONS
EASEOFFTHEGASPEDAL
RASSLE  OVERDUE  UNE
UNWISEINVESTMENT  ECCE
MTIDA  COE  SNEAKPEEK
POLO  CEREALS  PIA
SNL  NOEMPTYTHREAT  MEL
FRY  TENUOUS  SALE
GIVEALIFT  TOR  SEZME
ACID  YOUAREOUTOFORDER
IAN  WRIEST  BLEARY
UNENVIABLEPOSITION
STRAIN  YSL  ISH  SAUTE
GISELE  LEPEW  NOD
COP  WITHOUTANYWARNING
HOE  ENTERTAIN  INVITEE
INN  DEARSANTA  ZESTERS
```

77

```
MCS  SAMBA  LEICA  WORM
CHE  ALARM  ANNUM  FIXUP
GRAFFITIPROOFBUILDING
ROSIE  SOLO  ISSUED
AMOR  CELS  OCELO  IRT
WANTS  THREEBLADERAZOR
OHISEE  ARAL  ENEMY
ASP  DEC  SORRY  BISTRO
SPELLCHECKER  HENCE
CINDER  RAID  LORDE  JIB
ACES  ELUDE  FORGE  MONA
PER  TTOPS  KLEE  TOOBAD
RHETT  SNOWBOARDING
SPEEDS  STIES  VIA  NEE
SPUDS  WAIF  BALLOT
AUTOMATICREDIAL  BREWS
GNU  USERS  SUCH  TREO
PERONI  MEAL  CIVIL
ALJAFFEEOFMADMAGAZINE
LOOTS  TSARS  AARON  EEL
EBBS  STRAT  MSDOS  WRY
```

78

```
ESSAY  SCOT  BIBLE  GRAB
PIPPA  AUTO  AFFIX  OHME
SLEEPINTHEBUFFET  DEUS
OVER  OKIE  RBI  RASSLE
MADCOW  TRAILERPARQUET
UAE  LEERAT  MUST
NBA  TYPEAB  SALSA
COLDHARDCACHET  ADDLED
IDLES  OIL  ROSANNE  IVY
SEEM  AFT  ABA  ICANSEE
YOUVEHADYOURFILET
SPONGES  BRO  ETA  WINK
OHO  LESBIAN  WII  EMCEE
PIPPIN  LETSMAKEADELAY
ENOKI  OSIRIS  ELS
MORE  ONBASE  REF
BACKSTAGEPASSE  BLARED
LATISH  CPR  WAZE  MOJO
ALOE  UNSOLICITEDBIDET
MOPS  GRIME  ONES  ONICE
EXIT  SATES  BENT  GENTS
```

79

```
RAID  IDTAG  GRADIENT
ZELDA  NEALE  ROLEPLAY
JOLLYRANCHER  OUTCASTS
ARIEL  CIAO  TUGSON
IBEG  TELESCOPE  DEVIL
LASERS  TON  GEMINI
BLISSFULIGNORANCE
ASK  GANYMEDE  UFOS
UTEP  YELLS  WILD  BIFF
GREASE  TAMALE  TETRA
HAPPYDAYSAREHEREAGAIN
TITAN  MOULIN  ROILED
SNOW  JOSE  TAMPA  NINO
POOH  STONEAGE  ADM
CHEERYDISPOSITION
DEIMOS  HEM  NOSIER
CYNIC  CHEWBACCA  AMBI
TEARED  TALL  ARSON
STATELAW  MERRYGOROUND
LOVEDONE  NAIAD  HENRY
ROADSTER  ORATE  MAGE
```

80

```
SNARF  JUSTSO  MANNERED
WALDO  UNPACK  ITSALIVE
IDEALBREAKER  NEWHAVEN
FIX  KEY  ENAMEL  PARS
TRAUMA  BUNTSERIOUSLY
LUSHES  AVERSE
LAWNSTUDENTS  ARLO  SAW
SINAI  MERLOT  SYSTOLE
AMB  COB  SCRUBS  HASTE
TEAS  BED  SOFAIRSOGOOD
PEORIA  ONETWO
LINEDETECTOR  ETA  NCOS
THECW  SEADOG  IRE  ALA
DORSALS  LEBRON  GOMAD
SPF  ROOS  LABOROFGLOVE
ADULTS  ASLOPE
INVISIBLESINK  GLOBAL
CHOO  DARWIN  SIA  ERA
HOTWATER  EXTRAINNINGS
APIARIST  RARING  TRIOS
SETLISTS  SMOOTH  SANTO
```

81

```
CIRCE  ABRAM  OBJECTORS
UBERX  HUEVO  BEAVERHAT
LIFECOACHES  INBALANCE
DETER  SYRUP  TONEPOEM
RELAY  DYLAN  USS
UKE  TEAR  NOOK  TIBIA
SINGLESBARS  DRIVENUTS
UNDEAD  ATEAM  BEE  LIST
ADULT  SCEPTERS  STELMO
LAM  EMMA  ISO  SPUTTER
TROUBLESHOOTERS
MIGRANT  OAF  PARM  TSP
AQUILA  DOCILITY  OPINE
SUIT  CHE  HEIDI  MIAMOR
TIDEPOOLS  SPAMFILTERS
STORE  TIED  BAIL  CEE
ALE  ARROW  BLAIR
BARESALL  SIZED  ENNUI
ANIMATION  POLOGROUNDS
GETINHERE  UNLIT  DICES
SWELTERED  PESTO  ETHAN
```

82

```
LOCAL  THOU  JAKE
PARTI  AFC  HENNA  ATON
STARE  MOA  ELTON  WARD
MISSIONIMPOSSIBLE
ITSALOSTCAUSE  ENOLA
MRI  ISLETS  LIN
PENPAL  OLEELO  NEMEA
HIS  NOISEROCK  ANT
GMAIL  GUT  GASH  IDS
RIDS  PSST  OILSUP  NET
ANAHEIM  RATBITE  MAR
SIM  SCISSOR  FERRERA
POW  CATHAY  BAYS  ANEW
IRE  SHAY  RON  STUDS
NES  SASHAYING  TIE
GOTTO  SHAYNE  RASPED
OUI  HAYLEY  BRA
ICONS  NEEDLESSTOSAY
NEEDLEINAHAYSTACK
SELA  ALGER  SEE  LAILA
URLS  MMHMM  SSN  OLDEN
ETSY  STYE  NASTY
```

83

```
POEM  PHIL  TRIP  INFECT
ENTOURAGE  HURL  SOOTHE
PECORINOCHEESE  SCOTIA
PECLASS  HUH  AQUADUCK
ALTO  ELITESQUAD
ARI  SILK  ALEX  EEL  BIG
HAND  NOOB  LACED  SODA
ENCODE  RASSLED  HIYALL
ABIDE  SELL  GLUTENFREE
ABSOFREAKINGLUTELY
DYE  TUX  PAR  RAI  SIR
BESTRAPPERFORMANCE
THIRSTTRAP  EASY  BREED
VANITY  IMEANIT  SOYEAH
AIDE  COEDS  DOME  ARGO
DRY  RAH  BUTT  PUTS  YET
LATEPAPERS  SCAM
ROLLATWO  RAW  TRUESUP
ORIENT  BENICIODELTORO
DAMAGE  OPUS  MODELTANK
ELOPED  YANK  SHOW  APSE
```

84

```
LEGUP  AWARD  RANSACK
OPINED  BABOON  EPICURE
COVEREDBRIDGE  GETITON
ADE  GAIA  LINEAR  SOW
LESSONS  GINA  RELIST
AIL  MOET  POTTYMOUTH
GERMANARMY  PAY  NARNIA
ARI  AYES  PERFIDY  END
DADBODS  TERR  AMA  ARGO
STEELE  NOTE  BRA  OLSEN
GARDENAPARTMENT
SPRAY  OWE  PLAY  DEEPER
TEEN  BUD  SEED  MISRULE
ARM  SUREDID  POOF  TEE
VIEFOR  ARR  DIRTYTRICK
ELMERSGLUE  OTOH  RUN
BEETLE  NTWT  EDITORS
BED  ARISEN  ARES  ROC
CARLSJR  COMPASSNEEDLE
OREOPIE  UNPACK  SCREEN
LSDTABS  GOTHS  TAROT
```

85

```
DOC   SCAB  ACHES  TERMS
OPA   LORI  CHILL  ASIANS
REM   IGETAKICKOUTOFYOU
IRE   MITER      STAPLERS
CARRYTHATWEIGHT   HERES
  HAI  OAT  AXLE  ERA
COCO       TCELL  REGATTA
HURTSSOGOOD       PUSHIT
USE  PUPAE   TOMS  SKEET
MEW  EVERT  FINAL   EASY
   IWANNABESEDATED
USPS   TEPID  EELED  ZAP
REALM  ORSO   ADORE  ODE
SCREAM      IMCOMINGOUT
ATATROT  DENCH      MALE
   GNU  ALTA  ANA  ANT
AMEBA  BABYONEMORETIME
CANARIES      ABUTS  MOT
THEKIDSAREALRIGHT   AVA
SERENE  MARRY  TARO  LIP
  ROSES  ITSME  STOP  SEE
```

86

```
BRAH   EGGO  MERLE   APSO
LAME   TRON  PAEAN  CRUMP
UNEDUCATEDGUESS    TAPER
RUNGS  NOLO   VEE   SIEGE
  PSEUDO  BETTERMOU  RAP
  TRALA  RBI    BIPOD
HAI  PLANT  APPALL   GUMP
ATOMS   THE   TONE   BOPIT
MITE   GOODSORT   SEDERS
STAR  GENUIN  TICLE   RED
  SPAN   SAO   BURN
ISM  SILIC  RUBBER   IBAR
MAILIN  CAFENOIR    NONO
AURAS  COIF   DOE   TEXTS
CLAP  PANNED  PRIVA   YES
  COOED   CUE   STERN
SEL  BRICATING   STIFFS
ALEXA  LOT   ZONA   FILTH
ALBUM  LASTDITCHEFFORT
BERRA  ATEAM  MAIM   TRAM
NAYS   CIAOS  EATS   YAWL
```

87

```
DISCS   CATS   ASKS  VAMPS
ICARE   ACHY   UNIT  INOIL
MERYL   IRAN   TIME  GATOR
  DIFFERENCEOFOPINIONS
  OSLO    HALFNOTES
CLAROS  OWETO  OUST   IMP
HIGHWAYMEDIAN    TATTLER
ALIEN  OAT  TNUT   EVITE
TALL  CURIO   BOOT   MARS
SCEPTER  NERD  AVOCADOS
   STOCKDIVIDEND
HOTSAUCE   SODA  RATTRAP
OPAL   SKOR  SMELL   RELO
ORNOT  SNOW   SEA   HADIT
DAGWOOD  ANIMALPRODUCT
SHU  ALIA  ENEMY  AMEXES
  SPAREROOM    AFEW
  MODEOFTRANSPORTATION
ATARI  IAGO   HAIL  ENDOW
GOTIN  ETON   IKEA  ADELE
SHAFT  RENE   SSNS  MSDOS
```

88

```
RADNER   SOTS   SEAMS  BFA
ASIAGO   NCAA   CLIOAWARD
PHAROS   ITLL   HIMALAYAS
COLE   ADVOCATED    BETAS
DRIP  SEEM  DOMES   SCRIM
SENT    SLOG  PESOS   HEED
  IMAM   MAOJR   DABEARS
HOTCOCOA  RHO   DAVID
ANA  WENTBYEBYE   ONEIDA
RAM   DORIC   ANTIDOTES
ARE  TUT  INKER  IRS  ABC
SURFINUSA   MIDAS    LTE
SNAILS  INBADSHAPE  ION
  DETER  RTE  AMEXCARD
EGGDROP  MYERS   OATH
LEAR   WEIRD   SOTU   ALLY
ITSOK  ENJOY  JESU  LIEU
FLUES   DONOTOPEN   KONG
BRINGITIN  SHIF  CUANDO
TENDERAGE  HIRE  UNREEL
WFF   LEGOS   INNS  TITLED
```

89

```
ACTORS   ADREP   SCAMPERS
FROMEARTOEAR    POWERNAP
LINEITEMVETO    AMARETTO
AMEND  TOED  PARER   PIET
TESS  BASS  FERRIED   CAL
  BRIT  HOLDON    UNITE
SPATIAL  MELLOW   CRANES
HIGHESTBIDDER   COSIGNS
REHAB   HOGGED    MOOLA
IPAD  RENNER   SAILEDOFF
NAS  PERNOD  BARNEY   NIL
ENTERTAIN   WINKED   HALO
  COUPE   BONDED   DOULA
BIGOTRY  FORGETABOUTIT
ALANON   BROKER   PATRONS
LOGON   TEEMED    RHYS
DVR  SPEARED  HERS   LORE
NEET  ALTER  PEPA   MANIA
EYEROLLS   ASIWASSAYING
SOLARIUM  NOTEVENCLOSE
SUSPENSE   GLADE   LEANER
```

90

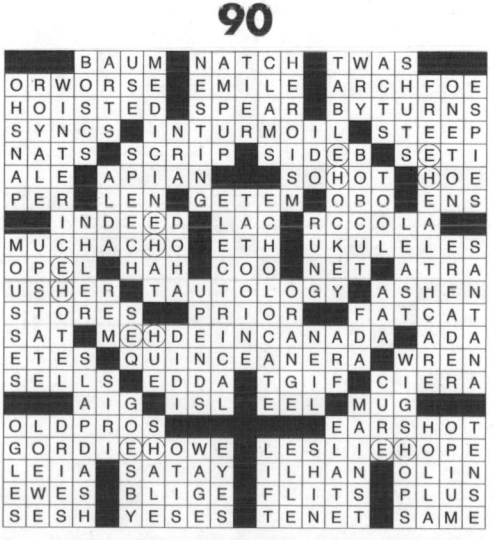

```
   BAUM   NATCH    TWAS
ORWORSE  EMILE   ARCHFOE
HOISTED  SPEAR   BYTURNS
SYNCS   INTURMOIL   STEEP
NATS   SCRIP  SIDEB   SETI
ALE  APIAN  SOHOT    HOE
PER  LEN  GETEM  OBO  ENS
  INDEED  LAC  RCCOLA
MUCHACHO   ETH  UKULELES
OPEL  HAH  COO  NET  ATRA
USHER   TAUTOLOGY   ASHEN
STORES    PRIOR    FATCAT
SAT  MEHDEINCANADA  ADA
ETES   QUINCEANERA  WREN
SELLS  EDDA  TGIF   CIERA
  AIG   ISL   EEL   MUG
OLDPROS        EARSHOT
GORDIEHOWE   LESLIEHOPE
LEIA  SATAY  ILHAN   OLIN
EWES  BLIGE  FLITS   PLUS
SESH  YESES  TENET   SAME
```

91

```
TAROT OGRE  BARRE HTML
ALARM OREL  FLEAS AHOY
CONCONFUSESFUSES  VICE
OHBABY  BEATSME  LARKS
SAY ILK ANO NATIONS
  ELONELONGATESGATES
LEAVENED REO  ELANTRA
ARIA ANS ACUMEN   RAT
MANMANDATESDATES CASE
ESTATE  ATE MED MOPED
    ROT CYCLOPS ION
CUMIN AHS MMA  DOGMAS
OPIE ANAANAGRAMSGRAMS
BTS  ADSITE IRA  ANON
ROSSSEA BYU ELECTORS
APPAPPRAISESRAISES
  ELITISM SEE ATV FAA
AFLAC SOANDSO  EIDERS
LOLA PROPROCURESCURES
POEM GOREY AMEX  HENNA
ODDS AETNA REST  ESSAY
```

92

```
SCAMS EVERGTREE  AKITA
HANOI PAPERHATS  WAGED
ANNUL ESOTERICA  AZURE
STANLEE  CREED UPROARS
TOLDYA  HONES  IDONOT
ASS MRT     RTE   ARE
    MELLOWY OLBEYES
ABBA  CRIEDWOLF  RAFA
BLOODO SILENTU IGIRLS
EAR ARLO LAA ERNO CUP
THEPLAY CONGO ODDJOBS
    HANDSAW ENQUIRE
PRODIGIES  BUGGYWHIP
FINS EARTH JAIHO SAME
FCC  ELO  OIL    SAT
THERPLANET ULTRAVRAYS
  DELIME SLR EELIER
GRADATES TON RAWONION
OUI CONTROVERSIAL GPA
ATL IUD ANEYE RYE HES
THY DTS MESSY SST TNT
```

93

```
RATEDR TUBMAN   RABID
BOBATEA APRICOT ELOPE
GUARDEDOPTIMISM LOTSA
ASTO PIU OMEN CLAPTON
MEET CATE LOCH   AXEL
EDS CULTURESHOCK CECE
  PAT OLAY  TEENIDOL
BBGUN TWOS GOOD SAUNA
YURTS HIGHANXIETY PAN
EGOT ZANY WAIL  ANWAR
  SWEDEN TOW DOCENT
  BIDEN NOOK AMES TGIF
DUN COMICRELIEF OBESE
ANGLO INTO ORGY BARTY
UNCARING  ALBA  HER
BYOB UNBRIDLEDJOY VAT
  NERD OENO DOUR DIVA
NOCLASS SFPD SIM AGES
OBELI CREATURECOMFORT
MIRED IPANEMA ENROUTE
SENDS  ITTEAM DETERS
```

94

```
DRESSAGE MYBAD  NAPLES
RESTATED COULD  OMEARA
UNPOISED BURDENOFPOOF
GOOPDYNAMICS  ENMASSE
    SMA ETA PETER
ODDJOB BRENDAN RAMPED
TERI ODE STILTS DRACO
IAMMALALA HEART IMRAN
SLOMO MILWAUKEEBOOERS
  SMOKE EVEN  EEL JED
    RICK ADDER POPO
SSR ITO LOAF  TORSO
TAMINGOFTHESHOO LITHE
ARISE WYATT MINUSSIGN
RAZOR NORTHS LON ICER
THENFL REPEALS DONKEY
    BARES TMI SEN
IMITATE BOOTSTRENGTH
PENELOPECOOS EUPHORIA
SAGELY SORTA EMAILING
ODESSA OPAHS NPRTOTES
```

95

```
ASCAP VOCE  SCOWL EVER
RHODE IRAN  TERRA VILE
BONAPPETIT ALMICHAELS
OVERPOWER ATLANTA FIE
RESNIK ANYTHINGISGOOD
  LED  EPA    AORTA
REALLYJUSTAMEETING
ACNE SEAAIR PARM EARN
GRAPH DENS OCTAD TRIO
AUTEUR IRONSON   EGG
  WHOSGOINGTOKNOW
BOO STARTED  EROICA
UNDO ALOAD MAIM MOTOR
BEER TOUR POROUS LOCI
  EVENPUTITINTHEFOOD
ASDOI   WET  TAU
THESTEAKTOCOOK SNUFFS
HAT AXLROSE FORTUNATE
EMAILALERT JULIACHILD
NECK MAMMA USAF  HIREE
ASHE SHEER TEST  STEER
```

96

```
ASP SAT OASES  TOM RDA
*PADPRO ALEVE ANTWERP
LIBRARY KEVIN *NFAVOR
ELLICE Y*ELD   EUGENE
STONEAGE AND FR*JOLES
  K*RIN NOE  LATIN
NORI  SAND*EGAN  OATS
BRONTE TIREDLY IFF*ER
CATGUT ICANSEE DAHL*A
  GREECE   ADSITE
MAJOR*S RAMEN POLAR*S
ALOUETTE SIR NATIVETO
COURT *SSARAE  PERIL
AULD GNAT LANE  NANO
ODE CUOMOS ATTILA NAS
  BASE ILANA *MDB
ODIUM *NCOGNITO JOYCE
PROSECCO WEE ONEUPPED
RAW DOUBLED*PPERS REI
AKA UPSETS ESPRIT ELF
HEN EYELET SUSANS SOY
```

97

```
LIFTUP  PFFT  PELT   SWAN
ACROSS  REARWIPER    CECE
SEAOFTRANQUILITY     HEIR
TBILL   AIDS  ROCS   SOUND
ILLS    APSE  SETSOFTONGS
NUT   SUPERVHS    NEAL
GEYSERED    ERASE  BROCHE
  TEAR  BROWED   REFLEX
UNLADE  JESUSLIKE   TEAT
NEARS   RUNED   TAZ  HAVE
DOCS  SANDSOFTIME    ONIN
ESTO  ORK   FAUNA  MUSED
ROOF  BADRATING   TIGERS
GUSTAF  NODULE    SETH
OLEOLE  ANDRE   FASTTALK
  MOST    WIDEOUTS   DEE
SONOFTARZAN   ARRS   PANE
AVERT   PEET   ARCO  GAMIN
LIAR  STATEOFTENNESSEE
ENTO  RADARTRAP   ANTONY
MEOW  SPYS   COGS   EXANTE
```

98

```
HOTTAMALE   TAFFY  CSPAN
ASIAMINOR   EMILE  OPERA
ROCKIDOLS   MOVIETROPES
ESSE  WISE  PREP   OGRES
  MIEN    STEPSONIT
POWERSTRIP    MIRY  SAL
ISH   ITSAMESS   DEADSPOT
VSIGN   ESCAPEES   IHEAR
OILPALM   KNEX   STORMY
TEES  IMDB  KLUM   ESPYS
  PEANUTALLERGY
JADEN   CLAP  THOU   BAMA
SAVORS    GRUB    WETONES
INLET   EGYPTIAN   WOODY
SEASHORE   STONEAGE   DIE
TBT   DIME   MIDDLESEAT
  OPENSPACE    RIDE
HIALL   TIER  ISIT   TOME
MENTALLAPSE   BLACKSTAR
PREEN   ATEIT  MANHATTAN
GAZES   GENRE  STAYLOOSE
```

99

```
WILT  OSCAR    NESS    RAE
ASEA  OWETO  YUCCA   BELL
RANK  HALOS  ETHOS   RAPS
MODEM   PENCILMOUSTACHE
  AHEM  BOOTL[EGG]ER  RITA
OPHELIA   FESSED    YEN
R[EGG]AFRAND  MAD  V[EGG]ESOUT
SEND  TEASET   BASSTUBA
ODD   ASSERT   POT   TOTEM
  AWAY  POETRY   MARINE
DEACON  L[EGG]OMY[EGG]O  ONMED3
RULERS  PILOSE    GODS
EBOOK  NGO   ORGANS   WSJ
SINFONIA  HANSEL    MILE
SEESFIT   LON   MAYBENOT
  PAL   PESTLE   STRANGE
KCAR  TAGTEAMS    DELI
B[EGG]EDTHEQUESTION  APPLY
IFDF  DRUMS  ELBOW  R[EGG]IE
ERES  TRIES  SIEGE   EELS
USD   VANS    TAROT   PROM
```

100

```
SCULPT  GNAW   DABS   INFO
NOMORE  MIRO   OSHA   TURK
APPLEJACKET    WHATMAKES
GAS   WATSONANDCRICKET
  GENE  NANO   AANDE
CARBOMB     MINTY   IBEX
COCA   POSTBAC    ATANY
SITTINONTHEDOCKET    DSL
INVADE  GARR   NULLVALUE
LVI   LAND   RAE   POEM
LIKEAMILLIONBUCKETS
MOTO  DOC   LEGO    STU
EATSPALEO   BOOS   ODISTS
RTE   UNDERGROUNDROCKET
CHART   WOODTAR     HOLY
HEMI  ALBEE   PITFALL
CANOE   TRAM   NEAT   TAU
FRONTOFTHEPACKET
YOUTIOKET   DARNSOCKETS
AINT  OILY   DRIB   FAERIE
MEGA  WELL   STAC   FTYPES
```

101

```
AHA  LTE   SCHMO   ISH  NIB
REXREED  SHOOINS   DUALIPA
PHLEGMY  FORTLEE   ABRAHAM
  WAP  GOOD[NOTHING]EATS  ADS
ANGELENO  PAPAL  WAR[NOTHING]ZONE
DEAD[NOTHING]HEAD  TOG  CASUALSEX
LASSI  PLANETEARTH   SOAMI
ITS  DOTIME   LOCALS    GET
BOYS  DUE  IBARS  HMO  SEAS
  OWEN   CLARION   ELON
ABASE  EWE  DMS  EID  SUGAR
LANAIS  TOOK[NOTHING]OVER  FIGARO
ARI  REEF  LAHTI  ETRE  SMU
B[NOTHING]SIDES  AERATED  HARP[NOTHING]ON
ABEFORTAS  MIO   ROCKSOLID
MATS   SOLARSAIL    DIRE
ACE  LUPINE   PEDANT   NED
KARATE  ENDUSER   GOOSES
  EBERT   OUSTS   SLOPE
SWEATS[NOTHING]IT  MAR  STAR[NOTHING]DATE
TILDE  SNOWPIERCER   HUMOR
ADAMS  ETPHONEHOME   ACELA
TENET  SEAN   TOTS   TENDS
```

102

```
IBMS  GOBUST    PDFS   SHOP
SISTERSISTER   ARIA   HOPI
MONACOMONACO   RANT   OMEN
  LOGON    HOMAGE    TEENS
FAWN   SITH   KUDO   PIBB
ALMA  ICEIN   LOUIELOUIE
TOURBUS  AGE   EXTRAEXTRA
SONTAG   HOTS   IRS    TET
ERR  ELK  OHNO  MPS   BONA
ASAP  YESNO  TSAR   HORNET
ETCETERAETCETERA
SURPRISESURPRISE
CRIKEY  USER   DOSAS   SERF
LEVY  NTH  IDES  MMA   LEO
ARE  AAA   AEON    APPALL
NAMESNAMES   ETD   KNEEPAD
KNOCKKNOCK   RINGS   ASIS
VOTE  FUEL   DART    CCED
GRECO   GOAWAY    IRULE
YODA  BEND   PEOPLEPEOPLE
MOOR  ARGO   DOUBLEDOUBLE
SSNS  AMOR   WISETO   TACK
```

103

```
METS   SISTINE   GERBIL
ETRE   SCREAMIN  SOLOIST
THEMOTHERROAD   MARMOTS
REVIVER  VON   PAOLO
ELITE  OMIT  FOLKSY  HIP
    ORDEAL  BASTE  CORA
PAINTEDDESERT   SQUALOR
STREAMER  ING   UNPACK
HOV  KOREAN   OKSHOOT
ANISE  GEM  HURT   INT
WENT  GATEWAYARCH  OARS
DEA  ICON  YAK   INTOW
  SILENTX  NIACIN  IPA
PUSHED   RAN  DONTDOIT
INVERSE  CADILLACRANCH
ETES  LLOYD   EATSAT
RON  ONMEDS  BAIT  NANAS
  PEEVE  PAN  ACETONE
CRAZIER  ROUTESIXTYSIX
DEPENDS  ENTHRALL  PITT
CARNEY   DETESTS   ERAS
```

104

```
MDPHD  BRO  POL   WHIM
AERIE  IAN  ERA  THINE
STOPSIGNS   REVERENCE
COGS  INCH  SOAMI  GUT
AXE  PIEHOLE  COPIERS
RENAL  WORE  ATOP
ASYLUMS  ETC  KENOSHA
    TMI  SHOES   PAS
  DEPOSITION   TORN
AMOR  CORNICE  ERODE
RAG  EBONY  RELEVANCE
ANT  GER   LTE   FAD
NOREGRETS  ASIAN  USE
CHESS  REACTTO  SLED
IMAC  ANIMATIONS
NAT  SPLAT   SRI
INSIDER  ARK  CHAPTER
  CECE  OATH  TERRA
BODYART  INSHAPE  IMP
APE  RERUN  HERR  SLIP
REVOLTING  MILESTONE
BRINY  ADO  IRE  PAGER
SALE  LOT  RSS  ABYSS
```

105

```
TVAD  SPAN   GOGH  SASH
HOBO  KEPT  TROU  TUTU
ANEWBIRTH   OFFREEDOM
INTERNET   EARCLIPS
  LINCOLNMEMORIAL
MASSEY   SOULS   CRAGGY
EVA  FDA  DOZEN  FAD  RAE
LOVESICK  BAG  BENSTEIN
TWIG  PER  SKY  RUE  HANS
  ORR  DOC   NOD   SET
BUREAU  CASHCOW   STRESS
EGOTISM  BEARD  BOOMMIC
ELF  LAP  AGREE  ATV  ANA
PITAS  HONESTABE  ERNST
  HOPS  WARHERO  SPEC
CELLARS    PACIFIC
CHU  ICU   TAP   POM
LENGTHS  PSE  OREGANO
AVIATES  RIN  MAHATMA
WROTETO  EDT  SBALOAN
SENORS      STERNS
```

106

```
FUSE  SPACE  BARB  OASIS
AHOY  MOREL  ABIT  PLANK
COMESOUTOFONESSHELLEY
THEMOORS  UTILE  UNEASY
  PART  IDOS   AMEND
GOESTHROUGHHELLER  FOG
AWOKE  AIDE  LOL  SCOWL
LIP  DAMN  MOMOA  ARLO
EELS  TAKESALONGWALKER
SEALE  SWORD  SERB  STY
  LEOI  WISPS  SOBE
OOH  GUNN  THATS  NARCO
PLAYSTHEFIELDING  ALPS
TIRE  AMISS  BOOB  ETA
ENDAT  LEN  TTYL  USAIN
DEL  BREAKSTHELAWRENCE
  YETIS  TWIX  ALAS
TVEXEC  SHOOT  STRAWHAT
GIVESAFAIRSHAKESPEARE
INERT  RINK  EVITA  EVAN
FORTS  ODDS  RENEW  DEBT
```

107

```
ASKS  COCO  TOOL  ELMER
THING  OAHU  EXPO  NAOMI
RODEO  ATIT  CHIN  LBOMB
ANDANOTHERTHING  IOTAS
IDIDNT  FEE  DEJAVU
NAE  AIMED  LIE  OVERSEE
  OSMOSES  SHINDIGS
THISISNTMY  ASANA  ATOP
RAMONE   RIYAL   TOY
ADULT  PERIL  VISOR  RNA
ITSDEJAVUALLOVERAGAIN
LOT  RAYON  BORAX  TYPED
  ANI  KOREA  SONICS
BABY  ARENA  FIRSTRODEO
UNROLLED   RUSSOLO
MARTIAL  REP  STYNE  GMO
  OPIATE  TAU  ENSUED
MIAMI  BABYONEMORETIME
ONSET  ELLE  IDEA  MELON
DITTO  LION  STAR  YETIS
STAIR  SAGS  EONS  LYRE
```

108

```
  SEPTA   SLIP   OAST
STARED  ATOMIC  GLOAT
THESILENCEOFTHELAMBOS
HITEM  LANE   COLA  UOFA
YPSI  BEVERLYHILLSCOUP
  MONAE   EAU   EACH
PANTSLABYRINTH   ISLAM
ETHOS  DUE  CAROMS  OGRE
TEA  DOSAS  ELATE  BMW
ESTADO  THIGHFIDELITY
  PERU  MOO   DEMO
JURASSICPARKA  DOUBTS
GET  FATAH  NARCS  OOH
REEF  LAMAZE  LGA  GLOBE
UPSET  BRIDGEOFSPIKES
  AREA  ONO   EATME
THISISSPINALTAPE  MAXI
AUDI  STAT  FOCI  DAKAR
THEBLAIRSWITCHPROJECT
SALTY  AMTRAK  EXHORT
LEES  EARN  TSARS
```

109

```
OSLO  UNFIT  HELP  BEAST
RHEA  NORAH  ETAL  ELLIE
BOTTOMLINE  ACRE  CAPRA
SOS  METE  OLDERBROTHER
 GRATED  TASTY  IMEASY
STEIN   ETHNIC  ONES
PUTTINGGREEN  ANDS  WAH
ATOZ  EAGER  ANTS  AHME
NUN  FALSE  TRUTH  FLAIR
 WHIRL  PEORIA  LETGO
ASIAN  INCONTACT  ARSON
BUTTE  VALUES  NASTY
USHER  APART  SPOCK  OAK
THIS  ANEW  BOOTH  MULE
SIT  ACTS  CHARLEYHORSE
 PSIS  ALECTO  ITSON
ATARUN  SMACK  SCATHE
GIVINGTHANKS  HULU  CON
AMEND  HANG  THIRDPARTY
TERCE  UNDO  AERIE  REIN
ESTER  STAR  BETON  ETSY
```

110

```
ROFL  AWED  TREAT  TEMPT
OURS  CALE  RASTA  ANAIS
STUDFARMS  AZTEC  BRINK
ARI  LIMIT  SEE  OOLONGS
 OTHO  URIAH  REBRAND
 BAS  PANIC  BAD  RIP
TEARSAT  EDAM  BROUHAHA
ARTDECO  DENIM  OCTAGON
DOORSTOP  SOLEMN  ELOPE
SSN  SNUG  NATO  CRONES
 STU  RIB  NOT  HIS
CATNAP  GARB  OHHI  WAS
ARIAL  SENIOR  SENDHELP
RESPECT  TAXED  AURELIA
LATESHOW  RITA  RAILCAR
ASH  IRA  NIGHT  FLO
 EVILEYE  GENUS  TOMB
HASIDIC  AWL  AMUSE  EAU
OREOS  OHGEE  BARCRAWLS
SCALA  UBERS  INGA  CASE
ESSAY  PORES  TEED  EGAD
```

111

```
AMARETTI  LOCH  SLABS
VENETIAN  REPAIR  AISLE
Q♦ ANNESL A♣  EMERGE  GETAC
 GUT  AESOP  NE 2♥ R K♣  EVENT
AAAS   ROASTHAM  RKO
HILT  INHASTE  NERDIER
INSOMNIA  TABU  DOEST
 INTURN  TYRA  YAKS
ASPEN  SLOE  10♥ DSBAR
MARAUD  SMIT 10♣  UTIL  PEP
PLOTTED  PI A♦ RO  INFLAME
SEW  ELAN 7♠ S♠AS  SLAVIC
 WHITE Q♥  RHEA  UBERS
FORA  ASHE  SUNUPS
 EVENS  TSAR  SNLHOSTS
BRENDAN  SUBSETS  PURE
AGR  MORTIMER  EPEE
SURF A♣ 10♠ SION  LOUIS  NRA
ISAAC  IDIGIT  SMO K♥ J♥ ETS
LOTTA  RELICS  ESTEEMED
SNEER  RENE  ROUNDERS
```

112

```
ACRES  AMID  TSA  ESS
PROMO  BASE  AHI  VEEPS
HEROWORSHIPPER  EGRETS
IDS  SPAS  ESA  FRETNOT
DOCK  IMPUGN  FRAGRANCE
 HOE  SIMON  SOIR  SKA
TRACER  KARYN  DREA  YGL
BICHROME  GLOBE  EVAL
ASH  ICE  SEADOO  NERVE
REC  ECLAT  NERD  TRIALS
 AERODROME  ARSE  ANKH
FORK  SULU  TIER  DISH
YODELS  BEFIT  VERONA
IFS  ETHANFROME  AYEAYE
 BEAU  ALE  ACE  VIV
IMPOSTERSYNDROME  ZEKE
TEACH  SUMO  GUY  TONER
STLEO  DAWDLES  PROUST
ALLROADSLEADTOROME
TIIERS  HEAD  ELOPE
 DISCS  DRY  REFER
```

113

```
MANORS  JAKOB  JOISTS
ANIMAL  SOCIALS  AGLARE
CINEMA  ALLTHAT  CRIMEA
ATANANGLE  UNIQUEUSER
WAS  GRANTS  CRUZ  MASS
 IDA  IDEATE  SIZE
SAMADAMS  FORM  TINHAT
IROBOT  TWOAM  ZEROG
ANN  STAR  SIDRA  BYLINE
MOES  APER  TERN  AMIDST
 TRIPLEA  DOUBLEU
RELYON  ISNT  WAIL  MAPS
EXALTS  ETNAS  LOON  LEI
FIVEO  FOURH  TEABAG
 TETRIS  NAPA  HUSHHUSH
 SPAS  LIMPID  IAM
ELLE  HUMP  TERROR  CAB
VOODOODOLL  OINOINONE
IBADAN  LAYDOWN  TRIVIA
TONITE  TIMELAG  HONEST
ASSESS  NEWER  SNORES
```

114

```
TRU  DDT  DIVAS  SLAVS
RESTORER  UNPAID  PANIC
ABSOLUTE  CASHREGISTER
MARK(O)MEARA  SEWON  EWE
 (E)OS  RATON  NADA  DEE
PLO  POMES  DOASLOWBURN
DANA  LIN  BOON  TWERPS
QUITCOLDTURKEY  NBA
ROIL  ISEE  WAS  WAR
DENTIST  ANNA  LOYALFAN
AND  CHAIROFTHEFED  TWO
STICKONS  SLOE  TRIDENT
SPA  TIM  NATE  EIRE
 RCA  TIMBER(I)NDUSTRY
COLONS  DEUS  REA  SAVE
MAK(I)NGALIST  GIRLS  XES
ETC  NOVO  ATEIN  MIA
STU  ORING  DO(G)HANDLER
CAPITALGAINS  OUTTHERE
ALICE  EEYORE  FRIEDEGG
LODES   RENAL  TAR  KOS
```

115

```
BLEAT·AFROLATINA·
PIERRE·PREPARATIVE
HATTREE·TIMEWILLTELL
REST·OATH·AIRBALL·MEA
EASEIN·HUN·TAO··DAMP
FDA·DEVELOP·SOLO·ORES
USC·BOHRATOM·KAT·NINE
SPAREUS·DOWEL·TILTAT
ARGOTS·FACETATTOOS
LILO·CONCRETEISLAND
SNIT·CONCURRENCE·SEES
GAYPRIDEPARADE··SOTO
·THEMARINERS·TAMPED
BIOLAB·SEGAR·MODERNA
KETO·MRS·DEDICATE·OTC
LAIT·SAUD·REVIVAL·NIA
ETSY··POD·RAT·LAGOON
INS·CATERED·LYRE·NUNS
NIAGARARIVER·MEDIANS
·KILLINGTIME·ADULTS
·DOMEASOLID··POPES
```

116

```
TARTAN·APES·ARID··PIN
ABUELO·GASH·SOME·LOSE
BREAKTHEICE·HODA·ALEX
SAD·AMANDA·WETBLANKET
··SLANT·PAWNS·MICA
PARKINGSPACE·THEMEDIA
ONEASY·ADE·TAMI·BOND
PITT·WATERMELONPATCH
AMIE·URNS·ARK··ASSAD
RUNSAMOK·GLAM·GAGS
TSA·BATHROOMSCALE·GMO
·INRE·OOPS·OVERCOOK
ALEVE·TBD·SPEC·ALAS
GENERALHOSPITAL·MENU
EARN·MOAT·IRA·PREFER
SHOOTOUT·GLOBETHEATRE
·LIEU·SIREN·ROOST
GOLDENGATE·GOATEE·CEO
ICEE·TILE·CROSSBREEDS
RHEA·TRIM·SINE·EVADES
LOS··ODES·IPAD·SERENA
```

117

```
SCRUBS·ADO··COBS·AGAR
PRESET·MEWS·INRE·LARY
OATBAR·PANT·LOOMLARGE
TMI·RIM·REO·ARTIE·LOB
SENECAS·EDMUNDH·SWINE
RANR·DRS·ABTEST·ACNE
·GALOOTS·ERR·WALKER
AKC·WASP·KARO··JOLLY
DEEPLY·EVILS·BUSES
LINUS·SWIPE·TELECASTS
IRAN·TTOPS·GREET·FLAT
BACKDOORS·CREEP·SEIKO
·BATIK·LHASA·SISTER
·PARAC·REIN·THUD·SIM
CHANEL·HOT·DREAMER
LORD·SIOUAN·ERS·IAMB
ANTSY·MALTOSE·NASTIES
MOI·ALFRE·EIN·TIS·NAH
BRATWURST·ALAS·SUTURE
EELS·MEET·ROCK·HEATED
DESK·PERE··STY·ASTERS
```

118

```
SWATAT·DOPE··DOG·FLASH
SOFINE·ILLS·OHOH·DITTO
ALFREDNOYES·FIFA·IGLOO
·FLAW·ERMA·POORRICHARD
AMID·TRAPDOOR·ERA·TSKS
FACETHEMUSIC·WEIMAR
TNT·ARIAS·LUPE·SWEARAT
·TOED·MYSELF·ORIOLE
APPOSE·TAO·ISR·MANURE
PAAR·PUNJAB·HIHAT·TOV
PIN·HEARTOFROMAINE·IKE
END·EARTH·CATERS·KNEE
ATOLLS·LIB·INS·CHEERS
SERAPE·ELECTS·SHAY
ERASMUS·LEAR·OTTER·PUP
·TEPEES·FIXBREAKFAST
BEAM·TAX·MEGAVOLT·LYES
ENDODONTICS·NELL·GARR
GEENA·CONK·KARLABONOFF
EMPTY·ELIA·MDSE·ANGLEE
MYTHS·STY·SUED·HEELED
```

119

```
ALGAE·PEAT·AFTS·ALPE
MOANA·EACH·BLUE·LOIN
ILLTURNTHISCARAROUND
DALI·ASSENT·GOSEE·KEA
·FOIE··AAS·WINGSPAN
SITUPSTRAIGHT·DIETARY
CARRIE·OUR·EAVE·LON
AGO··HUG·SERE··ATOM
DONTUSETHATTONEWITHME
·AMARETTO·NCIS·EST
OCTUPLE·SLOTH·OROURKE
TOW·ETTA·DOUBLEUP
ITOLDYOUAHUNDREDTIMES
SELA··DROP·DIS··ICU
EPA·SITH·FIN·WHENCE
ATFIRST·YOUREGROUNDED
GETSREAL·SHE·EWES
ELF·EERIE·UNABLE·INIT
LETSPLAYTHEQUIETGAME
MEET·INES·MULE·ANDOR
ETAS·TADA·YAKS·PSAKI
```

120

```
TWERK·BRAS·BABE·CATS
HAVEIT·BELT·ALUM·IMHO
ELECTRICALOUTLET·LARA
YESICAN·DUMPSON·RAZOR
·TACH·ERAS·FAKENEWS
LIBERIA·RECTO··EAT
ADO·NBA·SHAVINGCREAM
GEOLOGIST·STAVE·TOSCA
ATOZ·TIOS·ELFIN··TRI
·WAS·ARIE··NETGAIN
USERNAMEANDPASSWORD
SNLSKIT·DOOM··SYD
ABA··TABOO·CLEO·LOAD
NONPC·RALPH·INFLATION
EXTERMINATOR·SFO·DUE
·AAA·FILET·WATTAGE
DRIBBLES·CLUE·ENOS
WEARS·BOOKONE·GOTWISE
ALMA·WORKSWITHOUTANET
DESI·ANTE·ETES·TENORS
ETON·DYAD·DERN·RANBY
```

121

```
ASSHAT  FEELOKAY  SHIP
NIKOLA  ADVOCATE  STENO
TRICKLEQUESTION  HARPO
SEP  ALT  SEAN  HORMEL
YDS  LOEWS  SVELTE  TINS
AGIN  OLDIE  OHM  LOCI
URBANE  RIOT  STEP  ENID
SEEME  ADDS  DATA  ADELE
ILAY  NILE  PAYEXTRA
NIT  MIME  SOWER  NOTPC
GELCAP  OHHENRY  OMEARA
FELLA  FOOTS  PITA  LAB
ATTEMPTS  SINE  MANY
GRASS  FOES  KICK  HACKS
EARS  PLUS  HONK  HONEYS
STET  EAT  EASEL  ERIC
TEAR  ATHENS  WEANS  OKS
ADRIFT  CROP  APE  UAE
TAUPE  ALLOVERTHEMAPLE
EAGLE  DIABETES  CALLED
SASE  ALTEREGO  KNEELS
```

122

```
INACOMA  HSWEEP  SCOT
MILITIA  INHORROR  HART
SHARONA  MAHAYANA  RUDY
CHIMMEYH  DIESEL
TATA  BEAT  HCOMMANDER
UVA  CAMP  HONDA  USA
BEL  ARBOR  HPICKER  SFO
ARMOR  ELISHA  EGESTED
SUBMARINEH  CAMO  PILE
EDSEL  GAH  OVA  ARTS
CLIMBSTHELADDER
DIEU  ARI  HUB  ENEWS
USSR  DCON  HREPAIRMAN
NICEJOB  CHORAL  AESOP
ETA  CHERRYH  TULIP  AWE
PER  TOOTH  LILT  BIC
TELEPHONEH  OVAL  OINK
SCRAWL  HPAINTER
PEON  ULTRAHOT  CENTIME
CLOD  SEARCHES  ELBOWED
ALMS  HOUSEH  SLYNODS
```

123

```
MUCHO  SEMIMINOR  PAPAL
EBOOK  IRENECARA  ATARI
NEWTS  DEARMADAM  SHRED
RATIO  LEONA  OSAKA
BIGNEWS  LICHENS
BLUENILE  REL  RAMSDOWN
ION  TEACEREMONY  DIO
TOGA  CROISSANT  BARR
EMARKETING  TRADENAMES
LESSEN  IGOTIT
STREFT  RFHOUSE  ILIADS
THUSFAR  DUNST  DESKSET
EON  TAS  GUV  WON  AMA
MUSTIEST  USS  HONDAFIT
SANDSTONE  THEMEROOM
GTA  AWE  AYE  ALL
HER  HAS  TRITT  RBI  LAG
ISOGON  SCARIES  ANGOLA
AQUA  OTTOMANSETS  AWOL
LUNG  IHERONETTES  ZUNE
LEDS  ETDS  SOIL  APES
```

124

```
ANTI  QUEST  ORES  AROMA
LOOM  URGES  TAXI  CAPED
LION  ENOCH  ODIN  HYENA
OCTOPUS  TIME  TCBY  NAG
WESTIE  MIRA  CLEO  NICE
ALS  IOTA  HARP  ONES
SACRA  CONG  NONE  ARG
ALOOF  ACE  HYPE  MUSCAT
GARB  AGED  UMPS  CREEDS
ANNO  DIN  ISPY  BRA  RDA
BET  WEE  NIH  ELI  NES
PER  FAR  PALS  NOB  IMUS
HATTER  KALE  IDOS  COPE
INHOME  IRIS  NED  DENTE
ETA  TAKE  BDAY  RAYON
ACME  MESA  POOR  HON
DRAM  ALES  SONS  UNDOCK
MAR  EXED  FIRE  FRESHEN
INKED  COVF  ISAID  JADE
NIECE  ONCE  SISAL  ORAL
SATON  MART  HASTE  WART
```

125

```
STAIRS  GOITER  DESIRE
WENTUP  AIRTIME  USENET
ELNINO  MAITAIS  MELTED
ALANTURING  STEAM  FIX
ROW  SEENAT  ALKA  MAD
NISSAN  IMITATIONGAME
NUCLEI  IRONS  PORTIA
JITSU  GNU  APT  FRIEND
INUIT  EASED  EPI  APSE
GRUELS  TELE  LOOKS
SIR  EVERS  CLUNK  DAM
BYSEX  SHIN  SCHEME
AERO  ETC  PINGS  HITON
STRAYS  ANI  EEK  AVERS
MONGOL  CLARK  SISTER
ENIGMAMACHINE  CASSIS
WEE  ANAS  TURBAN  OLA
SPY  DRAGS  CRYPTOGRAM
OFYORE  BLINKAT  ADRATE
FOLDER  AAMILNE  NEATEN
TREADS  SMILED  ASSESS
```

126

```
ARTICLE  CFCS  PEARCE
TOOCOOL  PAWAT  DENIERS
OFFENSIVELINE  ARTROOM
PLUM  ESOS  WINDTURBINE
EMT  WON  CHA  ONLY
IGNEOUS  EMAIL  APB
OSO  GUS  EWELL  LAYSHIA
OLDMACDONALD  PIT  OGD
PACE  HARDG  AGREES  MED
SMORE  LOEB  LEGALFEES
MILITARYACADEMIES
HEPTAGONS  DESI  MATTE
ALL  LENDER  LSATS  SEAL
LIE  TAO  STEELGUITARS
FOXTAIL  KVASS  ICK  DOE
ENT  INPUT  AFCEAST
COED  BOO  ESL  OAT
SOUNDSYSTEM  PACT  ODOR
OUTPOUR  SPANISHARMADA
APRONED  UPTON  ASPIRIN
PEEPED  PSST  THICKET
```

127

```
CRUST  PERM  JANE  GOOFS
TUSHY  ASIA  ODOR  ADMEN
RECAP  RAPS  SOTS  MISDO
   PICKUPTHEPIECES
ARLENE  LEAPT  OTTAWA
TEA GOOVERTHEEDGE REC
OPIE  KIDS  SEGO  BATH
NORMARAE    OLDBETSY
   PLAYWITHMATCHES
PIGEONS  RAITT  ELATION
ADORE  SEEDIER  UPDOS
YOLO HOT BED IRA ALFA
FREEDOMOFASSEMBLY
   SERENE  POSIES
BAM GETITTOGETHER PAR
ARIAS TEARSINTO GNOME
LEND PARTIESDOWN EPIC
SWERVE       ALLPRO
AERIES PICTURE NOSEIN
MOVEIT PERFECT ABORTS
NANNY MOMENTS SENSE
```

128

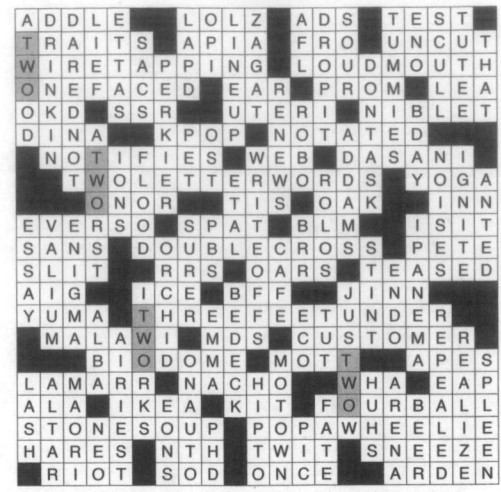

```
ADDLE  LOLZ  ADS  TEST
TRAITS APIA FRO UNCUT
WIRETAPPING LOUDMOUTH
ONEFACED EAR PROM LEA
OKD SSR UTERI NIBLET
DINA KPOP NOTATED
NOTIFIES WEB DASANI
TWOLETTERWORDS YOGA
ONOR TIS OAK INN
EVERSO SPAT BLM ISIT
SANS DOUBLECROSS PETE
SLIT RRS OARS TEASED
AIG ICE BFF JINN
YUMA THREEFEETUNDER
MALAWI MDS CUSTOMER
BIODOME MOTT APES
LAMARR NACHO WHA EAP
ALA IKEA KIT FOURBALL
STONESOUP POPAWHEELIE
HARES NTH TWIT SNEEZE
RIOT SOD ONCE ARDEN
```

129

```
MOAT  IFSO  RADAR  ENACT
ONME  MAID  IRULE  XENON
MEANGIRLS GREASEPAINT
SUNDANCE SHA NHLER
PARS ENTITY BOIL CAT
IKE TOROS EOS SHIA
MAGLEVTRAIN CATECHISM
ALLSTAR TUCSON LILLE
NEO SNUG SULA OLIVIER
EXAM ILS EACHTIME
DATINGSITE WHITEBREAD
ZOOMBOMB KEA SETI
AMAZONS KILO SWAY NWA
LADEN MERELY ASOCIAL
LIONESSES ADVENTURERS
ONUS TNN BRIEF OWE
WET DIEU AYESIR IATE
BLEEP NES LESSTHAN
CALLIGRAPHY GIFTHORSE
ONION AGAME ENID REEL
SAUTE TEPID SGTS SELL
```

130

```
TAD  OBAMA  EPIC  PEN
AWES PARED CENA ALTER
FANTASYSUPPORTS SUSHI
FRIED OPAH SEAOTTERS
YESWECAN GOFORBAROQUE
SNOB LENIN ARI
IDS NAPA ETNA DEET
FALCONCARESSED PEPSIS
SNEAK ILYA LEER ICKY
OOPSIE ANTES DISDAIN
THEROUXINTHETOWEL
PILESON NORAD RAMAPO
ETAS DEED ARGO MITER
RETIRE DERIDEAPRICOTS
MENU SPIT MRED REO
BIN APRES RAIN
GRAVYTERRAIN CASTANET
RECORDSET EGGO ADELE
ACUTE THUNDERCOLLAPSE
FARED EARN LOOFA LAIN
PAR ABEE SWATS LES
```

131

```
ACTAS GNARL STRIP ADES
HAITI MONEY ARENA SERA
SPELLCASTER DISCI LDRS
AER RICARDO UNLEASH
JOHNNYCASH ELDERLAW
CLATTER OSTEEN ETOILE
RIVALRIES AND RISEFROM
EVE EXHALE NOMSG ANE
WENT AREAR CHINA REIGN
WES SGS BUC GUESSED
ASSISTS REHASH ERASERS
LAWSUIT UNE HON GTI
LIETO AUGER ELISE ETSY
ODD HTTPS MIDACT HIE
THEASHES BIC SEATANGLE
SINGTO ELROYS RECOILS
ERUPTION TALKSTRASH
HOGWASH SCENERY TRE
OREO AIMTO ATONESELBOW
SCAR NAMED GHANA SCONE
EARN DLINE SORER SOWED
```

132

```
WINES NOTIN IFWE PHIL
ANODE AMIGO SNOOP RIDE
SPOUT SIDLE PAREIDOLIA
PUNCTUATIONMARK COTTON
STEALS NODICE NESTS
TEAEGGS LEAPFROG
VICES IRS SOB AAATEAMS
EMO SEA ITSABLUR HEN
RONS MIMOSA REESE HALL
BUGABOO HAM ROT NOM
STALAG HYPHEN ATHOME
LEG MME ARI EXHUMES
SHIM COOLS TREBLE MELT
PAN LOWLIFES IVS NEE
FLEABANE NED MOI AFTER
NEWSREEL WASSAIL
PHAGE CALAIS CRETAN
EUGENE ROTATECLOCKWISE
SMILEYFACE ONAIR IONIA
TILE EDGAR NERFS SUGAR
ODES SAUR ERATO STEMS
```

133

```
BEEFIER  LAPDOGS  HAREM
ECLIPSE  OHHENRY  AMARE
THOROUGHFAIRIES  HADES
HONE  RIOTS  MON  PANICS
     BRASS   PANAMAHAITI
ALTOON  ESAU   DANA
DORMICE  WILDCARD  UTNE
DOUBLEDIARIES  CARPOOL
EST  SHY  FIDO  AROMA
REHUNG  AZURE  ONETOTEN
   SHOULDERHAIRINESS
SWEATSIT  GOTTI  OREIDA
TORUS  BONE  ITE  EER
YOULOSE  BOOKSONTAIPEI
ELMS  CLEANUPS  GETSORE
     PREP  THOR  LOUPES
POLKAIDIOTS   ITEMS
EMINEM  GPA  ADREP  PAPA
CAMEL  FRESHPAIROFEYES
KNOLL  DARKISH  PROCESS
SISTA  AMASSES  STETSON
```

134

```
SAILS  BFF   BMAJ  OATER
OZZIE  LAI   IAMA  OLIVE
FUZZYWUZZY  ARROZ  HBEAM
TRY  FREEZINGDRIZZLE
     DRESS  POESY  DEANERY
ZEROIN  GEOG   GULLIVER
AGAZE  GTE  RAZZLEDAZZLE
LAZED  LOEB  PESETA  OAK
EDEN  DITZES  NAN  MANIA
SSS  PATIENCE    JADED
    ZIZZERZAZZERZUZZ
MAINE   DEERHIDE   MAT
HOSTS  SUE  RESINY  CANI
ETS  SAUTES  SANG  NANTZ
PRIZEPUZZLES  TOY  ORTIZ
TISAPITY  CHEZ   PAPACY
ANIMATO  GLEAN  EARNS
   BUZZFEEDQUIZZES  OSU
HAZEL  OLLIE  FORTYWINKS
BLAZE  NEIL   NAE  ELZIE
OPCIT  EDDA   ESC  RLESS
```

135

```
LAS  ATOMS  EEK  LADIES
ASA  SARAH  ELLE  ORONYM
PSYCHOANALYSIS  GIJOES
CUSHY   OREO   MONSOONS
ACME  ISWEARIT  SIS  EHS
THEREDCARPET  PANELSAW
      PIERS  GPA   EDDA
PELOTON  TSHIRTCANNON
ALOU  MEANIE  GLUED  AWK
CLAIMS  NONE  TABOOS
KANJI  SIMONSAYS  BORON
    ATHOME  OKIE  MORALE
AMA  RADAR  TOLDTO  ENDS
BINGEWATCHER  ORESTES
UNTO   OYE   IDIOT
JOBOFFER  CHANELNOFIVE
ARE  ALS  UKULELES  ONED
RESTUPON  MORT  BASTE
GOTHAM  FLYMETOTHEMOON
ALLELE  TIME  IRAIL  LEI
REESES  TAD  AORTA  ESC
```

136

```
OMITS  SCHWAB    ONSPEC
HADIT  TRAINOR  PREHEAT
SLIDE  ROGETSTHESAURUS
NADIR  OPS   NEUROTIC
ALIENS  WWI  SUN   HEM
PATRONOFTHEARTS  IMAGE
    LLBEAN  OLE  GONGS
STOIC  GIST  BAE  DEUCES
TOCCATA  SATAN  HATRED
ATHENA  WINES  LENIN
GOO  THEREINSPIRIT  UFO
   MOONY  GSPOT  ENURED
STONED  SHELL  BLOGGED
ECHOES  NET  ALOE  WHETS
TRESS  AOL  HYENAS
TUTEE  CHARTFREDPLANES
ABE  MRI  ISR   FOMENT
  ASSOONAS  SOU  WOODY
DOACONSTRICTORS  CECIL
ARCADES  INPEACE  ABOVE
ASTRAY   GASPAR  LANES
```

137

```
ALLAH   DEBIT  CDC  SPAT
MOIRA  TEXACO  LAO  HULA
OFFENSIVEREBOUND  ITEM
STEW  AMISS  IBET  CEASE
     EDGES   RAISEHELL
FLOOREXERCISE  OLDISH
RILKE  SUIT  DUNE  DEE
APA  WES  STARTINGBLOCK
YOYOTRICK  YOGI  SANTA
    HONDA  MADISON  RIOT
SHAW  SERVICELINE  ETRE
CODE  TRAILER  TRIAD
ORALB  OMAN  TEENMOVIE
UNPLAYABLELIE  PSI  INA
TIT  TADA  OKRA  DOORS
SNAPON  SEVENTENSPLIT
    TANGERINE   ELATE
ROILS  YURI  DELIS  NEWT
AWOL  DESIGNATEDHITTER
ZINE  JUT  MOUSSE  MONAE
ZEST  SPY  ARBYS  PEARS
```

138

```
PAT  RASCALS   PEN  SEP
ECO  EMMYLOU  WAGE  APE
THEW  EALBUM  HITORMISS
FETA  SRO  DEPORT  DIDIT
ODORS  TNT  REMEET  ABLE
OFT  ASISAY  PETRI  MOOR
DOORDIE  LIVERAN  NIONS
   READS  MUNI  PSST
     METRES  LOL  THRILL
IMPOSEON  BEHEAD  ODEA
MOUNTRUSH  MOREORLESS
POPE  EASELS  SURELETS
STASIS  NSA  NOSIDE
     SHAH  THON  ADDTO
MARCH  GORDERS  INOROUT
AVER  ARTIE  HEPCAT  UTE
DAZE  TONNES  SHE  SACHS
ERODE  NESTEA  ABC  SHOT
WINORLOSE  WHIRL  DTOUR
ACE  AIMS  USROUTE  FSU
YES  SPY  POSSESS  FEN
```

139

```
ATOMICREACTORS   APPS
CANADIANROCKIES  NARC
THELITTLEMERMAID TRIO
BIPED ACELA SCAT ANN
ITIS SOCIAL MAKEHASTE
GIN MCRIBS HOLODECKS
  MARINO DONT ASTI
 CODING VILE PLUS
NUTMEG CANDYCOUNTERS
DASHED TAPASBARS HAUL
RISEN BASE FEST AETNA
AVER FISHSCALE DIGSIT
MEDICINECHEST HEROIC
 NUNS ROOT COMBAT
 ELBA OOPS RANOUT
TRAILMAPS VALETS MAG
DRAWSLOTS NOWISE RAGU
WES MAIM GOTME BARRE
EMUS PRIVATEENTRANCES
LORE ELIMINATIONDIET
TREX KEYNOTEADDRESS
```

140

```
LASS OGRE BOAR ITSOUT
AUTO ROAD ARLO GRUNGE
PREGNANCYBRAIN NINTHS
PATOOTIE SOLIDFOOD
 ONEG EIN OUR ANIN
GLADE HOWDEDO NAMEONE
LOL STREETSMARTS MFA
EVICTING LIQUIDDIET
NEGRONI ADT TIN OUNCE
SYNOD GOFAR ASSETS
 MOTHERWIT AMY TEST
DREW ITD GASGIANTS
RESETS GAUDY ROSIE
AMPLE LIE ERY THEFEDS
POOLNOODLE SHUFFLES
EDU PLASMASCREEN MAI
RESUMED ONTOPOF STALE
YLEM AER ANG OAHU
 PANDERING FURIKAKE
REWIND MINDOVERMATTER
HEARYE ICET OTTO URNS
OKDEAR TAZO LAHR KATE
```

141

```
DILATES POGO ALT FEMA
ECOCIDE AWAY TOE AXIS
FROMDUSKTILLDAWN BONK
TYPEA AEON ELLS ITEM
 SLUMDOGMILLIONAIRE
ASS REST OWL FRANC
HATFUL CROSSE GOFOR
OCEANSELEVEN ASH IMO
OHARA GEMS DSL ITISNT
TAKELEAVE PEW TRYTHIS
 WEDDINGCRASHERS
CANARDS DOS NEEDALIFT
SHORTI YSL PEER NORAH
IOS ERE INHERENTVICE
SKIPS ESSAYS USENET
 RERAN ETS ACTI ADA
THEGODFATHERPARTII
ABEL SARA ERIE TOPAZ
TOBE PICTUREINPICTURE
AGOG ORE GULL INHALED
ROBS TED HESS DAYSPAS
```

142

```
MESS ECARDS GARB ODES
CRUE MANIAC OBOE NOME
CANTTURNTHATDOWN SOME
ASDOI ALTON TSTRAP
BEANSALAD TOOKASTAB
ERE GALORE AREARUG
 DROPEVERYTHING SUP
FABIO EXES EON EATIT
ASUSUAL ALPS ENDLESS
RHYMES PINA SIRI BRED
 NOSTRINGSATTACHED
ALOU ROTH EGOT HIREES
LAWNBOY EASE PEPTALK
EMPTY SAP TADA TALLY
SEA LIMITEDEDITION
 DYNAMOS INDEED NAY
 LOWPOINTS ITSAPLANE
ICANSO AURIC AORTA
MATE ROCKBOTTOMPRICES
DREW TRUE BLENDE ROUT
BARS SEED ELDEST ESPY
```

143

```
CBS ASLEEP UPSET GMC
LAID NEURAL NOONE OAR
ALLA NEVERENDINGSTORY
USEDCAR UAE LONE
SANSA BEARSREPEATING
EMT MARIMBA DRAG SEGA
 PERPETUALMOTION SOY
KANYEWEST AGENTS
FARMS EOS ASPCA
ETTA NANA POPART ISAY
TANS ADINFINITUM KERR
INES GOLDEN GEEZ HUME
DAREI WED TIDES
 SHARPE IMPOSESON
NBC RECURRINGDREAMS
ORAL RAFE NAMASTE CIT
NONSTOPFLIGHTS GUIDO
CIAO ACR ALGREEN
CONTINUITYOFCARE SNAG
ODE LETME URCHIN ACLU
YES STEPS POSIES ESE
```

144

```
ATOM TALE MASHUP TART
CORA ALOT ARCANA ODOR
LOCKSMITH MOUSER OLAY
UNSEAT RENAULT TVDADS
 MWAH LABSPECIALIST
COPE MOB DIET PELE
ORO NOSIR FIREOPAL
BAGGAGEHANDLER TOOLE
SLOUGH ODE AXILS LIP
 SLUED ALPACA BYTE
OUTPATIENTCOORDINATOR
URIS TOMCAT SLASH
NBC ONEAM STS OVIEDO
CAKED NAILTECHNICIAN
ENSNARED ORATE STY
 TREE WISE VAN STAX
CIVILENGINEER PORE
ANORAK REALTOR POETIC
TATE ICANSO BASECOACH
CNET NAVIES EGOT FLEE
HEDY GREECE SEWS FLEX
```

145

```
ACTS   ARI  PJS     HAITIAN
THRU  BUSROUTE    UNNERVE
PEANUT[BELL]BUTTER  DEGREES
   FINN  ANI   ARP   NORA
SLITS  SNICKER[HEART]DOODLE
   INITS   MOSDEF  DRYAD
GINGER[TREE]SNAP  LETS  ORG
ENG  ATANY  TOLL[ANGEL]HOUSE
ANAT  DANE  REM    TOAD
RAWR  ARC  KERNS    PETS
STAUB  THIN[STAR]MINT  ETHER
EYER   OTOES   ORB   TELE
   SAGS  TWA  FRAU  ABES
FIG[ELF]NEWTON  OLEIC  ENO
ILE  CLEO  SHORT[CANE]BREAD
DINAH  LOGJAM   SELES
OATMEAL[MAN]RAISIN   RACKS
   RADS  YES  MEA  SINE
COINOPS  COOKIECUTTERS
DRFAUCI  ONIONDIP   AERO
CRYSTAL    SLO  YDS  LSAT
```

146

```
ORDAIN   APACHE   IMIGHT
COULDA  USOTOUR   MOTHER
HORSEBACKRIDER   OPPOSE
OMAHA  PLS  TIVOS    RUSE
   ATSEA    NORTHPOLE
REGRET   TWIG    YEAS
PREP  ATRAIN  GERM   GEO
MITT  PUBLICHOUSE   SOAP
SCHOOLTIES  EWE   BOOZE
   INSET   BRISK  OBGYN
ART  TRUEFALSETEST   LES
BOCCE  TRACT   NICHE
ABHOR  IVE  MAINTHEMES
COED  SPEARHEADED  DATA
ITD  TEES  ENHALO   GPAS
   ANNA   SPAS   WRESTS
   SOFTDRINK    NANAS
PAIR  LOOIE  TOP   CANAL
ICLOUD  WORKOUTTHEBUGS
CHEESE  ANTENNA  AMENRA
SADDEN  NESSIE   GETSAT
```

147

```
SOCKO  AGOG  BASS   STOLI
ABOIL  DEAR  USMA   TOKEN
HOUNDSHAKE  DIEM   ALIEN
LENS  HER  NEDFLOUNDERS
   THEIR  HARI   TABLA
AAMILNE  EDGED  NIELSEN
SHIPMEN  YESSES  DELUXE
IOS   TAJ    FAD    PEC
SYSTEM  COUNSELEDCHECK
   ANO  MENTOR  REAIRS
  SMUDGE  TFI  IINARMS
STEREO  SISTER   LLB
MOUSEMARKETING  TOOFAR
ARA  DOO   LEI    ALI
YERTLE  WASABI  MAGPIES
INTEARS  LOBES  AVERRED
  QUITE  LINI  MEDOC
TROUNCESTATE  EAR  POST
RABID  ETON  FUZZYMOUTH
EMILE  LONG  INRE  OSCAR
SPEAR  EPEE  TOAD  NEHRU
```

148

```
INFO  SPAM  DONT  HAAGEN
TOIL  TORE  FREE  AREOLA
CHADLIBYA  LEWD  RAILON
HOTCOCOA  LAOSCAMBODIA
   OAKY  POT  CROESUS
ALCOVE  FEE  LUND    TIS
GUATEMALABELIZE   PEROT
AMC  SUPER  CUP   BRAINY
REAP  PEA  FIN  DOESKIN
SNOOT  BULGARIAGREECE
   PUBLANU  BEMUSED
AUSTRIAGERMANY   QUALM
INWARDS  EAR  ORK  PREY
SMORES  ENG  GUANO   ROB
HARTS  BRAZILARGENTINA
AND  DEER  ELS  ELIDED
   DIECAST  KIA  THAD
MYANMARCHINA  WHOTFOFF
YENFOR  IDLE  CHILEPERU
SOCUTE  NASA  POPE  ONUS
THENEA  DYAD  AMES  DOGE
```

149

```
ATPAR   ANCHOVY   SPEEDO
RHINO  APARICIO  PLANER
KENTCIGARETTES   LASTED
AVES  SERRATED  FUNTIME
NAT  WENTATIT   BARTERER
SUREBET  TIN  CONGOREDS
ALEXA    KINGHUSSEIN
STEI  STOVETOPS  SLATED
   RECIPE  HOPES  SUAVE
SEASONS  DETESTS   SHIN
OURLORD  SAPID  PISTOLS
USNA  NEBULAE  NATURES
THIRD  RESIN   IGUANA
SIEGEL  USAINBOLT  LIZA
   ECURRENCIES   BIDEN
ZEPPOMARX  BET  BELAIRS
AQUILINE  CULTHERO  TOW
MUZZLED  HOTSEATS  MAZE
FIZZER  HUNTERGATHERER
INLATE  ARGONGAS  SNORE
REESES  PLANSON   TUDOR
```

150

```
ATTACK   RACER   STAMEN
LEAGUE  REVILES  CIMINO
PATINA  OVERLAP  AKINTO
APTLYNAMEDCELEBRITIES
COLE  FALA  NICE   YORE
ATE  BLINI  SINGE   NOS
   WEARINGNAMETAGS
SWEEPEA  UAL   SORROWS
GERARD  GAGON  REREAD
RAINS  IMAC  UOFA  TESLA
AWN  SUM   FAR     TIM
BEGET  HYMN  FUNK  SCENE
SEENAS  ASIAN  AMANAS
DRYMOPS  ENV   OSMONDS
   APPLESWEATSHIRT
GTS  AHEAP  AMORE   TVS
OATH  ARUT  SKOR   CHET
THEONETOTHEWESTOFHERE
HIPPOS  ONEVOTE  AROUSE
ANOINT  MITERED  TASSEL
MINNIE   KAREN   STEADY
```

151

```
ETC   SPECK  ICED    SHUI
GOES  HELLO  MILE    CENT
GELT  ENIAC  PAIL  CELLO
 TIARAS  SHOO  TIEONEON
MOBRARIES  JUVENQUENCY
ITALY OPS  SNO  EUR  AKA
NOTI  SNAIL   DADAIST
TEENPOP  ZEAL  ITPEOPLE
  GILL  ENDORSE  CLUES
ATE  ETAS  AZTEC   REMAP
MEDICINTS   COMMETARY
OPINE   ROPES  SUED  SYS
NECCO  SABRINA   HAIL
GETAFLAT  ONIT  ANTEDUP
  SPYFILM  TOMMY  GENE
FAR  ASA  SEN  NAM  MATTE
INOPPORTUNT  ELABORAIL
NOBLELIE   AHEM  DAMMIT
ARBOR  HERD  RELAY  ONLY
LAID   AMIE  ANGLE  REED
EKES   TSPS  STAID   DDS
```

152

```
CATBERT  ABSENT  OPTICS
AQUIVER  REELIN  AIRMAN
SURGERYVERDICT  TRIFLE
SANDRA  ESTATE  CYANIDE
  SATIRE  RENAL  NINER
CMON  SURPRISEFIGHTERS
ZINC  ENSUES   INLAY
ANTES  ROMP  DIEGO   NBC
REO  HAIFA  SURLYMAJORS
  RIDOF  RAPID  LINEN
ATHEIST  MOVES  BILLOWY
SHEET   AILED   HEIST
SURFERBALLS  WOWIE  SHH
TSA  BACKS  MAUI  TOQUE
  SHISH   WAISTS  RULE
SURPASSEDPERFECT  DIAL
ATEAT   ONEIL   SHAKER
MATCHES  DELPHI  FORTWO
OHOKAY  SURFEITOFANGER
SALLIE  SCREED  DELOUSE
ANDERS  NEEDLE  DRAWNTO
```

153

```
OWINGTO  CHIA  FACEMASK
NOSERAG  HULU  ANATOLIA
CONTAMINATED  LITANIES
DST  NEVER   ISSO   ANNE
ADREAMWITHINADREAM
CLOVES   IMSET   TIC
GINA   BILKO  SYCOPHANT
IAMNOTACTIVE  EMS  TAO
RETURNED  IGLOOS  DENT
 TOFF  LEGUP   DEANS
FORTYFIVE  OVERFIFTY
TONKA   SIDES   ROAD
ALSO  HIHATS  BADRISKS
TIE  SOD  VACATIONTIME
ACTSPHONY  LUMEN  ALOT
 ACU  EULER   EWINGS
WHATAMIAMINDREADER
RAGA   STAN  ELGIN  SUD
IRONRULE  NOADMITTANCE
STRICKEN  ELMO  TEASELS
TEACARTS  YEAS  ADSPEAK
```

154

```
CARAFE  CHURNS   HASSAN
ACADIA  BAZOOKA  OPPOSE
RECAST  SWIMMINGTRUNKS
ELEPHANTS  ENDOW   DIET
DART  WAVETANK  BIB  ADS
   LAP  SSE   DINAR
OPENEYES  KREME  GSHARP
PITON  QATARIS  SMILES
EXTRADRUMSTICKS  ANIMA
DYED  CHICKENS  OUTOFIT
  STOOD     ANTIC
WESTEND  FOCACCIA  EELS
ACORN  ELECTRICCHARGES
NODOFF  CATSEAR  ROOST
ENAMOR  DRACO  ACCESSES
  SLAMS   ALB   HHS
TAD  DIA  HONEYBEE  ELSE
AVOW  DUGIN  FIREFLIES
LIGHTNINGSPEED  TAIPEI
CAMARO  CHEERED  ADZING
SNAPAT   STEELY  HEADON
```

155

```
COARSE    HASTE    ASPIC
APPENDS  COSSET  PLOUGH
THEDUDE  RAHRAH  ALUMNA
SEX  GALLERY  MIST  SPOT
PLAY  SLAVS  ROOTED  IRT
AIMEE   PIETA  PALMTREE
WASATCH  CROWDIN  CHOIR
  CHASE  PREACH  ENT
CUTS  OUTSET   INHELL
ALACRITY  REPO   RUBOFF
BASRA  EXPONENTS  NOLIE
SNEEZY   ISLE  OINTMENT
AZALEA   INSOLE   BONE
 TAM  WOLVES  CLOSE
THREW  SMELTER  STPETER
RETREATS   ASSAM   SNARE
IFS  BOTTOM  SWABS  CLUB
RACE  KORN  WELCOME  EDU
ETALIA  ELAINE  NEATNIK
MEMORY  EARNED  GAVOTTE
ESSIE   TYKES    REESES
```

156

```
TSP   PSAS  MECCA   BARE
APU  SOAP  IDOLS  TAMER
RET  HONEY  MEMOS  ICING
DESSERT  SCENES  TEASES
IDLY  MAFIA   SEAHORSE
SOIREE  ATM  HOTHAND
 PUP  SQUAREFOOT  ITCH
RESPECT  AREA  RSS  IOU
IN  EAR  TOOL  ATTICUS
AVOW  RAMI  STLO  HUNKS
SENIORPROM  HERDEDCATS
 LASSO  INON  TOY  ALEE
TOPHATS  STASH  LED  LAE
EPI  YAK  EDIE  ATEITUP
LEGO  NORELATION  ASH
 UNDRESS  SVU  UNLESS
ARTISTIC   BORON  ABUT
BLACK  MARTYR  FARMORE
RETRO  PAPUA  INTRO  XFL
ORION  AGENT  ENEMY  EEL
STOP  WEDGE  SENS   SRA
```

157

```
IGLESIAS  JEMIMA   ORATE
DUALROLE  OSIRIS   NOTAX
TAKEOUTTHETRASH    PATTI
AVEC   ARI  DOTHEDISHES
GARTH  ADS  SEA   ATTEST
       EINSTEIN   PONCHO
SWEEPTHEFLOOR    VSHAPED
OIL  SHA  VENICE     META
WIIG  MESA  POORAT    RON
NUMEROUNO  GOTOTHEBANK
      SIA  ADMITIT   ALE
SORTTHEMAIL   NIBBLESON
UDO  EUROPA  AGEE    NIKE
MIDI  AROMAS   SAY   LAW
ONENESS  PICKUPTHETOYS
      WEAKER   HERESHOW
SCARRY   AIG  DIE   HOSER
PAYTHEBILLS   CPA   SURI
INIGO  CLEANTHEGUTTERS
TONAL  CANDID   RUNSAMOK
SENSE  STEEPS   SECURELY
```

158

```
  ETS  THECOPA   PANICBAR
SARA   HEALSUP   IRONRULE
TRAPPARTISTS   CCTHEDAY
OFSORTS  NITES   SADE
RUHROH  AGEE  ICET   GRE
ELY  TUMS  DIZZCONTROL
   AIRDUCT  DEE   YAHOOS
STRIPTT  RETOUCH  BRUTE
TRIMS   BENE   PHOTOOP
EASE  OCTANES   WIRETAP
ALI  AMUUMENTPARKS  HIE
MANOWAR   RAPANUI   MILT
   GRANDMA  GABS  NONET
TATER  SORBETS  CLOCKYY
TRIADS  TMI   STRAINS
OLDDSTATION   ARKS  COM
POE  OBOE  ONCE   ELAINE
   LENA  SIDEA  DLISTER
GGLOUISE  SURPRIIPARTY
UPACREEK  ALTROCK   HOWL
SAWHORSE  YESISEE   INO
```

159

```
LASS  MANIC   LEAF   OVAL
ICON  ALERO  ETNA  BIOTA
SQUARECHIN  ASTI  ALLEY
PURGE  HISSED   ONESEC
INSIDE  HOSTINTHEDARK
LEO  DIME  LOOPIEST  NEE
EST  DIRGE  AND   WAIST
ACES DISMISSED   BOBCAT
ESAU  TAZ  ITSWAR   CALL
   ADS  MENU  AXIS   SEE
ABETAROUNDTHEDUOH
SAL  SAGA  BIEB    EMU
CREW  REJOIN  OOP  ACTI
ACCEDE  BEGINWATCHING
RABBI  CSA  MENSA   MDS
ADA  MAHIMAHI  STOW POT
BELOWMACARONI   OSAKAN
DMITRI  MILNER   RENEE
PAWAT  ALSO  OCEANDEIST
IVINS  DIOR  VALLI  PSIS
CANI  EASY  ESSEX   STAY
```

160

```
ICEBERG  SHARPTON   CUSS
MATINEE  COMEHERE   ASET
STANDINGROOMONLY   BEAR
   ENTRAPS  NAY   MEADE
ZANY  SLOP  JEN   SALLOW
EPEES  EVERLASTINGLOVE
DIRTII3  ERVINE   DEMOTED
RADIOCAR  TEIXEIRA
ASA  OAR  EROS  BOT  CAAN
FALLINGRAIN  MOM  JAYNE
IMEANI  AHP  SAO  SIRENS
SOROS  IIN  PARKINGRAMP
HATS  DMS  TRIX  RAG  YER
   LEGALAID   EAGLEEYE
SCAPULA  ONETON  SENSES
QUALIFYINGROUND   STIRS
UPLAST  NGO  CURE   ORSO
IRATE  PIO   ACHIEVE
SORT  FEAROFMISSINGOUT
HUGE  ANTIPODE  STOOPTO
YSER  THEATERS  YESISEE
```

161

```
FACADE   ARROZ   VAC  AAS
ERODED   SLOANE  IDA  SLO
NOODLE  MECHANICAL  SUN
CALLINSICK  PICKME   AMI
ERS  MITT  WRATH   NSYNC
LICE   BEERHAT   DESI
ORNOT  PRELL    TUPAC
LEOV  SKISLOPE   STRUTS
EDGE  AIMS  ALPHA   RITA
HOTRODS   ITSA  SKIMPY
WEARY  SHIPSHAPE  ATEIN
WARIER  ODOM   ANALYSE
IDEA  OTTER  CYTO   LIRA
SANCTA  STORYARC   INRI
GRILL   MASSE   INKED
SALE  CULPRIT   NYSE
TONED  PALIN  NCOS   CDS
NWT  INDIRA  FISHMARKET
OHI  TOWNSQUARE  AREOLA
TAC  OUI  OUTLAW  MAINLY
ETS  RNS  NEALE  AENEAS
```

162

```
MAOISTS  STAMPS   MORASS
UNPLAIT  IAMTOO   AVENUE
TWELVEANGRYMEN   RANKED
EAR  ARRANT  ICI   ALDA
DRAWN  THEAFRICANQUEEN
   ETTU  DRIED   PAULS
FLAN  UPI  NIL    ROTORS
DOCTORSTRANGE  SAT  CAT
IGETIT  DEPENDON  ASKME
COROLLA  NUYS  PAC  PSST
   BYEBYE    BIRDIE
AMIE  SOO  SMEE  EDHELMS
SANDL  UNTHAWED  RODEOS
PTA  ACT  WATERSHIPDOWN
SANRIO  YRS  LIV   INNS
   YELLS  LOUIS  TEVA
THELADYVANISHES  ALUMS
RAVI  BMI  SAVOIR   SAL
UNEEDA  AMERICANBEAUTY
CONFIT  NOLUCK  GESTATE
KITSCH  DRINKS  STEELER
```

163

```
BASK  ALLIN  BFF  CHEERS
ORCA  NUTRI  RAE  HOLDIT
AMAZINGDOGRACE  ENLACE
REMOTES  BITTE  FAKETAN
DEPOT  FORESTERPARENT
    YESITIS      ROOT
DIM  NPR    CROWS  AKIN
ORGANDOMINATION  GRATE
TAUTEST  MACRO  ANTLER
STEIG  INAPT  TYPO  EMO
  SCARFACERESOURCES
ADS  TOYS   ENORM  CRABS
DONKEY   MUSTI  MAHALIA
AVOID  PARASOLMILITARY
META  CAGER   EEG   ODD
    SOSO   SEAGRAM
GLAREATGRANDMA  SHAMS
REMORSE  ECIGS  WIRETAP
ONESET  THEPITIEDPIPER
ATNINE  OAR  NEPAL  SAVE
NODEAR  EBB  GLORY  TREE
```

164

```
SHOP  GOTTA  ULCER  ECON
TONI  ENEWS  NIHAO  SADE
ALEE  CHAOSTHEORY  SNIT
BESPOKE  AURAS  PCGAMES
   MANOR  CRYPT  SEEYA
MANA   TEMPO    TSKS
JUL  GARB  DEY  CALF  ETC
ESL  ELVES   MOVER  ARE
SIT  RASSLE  HECATE  LEN
SCHISM  TORNADO  BELLAS
IMIN  OFFTO  DIARY  ATMO
CANDO  ORCS  JAPE  ETHER
ANGER  SIA   TUE  SEERS
   BUTTERFLYEFFECT
STAT  BEN  LAO  FED  ORTS
PHI  BARD  ORR  SRTA  ERA
ARRAY   AWAKE   WIPED
DIFFERENCE  INTHEWORLD
EVAL  ADEER  EDITS  WILE
SERA  GEARS  SORTA  ASIN
  SET  ENTS   REPS  NES
```

165

```
STRAP  TOMBS  ROPES  IAN
IRINA  ORION  EXERT  RBI
LOFTS  MANGA  VIRGO  ELL
ONESELF  GER  IDA  LANES
  YOUONLYLIVETWICE
ODS  SPREES  BASIE  ECO
VEE   IDED  AIL  OLDSAWS
UNSEEN  WIZ    LAUREL
LITTLEBROWNANDCOMPANY
AREAS  LICIT  EWOKS
ROTS  ONO   HEP   ASIS
  SPASM  BUILT  CLINT
TINKERTOEVERSTOCHANCE
OMEARA   SNL   AUSTIN
INERTIA  LIE  CAMP  ATT
ODE  STIEG  TOBOOT  XES
  INTERCONTINENTAL
GENOA  IRT  REG  KEROUAC
RTE  SOFIA  ABASE  SUNRA
ITS  EULER  MAMIE  ASIAN
NAS  DREDD  PRESS  LETBE
```

166

```
OATH  AMP  ATARI  HEISTS
SLAY  LAO  LOREN  OLDHAT
HAPPILYEVERAFT  CALICO
ASSOCIATE  ABSOLUTEPOW
   ONSIDE    NOSED
PLAN   CAVITIES   MET
PHONIES   ADIOS  PAGODA
RECYCLINGCENT  TITANIC
INK   STATUS  AMENBROTH
COERCE  GOATS  ONSET
ELDER  POST  TWOS  SERFS
  GAILY  EMAIL  STREET
BRAINTEAS  ARMADA  FRA
REVOKED  CELLPHONENUMB
ANONYM  DANTE  GENESIS
NOW   FENESTRA   DOES
  PROOF   SALAMI
RELIEFPITCH  NOMINATES
UTOPIA  NOLAUGHINGMATT
SAVING  EMIRS  ANT  OKRA
TSETSE  SEPTA  SOY  SEEN
```

167

```
LOGO  PFFT  DRIP   SHALL
SURPRABLE  RUNE  ITALIA
DIETITIAN  JEST  PEGLEG
  EES   IUM  STERON  EDO
UNDEPARTY    ARI  CINES
ISH   ITSABET   ILLICIT
BRODATE    TRAVEGLOVE
ADREP   ICONCUR  SENECA
RANSOMNOTE  CLAM  DARTS
PLO  PROFEOFME   SOP
MOAT  TONI  REALTOR
CITRINE   LOKI  SEEN
SOX   FORTHEPIC  EDA
TIERS  ESAU  AWARDGALAS
ENDOWS  TANLINE  ECOLI
FRUITFFYING   LESTOIL
LETSLIE  GOOGLES  KEL
LIVES   LSU  ROOTOFLAN
OPI  MOLING  ELL  AOL
OPENIT  CARA  ICALLDIBS
FEWEST  AGOG  VANILEVIL
ARSES   NIKE  ETTU  SEXY
```

168

```
AJAR  PCP  ISPOSE  DRAPE
GODOFWAR  THENHL  RENAL
OHIDUNNO  BANKOFGUYANA
UNDID   THAW  PRIAM  KIP
TOLIVEANDDIEINLA  ENGRAINS
IRS  LAGGED  WAS  RONNIE
  SERGES   TAX  HULA
SPIN  EYE  BASEBALLCARD
ORGIES   BATH  EVE  INRE
FOOTPATROLS  ALE  ANNAL
ATT  PYRITE  GOLIMP  ATE
REYES  INS  BANANASPLIT
ASOF  LAS  MEME  SERENE
STUFFEDOLIVE  LIT  EEGS
  ERAS  AMY  REDOES
SPACER  OPI  CIALIS  IDO
LISTENUP   CHOPPEDSALAD
ARK  ZEPPO  OLAY  AMORE
MASHEDPOTATO  EASYWINS
OTTER   ESTHER  ARTSALES
NEONS  REOILS  REP  YODA
```

169

```
ADMIRE . ACTUP . HOTDATE
GODSEND . DIANE . TRUEDAT
OCTOBER . MAKINGMEBLUSH
. MUMBAI . EQUALS . ALTO
OUTOFYOURGOURD . . BYTES
WHARF . BLARNEY . OJOS .
LUMP . ALI . . SHOO . GAS
SHAHS . MISSINGTHEPOINT
. . THAT . DERAIL . ROAR
BOOHOOS . FLOWER . PETCO
INFORITNOW . DARNTOOTIN
GEHRY . IROBOT . OURSONG
TOES . HANGRY . STET .
ONLYASGOODASTHE . AMITY
PEP . BIOS . AHA . ACRE
. FLAG . DIALING . CREEL
CAMRY . COMPANYYOUKEEP
OTOE . SAIDNO . NURSES
SOMETHINGELSE . OATMILK
TWOPAIR . EXAMS . SKIAREA
ANARCHY . STRUT . APNEWS
```

170

```
DOTTEDIS . MOST . PUM[PIR]ON
ORNAMENT . ALLEN . IGUANA
CONS[PIR]ACYTHEORY . NANTES
. SEDALIA . USES . SELA
HOMES . ENLACE . PESTS
UNA . TWO . TISH . VAM[PIR]EBAT
BARGAIN . SATE . ANAEROBE
CULOTTES . ASSIGN . SOBA
ATONE . GOUT . INLAW . TIT
PONE . SPRUCE . ENO . YES
. RES[PIR]ATORYSYSTEM
SPA . MAO . INNATE . AMAL
HAW . USUAL . NAPS . BRAVE
AREA . SEPTET . S[PIR]OAGNEW
REIGNITE . LOCO . INBOUND
PENNANTS . LOOP . TOY . AGE
. SURGE . BITMAP . ABLER
TA[PIR]S . SOUP . FLONASE
OXIDES . MISSISSIP[PIR]IVER
RENEWS . ALIKE . ELSINORE
EDGIER . TSAR . REENGAGE
```

171

```
YOSHI . MAUDE . TOAST
ASTON . SLUGFESTS . ELBOW
LSATS . LIFEOFPIE . ADORE
LORD . DEAF . ICED . CUTE
. TENDERISTHEKNIGHT
INASNAP . NUKES . IDEATES
MONKEYS . NOM . TOEPICK
ARE . CANDIED . . MRI
YAWNS . ORLY . NUIT . TEEUP
. OHSTOP . ROOMED
INSEARCHOFLOSTTHYME
ADO . EGO . AWRAP . EVE . OOF
ROVER . SNIDE . ELENA
FLAX . GAP . ILL . AVA . ETSY
. THELITTLEPRINTS
SWEARSTO . HEADSLAP
HEARST . SPEEDOS . SHIRAZ
ENSNARE . GOTON . SCIENCE
ISA . JULIUSSEESHER . OKS
DEB . ODEON . SPENT . LET
III . BEAN . ALES . DRY
```

172

```
SLEPT . MMS . AIM . EMAILS
MANORS . MYLANTA . NESTEA
AUDIENCEHISSED . GNAWAT
CRINKLE . EPHEMERA . PANE
KANT . MARIO . IRV . STE
. BAREBONESRENDITION
DEB . GENL . TANGELO
AVARIETYOFPARTS . LUCAS
SECOND . BOLGER . SERAPE
. HUG . PAIGE . EATS . LIE
SPEX . WAHISANDALL . GLAD
EEL . WARM . SAUTE . IRE
TROJAN . HATERS . ANORAK
HURON . NOBODYTOACTWITH
. ETAILER . SINE . DMZ
REFLECTEDONHISROLE
ELO . DOT . OATES . SAGS
TEXT . LIVEOAKS . ERITREA
AVIARY . ATTHEWRAPPARTY
PEERAT . CARSFAT . MOTETS
ENRAGE . ALA . MRE . DETOO
```

173

```
ONSTAR . ICU . EBERT . CHUG
REPOSE . RAG . XAXES . ROME
SWAYUPHIGH . QUANT . ASIN
EMTS . ODE . SUMMERSWEAR
RESTAPLE . POI . SWANLAKE
. ORALS . ORSO . SPA
SWARMRECEPTION . SPITES
AONE . TREND . THOR . SNARK
MENSCH . DIKE . ROC . TERI
. SEADOVE . AIWA . OBOE
FORWANTOFABETTERSWORD
OPER . OEUF . OTHELLO
ARTY . NAS . OBIE . SUPERB
MARES . MEAN . CELIA . OLAY
SHORTU . SPARKLINGSWINE
. ANY . ACUE . ELATE
ISCARIOT . CDT . SANDREEF
SWEPTFORJOY . STY . DANO
LILI . OHYOU . SWISHLISTS
APTS . ROSIN . HAL . SEVERS
MESH . MOTET . ATL . TIEDYE
```

174

```
MICROLOAN . PATEL . SILO
ADHERENCE . ELUDE . IKNOW
YOUGOTTHATSTRUT . DEUCE
ALMS . HAY . ROOK . SERENA
. SAP . CUSSSENSITIVE
MORAL . WOE . ROTS . SOL
FOLEY . CHI . MIATA . DORM
WHYTHELONGFUSS . TBONES
IAM . IDEE . REDS . HERO
WIPE . GALPAL . UFO . ADD
. RUDDERSOFTHELOSTARK
SUE . LEI . SEDAKA . DOES
CARY . SPAR . TAME . PGA
ACCEDE . LOADEDTHEBUSES
HAHS . CSINY . IOS . BAILS
EPA . LIMA . IMP . BEETS
MUCKUPARTISTS . ROD
CHASER . HOPE . LEO . LADE
SHIFT . THENUMBOFTHEGUM
KINKS . TURIN . FREEAGENT
INGA . VNECK . FIREWORKS
```

175

```
BARTAB    DRAW  BBALL
IVORIES   CRASHCOURSE
NATURALS  TRICKORTREAT
ALOE  TEALEAVES  ATBAT
COURTREPORTER   AWLS
ANT RIP WREN JUDE  WWE
    MAX WEIR SUGARCOAT
FORAY GARB TUNED  HURT
AVER MOI LIENOR  SALMA
DELETEDSCENES   SPENDS
ERASER THINNED  RECIPE
SYNCED ADESTEFIDELES
RITES ARTERY TIM  SILT
AGES GRETA WHEN  WIELD
THATSOKAY  SEAR  PIT
ATM HUED SPED ARM  DUA
    DERN SKINNYDIPPING
ALARM SHOESTORE  REBA
SLUMBERPARTY  WEBSITES
PLANETEARTH   PUMMELS
FAUST  DYES    SHORTI
```

176

```
MENU RAGU CAPO  ICICLE
UNIT ATOP OARS  NOONAN
SONEOPOOL THELASONERD
EKE RANDOM SMILE  ETA
  IDBET GATS  ANACIN
  ELS HADAKID  SUNTRAP
BADE AIM RISES  REHIRE
ALBA STEFANI  THERULES
HEARTHS TROTTED  TRENT
TERSER ERAT OPTS   TSA
   DAYSOTWOLIVES
CAM MOTO OVEN  PEOPLE
LOGAN REPUTED  ATECROW
ILIKEIKE REROUTE  CEDE
SOLEMN MODEL NIT  USES
PRESETS OUTOFIT   GPS
   WAHWAH HOOT  BUYER
OAF EARLS KRAKEN   VAC
FRFOURTRAIN  BREAKZERO
USAUSA OLGA EDEN  ANEW
MORROW WANT SSNS  CTRL
```

177

```
 GMAIL  SWEEP   STINKO
EROICA BEAGLE  CUEBALL
NACRES RANGIN  UPDATED
EPHEMERALDS PEPE  RAPS
SHADE HISS BADPR   STA
  ALVIN   GILGAMESHOW
DEALTIN ORELSE  ATLAS
ETTE PEPPILL   RINSE
SHARD  REMINISCE  ESPN
ANTE BEN DYS  INAPILE
INE CHIVAS ETCETC  DUE
PONTIAC ITE HER   EWES
ALDO METRONOME   SIMON
   OOMPH REBUSES  SANE
 DANTE ARAMIS  LIVENED
FIRSTRATEGY  TIBIA
ESC IRISE ARIZ  SCRIM
SLAV NEST OBAMACARENA
TIDINGS ARRIVE  AVENUE
EKESOUT READER  MISERS
RESAVE TYLER    ESTEE
```

178

```
JAMSESH ABACI  ABLEST
ALITTLE WEIRDO  CLAMOR
BONECONTENTION  LATOYA
STD HARES ETES  DIJON
  BLINIS STROKEGENIUS
ALLEN  SAYSO  WAS
BOOKGENESIS PEZ  BLAM
BOWS VOWEL  PRIDEPLACE
ANN PINE  IRON  SLIMES
  IOTA DESISTS  UMBRA
 STREAMCONSCIOUSNESS
AWAIT EARTHEN  ICKY
GOSSIP PARE BTUS   DUI
FREECHARGE MRCUB  PEGS
ADDS OUI RITEPASSAGE
   ANG AMUSE    PARSE
COMEDYERRORS  AFLATS
HAUER REAR ICIER   AID
ISTRIA FRAMEREFERENCE
CITIFY SALIVA  TREETOP
ASSETS TEXAN   HYDRANT
```

179

```
DAN  FLAT  CAR  CABIN
IMAM LONGO POET  EPOCH
SITE IONIA LURE  SPOIL
RAIDERSOFTHELOSTARK
OBVIATE  HINDS  IROBOT
BLEAT SUNSETBOULEVARD
EES OUTRE YELP   EGGS
  CUT LABS  AAH
RICOTTA  PATRIOTGAMES
OSAY ERG SPURN  ELICIT
ALTO RIOTS SEOUL  DARE
NECTAR OVERT RPI  DREA
 THEGODFATHER  SMOLDER
  ATA  ODIN  INE
DAIS META CASTE    APP
ONTHEWATERFRONT  SAVER
MYSORE ONCUE  EPISODE
 HONEYISHRUNKTHEKIDS
CRETE ALEE PANSY  IDLE
HARES DEUS SPOOL  NEET
INERT ASP  ETNA   DRS
```

180

```
BAHT  BUSS  OREM  SANS
IDEAL ANTI EPOXY  ERIC
BARBIEDOLL TAMAGOTCHI
IMSOMAD  INTHEMOOD
  ROSAS CAA   SPATES
HAMS ETCHASKETCH  TIME
APR CLARO AEIOU  CECIL
SEPIAS ATL TRUETO  KLM
ADORN  TWISTER  AZALEA
TOTED OCALA   DOYLE
 MANY CHRISTMAS   COMA
 TILED  SAYSO   ONEIL
BROCAS PLAYDOH  USEME
AAH NLEAST SPA  APOLLO
SNEAD TRASH INONE  MON
STAT CHATTYCATHY  ROWE
IODATE  OPA   IMDUE
ROSSPEROT  SAMBAED
RUBIKSCUBE SILLYPUTTY
ERRS NANAS ASEA  STONE
FLAK ARTY  THAW   SPAR
```

181

```
MAMBA  FACTIS  ISAY  MOA
ABOIL  IDUNNO  NOTE  ART
JUDGEANDJURY  BUTTDIAL
STEP  REMOTE  GERE  ETNA
   OBESE  PARTON  LAGS
HARPIST  PEACEANDQUIET
AGAPE  VIVIEN  ETD
PENANDPAPER  ALTEREGOS
SEA  NOONE  CEOS  ONO
  CHIRP  SUCHAS  ROES
  BREAKINGANDENTERING
ZOOM  DELTAS  ADIOS
IDS  LORI  CEDED  QIN
TESTPILOT  BOOMANDBUST
  ADO  ZEALOT  LEASH
HUGSANDKISSES  SPEEDOS
UNIT  TENETS  SHIRR
MEME  AFAR  SPECIE  PLEA
BALSAMIC  ROOMANDBOARD
USE  WEEK  ALLURE  INDIE
GET  ERRS  GOOSED  OGEES
```

182

```
SCISSOR  SEASALT  CIDER
CONFINE  OMELETS  UNITS
INBOXES  FUTUREPERFECT
FAA  SILT  NRA  UFOS
INDEFINITEARTICLE  EPA
  TREE  FAT  YELLOWFLAG
SMART  TECHS  SLOG  IFWE
PASSIVEVOICE  BUY  GUNN
ACT  DOSE  COPPED  TWEED
SEEP  ILSA  RIO  AZALEA
  RELATIVECLAUSES
FEDORA  REC  OTTO  PACT
RAISE  OHYEAH  HERA  NAH
UTAH  ACA  PRESENTTENSE
MEMO  BEST  DUEIN  TACKY
PROPPLANES  RXS  MISO
SYN  SENTENCESTRUCTURE
  DRYS  TOR  CSIS  LIL
OBJECTIVECASE  FLINTMI
ISIAH  CORAZON  LINSEED
LAMPS  INSTYLE  ENGARDE
```

183

```
COSMIC  STARES  INFLOW
ONEACAT  ORNATE  CETERA
POWDEREDWIGWAG  HERNAN
  REPROS  IDTAG  OGLE
PIE  ORO  ANA  EPCOT
LAO  JOINEDATTHEHIPHOP
OLDPAL  ELO  AMAZON  WWI
ALIENEE  APT  CHEN  WINE
FINGERTIPTOP  HEVISIT
DEB  CDS  ASIA  NINETY
  OFTHEIJISINGSONG
MASALA  ASST  SUI  SEM
ELTRAIN  LETHERRIPRAP
GIRD  LEAF  RAO  SEMAINE
AKA  SOCCER  CCS  DONEIN
NEWYORKKNICKKNACK  PAD
  PAUSE  FRY  AGA  SAC
ICON  DAFFY  TRIVIA
BALKAN  TRIPLEFLIPFLOP
ALLEGE  WANTON  EASEOUT
RESEED  TUGSAT  ROSTRA
```

184

```
PLAYER  TOOLBAR  DEALER
OEUVRE  VAMOOSE  ARCADE
TERESA  SKABAND  LITMUS
TWOSTRIPER  SERVICEACE
EAR  MONEYTREE  ZEN
DYAN  LOT  POI  WES  BEST
  OBI  SPUNK  UFO
THREEBEARS  GIVEMEFIVE
COOLBEANS  DAYTRADER
BRO  ELSE  ELF  IRON  ONO
YAMS  TWENTYONE  ANTS
  TAFT  SERIF  LILT
BARRACKS  FACETIME
SIXDEGREES  CASHISKING
ATFIT  ANNTAYLOR  FENDI
YES  FOYT  EGG  FIFI  DOG
  AUTO  MIENS  SINS
JACKLONDON  ELITEEIGHT
AFAR  OBESE  TAKIN  DREI
MEMO  LONER  STEAD  EARN
IWIN  EXTS  SANS  BUST
```

185

```
POINT  STRAINED  STAND
ACMES  THISLIFE  CHLOE
DOETH  RADIOERA  RAINS
DNA  IRE  EASTON  ITSOK
INNEREAR  NEONS  PCT
NONETAKEN  ITHELP
GROK  DENOTE  TESSERAE
  DIDIWIN  CUP  NOVB
LEANIN  POCONOS
GUMBY  OSA  LATISH  MOO
BREAKTHEGLASSCEILING
TON  IAGREE  HIE  NADER
  TREERAT  SEXILE
SPAY  DEN  FOGGIER
COLORIZE  YOYOMA  ABLE
IMBUES  POSTERIOR
RIG  WINCE  FLEXAGON
SLIDE  ISEULT  ERE  EKE
LOGIN  DEGREASE  ROLOS
ADHOC  TEEINGUP  TROUT
BETTY  HAVEASAY  SAWTO
```

186

```
PAPER  SOLANGE  ELSA
AGREE  FOREWORD  GOTAT
REINDEERCALVES  OSIRIS
IND  TUNE  ICES  ERODE
STEWARD  DOGCOLLAR  NIX
  POGO  FAVRE  ITSABET
CARS  ALTER  SADE  NUDE
GERMANBEER  RENO  STRUT
IDA  LOADS  MARINECORPS
FADERS  FORUM  MIN
TREE  MENTALIMAGE  YAWN
  GPA  AIDAN  FRR  SRO
STARCLUSTER  PAIGE  TEA
HOLES  BALD  PEACEMARCH
ELMS  POLE  LITHO  IMOK
ADASTRA  BETAS  STAN
FAR  HOTCEREAL  LETSOFF
ELSIE  SILO  MARA  MEL
DIAPER  VEGETARIANMENU
  ELAND  INAPANIC  CIRCE
  ADDS  CANARDS  EASES
```

187

```
SOWN  GIF  NIMBLE  ADAGE
CREATIVE  ACHIER  BORAX
ANISETEA  JAZZVOCALIST
RAGTAG  ROAR  IDO  OGRE
ETH  MOUNTFUJI  ELTRAIN
ETC  TOT  SAM  DAH  TNT
YOUBET  DEO  DEFOGS
MMMBOP  GALAAFFAIR
SEAEEL  VIVO  NFL  REFS
RETORT  AGES  RAN  EONS
ATTN  EMPIRESTATE  FRAU
SUED  DIE  SLIM  WHACKS
PROD  EKE  TAMP  MELEES
WHENINROME  CARLOS
CATNAP  TOO  TERRIF
ALA  KID  KEN  WAR  NNW
TAXSALE  IGETITNOW  AAH
ABIT  OAF  WRIT  BOWTIE
LAWOFGRAVITY  LOOKOUTS
OMANI  TRICOT  EYESORES
GAYER  HECKNO  DES  LEDE
```

188

```
THEMAN  AMIGO  SMOG  AWW
BOVINE  TAROT  EIRE  BYE
SHESNOTTHERE  ALCAPONE
POSH  INI  ILLBEAROUND
AHAB  ALLIES  CUTEY
THEPOWEROFLOVE  CALF
HUM  PETUNIA  POSTAGE
AMES  ABET  CHROME  CAT
WARTORN  LIEIN  REBA
ENGAGE  DEVILINSIDE
DEEPEN  UNITING  LUSTER
LETSGOCRAZY  ICEAXE
RAKE  TUTEE  CATCHON
ELI  CRIPES  TERI  TIDE
FISCHER  SWEETIE  TUG
SAAB  JUDYINDISGUISE
DJINN  NOPEST  ZOOS
RUMOURHASIT  PRE  FARE
LIMEKILN  COMEONEILEEN
ACE  AMEN  ELATE  SMARTY
OYE  HERA  SEXES  PAGODA
```

189

```
ATTIC  TAB  TUBI  SCLC
FRODO  ARACHNID  STOOD
DRAWERSOFCHESTS  CAMPS
RADIANT  SHIFTS  JAIME
AMEN  PIP  EAR  AUDRA
BED  HONOROFMAIDS  WNBA
OPTION  PFFT  ADAM
ENBIES  SLID  OER  YOLO
MORNS  FOOTOFFLEET  FDR
INON  EON  ARID  LANCE
RETINUE  DAFOE  YAMAHAS
THEOC  NEIL  SEX  GAGE
BAE  MANOFRIGHTS  LAILA
OKRA  LOL  POOR  BOTNET
NEST  YETI  GOOGOO
KNOT  PLENTYOFHORN  WOO
FRATS  FAA  SOD  SAID
ABACI  OUTRAN  FERTILE
EXACT  ABSENCEOFLEAVES
GENTS  OVERSHOE  LAGER
ODDS  KIDS  END  OPEDS
```

190

```
SCREAMO  FOLDUP  FROS
INEXPERT  AVERSE  LEIA
BES[TRAP]ALBUM  CEASES  YANK
STU  OSMOSING  TRICKS
ROAN  OILSUP  ANTS
FORINSTANCE  EARWIG
ONEND  ESL  ORCHES[TRAP]ITS
SECT  [TRAP]PISTS  KOBE  TIE
SITSON  TWOBIT  SHEHER
ELS  ROOK  IRONED  AZERA
BADDEST  UNNERVE
ACORN  SPICER  TACO  PMS
DORAGS  TAHINI  ACCRUE
DNA  EXEC  ONECUP  HERA
S[TRAP]LESSGOWN  ALE  MADAM
MOWGLI  VON[TRAP]PFAMILY
TOAD  DISOWN  RIPS
SIMIAN  MISSOULA  POP
NOEL  ONTILT  TRAPDOORS
INGE  LEANTO  ESPOUSES
TSAR  ATRISK  SEXIEST
```

191

```
PHD  PALACE  ACCOST  HSN
RIO  AVATAR  YAHWEH  IPOS
EGO  REBELALLIANCE  TARA
THREERS  SOANDSO  LOCUS
ANDERS  ROEG  SUNNINESS
POOL  HANSOLO  PDAS  THY
EON  STEEL  APP  GRAPH
SNOWMAN  YARDSALES  REIN
THEISM  ROY  YEA  AFRO
STEAK  ASIA  WEAR  CLIOS
SAHARA  STAR  W/T A/R R/E S/K  SHINNY
ABETS  WHOS  RISE  NANAS
SIRI  HER  PAS  DIESEL
KNEE  WARMSUPTO  METSFAN
ISLET  SIR  BIORE  REA
IMS  GRIM  MRSPOCK  CORK
DONTBESAD  HUEY  DONNIE
BLOAT  TSELIOT  PRINTAD
ETTU  THEFEDERATION  ILL
TERN  MARINE  ISITOK  ELI
NYT  ITSBAD  DECALS  RYE
```

192

```
CDS  WINDS  CRAP  ASSUCH
PIANODUET  LIME  MURPHY
UNLIKABLE  UNINHIBITED
ICE  SIEGES  LOS  LORE
TWEENS  PLIE  INSTA
MANN  ABS  INDIGO  ENZO
INTERFACING  SHRINKING
YESAND  TOT  STAPLE
CARES  LLAMA  BAH  DON
WAVES  LEO  AUDREY  PROD
AROD  INVECTIVE  HIKE
SAGS  GREECE  STP  SEVER
ALA  ROE  OSCAR  FEWER
BADDAY  VAN  ORIOLE
IRRIGATED  COMPLEMENTS
MOVE  ENAMEL  SEC  OAHU
IDLED  AMID  KICKER
SEED  INE  PETERI  NEE
ALTERCATION  COMMANDED
AMTRAK  TOUT  ACAPPELLA
BOASTS  ANTS  YACHT  YIN
```

193

```
CHAW  WIELD  FEDS  BERT
LOLA  GENXER  AVOW  OREO
OUISHALLOVERCOME  UNIT
USB  OSCAR  SAIL  ATNINE
DEISM  HIC  DIEUPROCESS
     PBS  DINED  TRIPE
IMPERIL  SENS  ION  SLAP
BELLETOWER  ROW  TBILL
ITAL  INE  DIDIN  LEAPTO
SAY  NDA  IRIS  AIRCREW
  EAUFORHEAVENSSAKE
TURNSON  ESTO  ACT  AVE
IRONER  CATER  POI  VDAY
PANES  DAD  CESTCHEESE
SLEW  ERR  OKED  SLURRED
    IMGAY  UNDUE  EGG
LAITTOWASTE  CAB  GEICO
INTHAT  TARE  ATREE  HAN
VISA  REINECATSANDDOGS
ETON  INDY  ALEAST  EPEE
RAKE  PESO  PESTS  WEST
```

194

```
ATMCARDS  BUREAU  ATIT
POOHPOOH  EASESIN  LIME
PIRATESOFTHECARIBBEAN
SLR  TOOHARD  SCOURGE
   IPAS  ERE  CHESSSET
ITSAWONDERFULLIFE
LOOSELY  ONEUP  PEGS
LENS  VEG  PUTON  GARRET
   THETOWERINGINFERNO
YAHOO  NORSE  CARPARK
ESE  OLSEN  AKITA  TEE
STRIKER  SPADE  IPASS
THEDEVILWEARSPRADA
EMBODY  EARLS  TAB  YVES
RAYS  PASTE  KENDALL
   WHENHARRYMETSALLY
GLACIERS  HAI  SAYS
RECITAL  GORILLA  PCS
ANIGHTMAREONELMSTREET
PINA  HAYRIDE  EMPANADA
ENGR  SNARLS  TOYMAKER
```

195

```
APPETIT  IMOUT  PACIFIC
SHALALA  NAOMI  ATACAMA
SATIRES  SCONE  UPSELLS
ISH  P  TIPS  OPTS  A  LIT
SET  ESE  ORE  IKE
IROC  TRACY  GLOSS  ONES
  VITA  ATEALOT  WART
ISITON  C  ADO  H  ELWOOD
SACRED  HOW  ALEPPO
OCTOBER  BONUS  TRILLED
PHONEME  OKAPI  HAALAND
OER  ASFOR  I  LSATS  CEE
DRY  N  OBE  LAT  K  ERR
    RODS  SINS
SOD  NAMEOFTHEGAME  CHO
THEHELP  MOWER  BARGAIN
ALVEOLAR  O  DISGORGE
FOIA  ORAL  SEGO  OSHA
FOLLOWTHEBOUNCINGBALL
KEELEY  GOPRO  FINELY
   DRED  SWING  CURE
```

196

```
N(EARLY)LY  BROIL  MRT  LEST
H(EAR)YE  INONIT  OSHA  ALTO
L(EARN)T  GANGESRIVER  BLIP
(EAR)NING  NEATO  PAY  MENS
   SIEGE  HOW  NAMING
MPH  CREEPERS  SONIC
ELISE  ISLAM  WES  BELLOW
SUPPRESSED  FREES  ASH
ASTI  SELA  SLEW  TSETSE
HOTROLL  STASH  UTAHAN
   SAT  EMERITA  PAT
ABLAZE  EAGER  THEBACK
DIETER  GROW  FIEF  TEAM
MI(ND)FD  YOGIS  BUDDYHOLLY
TISNT  PSA  SELIG  INLET
OOZES  CALLDESK  ISH
YOUWIN  AXL  TRIED
PLUG  ISD  POACH  CROSS
AITA  CHETONGUECLUCK  WIIG
PERT  HOLA  SIRREE  EDDA
ABES  TIC  ODEON  LEES
```

197

```
CAMP  AMUST  ARLO  PEP
OBOE  PALLID  MOOR  TAPE
HADNOPRAYER  ETES  SLAW
ICE  OLIN  DIDNTWORKOUT
BULLPEN  OBEDIENT  OLE
ASTI  ESPN  MIN  BEAKER
KETONE  TONGUE  LATS
CAMETONOTHING  SAHL
ALOHAOE  ETS  GENESIS
RESELL  GULL  BAO  HTTPS
DUAL  LETMEDOWN  ASIA
STILL  ORE  BUNK  SIRENS
SCIENCE  COE  JUMBLES
TOOK  WOULDNEVERFLY
THAI  TENHUT  RELATE
HUSSAR  AIR  MEWL  APPS
EMU  BEATTIME  OSHKOSH
MISSEDTHECUT  OSHA  LYE
ADUE  ARAL  DIDTHETRICK
GOAT  MINI  SENIOR  ACHE
IRL  EASE  RASTA  PEEL
```

198

```
ATTESTS  SOCAL  ADASTRA
GROCERY  UNHIP  CONGEAL
EUROVAN  ITEMS  HECTARE
SET  ECCE  IOS  GERI  REX
  ISNT  RAMPAGE  SEND
ALLOW  LIMESTONE  NORMA
SYLLOGISM  RENTTOOWN
TRAINER  OFTHE  DOWNPAT
OAS  DRAW  ABE  TOGO  SHE
  TERSE  NAY  AWARD
STORY  ENCRYPT  SLEEP
KEEPS  EBAY  AAS  DFLAT
INES  LIP  MMA  TESH
NOB  CAST  SAP  INCH  CTR
GRANOLA  SPRAY  DRAFTEE
SALOME  CHAMBER  OLEOLE
SLUR  LOOT  SOYA  FIRS
GAMETES  THEBORG
BREADED  RHENIUM
IHATEIT  KHUFU  ANASAZI
TOT  SRO  MOD  NIA
```

199

```
T P S   C D S     P O S T E D   S U B
H U T   T R E A T Y   E S C H E W   W H O
E S E   H O N C H O   P H O E N I X A - Z
W H E R E A S   E D S   A U F   I T O O
B - L I S T E R P A C K   R E D F I S H
  U G L I   R I O   R I M   N O R
Y P R E S   G - R A T E D C H E E S E
E B A Y   W H I P U P   R U E   E V A D E
P R Y   T I E D O N   S I N S   W I V E S
  A S S I S I   W E A N S   L I N E N S
  A M E R I C A N G O T H I - C
M E W L E D   T O Y O U   A F F E C T
A R I A L   I S M S   A V A N T I   R A W
G I T M O   M O I   B R I N G S   T O K E
  C H I C K E N C O - O P S   T O P E D
  K O A   S O B   L O X   O R C S
  C H A S I N G   M O V I N G A - S I D E
F L A B   T U T   Y I N   A N D O R R A
L O - C A L H E R O   S E E M T O   C U T
A S H   W E A S E L   A S S E S S   L G A
P E A   W E T T E D   P S Y   E S T
```

200

```
E T T U   G O M A D   A S S A Y   S A D
G H O S T   A L A M O   S W I N E   Q U E
G O N E R   S A T I N   S A N T A   U G A
C R E D I T   F A S T I N G F O R W A R D
E E L   P E A   H A N   B U N   A R A L
L A O S   A L P S   S T E A L   G R E T A
L U C K Y S T R E A K I N G   C A P R I S
  I V E   E D S   M O S T L Y   O N T
C Y G N E T   L A S S E S   H A L L O
F O O D S   B I N E T   M A N E A T E R
O G L E   B U M S T E E R I N G   W I L E
S I D E B A R S   A B U S E   A N N I E
  I P A S S   D E M O N S   N U D G E D
G I N   K I T C A R   O S E   I R A
A N G L E S   S T O C K I N G M A R K E T
M S D O S   T I E T O   N T S B   T E C H
E P I C   O O M   I C Y   N U N   R U E
L I G H T S W I T C H I N G   S U B P A R
A R G   I H E A R   L E A R N   T I L D A
W I E   V E L M A   E L S I E   S T O O P
S T R   O A S I S   A D A P T   S P R Y
```

The New York Times

SMART PUZZLES

Presented with Style

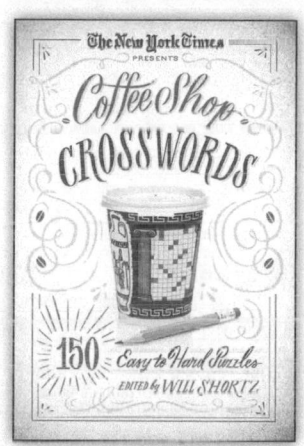

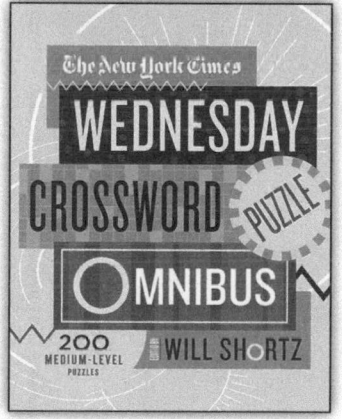

Available at your local bookstore or online at
us.macmillan.com/author/thenewyorktimes

 ST. MARTIN'S GRIFFIN